Contemporary Political Studies 1996

by Iain Hampsher-Monk

Founder & Editor, *History of Political Thought*
(Imprint Academic) [with J.Coleman] 1980-continuing

The Political Philosophy of Edmund Burke
(Longman) 1987

A History of Modern Political Thought
(Blackwell) 1992

Defending Politics: Essays on politics and pluralism in honour of Bernard Crick
(British Academic Press) [editor & contributor] 1993

by Jeffrey Stanyer

County Government in England and Wales
(Routledge & Kegan Paul) 1967

Understanding Local Government
(Fontana) 1976

Administering Britain
(Fontana) [with B.C.Smith] 1976

A History of Devon County Council, 1889-1989
(Devon Books) 1989

Centre and Periphery: Brittany and Cornwall & Devon Compared
(Exeter University Press) [edited with M.Havinden & J.Quéniart] 1991

Contemporary Political Studies 1994
(PSA) [edited with P.Dunleavy] 1994

Contemporary Political Studies 1995
(PSA) [edited with J.Lovenduski] 1995

CONTEMPORARY POLITICAL STUDIES 1996
Volumes I, II & III

Iain Hampsher-Monk

Professor of Political Theory
University of Exeter

Jeffrey Stanyer

Senior Lecturer in Politics
University of Exeter

THE POLITICAL STUDIES ASSOCIATION
OF THE UNITED KINGDOM

CONTEMPORARY POLITICAL STUDIES 1996

Volume II

edited on behalf of
The Political Studies Association
of the United Kingdom

by

Iain Hampsher-Monk
&
Jeffrey Stanyer

Foreword
Iain Hampsher-Monk

Introduction
Jeffrey Stanyer

Proceedings of the Annual Conference
held at the University of Glasgow
Glasgow
April 10th-12th, 1996

Political Studies Association
of the United Kingdom
1996

First published in Great Britain in 1996 by
THE POLITICAL STUDIES ASSOCIATION
OF THE UNITED KINGDOM
official address:
Department of Politics,
The Queens University,
Belfast BT7 1NN.

© I.Hampsher-Monk, J.Stanyer & the several authors each in respect of the paper contributed, 1996.

British Library Cataloguing in Publication Data
A catalogue record for this book is
available from the British Library
ISBN 0 9523150 6 8

Typeset in LaTeX by Jeffrey Stanyer.

Printed and bound in Great Britain by Short Run Press Ltd, Exeter.

Cover Design by Delphine Jones, Graphic Design Unit, University of Exeter.

Distributed by Blackwell, Oxford

All rights reserved.

THE POLITICAL STUDIES ASSOCIATION OF THE UNITED KINGDOM

Contents

Conference Organisation   inside front cover

PSA Executive, 1995-1996   inside back over

Foreword   vi

Introduction   vii

List of Papers   viii-xxv

Index of Convenors & Paper Givers   xxvi-xxviii

Papers: Volume I   1-633

Papers: Volume II   634-1271

Papers: Volume III   1272-1906

FOREWORD

by Iain Hampsher-Monk

This is the third annual *Contemporary Political Studies*, confirming its place in the life in the United Kingdom political studies community. For the first time, *CPS* will be marketed and sold by Blackwell beyond the Conference itself, displaying to a much wider audience this annual, panoramic, frozen frame of current activity in the discipline. For the wider audience it should be explained that all the papers here are to be presented to panels at the PSA Annual Conference at Glasgow and that, apart from the light editorial hands of the convenor and Jeff Stanyer, they have not been subjected to review or refereeing in the normal way. They represent work in progress and will doubtless mature as fully fledged articles or chapters or books (!) in the course of time. The combination of the Conference and the volumes offers an essential and, we hope, not too daunting stage in the career path of entrants to the profession and an incremental way of generating published research.

During the three years that *CPS* has been published the Annual Conference has transformed itself from a substantial yet moderate sized affair to a truly major undertaking. At the time of writing over five hundred delegates have registered for Glasgow, some four hundred and twenty of whom will be involved in delivering the programme. The programme itself has grown rapidly in the last three years. In York in 1995, itself a record year by some considerable margin, there were ninety-eight panels; this year there are one hundred and twenty-three. The number of papers submitted in time for publication in the Swansea volumes in 1994 was seventy-six, in 1995 one hundred and forty-six, this year it is nearly two hundred. It was a matter of considerable relief, even to my indefatigable colleague Jeff Stanyer (who unbelievably copy-edits, type-sets and proofs these volumes in less than a six weeks), that not all the paper-givers choose to publish in *CPS*.

The volume and diversity of intellectual activity presented here – much of which gratifyingly falls within the conference theme:

NEW BOUNDARIES, NEW IDENTITIES

– shows the continued tremendous vigour of United Kingdom Political Science.

IHM
15/3/96

INTRODUCTION

by Jeffrey Stanyer

When an organisation takes a new direction in its activities there are always some who predict that it will be a failure. In these cases only time can provide evidence supporting or undermining the claims of both pessimists and optimists and in the short run the PSA membership collectively has shown that it can get Conference papers ready in time – 140 were submitted not later than a few days after the deadline – and the innovation has not been ignored by the leading departments and individuals in the subject. There were also some who did not believe, on the basis of their experience with journals and commercial publishers, that it was physically possible to produce the papers in book form in little more than two months.

I am sometimes asked about the problems involved in publishing the volumes. The level of stress lies above that of facing West Indian fast bowlers and below that of fielding short leg to the bowling of some of my friends. This year there has been an additional pressure: the team manager ('Raymond' Hampsher-Monk) decided that we should bat for only 40 overs in a 50 overs match. The game is going to the last ball, but his decision promises to produce a large number of extra batting points for the profession.

Where will it all end? PSA has left Margaret Mitchell and Katherine Windsor well behind, up ahead lie the Webbs and ultimately Shakespeare and the Bible. The pessimists, therefore, were wrong and the PSA Executive faces the question of whether it has been too successful. They must not imitate Frederick the Great in not providing for the future. To this end I shall be preparing a more rigorous manuscript & disc submission format; the only factor that really threatens the speed of the publication process is the inability of many of the contributors to follow instructions. Some of this is my fault, some of it that of the panel convenors, but a considerable part must be assigned to the writers themselves – but I will not say any more about this today, except (as a summary of my reflections on three years):

'No writer is a hero or heroine to
his or her copy-editor and type-setter'

A postscript: as I was drafting this introduction I received a telephone call from an undergraduate doing a dissertation at another university. He asked how he could obtain a copy of a paper presented to the 1980 PSA Conference in Exeter by C.White. Nothing could highlight the difference between then and now better than this question. I played with a straight bat but ...

JS
18/3/96

Panels & Papers

The papers listed here are those that were sent to the editors in time to be printed. Other papers will be brought to the Conference by the authors and will be available for purchase from the Papers Room. Sessions for which no advance papers were expected and the panels which produced none are not included.

A full and revised timetable will be given to participants as they register.

First Session   Wednesday, 1.30pm

The Debate over American Decline (Bob Mckeever)

Ken Dark (Reading), 'United States' Decline in Global Perspective: comparing processes of change in the USA, USSR and China' [1-12]

Anthea Harris (Reading), 'Long Term Perspectives in International Relations Theory: the United States and the end of the Cold War' [13-20]

Historical Aspects of Britain's Relationship with Europe (John Young)

James Ellison (Christ Church College, Canterbury), 'Perfidious Albion? Britain, Plan G and European Integration, 1955-1957' [21-32]

Piers Ludlow (Balliol College), 'A Mismanaged Application: Britain and EEC Membership, 1961-1963' [33-44]

Business and English Regionalism (Jonathan Bradbury)

Dylan Griffith & Rod Hague (Newcastle), 'Local Economic Hegemony and Regional Policy Networks: the case of British Nuclear Fuels in West Cumbria' [45-52]

Chris Lanigan (Newcastle), 'Business and Regionalism in North East England' [53-61]

Simon Lee (Hull), 'The Betrayal of the Entrepreneur and Enterprise in England' [62-67]

Green Political Theory (Neil Carter & Brian Baxter)

Brian Baxter (Dundee), 'Must Political Theory now be Green?' [68-78]

Tim Hayward (Edinburgh), 'What is Green Political Theory?' [79-91]

Ethnicity: Concept and Meaning (Karl Cordell)

David Chapman (Democracy Design Forum), 'Electoral Systems Designed to Protect Minorities and their Use in Northern Ireland and Eastern Europe' [92-102]

David Chandler (Leeds Metropolitan), 'The Internationalisation of Minority Rights in Eastern Europe: an example of how the globalisation thesis recreates the East-West divide' [103-113]

Jeff Richards (Southampton Institute), ' "Them and Us": the reassertion of ethnic and national identity in the New Europe' [114-123]

The Stoney Path to Europe (Detlef Jahn)

Detlef Jahn (Nottingham Trent), 'Introduction' [124-126]

Andreas Bieler (Warwick), 'The Austrian Application to the European Community: social forces within the constraints of national institutions' [127-134]

Patricia-Roberts Thomson (Nottingham Trent), 'Referendums and Legitimacy – Myth or Reality?' [135-142]

Teija Tiilikainen (Åbo Academy University), 'Finland and the European Union: how the Finns became satisfied citizens of the European Union' [143-150]

Hegel (Howard Williams & Anthony Burns)

Kimberley Hutchings (Edinburgh), 'Hegel and Foucault on Politics and Truth' [151-158]

Mark Neocleous (Brunel), 'The Law Does Not Write Fiction: Hegel, corporations and the British state' [159-166]

Robert Bruce Ware (Keble College, Oxford), 'Self-Containment and Self-Consciousness in Hegel's Theory of the State' [167-175]

International Justice (Matthew Festenstein & Simon Caney)

Theresa Callan (Portsmouth), 'Realism and Communitarianism: transgressing the boundaries' [177-187]

Local Government Reorganisation (Steve Leach)

Stephen Cope (Portsmouth), Mark Bailey (Portsmouth) & Rob Atkinson (Portsmouth), 'Reinventing Local Government Boundaries: a question of community identity?' [188-197]

Steve Leach (de Montfort), 'The Local Government Review: an inter-organisational perspective' [198-209]

Political Theory and the Child (Andrew Lockyer)

Matthew Liao (Queen's College, Oxford), 'Improving Susan Moller Okin's Conception of the Family' [210-229]

Bureaucratic Gamekeeping (Chris Hood & Oliver James)

Rebecca Boden (Sheffield), Julie Froud (Manchester), Anthony Ogus (Manchester) & Peter Stubbs (Manchester), 'Controlling the Regulators: compliance cost assessment in United Kingdom central government' [230-231]

Christopher Hood (LSE) & Oliver James (LSE), ' "Regulation" inside British Government: the inner face of the regulatory state' [232-247]

South Asia Politics (Gurharpal Singh)

Bob Currie (Huddersfield), 'Liberalisation or Liberal Promises?: an examination of India's recent experiments with economic deregulation' [248-256]

Mohammad Waseem (St Antony's), 'Democratisation in Pakistan: the current phase' [257-264]

Andrew Wyatt (Bristol), 'Indian Christians and the 1966 Lok Sahba Elections' [265-272]

Third Session   Wednesday, 5.00pm

New Labour and Devolution (Jonathan Bradbury)

Jonathan Bradbury (Swansea), 'The Labour Party and the Politics of English Regional Reform: critical perspectives' [273-280]

Russell Deacon (Cardiff IHE), 'New Labour and the Welsh Assembly: "Shaping the Vision' or updating the Wales Act, 1978?' [281-288]

Peter Lynch (Stirling), 'Labour and Scottish Devolution: securing consensus and managing opposition' [289-297]

China Twenty Years on from Mao (Karen Henderson & Jane Duckett)

Jane Duckett (Manchester), 'State Restructuring for an Encroaching Market: China's experience of commercial system reform' [298-306]

Paul Wingrove (Greenwich), 'Twenty Years of Dealing with the Bear: China and the USSR, 1976-1996' [307-314]

Panels & Papers

Comparative European Public Policy (John Gaffney & Helen Fawcett)

Hugh Compston (Cardiff), 'Trade Unions, Policy-Making and Unemployment: a comparative study of 13 West European democracies' [315-327]

Helen Fawcett (York), 'Comparing the Support for the Unemployed and their Families in Twelve Member States of the European Union' [328-335]

Roxanne Powell (Independent Scholar), 'Public and Private Spheres in Britain and France: strict separation or blurred boundaries (1965-1995)?' [336-349]

Graham Timmins (University of Huddersfield), 'European Union Policy towards East-Central Europe: prospects for enlargement' [350-356]

Green Politics and the History of Political Thought (Neil Carter & John Barry)

Keekok Lee (Manchester), '*Homo Faber*: the ontological category of modernity' [357-368]

Piers Stephens (Manchester), 'Plural Pluralisms: towards a more liberal green political theory' [369-380]

Ethnic Minorities: Portrayals and Illustrations (Karl Cordell)

Gerd Nonneman (Lancaster), 'Muslim Communities in Post-Cold War Europe: themes and puzzles' [381-394]

Philip Payton (Exeter), 'Inconvenient Peripheries: ethnic identity and the "United Kingdom Estate" – the cases of "Protestant Ulster" and Cornwall' [395-408]

The Stoney Path to Europe (Detlef Jahn)

Tor Bjørklund (Oslo), 'The Dispute about Norwegian Membership in the European Union: a transformation of an issue from foreign to domestic policy' [409-416]

Detlef Jahn (Nottingham Trent) & Anders Widfeldt (Göteborg), 'European Union Accession and its Aftermath in Sweden: are the Swedes fed up with European Union membership?' [417-423]

Hegel (Howard Williams & Anthony Burns)

Ian Fraser (Nottingham Trent), 'Hegel and Modern Need Theory' [424-432]

David Sullivan (Coleg Harlech), 'Hegel on War and International Order' [433-441]

Deliberative Democracy (Matthew Festenstein & David Owen)

Andrea Baumeister (Stirling), 'The Dynamic Political Community: pluralism, conflict and negotiation' [442-451]

Local Government Reorganisation (Steve Leach)

George Boyne (Cardiff), 'Local Government Reorganisation in Scotland and Wales: a public choice perspective' [452-462]

Gerry Stoker (Strathclyde), 'Hearing but not Listening: the Local Government Review in West Sussex', [463-474]

Martin Stott (Oxfordshire CC), 'The Local Government Review: the Oxfordshire story' [475-487]

Citizenship and Mass Communication (Mark Wheeler)

Jill Hills (City University), 'Democracy, Public Service Broadcasting and Regional Identity' [488-501]

John Street (East Anglia), 'Remote Control: politics, technology and culture' [502-510]

Mark Wheeler (London Guildhall), 'Orbiting Your Living Room, Cashing in Your Bill of Rights? communications, politics and citizenship towards the second millenium' [511-519]

Political Theory and the Child (Andrew Lockyer)

David Archard (St.Andrews), 'The Age of Majority' [520-528]

Governance and Peripheral Regions in South Asia (Gurharpal Singh)

Alexander Evans (Bristol), 'Islamic Terrorism in the Kashmir Valley: insurgency or intervention?' [529-536]

Apurba Kundu (Bradford), 'Commissioned Officers in India and the Emergency, 1975-1977' [537-545]

Shinder Thandi (Coventry), 'Fighting Sikh Militancy: counterinsuregency operations in Punjab (India) 1980-1994' [546-554]

Panels & Papers

> **Fourth Session   Thursday, 9.00am**

New Labour and Devolution (Jonathan Bradbury)

Graham Leicester (The Constitution Unit), 'Journey without Maps: Scottish Devolution in the 1990s' [555-563]

James Mitchell (Strathclyde), 'From Unitary State to Union State: Labour's changing view of the United Kingdom and its implications' [564-572]

The Practice of Civil Society (Karen Henderson & Virginia Charles)

Adam Fagin (Middlesex), 'Transition to Democracy in the Czech Republic: the concept of civil society' [573-580]

Brian Slocock (Paisley), 'Interest Groups and the Post-Communist Policy Process: industry and the implementation of the Czech Clean Air Act' [581-588]

Political Legitimacy: Leadership and Institutions (John Gaffney)

Paul Taggart (Sussex), 'Political Legitimacy: leadership and institutions' [589-597]

Conceptual Boundaries in Third World Politics (Heather Deegan)

Helen Hintjens (Swansea), 'Structural Adjustments and Politics at the Grassroots: two West African studies' [598-609]

Robert Pinkney (Northumbria), 'Tanzanian Elections 1995: some snapshots of leaders, activists and voters' [610-622]

The Politics of Gender Law and Order (Adam Edwards & Anna Maclure)

John Hoffman (Leicester), 'Gender, Sovereignty and the Problems of Violence' [623-633]

Karl Popper: Conjecture and Refutation in Liberal Theory (Matthew Festenstein, Sally Jenkinson & Simon Tormey)

Jeremy Shearmur (ANU), 'Popper's Political Theory: a reassessment' [634-641]

Simon Tormey (Nottingham), 'The Problem with Problems: Popper, negative utility and the open society' [642-653]

Political Marketing (Dominic Wring)

Bruce Newman (DePaul, Chicago), 'The Role of Marketing in American Politics' [654-664]

Dominic Wring (Nottingham Trent), 'The Historical Role of Marketing in British Politics' [665-675]

Multiculturalism and the Public Sphere (Stuart White)

Don MacIver (Staffordshire), 'The State and Minority Separatism' [676-687]

Tariq Mohood (PSI), 'Race in Britain and the Politics of Difference' [688-695]

Politics and Health (Alison Hann)

Carla Koen (Warwick), 'The Boundary between the Public and the Private: a case study of the Japanese pharmaceutical industry' [696-706]

The Death of Conservative Party Local Politics (Peter John)

Josie Brooks (Southampton Institute), 'The Role of Right-Wing Think Tanks in Conservative Local Government' [707-718]

Ian Holliday (Manchester), 'Diversity and Conflict in Conservative Local Government, 1979-1996' [719-730]

The European Union: Rigid or Flexible Decision-Making (Juliet Lodge & Andreas Kintis)

José Magone (Hull), 'The Impact of Structural Funds on Southern Europe' [731-738]

Fred Nash (Southampton), 'The United Kingdom and the European Union: an essay in retrieval' [739-750]

Claudio Radaelli (Bradford), 'Harmonising What, How and to Which Effect: the politics of problem definition in European direct corporate tax harmonisation' [751-760]

Fifth Session   Thursday, 11.00am

The European Union: Rigid or Flexible Decision-Making (Juliet Lodge & Andreas Kintis)

John Peterson (Glasgow), 'Decision-Making in the European Union: the Single Market' [761-770]

Exploring Civil Society in Post-Authoritarian Regimes (Karen Henderson & Adam Fagin)

Joe Foweraker (Essex) & Todd Landman (Essex), 'Social Movements, Human rights and Civil Society in Latin America' [771-777]

Lucy Taylor (Sheffield), 'Civilising Civil Society: disassociating popular participation from politics itself' [778-785]

Mark Thompson (Glasgow), ' "Delayed" Democratisation: developmental states and civil society in the Asian Pacific' [786-795]

Comparing Political Parties (John Gaffney)

Kate Hudson (South Bank), 'Post-Communists and Social Democrats in Hungary' [796-805]

Conceptual Boundaries in Third World Politics (Heather Deegan)

Lesley McCulloch (Aberdeen), 'The Misallocation Phenomenon of Defence spending in South East Asia: a global political dilemma or a nation's prerogative?' [805-811]

Heather Deegan (Middlesex), 'The Middle East and Africa: an alternative development agenda' [812-821]

Defence and British Politics in the 1980s (Andrew Dorman)

Andrew Dorman (Birmingham), 'Defence as an Electoral Weapon: the case of the Conservative Party in the 1980s' [822-829]

Lucy James (Birmingham), 'Alternative Defence: the case of the Greenham Common women' [830-837]

Roger Wicks (Birmingham), 'The Case for Defence and the Labour Party, Political Ideas and Nuclear Disarmament in the 1980s' [838-844]

Local Government and the Environment in the 1990s
(Neil Carter & Stephen Ward)

Stephen Ward (Salford), 'United Kingdom Local Government and Environmental Agenda Change' [845-857]

Stephen Young (Manchester), 'Participation Strategies in the Context of Local Agenda 21: approaching a new watershed?' [858-870]

Fuzzy Boundaries and Policing Futures (Adam Edwards, Stephen Cope & Peter Starie)

Stephen Cope (Portsmouth), Sarah Charman (Portsmouth), Steve Savage (Portsmouth) & Peter Starie (Portsmouth), 'Redrawing the Boundaries of Police Governance: centralisation, the role of the Association of Chief Police Officers and policing futures' [871-884]

Alasdair MacIntyre (Matthew Festenstein, Mark Evans & Kelvin Knight)

Kelvin Knight (North London), 'Revolutionary Aristotelianism' [885-896]

Marx and Hegel (Mark Cowling)

Chris Arthur (Sussex), 'Capital: a compulsive-neurotic subject' [897-906]

Gary Browning (Oxford Brookes), 'Good and Bad Infinities in Marx and Hegel' [907-917]

Multiculturalism, Equality and the Public Sphere (Stuart White)

Elizabeth Sperling (Liverpool John Moores), 'Women and Quangos: a step backwards in the progress towards equality in representation in public service provision?' [918-923]

Stuart White (Nuffield, Oxford), 'Freedom of Association and the Right to Exclude' [924-932]

Politics and Health (Alison Hann)

Peter Falconer (Glasgow Caledonian), 'To Charge or Not to Charge: the politics of health charges in Britain' [933-943]

Ideology, Hegemony and Political Subjectivity (David Howarth & Aletta Norval)

David Howarth (Staffordshire), 'Theorising Hegemony' [944-956]

Local Governance (Gerry Stoker)

William Maloney (Aberdeen), 'The Regulatory Game in the Privatised Water Industry: complexity and conflict' [957-968]

Think Tanks in Comparative Perpective (Andrew Denham)

Donald Abelson (Western Ontario) & Christine Carberry (Western Ontario), 'In Search of Policy Advice: when Presidential candidates turn to think tanks' [969-979]

Sixth Session   Thursday, 2.00pm

Boundaries and Identities in Tropical Africa (Christopher Clapham)

Christopher Clapham (Lancaster), 'Territoriality and Statehood in Tropical Africa' [980-989]

Peter Woodward (Reading), 'Borders and Conflict in North-East Africa' [990-999]

The European Union in International Perspective (Juliet Lodge & Andreas Kintis)

Andrew Geddes (Salford), 'Racist Discrimination and the European Union' [1000-1006]

Lees Miles (Humberside), 'The Swedish European Parliamentary Election: are the Swedes turning their back on Europe?' [1007-1012]

Richard Whitman (Westminster), 'The European Union's Southern Flank: Euro-Mediterranean partnership or new-found pacifier?' [1013-1019]

Andreas Kintis (Hull), 'Two Years of CFSP: a review' [1020-1026]

European Citizenship and Justice and Home Affairs (Jörg Monar)

Jörg Monar (Leicester), 'European Justice and Home Affairs: deficits and reform possibilities' [1027-1040]

John Benyon (Leicester), 'Building Police Co-operation: the European construction site around the Third Pillar' [1041-1062]

Political Theory and the Foundations of Value
(Matthew Festenstein, Mark Evans & Kelvin Knight)

Mark Evans (Swansea), 'Foundationless Liberalism: coming to terms with contingency' [1063-1074]

Martyn Oliver (Westminster), 'Rorty and Rawls: contingency and political theory' [1075-1082]

Models of Community (Andrew Reeve)

Andrew Reeve (Warwick), 'Community and Industrial Society' [1083-1092]

The Political Science of British Politics (Fred Nash)

Jim Bulpitt (Warwick), 'Historical Politics: leaders, statecraft and regime at the accession of Queen Elizabeth II' [1093-1106]

Fred Nash (Southampton), 'Political Science and the Study of British Government and Politics' [1107-1132]

Politics and Health (Alison Hann)

Maggie Mort (Leeds), Stephen Harrison (Leeds) & Gerald Wistow (Leeds), 'The User Card: picking through the organisational undergrowth in health and social care' [1133-1140]

Christopher Nottingham (Glasgow Caledonian) & Fiona O'Neill (Birmingham), 'In Care of the European Union: problems and possibilities in the development of a European health care regime' [1141-1148]

Barriers to Full Employment (Jonathan Tonge)

Suzanne Blancke (Ruhr), 'Trade Unions and Employment Policy: the lack of consequences of proclaimed goals' [1149-1161]

Jonathan Tonge (Salford), 'Barriers to Full Employment Policies in Britain: problems of ideology, institutions and substitutions' [1162-1176]

Ideology, Hegemony and Political Subjectivity (Kate Nash)

Glyn Daly (Manchester Metropolitan), 'Who Stole Great Britain? Ideology and Nationalism in psychoanalytical theory' [1176-1182]

Jeremy Valentine (Lancaster), 'Subject and Subject-Position in the Concept of Antagonism' [1183-1190]

The Transformation of the State in Postwar Britain
(David Marsh)

Colin Hay (Birmingham), 'Labouring under a Misconception: the discursive construction of the "winter of discontent" ' [1191-1201]

Peter Kerr (Birmingham) & David Marsh (Birmingham), ' "Post-war Consensus" What Consensus? how misreading the past means misunderstanding the present' [1202-1213]

William Morris (Mark Bevir)

Mark Bevir (Newcastle), 'William Morris: romanticism and the rejection of politics' [1214-1224]

Ruth Kinna (Loughborough), 'William Morris: from art to socialism' [1225-1233]

Seventh Session   Thursday, 4.00am

Post-Structuralism and Radical Politics (Moya LLoyd)

Iain Mackenzie (Queen's, Belfast), 'Deleuze & Guattari's Poststructuralist Philosophy' [1234-1241]

James Martin (Queen's, Belfast), 'Organicism and Complexity in Gramsci's Social Theory' [1241-1249]

Do Constitutions Matter? (Richard Bellamy)

Richard Bellamy (Reading) & Dario Castiglione (Exeter), 'Normal Politics, Constitutional Politics and Political Constitutionalism in Bruce Ackerman's *We the People*' [1250-1256]

Cécile Fabre (Worcester College, Oxford), 'Jeremy Waldron on Bills of Rights' [1257-1263]

Identities, Boundaries and Voters (John Curtice)

Joy Squires (Wolverhampton), 'Revisiting "Internal Colonialism": the case of Shetland' [1264-1271]

Labour and Leadership (Tim Bale)

Tim Bale (Sheffield), 'A Cultural Theory of Labour Leadership' [1272-1279]

Richard Heffernan (LSE), 'Labour in the 1980s and 1990s' [1280-1290]

Issues in Contemporary Liberal Theory (Matthew Festenstein & Alan Apperly)

Kevin Magill (Wolverhampton), 'The Idea of a Justification of Punishment' [1291-1299]

David Merrill (Southampton), 'The Inadequacies of Dworkin's Equality of Resources as a First Principle' [1300-1309]

Glen Newey (Sussex), 'Recent Political Philosophy' [1310-1321]

Military Intervention in the Post-Cold War World (Andrew Dorman)

Andrew Dorman (Birmingham), 'Britain and Military Intervention in the 1960s' [1322-1328]

James Lewis (Birmingham), 'The Ethics of Intervention: a Kantian approach' [1329-1342]

New Boundaries, New identities (Fred Nash)

Andrew Beh (LSE), ' "Generations" and "Political Science" ' [1343-1351]

The Limits of Fiction (Susan Stephenson)

Peter Johnson (Southampton), 'Three Theories of Narrative Gaps' [1352-1357]

Liam O'Sullivan (Southampton), 'Identity and Authority in Henry James' [1358-1369]

Initiatives to Cure Unemployment (Jonathan Tonge)

Per Madsen (Copenhagen), 'Labour Market Policy Reform in Denmark: from rules and regulations to worksharing and decentralisation' [1370-1383]

Susan Milner (Bath), 'French Trade Unions and the Work-Sharing Debate' [1384-1397]

Post-Structuralism and Radical Politics (Moya Lloyd)

Moya Lloyd (Queen's, Belfast), 'Performativity as Politics: contesting the boundaries of identity' [1398-1405]

Property and Historical Context (Colin Tyler)

Colin Tyler (York), 'Context, Capitalism and the Natural Right to Private Property in the Thought of Thomas Hill Green' [1406-1414]

Ursula Vogel (Manchester), 'Boundaries of Modern Individualism: theorising property in marriage' [1415-1420]

Eighth Session   Friday, 9.00am

Citizenship in Early Modern Political Thought (Martin van Gelderen)

Geert van den Bossche (Sidney Sussex, Cambridge), 'Citizens and Subjects in the United States of Belgium, 1790' [1421-1428]

Richard Whatmore (Sussex), 'From Constitution Building to the Reformation of Manners: three theories of modern citizenship in France, 1783-1973' [1429-1437]

European Political Parties in a Comparative Perspective (Simon Lightfoot)

Charles Lees (Birmingham), 'The Ambivalent Left' [1438-1451]

Simon Lightfoot (Nottingham Trent), 'The Party of European Socialists: from nascent party to full party' [1452-1459]

Stuart Thomson (Aberdeen), 'The Social Democratic Dilemma' [1460-1468]

Identities, Boundaries and Party Representation (John Curtice)

David Rossiter (Oxford), Ron Johnston (Bristol) & Charles Pattie (Sheffield), 'New Boundaries, Old Inequalities: the evolution and partisan impact of old Celtic preferences in British redistricting' [1469-1482]

Herbert Spencer's Liberalism (Tim Gray)

Tim Gray (Newcastle), 'Spencer's Evolutionary Liberalism and the End of History' [1483-1492]

John Offer (Ulster), 'Spencer's Future of Welfare' [1493-1507]

New Public Management and Local Governance (Jim Chandler)

Neil Barnett (Leeds Metropolitan) & Robert Leach (Leeds Metropolitan), 'The New Managerialism, Community and the Local Government Review' [1508-1515]

Jim Chandler (Sheffield Hallam), 'What Might be New about New Public Management?' [1516-1524]

Howard Elcock (Northumbria), 'Leaders, Policy and Administration: some notes towards cross-national studies of local government leaders' [1525-1538]

The Political Economy of Gendered Exclusion (Carmel Roulston & Linda Watson-Brown)

Linda-Watson Brown (Stirling) & Graham Dawson (Open University), 'Misplaced Loyalty: women and the politics of economic exclusion' [1539-1550]

Reappraising the British State (Gita Subrahmanyam)

Andrew Chadwick (LSE), 'State and Constitution: ideologies of the left and proportional representation in Britain, 1900-1924' [1551-1565]

Public and Private Identities (Barbara McGuiness)

Stephen Buckler (Birmingham), 'Hamlet and Hannah Arendt's Theory of Action' [1566-1576]

Interest Mediation and Party Politics in Southern Europe (Kostas Lavdas)

Kostas Lavdas (West of England), 'Business Associability and Party Political Factionalisation: the case of Greece's SEV' [1577-1585]

José Magone (Hull), 'Neo-Corporatism and Trade-Union-Party Relations in the Southern European Semi-Periphery: a preliminary comparative study of Portugal and Spain' [1586-1595]

Maria Mendrinou (Manchester) & Ilias Nicolacopoulos (Athens), 'Party Identification, the Left-Right Dimension and Sympathy Scores for Interest Groups: the case of Greece' [1596-1601]

Orazio Lanza (Catania), 'Confidindustria and the Party System in Italy' [1602-1611]

Problems in Democracy (Keith Dowding)

Gordon Burt (Open University), 'Downs on "The Inherent Inequality of Political Power in Democratic Societies": towards a formal model' [1612-1619]

Maija Setälä (LSE), 'Agenda-Setting and Referendums' [1620-1630]

Developing Student Skills in a Politics Degree (Neil Stammers & Penny Welch)

Penny Welch (Wolverhampton), 'What Skills do Students Learn on Politics Course? n introduction to the workshop' [1631-1637]

Ninth Session   Friday, 11.00am

Contemporary State Theory (Peter Burnham)

Robert Ware (Keble College, Oxford), 'Set Theory, Self-Consciousness and the State' [1638-1649]

Discourse, Strategy and the Boundaries of the Political (Colin Hay)

Diane Feiler (LSE), 'Anti-Abortion Rhetoric and Cold-War Rhetoric: metaphor and strategy' [1650-1658]

Alan Finlayson (Queen's Belfast), 'Nationalism and Discourses of Sexuality' [1659-1666]

Colin Hay (Birmingham), 'The Tangled Web we Weave: the discourse, strategy and practice of networking' [1667-1674]

Joost van Loon (Cardiff), 'Infinite Re-Presentations: Michael Pêcheux's Theory of Interpellation' [1675-1684]

Education and Political Theory (Geraint Parry)

Tim Kenyon (Liverpool), 'Quasi-Markets and Quasi-Choice: the role of the state as education provider' [1685-1696]

Geraint Parry (Manchester), 'Political Liberalism and Education' [1697-1708]

Hobbes, Feminism and Liberalism (Rita Prokhovnik & Gabriella Slomp)

Raia Prokhovnik (Southampton), 'Hobbes' Leviathan: feminist interpretation and feminist theory' [1709-1721]

Gabriella Slomp (Strathclyde), 'The Impossibility of a Glory-Seeking Liberal' [1722-1732]

Charles Tarleton (Albany, New York), ' "The Word for Deed": Hobbes' two versions of Leviathan' [1733-1749]

Irish Politics (Alan Greer)

Joe Bradley (Glasgow Caledonian), 'Some Aspects of Orangeism in Contemporary Scotland: religion and politics' [1750-1758]

Paul Dixon (Leeds), ' "A Real Stirring of the Nation": the crisis of the British Army over Northern Ireland' [1759-1768]

Chris Gilligan (Salford), 'The New Constitutionalism in Northern Ireland' [1769-1774]

Daragh Minogue (Portsmouth), 'The Divorce Referendum in the Republic of Ireland' [1775-1783]

Policy Transfer (David Marsh)

David Dolowitz (Birmingham), 'Nothing New under the Sun: the development of British unemployment policy during the 1980s' [1784-1794]

Political Philosophy and Deeply Divided Societies
(Shane O'Neill & Richard English)

Shane O'Neill (Queen's, Belfast), 'Political Justice in Northern Ireland: the demands of overlapping consensus' [1795-1802]

Race and Politics (Rose Gann)

Randall Hansen (Nuffield College, Oxford), 'Citizens and Subjects: the British state and United Kingdom immigration policy, 1948-1962' [1803-1816]

Scandinavian Politics (Alastair Thomas)

Alan Bairner (Ulster), 'Sport in the Construction of Swedish National Identity' [1817-1827]

Jouko Huru (Tampere), 'Finland and Europe' [1828-1841]

Stuart Wilks (South Bank), 'New Left Parties in Scandinavia: the emergent politics of post materialism or the last line of defence for the social democratic state?' [1842-1852]

The Boundaries of Gender (Judy Evans)

Samantha Ashenden (Birkbeck), 'At the Boundaries of the Political: feminism beyond identity politics' [1853-1862]

Theories and Theorists of International Relations (Peter Lomas)

Peter Lomas (Dundee), 'Basic Rights and Basic Facts; the crisis of individualism and the end of human rights theory' [1863-1877]

Political Communication (Bob Franklin)

Bob Franklin (Sheffield), 'More Interested in Cantona than the Match: changing news priorities in newspaper reporting of Parliament' [1878-1884]

Papers to be Assigned to a Panel Meeting

Michael Harris (Sheffield), 'Citizenship – New Right and Labour' [1885-1896]

Andrew Jordan (East Anglia), 'From Brussels to Blackpool and Southport: "post-decisional politics" in the European Community' [1897-1906]

Page numbers 1-633: Volume 1;
Page numbers 634-1271: Volume 2;
Page numbers 1272-1906: Volume 3.

List of Convenors

Alan Apperly	1291
Tim Bale	1272
John Barry	357
Brian Baxter	68
Richard Bellamy	1250
Mark Bevir	1214
Jonathan Bradbury	45,273 555
Peter Burnham	1638
Anthony Burns	151,424
Simon Caney	117
Neil Carter	68,357,845
Jim Chandler	1508
Virginia Charles	573
Chris Clapham	980
Stephen Cope	871
Karl Cordell	92,381
Mark Cowling	897
John Curtice	1264,1469
Heather Deegan	598,805
Andrew Denham	969
Andrew Dorman	822,1322
Keith Dowding	1612
Jane Duckett	298
Adam Edwards	623,871
Richard English	1795
Judy Evans	1853
Mark Evans	885,1063
Adam Fagin	771
Helen Fawcett	515
Matthew Festenstein	117,442,634 885,1063,1291
Bob Franklin	1878
John Gaffney	315,589,796
Rose Gann	1803
Tim Gray	1483
Alan Greer	1750
Alison Hann	696,933,1133
Colin Hay	1650
Karen Henderson	298,573,791
Chris Hood	230
David Howarth	944
Detlef Jahn	127,409
Oliver James	230
Sally Jenkinson	634
Peter John	707
Andreas Kintis	731,761, 1000
Kelvin Knight	885,1063
Kostas Lavdas	1577
Steve Leach	188,452
Moya Lloyd	1234,1398
Simon Lightfoot	1438
Andrew Lockyer	210,520
Juliet Lodge	731,761,1000
Peter Lomas	1863
Anna McClure	623
Barbara McGuiness	1566
Bob McKeever	1
David Marsh	1191,1784
Jörg Monar	1027
Kate Nash	1176
Fred Nash	1093,1343
Aletta Norval	944
Shane O'Neill	1795
David Owen	442
Geraint Parry	1685
Raia Prokhovnik	1709
Andrew Reeve	1083
Carmel Roulston	1539
Gurharpal Singh	248,529
Gabriella Slomp	1709
Neil Stammers	1631
Peter Starie	871
Susan Stephenson	1352
Gerry Stoker	957
Gita Subrahmanyam	1551
Alastair Thomas	1817
Jon Tonge	1149,1370
Simon Tormey	634
Colin Tyler	1406
Martin van Gelderen	1421
Stephen Ward	845
Linda Watson-Brown	1539
Penny Welch	1631
Mark Wheeler	488
Stuart White	676,918
Howard Williams	151,424
Dominic Wring	654
John Young	21

Convenors & Paper-Givers xxvii

List of Paper-Givers

Donald Abelson	969
David Archard	520
Chris Arthur	897
Samantha Ashenden	1853
Rob Atkinson	188
Mark Bailey	188
Alan Bairner	1817
Tim Bale	1272
Neil Barnett	1508
Brian Baxter	68
Andrea Baumeister	442
Andrew Beh	1343
Richard Bellamy	1250
John Benyon	1041
Mark Bevir	1214
Andreas Bieler	127
Tor Bjørklund	409
Suzanne Blancke	1149
Rebecca Boden	230
George Boyne	452
Jonathan Bradbury	273
Joseph Bradley	1750
Gary Browning	907
Josie Brooks	707
Steve Buckler	1566
Jim Bulpitt	1093
Gordon Burt	1612
Theresa Callan	177
Christine Carberry	969
Dario Castiglione	1250
Andrew Chadwick	1551
David Chandler	103
Jim Chandler	1516
David Chapman	92
Sarah Charman	871
Chris Clapham	980
Hugh Compston	315
Stephen Cope	188,871
Bob Currie	248
Glyn Daly	1176
Ken Dark	1
Graham Dawson	1549
Russell Deacon	281
Heather Deegan	812
Paul Dixon	1759
David Dolowitz	1784
Andrew Dorman	822,1322
Jane Duckett	298
Howard Elcock	1525
James Ellison	21
Alexander Evans	529
Mark Evans	1063
Cécile Fabre	1257
Adam Fagin	573
Peter Falconer	933
Helen Fawcett	328
Diane Feiler	1650
Alan Finlayson	1659
Joe Foweraker	771
Bob Franklin	1878
Ian Fraser	433
Julie Froud	230
Andrew Geddes	1000
Chris Gilligan	1769
Tim Gray	1483
Dylan Griffiths	45
Rod Hague	45
Randall Hansen	1816
Anthea Harris	13
Michael Harris	1885
Stephen Harrison	1133
Colin Hay	1191,1667
Tim Hayward	79
Richard Heffernan	1280
Jill Hills	488
Helen Hintjens	598
John Hoffman	623
Ian Holliday	719
Chris Hood	232
David Howarth	944
Kate Hudson	796
Kimberley Hutchings	151
Jouko Huru	1828
Detlef Jahn	124,417
Lucy James	830
Oliver James	232
Peter Johnson	1352
Ron Johnston	1469
Andrew Jordan	1897
Tim Kenyon	1685
Peter Kerr	1202
Ruth Kinna	1225
Andreas Kintis	1020
Kelvin Knight	885
Karla Koen	696
Apurba Kundu	537
Todd Landman	771
Chris Lanigan	53
Orazio Lanza	1602
Kostas Lavdas	1577
Robert Leach	1508

Steve Leach	198	Claudio Radaelli	751
Keekok Lee	357	Andrew Reeve	1083
Simon Lee	62	Jeff Richards	114
Charles Lees	1438	Patricia Roberts-Thomson	135
Graham Leicester	555	David Rossiter	1469
James Lewis	1329	Steve Savage	871
Matthew Liao	210	Maija Setälä	1620
Simon Lightfoot	1452	Jeremy Shearmur	634
Moya Lloyd	1398	Brian Slocock	581
Peter Lomas	1863	Gabriella Slomp	1722
Joost van Loon	1675	Elizabeth Sperling	918
Piers Ludlow	33	Joy Squires	1264
Peter Lynch	289	Peter Starie	871
Lesley McCulloch	805	Piers Stephens	369
Don MacIver	676	Gerry Stoker	463
Iain Mackenzie	1234	Martin Stott	475
Per Madsen	1370	John Street	502
Kevin Magill	1291	Peter Stubbs	230
José Magone	731,1586	David Sullivan	433
William Maloney	957	Paul Taggart	589
David Marsh	1202	Charles Tarleton	1733
James Martin	1241	Lucy Taylor	778
Maria Mendrinou	1596	Shinder Thandi	546
David Merrill	1300	Mark Thompson	786
Lee Miles	1007	Stuart Thomson	1460
Susan Milner	1384	Teija Tiilikainen	143
Daragh Minogue	1775	Graham Timmins	350
James Mitchell	564	Jonathan Tonge	1162
Tariq Mohood	688	Simon Tormey	642
Jörg Monar	1027	Colin Tyler	1406
Maggie Mort	1133	Jeremy Valentine	1183
Fred Nash	739,1107	Geest Van den Bossche	1421
Mark Neocleous	159	Ursula Vogel	1415
Glen Newey	1310	Stephen Ward	845
Bruce Newman	654	Bruce Ware	167,1638
Ilias Nicalocopoulos	1596	Mohammad Waseem	257
Gerd Nonneman	381	Linda Watson-Brown	1539
Chris Nottingham	1141	Penny Welch	1631
John Offer	1493	Richard Whatmore	1429
Martyn Oliver	1075	Mark Wheeler	511
Fiona O'Neill	1141	Stuart White	924
Shane O'Neill	1795	Richard Whitman	1013
Liam O'Sullivan	1358	Roger Wicks	838
Anthony Ogus	230	Anders Widfeldt	417
Geraint Parry	1697	Stuart Wilks	1842
Charles Pattie	1469	Paul Wingrove	307
Philip Payton	395	Gerald Wistow	1133
John Peterson	761	Peter Woodward	990
Robert Pinkney	610	Dominic Wring	655
Roxanne Powell	336	Andrew Wyatt	265
Raia Prokhovnik	1709	Stephen Young	858

Karl Popper: Conjectures and Refutations

Jeremy Shearmur
Australian National University

'Popper's Political Theory: A Reassessment

Introduction

The broad lines of Popper's political thought are too well-known to require much explication. Popper is a fallibilist, and stresses that all our knowledge is tentative. He favours an approach to politics in which various ethical demands are impressed upon society, through political initiatives, and are subjected to critical feedback from citizens. He argues for the relief of avoidable suffering and for the remedying of injustice (his agenda including the provision of access to higher education). The promotion of happiness, or of a particular vision of the good life, is the task of the individual or of voluntary arrangements.[1]

Popper was egalitarian in his sentiments, and favoured the idea that a basic income should be provided to all, funded through income tax. However, as he got older he had doubts as to whether equality was compatible with individual liberty, to which he had a still greater attachment. It would be a mistake to place him, politically, on the right, although he certainly did think that Western societies were the best that had been achieved. For there is no reason to suppose that Popper ever went back on the harsh criticisms of conservatives, and of the proponents of laissez faire, which are to be found in his *Open Society*. Government, for Popper, should have the task of protecting its citizens, and this includes protection from economic exploitation.

In this paper, I do not wish simply to repeat Popper's ideas. I also do not have space to discuss how his work may raise problems for some of the intellectual fashions of our day. Instead, I will explore some problems and difficulties about his views. I will raise three points. The first two pertain to the structure of the social world and its relation to Popper's approach to politics; the third, to his conception of our duties to others.

Giving meaning to the meaningless?

Popper has argued that there is no intrinsic ethical meaning to history but that it is possible for us to give history a meaning, in the sense of imposing upon society an ethical significance, through political initiatives. I would agree that there is no intrinsic meaning to history in the sense of a Hegelian or Marxian teleology. But his own views are problematic because there are two senses in which the stuff with which political initiatives are concerned has an order of its own, the relationship between which and Popper's favoured initiatives is problematic.

---

[1] For references and argument relating to the claims made about Popper in this paper see, generally, my *Popper and Politics*, Routledge, forthcoming.

First, the social and economic world has a structure. This, to be sure, is a product of human action; but it nonetheless exists, and, at any point, it limits what it is possible for us to do. Consider Adam Smith's discussion of the disadvantages of commercial society. Smith is well-known for his discussion of the advantages of an economic system based on the division of labour. But he also discussed the way in which this brings with it disadvantages, which cannot be eliminated – they could, at best, be palliated – if one had such a form of social organization. The social sciences, at their best, inform us about such relationships, and thus about limits upon what we can achieve. Popper would not quarrel with this. Indeed, he referred to examples of such knowledge as things which his piecemeal social engineer would have to bear in mind. The problem for Popper's politics is that such knowledge is not, in general, going to be understandable by all members of a society. Claims about such knowledge are of course fallible. But that there are such limitations upon what we can do, and what they are, is not, on the face of it, something that can easily be made accessible to all citizens.

One might see this as the revenge of Plato upon Popper. For social arrangements which are in the best interests of all members of a society may have ineliminable defects, the rationale for tolerating which it may not be possible for the social theorist to make clear to them. This, in its turn, poses obvious enough problems about Popper's ideas concerning democracy and critical feedback.

My second point concerns meaningful human action. What Popper's social engineer is working upon is in large measure us, our actions and their various consequences. We do desperately need to improve our institutions, and to find ways in which we can remedy misery, and so on. But we face a major problem concerning how our wish to do such things relates to the fact that what we are dealing with are the products of the actions of many different people, all of whom are typically doing what they are doing for what seem to them the best of reasons. If we treat people as ends in themselves, and respect their moral judgement, we cannot also simply treat them as instruments in the achievement of our ends.

But what, in the light of this, are we to make of piecemeal social engineering?

Street-level political philosophy and filter mechanisms

In my view, rational choice theory is right about one thing, and wrong about two. It is right in that it draws our attention to the significance of the disaggregation of much of the activity upon which the kind of political agenda with which Popper was concerned depends. As Olson argued, from the simple fact that something is in the interest of a group we cannot conclude that each member has the motivation to bring it about. However, rational choice theory seems to me wrong in that it works with a model of rational agency taken over from economic theory; one in which we understand social phenomena as the products of the actions of individuals with perfect knowledge, taken on the basis of their preferences.

There are two problems with all of this.[2] First, it neglects the way in which human agents are limited in their knowledge, and in which they typically act in specific institutional situations on the basis of various routines and procedures. I am not claiming that people share norms, or trying to breathe life back into Parsonian social theory. My point, rather, is usefully illustrated by what Melvyn Lipsky has said about so-called 'street-level bureaucrats'. Lipsky discussed the role of those people within bureaucracies who interact with members of the public. Examples might include police on the beat, those who actually deal with people making claims for social security, and so on. Lipsky, in writing about his work, says: 'I argue that the decisions of street-level bureaucrats, the routines they establish, and the devices they invent to cope with uncertainties and work pressures, effectively become the public policies they carry out'.[3] His view seems to me very much to the point, but to apply not just to street-level bureaucrats, but to us all and, more generally, to the problematic of piecemeal social engineering. We have to make out in, and to find ways of coping with, the variety of social institutions and situations in which we find ourselves, and which make up our lives. Rational choice theorists are correct enough in their stress upon incentives. But the incentives that we can respond to, and what we can make of them, depends on our perception of these things; and this, in turn, depends upon our traditions, habits, and ways of coping with the world, and upon the forms of accountability to which we are subject. At the same time, our preferences and judgements obviously range not just over our own particular actions and their immediate consequences, but also over the large-scale consequences of the actions of ourselves and of others, including those issues which have become the agenda of public policy.

Second, it is important that we do not take too subjectivist a view of human action. To be sure, each of us acts upon our understanding of the world and of the situations in which we are acting. But our actions are also subject to constraints imposed upon us by the thing-like characteristics of the social world. These, of course, are the products of previous human actions. But given that these prior actions have taken place, their products may constrain us in much the same way as do objects in the physical world. One can no more easily obtain a loan at a rate significantly less than the going rate of interest, than one can put one's hand through a solid table. This, in its turn, means that in respect of certain issues, the details of people's subjective motivations become unimportant. Certain key features of the social world act as filter mechanisms, such that, if people are to be successful in what they are doing, they have no option but to comply with them, and we need not bother too much about the fine detail of what leads them to act in this way.

For our present purposes, what matters about all this is as follows. The objects which will concern Popper's social engineer will typically be emer-

---

[2] For some others, see my 'Schutz, Machlup and Rational Economic Man', *Review of Political Economy*, 5, 1993; 'Subjectivism, Explanation and the Austrian Tradition', in S.Boehm & B.Caldwell (eds), *Austrian Economics: Tensions and New Directions*, Kluwer, 1993.

[3] M.Lipsky, *Street-Level Bureaucracy*, Russell Sage, 1980; C.Ham & M.Hill, *The Policy Process in the Modern Capitalist State*, Wheatsheaf, 1984.

gent properties of the products – often of the unintended consequences – of meaningful human action. But these, in turn, must be understood as the products of actions like those of street-level bureaucrats, or of the operation of filter mechanisms, or of their interactions. It is not enough for us to think that some such product is desirable; we need, rather, to show how it can be brought about as a consequence either of action taken in the light of existing routines, ways of coping with tasks in various social institutions, and so on, or as the product of modifications to such routines, institutions, etc, as can feasibly be undertaken. Consider, say, some claim as to the rights that some class of persons is supposed to enjoy. That they can have such things will depend upon correlative behaviour on the part of other people. But there is no point in saying that people ought to have the rights or entitlements in question, unless others can be expected to undertake the correlative behaviour. And this means, that this behaviour can feasibly become part of their ways of undertaking the various tasks that they have to undertake on a day-to-day basis, or a product of their interaction with filter mechanisms. Rights have to be composed out of the disaggregated behaviour, or transformations of the disaggregated behaviour, of others. And unless this can be done, it matters not one iota how much general social agreement there might be that people should have the rights in question.

All this leads to some difficult problems, in that to demand that government should be able to act so as to produce such things, would look as if it is to be given not just powers to redesign institutions, but also to redesign us – to re-socialize us, to try to create new traditions and habits, and so on. And given that when we are talking about government, we are here talking about fallible human beings who are as much subject to the temptations of power as is anyone else, it might mean that we are calling for something which we would be uneasy about putting in anyone's hands.

All this, it seems to me, suggests that the social engineer faces certain difficulties which are not explicit in Popper's work.

Some problems about morality

In the previous section, I raised problems about the feasibility of certain of the activities of the social engineer. I wish, now, to consider the morality of those activities. My discussion will be brief. Popper's agenda for politics works, very much, at the public level: he is concerned with the relief of suffering, the remedying of injustice, and so on, by way of governmental initiatives. I wish to raise two problems.

The first follows directly from my discussion in the previous section. It is that, once we see what the meeting of such a goal would amount to in terms of the actions that people would have to take in order to bring it about, we may discover that something which at an aggregate level had looked morally attractive, is not, in fact, so at all. For it might involve people's having to take actions which, in their particular situations, are morally unreasonable. My concern, here, is not to raise issues of virtue ethics against considerations of morality. Rather, it is to insist, against both the utilitarian and the theorist of justice, that the most fundamental moral issue relates to the reasonableness or otherwise of what is being asked of someone, give the specifics of the situation that they are in, and who they – and the other people concerned – are. There is a perfectly good sense in which we can talk about whether or not an action is reasonable; and there is, for example, in the kind of approach to the understanding of morality offered by Adam Smith, and subsequently within 'dialogue-based' approaches to the understanding of the objectivity of ethics, an approach to the understanding of ethics to hand, which suggests how such judgements need not be arbitrary. My point here can be put very simply: just as, from a factual point of view, we must show how what we want to achieve can be composed on the basis of actions which it is feasible for people to take, so we must also show how it can be built up from actions which it is morally reasonable for them to take, given who they are, and the situations within which they are acting.

Second, I think that there is a problem about Popper's approach to political issues, concerning the relation between public and personal obligation. We expect, of a government, impartiality in respect of how it treats its citizens; for example, that it should treat its citizens with formal equality, or that it addresses those needs which are greatest, wherever they may be found. However, this may be contrasted with what we would expect of an individual, whose obligation is to discharge particular moral claims. The moral life of each of us involves special obligations towards those for whom we are responsible and who are dependent upon us. What is involved is in no way limited to the relief of suffering and the meeting of basic needs. We even have, rather, an obligation to do what we can to delight those who are close to us, provided that they can escape, if they do not find our efforts to their taste; to do what we can to succour and promote those things which seem to us valuable; and to make the best that we can of ourselves.

Now, public and personal obligations are in competition with one another, at least with regard to how they call upon our resources. For what the government takes from me to discharge 'public' obligations is no longer available to me to discharge personal ones. Popper puts forward an agenda for public action which combines concerns about justice and the relief of suffering, but also acknowledges personal responsibilities which can include trying to promote the well-being of ones friends. But he does not tell us about the relations between them. If someone is going to uphold Popper's views, they need to explain how claims upon our resources and upon our persons are to be divided between these two spheres. For, clearly, a concern for the relief of avoidable suffering, in a world of the kind within which we currently live, might lay claim to all of our resources, leaving nothing beyond the barest minimum for the discharge of personal obligations – which would, in my view, make a nonsense of our day-to-day lives.

I would like here also to offer a more radical challenge to Popper's view, although clearly its speculative character limits its critical force. For I would wish to suggest that, with certain exceptions which I will explain, public obligations have to be constructed out of personal ones. Clearly, the suffering, and so on, of others with whom we do not have any form of personal relationship does have some call upon each of us. But this, in my view, should be a matter for our personal judgement, and its call upon us has to be weighed against our more personal moral priorities.[4]

What we usually take to be a public obligation looks to me like a generalization of what are, in fact, obligations relating to roles in specific institutions; for example, of the judge and of the bureaucrat, who are given precisely the task of judging cases impartially on their merits. But these are institutions which people have brought into being because they value such services. As a result, such obligations are derivative from personal obligation, rather than having a priority over it, though those who staff such institutions have, of course, a personal obligation to behave in an impartial manner.

Indeed, in my view, the only obligations that we have of a genuinely public character, are two. The first is the obligation to preserve and to foster a public sphere – that sphere within which we may reflect together upon, and evaluate, other, more particular, moral claims. This, it seems to me, has in consequence a certain priority over them. The second concerns our obligation to make choices about large-scale social institutions which will, themselves, serve to form the roles that we hold, and form the situations within which more particular choices will then be open to us. That we need to make such choices points, again, to the importance of a public forum within which we can deliberate about them. However, what seems to me of importance about such a forum is that any pertinent criticism can be voiced, rather than that everyone can participate, personally, in it.[5]

What is to be done?

While I have offered a criticism of Popper, I have also opened up some problems to which I have not yet offered a solution. For while I have stressed the priority of the personal, and the problems of social engineering, I have not argued that the task of the social engineer is unimportant, and I have thus not explained how these issues are to be inter-related. I certainly would not wish to repudiate the concerns of the social engineer, just because our personal concerns range not just over our immediate actions, but also over the longer-term consequences of our actions. We may have various such concerns – from that of the individual to lose weight, to that of a family to live in a sociable neighbourhood, to our wish to live in societies in which people can make the best of themselves and be of service to others and in which people are free from poverty and, as far as possible, from avoidable suffering.

---

[4] Such judgements are, in my view, not arbitrary, for, as I have mentioned, they are open to the critical scrutiny of others, on the basis of whether or not they are reasonable in the situation in which we are making them. In addition, we may also have collective obligations to make large-scale changes in our institutions which will, in turn, affect the situations within which we subsequently act.

[5] For some argument, see my 'Liberalism Today', delivered at the APSA conference, Chicago, 1995.

At the same time, different people may have different judgements with regard to such things. Some may value community in some strong sense, while others value individual freedom; some may wish for the public cultivation of religious values, while others may wish to get away from any such thing, and so on. In addition, the realization of specific values, and of specific kinds of learning mechanisms, may call for socialization into specific kinds of behaviour, habits and traditions. There are also different kinds of choices to be made between different ways of life and different forms of social organization, each of which will bring with it their different mixtures not only of values and virtues which can be realized within them, but of worthy goals which can't. Finally, there is the problem of the lack of transparency, to all but the specialist, of what may be required to realize some social order that we may favour.

In my view, just because of the character of the disciplines involved, and the ways in which they may impact on our very characters and identities, and just because of the differences in the views that people might legitimately have about what is desirable, what is called for, here, is individual choice rather than the imposition, upon the individual, of the results of collective decision-making. But individual choice may include membership of a form of organization the broad characteristics of which people favour, and submission to its codes of conduct, the detailed rationale for which they do not understand. Such ideas might be realized by way of a combination of proprietorial communities within a minimal state, and critical accountability in a public forum. The details of all this, and arguments for it, I must spare you on the present occasion.[6]

I would like to conclude by raising one final issue which I believe to be important. Popper favours the protection of the vulnerable, including against economic exploitation. Subject to what I have said above, this seems to me an attractive ideal. But we are owed an account of how a society is supposed to function – of how people are to interact, to desirable social outcomes – if vulnerabilities are to be protected, as Popper would wish. I make this point not from the perspective of conservatism, but from that of classical liberalism. For one element of classical liberalism for which it has repeatedly been criticized for its inhumanity, relates to the relative harshness of the coordinative mechanisms and disciplines that it involves. From its perspective, people are free; but it explicitly makes provision for how they are, nonetheless, to be led to cooperate with other people, and to meet their needs, by – to put things at their most blunt – telling them that, if they are able-bodied, they will not eat unless they do so. This, to be sure, is not a lovely theory; but it does suggest how we may handle one key issue: it serves to direct people who enjoy a fair measure of autonomy and who cannot be relied upon to share judgements or attitudes or to like one another, into productive cooperation. A key problem for the proponents of modern or welfare liberalism – and, I believe, for Popper – is how the kind of society that they favour is supposed to function, unless, in the background, people are being constrained, prodded or indoctrinated into

---

[6] But compare my *Popper and Politics*, Routledge, forthcoming, and my *Hayek and After*, Routledge, forthcoming.

forms of compliance by means which liberalism cannot, as it were, 'officially' recognize.

Indeed, one major theme of this short paper is that those who favour such ideas must, at the same time, offer an account of how a society that realizes them is also supposed to function. This, in turn, means that the welfare liberal must also be a systematic social theorist. And this, it seems to me, is perhaps the greatest challenge that today faces those who find Popper's political philosophy attractive.

Liberalism

Simon Tormey
University of Nottingham

'The Problem with "Problems":
Popper, Negative Utility and the Open Society'

Abstract

> Popper's political philosophy can be summarised as an attempt to integrate a scientific approach to politics with a Kantian-inspired defence of the individual against the encroachments of the state. The claim of this paper is, firstly, that Popper fails to establish that the approach he recommends is a suitable one for the resolution of political issues, and secondly, that, far from complementing his concern for the individual, Popper's approach, if implemented, is likely to lead to injustice and a diminution of individual autonomy. In short, Popper's desire to put politics on a rational footing is likely to harm rather than safeguard liberty.

Towards a Rational Society? Popper's Negative Utilitarianism[1]

Popper, it is clear, does not like radical blueprints for social change which involve far-reaching or 'utopian' social engineering. Utopias are by definition unattainable and thus the attempt to perfect society is doomed to failure. Although Popper's critique is based primarily on *a priori* grounds in the sense that he feels it is a logical impossibility to plan holistically, it is clear that an important part of his objection to utopianism is the assumption clearly contained in the work of utopian thinkers that there is, ultimately, one model of human happiness and thus one model of the ideal society. Popper in his 'Kantian' mode is clearly hostile to this idea of uniformity, to the notion that we are all in this important sense the same. He wants to say that happiness is a subjective state of affairs; and hence that what makes one person happy might produce indifference or even unhappiness in another. It is for this reason that it is enormously difficult to, as it were, manufacture happiness, contentment, or fulfilment for all and it is the difficulty of doing so which makes such an ambition so fraught with danger. As Popper argues, 'of all the political ideals, that of making people happy is perhaps the most dangerous one ... the attempt to produce heaven on earth invariably produces hell. It leads to intolerance'.[2] The state is a powerful weapon; but like all weapons it can be used for good or ill. If allowed to

---

[1] The clearest formulation of Popper's negative utilitarianism is in chapter 9 of K.R.Popper, *The Open Society and its Enemies*, 2 volumes, fifth edition (revised), Routledge, 1984, hereafter *OSE I/IIrm* .

[2] *OSE* II, pp.237.

fall into the hands of those like Plato or Marx, those in other words with 'romantic' blueprints for collective happiness, it will surely be used as a weapon of despotism. As Popper reminds us, it is not so much the nature of the institutions of state which counts so much as who is 'manning' them, who is in charge of them. Leaving them manned by those thinking only of our happiness will lead to the creation of a society of happy slaves, not free men and women.

Politics must not therefore be about ultimate states of affairs, then, but about what needs to be done in the here and now. It must be concerned with the tangible problems and difficulties which we see around us. As Popper puts it, [p]ain, suffering, injustice and their prevention, these are the eternal problems of public morals, the 'agenda' of public 'policy'.[3] Problems, no matter how knotty, emit of solutions. Problems are the very stuff of human life, for we are in a sense problem-solving creatures, not only in our own lives, but in all worthwhile fields of human endeavour including politics. What is crucial is that a scientifically rigorous method be applied to the resolution of problems. Popper's complaint about political practice is that it lacks rigour or scientificity. Politics in societies such as our own is an arena of rhetoric, of ideology, of 'passion' and 'violence'.[4] Politics is like science before the Enlightenment: full of mystification, half-baked ideas, superstition and demagoguery. Politics lacks a standard against which to measure irrational from rational beliefs, good practices from bad, hocus-pocus from detached neutrality. Politics must therefore be placed on a new footing if it is to serve the true interests of society. It must be guided by maxims of reason rather than prejudice, and above all it must adopt a method which guarantees results and which gives a focus to the efforts of policy-makers. Politics must be divorced from ideology.

In place of the haphazard practices of current democratic practice Popper proposes introducing the inductive methods of the sciences into political practice. Politicians, or rather 'piecemeal engineers' as Popper would like to call them, should as in 'true' science start not with theories purporting to explain everything, but with particular problems, in this case 'evils' thrown up by society. Once a clear view of the problem is obtained, different solutions based on different hypotheses about the cause of the difficulty should be, like scientific hypotheses, submitted and tested in the open. In other words, it should never be assumed that a hypothesis does not need testing before it is put into action, because given the fallibility of knowledge how will we know in advance of trying it out that it will work? At the same time these experiments should be 'piecemeal' rather than holistic and carried out on a small scale first of all so as to limit any 'damage' caused by failed 'experiments'.[5] It is this unwillingness to take anything on face value which is of course the essence of the open society. Once it is clear which of the competing hypotheses seems to offer the best results it should be put into practice until further problems throw its findings into doubt. Thus we must, as in science, never assume that our results are final, that they represent

---
[3] *OSE* II, p.237. See also K.Popper, *Conjectures and Refutations*, fifth edition, Routledge, 1991, pp.345-6.
[4] *OSE* I, p.159.
[5] *OSE* II, pp.222-3.

the Truth. We should never become so attached to our findings that we are unable to cast them aside when better hypotheses and theories present themselves. This is the essential modesty of 'piecemeal social engineering' and the reason why it is less 'risky' and less 'controversial' than more ambitious forms of political practice.[6] It is an approach which by contrast to the engineering of the utopian variety is cautious, rigorous, and neutral. It is government by 'repeated experiments and continuous readjustments'.[7]

Problems, Problems ...

According to Popper what makes his account of politics as science rational is that it is in this fashion concerned exclusively with problems, with human suffering and evil. There is in his view something undeniable about the existence of problems. Problems are tangible; they are 'out there', and everybody can see them. Being happy, on the other hand, is something personal to me rather than being a property of the world or society. Experience has taught us that happiness is not produced by any one thing and thus there is no prospect for unlocking the key to happiness. Happiness is as often as not a fleeting or transitory moment and hence is intangible. Social problems on the other hand are not like this. Turning our backs on them will not get rid of problems but simply delay the day when a decision as to what to do with them needs to be made. For this reason it is in Popper's view much easier to mobilise support for the alleviation of suffering, of what is manifestly wrong, than it is to mobilise people in support of the 'good'.[8] People are, he thinks, more willing to come to the aid of someone in pain than they are to attempt to make him or her 'happy'.[9]

It seems clear from what Popper is saying that he is operating with a mechanistic account of the structure of society. Popper feels comfortable not only with deploying a vocabulary ('engineering', 'scientific politics', etc) which has, as he almost gleefully admits, 'objectionable associations', but with making direct analogies between the work of the piecemeal engineer and that of the mechanical engineer.[10] As we noted earlier, it is precisely his mechanistic view of society which reduces institutions and structures to mere instruments for the realisation of ends which has made conservative commentators hostile to Popper. Society, Popper seems to be claiming, is like a piece of machinery in the sense that at least some of the problems which develop with it are similar in their effect to problems which can develop in machines. It is in this sense that Popper urges us to develop a

---

[6] *OSE* I, p.159.

[7] *OSE* I, p.163.

[8] *OSE* I, p.158.

[9] Presumably what Popper is getting at is that people feel a greater sense of obligation or duty to those in need than to those who are not immediately troubled by anything other than unhappiness. Space precludes an examination of this issue, but I think Popper would need to tell us more about who is to benefit from our actions than he does. I don't think it is too far fetched to imagine a person saying that he or she would rather attempt to make members of hi or her own family happy than to come to the aid of a person unknown to him or her.

[10] See, for example, *OSE* I, pp.163ff; K.Popper, *The Poverty of Historicism*, Routledge, Ark edition, 1986, pp.64-5.

'social technology' to mirror scientific technology. He wants his piecemeal engineers to approach their task in much the same fashion that a mechanical engineer keeps an engine in good condition, 'ticking over' as it were.[11] Yet from our point of view there are serious objections to this analogy, ones which, if allowed to stand, would seriously question Popper's attachment to an ethic of individual choice and responsibility.

The main difficulty with the mechanistic conception of society is that we lack an immediately obvious model of how society should perform. When a machine develops a problem it affects its performance. We can tell that, for example, a car has a problem when fumes or loud grinding noises are emitted by the engine, when it refuses to respond to the brakes or accelerator or, finally, when it comes suddenly to a holt. We have a model, in other words, of what a 'healthy' car is like and we know when the car is malfunctioning by reference to it. If something goes wrong with the car we have a model to which we can refer in order to verify that what we are doing is in fact 'rational' in these terms. But what is the equivalent model of the 'healthy' or 'rational' society which we could use to locate the source of the problems and difficulties society throws up? Some of Popper's remarks might well lead us to the conclusion that he does possess such a model. He notes, for example, how important full employment is to a healthy society and it is clear that he feels it symptomatic of such a society that there be evidence of a greater equalization of incomes. It would also be entirely characteristic of Popper to add to that list the alleviation of obvious suffering of the sort associated with homelessness, ill-health and poverty (hence Magee's understandable insistence on claiming Popper for the social democratic tradition). We might expect that such a society would be one where there was little protest or discontent. Assuming for the moment that Popper is arguing that we have a model of a rational society available to us what we then have every right to ask is how in essence his approach differs from that of thinkers such as Marx and Plato who are castigated by Popper for putting forward just such 'finished' models of the good, happy or just society. We could also ask why, if we know what will produce the rational society, we must continue repairing our own flawed society in this rather pedantic 'piecemeal' fashion. Why not do all the 'repairs' at once (as of course the mechanical engineer or garage mechanic might do) and be done with the whole business of politics – at least until the next problem arises?

I think the only way Popper can get out of this conundrum whilst keeping the basic argument intact (assuming for the moment that this is his argument) is for him to claim that there is a world of difference between offering a model of a society without problems – or, let us say, fundamental problems – and offering a model in which people are supposed to be happy, fulfilled or content. The claim here is, as just mentioned, that suffering and pain are tangible, real 'things' which emit of solutions whereas the pursuit of happiness is far more elusive. But this is not a particularly convincing argument, nor one which puts as much space between Popper and his quarry as he might think. After all, is it not at least part of Marx's argument – and, in his own fashion, Plato's – that the advantage to humanity of a com-

---

[11] *OSE* II, p.222.

munist society is that it would be one in which the fundamental causes of suffering and pain have been eliminated or transcended? If Popper is willing to admit (as he seems to be) that we can identify certain conditions as causing unhappiness and suffering, for example, unemployment, poverty, etc., then it is difficult see why we would have to reject the arguments of those such as Marx who argue that the validity of their political programme or 'blueprint' is derived from an analysis of what makes men unhappy, what creates suffering and social 'evil'. In other words, we might want to say that the moral argument for communism is at least partly based on similar premises to Popper's argument for negative utility, which is that society has a duty to relieve pain and suffering. That Marx expected the abolition of wage labour, alienation and exploitation to lead to a more contented form of life is hardly in this sense a fantastic or even an unreasonable one taken on its own terms, for what, after all, is the *point* of relieving misery, suffering if not to make men happy or at least less unhappy than they currently are? Is not, in other words, the relief of pain and suffering merely the flip-side of the provision of happiness and contentment?

I think it unlikely that Popper really wants to say that it is possible to erect an ideal model of society against which to measure the rationality of our own arrangements and of course the efforts of piecemeal engineers to improve matters. It would, as is implied above, make a nonsense of his critique of holistic planning and indeed of his critique of radicalism more generally, for once we admit that it is possible to arrive at a model of the Good Life then the argument for incremental or piecemeal change is weakened. Although from his terminology we might expect Popper to defend a mechanistic conception of society, such an approach is inconsistent with certain other ideas he has about the character and limits of social engineering, and with the (quasi-) Kantian notions about the autonomy of the individual he holds as well. It seems more important for Popper to defend his argument about the incommensurability of concepts such as 'happiness' than to be fully consistent with the logic of his argument about the nature of social problems; and it certainly fits better with his more general scepticism about holism as an approach to reform. After all, if it *were* accepted that societies were actually like machines then this would open the door wide open to those who argue that a radically malfunctioning society with a proliferation of social problems is one that is crying out for radical reform. Popper of course wants to keep this door firmly shut.

Helping Popper escape difficulties in such fashion leads, however, to further problems in attempting to decide what constitutes a problem pressing enough to merit the attention of the state. As we saw earlier, I know when I have a problem with my car (or whatever) when it behaves in an abnormal way or, indeed, it refuses to move at all. There are, in other words, signs that tell us when a problem has appeared or is about to appear. Our view of what constitutes a problem is thus normally derived from our knowledge or memory of how a particular machine or object should operate. The car should start when I turn over the starter motor; the computer should run when I press the right button; the telephone should sound when I dial this number, and so on. Failure of the machine to operate in the way we expect it to leads us to think that there may be a problem with it, so if a machine appears to be behaving normally then there is little *prima facie* ground for suspecting that there may be something wrong. We start then with an idea of what the machine should be like, how it should be behaving and work from that model to problems as and when they occur. The difficulty with Popper's approach is that if we deny it is possible to describe the final form of society because of the objection that we all have different ideas about what this ideal society might be like, it surely makes it equally difficult to decide what constitutes a problem. How will we know whether to consider something a (social) 'problem' if we do not have before us a model of what a society *without* problems would be like?

Popper's claim is that problems, 'suffering', 'evil' or 'pain' are tangible, real and, in a sense, obvious, and with good reason. To assert that someone lying in a cardboard box under Waterloo Bridge does not represent a 'problem' for society seems to fly in the face of common nostrums about the nature of the obligations we owe to each other. The same or similar might be said about a whole range of other pressing matters from unemployment and poverty to inadequate transportation, from the destruction of the environment to low levels of educational attainment. Popper seems at one level quite justified in asserting that problems have a tangibility or objectivity which is lacking in concepts such as happiness, fulfilment or contentment. There are, nevertheless, good reasons for us to think that the tangibility of problems as opposed to concepts is more illusory than real. To take the example just mentioned, it might be claimed that whether one views homelessness as a problem or not depends on one's view of what it is that the individual minimally needs in order to live any kind of civilised existence. I can say that someone needs a roof over his or head because without it, he or she lacks somewhere permanent to put his or her possessions, to wash, eat or be a part of the community. Homelessness, I want to claim, is something pressing and immediate; it excludes and isolates individuals in a manner detrimental not only to themselves but also to society. But what is the defence against the view that, after all, this is just my opinion? What do we say to the objection that my view of homelessness has been informed by my attachment to prior notions about what constitutes 'need', 'civilised existence', 'exclusion' and so on, that these are value judgements derived from my own perception of what, ultimately, makes people 'happy'? If Popper really is a serious moral pluralist in the sense that he does not want to privilege any particular notion of the Good Life over another, then how is it possible unproblemmatically to locate problems in the first place?

Some critics have indeed seen this problem of incommensurability as one threatening the basis of his political philosophy.[12] Popper on this view is a moral relativist who simply contradicts himself when he says on the one hand that we must not chase the promise of happiness, while on the other urging us down the road of what will clearly approximate a welfarist social democratic state. There seem, however, to be good grounds for rejecting this

---

[12] I take this to be the thrust of, for example, Terence Burke's critique of Popper. See T.E.Burke, *The Philosophy of Popper*, Manchester University Press, 1983, especially chapter 5, 'Freedom and Values'.

critique, not least because Popper explicitly denies that he a moral relativist. To begin with, Popper rejects the view that all moral positions are of equal value and thus that moral judgements cannot be weighed against each other regarding such a position as based on 'faulty reasoning'.[13] He claims that in societies such as our own it is possible to talk about the existence of some sort of consensus regarding what is acceptable and unacceptable, good and bad behaviour, just and unjust states of affairs. It is this consensus, this shared moral understanding, which allows us to expect that people will react to a given situation – such as a person suffering – in the same way. People living in cardboard boxes constitute a problem not only for me but for society, because in Popper's view most people in our society regard homelessness as a moral evil. The tangibility of suffering is thus given in this shared moral horizon. Part of what it means to be a member of society is to share 'moral standards' with others in that society, to look upon people's behaviour in a similar light. Morality is thus conventional and part of our becoming a social subject is learning what these moral standards or 'higher values' are.[14] Popper argues that in a civilised society these moral standards form the bedrock of government action and ensure that the state's actions are regarded as legitimate by the population. There are of course limits to the degree to which this consensus is able to guide the actions of the state, the implication being that whilst it may be possible to mobilise opinion for particular objectives such as helping the unemployed it would much more difficult to get people to agree on an entirely new set of social arrangements. Our attachment to 'higher values' encourage us to act in a piecemeal fashion to help the disadvantaged, but evidently not to act so radically that we risk having to redesign current institutions and practices.

We can leave to one side the question of whether it is possible to identify 'moral standards' of the sort Popper discusses. This is of course firmly trampled ground in the literature of moral philosophy and is in any case only tangential to our concerns. What does need clarification is how, assuming that it is possible to talk about the existence of such standards, this helps Popper's case for a scientific, but non-utilitarian politics. Let us go back to the problem we were discussing above, namely homelessness. It is, as we saw, consistent with Popper's argument to say that few individuals in our society could be failed to be disturbed by homelessness or to view it as anything other than a form of unnecessary suffering. However, it is Popper's next move which is difficult, for what he seems to be arguing is that the identification of suffering (or social problems more broadly) goes hand in hand with the desire to want to do something about that suffering.[15] In other words, he thinks that because we share certain moral standards that we will feel the same degree of commitment to resolving situations that

---

[13] *OSE* II, p.381.

[14] Given the potential importance of the idea of 'higher values' to his political philosophy Popper devotes worryingly little time to developing it. The only substantial discussion of what he means is in the addendum to later editions of *OSE* II. See especially pp.381ff. On this issue see especially Jeremy Shearmur, 'Epistemological Limits of the State: Reflections on Popper's Open Society', *Political Studies*, 38, 1990, pp.116-25.

[15] My hesitation at this point is only a reflection of the undeveloped nature of this area of Popper's work. It is difficult, I think, to know with any great certainty what exactly it is that Popper wants to claim here.

we agree are bad, wrong or 'evil'. Yet, this assumption seems to fly in the face of political realities. Even if for the sake of argument we assume that the vast majority believe that homelessness is bad or wrong surely this should not be taken as indicative that they all accord the provision of facilities for the homeless the same priority. Of course some might be expected to feel very strongly about the issue and demand that it be dealt with as a matter of urgency; some others will feel that it is important, but not as important as, say, providing for the NHS, for schooling or old age pensions; and I think we have to assume that there may well be others who, though agreeing that homelessness is a bad thing, would not want to spend any great sum of money on the problem at all, preferring instead to keep taxation to a minimum. In short, it seems quite unwarranted to assume that the identification of problems is tantamount to the desire to want to resolve them.

All of which leaves Popper's assumption that the equation of politics with problem-solving puts politics on a new, more rational footing looking rather less radical than he thought it might. The identification of problems such as the suffering of particular groups and individuals is surely not a substitute for political debate as Popper seems to think, but rather the precursor to it. The identification of problems is not in this sense the end of the political process but rather the beginning, for, as I think is clear, it is one thing for us to agree that x is a problem, but quite another to agree on what, if anything, ought to be done about it. As Popper suggests, problems can emit of solutions, but the acceptability or otherwise of any given solution is the very stuff of political debate. Given that for Popper the essence of the Open Society is in a sense debate, it is more surprising to find a distinct lack of detail about the institutionalisation of these deliberations, about where this discussion is to take place and with whom. In view of his wariness about the 'violence' and 'passion' of debate in our tightly administered society I think we should wonder how extensive and participatory this 'public' discussion is likely to prove.

Negative Utility and the Individual

As I think should be clear from the comments above, it is at least part of Popper's claim that the advantages of negative utility as an approach to setting out the objectives for state action lie in the fact that following the maxim 'minimize suffering' is unlikely to result in transgressions against the rights or, more loosely, autonomy of the individual. Pursuing happiness is fraught with difficulty in Popper's view, because of the impossibility of legislating accurately for such an intangible objective (hence his objection to the traditional utilitarian approach). This is not the case with 'piecemeal social engineering' for two reasons. Firstly, state action is limited to tackling only those objectives which emit of a solution and, secondly, in being piecemeal rather than holistic, state action at all times proceeds with 'caution' and 'modesty' thereby limiting the impact of any faulty policies. Even with these caveats in mind, I think Popper's prescription for rational government is, however, just as likely to trample over the autonomy of the individual and to result in considerable injustice as would the implementation of more traditional forms of utilitarian practice.

We need, firstly, to imagine a situation in which any difficulties with establishing agreement about what constitutes an object for state action can be overcome, and hence where we have a clearly identified problem in front of us together with the political will to solve it. What next? Popper, as already noted, recommends that we 'test' in the manner of scientific theories the various hypotheses which interested parties proffer as proposed solutions to the problem. Exactly which parties or groups are thought to be fit or qualified enough to offer suggestions is not made clear by Popper – a worryingly relaxed stance for someone who has made it one of his life tasks to ensure the safety of an 'open society'; but I think we can imagine who he might be thinking of, that is, think tanks, institutes, academics and others who make it their business to study and, of course, influence social policy. Perhaps an example here might serve to show Popper's intent.

Let us assume that it is agreed by our political masters that the low reading age of children in state schools constitutes a problem sufficiently pressing to warrant immediate attention.[16] What Popper seems to have in mind is that the government would oversee a process of experimentation in schools to test competing theories about the best means of getting children to read. Children in area A would be taught according to one method, the children in area B according to another, children in C another, and so on. It would of course be difficult to decide exactly how much 'experimentation' was needed to produce 'satisfactory' data, but this is a problem which confronts anyone conducting experiments to test hypotheses, including scientists. The experiment would presumably run for a number of years and be as exhaustive as possible. At the end of the given period of time the results would be compared and the theory producing the best results adopted as the universal policy for teaching in schools. Gone, Popper hopes, the fraught ideological battle between the educationalists of the academy and hard-nosed traditionalists. In its place a rational process designed to promote the best results and, by extension, the interests of the public at large. Popper's point is that the public interest is better served by adopting a neutral, detached method of governing than it is by the existing see-saw between conflicting ideological positions. If there is a method available which transcends the harmful squabbles of politicians then why not apply it to all aspects of social policy?

For someone who professes himself to be an individualist and a lover of liberty it is surely curious for Popper to advocate the approach outlined above. The reason why we should be suspicious is that any talk of using people for experiments surely transgresses their autonomy as human beings. If we follow Kant (as Popper claims to) then autonomy is to be defined as being treated as an end in oneself rather than as a 'mere means' for the satisfaction of the needs or wants of another. No one is to be used as the vehicle for the happiness of others no matter how many others are involved. This is the essence of Kant's uncompromising individualism. Yet Popper's

---

[16] Popper himself mentions 'educational reform' as a problem of the sort which might be tackled by the means he proposes. See *OSE* I, p.159.

approach would appear to transgress these strictures. If we take the example discussed above, it is clear that on one level the children in the schools in which the experiments are taking place are being used for the purpose of finding the best means of teaching children to read. They are 'guinea pigs' in an experiment to improve the conditions and expectations of those who will follow them into the classroom. Whilst Popper might be justified in arguing that theories need to be tested, he still needs to show how testing is compatible with his own proclaimed individualism. He still needs, in other words, a response to those (for example the parents of the children involved in the testing) who might with some justification worry that the use of people in these experiments is tantamount to employing them as 'mere means' for the development of educational policy. Let us imagine that as a result of having been exposed to a 'flawed' theory concerning the acquisition of reading skill that some of the children are hampered from learning how to read and as a result they do poorly at school. Their poor results – let us imagine – feed through into poor self-esteem, into truancy and in some cases delinquency. Some of the subjects of the failed theories end up unemployed and marginalised. As a result of having been exposed to flawed theories, the life chances and expectations of some of the subjects are so severely diminished that they themselves become in turn a 'problem' not only for their parents but of course for society as well. The question is, would these people not have a justified claim to compensation for the injustice done to them?

If this case seems too extreme, we can turn the example around. Let us imagine that instead of certain groups of children failing, we can see how the testing produces enormous benefits for one group, say the children who went to school A. The children in this school master the rudiments of reading more quickly. As a result, they are able to make considerable progress in their school work and end up excelling in exams thereby securing places at the top institutions of higher education. Because of their academic success, many of these subjects find their life chances and opportunities considerable enhanced, with a higher percentage of them than normal ending up in prestigious and well paid employment. In other words, the experiment is a great success: it unearths a method of teaching children how to read which allows an acceleration of the learning process with all the advantages that accrue from it. Meanwhile the children in schools B, C and D do no worse than the average. Their capacity to learn how to read is not impaired but neither is it enhanced. Their life chances are thus unaffected by the experimentation and the state can with some authority claim that the experiment has only winners, not losers. But, again, does this encouraging result allow us to wave away the fear expressed above, which is that Popper's proposals remain utilitarian, instrumental and hence damaging to individual autonomy? Arguably not, since what in essence has changed? The fact that a minority does well will not surely diminish the justified concerns of the many that they are 'victims' rather than beneficiaries of the process of experimentation. They have been used for the benefit of others and made to suffer the consequences of not having been treated the same way as the children in school A.

Although in this case there are no victims in the sense that no one has been disadvantaged by the process of 'engineering', those who have not benefited from it are, I would have thought, quite likely to feel aggrieved and to feel that an injustice has been done them. In short, the experimental method advocated by Popper would not overcome the traditional objection to utilitarianism which is that it treats people in an instrumental and ultimately unjust fashion in the name of social good or, as in this case, in the name of minimising unhappiness. On this point at least I think Kant is more nearly right than Popper: people are unlikely to look favourably upon being used even if this results in a minimisation of suffering.

We can note, finally, that part of the difficulty with the experimental approach as applied to society is knowing what might count as a satisfactory set of results and hence knowing when the problem has been resolved. At what level does for example unemployment 'cease' to be a problem – if indeed we agree that it is a problem? Levels of unemployment that would have been considered outrageous twenty years ago look almost reasonable considered alongside the picture today. The success or otherwise of a policy is always relative; relative to what the situation was like before the policy designed to alleviate it was formulated; relative to the public perception of its importance when set against other problems; relative to the levels of funding available to central government and so on. What policy is counted a 'success' is more often than not determined by the ability of the government (and those sympathetic to its policies) to persuade people that, firstly, a problem can be identified which requires governmental action to resolve it, and, secondly, that the proffered solution to the problem has obtained results which ameliorate rather than leave the situation unchanged or even worsen it. Part of the problem with Popper's approach is that he makes the leap all too readily between laboratory and society, between a world of objective, detached observers and the world of ethical and moral contestation. The traditional utilitarian position has been criticised on grounds that it fails not only to recognise the contentious nature of public policy issues, but that contestation is the very essence of politics. The same objection can, I think, be made against Popper's approach.

Conclusion: Popper's Anti-Political Politics (or Saint-Simon Revisited)

As I think should be clear, Popper's Kantianism and respect for the individual sits uncomfortably with his belief in the necessity for the application of experimental methods to social and political life. On the one hand we have the view that it is never the state's task to define what the ends of life should be and on the other a method for resolving 'problems' which is likely to end up doing just that. The difficulty is in my view caused by Popper's belief that he can combine a meaningful defence of the individual with what is an essentially utilitarian – if 'negative' – account of what the state should be doing. Far from exhibiting a Kantian concern to ensure that each individual is respected for what he or she is, that is, a unique self with needs, rights and desires that cannot be subsumed within a greater entity or class than him or herself, Popper's philosophy exhibits a marked suspicion of the individual and in particular of the individual *qua* political actor. Popper's politics is about experts, social scientists and other techno-boffins working away behind the scenes on 'our' behalf. Ordinary people, their hopes, desires and expectations are part of the 'problem' of contemporary politics, not part of the solution. It is their 'passion' and the 'violence' of their views which presents a challenge to the 'rational', 'scientific' administration of society. How much better the machine would function, how much smoother the operation of institutions would be, if they – we – were kept out of the picture until it is safe for them to be ushered into the polling booth for the five yearly test of their contentment with arrangements.

Although Popper is critical of a number of aspects of Enlightenment rationalism in particular that trend which stressed the necessity for viewing society 'holistically', as something to be reformed 'wholesale', there is more of the Enlightenment in this vision than Popper might care to admit. Like Condorcet, Saint-Simon, Comte and Marx, so for Popper political questions are ultimately questions of administration. Politics is above all, a problem-solving activity rather than a contest between different conceptions of what should be, of the Good Life. It is about maximising the efficacy of 'outputs', of delivering results and ordering policies rationally. But as critics of this vision have long argued, this is a vision of an end of politics rather than of its elevation to something more rational or scientific. It is a vision which does not speak of confidence in the public realm, but of fear of the mob – of the horny handed, the uneducated, the ignorant and the 'untrained'. It must count as one of the more curious ironies of the history of political thought that a philosopher whose name is so readily associated with the defence of pluralism and individuality against the elitist and inegalitarian schemes of Plato *et al* should himself be charmed into surrendering the Open Society to a minority whose claim to govern rests on a suspiciously similar premise to that of the philosopher kings.

Political Marketing

Bruce I. Newman
DePaul University, Chicago

'The Role of Marketing in American Politics'[1]

Introduction

The Hershey Foods Corporation sells chocolate bars, hershey kisses, Reese's candy, and other items as well. The marketing of these products is handled by a department that includes sales representatives, marketing researchers, advertising specialists, direct marketing experts, and others. The marketing department is responsible for developing marketing plans for each of the existing products and brands as well as developing new products and brands. People buy Hershey products because they have an excellent reputation in the marketplace as a consistently good tasting candy. The Hershey Corporation brings in approximately $1.8 billion dollars in annual sales.[2]

The president of the United States also sells something, ideas! More importantly, the president is selling himself to the American people, and trying to convince them to follow his lead. Each of his ideas is formulated into programs that he must market to the American people and to Congress. For each of his major initiatives, a president enlists the help of several marketing professionals to convince Americans to support his causes.

Just as previous presidents have used the expertise of marketing experts, so has Bill Clinton. He had the help of a professional marketing researcher (called a pollster in politics) to help him choose the themes and policies he would stress in his sales pitch; advertising specialists to direct the development of commercials; direct marketing experts to help him get his message targeted to specific audiences; and of course his sales representatives, his wife Hillary, and the members of his Cabinet who fly around the country making speeches and appearing on the nightly news programs to push the president's latest agenda. No, Bill Clinton didn't rack up billions of dollars in annual sales, but instead tries to move public opinion, the currency in politics.

From 'Electronic Electioneering' to 'Electronic Governing'

Electronic governing is the new force in politics today! It relies on the use of the latest marketing technology that was formerly used in presidential campaigns, and is now being incorporated into the daily running of government by the president. However, due to the fact that this same technology is available to anyone who understands it's use and potential power, we see it being used by the new power-brokers in politics as a political weapon to

---

[1] For technical reasons the figure accompanying this paper is not reproduced here. It is derived from B.I.Newman, *The Marketing of the President: Political Marketing as Campaign Strategy*, Sage, 1994, p.12. Copies may be obtained from the author at the Conference.

[2] P.Kotler, *Marketing Management*, Prentice-Hall, 1991, p.128.

impact on the president's approval ratings in the polls. The new power-brokers in politics are the talk-radio personalities (such as Rush Limbaugh and Ross Perot), the media, the pollsters, consultants and hundreds of spin-doctors (slang for consultants) representing numerous interest groups who are affected by the outcome of legislation.

Marketing technology has altered the way business is conducted in industry after industry, from sports to politics. Herein lies the challenge to the president, and to our society in general, and that is the ability to control and manage the use and impact of marketing technology on politics. It is not possible to win in politics today without a market orientation, either during a campaign or after entering office.

Marketing is an Exchange Process

Marketing is often described as an exchange process between a buyer and seller, with the buyer exchanging money for the seller's product or service. When applying marketing to a political campaign, the exchange process centers on a candidate who offers political leadership (through the policies he advocates) and a vision for the country in exchange for a vote from the citizen. Once in the White House, the exchange centers on the same leadership and vision being offered to the American people in exchange for their vote of confidence (as measured through opinion polls that track the president's approval ratings).[3]

The exchange process becomes slightly more complicated when we apply it to a sitting president, as his leadership can only be effective if he is able to move legislation through Congress. However, as a president's approval ratings increase in the polls, there is an indirect pressure on Congressmen and Senators to work with the president to avoid alienating his constituency. Eventually, the exchange between a president and the American people moves to the next campaign when the president runs for re-election. A market orientation then requires that research and polling be done to help shape the policies of the politician, which become the product through which the exchange is consummated.

Bill Clinton is a marketer because of his ability to 'reposition' ideas, respond to constantly changing market conditions, and reformulate strategy in communicating his message to the American people. This does not mean that he has been a successful marketer, only that he definitely is using marketing to an extent that we have not seen in previous administrations. Ultimately, we will have to wait to see if he is re-elected to determine whether or not he has been successful in his use of marketing. Although the opinion polls reflect attitudinal shifts in the electorate, it is the behavior of the marketplace (in this case the act of casting a vote in the upcoming presidential election in 1996) that will serve as the most serious test of Clinton's efforts as a marketer.

---

[3]For a good review of the role of marketing as a campaign tool, see B.I.Newman, *The Marketing of the President: Political Marketing as Campaign Strategy*, Sage, 1994; B.I.Newman & J.N.Sheth, *A Theory of Political Choice Behaviour*, Praeger, 1987; B.I.Newman & J.N.Sheth, *Political Marketing: Readings and Annotated Bibliography*, American Marketing Association, 1985.

Anticipating Needs

Success in marketing goes beyond the simple identification of the needs of consumers, but also includes the ability to forecast what those needs will be in the future. Marketers must not only be able to measure and identify the needs and wants of their customers', but they must also have a vision which enables them to anticipate what those needs will be. Whether it is a candidate, issue or product, marketing is a critical component to understanding what voters, citizens or consumers want and need. Needs may be driven by both emotion and rationality, resulting in people desiring the same product or candidate for different reasons.

Marketing is a needs assessment approach to product innovation which relies on information from the marketplace to help guide research and development. This means that the most successful products are molded around the findings from needs assessment studies. Automobiles and gym shoes are just a few examples of product categories which follow a marketing orientation. The development of new car models and innovative gym shoes such as pumps were based on this type of research. Just as a smart marketer makes sure that there is a need for his product before he distributes it around the country, so must a politician be sure that voters are concerned with an issue before he decides to advocate it.

Whether it is the budget battle or sending American troops into Bosnia, President Clinton, like presidents before him, has relied on opinion polls to help steer his policy decisions with an eye towards how the public will respond to these initiatives. What separates this president from his predecessors is his adroitness in shifting positions as the mood of the country changes. Who would have thought that the Republican revolution started in November 1994, would have begun to be declared dead one year later by political analysts? The influence on public opinion by a whole host of actors, including the interest groups, the media, foreign leaders and others makes it very difficult to anticipate how the needs of the nation will change. This is unlike the 'commercial marketplace', where companies have a greater control over how their product is perceived by the public. There is of course a fine line between the actions of the President being interpreted as an anticipation or response to the needs of the electorate. The President's detractors have accused him of following the polls, and waffling on issues. However, a leader today must re-position his ideas and policies to respond to a marketplace whose anticipations are constantly changing, something the President has done very well.

Creating an Image

Politics relies extensively on imagery today. Presidents rely on image manipulation to keep their approval ratings up in the polls, the ultimate measure of effective leadership in today's society. So what exactly is an image? Technically speaking, it is the visual picture which appears in a consumer's mind at the mention of a brand or company name.

Small changes in the physical characteristics of a brand can change the image of commonplace products. For example, when Procter & Gamble introduced Cheer with a blue color, consumers associated the color with a cleaner and more effective detergent. However, the key ingredient in influencing a consumer's brand image is product positioning. Marketers try to position their brands to meet the needs of defined customer segments. They do so by developing a product concept that can communicate the desired benefits through advertising and by utilizing media that will reach the target segment. When Schweppes first came onto the market in America, it could have been positioned as a soft drink or as a mixer. Positioning it as a mixer guided the promotional direction. The use of Commander Whitehead as the dapper Englishman referring to 'Schweppervescence' produced an image of prestige for a product category that might otherwise be regarded as commonplace.[4]

Even when competing products and their accompanying services look the same to buyers, buyers may perceive a difference in the company or brand image. One of the best examples is Marlboro cigarettes. While most cigarette brands taste essentially the same and are sold the same way, the only way to account for Marlboro's extraordinary worldwide market share (around 30%) is that Marlboro's 'macho cowboy' image has struck a responsive chord with most of the cigarette smoking public. Marlboro has been given not just an image, but also a personality.[5]

In politics, an image is created through the use of visual impressions that are communicated by the President's physical presence, media appearances, and experiences and record as a political leader as that information is integrated in the minds of citizens. Early on in his tenure, President Clinton was constantly photographed in the media in his athletic shorts, jogging, and then stopping at McDonalds to eat a sandwich. Images such as these did not help the President to convey an image of statesmanship and authority. Questions raised in electronic hall meetings (a promotional staple during the campaign) after Clinton entered the White House proved to be embarrassing at times, again chipping away at the image of the President. All of these activities were soon replaced with a more selective set of photo opportunities for the press, and usually only when foreign leaders visited the President at the White House. Along with this change in public image came the start of a gradual but steady rise in the polls for the President.

Marketing Research Drives Strategy

In the business marketplace, consumers differ on several dimensions. They may differ in terms of their needs and wants, ability to purchase high priced products, geographical location, consumption patterns, and even manner in which they go about making their purchases. Companies operate in a global marketplace today, and the number of consumers are too broad and diverse to effectively serve all of them. Some companies are better able to satisfy the needs of certain groups of consumers over others. In order to select out those consumers they choose to target with their promotional campaigns,

---

[4] Henry Assael, *Consumer Behaviour & Marketing Action*, South-Western College Publishing, 1995, p.365.
[5] P.Kotler, *Marketing Management*, p.300.

companies have sophisticated computer models which identify and describe the exact profile of their potential buyer.

The importance of doing research rests with the notion that not all products can be sold to all consumers. Companies use marketing research to determine what to stress to different consumer groups. Take the case of a cruise ship which is seeking to build up its clientele. People who take cruises fall into different demographic groups, some being older couples with no children looking for a relaxing vacation, while others are parents with children looking to pick a cruise which has activities all day long to keep their kids occupied. Whether it is the choice of which movies to play on board, the choice of a menu, or even the kind of pool activities to promote, cruise ships must conduct marketing research to determine how best to satisfy the needs of each of these two key groups of customers.

This same logic applies to the decisions that a sitting president has to make has he tries to determine which issues to try and get passed through Congress. There are different interest groups, each with their own set of needs that a president has to attempt to satisfy. It is impossible to satisfy every interest group's needs, so careful marketing research is conducted to determine which issues are of more importance to each interest group. Clinton's choice of pushing for a bill to protect gays in the military at the start of his presidency was a strange decision, as it alienated so many different interest groups that he had to retreat from the promise he made on that issue during the campaign. It is easy enough to use research to identify the needs of different groups of citizens during a campaign, but a very different challenge to get them passed through Congress after entering the White House.

Market Segmentation and Candidate Positioning

Volvo has been selling its cars on the basis of safety features for years. They realize that they have to appeal to car buyers with a unique offering that allows them to make a good profit in the marketplace. They have been innovators in the structural design of bodies of cars to ensure the greatest safety possible for passengers. More recently however, they have tried to alter their image by bringing in new models that are promoted on the basis of safety and performance. So who is the typical Volvo buyer? Market segmentation is a process which would be used to make that determination, and targeting is the selection of the segment(s) to which appeals are directed to. The point here is that this results in a match between the buyer and seller, just as there has to be a match between a candidate and voter segments.

In business, market segmentation and targeting are used to identify those groups of customers who the marketer directs his product and promotional campaign towards. It is used by many companies who choose not to sell their product or service to every potential customer, but only those who are likely to buy it. Seven-Up chose to be the 'uncola' as a means of segmenting their market of potential soda drinkers who don't want to drink a cola. Avis adopted the motto 'We try harder' to differentiate themselves from the leading car rental company Hertz several years ago. Since then, companies like Dollar and Budget entered the car rental market by offering lower prices (as their names suggest) as a means of segmenting their market.

In politics, market segmentation has been traditionally used by each of the political parties to choose which segments of citizens they target with their appeals. Historically, the Democrats have been the party of the poor and minorities, and the Republicans the party of the rich and big business. Each party worked very hard at identifying the needs of their constituents, and developing programs and policies which were geared at satisfying those needs. However, as the marketing technology has become available to tailor meet the needs of all constituents, regardless of group identification, the segmentation of people along party lines has been blurred, with both parties trying to attract citizens from the competing party.

Once the multiple voter segments have been identified, the candidate has to position himself in the marketplace. Positioning is the vehicle which allows the candidate to convey his image to voters in the best light possible. The image is crafted through the media by emphasizing certain personality traits of the candidate, as well as stressing various issues. For example, in 1992, Bill Clinton created an image of himself as an outsider who would bring about change in Washington through a series of innovative economic programs. From a competitive point of view, he was contending with an incumbent president who was sitting on an economy in recession, and not getting results from his actions. Naturally, Clinton capitalized on his strengths and took advantage of his competitors' weaknesses.

The opinion polls reflect an electorate in America today that is not at all satisfied with the leadership of either of the political parties, and the President has responded to this by positioning himself as a leader who will answer to no one but the American people. This political orientation has been referred to as a 'triangulation' positioning strategy, pitting the President at the apex of a triangle, and the two political parties at the bottom corners. This is in direct response to the polls that suggest the President has a better chance of getting re-elected if he is perceived to be charting his own course independent of the political parties. It also positions the President closer to the center of the political spectrum, a position that his administration anticipates will be the place where the most votes will be won in 1996.

Ideology as a Branding Mechanism

Along with the constant shifting back and forth of people from one party to another has come a blurring of the definition of ideology in this country. In marketing terms, ideology is a labelling process, almost similar in nature to the use of branding for products. People have historically used ideology as a way of labelling both themselves and politicians, and then making a connection between themselves and the candidate (and political party the candidate belonged to) through the use of this label. However, instead of a majority of the people referring to themselves as liberals or conservatives, a majority of the people now refer to themselves as independents (forget about the ideological label called moderate).

These 'labels' are no different then the ones we see on products, as well as attached to services offered by a whole host of professionals who advertise in the hope of creating an image which defines who and what they stand for in the minds of consumers. Just look at what accountants did with H & R Block, or what lawyers did with Hyatt legal services, or what Schwabb did with financial services. Extensive advertising can be used to label and define who the provider is and what makes his services different than his competition. This is precisely what political parties and candidates do to sell their ideas to the American people.

As a result of this change, ideology is now driven less by party affiliation and more by marketing, and the latest poll results indicting the mood of the electorate. During Franklin D. Roosevelt's time, most Americans new what it meant to be a democrat (or a liberal), and Roosevelt's NRA (National Recovery Act) was used to help him implement his working ideology, which was that government should be used to get the country moving again after the Great Depression. But today, the labels liberal and conservative in politics are no longer defined by the political parties, but by the candidates themselves and the images their consultants craft for them. As President Clinton said early on in his administration, his ideas are neither liberal nor conservative, but both. Along with this change has come a dramatic shift in power from the political party to the consultants.

The Choice of Consultants

'We used to create heroes', says Bob Goodman, a veteran media consultant for Republican political candidates. 'Not any more, Dad,' says his son, Adam, a second-generation media consultant now working with his father-and teaching the old fellow some new tricks. 'We're all technocrats now', Adam Goodman says, 'reacting to the overnight polls, fighting against shorter and shorter attention spans out there among the voters. What counts now are tracking polls, focus groups, dial groups, and digital-TV editing machines, and of course the product, a candidate who is able to raise the huge amounts of cash needed to pay for the technology.'[6] The fact is that today, consultants sometimes take the center stage, and even determine the issues of a campaign. Technology and money are doing to politics what they have done to sports: making them more organized, more professional, more compartmentalized, and less improvised. Politics has become a big, profitable business. Some say the byproduct of these consultants is cynicism of the electorate, and growing armies of people involved in opposition research.

At the level of overall strategic thinking, the candidate is involved, but when it comes to creating a campaign platform, conducting polls, setting up a promotional strategy, very few candidates are involved. The services offered by consultants include several different activities, such as direct mail, fundraising, TV and radio spots, issue analysis, and print advertising, all essentially an effort towards raising funds and impacting on voter's choices.

---

[6] *Wall Street Journal*, January 10, 1994, p.1.

The ability to lead in the high tech age hinges on the careful selection of the right consultants to run the candidates political campaign, both before and after entering the White House.

The Republican Revolution of 1994

The 1994 election found the country yearning for more change, similar to the 'mantra' Americans voiced in the 1992 election. There was a desire for less government and both parties campaigned on this platform. The Republicans victory in 1994 was capitalized on by using the Contract as a 'post-election' marketing tool. In response to the successful marketing of the Contract after the election, the president introduced his Middle Class Bill of Rights, a 'new and improved' version of the Republican's Contract. Each of these efforts reflected a move towards the political center, where the most votes could be attracted.

In September, 1994, soon after Republican Newt Gingrich announced the Contract with America, the Republican National Committee lined up nearly 300 talk-radio interviews through the Virginia Contract Information Center, which has 500 radio talk show on its fax network. The hosts of these shows were sent pro-Contract press clippings and talking points for the Contract. Many of the radio show hosts usually read the clippings verbatim. The success of the Contract was due in large part to this marketing effort.

Just as consumers don't take the time to read labels on products, neither, do citizens take the time to listen carefully to what politicians say. On his first day as Speaker of the House, Newt Gingrich talked about Franklin D. Roosevelt with high praise for the way he made government work in his first 100 days, without mentioning of course that he is setting out to dismantle the very programs that were put into place during Rooseveltls time. Voters do, however, pay close attention to what politicians actually do. Promises may work to get a politician elected, but delivering is the essential ingredient for continued success in office, as is evident from the dramatic fall in the polls the Republicans witnessed one year after their contract was proposed to the American people.

In what would become one of the latest technological advances put forth in the 1994 campaign, Republicans used a technique that was mastered in the movie, *The Terminator*, called 'morfing' (where Arnold Schwartenager is turned into The Terminator over a 5 to 10 second period, making it seem as if Arnold and The Terminator are the same person). Republican candidates capitalized on Clinton's ebb in the polls, and 'morfed' their Democratic opponents into Bill Clinton. The impact of this use of imagery was felt at the polls by the Democrats, who went down in defeat in what many termed the Republican Revolution of 1994.

The mid-term election of 1994 was labeled by Ralph Nader as a 'turning point in the dissolution of the two-party system.'[7] Nader pointed out that it is increasingly difficult to distinguish between Democrats and Republicans, and that they in fact represent the same party with different names. Nader has even been known to make fun of the two parties on occasion by referring

---

[7] *Chicago Tribune*, December 19, 1994, p.12.

to them as the 'Demopublicans' or 'Republocrats.' Nothing could be closer to the truth as we witness leaders in both parties disregard party label in pursuit of the 'hottest' issues that will sell in the political marketplace.

The New Politics: 'CyberDemocracy'

Movement toward a more direct form of democracy has been driven by the latest developments in telecommunications technology. Newt Gingrich opened up proceedings of the House of Representatives to television cameras and stars in the National Empowerment Channel, a televised talk show. All of these technological changes are happening so quickly, it is hard for the ordinary American to keep track of them. It is very likely that in the upcoming 1996 Presidential election, the two traditional parties will be joined by a third party. It is also likely that the Internet will become the newest 'channel' through which information is coneyed directly to the American voter.

Newt Gingrich made the comment that 'all budget decisions be compatible with an emerging information-age Third Wave society that recognizes that the computer and all of the breakthroughs in telecommunications are going to change permanently our way of life.' So just what does this mean? This is hard to say when we're talking about a politician who has been referred to as a 'technonut', and who may now be the most powerful politician in the United States. Gingrich shares an excitement for futuristic scenarios such as colonies living on the moon by early next century.[8]

We are headed on a collision course on the super-highway as the two parties' futurists (Gingrich for the Republicans and Gore for the Democrats) have very different views of how democracy is going to be changed through the use of information technology. At issue is how the federal government is going to foster the growth of the information superhighway. The Republicans want less government involvement than the Democrats do. Gore would like to see universal access to the computer system through schools and libraries. On the other hand, Gingrich has talked about giving tax breaks to help poor kids get lap-top computers.

We as voters are so wired in to our federal government that interest groups have the power to change legislation in a matter of days. With lobbyists sitting in the balconies of Congress, listening to debate on issues sensitive to their interest groups, all it takes is one call on a cellular telephone to initiate a letter-writing campaign to flood a Congressman's off ice with enough mail to stop the politician dead in his tracks.

The information technology industry has spawned many cottage industries, with companies entering left and right. One such company is Bonner and Associates which can send out 10,000 faxes overnight to a Congressman's office. When Mr. Bonner is hired by his client, he isolates the swing votes in Congress, then does a scan of the corresponding districts, and identifies citizens whose profiles suggest that they are sympathetic with the cause. Then, after a critical committee hearing in Congress, Mr. Bonner's employees call the sympathetic citizens, explain what is happening, and

---

[8] *Wall Street Journal*, January 23, 1995, p.A18.

through the magic of telecommunications, put them directly in touch with the Congressman whose vote is critical to blockage or passage of the bill in question. The charge is $350-$500 per call.[9]

The dilemma politicians face today is that through the information technology that exists, citizens hear every utterance of a politician, and nothing can be said without the possibility of it getting into the news the next day. Furthermore, through the advent of talk radio and constant polling, politicians always know what is on the minds of the electorate. If they don't respond to the opinions of Rush Limbaugh and the polls, they're thrown out of office. On the other hand, if they are perceived to be too responsive, and thus seen as pandering (as Bill Clinton has been so labeled), they're punished for being reactionary.

The number of Americans who trust our leaders has plummeted from 70% in the 1960's. to around 20% today.[10] It could be a reaction to the alienation fostered by the talk radio movement. Or it might be a reaction to politicians who refuse to stand up and go 'against' the polls if they feel strongly about an issue. But most likely it is in response to a political system that has lost control of what it is doing, and reflective of a loss of power of the political party.

Political parties no longer carry the clout they used to. The absence of patronage armies and strong partisan leadership, as well as the advent of sophisticated, costly media strategies in campaigns, has lowered the value of the political party endorsement. In some cases, being a part of a slate assembled by party leaders could be a liability for candidates. This is the result of the mood of the electorate, and at the core of our problem as a democracy.

Ever since the procedural reforms of the mid 1970's, and the expansion of the primary system, investigative reporters have been expected to inspect the candidates platforms for the voters, giving the media a more powerful role in politics in the U.S. The fact is that it remains much easier to get a 'negative' message through the media than a 'positive' one through. This is a situation which will continue to make it very difficult for presidents to be successful in the White House.

Voters want people who aren't political, even though most government processes are political. What is alarming about today's high-tech political system is the swiftness that change is taking place. Change has become a way of life for voters. Voters are alienated and fed up with the way our two-party system operates.

Conclusion

There is no doubt that modern marketing practices have increased voter cynicism if we look at the dramatic increase in the percentage of voters who distrust politicians. As the campaigns become more slick and sophisticated, voters realize that it is increasingly more difficult to separate fact from fiction. It is difficult to discern whether politicians are doing their jobs

---
[9] *Time*, January 23, 1995, p.18.
[10] *Time*, January 23, 1995, p.21.

because they really care about the welfare of American citizens, or to make money.

The $4.5 million book deal that Newt Gingrich struck soon after becoming Speaker of the House is evidence of this problem. Let us not forget that in marketing, perception is often the reality! Citizens can only become apathetic and pull out of the political process by not voting if they feel as if they are being manipulated. Simply witness the extremely low turnout of democratic voters in the mid-term elections to understand what it means to have an apathetic electorate. Voters lose faith in a politician when his promises are forgotten after he enters office.

Finally, can a candidate or politician even think of campaigning or governing without the use of marketing? Unfortunately, the answer is no, and dictates why something drastic needs to be done about the direction information technology is driving our political system in. Clearly the most successful corporations in the world are customer driven, such as MacDonalds, General Electric, Toyota, etc. This same focus, or what is called a 'market orientation' in marketing has been adopted by politicians, and is here to stay.

Political Marketing

Dominic Wring
Nottingham Trent University

'The Historical Role of Marketing in British Politics'

Introduction

During the 1992 general election analysts took great interest in scrutinising the work of once largely neglected party strategists. On one occasion a routine ITN lunchtime news item featuring presenter John Suchet and experienced Westminster based journalists Julia Langdon and Michael White ended a discussion on the now imminent campaign alluding to the supposed ability of the 'marketing men' to dictate the likely course of events. By no means an isolated event, such interchanges help highlight the way in which some of the most informed political commentators now view the modern electoral process. Nevertheless this view is not necessarily shared by the candidates, at least in public. Dennis Kavanagh has noted that leading politicians are often loathe to admit the important strategic role that marketing plays less it detracts from their own status or else upsets influential elements in the party (Kavanagh 1995). For these and other reasons the history of political marketing in Britain cannot be necessarily found in official party sources.

Evolutionary Models of Marketing

In their important analysis of the increasingly prominent role given to management theory and practice in the work of non-profit making organisations, Crompton and Lamb argue: 'Marketing is about two things. First, it is a philosophy, an attitude and a perspective. Second, it is a set of activities used to implement that philosophy' (Crompton & Lamb 1986). This dichotomy is particularly useful when analysing the strategic development of a political party, itself an idiosyncratic form of non-profit organisation. Conceiving marketing as both a set of tools as well as a guiding philosophy helps identify the key historical stages in the evolution of electioneering, an activity which forms the principal manifestation of this management process within the political sphere. This also makes it easier to understand how alterations in campaign practices can be motivated by factors other than the mass media or technological innovation. Rather, by placing greater emphasis on parties' own strategic change, it is possible to compare the development of electioneering with that of a business marketing programme.

Several management theorists use a three phase model to explain the evolution of marketing as a commercial philosophy. From this perspective it is possible to view the process as more than the use of tools such as advertising and research. Within this framework the initial stage of 'production' orientation takes a classical Fordist view of business and assumes the customer will, with minimal encouragement, purchase what the firm makes. With the advent of the next phase, the more complex 'sales-led' approach, organisations begin to invest in market research in order to better target selected consumer groups with more refined communications. The third and most sophisticated orientation, the so-called 'marketing concept', is based around the organising principle that a successful business strategy starts as well as ends with the buying public. To use the standard Chartered Institute of Marketing definition, their subject of interest is: 'the management process responsible for identifying, anticipating and satisfying customer requirements profitably' (cited in Whyte 1988).

Whilst most historical accounts of political campaigning in Britain have tended to focus on the way media and technology have affected party organisation (Swaddle 1988; Cockerell 1989), Smith and Saunders utilise an evolutionary marketing model to identify key strategic changes (Smith & Saunders 1990). Similarly Avraham Shama adopts a comparable approach based on his analysis of American electioneering (Shama 1976). It is possible to apply a derivative model of the latter to illuminate the major turning points in British campaign history.

The Era of Mass Propaganda

Prior to the Second World War, commentators and political organisers regularly referred to the business of political communications work as 'propaganda'. The term, now somewhat antiquated in electoral terms, usefully described a one-directional communication process in which passive audiences found themselves subjected to the sometimes manipulative appeals of political elites. As an agency of persuasion, propaganda can be compared with the production orientation stage in the development of conventional marketing, both approaches being primarily concerned with accommodating their own organisational needs rather than those of their publics. According to Shama, this lack of concern with voters' wants manifested itself in an electoral strategy based around a simple principle: '...increased awareness would increase voter preference. The inputs to the promotion campaign to achieve increased awareness were designed on the basis of guess and intuition' (Shama 1976).

In Britain the development of modern mass propaganda dates from the Representation of the People Act passed in 1918. The Act, a defining moment in British history, nearly trebled the electorate to a size of 21 million (Swaddle 1990). Prior to then campaigning had largely consisted of canvassing, leafleting and meetings. There had been limited innovations, notably Gladstone's stump oratory during the 1880 Midlothian campaign which succeeded in attracting considerable press interest, thereby cementing the relationship between media and political elites (Hanham 1978). Interest in the way leaders communicated to people in the emerging 'mass society' was heightened with the onslaught of the propaganda intensive Great War and beginnings of radio broadcasting (Kornhauser 1959). The changing environment presented strategists with what leading Labour official Egerton Wake called a 'formidable problem in political engineering' (Wake 1929): the roots of modern political marketing lie in experimentation undertaken by electoral organisers during the inter-war years.

Four years after losing the 1906 election the Conservatives moved to embrace a propagandist orientation through the employment of their first press officer, Sir Malcolm Fraser (Cockett 1994). A Press Bureau was established in 1911. More re-organisation came later with the appointment of J.C.C. Davidson as Party Chairman in 1926. In reforming the Central Office party headquarters, Davidson appeared to take heed of one guide popular amongst Conservative agents at the time: 'Winning elections is really a question of salesmanship, little different from marketing any branded article' (cited in Swaddle 1990). In 1927 former MI5 officer Joseph Ball was appointed head of publicity (Cockett 1994). Together with Davidson he revolutionised party propaganda. The Press Bureau was expanded and specialist sub-sections formed to target stories at newspapers, many of whom were already pro-Conservative. During the 1929 election the Conservatives became the first party to use an agency, Holford- Bottomley Advertising Services, to help them design posters and leaflets later distributed in their millions (Hollins 1981). The agencies S.H. Benson and Press Secretaries Ltd also played a role in the campaign (Pinto-Duschinsky 1981). Benson's, soon to gain reknown for the 'toucan' advertisement 'Guinness is Good for You', faired less well in their first incursion into politics, receiving heavy criticism for the 'Safety First' campaign slogan. Despite this setback, the Conservatives re-employed the agency in the subsequent general elections of 1931 and 1935.

In preparing for the 1929 election, Central Office set-up a candidate training centre, the Bonar Law College. In addition Conservatives could also expect coaching prior to speaking in Party Election Broadcasts. At local level Streatham Association organised the first recorded telephone canvass (Swaddle 1990). There is also evidence of limited experimentation with direct mailing. But perhaps the most striking campaign innovation came in the shape of film propaganda. Guided by Albert Clavering, Alexander Korda and others, Conservative Central Office purchased a fleet of mobile cinema vans and made, distributed and showed films to thousands of voters during the 1929 election (Hollins 1981). By 1935 the programme had been extended, the vehicles' costs contributing to the most expensive British campaign of all time (Pinto-Duschinsky 1981).

The birth of Labour as a mass propagandist organisation was symbolised by the decision to set up a publicity department at headquarters in 1917. Head of the new section Herbert Tracey together with National Agent Egerton Wake were put in charge of party campaigning. Lacking in financial resources, Labour found compensation in the shape of strategic advice from assorted sympathisers such as leading Fabian intellectual Sidney Webb, founder of the LSE and joint author of the Labour party constitution. In 1922 Webb developed the thesis that electioneering could be improved by deployment of 'stratified electioneering', a process akin to the market segmentation and targeting techniques which later formed the hallmarks of good marketing practice. Citing another famous scholar, he wrote:

> '... it was an acute remark of H.G.Wells, twenty years ago, that modern Democracy was characteristically grey, not be-

cause any one of the units making up the mass was itself grey, but because the mixing of them together produced a dirty and unattractive grey. He looked forward to a time when we might be able to see Democracy, not as grey but as very highly coloured indeed, the units being all allowed their separate individuality of hue.'

Webb continued:

'Now, I should like to see a little variegated colour in electioneering, in addition to the common grey. Every elector has his own "colour", if we could only discover it. He differs in character and circumstances, temperament and vocation, religion and recreation – and in a thousand other ways from his fellow men. At present we tend to address them all in the same way, with the result of achieving everywhere a certain amount of "misfit".' (Webb 1922)

Webb's analysis is more than a matter of historical record: influential strategists including party secretary Arthur Henderson, the most senior official in the organisation, were keen for agents to operationalise the concept. Evidence suggests several did by targeting electoral groups according to their occupation, age and lack of strong partisanship (Wring 1996).

Many strategists, conscious of what one called the 'psychology of the electorate', were eager to promote 'party image' to use the phrase originally coined by Graham Wallas in 1908 (Wallas 1948). Symptomatic of this was Labour's decision to formally launch a logo in 1924. Writing on the value of political advertising in the party agents' journal the same year, another strategist offered theoretical insights later popularised in the non-profit marketing studies involving Kotler (Kotler & Levy 1969; Kotler & Zaltman 1972):

'Originally advertising was almost entirely of a commercial character, and was defined in many text-books as "printed salesmanship"; but this definition is no longer adequate, for in recent years a form of advertising which has little to do with the selling of commodities has been developed extensively. For want of better title we shall call it "Social Advertising", since it is concerned with arousing public interest in undertakings of a social character.' (Horwill 1924)

Despite such insight, advocates of advertising found themselves stalled by poverty coupled with the existence of a strong evangelical tradition in the party eschewing the use of 'manipulative' capitalist techniques. Together these factors help explain Labour's decision to abandon plans to use an advertising agency for the 1935 campaign and why attempts to develop film propaganda proved problematic (Hollins 1981). It was not until the 1937 local elections that the party, in the guise of London region, used agency professionals in their campaign preparations. London Labour leader Herbert Morrison proved to be instrumental in this process, persuading sympathetic contacts in public relations and advertising to volunteer their services to help what turned out to be a highly successful campaign (Donoghue & Jones 1973).

The Introduction of Media Campaigning

The post-war growth in the television and advertising industries had a profound impact on society: J.B. Priestley famously termed them conduits of 'admass' culture (Wiener 1981). Proliferation of these media had a particular impact on political communication in Britain, giving rise to a new kind of electoral strategy akin to the 'selling concept' stage in the development of conventional marketing. Like their counterparts in the commerical sphere, political parties began to embrace market research in order to better plan and target potential groups of supporters with more sophisticated advertising communications: '(Opinion polling) studies were conducted concerning the effectiveness of different promotion appeals and media in reaching the voters' (Shama 1976). Again the primary focus, though increasingly conscious of public opinion, remained geared to understanding organisational objectives. In recognition of the processes involved, commentators began to term the new approach 'media campaigning'.

The origins of the Conservatives shift towards media campaigning lie in their massive 1945 defeat by Labour. In the following two decades leading figures Lord Woolton, Lord Poole and R.A. Butler would be instrumental in reconstituting their party as a formidable electoral machine. An early sign of Conservative determination to infuse their electioneering with a more media conscious feel came with the appointment of leading advertising agency Colman Prentis Varley in 1948 (Rose 1967). It was the beginning of a longstanding and mutually profitable relationship. CPV executives proved to be the inspiration behind 'Life's better with the Conservatives- don't let Labour ruin it', the 1959 campaign slogan derived from 'You've never had it so good', itself a paraphrase of comments made by prime minister Harold Macmillan (Windlesham 1966).

Whilst links between the Conservatives and advertisers were largely in the public domain, almost unknown was the decision by Central Office to set up the Public Opinion Research Department in 1948 (Street 1992). Marking the first attempt by a British party to incorporate polling methods into electoral strategy, the PORD is additionally significant because it coincided with a major repositioning of the Conservatives which ended with the party taking office in 1951 having moved towards the electoral 'centreground' in recognition of the outgoing Labour government's popular public policies (Gamble 1974). It would be simplistic to view this shift solely as a product of survey research but it is noteworthy that R.A.Butler, the chief architect of post-war Conservative policy, was a patron of the PORD and keen student of public opinion. The service itself monitored polling trends, providing key figures in the bureaucracy and parliamentary party with regular briefing reports. In one of its most ambitious projects, the department commissioned Market and Information Services Ltd to undertake a largescale study of 5,000 electors in 1949. Entitled 'The Floating Vote', the report was significant in that it chose to analyse the newspaper readership, occupations, recreations, age and sex of uncommitted electors, thereby acknowledging the importance of this constituency (Street 1992). Though the PORD was disbanded in 1953 and its functions merged with other Central Office departments, private polling continued to be commissioned thereafter.

Under direction from a team led by Tony Benn and Woodrow Wyatt Labour began to produce sophisticated Party Election Broadcasts for television during the 1959 campaign (Cockerell 1989). More significant organisational change in favour of the new media campaign style came after this election defeat. One of the catalysts appeared in the form of an opinion research study commissioned by a magazine sympathetic to then Labour leader Hugh Gaitskell and his supporters on the centre-right, so-called 'revisionist' wing of the party. Entitled 'Must Labour Lose?', the report was interpreted as a call for the party to reshape its image in order to win support from a burgeoning middle-class (Abrams et al. 1960). Whilst many rejected the research findings, the fact that polling analysis managed to provoke a major debate provided support for those committed to integrating these methods into the formulation of promotional campaigns (Crosland 1962). Subsequently market researcher Dr Mark Abrams, co-author of Must Labour Lose?, became an integral member of Labour's strategic team in the successful general election campaign of 1964. Labour continued to use polling, contracting the services of MORI throughout the 1970s.

The period 1962 to 1964 was one of tremendous strategic change. After the untimely death of Hugh Gaitskell, Harold Wilson was elected to the leadership. The appointment of Len Williams and John Harris to the key posts of General Secretary and Director of Publicity helped further revitalise the party machinery culminating in the embrace of media campaigning (Rose 1967). Wilson proved to be an inspirational strategist, becoming pivotal in building links between his party and a group of sympathetic advertising and public relations professionals convened by David Kingsley, a London based executive, in preparation for the 1964 general election. Throughout his leadership Wilson maintained close links with professional advisers: on his retirement the party was left in something of a strategic vacuum.

The Advent of Political Marketing

Over the past decade it is possible to discern a trend towards the reporting and analysis of what is termed 'political marketing'. Interest in this phenomenom reflects the belief that electioneering in Britain has undergone a major transformation in recent times. This change can be seen to mirror the development of a marketing orientation in commerical terms. Unlike sales-led, media campaigning in which organisers are 'simply called to investigate voters' opinions', modern political marketing requires a more comprehensive, holistic approach to electoral strategy, one which: 'calls for research which goes far deeper than this. The new marketing concept is interested in the basic political needs and wants of the voters' (Shama 1976). Put simply opinion research, as representative of the electorate, begins to take on an important policy perspective in addition to its existing presentational role.

Margaret Thatcher's leadership proved to be a watershed in the development of political marketing in Britain. Elected Conservative leader in 1975, Thatcher set out to rejuvenate a party demoralised by defeat in the two general elections of 1974. Within four years a revitalised organisation had established a close working relationship with advertising agency Saatchi and Saatchi. At the heart of this arrangement lay a partnership between party communications director Gordon Reece, Saatchi executive Tim Bell and the leader herself. The trio provided the inspiration behind the implementation of a series of campaign initiatives, most famously the 'Labour Isn't Working' poster, aimed at further undermining public confidence in a Labour administration already besieged by problems. In her analysis of Conservative organisation during this period, Margaret Scammell contends the party was undergoing a major re- orientation:

> 'Most importantly there is evidence that the marketing concept shaped the manifesto and electoral strategy in all three elections under Lady Thatcher's leadership. This is not to say that market research dictated the details of policy but it did suggest the tone and tenor and indicate that certain policy options were electorally out of bounds.' (Scammell 1995)

The ability of the Thatcher leadership to transform Conservative strategy is partly explained by the nature of the party's internal structures. Because the Party Chairman, that is the chief bureaucrat, is an appointee of the leader the party organisation tends to operate on a hierarchical basis. Consequently on taking charge, Thatcher fundamentally restructured Central Office even though she was unable to initiate similar immediate surgery on her parliamentary frontbench team. Given Conservative leaders also draw up the party manifesto, keen polling analyst Thatcher was well placed to begin using the marketing concept to aid with policy development. Such a reading of recent history sits awkwardly with the popular perception of Thatcher as an ideologue led by conviction. However, as Scammell demonstrates, the new electoral approach understood the force of public opinion and exploited latent populist concern over crime and immigration, the Conservatives tying them to more orthodox policy appeals such as the commitment to allow council house tenants the opportunity to buy their homes (Scammell 1995).

Following their emphatic 1979 victory the Conservatives continued to reorganise their campaign machinery. In 1981 Central Office employed Christopher Lawson to head a new marketing department. Lawson, a former executive of sweet manufacturer Mars, committed himself to distilling the party message into a few readily understandable appeals (Elebash 1984). Research proved invaluable. Particularly important were polling findings indicating that though there was serious public concern over rising unemployment, most voters blamed the world recession not the government (Scammell 1995). In 1983 the Conservatives secured re-election by an increased margin.

Though the general election of 1987 resulted in a third consecutive victory, campaign management became the focus of heated debate within leadership circles. Essentially the row revolved around the role of the prime minister. Fearing she was becoming increasingly unpopular, some advisors cautioned against leader-centred campaigning. Aggrieved by this view, Thatcher took comfort from other strategists' belief in her value as an electoral asset. During the campaign itself these tensions exploded when, a week before voting, a rogue poll indicating Labour was gaining support ignited a furious row between the rival Central Office strategists on what became known as 'Wobbly Thursday' (Tyler 1987). Arguably these events, coupled with the dramatic Conservative leadership elections held in 1990 and 1995, reflect the power as well as the vulnerability of an office holder who is expected to deliver as both party chief and key strategist.

If the Labour electoral machine was ineffectual during the 1979 election it had virtually disintegrated by 1983 in a campaigning effort MP Austin Mitchell compared with the infamous marketing launch of the Ford Edsel (Mitchell 1983). This devastating defeat effectively marked the end to a long-running civil war which had prevented the development of a coherent political strategy and seen part of the Labour right-wing split off to form the rival Social Democratic Party in 1981. Following the 1983 debacle Labour elected Neil Kinnock leader. Because of a party structure which made the leadership formally accountable to an Annual Conference and its National Executive Committee, Kinnock's intention to reform Labour policy and organisation were always likely to face more formidable internal opposition than those piloted by Conservative counterpart Margaret Thatcher. Though initially fraught with problems, Kinnock's eventual success in operationalising the political marketing concept helped transform party campaigning and, arguably of greater importance, shifted the balance of power in favour of his leadership.

Streamlining of Labour headquarters in 1985 resulted in the appointment of two officials who became central to Kinnock's process of reform; these were General Secretary Larry Whitty and Director of Campaigns and Communications Peter Mandelson. The following year saw the launch of the Shadow Communications Agency (SCA), a voluntary network of sympathisers working in marketing and advertising (Hughes & Wintour 1990). Though they did not prevent the subsequent 1987 defeat, the SCA helped provide creative inspiration and rejuvenate campaign organisation. Some have concluded the election marked Labour's adoption of marketing but, as Nicholas O' Shaughnessy points out, it was perhaps more an object lesson in advertising (O'Shaughnessy 1990). Arguably events after the campaign proved to be of greater significance.

In strategic terms Labour embraced a marketing orientation during the Policy Review launched after the 1987 defeat. The initial stage of the Review involved the presentation of specially commissioned opinion research entitled 'Labour and Britain in the 1990s' to a meeting of senior leadership figures. The report concluded by arguing that Labour ought to radically change direction in order to win uncommitted voters alienated by what was perceived to be the party's outdated image (Hughes & Wintour 1990). Ultimately the Review enabled the leadership to effectively reposition itself nearer the electoral centreground, leading one analyst to conclude:

> 'Neil Kinnock is certainly to be congratulated for being the

first Labour leader to introduce marketing disciplines into his party's ideas and presentation' (Henley Centre 1990).

Arguably one legacy of the Review, and the shift to a marketing orientation, has been borne out in the party's collective decision to elect the apparently 'voter friendly' Tony Blair as leader and the subsequent support given him in his successful attempt to re-write Clause Four, Labour's 75 year old mission statement.

Conclusions

Rather than viewing the historical transformation of campaigning in Britain as primarily the result of media or technological innovation it is useful to see the process as one of strategic change comparable to the development of a company engaged in conventional business activities. Like the plan of a commercial firm, the organisation of party campaigning can be seen to evolve greater sophistication through three stages, namely the so-called 'production', 'selling', and 'marketing' orientations. In electoral terms these are the equivalent of what have been termed the 'propaganda', 'media' and 'political marketing' approaches to electioneering. With reference to the Conservatives, this three part sequence of strategic change can be traced through the implementation of initiatives launched following the party's most serious electoral setbacks in 1906, 1945 and 1974. Similarly Labour developed as a mass propagandist party in response to the expansion of the franchise in 1918, moved towards a media orientation after losing in 1959, and more recently has embraced a political marketing approach after the 1987 defeat.

The two main parties of government in Britain have long been engaged in marketing related activities. The business of political image making and public relations has a longer heritage in this country than is commonly supposed. It is not a product of American importation: witness the Conservatives' decision to hire Guinness advertisers' S.H. Benson during the inter-war years. Similarly the highly original analysis of Labour strategists like Sidney Webb, specifically his insights into market segmentation and targeting, help revise the notion that study of electoral organisation has little to offer the greater historical understanding of marketing ideas and practices.[1]

References

M.Abrams & R.Rose with R.Hinden, *Must Labour Lose?*, Penguin, 1960.

---

[1] The centre parties, mainly in the guise of the Liberals, have made some contributions to the development of campaigning. In 1929 and again in 1974 the party challenged the then legally understood electoral conventions and proceeded to publish newspaper advertising. The party also became the first to hire a professional advertising agent and former J Walter Thompson executive to head its publicity department in 1937. In 1981 the now defunct SDP pioneered the use of American political consultants by engaging agency help in launching an ambitious and successful direct mail service aimed at prospective members.

M.Cockerell, *Live at Number 10*, Faber & Faber, 1989.

R.Cockett, 'The Party, Publicity and the Media', in A.Seldon & S.Ball (eds), *Conservative Century*, Oxford University Press, 1994.

J.Crompton & C.Lamb, *Marketing Government and Social Services*, John Wiley, 1986.

A.Crosland, 'Can Labour Win?', in *The Conservative Enemy*, Jonathan Cape, 1962.

B.Donoghue & G.Jones, *Herbert Morrison: Portrait of a Politician*, Weidenfeld & Nicolson, 1973.

C.Elebash, 'The Americanisation of British Political Communications', *Journal of Advertising*, 13/3, 1984.

A.Gamble, *The Conservative Nation*, Routledge Kegan & Paul, 1974.

H.M.Hanham, *Elections and Party Management: Politics in the Time of Disraeli and Gladstone*, second edition, Harvester, 1978.

Henley Centre Comment, *Marketing*, 20th December 1990.

T.J.Hollins, 'The Presentation of Politics: the Place of Party Publicity, Broadcasting and Film in British Politics, 1918-39', unpublished PhD, Leeds, 1981.

G.Horwill, 'The Psychology of Political Advertising', *Labour Organiser*, 43, 1924.

C.Hughes & P.Wintour, *Labour Rebuilt: the New Model Party*, Fourth Estate, 1990.

D.Kavanagh, *Election Campaigning*, Blackwells, 1995.

W.Kornhauser, *The Politics of Mass Society*, Routledge, 1959.

P.Kotler & S.Levy, 'Broadening the Concept of Marketing', *Journal of Marketing*, January, 1969.

P.Kotler & G.Zaltman, 'Social Marketing: An Approach to Planned Social Change', *Journal of Marketing*, July, 1971.

A.Mitchell, *Four Years in the Death of the Labour Party*, Methuen, 1983.

N.O'Shaughnessy, *The Phenomenom of Political Marketing*, Macmillan, 1990.

M.Pinto-Duschinsky, *British Political Finance*, American Enterprise Institute, Washington, 1981.

R.Rose, *Influencing Voters*, Faber & Faber, 1967.

M.Scammell, *Designer Politics: How Elections are Won*, Macmillan, 1995.

A.Shama, 'The Marketing of the Political Candidate', *Journal of the Academy of Marketing Science*, 4/4, 1976.

G.Smith & J.Saunders, 'The Application of Marketing to British Politics', *Journal of Marketing Management*, 5/3, 1990.

S.Street, 'The Conservative Party Archives', *Twentieth Century British History*, 3/1, 1992.

K.Swaddle, 'Hi-Tech Elections: Technology and the Development of Electioneering since 1945', *Contemporary Record*, Spring, 1988.

K.Swaddle, *Coping with a Mass Electorate*, unpublished PhD, Oxford, 1990.

R.Tyler, *Selling the Prime Minister*, Grafton, 1987.

E.P.Wake, *Labour Organiser*, 93, 1929.

G.Wallas, *Human Nature in Politics*, fourth edition, Constable, 1948.

S.Webb, 'What is Stratified Electioneering?', *Labour Organiser*, 25, 1922.

J.Whyte, 'The domain of marketing – marketing and non-marketing exchanges', in M.J.Thomas & N.Waite, *The Marketing Digest*, Heinmann.

M.J.Wiener, *English Culture and the Decline of the Industrialist Spirit, 1850-1980*, Penguin, 1981.

Lord Windlesham, *Communication and Political Power*, Jonathan Cape, 1966.

D.Wring, 'From Mass Propaganda to Political Marketing: the Transformation of Labour Party Election Campaigning', in C.Rallings et al (eds), *Elections and Parties Yearbook 1995*, Frank Cass, 1996.

Multi-Culturalism and the Public Sphere

Don N.MacIver
Staffordshire University

'The State and Minority Separatism'

Introduction

The dominant form of political organisation throughout the world in modern times has been the nation state. The nation state as a term came into use after the first world war and is therefore a relatively recent addition to the vocabulary of politics. It is intended to indicate the coincidence of the nation and the state and thus purports to be the fulfilment of the liberal idea of the nation as a self determining group of people. The nation state, however, is a highly contested concept. The term itself is problematic since its practical meaning is in many respects confusing, being applied by some conventions to all states, whatever their ethnic and national composition. Moreover, it was a misnomer even as it was invented: not only is it a statement of political aspiration rather than reality, it is also ambiguous, as it simply begs the question of what is the nation that constitutes the nation state.

There are two concepts of the nation in general use in the history and political science literature. First, there is the civic concept of the nation in which the nation is defined through membership of a civil society with distinctive civil institutions, associations, values and interests. In this sense the nation is an association with a common history and a collective personality whose continued existence is an act of will expressed in the consent and participation of its members. The nation is therefore defined by its members who renew it every generation and may permit the entry of new groups to citizenship. This associational view of the nation evolved in Western Europe and was given its dynamic character and universal appeal by the Jacobins during the French Revolution. It became more influential with increasing democratisation as statesmen using nationalism and national symbols as instruments of state building, sought to secure and legitimise their regimes amongst newly mobilised populations by creating and fostering national cultures to provide a basis for integration and loyalty. Instead of the nation being the basis of the state, the state became the basis of the nation, which it manipulated and directed for its own ends. Thus the state nation claimed to be the nation state, a political community based on an officially sponsored national identity.

Second, there is the ethnic concept of the nation in which the nation is defined as an ethnic community with a distinctive culture usually expressed in a language peculiar to its members. The nation in this sense is an organic entity with an existence of its own, the repository of the traditions and experience of a community. The nation defines and gives identity to its members who are the bearers and custodians of its culture and values. This communal view of the nation was derived from ideas first proposed by Herder and developed by the romantics. Since then it has appeared in a number of different versions and has had a significant influence on the idea of the nation in European thought. It has always appealed to romantics who have seen the ethnic community as the 'natural' basis for the state.

Most states acknowledge both these concepts, at least to some extent, as principles of citizenship, but they are rarely operationalised in a pure form. The two principles do come into conflict from time to time, however, highlighting and sometimes sharpening the social divisions which they articulate. States generally find the associational concept of nationality and citizenship more compatible with the demands of administering a modern political economy. Ethnic communities, on the other hand, find the ethnic concept more effective in rallying support for their distinct identities and the political demands they build upon them. Thus the coexistence and interaction of these two divergent concepts of the nation, nationality and citizenship has a number of significant implications for the management of ethnic diversity within modern civil societies and states. First, divergent concepts of nationality and citizenship are likely to produce divergent approaches to ethnic pluralism which may create ambiguities and conflicts on matters such as immigration and minority rights. Second, it encourages a possibly false dichotomy between individual and communal rights which may increase the extent and intensity of ethnic conflict within plural societies. Third, the adoption and manipulation of these concepts by both dominant and rival aspirant élites may produce conflicting views of the basis of national community and encourage centrifugal pressures and fragmentation. This may compound the difficulties of the state by undermining its capacity to respond effectively to the demands of ethnic and regional minorities.

One of the major sources of political instability and conflict in the world today is that the boundaries of states and the boundaries of ethnic and national groups do not coincide. The boundaries of states are relatively rigid and only change as a result of very exceptional external pressures or cataclysmic conflicts. The boundaries of ethnic groups are more fluid and frequently cut across the boundaries of states. Ethnic groups generally have older pedigrees and often receive very much greater loyalty than states. They may also be the focus for an alternative national identity to that officially associated with the state. Moreover, while ethnic groups are exclusive and persistent, they are also resilient and forceful in the expression of their identities and interests. Their demands for political power and autonomy are a frequent source of rivalry and conflict within states. While this has been highlighted to some extent by some of the catastrophic conflicts of the early 1990s, this should not be allowed to obscure the fact that some form of ethnic pluralism is a feature of the vast majority of states.

This observation is affirmed and emphasised by the rise of ethnic and ethno-regional nationalist movements some of whose demands can be met only by restructuring or even dissolving existing states. There are about 200 states in the world today but thousands of ethnic groups. Few states are ethnically homogeneous; most include significant ethnic minorities. Many states have ethnically distinct regions with their own cultural identities which in some cases are politically active, with substantial popular support for autonomy or independence. Even regions without a distinct ethnic base may acquire a social and political cohesion which enables them to articulate their particular interests effectively within the state and even beyond, as the experience of Canadian provinces demonstrates. Some regions may believe themselves to be deprived relative to others and this may cement local identities and sustain the commitment of local interests. The existence of such disaffected, discontented or simply distinctive groups and regions within a state may not immediately threaten the state, but the mobilisation of ethnic minority and ethno-regional nationalism may challenge the political authority of the state and reveal shortcomings in its cohesion and legitimacy.

Ethnic pluralism, regionalism and multiculturalism thus have significant implications for the social cohesion, political integration and even the viability of states as well as for their structures and processes of government. Multinational states are usually characterised by fragmented political cultures, social pluralism and 'deep diversity'. They probably incorporate major ethnic, language or religious differences that reinforce or cut across socio-economic cleavages. There may be strong loyalty or identification with particular regions or ethnic groups, possibly expressed in commitment to distinctive symbols, traditions and institutions and sometimes in resurgent nationalism. Older and well established states may have had more time and opportunity to develop satisfactory procedures of conflict management and resolution, but they still do not escape the divisive effects of renascent ethnic and regional identities. The existence of such pluralities, therefore, is likely to produce divided communities with conflicting orientations to politics and disputed standards of legitimacy which may lead to serious civil conflict or even the disintegration of states as in Lebanon and Yugoslavia.

Pluralism and Identity

The argument that people should determine their own government and that the most appropriate basis for this is nationality or national identity was presented most succinctly by John Stuart Mill. There was 'a prima facie case', he wrote, that a national group should be united 'under the same government and a government to themselves apart'. This was an idea that had been evolving in western Europe, especially in England for nearly two hundred years, when Mill wrote. His demand that, if a people were free to do anything they should be free to choose their own form of government, was a culmination as much as a beginning in political thought. The strength of liberal ideas in the late nineteenth and early twentieth centuries, the influence of Anglo-American Liberal internationalism and the powerful advocacy of Lloyd George and Woodrow Wilson then ensured that this idea became well established in the thought and practice of international relations, though not so much of international law. Indeed in modern politics national identity has become almost the only acceptable basis for the legitimate exercise of political power and authority. In homogeneous societies with a uniform or a dominant culture and a high level of agreement about national identity, the basis of legitimacy is likely to be undisputed. Where these conditions are lacking and there is uncertainty or conflict about national identity, agreement about political legitimacy may be difficult to establish or simply unattainable. Then not only the foundations of legitimate political authority but the whole framework of political organisation are likely to be contested.

Mill took the view that it would be virtually impossible to maintain liberal democratic government or political unity within a multinational or polyethnic state. The common public opinion, the exposure to similar influences, the shared goals, the unity of purpose and leadership which Mill thought necessary to the proper functioning free institutions would be lacking. This would be compounded by the existence of widespread mistrust and suspicion, divided leadership and possibly even significant differences over fundamental values. In such a situation simple conflicts of interest would be turned into issues of principle and matters of right on which there could be no accommodation or compromise. This could be avoided if minorities were prepared to assimilate, which would in any case be in their own interest as it would give them access to a greater cultural and political system. It seems that Mill's model was not the nation state but the state nation whose official nationalism provided a sort of canopy for the cultural and political socialisation of all its members, however diverse their origins.

Mill's view was directly challenged by Lord Acton, whose famous paper on Nationality was conceived as a fundamental criticism of Mill's theory. Acton argued that any state which identifies itself with a particular idea or section, be it nation or class, tends to become absolute and unable to tolerate dissent. Thus, while the nation state (or the state nation) absolutises the 'popular' will, the values of particular communities tend to be marginalised or simply disregarded. Contrary to Mill, Acton thought that multinational states provided a promising framework for the success of pluralist liberal democratic institutions. The conflicting interests and divergent loyalties in multinational states would act as a focus and inspiration to particular communities and form a bulwark against the absolutist tendenceies of central government. Acton believed that the ideal society and the ideal state would include several national or ethnic communities each of which would be to some extent self-governing. He apparently did not consider the possibility that such a state could disintegrate into a number of separate absolutisms.

Acton's view was shared to some extent by Otto Bauer, the Austrian Marxist thinker who was at the centre of a school of thought which tried to explain ethnicity and nationalism and bring them into the Marxist framework. Bauer's views were based on a more fully developed theoretical foundation than Acton's, a lifetime of direct experience and a large body of empirical data gained from a long period of research. Bauer's approach did not condemn nationalism or attempt to marginalise it, but affirmed it as one of the great forces of history. Bauer, however, regarded ethnicity and national identity as essentially a cultural phenomenon which should be protected within the state by measures of autonomy and self-regulation. Together with Karl Renner, Max Adler and others Bauer developed a political and administrative scheme for this purpose based on the idea that national identity should be treated as a personal rather than a collective or group attribute and that states should provide a system of support to enable members of all ethnic groups to gain access to public life. For a multinational state to succeed on these principles, Bauer was acutely aware that the rights of individuals and ethnic communities would have to be guaranteed and national identity as far as possible depoliticised.

Mill did not deny that individuals are influenced by the groups and communities in which they live, but arguing that a political society which developed around rival or conflicting communities was not likely be a succesful democracy. Liberals in the tradition of Mill see political society as a collection of free and rational individuals guided in their behaviour by their own interests and obligations and the search for a good life. Liberals reject the idea of 'political society as a community because, among other things, it leads to the systematic denial of basic liberties and may allow the oppressive use of ... force'. Acton and Bauer offer rather different views of political society and the relation of individuals to it. Acton argues that as a matter of preference and Bauer as a matter of necessity individuals do not relate to society simply as individuals but through the communities in which they live.

A more thorough version of this communitarian view is offered by those who argue that it is not just as a matter of preference or circumstance that people belong to communities or groups. It is inevitable in the nature of human social relations that people exist in communities which not only influence their outlook and behaviour but actually determine who and what they are; the communities they belong to are 'not relationships they choose ... but a constituent part of their identity'. People, therefore, are not isolated individuals; moreover, the communities to which they belong play a crucial part in creating them and their needs, preferences and consequent demands. In dealing with issues of social and cultural diversity, therefore, it may be desirable not only to take account of communities, but to give priority to communities. The vital role of the community in shaping the individual means that the purposes of individuals are part of a common good that can only be validated by and within the community and its system of values. There is no political principle which gives universal validity to any political purpose and political purposes generally do not have any necessary validity outside the community which supports them and is affected by them. Thus the purposes and prevailing values of a society should not be imposed on one of its minority communities. Minorities may wish and be entitled to protect their own core values.

One of the implications of this is that, while it is necessary in the interests of social justice that all groups in society should be treated equally, it may be desirable in some conditions to treat certain particular groups differently. This is important to some ethnic, regional and minority groups who wish to protect their own culture and resist the assimilative pressures of a larger society or dominant culture. Such groups seek the opportunity to maintain a minority language, a distinctive civil society, a traditional way of life or even a combination of these. They may demand recognition for the distinctiveness of their community culture and seek some special treatment, such as a privileged status or a measure of local, sectional or functional autonomy or in some cases full territorial self-government, to enable them to protect it. These kinds of demands are more likely in multinational states, where they are likely to create difficulty for political authorities. Attempts to concede special treatment to any group is likely to produce a reaction, either negative or imitative or both, among other groups. It may also meet objection from the majority population who may feel that separate or different treatment can not be equal. On the other hand, such concessions may be the only way to avoid seething discontent or serious domestic conflict or even the breakup of the state.

While it is true that the social structure and ethnic composition of multinational states frequently presents them with particularly intractable problems of government, there is also considerable evidence that social pluralism need not be an obstacle to the development and maintenance of stable national polities. Indeed many states persist and succeed despite having fragmented political cultures (for example, Switzerland and Canada), while others adapt or change to accommodate plural identities (for example, Belgium and Spain). Thus the development of a national political community with an integrated identity and regime loyalty may be compatible with the existence of active regional and ethnic sub-cultures. In such conditions, however, it may be difficult on occasions to achieve consensus or to govern through the institutions and processes of 'normal' politics. Moreover, in these circumstances there is likely to be conflict over the constitution, composition of government, recruitment to the public service and official language policy, not to mention the recognition of minority cultures and the prioritisation of groups and regions in the allocation of resources. These problems have become increasingly visible in our time and recent events in several parts of the world have demonstrated that the consequences of political failure in these matters can be dreadful and savage.

Minority Separatism and the Response of the State

Many states face particular difficulties in dealing with ethnic minorities and regions which demand special treatment, cultural autonomy and self-government. The demands and objectives of ethnic and regional minorities are not all the same or even consistent from one time to another in a particular case. There is considerable ambivalence as well as uncertainty about the demands of such groups and movements, but they may be classified in three categories. First, there are demands which are mainly output oriented, that is they are concerned to win specific benefits from the political system, such as increased expenditure on regional projects, rather than change the system itself. Second, there are demands which are regime oriented, that is to make significant changes in the structure and organisation of the state within which they exist or in their relationship to the state. Demands for certain kinds of cultural autonomy, home rule and regional self government come into this category. Third, there are demands which appear to be community oriented, that is for fundamental changes in the identity and definition of the political community. Autonomist, secessionist, irredentist and independence movements are by definition community oriented in their demands. The rhetoric and activity of all minority nationalist groups tend to make some use of the vocabulary of nationalism and separatism, but ethnic and ethno-regional demands are not necessarily for separation, at least in the sense of independence. Separatism is an affirmation of a different identity and a demand for its recognition and for the political means to sustain it. Separatism, therefore, is a term which describes the attitudes and ideology of all minority and regional nationalist movements.

Figure 1
Separatism

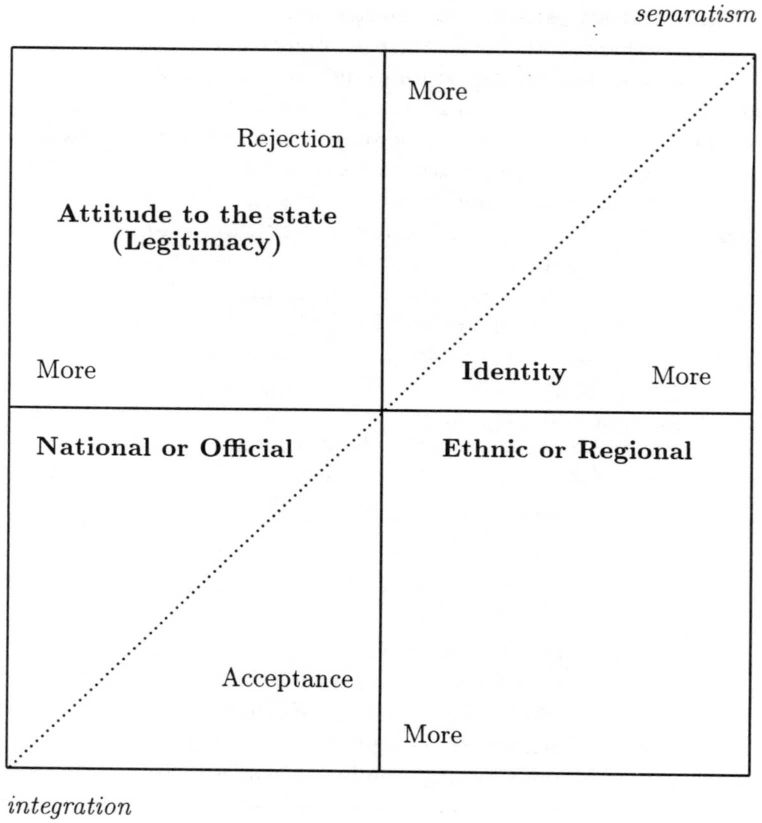

separatism

	More
Rejection	
Attitude to the state (Legitimacy)	
More	**Identity** More
National or Official	**Ethnic or Regional**
Acceptance	
	More

integration

In all political systems the articulation of society in relation to the state has two dimensions, identity and legitimacy, which together define the level of political integration of the state. In polyethnic and multi-national societies and particularly in the case of of minority groups and regions, these dimensions are especially sensitive and significant. The two dimensions are represented in Figure 1. Identity is an expression of the preferred identity of individuals and communities within the political system, that is, the relative strength of minority/regional as opposed to 'official national' identity. In many multi-national states people prefer to identify themselves in terms of minority or regional identities, for example, as Quebecois or Catalans or Scots rather than Canadians, Spanish or British. Legitimacy is an expression of the attitudes of people and communities to the state, that is their acceptance or rejection of the existing national state and its role in their lives as opposed to a preference for allocating some or more of its functions to a regional government. These two dimensions provide an index of national integration within the state and, conversely, of the strength of minority or regional nationalist demands for differential treatment or self-government.

Some states have low levels of legitimacy (due to incomplete acceptance) amongst minorities and low levels of identification with the official 'nation' (due to competing identities), and hence relatively low levels of national integration especially amongst minority or regional populations. Frequently this is expressed as a strong ethnic or regional identity combined with an ambivalence towards the state. The dimensions of this attitude are presented as the diagonal line in the Figure. This line plots the resultant of the identities of minority and regional populations and of the range of attitudes to the state from support for the existing 'nation-state' to a preference for regional autonomy and ultimately even secession to form an independent state.

National separatism, then, may also be considered as a political process in which the relationship between an ethnic minority or region and the state develops and changes to a more distant and more autonomous one. As a political process, it may be understood in terms of the conditions and factors which initiate and sustain it and subsequently determine its development. These may be identified as the social, environmental and moral conditions and the integrative capabilities of the sub-unit in relation to the political system as a whole.

Social conditions include the condition of the state before the beginning of the separatist movement, the ethnic composition and distribution of the population, the economic relationship of the subunit to the larger system and the extent to which the sub-unit could itself be objectively regarded as a distinct society and a separate political community, the exact nature of the separatist movement and the extent of its support and finally, the strength, mode and agencies of resistance to secession. The significance of these conditions is that, while ethnic, cultural and linguistic homogeneity may not be essential to maintaining a stable political community, they may be more important for a successful secession. A secession movement in a society with deep and politically active internal cleavages, for example on religion (for example, Ireland 1920-21) or clan loyalty (for example, Somaliland post 1992), may find its cohesion reduced and its prospects of success damaged.

Environmental conditions include the territorial definition and size of the sub-unit and its location in relation to the territory of the existing state. The quality of the physical and natural environment is also important, in particular whether it has experienced any significant recent change which would make separation more attractive as, for example, the discovery of North Sea Oil was supposed to have done in the case of Scotland. Environmental factors also include other states, which may encourage or support the secessionist movement, as it is said Germany did in the case of Croatia. If favourable social and environmental conditions are present in strength, there is a greater chance of a separatist movement being successful.

The possibility of gaining support for separatist claims or for effecting a successful secession may be considerably enhanced if the claims of the seceeding unit can be supported by a convincing moral case. Such a case can be made if the region and its people were incorporated into the state by force (Georgia or Estonia in the Soviet Union, Eritrea in Ethiopia); or if the region and its people are being oppressed, exploited or economically disadvantaged by the state (Biafra, Bangladesh, Singapore); or if the state or the central government consistently ignore the terms on which the state or the union was originally agreed, a claim sometimes made by Quebec and Scottish nationalists; or if the region has an historic experience of separate statehood which its people wish to restore (Norway in 1905, Poland in 1919, possibly Scotland. If such a moral case can be made, the claims of the separatists are more likely to meet a sympathetic response within as well as beyond the state.

In some cases territories and regions may be able to develop or deploy certain institutional and political resources in challenging the state. These resources may be described as coercive, instrumental and identive. Coercive resources are primarily autonomous institutions for maintaining authority, control and security in the form of a legal administration, courts, police and military forces. Instrumental resources are economic, technological, administrative and human resources and the ability to utilize them effectively for the provision and delivery of government services. Identive resources are values, symbols, traditions, religious and cultural institutions which endow the territorial unit with legitimacy, social cohesion and political coherence.

The crucial part of the process of secession is the internalization of these resources, especially the identive resources, within the sub-unit, ie their transfer from the existing socio-political system to the sub-unit. The internalization of integrative resources in sub-units not only strengthens the integrative factors themselves but may place additional stress on the existing system which may make secession more probable and more practical. This would suggest that some containment responses to ethno-territorial disaffection, especially the expansion of political autonomy in the form of home rule or devolution, may be counterproductive because the enhanced opportunity they provide for the internalization of integrative assets may actually increase the possibility of secession.

The failure of integration, especially of identitive and instrumental capabilities, and the internalization of integrative resources in sub-units challenges the continuation of the existing form of the state in some modern societies. Doubts on this point may be dispelled or at least reduced by consideralion of the case of Norway. In 1905 Norway seceded from Sweden after a non-violent Norwegian uprising following several decades in which the Swedish-Norwegian state had experienced progressive disintegration due mainly to the internalization of integrative, particularly identive and instrumental resources within the Norwegian sub-unit. Even when Norway was transferred to Sweden, after four hundred years of union with Denmark, a Norwegian nationalism was emerging based on a rapidly reviving Norwegian identity and the creation of Norwegian tradition from the legacy of a proud if distant heritage. The establishment of a home rule constitution for Norway made it possible to internalize coercive, instrumental and identive assets in the Norwegian sub-unit, which weakened the legitimacy of Swedish rule and reduced the integrative capability of the union. Latterly the separation of Norway was accelerated by the increase in instrumental and identive assets notably economic resources, political institutions and national consciousness. In the end the union became an obstacle to the further development of the Norwegian political community and the final separation was almost a formality.

Although few states are threatened with imminent disintegration, some do face fundamental conflict over the nature and structure of their regimes. In former Yugoslavia, ethnic conflict concerned the definition of the political community itself, whereas in some cases, such as the United Kingdom or Canada, the conflict may be more regime centred, but not necessarily any less intractable. Some ethno-regional groups claim to be resisting oppression and illegal annexation, but the more usual complaint of ethnic and regional minorities is that the state is remote and indifferent to their special concerns and cultural needs. What ethno-territorial groups generally seek is greater control over their own affairs in the belief that they can apply their own resources more efficiently in pursuit of their own interests. Ethnic and regional groups, therefore, tend to define their needs and their differences with the state in cultural and political terms, in the hope that this will more strongly legitimise their claims to special treatment and greater autonomy.

The state and central government, however, are more likely to define ethnic and regional problems in economic and administrative terms, hoping that they can contain the issues within parameters that they can more easily control. To the extent that ethno-regional discontents are generated by the unsatisfactory performance of regional economics and the insensitive administration of minorities and regional societies, this is reasonable. Governments have responded to these challenges in fairly consistent ways. They have tried to define their purposes more clearly, sometimes making concessions to special cultural demands and regional economic needs. They have tried to improve the effectiveness of their services by increasing consultation and participation in decision making. They have tried to relieve the pressure on government structures by various devices of functional and territorial devolution. Such reforms are presented as an expansion of regional autonomy and new contributions to more effective government In reality they are more likely to represent an effort to accommodate regional demands to the interests of central administration and to bring regional élites within the control of central government.

Attempts to deal with minorities and regional problems in this way ultimately place the state in a dilemma. From the point of view of the centre, the object of increasing regional autonomy is to broaden the area of consent and secure the integrity of the state. Economic development, however, requires more central control of resources to ensure the success of regional policies. From the viewpoint of the region on the other hand, the expansion of autonomy is meant to provide greater local control of decision making. As for economic development, regional economic needs are seen as reflecting the repeated failures of central government, the redemption of which must involve less central control of resources rather than more. For the regions this means that, while some of the benofits of state intervention may be eagerly sought, the state itself may be resented. The dilemma of the state then is that concessions to regional demands must mean yielding central powers to the regions, which might be seen as endangering the integrity of the state. On the other hand, witholding concessions may fuel regional identity and separatist sentiments whiclhwould simply reduce the legitimacy of the state in the regions.

Modes of Accommodation

In some cases it is possible to resolve this dilemma only by the moderation of regional and minority demands or by the breakup of the state. The breakup of the state is not always an objective of the nationalist groups and is not necessarily in their interest. Many ethnic and regional nationalist movements, such as home rule movements, employ the vocabulary of national separatism to pursue demands which can actually be satisfied by changes in the existing regime. Many ethnic demands, except on the part of a few extremists, are not for political independence, but for recognition of a cultural identity and the provision of the economic and administrative framework to sustain a distinct regional society. If this is the case the problem facing the state may be more tractable and solutions which could preserve the integrity of the state, while satisfying the aspirations of minority and regional demands may be more readily found. Such solutions involve the institutionalisation of political arrangements which recognise cultural diversity and facilitate the accommodation of plural identities.

The available solutions include various forms of territorial and communal autonomy based on the principles of federalism and consociationalism. These are essentially power sharing arrangements which enable two or more groups to avoid direct conflict and cooperate within the same state. They avoid domination by the majority, protect the rights of minorities and enable diverse groups to protect their own cultures and ways of life. By creating a measure of self government they may provide greater sensitivity to the demands of local and particular groups and reduce discontent by adjusting policy to their needs. Such systems of shared rule are intended to facilitate political integration and stability in polyethnic societies thus maintaining the integrity of the state while satisfying both the interests and ethno-territorial aspirations of some groups within it.

While the demands of regional and ethnic minority groups puts more pressure on the state, the state is itself increasingly expected to provide order, justice, economic development and social welfare to its heterogenous populations. This puts further pressure on the distributive and administrative capability of the state as well as on its economic resources. However, the state is today less expected to be the sole provider of its own security and is less able to behave as a wholly independent unit in the international economy. Indeed, sub-state units such as regions and provinces have themselves become increasingly active in the international economy. Some have sought to convert this to a basis for autonomy or limited independence in a new international environment. Hence proposals such as Quebec's 'sovereignty association' and the Scottish Nationalists' 'independence within the European Community'. It is possible that such ideas may provide an alternative way of reconciling the differences between the state and some of its ethnic minorities in the future.

Most states exist in multinational or polyethnic societies and it is possible that the extent and effectiveness of integration in these Tnation statesU may have been overestimated. Even those states which have declared themselves to be multinational and celebrated the fact in their constitutions have not been able to avoid the demands of minority and regional groups for autonomy. The revival of ethnicity and regionalism, by simultaneously challenging the state and impairing its capacity to respond effectively, may threaten the survival of the state as a coherent political community. This could have significant implications, not only for the persistence of the nation state as a community of rights, but also for the nature of political order in all parts of the world.

Multiculturalism and the Public Sphere

Tariq Modood
Policy Studies Institute

'Racial Equality and Multiculturalism in Britain:
The Progressivist Bias Against Some Minorities'

Introduction

Charles Taylor has argued, rightly I believe, that liberalism is not a 'neutral ground on which people of all cultures can meet and coexist' [1]. The only example he gives of where 'one has to draw the line' is 'incitement to assassination'. So far there is likely to be no conflict. He reaches this conclusion however by arguing that the controversy over *The Satanic Verses* shows that '[f]or mainstream Islam, there is no question of separating politics and religion the way we have come to expect in Western liberal society' (*Ibid*). My objection is that it is far from obvious that this is what the controversy showed or needs to show in order for anyone to reach the conclusion that liberalism ought not to tolerate incitement to murder. Taylor offers no evidence that 'mainstream Islam' involves an acceptance of incitement to assassination; nor that if you hold that politics and religion do not have to be separated (in the way that Taylor himself argues that politics and culture do not have to be separated), then you have no argument against incitement to assassination. The reference to mainstream Islam is in fact a *non sequitur*, but the impression is created that liberalism cannot accommodate mainstream Islam, that mainstream Muslims are not to be included in 'the politics of recognition'.

I suggest that some of the preliminary tasks in conceptualising a multiculturalism appropriate to Britain are to identify and remedy the ignorance-cum-prejudice against groups such as Muslims, and the structural bias against disadvantaged religious minorities in contemporary political philosophy.

My contribution here is two arguments:

- 1. Racial inequality in Britain cannot be characterised in terms of a black-white colour dualism: the distinctive forms of racism suffered by Asians and Muslims need to be identified and countered.

- 2. Notions of multiculturalism which attempt to confine culture and nationality to a private sphere are inadequate, but the new modes of affirming group difference, especially in some North American versions, seem to carry a bias against religious minorities.

---

[1] In A.Gutmann (ed), *Multiculturalism: Examining The Politics of Recognition*, Princeton University Press, 1994, p.62.

Racial Equality

From the 1970s onwards, in the wake of immigration into England from some parts of the former Empire, a growing body of opinion, especially expert opinion, came to the view that a racial dualism had emerged in Britain. It was most succinctly expressed in 1982 by Salman Rushdie:

> 'Britain is now two entirely different worlds and the one you inherit is determined by the colour of your skin'.

The truth in this view was somewhat exaggerated and is now increasingly inappropriate. Using the three key indicators of unemployment, job hierarchies and educational qualifications shows that there is a dualism, but that it is not a colour dualism. Bangladeshis, Pakistanis and Caribbeans have made some progress but continue to have the disadvantaged profile of a decade earlier. The Chinese, African Asians and Indians, on the other hand, have or are developing a socio-economic profile which is similar to or better than that of the White population.[2]

The most important fact the new data on socio-economic diversity should help us to see is that racial discrimination is not a unitary form of disadvantaging because not all non-white groups are discriminated against in the same way or to the same extent. Colour-racism may be a constant but there are other kinds of racism at work in Britain. Colour-racism is the antipathy, exclusion and unequal treatment of people on the basis of their physical appearance, above all on their not being 'white' or of European-origin appearance. Cultural-racism builds on colour- racism by using cultural difference from an alleged British or civilised norm to vilify or marginalise or demand cultural assimilation from groups who also suffer colour-racism. Post- war racism in Britain has been simultaneously culturalist and biological and, while the latter is perhaps essential to it being racism, it is in fact the more superficial aspect. As white people's interactions with non-white individuals increased, they were not necessarily less conscious of group differences but they were far more likely to ascribe group differences to upbringing, customs, forms of socialisation and self-identity than to biological heredity. So, for example, white people who continue to be racists towards some ethnic groups, can come to admire other ethnic groups. Several ethnographic studies have found for example that white working class boys who are anti-Asian admire Afro-Caribbean sub-cultures because of their positive masculine and class associations. Opinion surveys consistently record that white people think there is more extreme prejudice against Asians than against Afro-Caribbeans. The gap is most amongst younger people and is widening.[3] A survey we are currently analysing at PSI found that all ethnic groups believe that prejudice against Asians in general, and Muslims in particular, is much the highest of any ethnic, racial or religious group.[4]

Perhaps unlike in the United States, there has been a significant growth in black-white sociability and cultural synthesis, especially amongst young

---

[2] T.Modood, *Not Easy Being British: Colour, Culture and Citizenship*, Trentham Books, 1992.
[3] R.Jowell et al (eds), *British Social Attitudes*, Gower, 1986, p.163.
[4] T.Modood et al, *The Fourth National Survey of Ethnic Minorities*, 1996, forthcoming.

people. This is evident in the high prestige that black cultural styles are held in, and in the hero-worship of successful black 'stars' in football and sport, music and entertainment. As also in the high rates of black-white marriages and cohabitation: nearly half of Caribbean men under the age of 44, and nearly a third of women have a white partner, compared to less than 10% and less than 5% of Asian men and women respectively. It is particularly important to note that this sociability is not necessarily in a colour-blind assimilationist, 'passing for white' context in which racism is ignored. For some young people it can take place in ways in which black ethnicity and anti- racism is emphasised, indeed is the point. Black persons can be admired, not in spite of, but because of their blackness, for their aesthetics, style and creativity as well as for their anti-racist resistance. Of course, there is also much negative stereotyping and racism against black people (and some positive stereotyping of Asians). My point is that different groups suffer different, as well as similar kinds of racism, and one kind depends upon cultural acceptability.

I am aware that the concept of cultural-racism will seem perverse to some. It will seem yet another example of an 'inflation of the meaning of racism' by bringing together two things, racism proper and cultural prejudice or ethnocentricism, that are apparently quite distinct, thereby obscuring the real nature of racist thinking and practices. It is true there is no necessary connection between cultural prejudice and colour-racism; but there is no more a connection between racial discrimination and class inequalities, and yet when the two do come together the concept of racial disadvantage is a good one to describe the situation. Or again, there is no necessary connection between racism and sexism but we know they can be connected, and when they are, a distinctive phenomenon is created in the form of stereotypes about submissive Asian women and the strong black woman who cannot keep her man . So similarly, there may be only a contingent, as-a-matter-of-fact connection between colour prejudice and cultural prejudice, true for only certain times and places; nevertheless when the two kinds of exclusionism and oppression come together, we have a distinctive phenomenon worthy of its own name and conceptualisation.

In this conceptualising, far from obscuring racism we learn something about it. Namely, that contemporary British racism is not dependent upon any (even unstated) form of biological determinism. There must be some reference to differences in physical appearances and/or a legacy of the racism of earlier centuries, otherwise we would not be speaking of a racism but of an ethnicism. The reference however is not necessarily to a deep biology; a superficial biology is all that is required to pick out racial groups, to stereotype them and to treat them accordingly. Being able to pick individuals out on the basis of their physical appearance and assign them to a racial group may be essential to racism but physical appearance may stand only as a marker of a race not as the explanation of a group's behaviour. The racist will want to impute inferiority, undesirability, distinctive behavioral traits and so on to a group distinguished by the use of phenotypes; but the racist does not have to believe, and by and large in contemporary Britain it is not believed, that the behavioral qualities are produced by biology rather than by history, culture, upbringing, by certain norms or their absence. I suggest therefore that a notion of cultural- racism is essential to understanding and opposing racism in Britain.[5]

Multiculturalism

Minority ethnicity, albeit white ethnicity, has traditionally been regarded in Britain as acceptable if it was confined to the privacy of family and community, and did not make any political demands. Earlier groups of migrants and refugees, such as the Irish or the Jews in the nineteenth and the first half of the twentieth century, found that peace and prosperity came easier the less public one made one's minority practices or identity. Perhaps for non-European origin groups, whose physical appearance gave them a visibility that made them permanently vulnerable to racial discrimination, the model of a privatised group identity was never viable. Yet, additionally, one has to acknowledge the existence of a climate of opinion quite different from that experienced by the earlier Irish or Jewish incomers.

In association with other socio-political movements such as feminism and gay rights which challenge the public-private distinction or demand a share of public space, ethnic difference is increasingly seen as something that needs not just toleration but also public acknowledgement, resources and representation. Iris Young expresses well the new political climate when she describes the emergence of an ideal of equality based not just on allowing excluded groups to assimilate and live by the norms of dominant groups, but based on the view that 'a positive self-definition of group difference is in fact more liberatory'.[6] An example she gives is of the black power movement which 'encouraged Blacks to break their alliance with whites and assert the specificity of their own culture, political organisation and goals' (*Ibid*, p.159). Another is of the 'gay pride assertion that sexual identity is a matter of culture and politics, and not merely "behaviour" to be tolerated or forbidden' (*Ibid*, p.161); and certainly one of the most important movements to contribute to this contemporary climate of opinion is 'gynocentric feminism' which, with its emphasis on the positivity and specifity of female experience and values has successfully contested the gender blindness of an earlier wave of feminism so that '[m]ost elements of the contemporary women's movement have been separatist to a degree' (*Ibid*, p.161).

These movements have not had the same impact in Britain as in parts of North America, but are certainly present here. In particular I think there is an ethnic assertiveness in Britain which has parallels with North America, and which has been less evident amongst recent migrants and their descendants in other European Union countries, where cultural assimilation is still regarded as integral to citizenship and political equality. This assertiveness based on feelings of not being respected or of lacking access to public space, often consists of counterpoising positive images against traditional or dominant stereotypes, of projecting identities in order to challenge existing power

---

[5] T.Modood, 'Political Blackness and British Asians', *Sociology*, 28/4, 1994.
[6] I.M.Young, *Justice and the Politics of Difference*, Princeton University Press, 1990, p.157.

relations or to negotiate the sharing of physical, institutional and discursive space. At the very least one would have to say that a significant anti-racist challenge is taking place to the presumed stigma associated with not being white or conventionally British.

The movement is from an understanding of equality in terms of individualism and cultural assimilation to a politics of recognition, to equality as encompassing public ethnicity. Equality as not having to hide or apologise for one's origins, family or community but requiring others to show respect for them and adapt public attitudes and arrangements so that the heritage they represent is encouraged rather than contemptuously expected to wither away. This movement, including the tension between the older and newer versions of equality and attempts to achieve compromise or synthesis, has influenced British race relations and anti-racist debates. It has also influenced one of the newcomers to this debate, Muslim assertiveness. A study of some of Muslim activism shows close parallels with the main contemporary American and British racial equality perspectives.[7] Three broad approaches stand out: a colour-blind human rights and human dignity approach; an approach based on an extension of the concepts of racial discrimination and racial equality to include anti-Muslim racism; and, finally a Muslim syndicalism or Muslim-power approach. What is revealed is less obscurantist Islamic interventions into a modern secular discourse, but typical minority options in contemporary Anglo-American equality politics. Certainly, British Muslim community activism mirrors much more closely other related contemporary equality debates than it does any Muslim polity (past or present) or any particular sectarian differences (such as Shia or Sunni).

The multiculturalism that I see emerging in Britain or at least pushing its way into debates, is then, in some important ways similar to that being elaborated by some North American political theorists. It is developing a notion of public ethnicity, of redrawing our understanding of the private and the public. This is hardly a simple matter. Indeed, there is a body of theoretical opinion which argues that the public-private distinction is essential to multiculturalism. John Rex, for example, argues that the fundamental distinction between a pluralist society without equality and the multicultural ideal is that the latter restricts cultural diversity to a private sphere so that all enjoy equality of opportunity and uniform treatment in the public domain.[8] He readily recognises that this is a far from watertight distinction; education, for example, is an area in which both the claims of the public (the teaching of a civic culture) and the private (the teaching of minority religious and linguistic heritages) have to co-exist, and Rex is open to the idea of state funding of schools which besides teaching a core curriculum are designed to meet the religious and cultural needs of minorities. He sees such state support for minorities as analogous to the many welfare and economic responsibilities assumed by the modern social democratic state. For him, therefore, the public-private distinction is not about a policy of laissez-faire

---

[7] T.Modood, 'Muslim views on religious identity and racial equality', *New Community*, 19/3, 1993.

[8] J.Rex, *The Concept of a Multi-cultural Society*, University of Warwick, 1985.

in relation to culture, a state neutrality about conceptions of the good, but an insistence that while there may legitimately be a sphere of differential rights, it does not extend to law, politics, economics and welfare policy. Yet Rex believes that as a matter of historical fact, European societies have managed to extract a 'rational', 'abstract' morality and legal system out of the various 'folk' cultures, and that all citizens can share this without betraying their folk culture, for all folk cultures have been subordinated to this civic culture, which is the basis of the modern state and capitalist economy. 'Thus multi-culturalism in the modern world involves on the one hand the acceptance of a single culture and a single set of individual rights governing the public domain and a variety of folk cultures in the private domestic and communal domains'(*Ibid*, p.6). On this view the multicultural state might be supportive of some or all folk cultures, but it effectively limits their scope and makes itself immune to folk criticism.

An important implication of this way of seeing the public-private distinction is found in a discussion by Habermas. To the question of to what extent a recipient society can require assimilation from immigrants, he answers that immigrants cannot be required to conform to the dominant way of life, but a democratic constitutional state must

> 'preserve the identity of the political community, which nothing, including immigration, can be permitted to encroach upon, since that identity is founded on the constitutional principles anchored in the political culture and not on the basic ethical orientations of the cultural form of life predominant in that country'.[9]

But surely there is not a valid distinction here: politics and law depend to some degree on shared ethical assumptions and inevitably reflect the norms and values of the society that they are part of. In this sense, no state stands outside culture, ethnicity or nationality, and changes in these will need to be reflected in the arrangements of the state. Indeed, Habermas goes on to recognise that, following immigration, 'as other forms of life become established the horizon within which citizens henceforth interpret their common constitutional principles may also expand' (*Ibid*, pp.139-140). But then, what is the point of his initial distinction? It cannot simply be to state that the status of law is different from customs and lifestyles, that immigrants must obey the law and (like everybody else) use constitutional means to change it and the political system, because that neither requires nor implies that the preservation of a recipient society's political identity is more essential than other collective identities, say, the recipient society's linguistic or religious identity.

It seems to me that to participate in political institutions presupposes a great deal of commonality; language or languages, for instance, including an understanding of the rhetorical and symbolic force of words, gestures and silences, the evocation of names and so on. The open and complex character of a rich and varied nationality must not be essentialised into to a few quaint customs; but nor can it be reduced to a political system.

---

[9] J.Habermas, 'Struggles for recognition in the democratic constitutional state', in A.Gutmann (ed).

People have a sense of constituting a society or a nationality or, as it were, a federation of communities by living and working and knowing each other in numerous and complex ways, from using the same local shops to reading the same newspapers; admittedly, none of these has the same formal status of membership as the rights of citizenship, and the points of trust and shared interests usually exist within a political and legal framework. My point is that even if some conditions are necessary to a participation in a shared public culture, such as the rights of citizenship, a public culture or a national identity cannot be equated with the formally legal or institutional. A sense of society, of effective as opposed to nominal membership in a shared public culture, over and above private and communal affiliations, may be dependent on many different points of contact and of sharing different things with different people. It may be like the philosophically proverbial cord, the strength of which does not depend upon a single thread.

Public and private, national and ethnic, then may mark different spheres of activity, and different ways in which we relate to people, but they are not strict divisions. There are bound to be dialectical tensions, and , as Rex recognizes, points of dependency; communities may look to the state to support their culture, for example through schools and other educational institutions, and the state may, for example, look to communities to inculcate virtues such as truth-telling, respect for property, service to others and so on without which a civic morality would have nothing to build on. If the public and private mutually shape each other in these ways, then however 'abstract' and 'rational' the principles of a public order may be, they will reflect the 'folk cultures' out of which the particular public order has grown, which provide its personnel and sustain it in all kinds of ways. There can then be no question of the public sphere being morally neutral; rather, it will appeal to points of privately shared values and sense of belonging, as well as to the superstructure of conventions, laws and principles. Those whose ethnic or community identities, for reasons of conquest or genius, are most reflected in the national, those who are most comfortable in these complementary identities, will feel least the force of a public-private distinction; they may feel it more when they have to share the public domain with persons from other communities, persons who also wish the national to reflect something of their own community. The elaboration of a strict public-private spheres distinction at this point may act to buttress the privileged position of the historically 'integrated' folk cultures at the expense of the historically subordinated or the newly migrated folk. In this context the public-private division, far from underpinning multiculturalism will work to prevent its emergence.

If we recognise that the public order is not morally neutral, is not culture or ethnic-blind, we can understand why oppressed, marginalised or immigrant groups (in Britain if not in North America, immigrants and former subjects of the Empire will be synonymous terms) may want to see the public order, in which they may for the first time be coming to have rights of participation, to 'recognise' them, to be user-friendly to the new folks. The logic of demanding that public institutions acknowledge the gender-bias of their ways of doing things, and allow for female insights and perspectives, becomes readily intelligible, as does the whole phenomenon of minorities seeking increased visibility, of contesting the boundaries of the public, of not simply asking to be left alone and civilly tolerated. To recognize what lies behind challenges to the public-private distinction is not however to necessarily know how to meet the various challenges in a principled way, what kind of institutional recognition or political representation is merited by the various claims. One normative ideal of a plural public is where 'each of the constituent groups affirms the presence of others' (Young, *ibid*, p.188). Committed people sometime speak of 'celebrating' diversity. For Taylor the critical 'recognition' is for a polity to commit itself to ensuring the survival of cultures or nations within its boundaries, as he would like Canada to guarantee the cultural survival of the Qubecois (Taylor, *ibid*, pp.58-61).

While I too strongly feel that multiculturalism means something more than negative tolerance or 'benign neglect', a cultural laissez-faire, it seems certain that while we all have to learn to live with groups of people and their norms that we may in various ways disapprove of, many people will not want to affirm or celebrate or publicly fund other people's religions or their hedonism, and I do not know what argument there is which says that one ought to celebrate ways of life that one regards as wrong or irresponsible. Perhaps, as the challenge of the politics of recognition is at many different points of the public-private boundary, such as gender, race, religion, sexuality, the normative character of the challenge may vary, and so then ought the institutional response. But if so, we must seek principles to guide us here. For otherwise what we may have in practice is a kind of 'differential incorporation', a pragmatic-cum-prejudiced response based on how much power a minority is able to exert, how much hostility there is to it, the structure of existing institutions, and so on. Thus a political party might find the will to address the under-representation of women in public office but not of ethnic minorities. Or, as Amy Gutmann suggests, public institutions should actively recognise the particular cultural identities of those they represent, but should be neutral as regards religious identities.[10] Perhaps this is just realism, but Gutmann believes that there is a principled basis for treating cultural and religious identities differently. I can see that there is a principled argument in favour of state neutrality, and there is another principled argument in favour of public recognition. Gutmann applies the former to religious identity, the latter to other identities, but no criteria are offered which justify this differential application. The pragmatic approach may be the best that we have, but I worry about a politics of recognition that begins with a structural bias against disadvantaged religious minorities.[11]

---

[10] A.Gutmann (ed), *Multiculturalism: Examining the Politics of Recognition*, Princeton University Press, 1994, p.12.
[11] A fuller version of this paper appears in *Philosophy*, Supplement 40, 1996.

The Politics of Health

Carla Koen
University of Warwick

'The Boundary between the Public and the Private Arena:
A Case Study on the Japanese Pharmaceutical Industry'

Acknowledgements

I am grateful to Professor Wyn Grant, Ed Page and Dallal Stevens for their help and suggestions. I also want to thank Roel Vestraeten, Jeannine Van Hoek and several officials in the Japanese Ministry of Health and Welfare and the Japanese Pharmaceutical Manufacturers Association for their stimulating interviews and useful information.

Introduction

Much of the extensive literature on the Japanese industry, and in particular on the Japanese high-technology industry, explains Japan's superior industrial performance mainly as the consequence of its particular structural features, that is to say, as the consequence of the particular relationships between the government, organised business, and the administrative bureaucracy (thereby referring to 'Japan Inc.'). An important question that informs this research, therefore, is whether and how the Japanese government is involved in the performance of its pharmaceutical industry. The Japanese pharmaceutical industry, although a major high-technology industry, does not demonstrate superior performance. More than a quarter of the medicines consumed in Japan originate from abroad; Japan imports three times more than it exports;[1] and for most of the post-war period, the Japanese pharmaceutical industry has exported only about 3 per cent of total production.[2] Furthermore, until recently, the industry's research efforts lagged far behind those of their competitors.[3]

Currently, however, some important developments have taken place. Although the export level of Japan's drug sector remains low, the composition of pharmaceutical exports – the quality of the products, the target markets, and technology sales – has changed significantly.[4] The pattern of pharmaceutical exports has shifted from an emphasis on non-patented bulk

---

[1] J.Howells & I.Neary, *Intervention and Technological Innovation*, Macmillan, 1995.

[2] In comparison, during the 1980s and 1990s, the United States (the largest drug market) has exported approximately 9 per cent of its pharmaceutical production, France 21 per cent, United Kingdom 55 per cent and West Germany 24 per cent.

[3] For a discussion of the Japanese pharmaceutical industry's research and development strategy (R&D) see amongst others: R.Ballance et al, *The World's Pharmaceutical Industries*, Edward Elgar, 1992; Scrip, 'Japan R&D Strategies for Success', *Scrip Magazine*, December 1994; International Marketing Services (IMS), *Japanese Globalisation*, IMS, 1989.

[4] M.R.Reich, 'Why the Japanese Don't Export More Pharmaceuticals: Health Policy as Industrial Policy', *California Management Review*, 32/2, 1990.

products to patented products. Moreover, the major Japanese pharmaceutical companies have upgraded and reoriented their domestic research programmes in order to develop drugs that are both profitable and have export potential. Additionally, the target countries for exports have shifted from Asian countries to Europe and the United States, although Asia remains the most important market. Finally, there has been an increase in the value of exports of pharmaceutical technology, exceeding the value of technology imports in the mid-1980s. These developments indicate the growing international acceptance of Japanese drugs, as well as the increasing technological capability (albeit, to a large extent, related to process technology) and, hence, increasing competitiveness of Japan's drug makers. Indeed, different sources argue that the majors have already achieved so many international successes that it is hard to doubt their emerging global competitiveness.[5]

Much of the available literature indicates that Japanese industries have typically followed a pattern of first developing products for the large domestic market, under government policies of protection from direct international competition, and then moving into foreign markets with relatively inexpensive but good quality products. Moreover, Porter asserts that, in nearly every Japanese industry he studied exports increased substantially only when the domestic market became mature. Domestic saturation, he argues, is invariably the impetus for a major export drive, as companies scramble to replace lost domestic volume and fill excess capacity.[6]

It is my contention that the Japanese pharmaceutical industry demonstrates a similar development path. This industry has not only followed the domestic stage of this pattern, but, in recent years, it is also adopting a global or outward-looking strategy. Moreover, this study demonstrates that Japanese public policy has largely shaped the performance of the domestic pharmaceutical industry. This does not imply that this study, therefore, supports the so-called 'bureaucratic regulation thesis'. Neither, however, does it recognise the ability of the 'market regulation thesis' to account for Japan's industrial development. Instead, the study emphasises political economy, that is to say, the political structuring of the economy, as an approach for analysing industrial development in Japan. The discussion of these issues is divided into three parts: the first part attempts to legitimise the choice of the analytical framework; the second part explains how the Japanese government health policy has influenced the domestic pharmaceutical industry's development path; and finally, the third section of the paper concentrates on the impact of the national industrial policy.

---

[5] For example, Tanabe with the product Diltizam, Daiichi with Quinolone antibiotics, Fujisawa with FK-506 (Prograf) and Takeda with Lanzoprazole. Sapienza's analysis of the direction of the research and development (R&D) efforts of major Japanese pharmaceutical companies confirms this conclusion of increased international competitiveness of Japanese pharmaceutical companies. A.M.Sapienza, 'Assessing the R&D Capability of the Japanese Pharmaceutical Industry,' *R&D Management*, 23/1, 1993.

[6] M.E.Porter, *The Competitive Advantage of Nations*, Macmillan, 1990; see also Reich.

I

To explain the developments in the Japanese pharmaceutical industry since the 1950s, one could rely on the two main perspectives that have dominated contemporary thinking about Japan's industrial development. The first, which Friedman calls 'the bureaucratic regulation thesis',[7] sees Japan as embodying a state-guided capitalist system in which the Ministry of International Trade and Industry (MITI) and industrial policy have played a leading or dominant role. In this view, government leadership has been the key to Japan's economic success, with business a willing follower. This model holds that Japan's élite bureaucrats intentionally created internationally competitive industries through measures designed by MITI with long-range strategic planning and a strong export orientation.[8] The second, 'the market regulation thesis' contends that Japan's post-war economic successes were the result mainly of market forces. This school sees the basic source of Japan's economic growth as being in a vigorous private sector which responded to the private market mechanism and intense domestic competition. The Japanese government, it argues, helped contribute to a favourable economic environment – as did the post-war international economic system – but the major impetus to growth was from the private, market-oriented sector.

However, as particularly demonstrated in Friedman's study of the Japanese machine tool industry, neither model proves able to fully account for both the performance and the transformation of the Japanese industry. Friedman argues that one of the basic problems with studies that rely on the bureaucratic regulation thesis is that in most accounts the actual behaviour of manufacturers themselves is not examined at all. Most studies, he contends, simply assert that a given policy leads to the desired economic outcomes, assuming that the promulgation of a regulation or a law is the same as proof of its effectiveness. The difficulty here is obvious. In any given case directives or legislation might be wholly superfluous to what industrialists actually do to produce growth. Moreover, it is possible that the bureaucracy's policies are either initially proposed by the firms which the regulators are supposed to be controlling, or are even foisted on the regulators by such firms. Friedman, therefore, argues that 'the failure to show that state control causes growth independently and effectively is the most serious objection to the bureaucratic regulation thesis.'[9]

The market regulation thesis, on the other hand, encounters problems because it downplays or even ignores the effect that politics can have on industrial expansion. The most serious objection in this case is that references to market forces and/or market efficiency really provide no explanation for Japanese industrial development at all. If, as this model claims, Japan's producers are able to meet the challenges of the market more effectively than manufacturers elsewhere, it is essential to know why this is so. Also, if the market operates more efficiently in Japan and hence disciplines pro-

---

[7] D.Friedman, *The Misunderstood Miracle. Industrial Development and Political Change in Japan*, Cornell University Press, 1988.
[8] Reich, p.125.
[9] Friedman, pp.3-6.

ducers more effectively, there has to be an explanation for this.

The inability of both models to explain Japan's industrial performance becomes even more pronounced when analysing the developments in the Japanese pharmaceutical industry. First, as is the case in all western countries, regulation in Japan of health policy appears to be an inescapable feature of the environment in which the pharmaceutical industry operates. It would be wrong, therefore, to assume that industrial development occurred as the sole result of unbridled competition under a free market. On the other hand, the Japanese government, or more specifically the Ministry of Health and Welfare (MHW), did not develop a clearly articulated sector-specific industrial policy for the pharmaceutical industry. Rather, policies adopted for protecting and enhancing the welfare of the Japanese people also worked to promote the industry. Whether health policy was intended to serve as industrial promotion policy remains a point of debate. What is clear is that, until the 1980s, the combined effect of several government health policies created a rapidly expanding domestic market of enormous benefit to the Japanese pharmaceutical industry. This, in turn, reduced the incentives for developing exports, while it served to strengthen the industry. In addition, national industrial policy on patents and capital liberalisation restricted foreign competition within Japan and thereby directed the benefits of the growing domestic market primarily to domestic companies.

Similarly, until now the MHW has not designed a clear policy on pharmaceutical exports or industry structure. By and large, the developments that have taken place in the Japanese drug industry from the 1980s onwards – that is to say, the drive to internationalisation and the change in R&D focus, as well as the expected large industrial restructuring – do not seem to be the result of carefully thought-out plans; rather, as will become clear from the discussion below, they seem to be determined by policies that were developed in response to immediate problems and contradictory pressures. This study, therefore, consistent with Friedman's conclusion,[10] contends that industrial development in Japan has resulted neither from bureaucratic guidance (the public arena) nor from market forces (the private arena), but rather from political structuring of the economy. In particular, this study demonstrates that a complex political process that combines the interests of the Japanese government with those of the agencies that have some involvement in the health sector, has provided the background conditions for the pharmaceutical industry's performance.[11]

---

[10] Ibid.

[11] To explain the above statements the study draws mainly on Reich, pp.124-150; I.J.Neary, 'An Industrial Policy for the Pharmaceutical Industry', Japan Forum, 1/1, 1989; Y.Hisaaki, 'Facing a Turning Point', Journal of Japanese Trade and Industry, 14/3, 1995; D.Macarthur, Japanese Pharmaceutical Expansion into Europe, Financial Times Business Information, 1991; IMS, Japanese Globalisation, pp.22-56; and on interviews and telefax communications with Mr.Roel Verstraeten (Director, New Business Development, Janssen-Kyowa, Tokyo), Mr Morton (President of Janssen-Kyowa), Ms.Jeannine Van Hoek (Country Manager Japan for Janssen-Cilag, Belgium) and with officials in the MHW and the Japanese Pharmaceutical Manufacturers Association.

II

In a given country, the pattern of demand for drugs is determined to a large extent by the incidence of disease, the composition of the population and by the tradition of medical practice. The unusually high level of drug consumption in Japan, however, is said to result from four key health policies which, until the 1980s, combined to produce a rapidly growing domestic medical market. The first policy concerns national health insurance. Changes in Japan's health insurance policy have progressively reduced patient restrictions on access to medical care, thereby providing the basis for continued expansion of the domestic pharmaceutical market through the 1970s. In the late 1950s the Japanese government adopted the goal of health insurance for the entire nation. It wasn't until 1961, however, that universal health insurance coverage was achieved. Throughout the 1960s, in the context of rapid economic growth, the government reduced the level of patient copayments for various health insurance plans. These policies of universal coverage and reduced copayments contributed to the rapid expansion of domestic consumption of pharmaceuticals in the 1960s. In 1973, the government introduced free medical care for the elderly -70 years or more or those aged 65 years or more if bedridden – which contributed to increased utilisation of medical services by this growing population segment in Japan.

The second and third policies that underlie the high level of drug consumption in Japan, that is to say dispensing practices and pharmaceutical pricing, are strongly related and are, therefore, discussed together. Throughout the post-war period, Japanese general practitioners and hospitals have both prescribed and dispensed pharmaceuticals to patients, with the difference between the purchase price from the supplier and the reimbursement price set by the government serving as additional income. In Japan, the official reimbursement prices for all pharmaceuticals are set by the government on the Drug Tariff. The National Health Insurance (NHI) drug price functions both as the reimbursement rate paid by all health insurers to all medical institutions, and as the official acquisition price recognised by the MHW for budgetary purposes. There is, however, a considerable difference between the official reimbursement prices for pharmaceuticals, and the actual prices paid by the physicians and hospitals. Pharmaceutical companies, as a matter of marketing strategy, offer drugs to hospitals and private physicians at a discount. This system, together with a lack of effective controls over prescribing patterns by physicians, has contributed to the expansion of the domestic market, by creating economic incentives for private physicians and hospitals to prescribe liberally and to choose products with higher margins.

In addition, Reich claims that under the health insurance system, the prices set by the government for pharmaceutical reimbursement (the fees for diagnostic tests and drugs) are overvalued in relation to costs, while technical skills (the fees for consultation, treatment, and operation) are undervalued. The discrepancy between material prices and technical prices has provided an additional incentive for physicians to excessively prescribe pharmaceuticals in solo practices and medical institutions. Furthermore, the generous reimbursement rates for pharmaceuticals prior to the 1980s allegedly served as an indirect support mechanism for the domestic industry.[12]

Although pharmaceuticals are in fact priced much higher in Japan than in the rest of the world,[13] according to contacts in the industry and the MHW, this has less to do with an intentional government policy to subsidise the industry than with the reimbursement price system. An NHI reimbursement price for a new medicine is set by comparison with the price of a product from a similar therapeutic category already established on the market in Japan (called reference drug pricing). In addition, however, the health insurance reimbursement system rewards minor improvements of established drugs with premium prices, thus driving the wheels of small step innovation (something in which the risk-averse Japanese pharmaceutical industry has excelled) and thereby causing an upward price spiral.[14] In any event, whether intentional or not, until the 1980s government price policy contributed to produce a rapidly growing domestic market as well as to increase the profits of the pharmaceutical industry.

However, the 'subsidised growth' of the pharmaceutical industry created huge public expenditures which were tolerated in Japan's period of high economic growth, but not in the 1980s. Hence, under pressure from the Ministry of Finance (MoF), the MHW has introduced several policies to discourage excessive spending on health. Amongst others, the MHW abolished the free-of-charge system for the elderly and, with considerable effort, is attempting to separate dispensing from prescribing by physicians (a policy which is known as 'bungyo'). In addition, from the beginning of the 1980s onwards, the MHW has drastically cut reimbursement prices. According to Reich, the reimbursement rate for pharmaceuticals represented a prime area for cutbacks.[15] The political strength of the Finance Ministry could easily defeat the declining power of the Japan Medical Association (JMA). In addition, the pharmaceutical industry, which depends on the Japanese Pharmaceutical Manufacturers Association (JPMA) as its political channel, was unable effectively to oppose the price revisions by the MHW.[16]

The declining power of the JMA from the 1980s onwards is widely thought to be prompted by the death of its charismatic president, Dr.Taro Takemi, and by the consequent dissent within the organisation.[17] Takemi's power can be attributed to two factors: first, the fledgling state of the pharmaceutical industry in Japan in the 1970s together with an MHW which, at that time, had little experience in real research, resulted in Takemi's advice being widely sought; second, Takemi's undisputed ability to organise massive strikes by physicians. The MHW officials feared Takemi's charismatic impact on the health sector, and, consequently, succumbed to the JMA's opposition to reforms. Amongst others, Takemi managed successfully to oppose 'bungyo', as well as strong reimbursement price cuts, both of which

---

[12] Reich, pp.132-133.
[13] Confirmed in IMS, p.50.
[14] Communication with Tokyo, August 1995.
[15] Reich, p.136.
[16] Although Reich asserts that the JMA was the political channel of the Japanese pharmaceutical industry (Reich, p.136), my contacts in Tokyo deny that this has ever been the case. Instead, they state that the JPMA has always represented the industry.
[17] The following discussion on the JMA and the JPMA is based on a telefax communication with Mr.Verstraeten and Mr.Morton, August 1995.

would have reduced the income of most physicians. The inability of the JPMA to oppose the recent price cuts, on the other hand, stems from the fact that it is heavily influenced by the MHW itself. Friendly ties between the industry and the ministry, which are strengthened by 'amakudari' ('retirements to heaven') by government officials who move to high positions in pharmaceutical companies and trade associations, underlie the MHW's impact on the JPMA.

The sharp reimbursement price cuts from the 1980s onwards inevitably had an enormous impact on the pharmaceutical industry. Unaffected by the oil shocks, the industry grew by over 12 per cent p.a. in the 1970s, with annual growth rates varying between 3 per cent and 24 per cent.[18] Only in the early 1980s did growth in the pharmaceutical industry weaken, actually showing a decline in production in 1984 and 1985 for the first time in the post-war period. In fact, the net result of the MHW health policy changes has been to reduce the pharmaceutical industry's profits, slow down its growth, and, as a corollary, to precipitate its overseas expansion. According to Mr Verstraeten and Mr Morton this was not a deliberate policy. They assert that the main, if not sole concern which led the MHW to introduce the reforms was to limit the growth in national medical expenditure to within the economic growth rate.[19]

The price interventions, however, have also created incentives for products whose prices were not lowered to the same extent as the prices of other products, namely, for new and innovative drugs. Government policy has had the effect of driving down the prices of older products, giving technologically advanced preparations a better price and a marketing advantage (in the eyes of dispensing doctors) over less expensive drugs in the same therapeutic class.[20] The MHW's price policy has thus created incentives for a strategic reorientation in corporate research. Firms responded by shifting their research focus away from the therapeutic segments in which prices were sharply cut (such as antibiotics) to other less-cut categories (such as cardiovasculars and anticancer drugs). According to Reich, reimbursement price policy has always played a major role in determining the strategic allocation of corporate R&D funds. He argues that in providing signals to private companies and in defining the market, pharmaceutical price policy has served as an important implicit form of industrial policy[21] A clear illustration of this statement is the fact that, from the mid-1970s onwards, downward price revisions for older drugs combined with significant price premiums for minor modifications induced companies to concentrate on merely altering existing drugs slightly, rather than on producing new innovative drugs. In recent years, however, the Japanese government has only offered premium prices to drugs with a significant therapeutic advantage, thus driving research programmes toward 'breakthrough' drugs.[22]

It is also important to mention, particularly because of the assumptions

---

[18] Neary, p.24.
[19] Telefax communication with Tokyo, August 1995, confirmed by government documents.
[20] IMS, p.45.
[21] Reich, p.135.
[22] Datamonitor, *The Pharmaceutical Industry in the 21st Century*, Datamonitor, 1994.

that are made with respect to this issue, that government cost-containment measures, especially the price cuts, have produced a differential impact on Japanese firms. Inevitably, the changes in the laws and regulations have hit the smaller companies, that have no significant research capacity and rely mainly on the production of over-the-counter (OTC) and generic preparations, the hardest. The reforms are said to have either worked to the benefit of the major producers, or these big firms suffered minimal inconvenience. In recent years, it is feared that, as a by-product of government cost-containment measures, the medium- to small-sized companies have been driven into great financial trouble. Not surprisingly, observers predict that the desire to survive will prompt mergers and acquisitions. Contacts in Tokyo assert, however, that this will happen only after MHW has given the signal, that is to say, only after the ministry has approached the big companies and induced them to initiate the restructuring process. They state that for cultural reasons restructuring in Japan is very difficult. Firing people is impossible and Japanese business practices – stable share holdings, cross-ownerships, corporate culture, and so on – make acquisitions and mergers a difficult strategy.[23] Hence, until the MHW encourages action, the big actors play a waiting game.[24] In view of the above, it is not difficult to understand that some writers suggest the possibility that the MHW is pursuing a policy aimed at the restructuring of the industry.[25] Again, there is no evidence that the MHW has deliberately designed its health policy in order to drive forward the restructuring of the pharmaceutical industry.

A last issue that is worth mentioning in the area of government health policy concerns drug approval policy. It is argued that when the Japanese pharmaceutical industry was only in its developing stage, drug approval policy not only facilitated the import of foreign pharmaceutical technologies but also hindered access to the Japanese market by foreign firms. Until the late 1960s, relatively low barriers to entry existed for Japanese companies to introduce foreign drugs that were already approved overseas. Until 1967, all medicines approved by the United States Federal Food and Drug Administration (FDA), or by a major west European regulatory authority, were given automatic marketing rights in Japan.[26] Consequently, until approximately the mid-1960s, Japanese pharmaceutical firms mainly focused on identifying foreign products to license for manufacture or importation. In the late 1960s, imports accounted for 35 to 40 per cent of final products of ethical pharmaceuticals in the Japanese market; this trend has declined slightly, but even in 1983 the figure remained at 31 per cent.[27] On the other hand, drug approval regulations also prohibited foreign firms from applying for the first step of drug approval, the demonstration of efficacy

---

[23] The same observation is made by Porter, p.407.

[24] Telefax communications with Tokyo, August 1995.

[25] Neary made this argument in 'An Industrial Policy for the Pharmaceutical Industry', Japan Forum, 1/1, 1989, p.25; Reich also suggests that government policy from the 1980s onwards could drive a restructuring of the Japanese pharmaceutical industry. It is not clear, however, whether Reich sees restructuring as a deliberate or accidental consequence of the reforms.

[26] D.Macarthur, Japanese Pharmaceutical Expansion into Europe, Financial Times Business Information, 1991.

[27] Reich, p.129.

and safety review, and stipulated that clinical trials had to be conducted in Japan on Japanese native citizens. Whereas it remains essential to conduct some elements of clinical trial work locally, from the mid-1980s onwards, pressures from the United States in bilateral trade negotiations compelled changes that allowed foreign firms to apply directly, thus increasing the independence of western manufacturers.

III

Apart from governmental health policy, national industrial policy in Japan has also affected the pharmaceutical industry and its approach to exports. Through the mid-1970s, two policies in particular, for capital liberalisation and for patents, served to protect Japanese pharmaceutical companies from direct competition by foreign companies within the domestic market, while giving domestic firms the benefits of foreign products through licensing.[28] The combination of a protected domestic market, through general industrial policy, with assured growth through national health policy, reduced the incentives for Japanese pharmaceutical firms to seek out overseas markets.

Before the mid-1970s, Japanese government controls on foreign direct investment (FDI) made the establishment of wholly owned subsidiaries extremely difficult. From 1964 onwards, when Japan joined the Organisation for Economic Co-operation and Development (OECD), the Japanese government began to gradually loosen foreign capital restriction. In 1967, 50 per cent foreign ownership of pharmaceutical companies became legal, with 100 per cent foreign ownership receiving authorisation in 1975. The restrictions on ownership, together with regulations for drug approval described above, meant that pharmaceutical firms located abroad generally had to license their products to a Japanese company in order to enter the Japanese market. Once a product was licensed, the royalty fee, often about 3 per cent, represented a relatively low return to the foreign company. As a result, the high benefits of the rapidly growing Japanese medical market were largely reserved for Japanese firms.[29]

The removal of government controls on foreign investment contributed to a surge in the number of foreign pharmaceutical companies in Japan. Reich states that from 1975 to 1983, the number doubled to over 300 companies with direct investment. In the 1980s, these investments diversified, including the creation of wholly owned subsidiaries, the expansion of sales forces, the construction of research laboratories and production facilities, and outright purchase of Japanese companies.[30] IMS contends that the arrival of significant foreign investment, while leading to increased competition in the Japanese market, gave strong impetus to Japanese R&D.[31] Furthermore, the increased competition in the home market, in combination with more expensive and innovative R&D, also contributed to push Japanese companies into overseas markets.

---

[28] IMS, pp.55-56; Neary, p.23.
[29] Reich, p.133.
[30] Ibid.
[31] Ibid.

The Japanese government patent policy for pharmaceuticals, on the other hand, demonstrates the same pattern as followed in most other countries. More specifically, the government initially provided only weak patent protection to allow for the development of the domestic industry which is based at the start on the copy of foreign drugs. Hence, prior to its revision in 1975, the Japanese patent law offered protection only to 'processes' and not to 'substances'. It did not recognise product patents. Firms could produce imitations of drugs sold by other firms so long as a different process for production could be found. In this way, the large benefits of the growing domestic market were reserved for the domestic companies. In 1976, the law was revised to also protect compound patents, which provided protection for unique compounds, regardless of manufacturing process. It is alleged that the main reason for the introduction of full patent protection derived from the government's recognition that the level of development reached by the pharmaceutical companies at that time necessitated the grant of a patent monopoly to permit them to launch into R&D and innovation in a major way.[32]

Both Reich and Neary contend that the transformation of Japanese patent policy for pharmaceuticals as well as the price cuts of the 1980s also reflect a shift in the balance of groups within the MHW.[33] Within the ministry there are two conflicting views. On the one hand, there are the 'traditionalists' who emphasise the regulatory role of the MHW and who are based mainly in the Health Insurance Bureau. Since the late 1960s, however, the other more economically and internationally oriented bureaucrats, based in the Economic Affairs Division of the Pharmaceutical Affairs Bureau (responsible for official contacts with the industry on production issues), have assumed more influence within the MHW. This shift in power relations seems to have been responsible for the policies of the 1970s and allegedly helped to produce the more explicit stick-and-carrot approach to the pharmaceutical industry in the 1980s.

Clearly, the above discussion confirms the statement made in the beginning of this study: the Japanese pharmaceutical industry conforms to the more general picture of the Japanese major high-technology industry in that it follows a similar, although as yet not quite as successful, line of development. In addition, the paper aspires to have established three important points. First, Japanese government policy has not always been as successful as some authors claim. The case study that is presented in this paper is a clear example of this. The paper, in accordance with Porter's study, contends that the regulation and central control of health care in Japan, while creating a rapidly growing domestic market and protecting the domestic industry from outside competition, also had the effect of dampening innovation and, hence, undermining competitive advantage.[34] As explained above, until the 1980s government price policy encouraged companies to concentrate efforts on incremental rather than breakthrough research. The efforts sought to develop 'me-too' drugs[35] that would be quickly approved

---

[32] OECD, *The Pharmaceutical Industry. Trade related Issues*, OECD, 1985.
[33] Neary, pp.22-26; Reich, pp.137-139.
[34] Porter, p.416.
[35] 'Me-too' drugs are imitative products which have marginal advantages, if any, over

and placed on the NHI price list, thereby reducing the risk of research and assuring financial returns. Additionally, the process patent system induced companies to focus on developing new processes for existing drugs. Furthermore, until the late 1960s, drug approval policy stimulated the import rather than the development of pharmaceutical technologies. This study, therefore, asserts that these policies have actually discouraged companies from initiating serious research efforts. Consequently, these policies have contributed to Japan's delay in developing pharmaceutical products capable of international competition. Second, Japanese government policy is not the most important determinant of successful Japanese industrial development. As Porter argues, there is a role for the Japanese government in this process, but it has been a shifting role whose significance is rather different from what has emerged as the accepted view.[36] Thirdly, the paper has underlined some concerns that have been expressed in the recent literature. In particular, it has shown that it is problematic to make firm statements concerning national-level patterns of industrially related policies on the basis of meso- or micro-level analysis. Equally misleading, however, would be to explain meso- or micro-level policy paths on the sole basis of macro- or national-level analysis. The use of general terminology such as 'Japan Inc.' or Japan's 'neomercantilism' to explain, again a far too general term, Japan's economic success is clearly not satisfactory. A better understanding of Japan's success in certain economic areas requires an understanding of the less successful sectors and their relationship to the government. Most importantly, one has to take account of the many variables, other than government policy, that are probably more decisive in industrial development.

---

existing drugs.
[36] *Ibid.*

The Death of Conservative Party Local Politics

Josie Brooks
Southampton Institute

'Waving the Magic Wandsworth: Right Wing Think Tanks and the Decline of Conservative Local Government'

Introduction

The local election results in May 1995 were among the worst ever for the Conservative Party but merely the latest in a trend which began in 1990 with the 'Poll Tax' débâcle. It was initially thought that the 1990 results were unusual and the Conservative Party's performance in local elections would stabilise. This has not proved the case and since 1990, local government elections have been an uncomfortable experience for the Conservative government. However a small number of Conservative councils remain; Wandsworth Borough Council, a model of Conservative local government is one example.

Explanations of why the Conservative Party has fared so badly in local elections vary. An analysis of whether shifts in the ideological alignment of the Conservative Party, illustrated by Thatcher's elevation, was the beginning of a return to the true tenets of the Conservative Party or the end of a great British institution (to take the extremes of the debate), offers little explanation of the manner in which the Conservative Party view of the sub national evolved during this period. The interpretation of events explored in this paper identifies changes in the Conservative Party in two distinct yet related ways. First, there has been a shift in how the Conservative Party views local government. Previously local government had been an important source of support for the national party. It acted as a recruitment ground for new MPs, implemented Conservative Party policy at a local level and most importantly, provided an important means of contact between the Party and the electorate in non general election years. However the ideologisation of the Conservative Party which began in the seventies and increased in importance during the 1980s was one source of change in the Conservative Party's view towards elected sub national government (ESNG). With government irritation with Labour local government, Conservative support for ESNG declined even further. Graham Mather explained,

> 'Councillors and officers may find that a new contest opens up, between elected bodies which seem cumbersome, disputatious, prone to capture by political extremists, excessively responsive to the "vote motive", and in the sway of powerful local interests. At best, it may seem, they represent a bureaucratised parody of an early model of local government and civic responsibility, slowing down new development and presenting a thousand niggling obstacles to reform: at worst, they frustrate adaptation, deter business investment, embark on dubious financing, enjoy gesture politics and offer a constant political and

economic challenge to the central government.'[1]

Faced with hostility from Labour and increased politicisation of ESNG, Government reconciled instinct with political need and became more receptive to proposals to transfer ESNG functions to agencies free of blatant interference.

Whilst acknowledging the deficiencies of mono causal explanations, this paper takes as its focus the particular view taken by three right wing think tanks of ESNG. It then examines whether there was convergence between the ideas promulgated by the think tanks on ESNG and trends within the Conservative Party. This involves much that is enigmatic; researchers who attempt to test the exact nature of the impact of think tanks on new policy formation find the evidence is confused and even contradictory.[2] It is difficult to disentangle specific influence from a number of other factors such as increased centralisation and a changing societal perception of the role of local government. Moreover influences on the policy making process are disparately dispersed, orbicular, even metamorphosed from their source, while organisations whose raison d'etre is policy development and advice are enthusiastic to claim successes.

This paper acknowledges the dangers of this approach and argues that an alternative method of investigation may be possible, namely the examination of whether New Right Think Tanks (NRTT) activities played a role in establishing a 'common sense' view of local government, articulated by ministers, shared by a number of Conservative councillors and joined with other factors to inform specific policy implementation. However Conservative councillors were caught in a cleft stick; should they defend the Government local government policy or the needs of their locality? The rapid reduction in numbers of Conservative Councillors in recent years, thanks to electoral losses, was accompanied by a view among Conservative activists that the reduction in the power of local government made it an unattractive area within which to become active in any case. A countervailing 'voice' in the Party arguing against the NRTT 'common sense' view of ESNG currently appears to be muted or even nonexistent. However the decline of Conservative local government is not uniform. Despite losses in many traditional strongholds, the Conservatives have successfully retained control of a number of 'flagship' authorities. The final question addressed by this paper is why the Conservatives have been successful in retaining control of Wandsworth and what lessons this might have for their future local government strategy.

New Right Think Tanks and Local Government

A number of writers on Thatcherism and the nature of Conservative politics since 1975 acknowledge the role and influence of NRTT on government policy.[3] The Institute of Economic Affairs (IEA), the Centre for Policy

---
[1] G.Mather, 'Thatcherism and Local Government: An evaluation', in Stewart & Stoker, *The Future of Local Government*, 1989, p.220.
[2] D.Butler et al, *Failure in British Government*, Oxford University Press, 1994.
[3] D.Kavanagh, *Thatcherism and British Politics*, Oxford University Press, 1990; R.Crockett, *Thinking the Unthinkable: Think Tanks and the Economic Counter Rev-*

Studies(CPS) and the Adam Smith Institute (ASI) have advised and reflected on the nature of government. Articulating a popularised and simplified version of Public Choice theory in defence of their claims they have broadly argued that the role of the state must be radically reduced. Although it is difficult to identify with precision specific inputs into the policy making process, these organisations involved policy makers in the writing of many of their documents,[4] whilst their intended audience was other policy makers and opinion formers.[5] These organisations were evidently much more than pressure groups, instead they shared an ambition to influence the opinions of the next generation of policy makers; they could thus be described as being engaged in the redefinition of the 'locus of common sense'.[6]

Although the history of these organisations has been written elsewhere,[7] it is worthwhile to briefly recap. The longest established organisation, the IEA, prided itself on academic impartiality and being distanced from the policy making process. Although policy makers were invited to and participated in their seminars and discussion groups, their target audience also included commentators on policy formation, so called 'second hand dealers'.[8] They claimed local government involvement in universal provision of welfare goods was wasteful and inefficient, and should be replaced by greater use of targeting; the introduction of the market mechanism would remove inefficiency and increase choice for consumers.[9]

Established by Keith Joseph and Margaret Thatcher, the CPS history is intertwined with the ideological shifts within the Conservative Party and, according to one writer, its mission by 1982 had seemed completed.[10] Yet under subsequent directors the CPS often identified areas where government action was necessary to curb the 'excesses of local government' or to praise the successes of Conservative run Councils.[11] A number of their publications concentrated on the misuse of local government and its functions by Labour councillors, whom it was claimed, were intent in meddling in national or even international politics [12] This is not to claim the publications of this organisation were wholly negative. The publication of The Good Council

---

olution 1931-1983, HarperCollins, 1994; A.Denham, Think Tanks and the New Right, PhD thesis, Southampton University, 1993; S.James, 'The Idea Brokers', Public Administration, 71/4; R.Desai, 'Second hand dealers in Ideas: Think-tanks and Thatcherite hegemony', New Left Review, 20, 1994.

[4] ASI, The Omega File, ASI, 1985; E.Butler & M.Pirie (eds), The Manual on Privatization, ASI, 1989.

[5] Crockett, op cit; K.Joseph, 'Introduction', Bibliography of Freedom, first edition, 1976; M.Pirie, Micropolitics, Wildwood, 1988.

[6] Pirie, ibid; Joseph, op cit; Harris & Seldon (eds), The Emerging Consensus, IEA, 1981.

[7] Crockett, op cit; A.Denham, op cit.

[8] Crockett, ibid, p.131; Desai, op cit.

[9] A.Seldon, Whither the Welfare State, IEA, 1981; A.Seldon, Charge, Maurice Temple Smith, 1970; R.Harris & A.Seldon, Welfare without the State, IEA, 1987; Harris & Seldon, Overruled on Welfare, IEA, 1979; Harris & Seldon, Not from Benevolence, 1977, IEA.

[10] Crockett, op cit, p.316.

[11] C.Goodson-Wickes, The New Corruption, CPS, 1984; M.Ivens, The Disease of Direct Labour, CPS, 1992; P.Beresford, Good Council Guide, CPS, 1987.

[12] D.Regan, 'The Local Left and its National Pretensions', in Hass & Knox (eds), The Politics of Thatcherism, 1992.

Guide by Paul Beresford, leader of Wandsworth Council and The Local Right: Enabling not Providing by Nicholas Ridley gave definition to what became models of good Conservative local government.

The Adam Smith Institute is an excellent publicity machine, imaginatively run by Madsen Pirie and Eammon Butler. The ASI approach has been to involve the current generation of policy makers in their activities; it also has paid attention to developing links with those who went on to become policy makers.[13] At first their publications focused on local government, quangos, privatisation.[14] From the outset Pirie and Butler focused on the removal of functions from government to the private sector.

Prototypes of a new Conservative local government was promoted by the think tanks; Beresford's *The Good Council Guide*, was described as a blue print for the management of Conservative local government.[15] Other publications include Ridley's model of the 'Enabling Authority', and more recently, an interesting defence of the quangoisation of local government functions by the current leader of Wandsworth, Edward Lister.[16] The ASI's policy recommendations, could be broadly paraphrased as 'privatise everything'. The IEA continued its policy of distance from the policy decisions made by the Conservative government, their recommendations, muted and of greater abstraction.[17]

How did the think tanks respond to elected local government? Mostly their reactions were mixed and depended on the author, the current political climate and the latest antics of Labour local government. Despite this there are a number of discernable themes: the end of big interventionist government,[18] the depoliticisation of local government[19] and the introduction of the market mechanism into the provision of goods hitherto directly supplied by local government.'[20] In its place, the think tanks proposals included demands for privatisation,[21] economic, efficient and effective local administration,[22] run prudently along business like lines. Local government should, it was argued, be focused on the strategic, making broad policy decisions, awarding contracts and little else.[23] Greater accountability of ESNG could be found by increasing the amount of revenue to be raised locally and making local taxes more visible.[24] Others argued for elected local government to continue to lose functions to government agencies or quangos.[25] or

---

[13] M.Pirie, op cit; ASI, *The Omega File*, ASI, 1985.

[14] For example ASI, *The Omega File*, ASI, 1985; E.Butler & M.Pirie (eds), *Economy and Local Government*, ASI, 1981; M.Forsyth, *Re-servicing Britain*, second edition, ASI, 1981; M.Forsyth, *The Myths of Privatisation*, ASI, 1983; P.Holland *Quango, Quango, Quango*, ASI, 1978.

[15] Ridley, *The Local Right* 1988.

[16] E.Lister, *Local Limits*, CPS, 1995.

[17] R.Carnaghan & B.Bracewell-Milnes, *Testing the Market*, IEA, 1993.

[18] W.Mitchell & D.G.Green (eds), *Government As It Is*, IEA, 1988.

[19] P.Minford, 'How to depoliticise local government', *Economic Affairs*, 9/1, 1988, pp.12-16.

[20] Carnaghan et al, op cit; M.Pirie, *Privatisation*, Wildwood, 1988.

[21] ASI, *Omega Report* 1985.

[22] N.Ridley, *The Local Right*; E.Lister, *Local Limits*.

[23] Ridley, op cit.

[24] C.Taylor, *Bringing Accountability Back to Local Government*, CPS, 1985.

[25] Lister, op cit

even to be replaced by community companies,[26] However although the preferred policy proposals of IEA, CPS and ASI differed in degree, they united around a common theme of condemnation of the excesses of Labour councils. Moreover these arguments also included a critique of the structures of ESNG and its inherent collectivist nature[27] and claims that the pressure from vested interest groups is greater than the amorphous mass of rate and tax payers. However differences did exist between the IEA, the CPS, and the ASI over the solution to these problems. For example Harris and Seldon argued for charges to be introduced to local government services, whereas writers published by the CPS tended to argue for more routine solutions, for example sound budgets and efficient and economic management of services. Madsen Pirie of the ASI argued for policy engineering and the application of public choice theory, in order to neutralise objections and opposition from stake holders.[28]

The think tank attack on big government was bifurcate. Increased centralisation and interference from the centre was criticised as was the fact that local government activities were historically diverse and broad in scope.[29] Central controls, linked to social engineering meant that ESNG was inefficient, wasteful and provided goods which were not linked to demand. Thus the IEA argued the solution to wasteful bureaucratic oversupply was the end of universal 'free' benefits.[30] Private suppliers would be encouraged to offer alterative supplies. For those who were not able to pay the full market costs there would be a system of targeted vouchers. The removal of many local government functions would also reduce the demand for central government grants. For those services which continued to be provided by local government, charges, fees and other means of alternative funding would be sought.[31]

The CPS, however adopted a more pragmatic approach, with less emphasis on grand solutions. Embroiled in the Joseph-Thatcher mission to change the nature of government it had little time for the minutiae of local government. Alfred Sherman the first director of the CPS, was for a time a member of Kensington and Chelsea council and published his comments on Wandsworth elsewhere.[32] In the 1980s a number of documents which were critical of the nature of local government and which were influential at the time of publication, were published. For example, Charles Goodson-Wicks identified practises in Labour local government, which he described in his booklet entitled *The New Corruption*.[33] His complaint was that Labour councils had eroded certain conventions which had previously governed ESNG.[34] Goodson-Wicks' pamphlet was published on the eve of the 1984 Conservative Party conference and, according to Gyford's account, influenced the terms of reference of the Widdicombe Commission announced

---

[26] D.Mason, *Wiser Counsels*.
[27] Mason, *ibid*.
[28] Pirie, *Micropolitics*.
[29] Lister, *op cit*; Seldon, *Charge*, 1977; Forsyth, *The Myths of Privatisation*, ASI, 1983.
[30] Harris & Seldon, *Welfare without the State*, 1987.
[31] Harris & Seldon, *ibid*.
[32] A.Sherman, *Waste in Wandsworth*, Aims for Freedom and Enterprise, 1976.
[33] Goodson-Wickes, *The New Corruption*, CPS, 1984.
[34] Goodson-Wickes, *op cit*.

during the conference.[35]

Conservative anger with Labour local government was well articulated by David Regan.[36] He argued that Fabian municipalisation, in conjunction with Municipal Marxism and Guild Socialism was deeply destructive to the fabric of British system of unitary government. Labour local government also intervened in national government affairs. Moreover Labour councils exploited 'municipal services wide scope for social engineering'.[37] The willingness of Labour councillors to break the law, effectively destroying the conventions of local government, meant Regan supported legislation to restrict illegal or unlawful activities. However, he cogently argued for the retention of local government, within a unitary state.

Ridley, on the other hand, used his publication to draw out the conclusions of the radical legislative programme introduced in Thatcher's last term. His booklet unwittingly opened up a debate on the role and purpose of local government. He claimed there were major savings if ESNG increased competition, sought out greater efficiencies and better value for money by the reintroduction of alternative suppliers of local authority goods. Central to the paradigm defined by Ridley was the end of the overt politicisation of elected sub national government by Labour politicians. Introducing the role of councillors as strategic planners enabling local enterprise to deliver priority needs, Ridley's vision of ESNG was of a mere provider of goods, accountable by the price mechanism and subject to monitoring by central government. According to Ridley's vision of good local government was within a unitary state and a well defined legal structure.

The ASI's director, Madsen Pirie, cautiously endorsed IEA arguments in favour of charges for local government services as payment at the point of consumption would increase awareness of the actual cost per item, ensure greater efficiency and value for money. But the introduction of charges would not impede self seeking actions by producer and interest groups. Every minority group which benefited in some way from local government involvement in the production of their preferred good or service would campaign for their subsidy, thus Pirie argued 'user charges would work against the grain of the political market place instead of along with it'.[38] Pirie preferred the removal of the monopoly of supply from ESNG service producers. Contracting out or privatisation would make local government services more efficient and increase productivity.[39] Strict monitoring of carefully drawn up contracts would, it was argued, improve the quality of local government services. The Audit Commission, lengthy contracts and a privatisation ombudsman were the means by which standards could be enhanced and costs kept to a minimum.[40]

The organisations discussed here postulated a paralogical interpretation of Public Choice theory. Germane to this debate is how their view seeped in to problem definition in the policy process. Thus, for example, the work

---

[35] J.Gyford et al, *The Changing Politics of Local Government*, Unwin Hyman, 1989.
[36] Regan, *op cit*.
[37] Regan, *ibid*, p.41.
[38] Pirie, *Micropolitics*, p.139.
[39] For example E.Butler & M.Pirie (eds), *The Manual on Privatization*, ASI, 1989.
[40] ASI, *Omega Report*, 1985, pp.349-356.

of Tullock,[41] Buchanan[42] and Niskanen[43] on the interest seeking activities of bureaucrats and politicians was translated into claims that Labour politicians, operating in conjunction with Town Hall trade unions, pursued policies which only benefited their supporters.[44] The seemingly bizarre financial arrangement for ESNG (rates) meant those in Labour run authorities who stood to benefit most from the generosity of municipal socialism, contributed least to its cost, a situation Henney describes as 'the calculus of patronage'.[45]

It was believed ESNG was failing for other reasons. By the 1980s Conservative ministers were concerned that the bureaucratic structures, procedures and methods, especially in planning and development were a barrier to enterprise.[46] The approach of the Conservative government was to bypass the bureaucracy and to develop new methods of solving a number of hitherto intractable problems.[47] Thus for example, Urban Development Corporations (UDC) were to harness the verve and flair of private enterprise. When opponents of UDCs argued that these bodies disenfranchised local communities from the policy process, writers from the think tanks and government countered this claim by pointing to disenfranchised business interests who were regularly asked to pay for projects over which they had no control or influence.[48]

Conservative Local Government

Many of these criticisms of local government are fairly well known today. Most of the current members of the Cabinet, or their predecessors have articulated a number of these points in recent years. However this is not to claim that there is empirical evidence demonstrating that the origins of these ideas may be traced back to the NRTT. At best, Conservatism and the Tory Party have tended to be ambiguous towards local government. Defining shifts within central-local government relations as a strategy for Conservative Party electoral success, Bulpitt's model of a dual polity placed ESNG at the periphery, whilst the centre concentrated on the economic and foreign policies. An aspect of Conservative statecraft therefore was the realignment of the role of sub national government in order to maintain the Party's electability.[49] Thus the apparent obliviousness of Margaret Thatcher and her government towards elected local government was in fact part of Conservative statecraft. ESNG's existence even at the at the periphery became more tenuous during the eighties; local government was not to be regarded as an institution of government, merely as an administrative

---

[41] G.Tullock, *The Vote Motive*, IEA, 1976.
[42] J.Buchanan, *The Economics of Politics*, IEA, 1978.
[43] W.Niskanen. *Bureaucracy: Master or Servant*, IEA, 1973.
[44] (A.Henney, *Inside Local Government*, Sinclair Browne, 1984.
[45] Henny, ibid, 1984, p.316.
[46] Conservative Party Manifesto, *The Next Moves Forward*, 1987, p.64.
[47] A.Thornley, *Urban Planning Under Thatcherism*, second edition, Routledge, 1994.
[48] ASI, *Contracting the Council Empires*, ASI, 1985.
[49] J.Bulpitt, *Territory and Power in the United Kingdom*, Manchester University Press, 1983; 'The discipline of the new democracy: Mrs Thatcher's domestic statecraft', *Political Studies*, 34; G.Stoker, 'Intergovernmental Relations', *Public Administration*, 73/1.

offshoot. Still more negatively, it was argued that local government was part of the problem of welfarism, a source of dependency on the state, for example by the supply of housing.[50] To encourage self reliance Conservative manifestos promised legislation on the sale of council homes, proposed new rights for parents in their children's education and proposed initiatives for the inner cities. Yet any mention of ESNG which would traditionally have been empowered in these areas was mostly negative and often critical.[51] Conservative governments implemented a number of measures to control, restrict and even abolish sections of ESNG. Local government, therefore, was to be no more than a vehicle for the implementation of nationally decided polices.

By different routes, think tanks and other ideologues explained government devolved to the local level was vulnerable to capture by those opposed to the tenets of the new Conservatism. There were other dangers too; ESNG could be used to confront national government policies.[52] Even if those who ran ESNG were sympathetic to national policies, there was the threat of localism and civic aggrandizement.[53] Thus the Conservative Party 's attitude towards ESNG since 1970s may be explained by its view of the British unitary state and how the party of government should deal with threats to its hegemony. No longer was elected local government an essential dimension of a pluralist democracy [54], but merely through delegated powers, part of national politics.

It has been acknowledged that the New Right project within the Conservative Party drew on middle class dissatisfaction with the post war settlement and the cost of welfarism. One of the sites of disaffection was in the wake of the 1974 reorganisation of local government and the revaluation exercise. These criticisms were linked to other complaints: the fondness of ESNG for over regulation, the expense and local government's apparent excessive autonomy. These concerns were central to the Rates Rebellion during the 1970s. Campaigns by the established ratepayers' organisation National Union of Rate Payers and the new, more militant National Union of Ratepayers Action Groups shared demands for the rating system to be reformed and that nationally determined polices, for example education, should be funded and even managed centrally.[55] Overriding these demands was resentment caused by the expense of local government reorganisation, revaluation and the alleged inefficiency of many councils. These pressures within the political mêlée of the seventies which spilt into the politics of the new decade, (which we now know as 'Thatcherism'), included strands of resentment with the perceived malaise of local government.

However, whilst the Government was busy ending with Keynesanism and introducing monetarism nationally, in local government circles, ideol-

---

[50] N.Ridley, *My Style of Government*, Fontana 1992.
[51] Conservative Party Manifestos 1979, 1983, 1987 & 1992.
[52] Regan, op cit
[53] Ridley, *Local Right*, p.74.
[54] K.Young, 'Local Government', in Kavanagh & Seldon (eds), *The Thatcher Effect*, 1989, p.132.
[55] Nugent, 'The Ratepayers', in King & Nugent, *Respectable Rebels*, Hodder & Stoughton 1979.

ogy was confined to a minority of Labour and Conservative councils. The Conservative national government focused its attention on cutting public expenditure, especially in local government, and on encouraging rate reductions. Only after it became obvious that this policy direction was flawed, did the government return to a previous policy commitment to abolish the rates and introduce the Community Charge. Elsewhere Government myopia on local government matters was expressed by their adoption of 'inappropriate policy instruments...used inappropriately';[56] for example the Local Government Act 1980, (which introduced block grants) could be described as a remnant from the last gasps of centralising corporatism. Even allowing for the new privatisation measures, the 1980 legislation may be seen as an act by a government whose view of the sub national was ill defined and incomplete. The legislation was important for another reason: for it could be argued that it was a factor which fixed the terms of engagement between central and local government that dominated the political agenda for most of the eighties. For the IEA it was unwelcome meddling and an example of unnecessary central government interference.[57]

New Model Councils

What was to be the new vision of Conservative local administration? One council which appeared to fit the bill was Wandsworth in south London. Usually a Labour borough since its formation in 1964, the Conservatives won the 1978 Wandsworth elections and set about consolidating their victory. Most of the evidence for Wandsworth's success comes from Paul Beresford, leader of Wandsworth from 1983-92. A close colleague of Chope, the former leader, Beresford was involved in the management of the authority between 1978-1992.

Beresford claims his party's electoral success in Wandsworth Borough Council (WBC) was due to its pragmatic approach, which enabled Wandsworth to reverse the socio-economic decline of the borough and keep the Conservative councillors in office. Beresford also argued the policies adopted by the Conservatives evolved in responses to the difficulties experienced by the Borough and were fruits of the application of common sense solutions. Privatisation was developed in response to the expense of the in house operation and poor industrial relations. In Wandsworth Conservative policies reflected people's ambitions; in other words, the Council set prudent budgets and sensible policies based on common sense.[58] There was a three pronged approach to the business of the authority: the efficient management of services, including the elimination of waste and market testing all council services; a vigorous sales policy of homes and all land where economically efficient to do so; and the rebuilding of the local commercial infra structure.[59] Policy was defined by its effect on the rates bill and a hallmark

---

[56]Rhodes, 'Local Government Finance', in Rhodes & Marsh (eds), *Implementing Thatcherite Policies*, Open University Press, 1992, p.62.
[57]IEA, *Town Hall Power or Whitehall Pawn?*, 1980.
[58]Beresford, *op cit*; see also WBC Paper 5159 Policy and Finance Committee, 28.6.88, Paper 6747 Special Policy and Finance Committee, 30 May 1990.
[59]Beresford, *ibid*.

of Wandsworth's policies successes was its boast that it levied the lowest rate demand in inner London.

Beresford's claim is that the management of Wandsworth was adroit and pragmatic, based on common sense. This may be true but it begs the question of what defined his and the Conservative's group notion of common sense. Most people would readily agree that they want efficient and effective services run economically, and that local authorities should give 'value for money'. However these expressions take on different meanings within competing political definitions. By claiming his world view as 'common sense', Beresford enabled other beliefs to be labelled 'extremist' or 'nonsense', and therefore dismissed with facility.

According to Ridley, Wandsworth was a model new Conservative authority, yet a careful survey of the council's records provides evidence that the authority was able to benefit from a number of policies designed to maximise their grants from government and to behave like other (mostly Labour) authorities. For example, the authority investigated methods of maximising their share of 'Section 11' money, the introduction of a welfare rights advisory service (unlike comparable services run by Labour authorities, it purpose was to advise the authority on methods to maximise welfare grants to WBC) and the capitalization of revenue.[60] At the same time demographic change reduced demands on council spending; the elderly population of the area has been declining and according to projections will continue to fall[61] The school age cohort was static with major growth in the 25-44 age group and small increases in the under school age range. This meant Wandsworth council was in an unusual position when compared with other inner city boroughs. These factors are quite separate from any suggestion of favourable treatment in the annual grant settlement, an allegation later disputed by Lister.[62]

Why were Wandsworth Conservatives so successful? They have held control of the borough since 1978, and bucked the national trend towards Labour in 1990 and in 1994. One explanation has been the interconnection between demographic change brought about by the structural changes caused by the Authority's council house sales policies and the propensity to vote Conservative. An alternative explanation of the successes of Wandsworth is that the nature of the council and its policy implementation was unlike other Conservative authorities. The councillors who took control in 1978 were mostly new to the Conservative Party and joined when Conservative radicalism was centred in the New Right. Chope was an advisor to the Adam Smith Institute Omega project. Michael Forsyth was a councillor in Kensington and Chelsea, (as was Alfred Sherman), was closely associated with WBC, a consultant for Pritchards and published by the ASI. This of course is tangential, but it can be concluded that new Conservative councillors who were inexperienced or were not socialised into the post war traditions of the Party were thus open to persuasion to the ideas of the think tanks.

---

[60] WBC papers 2283 3/5/84 (section 11), 1944 9/11/83 &2199 6/3/84 (benefits take up) 5300 4/10/88, especially paragraphs 22 & 23 (capital controls).
[61] WBC paper 6746 30/5/ 90, Special Policy and Finance Committee.
[62] Lister, *op cit*.

A second conclusion is the Conservative leadership was adroit in the development and presentation of policies which were attractive to the electorate, what Pirie would describe as policy engineering.[63] Two such policies were the 'Brighter Borough' and the 'Crimewatch' initiatives. Both projects were relatively cheap to implement but highly visual. The removal of graffiti, cleaning public areas and introducing public seats and flower beds was, as Paul Beresford remarked, 'ensuring the profile of the Council as an important (but not the only) agent in promoting and providing for the welfare of all sections and groups of the population in the Borough is kept before the public'.[64] Thus the leadership of Wandsworth successfully projected what good Conservative local government ought to be. 'Common sense' local government policies were described as low rates, value for money and efficient, economic and effective services and became the main tenets of Conservative local government. Labour, its main rival in the borough, was unable to mount a successful challenge to the hegemony developed by the Conservatives as its local government policies were not seen as sensible or within the boundaries of what was perceived as common sense, which was of course defined by the Conservative hegemony.

Finally the Conservatives in Wandsworth were fortunate in having a long period of time to develop their policies, gain government favour and, most importantly, the tide of national politics was running in their favour. The importance of this factor can be seen by examining the case of Eric Pickles and his colleagues in Bradford, who had none of these advantages. Their efforts to carry out in eighteen months what Wandsworth had built in twelve years, largely failed because in that small time period they were unable to establish their own common sense definition of good local government. Moreover the enthusiasm of the force behind the Conservative Bradford revolution allowed a coalition of opposition to develop and sustain a counter hegemony to the electoral benefit of Labour.

What lessons are there to be learnt by the Conservatives from the their experiences in Wandsworth? Possibly the most important is their treatment of ESNG nationally will have strong negative consequences which may only be resolved at a local level. The Conservative view of the local as being unimportant was expressed by Ridley:

> 'When people vote in local elections they tend to vote on national issues. This is regrettable – but it is so. They tend to vote according to their perceptions of the aims of a party expresses and implemented by national politicians ... (that) Conservative controlled authorities who try hardest to support the aims of the Conservative government are the ones who do better than average in local elections is no accident.'[65]

Ridley's conclusion identified the conundrum which faces Conservative local government. Devaluing local government means local elections are decided by national party issues. Research carried out by Whiteley et.al.

---

[63] Pirie, *Micropolitics*.
[64] Beresford, WBC paper 5159, 28/6/88.
[65] Ridley, *The Local Right*, p.80.

led the authors to claim increased centralisation by government and the restrictions of local government, during the eighties, coupled with increased ideologisation of the Conservative Party, has removed incentives for Conservative supporters to become active in local government.[66] Moreover those most inclined to become Conservative councillors are those from the 'Progressive' wing of the Party, those who are politically most distant from the ideologues from the think tanks. There is a further point here, namely the mission of the think tanks was in the first instance directed at the Conservative Party itself and particularly at those politicians who were involved in the compromises of the post war period. By crowding out those voices who opposed the new radical ideology, the Conservative Party had few supporters of a robust sub national tier of government. Moreover, support for central Government actions meant promoting the reduction of ESNG functions and denial of democratic representation for local communities. There seems to be an apparent contradiction in the behaviour of Conservative local government candidates, who presumedly want to be elected, but support greater centralisation and diminution of ESNG's powers. Yet according to Beresford, Lister and Ridley robust support for national government policies could be electorally successful for Conservative councils. In the case of Wandsworth, this was done in conjunction with successful actions in maximising government grants and promoting a high profile role for local government, ironically mimicking the actions of a number of Labour run authorities.

The importance of NRTT to the success of the Conservatives during the last twenty years is disputed.[67] In the world of ESNG their role is also less than certain. The CPS and ASI promoted privatisation, council house sales and competitive tendering, which were adopted by government, yet the lack of substantive evidence weakens the case for claims of their importance. However by the NRTT adding their voice to the cacophony against ESNG, a new 'common sense' definition of good local government was constructed. This vision incorporated concepts of 'value for money', efficiency, economy and effectiveness underpinned by low rates and privatisation. The pursuit of these goals by national government, in combination with Conservative statecraft objectives have translated into the loss of local government functions, increased centralisation and the reduced peripheral role of ESNG. Ironically what was missing from the new common sense view of local government was the role Conservative councillors were expected to play, or indeed, whether they were even necessary. For Conservatives keen to regain Tory influence in ESNG will have to do address some of these issues and not simply 'wave the magic Wandsworth' of their (non-interventionist) ideal council if they are to promote a substantive counter concept of local government.

---

[66] Whiteley et al *True Blues*, Oxford University Press, 1994.
[67] Denham, *op cit*; Crockett, *op cit*.

The Death of Conservative Party Local Politics

Ian Holliday
University of Manchester

'Diversity and Conflict in Conservative Local Government, 1979-96'

Introduction

Conservative local government has always been diverse. When British local government was slowly being reformed in the nineteenth century, activist Conservative councils inspired by the public health movement in some towns and cities contrasted with quietist Conservative councils inspired by economist and ratepayer ideals in others. Both types of urban Conservative council contrasted further with the largely instinctive, and often unselfconscious, conservatism of councils in rural parts of the country which organised Conservative party politics did not begin to penetrate until the very end of the Victorian era. This diversity was subsequently reduced by institutional reforms sponsored by central government but often prompted by local criticism of existing arrangements. Increasingly in the nineteenth and twentieth centuries governments not only democratised local government, but also set and monitored standards which all reformed councils were required to meet. Diversity was reduced further by the spread of party in local government, again often prompted by local demands for central intervention. In the twentieth century in particular, national party intervention in local affairs slowly ensured that a further measure of uniformity was generated among councils. However, despite many standardising pressures, it would be difficult to argue that Conservative local government has been reduced to a single pattern, or even a small set of similar patterns, at any stage in its development. Even in the post-war years, when pressures of standardisation have been most intense, local politics and local policy in spheres such as education, housing and planning have often differed across the spectrum of Conservative councils. This diversity continues in the 1990s.

What has changed in recent years is the effect of diversity on intra-party relations. Whereas for many years diversity in Conservative local government was partnered by an underlying harmony and toleration of difference,[1] in the recent past intra-party relations in the local government sphere have become more conflictual. This conflict is not always visible, and frequently finds expression only in intra-party channels. Often it is strictly latent. Sometimes it results in nothing more public than quiet dissociation from the Conservative local government cause. However, in none of these manifestations is it unproblematic for the Conservative party, for in each it reduces its effectiveness in the local government arena.

Explanations of contemporary conflict in Conservative local government are therefore important. They are presented here in the context of Conservative local government development since the mid-1830s, when the Poor

---

[1] J.Gyford & M.James, *National Parties and Local Politics*, George Allen & Unwin, 1983, p.43.

Law Amendment Act 1834 and the Municipal Corporations Act 1835 inaugurated the modern age of local government. Analysis of the key factors which have generated intra-party conflict proceeds from investigation of the Conservative tradition of local autonomy, which for many years underpinned toleration of diversity and harmonious intra-party relations. Revision of that tradition, from the 1830s onwards, is the first factor in the process of change examined here. The second is Conservative party politicisation of local government, a factor traceable to the 1890s but significant only from the 1940s. The third is élite reorientation of Conservative party doctrine, partially visible in the 1930s and 1940s, more evident (in an absent-minded sort of way) in the 1950s, and highly prominent since the early 1960s. The fourth and final is élite re-reorientation of Conservative party doctrine undertaken in the 1970s, 1980s and 1990s. Technically, this is a subordinate aspect of the third factor, but because it is interesting and important in its own right it is considered separately here. Together, these factors explain the shift from relative harmony to significant conflict in Conservative local government. They also indicate that the future of Conservative local government is problematic. Ways forward are considered in the final section.

The Conservative tradition of local autonomy

A localist dimension was for many years integral to British (more accurately English) Conservatism. The very process whereby the Conservative party assumed its present form was marked by local voluntarism. In the local government sphere, councils possessing important degrees of autonomy long pre-dated formation of the Conservative party, were often active in prompting its move into the local government sphere, and strongly influenced its conception of the correct constitutional place of local government.

Although the Conservative party's Tory pre-history was characterised by ambivalent views about local autonomy, localism had thus become predominant within the Conservative tradition by the time the Conservative party was formed by parliamentary Tories at the start of the 1830s. A strong absolutist strain certainly managed to survive intact both the collapse of the Stuarts in 1688 and the ensuing Whig ascendancy of the eighteenth century.[2] However, political reality and political advantage combined to ensure that a localist strain was primary within the party by the time debate of significant local government reform was placed on the political agenda by Whigs and Radicals in the 1830s. The political reality was that England was in large part – and in many ways increasingly – governed locally for most of the years between 1688 and the 1830s. The political advantage was that in this period the local sphere was increasingly colonised by Anglican Tories, to the extent that the exclusivity of both rural and urban councils became a national scandal.[3] The strength of localist opinion in the Conservative party is reflected in the line taken by it in the reform debates of the mid-1830s. Conservatives, while not being wholly opposed to change, sought

---

[2] J.A.W.Gunn, *Beyond Liberty and Property: The Process of Self-Recognition in Eighteenth-Century Political Thought*, McGill-Queen's University Press, 1983, Chapter IV.

[3] S.& B.Webb, *The Parish and the County*, Longman, 1906.

to defend local automony and tolerance of local diversity. It is true that some Tory Ultras saw in proposals to reform the poor law and the municipal corporations something very close to the end of civilisation as they knew it, but even in the House of Lords where it was most prominent this turned out to be a minority view. With not a little cajoling, those resistant to change were persuaded that the Conservatives' best interests were served by taking a positive approach to reform.[4]

In doing so, Conservatives were well aware that in addition to political advantage deep ideological issues were at stake. A large part of the early drive to reform English local government was provided by the institutional philosophy of Benthamite radicalism. It was taken to the heart of the reform process by men like Edwin Chadwick and Nassau Senior, close friends of Jeremy Bentham who in 1833 became dominant members of the royal commission on the poor law.[5] The doctrine to which Benthamites subscribed promoted the ideal of uniform national standards, sometimes minimum, sometimes not, and the principle of inspectability as a means of realising it. Taken to its logical limit, which in time it often was, this was the antithesis of the Conservative doctrine of local autonomy.

Revision of the Conservative tradition of local autonomy

That doctrine was, however, itself changed during development of the reform process. As control of local government slowly shifted from a 'natural' and self-replenishing élite to the democratic multitude, so Conservatives sought to revise their understandings of the local autonomy to which they remained committed. From the very start of the modern period of local government, in fact, they advocated a form of protected local democracy which quickly became central to Conservative conceptions of the local state. From the 1830s onwards, therefore, Conservatives were engaged in a dual operation: restriction of the spread of reform, and revision of their understanding of local autonomy. In the long term, the latter was the more important.

Restriction of the spread of reform was probably as successful as could have been expected. Only 178 municipal corporations were reformed in 1835, though many industrial towns were incorporated thereafter. Rural government remained unreformed until the late 1880s. It is true that the county society which underpinned pre-reform rural government was in many respects real and vibrant to the last,[6] but in an increasingly democratic age local government by justices of the peace was highly anomalous. Its survival reflects in large part Conservative success in resisting reform.

Revision of the Conservative understanding of local autonomy saw two types of protection become particularly favoured by Conservatives. One was restriction of the franchise to ratepayers, however defined (itself a major

---

[4] G.B.A.M.Finlayson, 'The Politics of Municipal Reform, 1835', *English Historical Review*, 81, 1966.
[5] B.Keith-Lucas, *The English Local Government Franchise: A Short History*, Blackwell, 1952, p.5.
[6] H.J.Hanham, *Elections and Party Management: Politics in the Time of Disraeli and Gladstone*, second edition, Harvester, 1978, p.3.

nineteenth-century debate).[7] In the 1830s, a cross-party consensus underpinned this restriction, and in mid-Victorian times even John Stuart Mill advanced arguments for it.[8] Its retention until 1945, when its almost accidental abolition by the Attlee government added eight million voters to local electoral registers, was, however, largely the result of Conservative refusal to countenance change in this sphere. Indeed, in reforming rural government in the late 1880s the Salisbury administration sought to create a yet more restricted franchise than that which had existed since 1835 in municipal corporations. In this it failed, but in doing so it managed to ensure that potentially controversial elements of local policy, such as control of education, poor relief and the police, were not (yet) made county council responsibilities and were therefore afforded special protection from the masses.[9] The second type of protection favoured by Conservatives was general control of local government finance. For many years the predominant Conservative view was that local authorities' overall spending should be controlled by the Exchequer through the grant mechanism.

It was then strictly a revision of local autonomy, rather than its supersession, in which Conservatives engaged in the long period after 1835 which saw control of local government gradually transferred from aristocrats and bourgeois to the mass of the British people. Indeed, in line with their commitment to local autonomy there were two ways of restricting local government which Conservatives tended not to favour. One was regulation, in the form of imposition of standards, which was all too closely linked to Benthamite radicalism for Conservative liking. The other was detailed control of local expenditure through provision of specific grants. Indeed, in the twentieth century the Local Government Acts 1929 and 1958 both sought to increase local discretion in management of local budgets by switching funds from specific to block grants. However, Conservative resistance to the spread of these mechanisms of control was not always successful. One of the few Conservative measures enacted in the mid-nineteenth century wilderness years of almost unceasing House of Commons opposition to Whig governments was the Local Government Act 1858. In an attempt to revive local initiative and restore local autonomy in the public health sphere, this Act abolished the Chadwickian General Board of Health created by the Public Health Act 1848. It was, however, a complete failure, and within a decade resulted in passage of the yet more coercive Sanitary Act 1866.[10]

Ratepayer democracy combined with general Exchequer supervision of local spending was, therefore, the essence of the Conservative view of local government developed in the nineteenth century and held for much of the twentieth. At local level it was partnered by an increasingly predominant view of what a local council should look like. Instances of Conservative activism surfaced in Liverpool and Bristol in the 1850s and 1860s,[11] largely

---

[7] Keith-Lucas, op cit, p.224.
[8] Ibid, p.7.
[9] J.P.D.Dunbabin, 'The Politics of the Establishment of County Councils', Historical Journal, 6, 1963.
[10] R.Lambert, 'Central and Local Relations in Mid-Victorian England: The Local Government Act Office, 1958-71', Victorian Studies, 6, 1962-63.
[11] D.Fraser, Power and Authority in the Victorian City, Blackwell, 1979, pp.44, 117.

disappeared from view in the 1870s and 1880s,[12] and were again visible in Liverpool, Bristol and Leeds in the 1890s and 1900s.[13] The rise first of Chamberlain's civic gospel and then of the gas and water socialism which it inspired ensured, however, that by the start of the twentieth century (often earlier) ratepayer democracy was also strongly predominant in Conservative local government. Here it favoured policies which had a minimal impact on the rates, a committee structure which elevated resource and controlling over service and spending committees,[14] and a culture (both member and officer) which was as 'non-political' as possible. The spread of 'non-politics' was often extensive and durable. In Warwickshire, candidates for election to the county council were not allowed to employ party labels until 1970.[15]

Conservative party politicisation of local government

Revision of the Conservative understanding of local autonomy which took place during the nineteenth-century democratisation of local government certainly limited the sphere of local initiative. It did not, however, undermine it. Conservatives' chief concern was to ensure that local autonomy operated within certain general limits, most of which were centrally prescribed. It was not part of party doctrine to seek to curtail local discretion by means of detailed central intervention in local affairs. A drift towards such intervention did nevertheless start to take place in the mid-twentieth century, and was indirectly driven by Conservative councillor demands. Those demands related to party politicisation of local government, which was subsequently to play a part in diminishing local autonomy. On the Conservative side it was chiefly as a result of local demands for central intervention that the central party machine became involved in local elections.

The first central intervention took place in London, which for many years was recognised to be a special case in this regard. The national visibility of London County Council (LCC) elections was certainly one reason why Conservatives chose to deploy the central party machine to fight them. The proximity to national party headquarters was probably another. More important than either was the party politicisation emanating from opposition ranks. This was also to be the key factor in driving Conservative party politicisation in councils outside London after the second world war.

Conservative insistence on this point is often treated with scepticism.[16] There is, however, little reason to believe that Conservative leaders from Salisbury to Churchill were anything other than sincere in declaring that they would rather not allow national politics to intrude into local government. In

---

[12] B.Coleman, *Conservatism and the Conservative Party in Nineteenth-Century Britain*, Edward Arnold, 1988, p.182.

[13] Fraser, *op cit*, p.120; E.P.Hennock, *Fit and Proper Persons: Ideal and Reality in Nineteenth-Century Urban Government*, Edward Arnold, 1973, p.285.

[14] A.Alexander, *Borough Government and Politics: Reading 1835-1985*, George Allen & Unwin, 1985, p.208.

[15] D.J.Mitchell, *A History of Warwickshire County Council 1889-1989: A Century of County Government*, Warwickshire County Council, 1988, p.187.

[16] K.Young, *Local Politics and the Rise of Party: The London Municipal Society and the Conservative Intervention in Local Elections 1894-1963*, Leicester University Press, 1975, p.29.

line with historic Conservative commitments, many members of the party élite felt that (within limits) local affairs should be locally managed, and that national parties had better not intervene in them. Only when excluded groups, represented chiefly by the Labour Party, demonstrated that national party politics was becoming an inherent aspect of local political life did Conservatives launch themselves with full vigour into local elections.

Most of the running on the Conservative side was made at the local level. The London situation is difficult to read. Here it seems that the visibility of LCC elections ensured that national leaders realised as quickly as their local counterparts that intervention was necessary. Elsewhere, local Conservatives were prime movers. At party conferences in 1927, 1929 and 1936, motions calling for national party political intervention to counter the rise of municipal socialism and the expenditure associated with it were submitted by Conservative associations and carried. Only slowly did the party élite concur with the groundswell of opinion from the party grassroots. However, by the end of the 1930s it was ready to sponsor party politicisation of local government, and would probably have done so had the second world war not intervened. In the event, the step was taken in the mid-1940s, with creation of a Local Government Advisory Committee (LGAC) of the National Union Executive Committee in 1945, a Local Government Department in Central Office in 1946, and a Conservative local government conference in 1947. Area and constituency committees, and 'schools' for prospective councillors, were also established at this time. Having taken the decision to play a full part in local elections, the Conservative party machine rapidly became very active. The second world war and reorganisation in 1974 provided two important break points in local government development after which Conservative party activity increased markedly.

The impact of Conservative party politicisation of local government on local autonomy was indirect but important. Once local government became viewed as part of Conservative electoral strategy, which from 1945 onwards was invariably the case, the possibility of its subordination to national political priorities was increased. So great is the subordination that in fact took place under Conservative governments in the post-war period that significant reduction of local autonomy may in any case have been the result. At the very least, however, it can be argued that party politicisation did nothing to impede this change and in all probability contributed to it.

Elite reorientation of Conservative party doctrine

At much the same time as Conservative party politicisation of local government was taking place, Conservative élite revision of party doctrine was also under way. It comprised subscription to a deeply instrumental view of politics in which some historic Conservative commitments were substantially downgraded and elements which previously were to be found only on the fringes of the party and the tradition of which it is the primary institutional representative were placed at centre-stage. In Oakeshottian terms, it involved a supersession of the procedural ideals of civil association by the instrumental ones of enterprise association.[17] In more familiar terms, it amounted to a shift in party orthodoxy from a predominant concern with the framework of law necessary to proper functioning of the economy, polity and society to a primary interest in means by which national economic progress (and usually renewal) may most effectively be promoted.

Instrumental conceptions of politics were certainly visible in the Conservative tradition even in the nineteenth century – though they were perhaps never as developed as Greenleaf argues[18] – and their increasing hold on élite Conservative opinion can convincingly be demonstrated in the interwar years, notably the 1930s.[19] However, they were not properly cemented in place until after the second world war. The circumstances in which this happened were highly specific. Their two most important elements were, first, a landslide Labour victory at the 1945 general election which was taken by the party élite to be more significant than in fact it was. Indeed, by the close of Labour's six years in office it was clear that traditional Conservative themes retained a good deal of resonance, and it was by prioritising the theme of freedom that the party was returned to power in 1951. Yet at this point the second key element became crucial. Churchill's decision to retain the position of prime minister for a substantial part of a full Parliament, and to construct his government in approximation of a wartime spirit of apolitical national unity, meant that the party was set on a course of quiescent concurrence in Labour's political agenda that gave instrumentalism a primacy in party doctrine never previously witnessed.[20]

The result was that Conservative governments of the 1950s almost totally failed to reverse a programme of centralisation undertaken by the Attlee adminstration between 1945 and 1951. Among other things, this programme removed from local control hospitals, public utility undertakings in the electricity, gas and transport sectors, outdoor relief and valuation. It was partnered by an increase in detailed central supervision of local finances. Despite being roundly denounced in Conservative party circles – motions highly critical of Labour policy were overwhelmingly carried at the Conservative party conferences of 1948 and 1949 – a policy of reversal was always viewed with some ambivalence by the party élite. Party propaganda of the late 1940s certainly declared in ringing terms that 'The governing principle of Conservative and Unionist policy on local government is that local government should be local, and that it should be government'.[21] Debates at the peak of the party at this time were, however, marked by a wide spectrum of views stretching from a desire on the part of the LGAC to promote a policy of return of functions, to a feeling on the part of the Conservative Parliamentary Secretariat that no real retransfer was likely to be possible.[22] It is therefore unsurprising that the Churchill administration

---

[17] M.Oakeshott, *On Human Conduct*, Clarendon Press, 1975.
[18] W.H.Greenleaf, *The British Political Tradition*, Methuen, 1983.
[19] S.H.Beer, *Modern British Politics: A Study of Parties and Pressure Groups*, second edition, Faber & Faber, 1969, Chapter X.
[20] A.Roberts, *Eminent Churchillians*, Phoenix, 1994.
[21] Conservative Party Archive, Bodleian Library, Oxford, 'Official Statement of Conservative and Unionist Policy on Local Government', CRD 2/22/2.
[22] Conservative Party Archive, Bodleian Library, Oxford, CRD 2/22/1; CRD 2/22/5.

of 1951-55, never in any case active or reforming, took very few steps to reverse these elements of Labour centralisation.

When combined with Conservative party politicisation of local government, élite reorientation of party doctrine thus generated a situation which could – and as it turned out did – prove highly injurious to local autonomy. Once Harold Macmillan, author of The Middle Way and allegedly on the point of joining the Labour Party when the second world war broke out,[23] had become Conservative prime minister in 1957 enthusiastic promotion of the politics of British economic renewal became the centrepiece of Conservative party policy. It could only be a matter of time before local autonomy experienced the consequences of this further change from meek acceptance of Labour reforms to determined pursuit of a similarly instrumental agenda.

This further change was certainly evident by 1961, the year from which Bulpitt dates sustained attack on the dual polity.[24] Under Conservative governments it generated major reform first of London government in 1963-65 and then of the rest of the local government system in 1972-74. Across Britain, an attempt was made to create strategic units in line with contemporary business orthodoxy which emphasised the importance of rational planning. As it happens, limitation of local autonomy was not a significant feature of these instrumentalist reforms. Parallel changes – to, for example, the NHS in 1972-74 – meant further loss of function, but in themselves the institutional reforms of the 1960s and 1970s were not particularly damaging to local autonomy. At the time they were defended on these grounds by government ministers. In retrospect, the years in which they were introduced are sometimes seen as something of a golden age for local government.

Elite re-reorientation of Conservative party doctrine

Only when further élite reorientation of Conservative party doctrine took place in the 1970s and 1980s did local autonomy suffer additional reverses. The re-reorientation was itself central to this change. In place of the Heath government's faith in large-scale, strategic units, Thatcher governments put their faith in fragmentation into a competitive market. Business orthodoxy having changed, so too did the predominant Conservative paradigm. In Greenleaf's terms, it could be argued that the party had made a move towards the libertarian end of the libertarianism-collectivism spectrum. This, however, would be a serious distortion of the change that actually took place, which is better captured in Oakeshott's terms. These focus on the fact that Conservative party doctrine remained deeply instrumental, and hold that individualistic values were simply put in the service of national economic renewal. Although the means changed drastically, Thatcher's ends were continuous with those held by Conservative governments for decades. It is in this sense that this shift in Conservative doctrine is properly viewed as a subordinate aspect of the more important shift from proceduralism to instrumentalism made by Conservative leaders earlier in the century.

[23] A.J.Davies, *We, The Nation: The Conservative Party and the Pursuit of Power*, Little, Brown & Company, 1995, p.88.

[24] J.Bulpitt, *Territory and Power in the United Kingdom: An Interpretation*, Manchester University Press, 1983.

However, one key reason for separating it out here is that this shift within a shift had significant consequences for local autonomy. Part of the explanation for this is that it took place at a time – and was arguably at least in part a product – of international recession and economic crisis. This crisis fed directly into the fiscal sphere, and in the late 1970s set Labour chancellor Denis Healey on a path of local expenditure restriction which Conservative chancellors in the 1980s sought, but rarely managed, to emulate. In turn, their failure fed directly into local expenditure controls of an unprecedented kind, and a major curtailment of local autonomy.

Quite independently of the entire saga of local government finance in the 1970s, 1980s and 1990s, the Conservative doctrine associated with Thatcherism was more calamitous for local autonomy than had been its predecessor. This was a consequence of the distinct nature of the two forms of instrumental politics. The drive to build strategic capacity in the 1960s and 1970s happened to be something which British governments could do on their own if need be, possibly not well, but at least in some fashion.[25] Furthermore, whilst they certainly upset local Conservatives in the process, they did not have to engage in significant limitations of local autonomy at an operational level. By contrast, the drive to infuse local government with a competitive ethos was something for which British governments needed the active assistance of local government to do at all. Furthermore, in addition to upsetting local Conservatives in the process, they had to engage in substantial limitations of local autonomy at an operational level.

Indeed, Conservative governments since 1979 have engaged in multiple encroachments on local autonomy in a wide range of policy sectors. In defending those encroachments, Conservative proponents of the new policy line prioritise many values, but local autonomy is rarely one of them. Instead, this tends to be downgraded in contemporary Conservative doctrine.

Conflict in Conservative local government

The rise of instrumentalism is Conservative party doctrine has resulted in a substantial downgrading of local autonomy. As the Macmillan/Heath experience demonstrates, this downgrading was not inevitable. It is in fact possible for local autonomy to survive a shift to instrumental politics. Crucially, however, that survival can never be more than contingent. When British economic circumstances continued to deteriorate in the 1970s, Conservative instrumentalism developed a new agenda for British economic renewal and had few qualms about the curtailment of local autonomy which resulted.

The impact of this curtailment on Conservative local government has been substantial. Restriction of the political space within which the party leadership is prepared to tolerate political difference has generated discontent and conflict in the ranks of Conservative councillors. In part this reflects social change within the party, and a gradual withering of the norms of courtesy and deference which once ensured that even important intra-party disagreements about local government policy could be smoothed over

---

[25] D. Ashford, *British Dogmatism and French Pragmatism: Central-Local Policymaking in the Welfare State*, George Allen & Unwin, 1982.

with relative ease. In part it reflects ideological change within the party, and an increase in self-consciousness all round. On top of these factors, it reflects the fairly brutal attack on local autonomy which has taken place in recent years. There is, then, a real crisis in Conservative local government. It extends beyond the numbers game which has seen Conservative representation fall to unprecedented levels in the 1990s. Examination of it requires analysis of the Conservative councillor corps.

Like Conservative MPs,[26] Conservative councillors can probably be categorised mainly as party faithful. Indeed, many Conservative councillors continue to fly the flag for the national government, despite the fact that this has become an increasingly unrewarding occupation. There are of course elements of national local government policy since 1979 with which Conservative councillors are naturally in broad agreement. Council house sales, some efficiency reforms and measures taken to depoliticise officers probably have majority support among Conservative councillors. Furthermore, the fact that non-Conservative elements of the local state have been worse hit than Conservative elements usually gains Conservative councillor approval. However, there are also important differences between central and local government which ensure that Conservative local government is experiencing an internal crisis that does not have an equivalent at the national level. One is that the fringe benefits of being a councillor are nowhere near as great as those of being an MP, with the result that councillors are more prone simply to abandon politics. In a reasonably quiet way, this has certainly been happening. A second is that communication channels into the party élite are far more accessible for an MP than they are for a councillor, again prompting more resignation among the latter. A third is that there is an additional dimension to local government debate. In addition to the core policy debate which in classic early 1980s terms divided wets from dries, there is in the local sphere a debate about local autonomy which stems directly from the Conservative tradition analysed here. It is, moreover, this extra dimension to debate which contributes most to the conflict which now exists in Conservative local government.

Among Conservative councillors, dissent is to be found at a number of points. Small 'c' conservative councillors, committed to local autonomy above almost anything else, are alienated by Conservative restriction of it. Similarly, councillors inspired by the enabling agenda associated with the rather quixotic pamphlet issued by environment secretary Nicholas Ridley in 1988 are frustrated by limitations imposed on them.[27] Even councillors who find merit in the agenda of competitiveness promoted by recent Conservative governments would in many cases rather not be faced with quite so many ministerial decrees. In regaining the faith of all these types of councillor, then, the Conservative leadership faces problems. It should perhaps be most worried by criticisms emerging from the ranks of 'enabling' councillors, for this is its primary source of new ideas in the sphere of local government.

One irony of the present situation is that it was Conservative council-

---

[26] P.Norton, 'Margaret Thatcher and the Conservative Party 1979-89', *Parliamentary Affairs*, 43, 19??.

[27] N.Ridley, *The Local Right: Enabling not Providing*, Centre for Policy Studies, 1988.

lors, candidates and activists who dragged a rather reluctant central party machine into the local political arena and thereby increased the likelihood of local government's subordination to a national political agenda. Despite this partial sharing of responsibility between local and central actors, most responsibility for change lies with the party élite. Indeed, a key condition of change is a shift of opinion and policy within that élite. Conservative local government is not quite dead yet, but its vitality has been substantially sapped. Means by which it might be restored are hard to identify, but necessary to find. Unless the Conservative party can restore its local government fortunes, a process of substantial disintegration could ensue.[28]

Conservative local government and the future

In considering the future of Conservative local government, sight must not be lost of political reality. Crucially, it is highly unlikely that the instrumentalism which swept the Conservative élite almost by default in the 1940s and 1950s, and which has been promoted ever since, will be abandoned by the present or any conceivable future leadership. For this reason it is hard to envisage ways in which the local autonomy necessary to revitalisation of Conservative local government can be promoted by the party, even if it moves into an extended period of opposition. Few elements of contemporary Conservative doctrine provide a basis for such a possibility. Indeed, a large part of the problem which the party now faces in seeking to develop a satisfactory understanding of the proper nature of the local state is that much contemporary Conservative thought pays little or no attention to territorial politics. For men like George Canning and Benjamin Disraeli, the structure of English politics was essentially territorial, and the nature of English Toryism differed by county.[29] This is clearly no longer the case, and is reflected in widespread neglect of the local sphere in the writings of modern Conservatives.[30]

Indeed, some go even further and pay little heed to intermediate institutions of any kind. In the case of Roger Scruton, the neglect is deliberate. For him, restoration of an organic national community is the way forward. In the case of Jonathan Clark, intermediate institutions are also intentionally dismissed. His reading of the English political tradition focuses on an antithesis between 'economic individualism' and 'the corporatism of intermediate agencies, from medieval barons and guilds to twentieth-century local government units and trade unions'.[31] Local government and other intermediate institutions simply feature on the wrong side of the tradition for him. Finally, to the extent that a consistent body of thought can be distilled from it, Thatcherism also tended to take this view. It was essentially an exercise in recreation of an authoritarian individualism held by the likes of Alan Macfarlane and Clark to comprise the dominant feature of the

---

[28] P.Whiteley et al, *True Blues: The Politics of Conservative Party Membership*, Clarendon Press, 1994.

[29] R.L.Hill, *Toryism and the People 1832-1846*, Constable, 1929, p.vi.

[30] A good example is D.Willetts, *Modern Conservatism*, Penguin, 1992.

[31] J.C.D.Clark, 'The History of Britain: A Composite State in a Europe des Patries?', in Clark (ed), *Ideas and Politics in Modern Britain*, Macmillan, 1990, p.34.

English political tradition since at least the thirteenth century.

Some Conservative writers have, however, sought to extend into the contemporary period that central strand of traditional Conservatism which focuses on the integrative function of a wide range of intermediate institutions. For them, Hobbes' interest in the basis on which government can be constructed in the absence of community is all too pertinent, and his solution all too unpleasant. They believe their task to be resuscitation of Burke's 'little platoon' of fellowship, and seek to focus not merely on the high politics and individualism which have preoccupied contemporary Conservatism, but also on intermediate institutions. This is not to say that local government is necessarily a central interest for them. Writers such as John Gray place their main emphasis in this regard not on the state but on civil society. 'The formation of individual character cannot be a concern of government – it is rather the task of intermediary institutions, families, churches and voluntary associations'.[32] Local authorities, being part of government, have little to contribute. However, incorporation of local government in a positive Conservative account is marginally less difficult if the starting point is Gray's analysis rather than Scruton's or Clark's.

The project is therefore not easy to conduct. Joshua Toulmin Smith's attempt in the 1840s and 1850s to promote what he saw as the libertarian spirit of a gothic constitution embodied in local self-government was a failure. His belief that 'primary institutions' could trace an unbroken heritage to Anglo-Saxon times did little to provide a foundation for their development in Victorian England. The Local Government Act 1894, which among other things created parish councils, never realised one of its central aims. 'The Act failed in the majority of parishes to create a new and active village democracy, or to revive the spirit of self government which had pervaded some at least of the open vestries'.[33] However, if implementation of the concepts of the active citizen or of civic Conservatism which have appeared in Conservative party circles in recent years is seriously sought, a revived local government should be considered as a way forward. It could be one way of recreating the 'neighbourhood and provincial connections' which Burke believed to be a necessary bulwark against centralisation and tyranny.

The only one of contemporary Conservative understandings of local government which could form the basis for its rebirth as an integrative force is the enabling council. Only as a genuinely governmental institution is local government likely to be able to contribute to reintegration of disintegrating local communities. The facts that the present institutions of local government were established on a highly inorganic footing by a Conservative government in the 1970s, and that the recent Conservative-sponsored inquiry into local government boundaries has made only marginal recommendations for change, mean that the raw material out of which any change must be fashioned is scarcely ideal. Nevertheless, if Conservatism is to take seriously the integrative function which has long been one of its principal concerns, a revival of local government is likely to be necessary.

---

[32] J.Gray, *A Conservative Disposition: Individualism, the Free Market and the Common Life*, Centre for Policy Studies, 1991, p.14.

[33] Keith-Lucas, *op cit*, p.42.

European Union: Rigid or Flexible Decision-Making

José M. Magone
University of Hull

'European Regional Policy and Southern Europe: Some Exploratory Notes'[1]

European Regional Policy and Southern Europe

Southern Europe contributed considerably to the emergence of a more consistent European Regional policy. This has been recently acknowledged by Lord Cockfield, who was the architect of the Single European Market (SEM). In his book on the genesis of the SEM he acknowledged that the allocation of additional structural funds was the price that he had to pay to achieve the support of the South European countries and the 'honorary Mediterranean' Ireland for the SEM. The main argumentation of the south European countries is that the SEM will bring more prosperity to northern Europe at the cost of the less developed countries. Such argument is not shared by Lord Cockfield, but he saw that to achieve an even development across the European Union, the south had to be helped to modernise infrastructures and improve human resources. Since 1985 Competitiveness and Cohesion became two inseparable notions.

In this contribution, it is intended to sketch out how this European Regional Policy is transforming the South European periphery. Most of the following pages will be dedicated to the new European architecture related to the emergence of the European Regional Policy. Afterwards some notes on the experiences of Greece and Portugal will be presented. This will be followed by some tentative conclusions on the impact of European Regional Policy on Southern Europe.

The Rise of the Region as a Subnational Actor

In the past two decades European Integration has developed from a process exclusively dominated by the member-states to a more complex political system, which now includes different levels of decision-making. The socalled 'multi-level' community comprises supranational, national and subnational actors. One can speak of a development towards an 'horizontal' and 'vertical' integration of policy fields. The need for policy-integration is related to the fact, that policy-making has become more complex over the past two decades.

In this regard, European regional policy can be mentioned as an example of such horizontal and vertical integration. In the early 1970s European regional policy was limited to assisting financially to projects developed by the member states. The main instruments used for that purpose were the European Social Fund (ESF) and the European Investment Bank (BEI). Although the European Regional Development Fund was created in 1975,

---

[1] For technical reasons it was not possible to print the footnotes to this paper. Copies of them may be obtained from the author at the Conference.

an integrated European regional policy dominated by the supranational commission came only into being in the mid-1980s.

The call of the European Parliament for integrating the regions into the decision-making framework was not a novelty. It was a mere continuation of a policy starting in the 1970s. Nevertheless, the demand became stronger and more successful in the 1980s. In the draft Constitution of the European Union, adopted by the European Parliament in 1984, the idea of a Council of Regional and Local Authorities was included.

Simultaneously, the programme of the Single European Market (SEM) in 1985 slowly integrated the ideas of 'Social Europe' and a 'Europe of the Regions' into the general framework.Policies became horizontally and vertically more integrated, creating a more coherent framework for the allocation of funds. The enlargement to Greece in 1981 and Portugal and Spain in 1986 increased the need to rationalise structures. European policy-making began to develop slowly into a taken-for-granted reality.

The reform of the structural funds in 1988 recognises the region as an important subnational actor. It became clear after 1988, that integrating subnational authorities would increase the ability of the small bureaucratic structures of the Commission to deal with the growing complexity of European policy-making. The reform led to a simplification of the allocation of funds. Moreover, three further principles should prevent an excessive delay at decision and implementation levels. The principle of partnership upgraded the role of the regions in decision-making and the implementation framework. The principle of a better administration of funds by a higher level of decentralization clearly gave more powers to the subnational actors.

A further principle is the consistency of European Union policies with the economic policies of the member-state, which I would dare say after Maastricht has been inverted . The growing pressure on the governments of the member states to fulfil the Maastricht criteria changes the whole rationality of national regional policies. They have become part of a larger whole, which is not visible today, but can be read in the document 'Europe 2000+' of the European Commission. The kind of flexible framework should contribute to a better implementation of the regional policy of the European Community, which was now formulated around five priority areas: (1) promotion of lagging behind areas (objective 1); (2) revitalisation of declining industrial areas (objective 2); (3) combating long term unemployment (objective 3); (4) facilitating the occupational integration of young people and (5) adapting production, processing and marketing structures in agriculture and forestry (objective 5a) and promoting the development of rural areas (objective 5b). After the integration of Sweden and Finland in the European Union a further objective 6 was included for regions with a very low density of population.

This horizontally and vertically further integrated policy was upgraded in 1989, when Common Support Frameworks (CSF) – the detailed support programmes of the European Community/European Union to the member states – were finally approved and implemented between 1989 and 1993 in the twelve member-states of the European Community/European Union. A long-term strategy of territorial evenness became the main objective of the new Community regional policy. The role of regional policy was upgraded in the budget, because it became the second largest policy area after the Common Agricultural Policy (CAP). The Delors-II Package endorsed by the European Council in the Edinburgh summit of 1992 and later on approved by the Council doubled once more the funds available for restructuring the European territory. The creation of a new fund of cohesion for member-states with a GDP below 80 percent of the community's average further consolidated the framework of European regional policy. Since November 1993, the Treaty of the European Union has upgraded European Regional Policy by declaring 'Economic and Social Cohesion' one of the 'pillars of the Community Structure'.

The Region as a Subnational Actor

The integration of the regions into the decision-making process is an important factor to achieve a successful implementation of the structural funds. It provides the European Commission with updated information on implementation problems. This could be observed after the Interreg conference in 1992, when several regional representatives came to Brussels to discuss about their experiences with the programme. Afterwards these reported experiences were considered by the European Commission in the elaboration to draft the new Interreg II for the period of 1994-99 Another element of the new European architecture is the Committee of Regional and Local Authorities (short Committee of the Regions-CoR). This new institution created by Maastricht is still subaltern to the Economic and Social Committee. It has only consultative rights in certain matters related to education, vocational training, structural funds and environment. The CoR is still a new institution and one does not know , how it will evolve. For the moment, the very heterogenous composition of the members prevents a coherent image of this new body. A third phenomenon related to the regions as a regional actor are the representations of regions at European level, The main task of this regions is to lobby in the European institutions. This is still in the beginning and is characterized by a high level of heterogeneity.

Competitiveness and Cohesion

In 1994 the fifth report on the socio-economic situation and development of the regions gave special emphasis to the lagging behind regions. The share of funds allocated to this priority area has increased from 62 to 65 percent from 1988 to 1993 and will increase to 73 percent in 1999. In this sense, 'lagging behind regions' became a crucial category in the new European regional policy. Portugal and Greece are two member-countries, which are eligible to receive support across the whole territory by the European Union.

Another aspect is that the Delors II-Package has led to a doubling of the funds from ECU 70 to 140 billion. This concentration of funds in the poorest regions mirrors the attempt of the commission to create equal social and economic conditions across the Community' s territory, which is regarded as an essential condition to improve the quality of life in (semi-) peripheral member-states such as Greece or Portugal. Specific Operational

Programmes such as Interreg II, Resider or Retex complement a project, which intends to modernise the territory of the union.

A chapter on the regional policies of the member-states highmarks that regional policy has changed considerably in the 1990s. In Southern Europe, one experiences that expenditure in the area of regional policy has risen considerably, while in northern European countries it has shifted to a more selective regional incentive approach. Such comparative differences matter to adjust regional policies to the specific realities of the countries. It seems that this is the direction to where European regional policy is moving.

Economic and Social Cohesion in Greece and Portugal

All south European countries have been major supporters of the European Integration process. The long tradition of a highly centralized state and the lack of resources to implement public policies have been negative factors undermining the modernization of these semiperipheral countries. A further feature has been the discontinuity of a democratic state. In the nineteenth and twentieth centuries periods of democratic rule were interrupted by authoritarian experiments. Portugal and Greece are not exceptions to the rule. On the contrary, both states are characterized by strong centralised states, which prevent the modernisation of the country. Europeanization has been regarded as a form to overcome this deficit. The new European regional policy clearly concentrates most of its resources on Southern Europe. The whole territory of Portugal and Greece is included as objective 1 regions.

This changes considerably the relationship between the South European countries and the European Union. The former nationally oriented regional policies are now much stronger influenced by a European rationale. The restructuring of the Greek and Portuguese territories is induced by a long-term logics of planning which had been incipient in both countries until now. It changes mentalities and culture in the two countries. The submission of Regional Development Plans to the European Union by the member-states is an important exercise to understand the problems existing across the national territory. The approval of the CSF to support this Regional Development Plans helps to transform mentalities in territorial planning. Evaluation and monitoring procedures further consolidate new patterns of behaviour, which will coexist with old ones for a long period of time. The long-term development strategies since 1989 may help to transform and modernize both culture and structures in Greece and Portugal.

Although, the first CSF in Greece and Portugal implemented between 1989 and 1993 did not lead to a convergence within the national territory, but it seemed to perpetuate the cleavages inside both countries, one must acknowledge, at least for the Portuguese case, that the disparities between the European Union average and the national average has not widen.

Assessments of the impact of structural funds in Greece since 1981 and in Portugal since 1986 emphasise that the economic disparities between the regions continue to persist. In the case of Portugal, the western coast around the two big urban centres Lisbon and Oporto were able to attract most of the funds, while Eastern regions were characterized by a further decline.

One of the main reasons is, that most of the projects are submitted in the more developed areas. A culture of project-planning is still in the making in Portugal. The recent CSF 1994-99 was approved only in 1994, although the Portuguese government was one of the first to submit its Regional Development Plan.

In Greece, the first ten years meant an adaptation to European Community procedures. There was a considerable impact on the administrative structures and culture of the Greek state. Nevertheless, the first CSF 1989-1993 was only approved after long negotiations between the Greek government and the European Union in early 1990, one year after the scheduled five-year plan. This has to do with the fact that in the crucial years, the PASOK government which had ruled the country since 1982, was replaced by a coalition government of the rightcentre New Democracy (ND) and the coalition of the left.

This delay led to a late allocation and implementation of funds. Such problems have been experienced in the second CSF 1994-99 too, when the fully negotiated CSF by ND was changed by the Socialist government, which came to power after the elections of October 1993. Both the Greek as well as the Portuguese CSF2 stress the need to invest in human ressources and modernise infrastructures. Neverthless there are some differences.

The Portuguese CSF2 is organised around four priorities:

- Priority 1: Developing Human Resources and Employment;
- Priority 2: Improving economic competitiveness;
- Priority 3: Improving the quality of life and social cohesion;
- Priority 4: Strengthening the regional economic base.

Ad Priority 1

It is intended to improve the educational, scientific and technological system. Furthermore, a pre-condition will be the improvement of the school network, the quality of teaching and the interface of productive activities. Simultaneously, a system of initial vocational training complementary to the educational system and an effective system of continuing training is to be further developed. Last but not least, the need to adapt employment to changes in production system is emphasised. On the whole, all these subpriorities foresee a major investment in the quality of education, which shall achieve an increase of persons engaged in continuous training measures from 5.2% in 1992 to 8% in 1999; the number of research workers per 1.000 persons should increase from 1.2 in 1992 to 2.5 in 1999; Expenditure by firms on R&D should increase as a percentage of total expenditure in this field from 26% to 40% .

Ad Priority 2

It will focus on the creation of economic infrastructure, particularly in transport, telecommunications and energy and the modernization of the economic fabric, principally by structural adjustment and greater competitiveness. It is intended to achieve an increase of coverage of imports by exports from

66.8% in 1992 to 70% in 1999 and the percentage of Transeuropean Road Networks (TERNs) completed from 42% in 1993 to 100% in 1999.

Ad Priority 3

It gives special emphasis to integrated assistance in the field of the environment and support for urban renewal measures and improvements to the health system and the launch of measures to support the economic and social integration of disadvantaged social groups. This priority attempts to reduce the deficits in public services supply. It intends to increase the percentage of the population served by the public drinking-water network from 77% (1990) to 95% (1999);increase the coverage of the population with a system for the collection of urban waste from 75% (1990) to 98% (1999);increase of the percentage of the population served by main drainage from 55% (1990) to 90% (1999);increase the percentage of waste water receiving secondary treatment (in communities with more than 2 000 inhabitants) from 20 to 90% (1999); to reduce the ratio of inhabitants per doctor from 345:1 (1991) to 327:1 (1999); to increase the number of hospital beds per 1000 inhabitants from 2.94 (1991) to 2.95 (1999) and reduce long-term unemployment as a percentage of total unemployment from 29.7% (1993) to 25% (1999).

Ad Priority 4

It is dedicated entirely to regional development.

The funds will be directed towards the seven NUTS II regions (five in continental Portugal plus Acores and Madeira). Quite crucial will be the support of inter-municipal planning. The three general objectives are 1) the strengthening of the regional economic base, particularly by providing support for the economic infrastructures (transport, equipment) and business infrastructures, as well as for economic operators in the regions concerned;2) the help to maintain population in the less developed regions so as to prevent desertification of the interior and to find the beginnings of a solution to the excessive demographic concentration around Lisbon and Oporto and 3) the improvement of the living conditions of the populations concerned, particularly with regard to the environment. The recent changeover of government after elections on 1 October 1995 may lead to a stronger emphasis on regionalisation. The present Socialist government hopes to implement the regionalisation as a in-between level between central and municipal government in 1997, so that decentralisation may lead to a more efficient administration and implementation of the structural funds. Europeanization is, in this sense, changing the whole structure of the Portuguese political system.

The Greek case shows similarities to the Portuguese CSF. It is organised around three main axis:

- Axis 1: Reduction in the degree of peripherality and promotion of internal integration by the development of large infrastructures;

- Axis 2: Improvement of living conditions;
- Axis 3: Development and competitiveness of the economy.

Ad Axis 1

It focuses on the development of transport, communication and energy infrastructures. Road networks and extension of the rail network will become priorities in the CSF. In the field of the communications, telecommunications and the restructuring of the postal service are mentioned as important for the further development of the country. In the energy sector, it will be central to continue the project on the introduction of natural gas in Greece financially supported by the European Union operational programme RE-GEN. In CSF2 the work done in CSF will be continued with support from the operational programme Interreg II. There were many implementation problems in CSF1 and it is expected that difficulties will continue throughout CSF2.

Ad Axis 2

The present CSF concentrates on the improvement of urban areas. it will give priority to the modernisation of public infrastructures. Moreover, it is intended to extend the underground in Athens and to build a new small one in Salonika of 9.5 kilometres comprising 14 stations.

A further area will be health and welfare focusing on the modernisation of the infrastructure and scientific equipment of health establishments in regions suffering inadequacies at this level; integration of actions to modernize the management of hospitals and other services, including the development of a data-processing system covering health services;training of health-care staff and creation and launching of a national centre for the collection of blood. A further major area is the improvement, monitoring and management of the environment. In this sense, infrastructures shall be set up to improve environmental conditions in Greece.

Ad Axis 3

It intends to relaunch the competitiveness of the Greek economy, therefore it covers all areas of Greek economy. In the past years the Greek economy was not able to catch up in relation to the European Union average. This axis intends to improve infrastructures in industry and services, r&d, tourism, agriculture and fisheries.

The success of the strategic priorities of CSF will be supported by actions to assure the development of human resources and employment promotion and to reduce regional disparities and opening-up of regional areas. Recent developments seem to assure that the CSF funds are being absorbed as scheduled, inspite of the delay at the very beginning. It is still too soon to make a final assessment. The administrative structures are under big strain to become more efficient in dealing with the implementation and monitoring of the structural funds.

Conclusions

The ongoing transformation of Southern Europe is intertwined with the process of European Integration. The South European semiperiphery has been so far the strongest supporters of the European Union. The South European countries have been major contributors to the idea that competitiveness has to be balanced with the principle of social and economic cohesion. The transformation of the European political system since the Single European Act in 1987 gave a special place to structural policies. Such policies are, in the end, territorial policies of the European Union, which intend to create a new European multi-level polity. South European countries are more vulnerable to this European rationale of policy-making, because its legacy is one of discontinuity of policy-making and implementation. Democratic long-term planning which takes the view of the population into account is a new development, that may lead to a self-generating pool of European supporters. In this, the CSF1 and 2 in both Greece and Portugal are important catalysts to recreate the spatial dimension and condition of democracy.

European Union: Rigid or Flexibile Decision-Making

Fred Nash
University of Southampton

'The United Kingdom and the European Union: An Essay in Retrieval'

Abstract

This essay offers a view of the nature and place of the European Union in the politics of the United Kingdom. In a discursive manner four characteristics of the subject, indicating the range of its complexity, are identified. The argument is that there is need for a more comprehensive approach to the study of the European Union, with some attention to constitutional issues. There is need to examine in some detail the constitution making powers and processes of the European system, such as the next IGC in April 1996.

Introduction

The European Union has become an increasingly popular subject of study at universities and elsewhere. This is as it should be: it is the immediate and relevant setting and, thus, the proper context within which to understand British politics.

The British context

An abiding legacy of the pre-1914 era is the image of Britain as the leading commercial and military power in the world, safe because not invaded in its island home, with its industrious and prosperous 'Island Race'. It is difficult to see how this self-image might apply to the inter-war period; it certainly does not apply to the post-1945 era. Problematically, the image of the United Kingdom as a proud and invincible nation was re-enforced because she was victorious in 1945.

As a matter of fact in 1945 Britain was in a position which, relative to its former glory and power, indicated a coming down. We could no longer rely on our own resources for defence, or seek to set the agenda of world politics. Even the Sterling was fast losing its role as an international currency. Britain was, at best, a poor third behind two 'super-powers'. Yet, British policy seemed to be informed by a sincere hope that it was still possible for her to continue as heretofore and, if not capture her former glory and dominating position of power, then at least be a leading nation among the top few, playing the Greek to a world of Romans.

It is not altogether correct to claim that British refusal to join the negotiations leading to the Treaty of Rome was informed exclusively by this nostalgic attitude, for the rather important reason that the provisions of the Treaty of Rome did not offer a solution to this problem, but only held out the promise of a better, though different, world.

But soon it became all too obvious to those who knew that, despite all the reservations about the truly political and supra-state character of the emerging institutions of the European Economic Community, as it was then, we really had to join it as an equal partner, and pretty damn quick at that. The next dozen years are normally explained away in terms of two ideas. Firstly, the fact that politics in the United Kingdom was dominated by a succession of economic and fiscal crisis, often made more complex by institutional innovation. And, secondly, in terms of the intransigence of De Gaulle in keeping us out of the European 'Nirvana', as well as imposing a phlegmatic pace upon the process of changes in the European system. As a result, and in part because in the meanwhile the economic and industrial condition of the United Kingdom had worsened, and the EEC had become all but paralysed, when we eventually joined, we found ourselves in a very difficult situation. To many our membership in the European system is a reminder of the painful fact that we could not succeed on our own. To others, our membership is *the* problem, in that it holds us back and ties us to 'foreign' practices. Despite various attempts to tell a positive story, our continued membership is, in one way or another, a permanent reminder of the fact of change and decline. Moreover, the fact that soon after we joined, world economic conditions took a sharp turn for the catastrophic, exacerbated by a growing crisis of governing in the 1970s, made it a uniquely inopportune moment to experiment with new institutions and relationships.

Lest this last statement should be taken to mean that it is possible to judge the right moment and act accordingly in the world of the political so as not to experience untoward consequences, two points ought to be made. Firstly, that the quip 'if men are to wait for liberty until they are ready for it, they will never be free' applies, *mutatis mutandis*, to the matter of making judgements about the timing of political decisions. In the light of this, the issue of Monetary Union and the so-called British 'opt-out' – or, in the view of some, the freedom to 'opt-in' when it suits – bear further thought and examination. Secondly, on what basis is one to determine whether the time for a certain action is right? Promises and objectives are a matter of judgement, whereas the extent to which they have been achieved are a matter of contingencies and consequences. Decisions can only be evaluated in the light of the fullness of the events, which also means in the light of the now known but at the time unforseeable contingencies, which may have had a role in determining the consequences we wish to examine. Politicians must be judged in terms of their promises; what they deliver will have to be judged in terms of consequences. In political science both intentions and consequences matter.

Four characteristics of the subject

1

The first characteristic of our subject is that it is too close to us; it is very much part of our present. A great deal of effort is expended to make information about the European system available to any one who may be interested, as well as establish and service documentation centres at various research institutions – such as at the Hartley Library, University of Southampton. These are, nevertheless, contemporary history materials, news-sheets and public documents, offered as 'official' factual information.

However, documents are becoming available at the European Archive in Florence. This, in conjunction with the release of British government papers, has enabled meaningful research to be initiated but only into the earlier stages of the creation of the European system, and policy in the United Kingdom, including the initial decision not to participate. Importantly, we now know that the British decision was based on a sophisticated understanding of the longer term political and economic implications of the European system. With prescience, it was understood that the idea of such a system had a propensity to integration within a kind of European federation. Curiously, it was against the background of this knowledge that, only two years later, it was decided to join the system, which decision was presented in mostly economic and political, though never constitutional, terms. But the constitutional issue was present from the start, and its implications were examined and clearly stated in the Foreign Office working papers before 1956. And when this issue inevitably surfaced in 1971-2, it was presented as a dry and not really important constitutional matter, the answer to which was rather very simple: Parliament retains its Sovereignty, indeed we can only join and accept European legislation when this Sovereign Parliament so decrees. Accordingly, European legislation was merely delegated legislation. This meant that the fiction of Sovereignty, and with it the ultimate option of withdrawing from the European system by simply repealing the 1972 Act, remained wholly intact. In short, the subject was not aired and examined, it was obfuscated and buried. It has, of course, come back to haunt and bedevil British politics.

Ignoring the known fact that the European system was likely to lead to a federal outcome, and ignoring the closely related issue of Sovereignty of Parliament by burying it in a legal formula and, thus, on the face of it, permanently defusing it, are the two central reasons why British participation in the European system has become a festering problem.

2

We have inadvertently identified the second characteristic of the subject: that it is intensely political, *qua* divisive, in a way that no other British involvement overseas has ever been.

In an obvious sense, this is how it should be. After all, joining the European system was never anything less than enlarging the context of British politics, albeit in some rather unexpected ways. Of course, it meant the addition of a further set of institutions empowered to legislate for the United Kingdom. Problematically, as a set of institutions they are not easy to categorise. Despite the fact that they are supra-state, they do not amount to a distinct and new tier of government. Furthermore, their effect is not directly and exclusively on national institutions and processes, nor identifiably local, while they certainly have a significant regional impact. More than that, their introduction has had a serious effect upon British constitutional arrangements which to-date remain un-articulated. This is confounded and made more difficult to identify and examine because the introduction of these institutions has had very little, if any, obvious impact upon the *every-day* working of our political system.

All this is further complicated by the fact that, since 1979, we also have another electoral cycle and level of representation in a Parliament physically remote from the confines of the United Kingdom, elected in constituencies which do not coincide, in size and identity, with our existing parliamentary constituencies. Incidentally, the fact that regional representation was, in the event, denied to Scotland and Wales, has made the idea of an extra-state level of representation even less understandable. However, persistent low turn-out is seen by some as the real face of public apathy to 'Europe', while the proponents of European integration see it as the result of a lamentable low profile of the European Parliament. The first argument is predicated on the premise that people do not really want to know about it – after all we are an 'Island Race' for whom such extra-state involvements are remote, if not altogether anathema – while the second implies that the lamentable condition can be corrected with a better dose of information and publicity. Either way, the reasons for low turn-out, the evident apathy and the low profile of the European Parliament are not explained. Moreover, the fact that one set of factual material is capable of being used to support opposing interpretations casts doubt on the claims of both sides.

This deeply, if not fundamentally, divisive character of the subject is further exemplified in the dichotomy and the on-going debate about the future of the European system. Two points are relevant.

Firstly, that the working British political system is rather peculiar in the manner in which it politicises and resolves issues. Normally speaking – even though there is no such thing as 'normal' in British politics – issues are capable of settlement if they can be turned into effective party policy. The so-called 'post-war consensus' period, creating a set of institutions which the opposing party when in government accepted and worked with, is a good example. This idea may be set to come back: a metamorphosed Labour party has evidently come to terms with the fact that four successive Conservative administrations since 1979 have settled the terms of British politics such that a new 'consensus' will be marked by the election into office of the next Labour government. And this consensus will be shown most clearly in the extent to which the next Labour administration will not 'un-do' the Conservative settlement: not that they will pursue Conservative policies, but that they must run a Conservative created system, at least for some time. Paradoxically, it may be argued that a fifth Conservative government in succession will probably be the worst thing that can happen to the settiement that they have, willy-nilly, put in place: it is seriously doubtful if a party of change is ever capable of consolidating its 'achievements' and can settle down simply to run the system in terms of that new settlement. The propensity to innovate is hard to resist for a party which has come to power with the promise of change, else its very reason has gone.

But the settlement that the present Conservative government is expected to bequeath to the next Labour administration does not include a settled perspective on the European system. Neither of the two larger national parties have managed unambiguously to turn the issue of policy on Europe into party policy, thereby settling the issue for a meaningful duration in the politics of the United Kingdom: a shift inside either party can change the existing party line on Europe. Incidentally, Europe is not an exception that probes the rule. A number of other issues, such as feminism, race, the environment and the like, are also not capable of articulation in strictly partisan terms, for which the 'normal' mode of British politics cannot produce 'permanent' settlements either. Evidently the shape of politics is changing.

Secondly, any end-related statement is a political, meaning partisan, argument. It is not the business of social science to determine the shape of things to come, but it can contribute by clarifying the likely consequences of policies already in train, or the meaning of options on offer. Significantly, such analysis must fall short of becoming vehicles for the partisan desiderata of the analyst. This is not asking for too much: of course analysts are entitled to their partisan preferences, but the place for the expression of partisan preferences is the public forum of debate, where the opinion of each has an equal right to be heard.

The point is this. Many analyses of the possible federalist or truly intergovernmental nature of the European system tend to become a 'nationalist' attack on a caricature of federalism in favour of intergovernmentalism or seek to convince that a European federation may be an important good to pursue. But the real meaning and the true implications of both are lost in the haze of the arguments. The issue of 'democratic deficit' is a case in point. Unless and until 'democracy' and 'democratisation' are unambiguously understood, they ought not to be proposed, at any rate not by academics whose interest is to expound the meaning of these concepts. Moreover, democracy has its own requirements. Without labouring the point, proponents of 'democratisation' do not admit, though they must see it, that in advocating it they are actually seeking to change the European system into a European state, albeit a federal one. The recognition that the very phrase 'democratic deficit' is a misnomer when used in relation to the European system is missing. It is not a concept that applies to it, for the European system is not a structure of that type: it is not yet a state; it has no claim to 'popular sovereignty'; and it is not, as such, a government to admit of democratisation. In short, such analyses are a part of the problem, not contributions to its understanding.

3

This discussion has naturally led to the third characteristic feature of the subject: namely the fact that the very nature of the European system is less than clear.

Even though there are numerous global and regional international organisations, they are, nevertheless, capable of being reduced to a dichotomous category. Typically, international organisations are intergovernmental fora in which, quintessentially, the player is the Sovereign state. Here the state is defined in Realist terms, predicated upon the assumption of their equal Sovereignty irrespective of all else. This simplifies matters a great deal, although, of late, we have had two types of exceptions to this rule: a people not yet organised into a Sovereign state, such as the Palestinians, have, nevertheless, been recognised as a unit with a distinct identity for purpose of association with the United Nations, while the role of some non-state actors has also been recognised. Exceptionally there are a few functional international organisations characterised by their distinct supra-state nature and form. The supremely successful example, and for that reason completely out of site, is that of the International Postal Union, now a part of the United Nations.

This simplified stereotypification serves to highlight the fact that the European system is neither the one nor the other. It is often said that the European system is unique in its own right, but this statement is, as such, also empty. Two important question arise: firstly, what sort of an organisation is it, and, secondly, what are the implications of it being what it is.

The difficulty here arises out of the fact that it is an intergovernmental system with a strong propensity incrementally to become a supra-state system, not that it was created as an intergovernmental system and has now metamorphosed. From its inception, its essential intergovernmentalism was infused with a necessary element of 'supranationalism'. There is no gain-saying that its predecessors, and the motivation of its originators, were strongly integrationist, desiring a permanent combining of European resources under the authority of a body invested, so to say, with pooled sovereignty of its 'High Contracting Parties'. It is also true that the European Economic Community did not embody these principles, and did not replicate the form and *modus operandi* of its predecessors, but it embodied enough policy objectives and created the necessary mechanism for the pooling of powers and the central direction of policy so as to make the principle of supra-state system a permanent feature of the new venture. Indeed, it is true to say that the first decade of its history tells the story of French resistance to the implications of this dual nature, which was not resolved even after the infamous Luxembourg Compromise, nor has the Ionian Compromise tipped the balance in the opposite direction.

This complicated hybrid nature of the system is the core of the problem. Of course, neither the 'debate', that is to say the partisan talk, nor academic contributions to it are couched in these terms. Rather, they are always couched in popular terms of loss of sovereignty and the possibility, and/or desirability, of a future federal European system. Meanwhile various amendments to the Treaty of Rome have emphasised its supra-state character to such an extent that we can now meaningfully describe it as intergovernmental in form but a 'federated system' in fact. It is in this sense a uniquely supra-state organisation. This has serious and interesting implications, four of which are worth a mention.

• In speaking of its incremental tendency to a supra-state system one does not mean to imply some mysterious process of inappropriate enlargement, amounting, well-nigh, to an encroachment by European Union institutions of powers and competencies that do not belong to it. Rather the pursuit of the 'logic' of its idea necessitates the pursuit of incrementally more extensive range of policies. A good analogy here is the history of the powers of the federal government in the United States of America: the pursuit of one phrase in the American Constitution empowering it to regulate inter-state trade, in effect, changed the balance between the federal and the state levels.

- The essential ambivalence of the nature of the European system is reflected in the fact that it is neither excluded from the immediate arena of British politics, nor is it directly and manifestly incorporated into the body of domestic politics. This uncertainty is given institutional form in the fact that, as a matter of routine, the Foreign and Commonwealth Office is the conduit of relations with the European system, whereas, depending on the subject matter, other ministers attend the Council of Ministers. Moreover, while European Union Regulations, Court decisions, and, in their effect, also Directives, have an inescapable impact upon the average Briton, such measures are not seen as products of, so to say, the 'normal' British political processes. Even its laws are not really laws in the ordinary sense of the term: true, Regulations are directly applicable, and Directives set objectives which the nation state must enact, but these are not seen as 'real' laws, only as impositions or, benignly, as importation of rules and regulations, albeit according to the wishes of the 'real' Parliament here at Westminster. This essential distancing is punctuated by moments of sensational outrage when the turn of events demonstrate the extent to which the 'real' Parliament has been divested of its 'real' powers. It comes as a shock to many that today we cannot regulate the export of live animals as we wish, nor control fishing in British waters. Equally, a few decisions of the European Court have received undue publicity because, supposedly, they stipulate the primacy of European laws to that of the home made variety. What is clearly disturbing in such instances is the fact that the 'debate' is so ill-informed: an impression is created that all European policies and laws take precedent over all British policies and laws. Indeed, the fact that even now, some twenty years on, we have such moments of incredulous sensation is proof positive of the extent to which there still is real confusion about the nature of the European system in this country.

Another implication is, as was mentioned before, that the issue of Europe, that is to say the desideratum of its future shape – the wider-deeper argument – is one that has so far defied the lure of 'normal' politics. It remains an issue, alongside that of devolution, precisely because it has not been possible for either party to turn it into an unequivocal partisan policy and, when in government, give it a settled form.

A further implication of its hybrid status is that it is not clear, when we discuss the European system, whether we are examining the issue of British politics, or issues of European Union politics. This, in part, is the reason why those who see it all as a part of ordinary British politics also cannot avoid the fact that such a manner of attending to it always includes, even if by unspecified implication, the question of continued British membership in it. The politics of European Union is routinely reduced to the question of British membership; the extent of our co-operation; 'opting-out' or 'opting-in'; our financial contribution and the extent of our visible benefits from it; the problem of borders, that of Europol, and its implications for our traditional 'liberties'. The fact that now there are fourteen other members – our consociates in our European Union – and that, therefore, there are fifteen other arenas of political activity and interest is all but ignored. There are short-lived exceptions: general elections in another member state stimulate our interest to the extent that the political colour of their next president or prime minister will determine the shape of their policy and, therefore, the balance of views about the future of Europe. But this interest is defined in terms of British partisan interests. We must take care not to extend this point unduly: the choice of the President of the Commission is not a similar issue, and has its own imperatives. Of course it is not being said that we ought to have an equal interest in the political processes of all the member states: but it is also true that there is no interest, not even in the political processes of the European system as such, except from within the confines of the British perspective.

4

This leads to the fourth and the final characteristic of the subject, which requires a brief introduction.

It is an abiding principle of British politics to ignore principles, and to proclaim the fact as a political virtue. This desire to act 'pragmatically' is, perhaps, the only constant in the history of British politics. And it amounts to the claim that we act according to a manner of governing that has been historically evolved and sanctioned. The features of such a manner of governing are not deduced from abstract principles, but have became established because they have proved useful and are in line with British practice. More than that, precisely because this manner of governing has 'evolved' in response to felt need, any changes thereby incorporated are also historically and pragmatically justified and sanctioned. The circularity of this view is obvious and interesting.

Now, this view presages two necessary claims. Firstly, that the core of this system is the seat and the summation of the power that can change the system, summed up in the claim of the rolling Sovereignty of Parliament. Secondly, that it is in the nature of this claim that it cannot be contained in any document, or statement of principles, else the very essence of Sovereignty of Parliament will be compromised. In short that we have no constitution as such other than the assertion of the ultimate Sovereignty of Parliament, plus whatever Acts of constitutional importance it deems to pass. But knowing these does not amount to knowing the British political system, for its guiding essence is to be found in the 'practices' which inform the working of the system. And this entire edifice is built on a Common Law tradition, albeit that ours is no longer exclusively, or even largely, a common law system.

This view of 'the political' and 'the constitutional', it may be thought, has a natural international extension in The (British) Commonwealth of Nations, which, as such, has never been 'constituted'. In its former bifurcated manifestation of Empire and Dominions, it was run respectively by the Colonial Office and the Dominion Office. Over the years, institutional amalgamation produced the Foreign and Commonwealth Office, which ran the Commonwealth since its inception in 1947. And it was only in 1964 that, at the instigation of some African members, the Commonwealth was given a Secretariat, headed by a normally non-British politician. Now, there is a constitution for The Commonwealth buried somewhere in the various communiquis of its Prime Ministers and Heads of States, and a few Acts of Parliament of one sort or another, amounting to rules, understandings and practices; typically British to the core. Yet, every member of the Commonwealth, except the United Kingdom, has a 'written' constitution of one sort or another, even if only in the form of a (British) Act of Parliament.

This account of the British approach is offered in order to facilitate the identification of the final characteristic of the subject. For, habitually, this tradition of politics, law, and constitutional thinking is contrasted to that of the Canon Law system on the continent – conveniently the matter of Scotland is ignored. To be sure, such a contrast is historically true, but it is also much overdone. Clearly all the other fourteen members of the European system have codified constitutions, and their legal system is different from ours. But this historical difference is often proclaimed as though, in itself, it can explain the evident problem of the United Kingdom in the European system.

Britain has no problem being a founder and a good and active member of the United Nations, and takes delight in its membership of The Commonwealth, but the European system is an altogether different matter. Our final characteristic should, therefore, be the nuance of constitutional implications of the European system, which is to say the evidently un-British nature of the system. But the problem is not that simple.

British membership in an obviously supra-state organisation with governmental and political functions is simply unthinkable. Britain would never become a part of such a folly; after all, British policy over the centuries has been informed by an unspecified attitude of the 'defence of the centre'. On the other hand, the Treaty of Rome produced a hybrid system, not an exclusively supra-state one. This was well-understood, which explains why British participation was highly improbable. The decision to join is, therefore, particularly interesting, but it is not enough to say that this was a necessary response to the fact of decline and need for larger markets. Such 'stuff of politics' matters were obviously important, but do not satisfactorily explain the paradoxical decision. However, the decision becomes less of a constitutional problem when we focus upon the not so obvious fact that the evident dissimilarities between the European and the British practice hide an important similarity between the core principle of British constitutional theory and that of the European system.

Now, it is common knowledge that the European system is the result of a number of treaties. What is not clearly understood, although it is becoming more widely recognised, is that the European system has not just a constitution, but a codified one. But a strictly intergovernmental system does not have, nor can it accommodate, a judiciary and a court whose decisions are binding. International law suffers from two crucial defects: its legitimacy and recognition as law depend upon the actions of states, and in a world of States it is not possible to speak of international law as a necessary set of enforceable rules. Norm-led voluntary acceptance of international law is the essence of such a system. This is precisely otherwise with the European system. Not only does it have a constitution – the Treaty of Rome as amended by subsequent treaties – but it also has a constitutional court, regulating the relations between its various institutions by interpreting the terms of its 'constitution', clarifying the implications of its various articles and European Laws for the member states, and, significantly, of late, with limited powers to impose 'fines' on member states.

Although the European system has a codified 'constitution', and although all its other members also have codified constitutions, the theoretical structure of power and seat of 'effective' authority in the European system is dissimilar to that of its member states which have a codified constitution but is similar to that of the United Kingdom which does not. The point can be simply put: the British system, despite much partisan rhetoric and political hype, is top-heavy. With us Sovereign power is in the gift of the Crown; 'democracy' is only a procedure whereby the populace select the personnel of Parliament and, indirectly, of the government who are then invited to wield the authority of the Crown for the duration. This must be contrasted with the principle of post-revolutionary France – now applied throughout Western Europe – which uses the hortatory terminology of 'democracy' to describe the seat of Sovereign power, not the procedure whereby an historical conception is made to work in a 'modern' setting. Dicey's attempt to produce a dual legal-political theory of sovereignty which would explain nineteenth century changes in the British system was disingenuous and remains analytically inconsistent.

In the European system, ultimate power – but not Sovereign power as such, for there is none – is located at the top: this system too is top-heavy. Its effective power is defined by unit-veto decision of its member states at meetings which are, importantly, not part of the constitutional European system as such, but which are, in fact, its constituent assembly, capable of changing any aspect of it, provided all agree. Curiously, this procedure is a rare example of 'non-majoritarian direct democracy', with all its disadvantages in practice. These assemblies are rule making meetings; they are not bound nor guided by the rules of the European system, and they have no rules except one: unit-veto. It is here that they can also agree to disagree. The European system is unique amongst the bodies with a confided constitution in that it does not have a set process for amending its constitution and changing the nature of its power. The impact of this absence is moderated by the further and equally unique fact that it has evolved a more or less continuously in-session constituent assembly of its finite number of sovereign members.

Furthermore, democracy is not the legitimating touch-stone of the European system, just as it is not that of the British system. This is most clearly shown in the history of the European Parliament over the decades, and the powers it has been given, but especially those it has not been given, by its constituent assembly. In both cases, though to vastly differing degrees, elections and claims to democratic accountability, and the like, are only the icing on the cake. In the United Kingdom claims to democracy are the historically important integument for the real nature and location of power; in the European system, circumscribed democratic elements are a necessary add-on which have also become a problem. This kind of thinking explains not only the British satisfaction with keeping the European Parliament in a condition of political impotence, but also the desire of the continental members to transform it into the seat of 'delegated' sovereign power.

It is not that we are a member of a European system which bears no resemblance whatever to our practices. Rather, it is the case that all the other members of the European system are distanced from both Britain and the European system in this respect. We are unique among the members of the European system in that the theory and practice of effective powers of the European system are in tune with our views more than with that of any other member state. This also puts a different gloss on the 'minority of one' position we have often found ourselves in, and amounts to the claim that the final characteristic of the United Kingdom in the European system needs to be drastically revised. For the democratisation of the European system will undermine the nature of the United Kingdom Union and the essence of British Parliamentary 'democracy'.

The Study of the subject

The above account is far from that of a simple set of institutions created by a number of mutually agreeable states for a specific functional purpose. In an obvious sense the European system is, properly, an international relations subject. But it is also more than that, except that it is not clearly and unambiguously a domestic politics subject. To say that it is *sui generis* does not resolve the issue. How ought it to be studied?

Clearly it is as yet not a fit subject for history; equally clearly it is, nearly as a whole, a contemporary history subject. Problematically, neither of these approaches will suffice; for it is a political science subject, while other social science disciplines, especially economic, also have important contributions to make.

This may be taken to mean that to understand the European system one must approach it from the perspective of every nuance that makes a contribution to it. This is true, but extremely unhelpful. Clearly we need to understand historically the reasons for the emergence of a strongly felt need for trans-state co-operation in Europe after 1945, and must locate it within its proper context. The historical context will enable us to understand its paradoxical nature. Clearly, that must be our starting point. But its so-called *sui generis* nature only draws attention to the features that make it so. Here we shall certainly need to come to terms with constitutional theory and institutional analysis. And because it is a working system, we must examine its working arrangements, and its input-output procedures and processes. Clearly, an element of public policy analysis is also necessary. Finally, it is a recent creation, without any meaningful historical antecedent, while it also tends to change relatively rapidly. No other political system has undergone this scale of change without experiencing paralysis, breakdown, or precipitating revolution. And the kind of change that we must examine are not simply phlegmatic reform of its procedures or institutional relationships, but also its size and membership, nature and shape. And yet, we are not dealing with a 'super' state. A good deal of political theory is obviously required.

Meanwhile, the European system is studied at many different levels, by students with different educational and academic backgrounds, and indeed for vastly different purposes. Superficially, there is a broad similarity between this and the debate concerning civics and the teaching of citizenship which was the rage not too long ago, and is always an important point in a 'democracy'. The European system is our broader immediate context: we live locally in time and space, and the local context for the determination of matters that affect us is not only the immediate place where we are, but must also be understood in terms of the effective decision-making and decision-taking powers that have a direct bearing on our lives, and on which, even according to the ineffectual terms of democratic theory, we ought to have an effect. Historically the context for our political locality has been the state, now it is the European system. There is, therefore, an obvious need that those whom it affects ought to know about it. Civics of the European system ought to be part of everyone's general education. That of course does not say anything about how it may successfully be done.

Social science has a direct claim on the subject; but so do Humanities. Students of Humanities do not bring the same kind of academic background and armoury of concepts as social scientists are expected to do. This problem is confounded when we consider that semesterisation is making this increasingly popular subject available as an option to an ever wider range of students from across many faculties. But to offer a more general account is in fact to offer a *different* account, and the difference is marked by the degree of inaccuracy which is in direct ratio to the degree of generality achieved.

Only social science is truly equipped to examine and meaningfully account for the European system, which is fast becoming a specialised subject, about to spawn its own specialisms. A detailed and focused literature review is the next necessary step in the pursuit of this attempt at retrieval.

But we live in interesting times: the present Inter-Governmental Conference is set to decide on important issues and changes to Maastricht. The President of the Commission wishes to regain the ground for the 'one for all' principle, not only by disposing of the 1992 'opt-outs', but also negating it as a principle of action for future IGC meetings. The European Parliament is hopeful that public pressure and demand for democratisation will work in its favour, and of course a few high profile successes – such as contributing to the solution of the Europe-wide problem of football hooliganism – will not go amiss. And a British Government White Paper has declared the limits of its tolerance.

The outcome of the present IGC must be examined from every possible angle. But it is perhaps more important to examine the constitution making powers of the European system.

European Union: Rigid or Flexible Decision-Making

Claudio M.Radaelli
University of Bradford

'Harmonising what, how, and to which effect?
The politics of problem definition
in European direct corporate tax harmonisation'

Introduction

The problem of European direct corporate tax harmonisation is addressed in different ways by distinct perspectives of analysis. When conceptual lenses vary, European tax harmonisation acquires changing meanings, suggests diverse policy implications, and, most importantly, implies alternative approaches to European governance of corporate taxes. This paper considers four approaches (namely, tax neutrality, fiscal implications of monetary union, fiscal federalism, and international mobility of capital) with the aim of arguing three analytical points: firstly, tax policy problems are not incontestable givens, but are the result of an interpretative act which makes problems amenable to human action: this is consistent with the literature on the politics of problem definition.[1] Secondly, problem definition has implications in terms of the structuration of the policy process as shown in the literature on advocacy coalitions, target populations, knowledge utilisation, and interpretative frames.[2] Consequently, the paper investigates how the politics of problem definition amalgamates actors, policy instruments, and policy solutions in the European direct corporate tax process. Thirdly, not every approach has entered the European tax policy process. Therefore the paper considers the potential of a wider discourse on European tax harmonisation, showing some inconsistencies of the current strategy pursued by the Commission.

A preliminary delimitation of the field of analysis is needed at this point: all the approaches considered in this paper have been developed within public economics. Hence they belong to the same family, share the same theoretical foundations, and proceed with similar assumptions relating to economic behaviour. Yet their policy conclusions differ markedly. This renders the investigation of the policy solutions advocated by these approaches an intriguing intellectual exercise.

The organisation of the paper is as follows: in section 1 the policy implications of the four approaches to European direct taxation will be presented, and in section 2 the evolution of this policy process will be considered. An

---

[1] D.A.Rochefort & R.W.Cobb (eds), *The Politics of Problem Definition*, University Press of Kansas, 1994.
[2] P.A.Sabatier & H.C.Jenkins-Smith, *Policy Change and Learning. An Advocacy Coalition Approach*, Westview, 1993; A.Schneider & H.Ingram, 'Social Construction of Target Populations: Implications for Politics and Policy', *American Political Science Review*, 87/2, 1993; C.H.Weiss, 'The Many Meanings of Research Utilization', *Public Administration Review*, 39/5, 1979; D.A.Schon & M.Rein, *Frame Reflection*, Basic Books, 1994.

assessment of the strategies available for policy development will conclude the paper, placing emphasis on the need to re-structure the policy process.

Table 1
Problem Definition:
Four Approaches to European Corporate Taxation

APPROACH	Dependent variables	Independent variables	Focus	Policy instruments
Tax neutrality	Tax wedges	Taxes on the income from capital	CEN CIN	Removal of cross-border withholding taxes
EMU	Fiscal implications of EMU	Monetary union	Anchor-tax Spatial disparities Second best	Euro-budget
Fiscal federalism	Tax assignment	Externalities Economies of scale Indivisibilities	Non-centralisation	Side payments
Tax base mobility	Tax regimes	Capital flows	Globalisation	Global agreements Institutional reforms

Four definitions of European tax problems

Even though no systematic attempt to highlight the different analytical perspectives on international tax policy problems has been presented in the literature, it is argued here that pointing out differences rather than similarities is extremely useful for the understanding of this policy domain. Admittedly, the perspectives analysed here reveal contiguities and can be joined by means of bridge-propositions. However, stressing diversities has three advantages. To begin with, the choice of underlining differences shows that policy problems can be defined only through conceptual moves (an approach, a model, a series of causal propositions concerning the economy). In the absence of an interpretative act, a policy problem cannot even be detected. Secondly, not only is defining policy problems an interpretative act, but problem definition is not univocal: distinct analytical moves do not lead to the same policy conclusions, notwithstanding the analytical contiguity of the approaches considered here. Given these two arguments a third proposition follows: what is presented in this paper is not a review of the literature, but an exploration of how problem definition brings about identification of chains of phenomena, problems, and solutions around which political action evolves.

A cursory view of alternative problem definitions is provided by Table 1. It can be seen that the four approaches do not share the same causal structure, as illustrated by the selection of independent variables, dependent variables, and analytical foci. To be sure, the notion of dependent and independent variables should not be considered strictly; indeed, this notion is employed in this paper only for shedding light on the causal chain which represents the backbone of each approach. Obviously, the most important column is the fifth (labelled policy instruments) as it illuminates the consequences of distinct causal models in terms of political action: it is here that the politics of problems definition becomes visible and politically salient.

Tax neutrality

This approach is extremely important as during the late 1980s it introduced a common set of beliefs and arguments in the European tax policy process. However, the concern for tax neutrality is not limited to European issues; indeed, public economics as a whole has exhibited an amazing paradigm shift, from the goals of re-distribution and fairness to allocative efficiency.[3] However, in the field of international taxation the concept of neutrality has peculiar connotations. Indeed, the policy discourse on international neutrality is based on the notions of capital export neutrality (CEN) and capital import neutrality (CIN). When CEN is achieved there is not a tax incentive to locate an investment in one country rather than another; CIN instead assures that in a given country there is not a tax-induced competitive advantage of a domestic company over a foreign company.[4] CEN and CIN can then be employed as a yardstick for assessing the efficiency of taxes affecting cross-border company activity in the single market. Besides, CEN and CIN can be conceived as intimately linked to the essence of the Single European Act whose thrust is to eradicate obstacles to the free movement of workers, capital, and goods. Similarly, CEN and CIN can be seen as an extension of this principle to cross-border tax obstacles.

During the 1980s a model capable of measuring the distance of existing tax systems from the benchmark of neutrality became available. This model, originally developed by King & Fullerton for the analysis of the cost of capital in closed economies,[5] was later extended to the analysis of open economies. In a nutshell, the open-economy version of the model allows the measurement of tax wedges, which represent synthetic measures of the tax incentives and disincentives originated by the impact of different tax systems on transnational economic activities. The advantage of this model

---

[3] See J.M.Quingsley & E.Smolenski (eds), *Modern Public Finance*, Harvard University Press, 1994.

[4] M.Devereux & M.Pearson, *Corporate Tax Harmonisation and Economic Efficiency*, London, Institute for Fiscal Studies, 1989.

[5] M.A.King & D.Fullerton (eds), *The Taxation of Income From Capital*, University of Chicago Press, 1984.

is that the impact of several taxes (for example, national and local taxes, corporate taxes and income taxes on the individual who receives dividends from companies) is condensed into one synthetic measure of the tax burden on investment. The policy implications of this model are evident and can be articulated in the following steps: in the place of abstract models of optimal taxation, tax wedges measure concrete tax distortions present in the European market; in their turn, distortions can be ascribed to specific taxes, particularly withholding taxes on cross-border company profit, interest, and royalty flow; finally, the need for European tax harmonisation can be proven on a case-by-case basis because the analysis of tax neutrality sheds light on specific taxes which are the major impediments to the completion of the internal market. Thus the approach has potential for structuring the discourse on European direct tax harmonisation in a pragmatic way: instead of harmonisation for its own sake, the approach advocates the removal of specific cross-border withholding taxes. Mitigation of tax distortions through limited intervention of the Commission, rather than full harmonisation of European tax systems, appears the most straightforward policy consequence of this approach.

Fiscal consequences of EMU

The independent variable is defined in another way by this approach, as shown by table 1. Whilst the approach of tax neutrality detects its own independent variables by looking at the interwoven mechanisms of different domestic tax regimes, for the economic and monetary union (EMU) approach the process leading to a single currency is the area in which independent variables work. Consequently, it investigates the repercussions of monetary variables upon fiscal variables. Obviously, it is impossible to sum up the huge debate on EMU. Thus it seems better to focus upon the following critical themes illuminated by this debate: the identification of anchor-currencies, as opposed to anchor-tax systems; the second-best implications of EMU; the issue of spatial disparities, and the fiscal prerequisites of an optimum currency area.

The 'anchor' theme points out the differences between the creation of a single currency and corporate tax harmonisation. It argues that harmonisation makes sense when there is an indisputable centre of gravity – an anchorage of the policy process – around which national systems converge. The anchor can be represented by one European system which possesses greater power and is regarded as somewhat virtuous. In the case of monetary policy it seems sensible to argue that the German system (independence of the central bank, credibility of monetary policy, structural power of the Deutschmark) could be the anchor for harmonisation.[6] By contrast, there is not a tax-anchor in Europe, which, thanks to its desirable properties and its structural power, can inevitably attract the other tax systems. To make things worse, the alternative choice of harmonising around the mere average of existing tax systems (for example, selecting an European tax rate which

---

[6] The political implications of this argument are considered by K.Dyson, *Elusive Union*, Longman, 1994.

is the average of the current 15 rates) is not efficient as the average of a series of non-optimal units is itself non-optimal[7] In conclusion, if a centre of gravity does not exist, the European Union could be better off without tax harmonisation. This leads Cnossen to argue that a more or less complete tax harmonisation is neither necessary nor desirable:

The crucial question with regard to taxation is not, it appears, how the various taxes can be equalised as soon as possible, but, on the contrary, how much tax diversity can be permitted without interfering with the establishment of a common market and further down the road to a monetary union.[8]

A second theme linking European taxation and EMU has to do with the second-best implications of the single currency. Briefly, the theory of second-best, when applied to EMU, states that removing monetary barriers in a market in which other barriers are still present (cross-border withholding taxes are a case in point) can decrease the degree of economic welfare.[9] Therefore monetary union must be implemented in conjunction with the removal of tax distortions; otherwise the efficiency of the single market would be put in jeopardy. Here there is a case for constructing a bridge proposition between second-best analysis and tax neutrality as the latter can be seen as the necessary complement to EMU.

The themes of spatial disparities and fiscal prerequisites of currency areas have a long history which dates back to the renowned MacDougall Report (1977), but they have been rejuvenated by the economic analysis of the monetary provisions enshrined in the Treaty of Maastricht. The school of spatial disparities[10] argues that the unification of monetary policy in Europe can exacerbate spatial differences in Europe. Even though these gloomy perspectives are not considered real threats[11] there is still concern that (i) the loss of flexibility in economic policy associated with the renounce to exchange rates, together with (ii) the elements of regressivity currently present in the Community budget could aggravate spatial disparities in the European Union. Consequently, the Community budget should be restructured in two directions: firstly, more effective transfers (compatible with a limited increase of the budget) and, secondly, less regressivity, with more emphasis on European corporate tax harmonisation and on the so-called European green taxes. Whilst students of spatial disparities tend to focus upon the re-distributive functions of the budget, the theory of optimum currency areas – originally elaborated by Mundell in the 1960s – when applied

---

[7] V.Tanzi & A.L.Bovenberg, 'Is There a Need for Harmonising Capital Income Taxes within EC Countries?', in H.Siebert (ed), *Reforming Capital Income Taxation*, Tubingen, J.C.B.Mohr, 1990.

[8] S.Cnossen, 'The Case for Tax Diversity in the EC', *European Economic Review*, 34, 1990, p.473.

[9] J.A.Frenkel et al, *International Taxation in an Integrated World*, Cambridge University Press, 1991.

[10] R.Proud'Homme, 'The Potential Role of the EC Budget in the Reduction of Spatial Disparities in a European Economic and Monetary Union', *European Economy*, Series 'Report and Studies': The Economics of Community Public Finance, 5, 1993.

[11] P.Santos, 'The Spatial Implications of Economic and Monetary Union', *European Economy*, Series 'Report and Studies': The Economics of Community Public Finance, 5, 1993.

to the EMU policy process points out the need to empower the stabilisation function of the Euro-budget. Accordingly, the federal budget ought to absorb a-symmetrical shocks which, in a single currency scenario, cannot be stabilised by means of flexible exchange rates.

Spatial disparities and optimum currency areas analyses hence advocate tax harmonisation for reasons which are not the same used by the tax neutrality approach. The key policy instrument within which tax harmonisation has to be considered is the Community budget. Furthermore, the study of spatial differences and currency areas lends weight to the arguments of fiscal federalism in that a federal budget is considered indispensable for coping with these problems.[12]

Fiscal federalism

The point of arrival of optimum currency areas studies, that is fiscal federalism, can be conceived of as a point of departure for the understanding of European taxation. The strength of fiscal federalism is that it provides a comprehensive analysis of all the Musgravian functions of economic policy, namely allocation, stabilisation, and re-distribution. To these a fourth federal function, regulation, has more recently been added.[13] The classic argument for federal tax assignment is the presence of externalities, economies of scale, and indivisibilities. However, recent research on fiscal federalism in the European Union has steadily progressed beyond classic arguments, and has stressed the peculiarities of tax assignment in the European Union.

It should never be forgotten that fiscal federalism is not a theory for centralisation, but a stock of economic and political arguments for noncentralisation. As such, fiscal federalism should be considered as intimately melded with the principle of subsidiarity. This is way recent research on fiscal federalism does not advocate the introduction of a federal corporate tax in Europe. At the same time, specialists on fiscal federalism do not show any hesitation in recommending a more incisive tax harmonisation, articulated along the following lines: economic conditions appear therefore united for recommending the establishment in the medium term of a single corporate tax regime characterised by a harmonised tax base, a minimum statutory rate and a common country-apportionment formula relative to the profits of enterprises operating in more than one Member State.[14]

More importantly still, the approach maintains that the creation of a fiscal federal structure in Europe cannot be achieved without side-payments. Existing federal systems contemplate a flow of equalisation grants. These inter- governmental grants preside over consensus among members and compensate for the absence of state-level flexibility in absorbing a-symmetrical shocks. By the same token, fiscal federalism in the European Union is simply inconceivable without side-payments deliberately planned for mitigating

---

[12] B.Eichengreen, 'Fiscal Policy and EMU', in B.Eichengreen & J.Frieden (eds), *The Political Economy of European Monetary Unification*, Westview, 1994.

[13] W.Oates, 'Federalism and Government Finance', in J.M.Quingsley & E.Smolenski (eds), *Modern Public Finance*, Harvard University Press, 1994.

[14] *Stable Money, Sound Finances*, Report for the Commission, published in *European Economy*, 53, 1993, p.88.

the huge political and economic costs (from the point of view of member states) of tax harmonisation. Side payments are a relevant aspect of many EU decisions, as illustrated by the political mechanisms at work in the Single European Act negotiations and in the Social Protocol of Maastricht.[15] Simply put, fiscal federal arguments insert the political logic of side payments into the discourse on European tax harmonisation.

Tax base mobility

Never has capital been more mobile than in the contemporary global economy. This is not just a consequence of the 1988 directive liberalising capital movement but is a more general trend in the international economy. In the past world of limited capital mobility, the problems of international taxation were more or less effectively governed through the residence principle and the time-honoured network of bi-lateral tax treaties.[16] The situation has now changed dramatically to the point that for some economists the mere existence of one tax haven somewhere in the world can trigger a process of unbridled tax competition.[17] In its turn, this race to the bottom can bring about a downward pressure on capital and skilled labour taxes. At the end of the process the whole tax burden will be placed on unskilled labour, which can provide a very limited revenue. Thus capital mobility seems nothing less than a political time-bomb which will soon disintegrate welfare state policies.[18]

Intriguingly enough, as far as policy conclusions are concerned this approach does not necessarily recommend harmonisation. Harmonising taxes in Europe is not a solution to the problem of tax base mobility because attractive tax regimes outside the European Union can thwart any effort to limit unbridled tax competition through European legislation. Controlling foreign controlled corporations' income and capital movement – the approach goes on – requires a global multi-lateral initiative under the auspices of an organisation such as the World Trade Organisation. The European Union could be, at best, a catalyst of a multi-lateral initiative, possibly in concertation with the United States and Japan. In any case, European institutions (in particular the Commission) should look outside Europe (global initiatives) and not inside (tax harmonisation) in their search for ways of governing international tax problems.[19] Giovannini instead seems to prefer the road to institutional reforms, such as, say, persuading Switzerland to abolish secrecy laws, or promoting a co-ordinated international campaign for dismantling laws which favour fiscal arbitrage of transnational corporations.[20]

---

[15] G.Marks, 'Structural Policy in the European Community', in A.Sbragia (ed), *Europolitics*, Brookings; P.Lange, 'Maastricht and the Social Protocol: Why Did They Do It?', *Politics & Society*, 21/1, 1993.
[16] S.Picciotto, *International Business Taxation*, Weidenfeld & Nicolson, 1992.
[17] Frenkel et al, *op cit*.
[18] H.W.Sinn, 'Tax Harmonisation and Tax Competition in Europe', *European Economic Review*, 34, 1990.
[19] J.Owens, 'Globalisation: The Implications for Tax Policies', *Fiscal Studies*, 14/3, 1993.
[20] A.Giovannini, 'National Tax Systems versus the European Capital Market', *Eco-*

Problem definition and the European policy process

Having shown that the construction of tax policy problems can proceed from a variety of analytical approaches, which entail different policy implications, the connection between problem definition and the structuration of the policy process has to explained. Political scientists are persuaded that arguments and economic policy paradigms are crucial elements of the policy process.[21] Moreover, as argued recently in the analysis of the so-called European green taxes, there is a relationship between arguments and policy instruments:

The features of arguments ... and the way arguments are utilised by the various actors will play a crucial role in the choice of instruments and influence their effectiveness. This does not mean that arguments are regarded as substitutes of power relations; rather they are powerful resources in the policy process.[22]

It is not inconceivable then to assess the development of the European corporate tax policy process by looking at the structure of its arguments and policy paradigms. In addition, arguments are potential catalysts of policy learning and ultimately policy change. Corporate tax harmonisation – which has been described in detail in another study[23] – provides a striking example. From the early 1960s to the late 1980s the policy process was stymied, notwithstanding many proposals for tax harmonisation put into the pipeline by the Commission. However, the rationale behind these proposals was weak in that tax harmonisation was advocated as a necessary element of the Community, without further elaboration. This brought member states to accuse the Commission of demanding tax centralisation and harmonisation for their own sake. The situation was changed by the re-definition of policy problems operated by the Commission at the end of the 1980s. In that period the approach of tax neutrality made its way into the European tax policy process. The Commission learnt that a head-on approach was not viable and therefore encased its old proposals (originally drafted in 1969) in the new conceptual framework of tax neutrality. This was an acceptable framework from the point of view of member states. As shown earlier, the tax neutrality approach avoids tax centralisation and – being rooted in efficiency arguments – is fully compatible with a subsidiary and limited intervention of the Commission.

This process of learning facilitated an important policy change, consisting of two directives and one convention approved by the Council in 1990. Yet after that event the policy process has suffered from a prolonged stalemate. Few dossiers are now open, after the withdrawal of a draft directive in 1994,

---

nomic Policy, 9, 1989.

[21] G.Majone, *Evidence, Argument and Persuasion in the Policy Process*, Yale University Press, 1989; P.Hall, 'Policy Paradigms, Social Learning, and the State. The Case of Economic Policy-Making in Britain', *Comparative Politics*, 25/3, 1993.

[22] A.Liberatore, 'Arguments, Assumptions and the Choice of Policy Instruments', in B.Dente (ed), *Environmental Policy in Search of New Instruments*, Kluwer, 1995, p.55.

[23] C.Radaelli, 'Corporate Direct Taxation in the European Union: Explaining the Policy Process', *Journal of Public Policy*, 15/2, 1995.

and momentum on tax harmonisation has been lost. At the moment there is no systematic interaction between the Commission and other European institutions, to the point that one could wonder whether the European arena will have any future prominence as far as international direct corporate taxation is concerned or, alternatively, other policy arenas (such as the OECD) will be ultimately preferred.

Problem re-definition and policy development

The previous analysis of alternative approaches to problem definition can contribute to the understanding of the current stalemate. The cognitive dimension of the European tax policy process appears under-developed. Of the four approaches under examination, only tax neutrality has been employed by the Commission for building up a rationale for European corporate tax measures. The definition of tax issues in terms of neutrality has stimulated policy learning and change, but it seems inadequate for a major re-launching of European tax initiative. Presumably, the link between taxation and monetary union (via the Euro-budget) has potential for bringing taxation into the core of European integration. It is true that the Treaty of Maastricht does not even mention tax harmonisation, but the rough road to monetary union which has followed the signing of the Treaty and the consequent need for a major overhaul of monetary policy in the context of the inter-governmental conference represent a formidable 'policy window' for the re-definition of tax problems. Re-defining European taxation as a crucial implication of the EMU project can secure saliency to this otherwise almost certain candidate to political wilderness.

Fiscal federalism has been surprisingly ignored by actors involved in the making of European tax policy. Yet this approach, when encased in a coherent logic of subsidiarity, could be the most obvious backbone of a prudent strategy focused upon non-centralisation (hence compatible with member states' fiscal sovereignty) and limited but incisive intervention of the Commission. The main message of fiscal federalism is that tax harmonisation cannot make progress without a deliberate attempt to modify the policy stake through the introduction of side payments in the policy process. As the political costs of harmonising taxes are extremely high, a side payment strategy has to be devised. When judged against the yardstick of fiscal federalism the current proposals of the Commission appear too narrow (because they are limited to the removal of a few withholding taxes), and at the same time too ambitious (because they do not contemplate any side payment for building up consensus).

The tax base mobility approach illuminates the narrowness of the Commission's strategy. By allocating too much attention to taxes in Europe, the Commission has forgotten that the credibility of European tax harmonisation proposals will increase only if the links with the rest of the world are seriously taken into account. It is not sensible to advocate for a common European withholding tax on savings when capital can flow so easily outside the European Union. Most fundamentally perhaps, the Commission has not gained much credibility in this field because it is not as yet perceived as an important actor in the world tax scene. Never has the Commission launched global initiatives, such as a GATT for taxation or, more modestly, more synergy with influential policy fora such as the OECD.

Policy development in European taxation requires many pre-conditions, and problem re-definition is just one of these. However, in opposition to the conventional wisdom, which argues that institutional reforms (precisely, the introduction of qualified majority voting in the Council) are the only way to policy development,[24] this paper has argued that the cognitive dimension of the policy process has potential for policy change: it may be true that actions speak louder than words, but knowledge is the fundamental track along which action proceeds.

---

[24] The conventional wisdom is epitomised by F.Vanistendael, 'Some Basic Problems on the Road to Tax Harmonisation', *European Taxation*, 1993.

European Union: Rigid or Flexible Decision-Making

John Peterson
University of Glasgow

'Decision-Making in the European Union: the Single Market'[1]

Introduction

Three years after the target date for the creation of a single, barrier-free market spanning the European Union by 31 December 1992, the legislative programme designed to bring the market into being is essentially complete. There remain wide swathes of the European Union's economy where a single market simply does not exist. Taxation and professional qualifications are two amongst many prominent examples. However, European Union legislation now has been passed in response to nearly all of the 282 proposals contained in the European Commission's original 1985 White Paper on the completion of the single market. Despite gaps in the original programme and severe problems of implementation, the 1992 project has been a raging success, and may be the most important achievement of post-war European institution-building (leaving aside the absence of war in Western Europe).

This paper focuses on the decision-making structures which facilitated the construction of the single market. It argues that the single market is, in many respects, a European Union policy sector in its own right, albeit a very eclectic one with varying degrees of rigidity and flexibility. Treating single market policy in this way allows us to explain why further market liberalization has been very limited in the wake of the completion of the 1992 project.

The Single Market & Political Science

Curiously, there is very little political science literature on the single market *per se*: that is, as a coherent 'sector' of European Union policy which gives rise to certain common and identifiable decision-making structures.[2] Of course, the economics of the single market – which are complex and subtle – are the natural domain of economists. Moreover, a rich literature exists under the broad rubric of 'political economy' which often sheds light on the politics of market liberalization in Europe and European Union policy-making structures.[3]

For its part, the political science literature tends to divide into three. A first group of work focuses on the single market very broadly in terms of

---

[1] Draft: please do not cite without author's permission.

[2] To illustrate the point, there is no chapter in any of the following sourcebooks which is truly appropriate to assign to students for the inevitable week of any European Union politics course on the single market: S.S.Andersen & K.A.Eliassen (eds), *Making Policy in Europe*, Sage, 1993; A.Duff et al (eds), *Maastricht and Beyond*, Routledge, 1994; C.Rhodes & S.Mazey (eds), *The State of the European Union*, Volume 3, Lynne Reinner & Longman, 1995.

[3] See for example D.Swann (ed), *The Single European Market and Beyond*, Routledge, 1992; idem, *The Economics of the Common Market*, Penguin, 1995; M.J.Artis & N.Lee (eds), *The Economics of the European Union*, Oxford University Press, 1994.

its implications for European institution building.[4] A second, much larger literature analyses European Union policy-making related either to specific economic sectors (such as the securities or pharmaceuticals industries) or broad horizontal goals embraced by the 1992 project (such as deregulation or mutual recognition of standards).[5] A third and final body of work concentrates on interest group structures at the European Union level.[6] A recent Economic and Social Research Council (ESRC) initiative on 'The Evolution of Rules for a Single European Market' promises to yield important contributions to all three of these 'sub-literatures', and indeed already has produced works which transcend these somewhat narrow categories.[7] However, remarkably little thematic or theory-based work has been done which focuses firmly on the single market as a distinctive 'project' or sector.

The 'micro' nature of most political science scholarship on the single market is in many ways understandable. The single market – until very recently – accounted for as much as 70 percent of all European Union legislation. Generalising about decision-making surrounding such a wide and diverse range of policy initiatives is difficult. A perfectly justifiable research strategy is to 'unpack' the single market and study bits of it intently. Many policy analysts who have chosen this research strategy probably would question the notion that there exists any such thing as a 'single market' European Union policy sector.

Yet, it must be recalled that the internal market has its own 'dedicated' institutions: the Internal Market Council, a Commissioner who assumes a single internal market portfolio, a Directorate-General (15) with (at least primary) responsibility for the single market. Although a very wide variety of Treaty articles can be used to legislate in the name of the single market, the so-called 'co-decision' procedure introduced by the Maastricht Treaty provides what is, for most intents and purposes, a single formal method of decision-making for single market questions.

Thus the single market can be seen as a sector of European Union policy

---

[4] D.R.Cameron, 'The 1992 Initiative: Causes and Consequences', in A.Sbragia (ed), *Euro-Politics: Institutions and Policymaking in the 'New' European Community*, Brookings Institution, 1992; J.Pinder, 'The Single Market: a step towards union' in J.Lodge (ed), *The European Community and the Challenge of the Future*, Pinter, 1993; D.Allen, 'European union, the Single European Act and the 1992 programme', in Swann, *The Single Market and Beyond*.

[5] Recent examples of work whose focus is mostly sectoral are W.D.Coleman & G.R.D.Underhill (eds), 'The Single Market and global economic integration', special issue of *Journal of European Public Policy*, 2/3, 1995; J.Greenwood (ed), *European Casebook on Business Alliances*, Prentice-Hall, 1995. More 'horizontally' focused works include G.Majone (ed), *Deregulation or Re-regulation?*, Pinter, 1990; J.-M.Sun & J.Pelkmans, 'Regulatory competition in the Single Market', *Journal of Common Market Studies*, 33/1, 1995.

[6] See A.McLaughlin & G.Jordan, 'The rationality of lobbying in Europe: why are Eurogroups so numerous and so weak?', in S.Mazey & J.Richardson (eds), *Lobbying in the European Community*, Oxford University Press, 1993; M.Mason, 'Elements of consensus: Europe's response to the Japanese automotive challenge', *Journal of Common Market Studies*, 32/4, 1994; K. Hayward, 'European Union policy and the European aerospace industry', *Journal of European Public Policy*, 1/3, 1994.

[7] See especially Mazey & Richardson, *Lobbying in the European Community*; K.Armstrong & S.Bulmer, *The Governance of the Single European Market*, Manchester University Press, 1996.

in its own right. A research question worth asking is: what (if anything) makes decision-making concerning the internal market unique or distinctive? The purpose of this paper is to offer findings from an ongoing research project on European Union decision-making which may move us towards an answer to this question.[8]

Decision-Making and the Single Market – an Analysis

To understand the recent evolution of single market policy, we must take care to distinguish between both different levels of European Union governance and different stages in the Union's policy process at which decision-making occurs. Change in policy outcomes may be a consequence of changing patterns of decision-making at only one level or stage, or of many. This section deploys a framework for analysis that is sensitive not only to the multi-layered character of European Union governance, but also to the inability of any one theoretical model to explain all outcomes at every layer of the Union.[9]

A first observation concerns the 'high politics' of the single market. Clearly, considerable change has occurred in the broad political and economic environment in which the European Union operates generally. At a 'super-systemic' level of analysis – one which transcends the day-to-day operation of the European Union as a system of government – much of the symbolic potency of the single market has waned. For a time in the late 1980s and early 90s, the single market as a project to enrich and unite Europe – and, crucially, to bring benefits to all – captured the popular imagination as well as the fancy of Western Europe's political class. Crucially, the 1992 project was launched at a time of relative prosperity and high rates of economic growth in Europe. As late as 1993, one could argue without hesitation that 'no serious contender for power in any of the [then] 12 EC Member States could credibly urge that the 1992 project be abandoned or that national support for its core objectives be withdrawn'.[10]

Three years later, after the deepest economic recession in post-war European history, the President of the European Parliament, Klaus Hansch, hinted starkly at the degree to which popular perceptions of the single market (and the European Union more generally) had changed: 'More and more people associate the European Union with social breakdown and the destruction of jobs. We must link it again with the creation of jobs and social progress'.[11] Amidst criticism, especially of Internal Market Commissioner Mario Monti, that no major new single market policy initiatives had been launched in some time, the Commission developed a wide-ranging campaign to 'promote the benefits of the single market and...clamp down

---

[8] This paper forms part of a research project on European Union decision-making, funded by the ESRC (grant R000235829), the European Commission and Joseph F. Rowntree Foundation.
[9] The framework is developed in J. Peterson, 'Decision-making in the European Union: towards a framework for analysis', *Journal of European Public Policy*, 2/1, 1995.
[10] J. Peterson, *High Technology and the Competition State*, Routledge, 1993, p.199.
[11] *Financial Times*, 16-17 December 1995.

on member states which refuse to apply European Union laws'.[12] But the heady days when the European Union legislated quickly and decisively on the measures contained in the 1985 White Paper– as if it were a national system of government presided over by a majority governing party – clearly had gone.

Thus, even if neofunctional treatments offered convincing explanations for the 'high politics' of the single market in the period following the acceptance of the Single European Act, then neo-realist or 'intergovernmental' explanations became more seductive in the post-Maastricht period (that is, after 1993). Political executives heading insecure governments and presiding over 'jobless' economic recoveries at home were generally less willing to embrace new initiatives which traded off short-term economic pain for long-term economic gain. What is often the earliest stage of European Union decision-making – the pre-legislative stage when the European Council endorses very broad policy goals to be pursued at the European Union level – was marked by summit declarations which endorsed little in the way of concrete action to kick-start the Union's economies through further liberalisation.

At a systemic level of analysis, where single market policies are 'set' after one of several versions of the Community method of decision-making (the Commission proposes, the Council disposes, the European Parliament amends), the 'new institutionalism' – applied to the European Union most notably in the work of Simon Bulmer[13] – helps shed considerable light on the recent evolution of relations between European Union institutions on questions concerning the single market. The most striking change in the balance of power between the European Union's institutions has been the profound weakening of the Commission on single market policy. Under the capable leadership of the Commissioner for Competition Policy, Karel van Miert, the Commission recently has made creative use of the tools available to it (such as Article 90 of the Treaty of Rome) in seeking to pry open the European Union's telecommunications market and setting tighter conditions on state aids.[14] Effective policing of European Union competition policy is a critically necessary, if not sufficient condition, for the single market to exist.

However, the Commission has been considerably weakened as an institutional player in single market policy, because it has been reduced mostly to policing the single market and exhorting Member States to embrace a faster pace of implementation of European Union directives. The days in the late 1980s when the Commission President, Jacques Delors, and its highly effective Commissioner for the Internal Market, Lord Cockfield, could bludgeon reluctant Member States into accepting radical liberalization measures often

---

[12] R.Watson, 'New crusade for border-free European Union', *European Voice*, 1/3, 19-25 October 1995.

[13] S.Bulmer, 'The Governance of the European Union: a New Institutionalist Approach', *Journal of Public Policy*, 13/2, 1994; idem, 'Institutions and Policy Change in the European Communities', *Public Administration*, 72/3, 1994.

[14] Van Miert's record as Competition Commissioner would seem to defy much of the analysis in S.Wilks & L.McGowan, 'Disarming the Commission: the debate over a European Cartel Office', *Journal of Common Market Studies*, 33/2, 1995.

appear to be gone for good.

In this context, one of the most enduring myths in the study of the European Union is that the Commission is a purposive, single-minded institution which remains bent on increasing its powers at any opportunity. In fact, the Commission is a highly fragmented bureaucracy and really a political system in itself, where virtually every political interest in the Union at large can find support somewhere. Moreover, the Commission as other bureaucracies often engages in bureau-shaping, not resource maximisation as public choice theory teaches.[15] That is, they seek high status and agreeable work tasks. By their nature, enforcing the rules of the single market and seeking to 'shame' Member States into proper implementation of European Union legislation are far less satisfying policy tasks for the Commission, compared to the task of leading the European Union to embrace bold new initiatives designed to unite Europe economically and politically.

Meanwhile, the Internal Market Council has become a far less busy and dynamic forum for decision-making. It has seen new, politically interesting and 'sexy' areas of policy – especially audiovisual and telecommunications – become the prerogative of other Councils (Culture and Research, respectively). The Internal Market Council generally has shown itself to be the most liberal permutation of the Council. However, it has failed to keep a tight grip on decision-making related to the single market. As a policy sector, the single market illustrates Ludlow's observation that although the two often seem incompatible, a strong Commission actually requires a strong Council.[16]

The role of the European Court of Justice (ECJ) in making the internal market a reality generally has not received due attention from political scientists. However, with arguable exceptions, the Court has not handed down any landmark decisions of the same magnitude as *Van Gend en Loos* or *Cassis de Dijon* in recent years. The Commission thus has lacked entrepreneurial opportunities in the form of ECJ decisions which could be used to justify radical policy initiatives concerning the internal market, after making profitable use of such opportunities at the systemic level in the 1980s.

At a 'sub-systemic' or meso-level of analysis, much recent scholarship has deployed – often quite profitably – the 'policy networks' model which emerged in the early 1990s from mostly unrelated literatures on (British) intergovernmental and business-government relations.[17] Simply stated, the model understands decision-making outcomes as bargains struck between

---

[15] P.Dunleavy, *Democracy, Bureaucracy and Public Choice*, Harvester Wheatsheaf, 1991.

[16] P.Ludlow, *The Treaty of Maastricht and the future of Europe*, Centre for European Policy Studies (Brussels) Working Document, May 1992.

[17] See S.Mazey & J.Richardson (eds), *Lobbying in the European Community*, Oxford University Press, 1993; idem, 'Promiscuous Policymaking: the European Policy Style?', in Rhodes & Mazey (eds), *The State of the European Union*; E.Bomberg, 'Policy Networks on the Periphery: European Union Environmental Policy and Scotland', *Regional Politics and Policy*, 4/1, 1994; C.Altenstetter, 'European Union responses to AIDS/HIV and policy networks in the post-Maastricht era', *Journal of European Public Policy*, 1/3, 1994; J.Peterson, 'Policy Networks and European Union Policy Making', *West European Politics*, 18/2, 1995.

actors whose power is determined by the quantity and value of the resources they possess. The internal characteristics of policy networks in different sectors often have powerful impacts on eventual outcomes, particularly because many 'policy-shaping' decisions are taken early in the policy process in informal, non-public settings after bargaining between effective actors.

There exists no single 'internal market policy network'. Rather, networks correspond – in vertical terms – to virtually every product or service which is in any way regulated, supported or impacted by the European Union. The extent to which such networks cross-cut or overlap with 'horizontal' networks structured around stages in the production process (that is retailers, the haulage industry) or role-players in that process (capital, labour, consumer) varies enormously between product sectors. Generally, networks which are broadly inclusive of most effective actors in any sector, yet still purposeful, tend to keep a tight grip on European Union decision- making which affects their sector.

For example, the European pharmaceuticals industry, one of the European Union's only world-class advanced technology industries, traditionally has enjoyed close ties to and strong support from the Commission, national industry ministries, and other lobby groups such as the Union of Industrial Employers' Confederations of Europe (UNICE). Crucially, the main pharmaceuticals 'Euro-group', the European Federation of Pharmaceutical Industry Associations (EFPIA), not only manages to unite both big and small firms in support of collective action, but also is responsible for a significant amount of self-regulation of the industry as a whole. What Greenwood[18] describes as a 'European business alliance that works' is at the centre of a tightly-integrated policy community.

By contrast, the European air transport industry is made up of (mostly) loss-making national airlines, many of which maintain very close ties to their home governments. The landmark *Nouvelles Frontiéres* decision by the ECJ in 1986 gave the Commission license to seek more robust measures to create a single market in transport than previously had been imaginable. However, the Association of European Airlines (AEA) is a conservative organisation which mostly works to preserve the protected privileges of its members *vis-à-vis* non-European carriers and tends to take a go-slow attitude towards liberalisation. National airlines, particularly British Aerospace, maintain their own independent links to the Commission. Recent attempts by the Commission, particularly under Neil Kinnock in 1995, to take centralised authority for negotiating a single 'Open Skies' agreement with the United States for all of the European Union have been resisted by Member States and national carriers alike. More generally, aviation markets are becoming globalised while the national champion ethos of the early post-war period lives on in European aviation to a greater extent than in any other industrial sector.[19] Thus, the aviation sector is marked by a relatively open,

---

[18] J. Greenwood, 'The pharmaceutical industry' in idem. (ed), *European Casebook of Business Alliances*.

[19] H.Kassim, 'The impact of European Union action on national policy and policy-making in the air transport sector', in H.Kassim & A.Menon (eds), *The European Union and National Industrial Policies*, Routledge, forthcoming; M.Staniland, 'The United States and the external aviation policy of the European Union', *Journal of European*

unpredictable issue network, which itself has little capacity for mobilisation of all effective actors to change the status quo very much.

Co-decision: How Much Change?[20]

Part of the rationale for treating the single market as a distinct sector is the application of the 'co-decision' procedure, which gives the European Parliament previously unprecedented powers to actually veto Council decisions related to most aspects of the single market (for example, free movement of workers, right of establishment, mutual recognition, harmonisation measures, etc.)[21] In the first 18 months after the coming into effect of the Maastricht Treaty, approximately 130 proposals for 'co-decision acts' were sent by the Council to Parliament.[22] The extent to which the European Parliament was able to force its agenda on the Council under co-decision varied considerably. To a considerable extent, the jury is still out on the question of how much co-decision has empowered the Parliament.

Yet, early experience of the co-decision procedure invites three observations. First, provided its relevant committee chairs and rapporteurs show sufficient political *nous*, the co-decision procedure can be exploited by the European Parliament to force far more concessions out of the Council than was the case under the cooperation procedure. For example, on directives related to voice telephony and the Socrates programme, the European Parliament's criticism of comitology procedures led the Council (and by extension, the Commission) to concede amendments which it almost certainly would have rejected if the co-decision procedure did not exist.

Second, co-decision has not only empowered the European Parliament at the latest stages of decision-making – or at a 'systemic' level of analysis – through the joint European Parliament-Council conciliation committees (which must be convened when the two institutions cannot agree). At the meso-level, sectoral policy networks have become far more open to members of European Parliament and their supporters at the early stages of the policy process. In several instances, the Council (usually through the Council Presidency) has gone to great lengths to consult informally with key MEPs after a Commission proposal has been tabled in order to try to avoid conciliation later on. Moreover, the Parliament has basked in its independence from the Commission, upon which it was dependent under the cooperation procedure if it sought to force amendments upon the Council. The cases of directives related to motorbikes and lifts showed that the European Parliament can act as genuine check on Commission's executive power. For example, the rapporteur of the European Parliament's internal market committee, Roger Barton (MEP for Sheffield), almost single-handedly organised European motorbike enthusiasts into a large and effective lobby group to

---

Public Policy, 2/1, 1995.
   [20]The argument developed in this section is fleshed out considerably in J.Peterson & E.Bomberg, *Decision-Making in the European Union*, Macmillan, forthcoming, 1997.
   [21]A clear and readable treatment of the co-decision procedure is R.Corbett, 'Representing the people', in Duff et al (eds), *Maastricht and Beyond*.
   [22]European Parliament delegations to the Conciliation Committee, 'Progress report for the second half of 1994', PE 211.522/rev. 2/ann, 1 March 1995.

scuttle proposals vigorously advocated by the Industry Commissioner, Martin Bangemann, to limit the power of so-called 'superbikes', despite scanty evidence to suggest a relationship between lowered power levels and increased safety.

Third and finally, debates which preceded the 1996 IGC saw numerous proposals for the extension of the co-decision procedure to more policy sectors than covered by it in the Maastricht Treaty.[23] These proposals reflected a general consensus that the co-decision procedure was working quite well, in fact much better than many had anticipated. To illustrate the point, one Deputy Ambassador, representing a Member State which firmly and instinctually opposes further empowerment of the European Parliament, offered the comment that 'co-decision has made [the Council's] life tedious, but not overly difficult. There are far too many unproductive meetings ... But sure, we can work with it and we do take more account of European Parliament's amendments now'.[24]

These are still early days in the history of co-decision, but there is considerable evidence to suggest that the procedure has made the European Parliament a much more powerful actor in areas where it applies. One effect is that consumer interests now appear to be more clearly represented via the European Parliament in decision-making related to the single market. More generally, it would be surprising if a future analysis in, say, 10 years time did not conclude that co-decision had made the European Union a significantly more pluralistic, if not necessarily democratic, system of government.

The Single Market in the 1990s – a Kinder, Gentler Debate

If decision-making concerning the single market has become more pluralistic, it also has become more consensual. At the 'super-systemic' level, the wider political environment within which single market policy is made has evolved considerably in the past 10 years. The extent to which the hard 'edges' have been rounded off policy debates concerning the single market is striking. Traditional economic interventionists in Western Europe have become more willing to accept market liberalization of the kind embraced by the 1992 project. The French Socialists' economic 'u-turn' in 1983, with Jacques Delors as French Finance Minister, was a crucial first step in this respect. The general vigilance and tough application of competition rules by van Miert – himself a lifetime Socialist – also illustrates the point.

Meanwhile, economic liberals have become far more tolerant of – even supportive of – selected acts of public sector economic intervention. In some respects, this change is a consequence of the very severe recession of the early 1990s and the ensuing social costs. It also has been encouraged by growing consensus on the need for large public investments in new technological

---

[23] See for example P.Ludlow et al, *Preparing for 1996 and a Larger European Union*, Centre for European Policy Studies, 1995; J.Peterson & M.Shackleton, 'Institutional reform and enlargement', Proceedings of the IGC Revision Conference, 9-10 June 1995, Europa Institute, University of Edinburgh.

[24] Interview, Brussels, 19.10.95.

infrastructures and worker retraining in order for the European Union to compete in an increasingly globalised economy. Finally, the somewhat mercurial conversion of Bangemann, a former German Economics Minister with strong liberal credentials, to advocacy of an European Union 'industrial policy' has had considerable influence on liberal thinking in Europe.[25]

This convergence of views about what sort of market the single market should be certainly has been encouraged by exchanges between advocates of both philosophies at the nitty-gritty, 'meso-level' of European Union policy-making. Intuitively, it makes sense that actors who regularly interact within policy networks become socialised to each other's views. Regular contact will not necessarily make them agree, but it at least promotes mutual understanding.

More generally, the European Union ultimately is a highly consensual system of decision-making, particularly compared to American governance.[26] British paranoia about the phenomenon of national officials who 'go native' actually may have some basis in reality. The advice of one long-established European Union lobbyist is that, 'You should never criticise the idea of European-level action when lobbying, because everyone you're lobbying is favourable to European action. What you lobby about is details of action.'[27] It may be that support for the single market from both the left and right 'free rides' on support for the idea that the European Union can usually accomplish more together than separately on most economic matters.

At first blush, it appears that increased élite consensus concerning the single market has not translated into a new 'permissive consensus' amongst voters, which might allow European executives to pursue new market-opening initiatives with the assurance of public support. The severity of the recession of the early 1990s led many European voters to become increasingly sceptical about the benefits of economic liberalization, particularly when domestic groups opposed European Union measures on grounds of protecting domestic employment. Public support for European integration more generally declined markedly.

Yet, in fact, popular views concerning the Single Market remained surprisingly stable in the early 1990s. Clear majorities of European Union citizens continued to express hopeful views of the Single Market between 1993-5. Anderson's careful analysis of trends in public support for the European Union not only suggests that popular support for the single market has 'reached some sort of equilibrium', but also that 'the European public may become more supportive of the integration process the more familiar they are with the workings of European institutions and the consequences of European Union membership'.[28] The symbolic potency of the 1992 project

---

[25] M.Bangemann, *Meeting the Global Challenge: Establishing a Successful European Industrial Policy*, London: Kogan Page, 1992. Interestingly, United States conservatives have cited Bangemann's affinity for interventionism as an obstacle to the creation of a single North Atlantic market. See T.J.Duesterberg, 'Prospects for a European Union–NAFTA free trade agreement', *Washington Quarterly*, 18/2, 1995.

[26] On this point, see W.Grant, 'Pressure groups and the European Community: an overview', in Mazey & Richardson (eds), *Lobbying in the European Community*.

[27] Interview, 1 February 1994.

[28] C.Anderson, 'Economic uncertainty and European solidarity revisiting: trends in public support for European integration', in Mazey & Rhodes (eds), *The State of the*

thus may have waned, but the European Union's political class retains the notion of 'preserving the single market' as a weapon to use in justifying further moves towards integration.

Conclusion

The single market was the European Union's 'big idea' in the 1980s and early 90s. Nothing has been found to replace it since the 1992 project was completed. The Common Foreign and Security Policy may once have been a candidate, but Bosnia and bickering between Member States over paying for it have made it a shambles. EMU may still mark a step-level change in the unification of Europe, but it appears unlikely that the Maastricht timetable can be met. In any event, recent concerns raised by Member States who clearly will not be in the first group of countries to qualify for a single currency show that EMU cannot match the single market's promise of benefits to all.

This paper has argued that the single market may be analysed as a distinct sector of European Union policy, and that interesting insights emerge when it is considered in this way. For example, consensual habits generally have emerged at the meso-level within many European Union policy networks which correspond to specific economic sectors. However, the power and single-mindedness of both the Commission and Council as actors has diminished at the single market 'policy-setting' level of analysis. Above all, European Union governments have lacked the will – perhaps the courage – to embrace bold new initiatives to further liberalise the single market at a 'super-systemic' level. Crucially, and perhaps surprisingly, it appears that public support for the single market has held up rather well despite the depth of the recession and its apparent association in the popular mind with European integration. Single market policy thus might be considered as one illustrative case amongst many of the way in which European Union governments have tended be led by domestic opinion instead of attempting to lead it in the 1990s, even when European citizens appear willing to follow.

Exploring Civil Society in Post Authoritarian Regimes

Joe Foweraker
University of Essex
&
Todd Landman
University of Essex

'Civil Society and Democratic Transitions'

Introduction

In his seminal article on democratic transitions Rustow argued that most transitions are 'set off by a prolonged and inconclusive political struggle',[1] and further suggested that one generation is usually the minimum period required to achieve such transitions. The subsequent literature tends to see democratic transitions as a critical moment in political time, characterized by decision making between competing élites, who weigh the costs of further authoritarianism against the costs of political liberalization.[2] This body of literature makes useful and sometimes essential contributions to the analysis of democratic transition, but it tends to ignore the question of popular agency, and so misses an important aspect of the making of democracy.

By focusing on social movement activity over time in the four politically authoritarian contexts of military Brazil, Pinochet's Chile, the one-party dominant system of Mexico and Franco's Spain, this paper adopts the notion of popular political struggle over the *longue durée* found in Rustow, and argues that the 'resurrection of civil society'[3] in all these cases actually precedes the moment of democratic transition. Instead of looking at whether a country is democratic or not, this paper analyses the evolution of individual rights in each of the cases and shows that social movement activity has a positive association with the extension of individual civil and political rights of citizenship. This process of 'democratic transformation'[4] is far from smooth or automatic, rather, it is both halting and contradictory. In order to examine the rebirth of civil society under authoritarian conditions and the process of democratic transformation, this paper outlines briefly the evolution of individual rights and patterns of social mobilization within the four cases. It then demonstrates the tentative connections between social mobilization and rights, which informs the larger arguments on the role of civil society in democratic transition.

---

[1] D.Rustow, 'Transitions to Democracy: Toward a Dynamic Model', *Comparative Politics*, 2, 1970, p.352.
[2] G.O'Donnell & P.Schmitter, *Transitions from Authoritarian Rule*, volumes 1-4, Johns Hopkins University Press, 1986; J.Higley & R.Gunther, *Elites and Democratic Consolidation in Latin America and Southern Europe*, Cambridge University Press, 1992.
[3] G.O'Donnell & P.Schmitter, 4, p.26.
[4] J.Foweraker & T.Landman, *Citizenship Rights and Social Movements: A Comparative and Statistical Analysis*, Oxford University Press, for theorising.

Rights and Movement Activity under Authoritarian Conditions

All the cases in this study are instances of repressive regimes that undergo political liberalization and that exhibit the rise and fall of social movement activity, placing them squarely in a comparative framework which Faure calls the mirror image of the 'most-similar systems design'.[5] Since the paper seeks to trace the relationship between rights provision and movement activity during periods of authoritarian rule and through moments of democratic transition, the time period for the four cases varies according to the particular political histories of them, as follows: Brazil, 1964-1990 (N= 26); Chile, 1973-1990 (N=17); Mexico, 1963-1990 (N=27), and Spain 1958-1983 (N=24). This section of the paper considers the relevant political histories of the cases, the evolution of rights, and the patterns of social mobilization, all of which are then summarised below in Table 1.

Brazil

For the years included in this paper (1964-1990), Brazil was ruled by a military authoritarian government that slowly returned power to civilians. The authoritarian period extended from 1964 to 1985 at which time the junta chose a civilian leader. In 1989, Brazil held its first democratic election for the president since 1960. From 1966-1979, the regime maintained a two-party system with the ARENA party representing the military and conservative interests and the MDB representing the so-called 'benign opposition.' The bicameral Congress was closed only briefly during the period and the MDB enjoyed increasing electoral gains in the both the Seanate and the Chamber of Deputies. From 1974 onwards, the military, beginning with General Ernesto Geisel, gradually liberalized the regime that ultimately allowed the formation of new political parties (1979), a relaxation of press censorship, the direct popular elections of all state governors (1982), and culminated in the promulgation of the 1988 Constitution, followed by the 1989 Presidential elections.[6]

In the early years of the regime, political and civil rights were systematically denied with the military's use of the Fifth Institutional Act (AI-5). All forms of civil unrest and social mobilization were effectively eliminated until 1978, when the trade unions in the South led the first mobilizations against the regime. The 1980s witnessed a dramatic surge in social mobilization by urban and rural unions, urban neighbourhood associations, ecclesial base communities, and women's groups. The wave of protest in the 1980s featured the *diretas já* campaign for direct presidential elections in 1984 which mobilized millions of Brazilian citizens.[7]

---

[5] A.Faure, 'Some Methodological Problems in Comparative Politics', *Journal of Theoretical Politics*, 6/3, 1994.

[6] M.Alves, *State and Opposition in Military Brazil*, University of Texas Press, 1985; T.Skidmore, *The Politics of Military Rule in Brazil*, Oxford University Press, 1988.

[7] M.Alves 'Grassroots Organizations, Trade Unions and the Church: a Challenge to the controlled Abertura in Brazil', *Latin American Perspectives*, 11/1, 1984; S. Mainwaring, 'The Transition to Democracy in Brazil', *Journal of Interamerican Studies and World Affairs*, 28, 1986.

Chile

On 11 September 1973 a military junta that included General Augusto Pinochet overthrew Popular Unity president Salvador Allende Gossens, ending virtually 140 years of uninterrupted democratic rule. After the coup, the military quickly consolidated its authority and General Pinochet emerged as the undisputed leader, effectively declaring himself the president of the republic of Chile in 1974 and promulgating the 1980 Constitution, which is still in effect today. In a bid to remain in power, Pinochet held a plebiscite in 1988 in which he garnered only 45% support. This defeat ushered in a rapid transition back to democracy with elections in 1989 and the victory of Christian Democrat Patricio Aylwin; however, Pinochet remains in control of the armed forces and the political right maintains a disproportionate amount of control over political institutions.[8]

In the early years of the military regime, dissidents and suspected subversives were routinely detained, tortured, exiled, and executed. The pattern of outright execution continued into the early 1980s when it was replaced by a strategy of forceful intimidation of civil society through the use of arbitrary arrest, detention, and torture. Social mobilization was virtually non-existent in the 1970s but started to build in 1980, reaching its peak during the 1983-1984 'days of national protest.' At the end of the decade, mobilizations increased surrounding the 1988 plebiscite and the subsequent elections in 1989.[9]

Mexico

Mexico is a one-party dominant political system, and the Institutional Revolutionary Party, the PRI, has been in power for 65 years. For the period in this paper (1963-1990), in an attempt to maintain its political longevity, the PRI has continued to dominate the political system with a combination of co-optation and repression of political opponents, and manipulation of electoral results. The presence of elections, albeit unfair, and the maintenance of some political and civil rights qualifies Mexico during this period as a 'semi-authoritarian' regime. After the massacre of student protesters in the Plaza de Tlatelolco in 1968, the regime has made attempts to liberalise the system with improvements in laws and procedures that govern the ability for citizens to contest government authority and participate in national elections.[10]

The denial of political and civil rights is carried out selectively against regime opponents throughout the period, but from the middle of the 1980s, there appears to be a downward trend in regime behaviour. Since 1986, human rights organizations such as Americas' Watch and Amnesty International report increases in the number of those people who have 'disappear-

---

[8] J.Valenzuela & A.Valenzuela, *Military Rule in Chile*, Johns Hopkins University Press, 1986; P.Drake & I.Jaksic, *The Struggle for Democracy in Chile, 1982-1990*, University of Nebraska Press, 1991.

[9] P.Oxhorn, *Organizing Civil Society: The Popular Sectors and the Struggle for Democracy in Chile*, Penn State University Press, 1995.

[10] W.Cornelius & A.Craig, *The Mexican Political System in Transition*, Center for US-Mexican Studies, 35, 1991.

ed.'[11] Undeterred by the increasing repression of the regime, social movements representing labour, peasants, students, women, the urban poor, and middle class professionals (particularly teachers) have challenged the Mexican state throughout the 1970s and 1980s. The most significant social mobilization during the entire period has occurred in 1965, 1968, 1972, 1975, 1979-1982, 1985, and 1988.[12]

Spain

Franco's Spain was corporatist-authoritarian with all power concentrated in the executive for most of the period (1958-1975); however, with his death in 1975 Spain made the transition to democracy, which is officially represented by the 1978 Constitution and subsequent democratic elections. The Francoist state was constructed legally out of a series of 'organic laws' which extended from 1938 to 1967. Although these organic laws established the rights and duties of all Spanish citizens, through a series of emergency clauses, Franco was able to deny selectively political and civil rights to citizens throughout his dictatorship.[13] The first right won back by civil society was arguably the right to association which shortly preceded Franco's death. Political opposition to the Franco regime was initially weak at home but was strong abroad. Waves of social mobilization began to appear in the early 1960s and then increased throughout the next decade and a half, culminating in the massive uprisings led by labour and students surrounding the death of Franco and the democratic transition.[14]

The Cases Compared

Given space limitations, this paper draws on previous research that provides quantitative time series measures of rights provision and social movement activity[15] in order to construct a comparative table of rights and movements in the four cases from which tentative conclusions can be drawn. The rights measures, divided into rights-in-principle (those guaranteed legally) and rights-in-practice (those actually enjoyed by the population), help show the rise and fall of rights provision over time. The social movement activity measures are divided between labour and other social movements. Table 1 below shows the years in which major positive and negative shifts in rights provision occurred in the four cases, and aligns these shifts next to major moments of social mobilization.[16]

---

[11] Americas' Watch, *Human Rights in Mexico: A Policy of Impunity*, Washington, 1991; Amnesty International, *Mexico: Human Rights in Rural Areas*, London, 1986.

[12] J.Foweraker & A.Craig, *Popular Movements and Political Change in Mexico*, Lynne Rienner Publishers, 1990; J.Foweraker, *Popular Mobilization in Mexico: The Teacher's Movement, 1977-1987*, Cambridge University Press, 1993.

[13] R.Carr & J.Fusi, *Spain: Dictatorship to Democracy*, second edition, Allen & Unwin, 1981.

[14] J.Maravall, *Dictatorship and Political Dissent: Workers and Students in Franco's Spain*, Tavistock Publications, 1978; J.Foweraker, *Making Democracy in Spain: Grass-Roots Struggle in the South, 1955-1975*, Cambridge University Press, 1989.

[15] J.Foweraker & T.Landman, forthcoming.

[16] Note that rights-in-principle shifts are marked with *, and rights-in-practice are marked with **.

Table 1
Rights Provision and Social Mobilization

Cases	(1) Rights Provision Positive	Negative	(2) Social Mobilization Labour	SMs
Brazil	1974*	1965*	1978-82	1968
(1964-90)	1978*	1967-69*	1987	1973
	1979*	1977**	1990	1979
	1985*	1987-90**		1983
	1988*			1985
Chile	1977*	1973*	1980	1980
(1973-90)	1980*	1985-86*	1987	1983-84
	1981*		1989-90	1989
	1988-90*			
Mexico	1970*	1985-90**	1962	1968
(1963-90)	1972-75**		1974	1972
	1977*		1978-82	1975
	1987*		1984	1982
			1986	1986
				1988
Spain	1970*	1969*	1962	1958
	1974*	1979-81**	1970	1962
	1975-78*		1975-77	1965
			1979	1968
				1975

* = rights-in-principle; ** = rights-in-practice

Close examination of the table shows a strong correspondence between positive shifts in rights-in-principle and both forms of social mobilization, and in most cases in most years, that social mobilization tends to precede the changes in rights. For Brazil, the increased mobilization from labour in 1978 coincides with the abolition of the Fifth Institutional Act. When labour is joined with other social movement activity, positive changes in rights-in-principle follow, eventually leading to a full transition to democracy. In Chile, rights-in-principle tend to respond to the increased labour and other social movement activity during the 1980s. The only exception in Chile is with the 1985 state of siege which put an end to the 'National Days of Protest.' The Spanish case is similar to Brazil and Chile in that social mobilization coincides with changes in rights-in-principle, but the transition is more concentrated in the years surrounding Franco's death in 1975. Finally, Mexico appears to have positive shifts in rights-in-principle that do not necessarily correspond to increased mobilization.[17]

For rights-in-practice, the relationship is less clear, where increased social mobilization can often invoke a repressive response from the regime, when

---
[17] For a complete statistical analysis of these relationships, their direction, and significance, see J.Foweraker & T.Landman, Chapters 6 & 7, forthcoming.

it has not altered the provision of rights-in-principle. In short, there exists a gap between what the regime guarantees in principle and what it delivers in practice, and it is this gap that is often associated with the rise and fall of social mobilization. For Brazil, rights-in-practice improved in 1974 with General Geisel's policy of political liberalization, but exhibited a negative shift in 1977 and in the late 1980s. For Chile, rights in practice remained at a very low level throughout the 1970s and 1980s, despite the positive improvement in rights-in-principle in 1977 and 1980. The state of siege saw a negative shift in both forms of rights, and the plebiscite and subsequent transition saw an improvement in both. It is clear in Chile that the 'days of national protest' provoked the full repressive capacity of the military regime, which some have argued led many sectors of the opposition to pursue more moderate, institutional strategies.[18]

In Mexico, the gap between principle and practice increases throughout the period. Positive improvements in principle are accompanied by negative shifts in practice, a trend that is punctuated by the rise and fall of social mobilization. The sharpest negative turn in rights-in-practice begins in 1985 and continues throughout the period as mobilization builds around the aftermath of the 1985 earthquake and the contested elections of 1988. The gradual, halting, and prolonged, struggle for democratization in Mexico is similar to the process in Brazil and clearly fits within Rustow's notion of democratic transition and this paper's notion of democratic transformation. Spain, on the other hand, is most similar to Chile, in that the moment of transition is more concentrated. Rights-in-practice and rights-in-principle in Spain tend to 'track' one another as the Franco regime carried out in practice what it had established in principle. The rise of social mobilization from the 1960s through the death of Franco and the transition itself challenged what was established in principle. By 1978, Spain had promulgated a new democratic constitution.

Tentative Conclusions

The brief review of these four cases and the rather synoptic evidence presented in this paper suggests that the resurrection of civil society is a long and difficult political struggle, that is neither an automatic effect of élite decision-making nor a spontaneous uprising that suddenly transforms the authoritarian regime into a democratic one. By focusing on the evolution of rights (in principle and in practice), this paper has shown that rights can be extended and taken away, but the evidence suggests (with the possible exceptions of the two states of siege in Spain and Chile), once rights in principle become re-enshrined by the regime, they tend not to be rescinded.

By focusing on the popular agency of social movements, the paper illustrates the development of popular social forces which are often ignored in élite- centred accounts of democratic transition, and it argues that this social mobilization is in part a struggle for rights. It is clear that the waves of social mobilization that describe these periods are motivated increasingly

---

[18] P.Oxhorn, 'Where Did All the Protesters Go? Popular Mobilization and the Transition to Democracy in Chile', *Latin American Perspectives*, 21/3, 1994.

by the struggle for rights, and it is the dissemination of a sense of individual rights through new forms of collective action that educates popular political actors and catalyses the creation of a new political culture, which is a 'rights' culture.[19] Since rights can exist in principle and in practice, all members of civil society must be ever-vigilant that the new democratic regimes in Brazil, Chile and Spain, and the liberalizing regime in Mexico, protect in practice what they have established in principle. The struggle for rights does not cease at the moment of transition but remains an active part of democratic consolidation and democratic life.

---

[19] J.Foweraker, *Theorizing Social Movements*, Pluto Press, 1995.

Exploring Civil Society in Post Authoritarian Regimes

Lucy Taylor
University of Sheffield

'Civilising Civil Society:
Distracting Popular Participation from Politics Itself'

The strengthening of civil society and citizen participation are two of the leading rhetorical instruments of democratic discourse in contemporary Chile. However, the nature of that civil society and the object of that participation have been moulded by a specific interpretation of what it means to be a citizen. During the dictatorship, these dominant ideas were challenged by social movements, but have now secured their hegemonic position within the public mind. This paper charts that ascendency, discussing the ideological roots of the two interpretations, the policies of the democratic government in relation to civil society and the twin demise of the social movements and the alternative model of civil society.

The dictatorship spanned 17 years, from 1973 to 1989, and introduced neo-liberal concepts, not only as an economic policy but also as a political ideology seeking to change the role of the citizen in politics and the relationship between the citizen and the state. The government which followed it has ameliorated the economic package to a certain extent, yet it has maintained crucial aspects of the ideology which have been absorbed within Chilean political culture and which, along with the reassertion of élite rule and the requirements of political expediency, have shaped a new form of civil society.[1]

The period of military rule saw the coexistence of two concepts of civil society. The first is a notion based on a neo-liberal interpretation and was proffered by the military government and the second is a concept founded on active and politicised participation and with a global, broadly left wing vision of state/society relations.

The military government, headed by General Pinochet, sought to impose a neo-liberal interpretation of the citizen and her relationship to the state.[2] Neo-liberalism seeks to strengthen the rights of the individual over those of the community and sets as its goal the maximisation of individual liberty. This implies the strengthening of negative rights *vis-à-vis* the interference of the state. Concomitantly, there is a relative increase in the responsibility of the individual over a larger portion of her own life and a decrease of state responsibility for the well-being of its citizens. The role of the state is to facilitate a person's ability to advance by ensuring the maintenance of negative liberties and thus maximising their freedom.

---

[1] This article is based on Ph.D research conducted in Santiago, Chile between November 1993 and May 1994.

[2] See, among others, M.A.Garretón, *The Chilean Political Process*, Unwin Hyman, 1989; P.Drake & I.Jaksić, *The Struggle for Democracy in Chile 1982 – 1990*, University of Nebraska Press, 1991.

The prime arbiter between citizens is not politics but the market and, along with the state, politics is highly restricted in its sphere of influence. Politics leads to the suppression of the individual by the tyrannical majority and is especially disruptive in the social sphere, distorting and hampering the actions of the invisible hand. In order to unburden the citizen, then, the government's anti-politics strategy involved not only highly coherent policy packages but also the cleansing of politics itself via closing down the parliamentary structures, banning the existence political parties and purging the nation of left-wingers. The concept of civil society reflects this individualism and the highly restricted arena of political activity. While it is perfectly acceptable that recreational groups should flourish, those with a political perspective are anathema to the project and jeopardise the future for Chile.

The second concept of civil society finds its roots in the pre-coup concept of the citizen. The Chilean citizen before the coup was a party political creature, engaged in fierce ideological battles and fighting for power through formal institutional channels – elections, party hierarchies, trade union structures. Chile's long democratic traditions, its penchant for legal procedures and the deep penetration of political education created a politicised and party oriented citizenry. The social movements which emerged during the military regime built on this tradition of political activism and holistic interpretations of political events, developing an alternative model of civil society. The model was based on notions of solidarity and of uniting as a community against a common enemy, and it was also founded on a strategy of conflict, of opposing and irreconcilable factions and of black and white arguments and positions. The most influential of these movements was the shanty town dwellers or *pobladores* movement.

The *pobladores* movement was driven by two goals, firstly, the exit of the military from politics and secondly improvements in living conditions; it was the *pobladores* who bore the brunt of the neo-liberal economic project. These goals were translated into two identities and two concomitant roles. Firstly, they saw themselves as the popular bastions against military rule, as groups of active citizens campaigning for the restitution of their civil and political rights. Yet they also defined themselves in terms of their socio-economic problems and their shanty town environment, the struggle spawning self-help initiatives, such as soup kitchens or health cooperatives, and other community bodies – youth, theatre and women's groups.

What was under organic construction was a very active and very politicised civil society, founded around closely knit communities bound by a common bond and extensive networks were being built up within the social arena creating real achievements. Activists formed alternative structures of community government in the form of democratically elected neighbourhood committees and, with the help of NGOs, set up alternative social services – healthcare centres, nurseries, training workshops.

This was a form of civil society in which the community appeared to unite behind a broad political position, in which a global analysis of the political context and social requirements dominated and where the link between reality, practicalities and political thought was strong.[3]

The *pobladores* played an important role throughout the transition process in maintaining its dynamic and in keeping the issues of poverty and human rights to the fore. The fact that they were key actors during the process of transition encouraged them to hold two clear expectations: firstly, that the issues they were fighting for would be addressed by the new democratic government; secondly, that although they would function in the social sphere and would allow the political parties to function as governors, their power and status would not be eroded.

However, the new democratic government of President Aylwin was in no position to answer all their demands and it did not wish to share any of its power, least of all with citizens who had a shopping list of urgent demands. Its hands were tied by Pinochet's constitutional and parliamentary legacy, and it did not wish to upset the still powerful military. Furthermore, the economic policy would not allow for an increase in public expenditure sufficient to meet their demands. Negotiation with the military was inevitable, and their position required dialogue and the construction of a consensus; the conflict-driven intransigence of the *pobladores* could upset delicate discussions. On the other hand, they could not be overtly side-lined or ignored; levels of poverty had worsened over the years and the grievances expressed by the *pobladores* were well founded. Moreover, the movement still commanded respect and a certain political clout among wide sections of the population.

The answer to this problem lay in the construction of a new definition of civil society, a highly participatory civil society yet one stripped of political content. It must be geared towards finding local solutions to social problems perceived through an analysis of the particularities of the local environment. The key to its success would be to ensure that the local solutions produced results and that participation in the new type of social organisations was high. The *poblador* movement, caught up in this trend, would be shunted sideways shifting its focus from the political arena to the social arena and encouraged to concentrate on improving the immediate environment. This would serve to keep the activists busy and to turn their focus towards harmless local projects and away from delicate issues at the national level. It would also bind them into the work of reconstructing the Chilean nation and as such bind them more closely to the government and to the democratic project. If the strategy worked and local participation reaped results for the local population, the momentum would become self-sustaining.

The government sought to impose its interpretation of civil society and the role of the citizen by utilising the twin strategies of incorporation and marginalisation. The process was to be developed through two policy initiatives; decentralisation and self-help projects set up through the auspices of FOSIS, the Social Investment and Solidarity Fund.

---

[3] See P. Oxhorn, 'The Popular Sector Response to an Authoritarian Regime: Shantytown Organisations since the Military Coup', *Latin American Perspectives*, 67/18/1, 1991; V. Espinoza, *Pobladores, Participación Social y Ciudadania*, Proposiciones 22, Ediciones SUR, Santiago, Chile, 1993.

The policy of decentralisation was to forge new links between civil society and the state, regulating and controlling that relationship. The social organisations created were to become the favoured interlocutors between citizen and state, replacing the *pobladores* in their role as representatives of the people and making their organisations redundant.[4] Decentralisation was implemented under military rule and although the structures laid down have remained intact, local government was democratised in 1992. The policy enhanced the power of the municipalities in terms of decision making and greatly increased their importance as a vehicle for policy implementation; key to this, two types of organisation were to be reinvigorated and encouraged. The first of these are the *Juntas de Vecino* or Neighbourhood Committees which are the permanent channel of communication between the people of the districts and the central municipality, a conduit through which they could petition to move a bus-stop as well as being a focus of community organisation. The second neighbourhood body stimulated by the policy was the *Comité de Adelanto* or Improvements Committee which is a temporary body, formed in order to rectify a given problem in a locality, such as unpaved passageways; once the paving slabs are down, the organisation ceases to exist.

The democratisation of this intermediate level of government was a priority for the *pobladores*. In seeking to democratise local government, especially the ıJuntas de Vecino, they aimed to join a democratic hierarchy and as such gain recognition and political power. However, instead of substituting themselves for the right-wing incumbents and superimposing their own organisation onto the network of Neighbourhood Committees, they were themselves superseded by this official structure.

Why had the *pobladores* movement not succeeded in capturing this new institutional arena? The answer to this lies in the deceptive and changing political environment and the new concept of civil society which dominated political discourse and which had permeated the public mind.

Firstly, the *pobladores* movement was weaker than it had appeared; although it had dominated the shanty towns, it did not necessarily involve all the residents and a substantial minority had in fact quietly backed the military during the dictatorship. More importantly, many of the activists had been only peripherally engaged in their actions and with the return to democracy, they willingly handed over political power and responsibility to their elected representatives. Many were exhausted and were relieved to turn their attention to their own lives which had remained on the back burner for too long. Finally, the *pobladores* movement was associated in the public eye with its fight against the military regime – while their struggle might have been appropriate in these circumstances, behaviour in a democratic context required different strategies.

Secondly, the now dominant notion of civil society did not allow for political activism within the social sphere. The rhetoric emerging from government circles emphasised that the old polarisations and head-on political

---

[4] Assertions based on interviews with representatives at all levels of the Municipalities of Conchalí and Pudahuel, Santiago. Also see *Modernización y Participación Social*, Ministerio Secretaria General de Gobierno, División de Organizaciones Sociales, Santiago, 1994.

conflicts were now obsolete. A modern and forward looking nation required more mature and reasoned political discourse, which included listening to the opinions and demands of other interested parties and seeking to reach a compromise. It was not enough to march angrily and make demands, citizens should participate in a more responsible way by reflecting on the realities and practicalities of pursuing a certain policy and putting forward realistic proposals. Moreover, it was no longer necessary to engage with the issues of national politics – this was the task of the elected representatives. The role of the good and responsible citizen in this new civil society, was to work for the good of her community and to share the task of improving conditions in order to speed up the process of economic and social development. This image was also completely compatible with Chilean neo-liberalism; the citizen must take responsibility for her own destiny and she must work hard to improve her own life chances and living environment. However, this did not preclude the creation of interest groups, on the contrary, the new organisations and networks of civil society, anchored around the municipality and directly linked to the state, should be actively encouraged.

In this ideological context it was not surprising that when elections were held for positions in the *Juntas de Vecino*, the residents elected are those who would work to build the community centre, not those who wished to march and demand and bring politics to the people. It was natural that they should participate in the Improvement Committees to gain tangible results yet these groups stand in stark contrast to the *pobladores* movement with its politics and its holistic political visions.

Could these social groups create any kind of social movement? Could they come together to alter policy priorities or to create a substantial pressure group to lobby the municipality? While the relationship between the individual groups and the municipality was being facilitated, the relationship between groups was strained and competitive, precluding the creation of a movement.

Firstly, the Improvement Committees, formed to fulfil a particular task, were in indirect competition with similar groups for the scarce resources available within the municipality. As such, they attempt to strengthen contacts more with the relevant officers in the municipality than with other groups. While local government provides some of the funding, it requires that a variable amount be raised by the group itself from donations of the residents affected. Not surprisingly, some of the residents contributed erratically, while others were hostile to the idea or the organisation and refused to participate at all. Moreover, the groups are often riddled with personal conflicts between neighbours – conflicts just as vehement and divisive as if they were political. As such, those heading the group spend a great deal of time visiting the residents to chase up their contributions or to further their cause in an inter-personal dispute.

The *Juntas de Vecino* also engage in competition and conflict, this time with other *Juntas de Vecino* in the same division of the municipal district. Some divisions have three or perhaps four alternative *Juntas de Vecino* and they compete for adherents, prestige and funding. On the other hand, they do have more force within local government, belonging to a central body which brings together representatives from across the district. The degree of representative clout within the municipality is highly variable, though, and their relationship to local government is not regulated through formal structures, depending entirely on the willingness of the mayor to listen to their opinions and requests.

The local groups, therefore, are riddled with internal conflicts which are encouraged by their structural relationship to the municipality. While they are successful in terms of creating social improvements – the passages are eventually paved, and neighbourhood centres are eventually built – their time and energies are directed towards achieving these improvements despite the environment of competition and disputes. Both types of group are obliged to fulfil complex administrative tasks and to file detailed reports of their progress and they become absorbed in the minutiae of their tasks to the detriment of any global analysis of their positions and relationships.

The second major policy area which has remoulded civil society is the FOSIS project. The FOSIS initiative sought to capitalise on the existing self-help projects and social networks within Chilean society, projects and networks created by community groups and NGOs with strong original links to the *pobladores* movement.[5] FOSIS is geared towards solving concrete local problems through state funding of specific community projects, and though the state does not deny its responsibility, it insists that well-being is primarily the responsibility of the citizen and the autonomous community groups. Organisations working in the shanty towns are thus invited to tender for funding, giving a detailed outline of the proposed project, its aims, a profile of those who might benefit, forms of community participation that it might utilise etc. Examples of projects range from youth training schemes to street lighting to simple sports arenas.

The FOSIS initiative is, in many ways an efficient, even cheap solution. It utilises organisations which are already established, such as NGOs, and which require no set-up costs and little further training. In the case of community organisations, the labour costs are minimal or nil. It is also an effective solution. Specialist organisations, especially NGOs, have often been working in the area for a considerable time, they understand the social and cultural particularities of those they aim to assist, they are embedded in the network of official and personal contacts and they, or their institutions, may be known by their potential beneficiaries and as such may inspire more confidence than an outsider. The state can therefore utilise their experience and expertise in order to create a more efficacious use of scarce resources. The projects are also seen by the public to be effective as the return on investment has an immediate and direct impact – training schemes begin, roads are paved, workshops spring up, waste ground is cleared and gardens are planted.

FOSIS is at the forefront of the government's interaction with the poor and in this arena it is tackling both economic and social hardship and is directing social participation. As such it is also a key agent in disseminating the twin identities: active citizen as socially responsible individual;

---

[5] Information based on interviews with NGOs, also *Participación de la Comunidad en el Desarollo Social*, Ministerio de Planificación y Cooperación, Santiago, Chile, 1992.

individual as responsible for her own destiny. This is also the field in which the citizen will encounter, at first hand and most frequently, the reformed identity of the state as facilitator, but not provider, of social and individual betterment.

The *pobladores*, though, found that they did not fit the mould. Firstly, FOSIS grants are intended to deal with circumscribed, specific social needs in defined communities and it is geared towards organisations which have been formed with specific tasks in mind: they deal with training for work, not the right to employment. Secondly, FOSIS responds not to demands, marches and speeches but to proposals; they require a detailed analysis, including costing, timescales and tangible benefits. Thirdly, in order to become a recipient, an organisation must have legal recognition, a list of members, an identifiable structure and mechanisms of accountability; in contrast the *poblador* groups are often difficult to legally characterise and have an inconstant, fluctuating membership.

Most fundamental are problems related to ideology. *Poblador* groups perceive a key role for the state in the provision of social welfare which lies in sharp contrast to the anti-statism and community responsibility of the government. Moreover, those who select the projects for FOSIS are unlikely to fund activities which would clash with the dominant ideological perspective, which includes political activism in the social welfare sphere. Finally, the identity of the *poblador* movement has become confused. During this dictatorship, the movement was defined by its struggle against a dual enemy, the military and the policies it pursued and the two issues became inexorably intertwined. Some activists have maintained this contiguity, denouncing this government as merely an official version of the last. Others, though, feel a loyalty to the new democratic regime, even though they remained opposed to its policies, and in this case are required to separate government and policy and to rethink their clear black/white, evil/good characterisation of politics; they have been forced to redefine themselves, not in relation to the enemy, but in relation to a more complex set of priorities, needs and political positions.

The fate of the alternative, political concept of civil society and the role of the citizen has gone the way of the social movement which championed it. The *poblador* movement, already in decline, has been successfully marginalised by structures into which it doesn't fit and a discourse which brands its approach as immature and obsolete. Its decline has hastened the ascendency of the replacement structures and has allowed the adoption of depoliticised state/society relationships to go unchecked.

The now dominant model exhorts citizens to participate in their local community, but this participation must complement and not conflict with the policies laid down by the government and the municipality. From being a possible source of difficulty, groups active in the shanty towns have become valuable instruments of policy implementation and are inadvertently working to secure the government's position.

Part of the strategy's success is linked to the fact that in material terms both the FOSIS initiatives and the development schemes channelled through the *Juntas de Vecino* work well and produce tangible results. Crucially, it *appears* that the government is committed to improving infrastructure, training opportunities and the general well-being of its poorest citizens, and this serves to bolster support for the government and for the democratic process in place in Chile.

The government cannot take all the credit for this, though; Presidents Aylwin and his successor, Frei have simply taken the lead from military president Pinochet whose dedicated imposition of neo-liberal policies and whose rhetoric of individualism laid down the foundations upon which Chilean society is being rebuilt. Despite a commitment to alleviating poverty and despite a genuine willingness to encourage participation, the ideological terms of reference which determine the way in which that poverty is alleviated and the way in which it is possible to participate are set by a neo-liberal regime which sought to eradicate politics from the process of government.

The contemporary interpretation of this goal is the seclusion of politics behind the highest structures of the political élite. Those outside these walls, however, have not forgotten their politicised past, and it is essential to keep them busy and out of harm's way, distracted from wider political considerations and submerged within the minutiae of issues in their own backyard. Whether the consequences of the government's policy are merely serendipitous or were designed as an exercise in civilisation, we cannot yet say. Certainly a political process without rancour and intransigent opposition allows the political élites to engage in civilised dialogue with the military. Certainly there is very little opposition to an economic policy which follows the civilised trend of the western world and which has changed little since General Pinochet occupied the Presidential Palace. And most certainly, a city without marches and demonstrations appears to be more civilised to the foreign investor.

Exploring Civil Society in Post Authoritarian Regimes

Mark R. Thompson
University of Glasgow

' "Delayed" Democracy: Developmental States
and Civil Society in the Asia-Pacific'

Introduction

Commentary on the economic success of the so called Asia-Pacific – itself a booming academic industry – has tended to overshadow the region's political peculiarity. The 'third wave' of democratization (Huntington 1991) has swept away authoritarian and post-totalitarian regimes over entire geographical areas: in Southern Europe, Latin America, and Eastern Europe. Much of the Asia-Pacific, by contrast, has remained politically becalmed. The first and most dramatic democratic transition in the region – the overthrow of dictator Ferdinand E. Marcos through 'people power' in the Philippines in 1986 – found a few successful imitators in the Asia-Pacific (Thompson 1995). Philippine events provided encouragement to South Korean and Taiwanese activists in the late 1980s – and perhaps even to Thai demonstrators in the redemocratization of 1992 – but there was no 'chain reaction' of democratic transitions as in Eastern Europe. Moreover, the Burmese and Chinese democratic movements were violently suppressed in 1988 and 1989, respectively. Outside of Africa, these were the only non-democratic regimes able to successfully crush major pro-democratic protests in a period since the mid-1970s characterized by over 50 (mostly remarkably peaceful) democratic transitions around the world. The other major countries of the Asia-Pacific region – Indonesia, Malaysia, Singapore, and Vietnam – continue to be ruled by stable authoritarian regimes. The 'global resurgence of democracy' (Diamond & Plattner 1993) has been relatively weak in the Asia-Pacific.

Ironically, explanations of political transition in the Asia-Pacific have not stressed this distinctiveness. Instead, in a major recent study (Morley 1993), the nine major countries of the region excluding Japan (China, Indonesia, Malaysia, the Philippines, Singapore, South Korea, Taiwan, Thailand and Vietnam) were shown to conform to the predictions of political modernization theory. This is the claim that economic growth first leads to social transformation – urbanization, mass communication, growth in literacy and the degree of formal education, the creation of new social classes (particularly the working, middle, and business classes), etc. – which in turn results in new forms of political activity. This political mobilization involves the organization of new groups and strata into political bodies – including labor unions, student groups, professional associations, chambers of commerce, etc. Such changes create conditions highly favorable to the existence of democratic government (Lipset 1959; Cutright 1963). As table 1 shows, two of three high Newly Industrialized Countries (NICs) have established democratic government and one of the two middle income countries. But only one of the four low income countries (the Philippines) can be classified as democratic.

But this rather 'close fit' of the political modernization theory to political developments in the Asia-Pacific is, in comparative perpective, itself rather unusual. Recent democratizations in Africa, Eastern Europe, and Latin America have tended to follow economic crisis or even financial collapse under authoritarianism regardless of the level of economic development (Haggard & Kaufman 1995; on Africa – Decalo 1992). There has often also been considerable political unrest preceding democratization. Transitions in South Korea, Taiwan, and, to a lesser extent Thailand, by contrast, belong to a smaller category of democratizations in which authoritarian regimes yielded to demands for democracy *only after* a long a period of political order, financial stability and economic development. South Korea and Taiwan were for approximately a decade (from the late 1970s to the 1980s) the wealthiest non-oil producing countries that were not democracies.[1] This led Robert Wade, writing about Taiwan, to suggest:

> '... what is striking, I think, is how late this (political) softening comes – long after the regime was well formalized and institutionalized, long after the threat from the mainland receded, long after the period of economic breakthrough, long after living standards began to rise for everyone.' (Wade 1990, p.254)

Singapore is currently the only non-oil producer in the World Bank's 'high-income economy' cateory that is not a democracy (World Bank 1992). (By one measure, Singapore's GDP in 1994 was higher than New Zealand's and comparable to Australia's.) Malaysia is the second wealthiest non-oil producing country that falls short of democratic rule. (Malaysia's per capital is similar to Spain's, Greece's, and higher than the Eastern European countries') (United Nations 1994).

Seen comparatively, then, democracy in the Asian-Pacific has, when it has occurred at all, been 'delayed'. To better understand why this is the case this paper focuses on 'developmental states' and civil society, particularly in Malaysia, Singapore, South Korea, and Taiwan. Economic development is a key factor in 'deepening' civil society. But another is the effectiveness and timing of state intervention. It will be suggested that 'strong' states demobilized civil society earlier and more effectively than in Latin America. In particular, labor movements and big business were depoliticized early and comprehensively by state action. The growth of a strong middle class contributed to the strenthening of civil society, but the attitude of the developmental state still shaped democratization.

Demobilizing Civil Society

A missing variable in political modernization theory is the developmental state (White & Wade, 1985). Modernization theory is entrenched in civil

---

[1] The wealthy but non-democratic oil producing countries of the Middle East and North Africa do not constitute a strong challenge to the expectation that development will lead to democracy. Almost totally dependent on the export of oil, there is little or no need for state élites to tax, and thus be accountable, to their populations. See Huntington 1991, p.65.

society: it predicts a chain reaction of social change (education, urbanization, unionization, professionalization, etc) that follows industrialization and leads, in turn, to more open, participatory politics.[2] Yet a strong state can shape social mobilization and the political consequences that accompany industrial development. The character of civil society – which is at the heart of modernization theory's premise that economic development leads to democracy – is influenced by the timing and type of state-led late industrialization, a phenomenon the modernization school has tended to neglect. For a variety of reasons – longer colonization, a less severe depression in the interwar period, etc. – Asia-Pacific countries, aside from Japan, did not commence import substitution industrialization (ISI) as early as the major Latin American countries did. When ISI was launched after the Second World War it was generally shorter and had shallower social roots. Authoritarian governments in Singapore, South Korea, and Taiwan (and an increasingly autocratic Malaysian regime after 1969) were able to thoroughly repress weak trade unions and small Left parties. This labor repression in the Asia-Pacific, in turn, was closely linked to export drives.

Big business in these Asia-Pacific countries grew up under export-oriented industrialization, not ISI, making it more sympathetic to labor-repressive policies and state intervention and less open to democratic rule and reduced state size. Also, of course, the importance of the sustained success of Asia-Pacific industrialization compared to the troubles of Latin America should not be underestimated. In times of economic crisis under authoritarianism, labor often found allies even among the business class for the restoration of democracy in South America. The economic success of Pacific Asian developmental states can, along with the weakness of labor and the pro-regime stance of most businessmen (and thus the lack of potential democratic alliances between these classes), help explain this slowness to democratize.

In South America, periods of ISI have been closely correlated with democratic (or, in Rueschemeyer, Stephens, and Stephens', 1992, terminology, restricted democratic) government. Following Rueschemeyer et al. further, the beginning of ISI in the 1930s in some South American countries contributed to the rise of at least limited pluralism. An industrial bourgeoise emerged which, in alliance with a growing working and middle class, began to challenge the traditional oligarchy, usually made up of landowners. Growth under ISI allowed the state to distribute more patronage, which contributed to political consensus and allowed that privileges be given to the new classes without endangering those of the old. Significant industrialization in Brazil, Chile, and Venezuela before and during the Second World War were followed by state efforts to incorporate and control the working class. State intervention was often extensive but unionization was generally legalized and workers rarely directly suppressed. While severe economic crisis was the precipitating factor behind most post-World War II democratic breakdowns in the region, the exhaustion of the 'easy phase' of ISI was often an underlying cause (Rueschemeyer et al, pp.210-212). Because

---

[2] Political modernization is largely an offshoot of Parsons' sociological theory. For an interesting discussion of the role of civil society in Parsons' work see Cohen & Arato 1992, pp.118-32.

ISI had strengthened the labor movement, which had a large stake in the continuance of this economic policy, authoritarian regimes in economically advanced countries in the region repressed the working class in order to impose austerity policies and undertake export promotion. Civil society was weakened but not destroyed, however. With the advent of economic crisis, political parties were quickly reestablished and working class organizations reinvigorated even if they did not reach their pre-dictatorial strength (*ibid*, pp.214-215).

Rueschemeyer et al argue that compared to Western Europe union organization in Latin-America remained weak and working class influence limited. But comparison with Asian-Pacific countries leads to a different conclusion. Unions, which arose largely during brief periods of ISI, were repressed in Singapore, South Korea, and Taiwan. Malaysia's trade unions remain formally independent but are severely restricted by tight labor laws (World Bank, 1993, pp.164-5, 271). Not facing an old and established labor movement as authoritarian regimes did in South America, export oriented industrialization could be launched in Asia-Pacific by putting a stop to the nascent spread of unionization and linking labor closely to the state.

Though political exclusion of labor was most extreme in Singapore, it illustrates an authoritarian political stragegy to further an export drive that was pursued in other Asia-Pacific countries, albeit somewhat less coercively. The repression of the Barisan Socialis Party in 1963 was accompanied by the demobilization of organized labor in Singapore. The National Trade Union Congress (NTUC), little more than a transmission belt of the ruling PAP, was forcibly substituted for the left wing radical Singapore Association of Trade Unions in 1965 (Regnier 1987, pp. 245-246). This corresponded to the beginnings of the state-led export strategy, in which 'reliable' labor not demanding 'unreasonable' wages was an essential part of the strategy. In return, government promised to achieve full employment, keep inflation low, and provide generous social programs. These promises were (astoundingly) kept – unemployment was effectively ended between 1971-73, the country enjoyed price stability, and public housing and education opportunities were provided. But, of course, the cost was the absence of free union organizing. The Singaporean state did not hesitate to punish deviating workers or pushed down wages if they seem to threaten development plans.

The repression of labor in Asia-Pacific did not mean that workers of these countries were worse off economically than their South American counterparts. In fact, real wages of nonagricultural workers in Taiwan almost doubled between 1970 and 1984 while those in South Korea nearly tripled. Real wages in Brazil actually declined in the same period and in Argentina they grew only by 12% (See table in Amsden 1989, p.196). This payoff to workers was the affordable spinoff of the Asia-Pacific miracle economies. While labor repression did not impoverish workers, it strengthened authoritarianism. To paraphrase Barrington Moore, Jr., workers exchanged the right to political participation for the right to earn higher wages.

This is not to say workers were always politically passive. They played a role in South Korean democratization, for example. But the lack of organization structures and long traditions made it harder for worker mobilization to take place. Not only were old unions washed away, most members of the working class joined the labor force under the new industrial-political order. Docile labor was the cornerstone of Asia-Pacific countries' export drive. Knowing neither democratic freedoms nor independent unions, workers were tamed by a system of generous rewards and ungentle restraints. The working class – at the center of Rueschemeyer et al's argument about societal pressures for democracy in the European experience, and important to the explanation of the Latin American cases as well – was consigned to the political backseat in the Asia-Pacific .

A similar argument can be made about the political passivity of the industrial bourgeoisie. Because industrial 'take off' took place under an authoritarian political system with an export-orientation, there were fewer conflict of interests between the state and factory owners than in South America. The industrialists of Asia-Pacificwere caught in the web of government-business cooperation that was spun tightly by the NIC states. Economic austerity, state intervention in business, military terror, and government favoritism had led to widespread unhappiness in the upper class in South America. Such discontent has seldom emerged in Asia-Pacificwhere there are few examples of business abandoning 'developmental dictators' (a notable exception is the Philippines where the economy faltered). Given the weakness of labor and the loyalty of business, civil society was unlikely to emerge until a new middle class created by a flourishing economy came of political age.

Democratic Transition in South Korea and Taiwan

Why then did democratization take place at all in South Korea and Taiwan? In large part because, as modernization theory predicts, an emerging middle class demanded it. I cannot provide a detailed description of these two democratizations here. But it is important to distinguish 'contingent' factors – particularly the role of students active in the last three decades of South Korean politics and the alienation of the native Taiwanese from the 'colonizing' KMT – from 'structural' ones. In both South Korea and Taiwan three decades of sustained development had produced large middle classes whose support was essential for successful democratic transition in these countries. Defining the middle class is notoriously difficult but a South Korean survey in 1987 showing 65% of the population identified itself as middle class can serve as a rough measure (Han & Park 1993, p.185.). Middle class backing for students and political parties helped these proponents of political reform win the struggle for democracy in the late 1980s after earlier battles, in which these protagonists were more socially isolated, had been lost.

In South Korea, the working class also entered the process of political change, but only after the transition had already begun. (Labor mobilization resulted in generous wage increases in the 1988-1989 period.) In Taiwan unions played a less significant role. Most 'captains of industry' remained skeptical about change in these two countries. In Brazil, by contrast, labor had been at the forefront of the democratization campaign (Keck 1989). It even won surprising support from some business quarters in the early 1980s (Cordoso 1989, pp.307-308). Thus, in Brazil, democratic transition was a cross-class phenomena. In South Korea and Taiwan, by contrast, the role of the middle class proved crucial to democratization because of the limited support labor could provide and the hostility of most big businessmen.

While a growing middle class strenthened civil society, the ideology of authoritarian development was weakening in South Korea and Taiwan. As self-defined security states, the lowered danger of invasion was bound to undercut the rationale for dictatorial rule. In addition, a factor not explored here – international (particularly the United States) pressure for democracy – also had an impact. However, this was arguably quite similar to the situation of most Latin American countries. More important perhaps is that almost uniquely among 'Third World countries' (if South Korea and Taiwan can still in any sense be assigned to this category), the goal of substantial economic progress had clearly been reached. The authoritarian ideology of development was undermined by the achievement of development. In South Korea and Taiwan regimes yielded to societal demands once the 'luxury of democracy' could be afforded.

Continued Authoritarianism in Malaysia and Singapore

Malaysia and Singapore have not yet fully democratized (for an earlier analysis see Thompson 1993). Parliamentary systems are in place but the political system is not democratic. In both Malaysia and Singapore the media is tightly controlled. Electoral opposition is penalized, sometimes even with imprisonment. Powerful ruling parties dominated by strong prime ministers run the state, not different parties rotating in power through elections.

The crucial difference between Malaysia and Singapore, on the one hand, and South Korea and Taiwan, on the other, is that in the first two countries the state has effectively demobilized a middle class-based civil society. Rapid economic growth in both countries has led to impressive social differentiation. Upon independence in 1957 Malaysia had a 'middle class,' broadly defined, that constituted 15% of the population (data cited in Crouch 1993, pp.142, 156). Rapid economic growth in the 1960s pushed this total up to 20% by the end of the decade. By 1990 it composed nearly one third of the population (*ibid*). In Singapore, the 'broad middle class' – which includes service (clerical and sales) workers as well as professionals (doctors, lawyers, managers, executives, etc) made up nearly half of the total population by the mid-1980s. (Professionals alone were 17% of the Singaporean population with the comparable figure being over 11% in Malaysia.) Members of the middle class were represented in, and supportive of, nascent democracy movements in the early 1980s in both countries (Rodan 1993, Vennewald 1994, Case 1992, Zakaria 1989).

An electoral swing away from the ruling People's Action Party (PAP) in Singapore – down 16.7% since 1980 to 'just' 60% in the vote of 1992 – and the election of a handful of opposition MPs prompted a state crackdown. Opposition candidates were attacked in a highly personal fashion and several were convicted of various offences and banned from parliament or encouraged to go into exile. The internal security act was invoked in 1987, NGO leaders were arrested, and the independence of the regime-critical Law Society undercut. In Malaysia, the rise of a serious challenge to the ruling UMNO party in the late 1980s was handled in a similarly authoritarian fashion with a media clampdown, prosecutions of oppositionists, the use of the internal security act, and so on.

Stable authoritarianism, based on an institutionalized secession and disciplined ruling parties, played an important part in the success of this demobilization of largely middle class opposition in these countries. As a justification, however, the invocation of 'Asian values' was crucial (*The Economist*, May 28, 1994, pp.13-14). The rise of this discourse in these two countries corresponds closely with nascent democracy movements (Vennewald 1994). One analyst has described the thinking of the Singaporean regime this way:

> 'Democracy "Singapore style" recognizes the rights of individual citizens to participate in and dissent on all policy-making but not the claims of organized interest groups to participate except in their specifically defined areas of interest and never in a style of confrontation' (Chee cited in Schumacher 1993, p.162).

The Singapore Prime Minister Goh Chok Tong has argued that 'Singapore's economic success could be undermined...if it followed the ways of the West.' He urged Singaporeans to avoid materialism, 'Western' democracy, a free press, foreign television, and pop music 'which could bring the country down' (cited in *The Economist*, 1994). In short, *the Singaporean state has created an authoritarian ideology that retained relevance despite the country's advanced state of economic development.* Malaysian Prime Minister Dr. Mahathir Mohammad has urged his countymen to 'Look East,' not only in terms of economic but also political values. Moreover, Mahathir has accused the West of 'ramming an arbitrary version of democracy down the throats of developing countries' (*Far Eastern Economic Review*, August 20, 1992, p.17) This 'anti-imperialist' ideology has also won these governments points at home while weakening domestic opposition.

Conclusion

Civil society was largely demobilized at an early stage of development in the Asia-Asia-Pacific countries considered here. In the interest of an export strategy, there was a crackdown on labor while the bourgeoisie was very dependent on state incentives. As the middle class grew in South Korea and Taiwan a consensus gradually emerged between state and society that economic development had advanced sufficiently for a democratization to be undertaken. In South Korea, for example, the military rulers reached a point when they finally chose to accomodate the insistent demands of civil society rather than again turn to repression (Han & Park, p.185). An authoritarian developmental ideology was gradually undermined by the success of economic development.

By contrast, in Malaysia and Singapore middle class demands for more democracy have been quashed. Here a justification was offered for continued non-democratic rule despite high levels of economic values. Although the genealogy of ideas is a murky realm, striking similarities can be seen between the current stress on distinctive 'Asian values' and the ideology of quasi-democratic Meiji Japan, and thus indirectly Prussia-Germany (Martin 1987). The call for Asian values parallels the Meiji slogan 'eastern ethics, western technology' (Morris-Suzuki 1992). Defeat in World War II undercut discussions of non-Western (and implicitly anti-democratic) values in Germany and Japan, or a least pushed them to the periphery of national discourse. They are no longer state ideologies. Continued insistence on Asian distinctiveness in Malaysia and Singapore demonstrates, however, that such developmental authoritarianism is far from dead. The recent spectacular economic successes of the largest Asia-Pacific states, China and Indonesia, points to the global impact this authoritarian path to the modern world may have once again.

Table 1
Level of Economic Development and Regime Type

Country	GNP per capita (1990 dollars)	Regime type (as of early 1996)
Newly Industrialized Countries		
Singapore	11,160	Quasi-authoritarian
Taiwan	7,332	Democratic
South Korea	5,400	Democratic
Middle Income Developing		
Malaysia	2,320	Quasi-authoritarian
Thailand	1,420	Democratic
Low Income Developing		
Philippines	730	Democratic
Indonesia	570	Authoritarian
China	370	Authoritarian
Vietnam	330	Authoritarian

Source: Adapted from Crouch & Morley 1993, p.279. Data, except for Taiwan, from World Bank 1992. Taiwan GNP per capita from 1991 World Population Data sheet, cited in *Far Eastern Economic Review*, Asia 1993 Yearbook (Hongkong, Review Publishing Company, 1993), p.7.

Bibliography

A.H.Amsden, *Asia's Next Giant: South Korea and Late Industrialization*, Oxford University Press, 1989.

W.Case, 'Sources of Legimacy in the Case of Malaysia: Stateness, Regime Form and Policy Performance', unpublished manuscript, 1992.

S.Chai-Anan & S.Paribatra, 'Thailand: Liberalization without Democracy', in James W. Morley (ed), *Driven by Growth: Political Change in the Asia-Pacific Region*, Armonk, New York, M.E.Sharpe, 1993..

T-J.Cheng, 'Taiwan in Democratic Transition', in J.W.Morley (ed), *Driven by Growth: Political Change in the Asia-Pacific Region*, Armonk, New York, M.E.Sharpe, 1993.

J.L.Cohen & A.Arato, *Civil Society and Political Theory*, The MIT Press, 1992.

F.H.Cordoso, 'Associated-Dependent Development and Democratic Theory', in Alfred Stepan, ed. Democratizing Brazil. Oxford: Oxford University Press, 1989.

H.Crouch, 'Malaysia: Neither Authoritarian nor Democratic', in K.Hewison et al (eds), *Southeast Asia in the 1990s: Authoritarianism, Democracy and Capitalism*, St.Leonards, Australia: Allen & Unwin.

H.Crouch & J.W.Morley, 'The Dynamics of Political Change', in J.W.Morley (ed), *Driven by Growth: Political Change in the Asia-Pacific Region*, Armonk, New York, M.E.Sharpe, 1993.

P.Cutright, 'National Political Development: Measurement and Analysis', *American Sociological Review*, 28, 1963.

S.Decalo, 'The Process, Prospects and Constraints of Democratization in Africa', *African Affairs*, 91, 1992.

L.Diamond & M.F.Plattner (eds), *The Global Resurgence of Democracy*, The Johns Hopkins University Press, 1993.

S.Haggard & R.R.Kaufman, *The Political Economy of Democratic Transitions*, Princeton University Press, 1995.

S-J.Han & Y.C.Park, 'South Korea: Democratization at Last', in J.Morley (ed), *Driven by Growth: Political Change in the Asia-Pacific*, Armonk, New York, M.E.Sharpe, 1993.

S.P.Huntington, *The Third Wave: Democratization in the Late Twentieth Century*, University of Oklahoma Press, 1991.

M.E.Keck, 'The New Unionism in the Brazilian Transition', in Alfred Stepan (ed), *Democratizing Brazil*, Oxford University Press, 1989.

S.M.Lipset, 'Some Social Requisites of Democracy: Economic Development and Political Legitimacy', *The American Politican Science Review*, 53, 1959.

B.Martin, 'Japans Wege in die Moderne und das deutsche Vorbild', in B.Martin (ed), *Japans Weg in die Moderne. Ein Sonderweg nach deutschem Vorbild?*, Frankfurt am Main, Campus, 1987.

J.W.Morley, *Driven by Growth: Political Change in the Asia-Pacific*, Armonk, New York and London, M.E.Sharpe, 1993.

B.Moore Jr, *Social Origins of Dictatorship and Democracy: Lord and Peasant in the Making of the Modern World*, Boston, Beacon Press, 1966.

T.Morris-Suzuki, 'Japanese Nationalism from Meiji to 1937', in C.Mackerras (ed), *Eastern Asia*, Melbourne, Longman Cheshire, 1992.

P.Regnier, *Singapore: City-State in South-East Asia*, University of Hawaii Press, 1987.

G.Rodan, 'Singapore: Preserving the One-Party State', in K.Hewison et al (eds), *Southeast Asia in the 1990s: Authoritarianism, Democracy and Capitalism*, St.Leonards, Australia, Allen & Unwin, 1993.

D.Rueschemeyer et al, *Capitalist Development and Democracy*, University of Chicago Press, 1992.

K.Schumacher, *Politischer Opposition und politischer Wandel in Singapur*, Muenster, Lit Verlag, 1993.

M.R.Thompson, *The Anti-Marcos Struggle: Democratic Transition and Personal Rule in the Philippines*, Yale University Press 1995.

M.R.Thompson, 'The Limits of Democratisation in ASEAN', *Third World Quarterly*, 14, 1993.

United Nations, *Human Development Report*, New York, United Nations, 1994.

W.Vennewald, *Singapur: Herrschaft der Professionals und Technokraten – Ohnmacht der Demokratie?*, Opladen: Leske und Budrich, 1994.

R.Wade, *Governing the Market: Economic Theory and the Role of Government in East Asian Industrialization*, Princeton University Press, 1990.

G.White & R.Wade, *Developmental States in East Asia: A Research Report to the The Gatsby Charitable Foundation*, Gatsby Cheritable Foundation, 1985.

World Bank, *The East Asian Miracle: Economic Growth and Public Policy*, Oxford University Press, 1993.

World Bank, *World Development Report 1992: Development and the Environment*, Oxford University Press, 1992.

H.A.Zakaria, 'Malaysia: Quasi Democracy in a Divided Society', in Larry Diamond et al (eds), *Democracy in Developing Countries: Asia*, Boulder, CO, Lynne Rienner Publishers, 1989.

Comparing Political Parties

Kate Hudson
South Bank University

'Continuity and change:
the post-communist left in contemporary Hungary'

The Hungarian parliamentary elections of spring 1990 were a resounding victory for Hungary's conservative forces: the Hungarian Democratic Forum went into coalition with the Independent Smallholders Party and the Christian Democratic People's Party to secure a conservative, nationalist, Christian majority to chart Hungary through its political and economic transition.

The four years of political, social and economic dislocation brought about during the Antall and subsequently Boross governments led in 1994 to a dramatic reversal of the 1990 election results. The Hungarian Socialist Party, which had secured only 32 seats in 1990, surged ahead with a total of 209 out of a possible 386 seats, giving them an overall majority of 16 seats. Second place remained the same, held by the Alliance of Free Democrats, although with their seats dropping from 91 to 69. The former ruling coalition parties were reduced to 38 seats for the HDF, 26 seats for the ISP and 22 seats for the CDPP.[1]

Whilst the scale of the victory was surprising even to the Socialists themselves, the move towards the left by the electorate was already an established feature of political life in central and Eastern Europe, largely provoked by discontent arising from an increase in poverty and unemployment and a decline in living standards.[2] The victory of Aleksander Kwasniewski in November 1995's Polish presidential elections consolidated political power in the hands of the Democratic Left Alliance (SLD) by adding control of the Presidency to their existing control of the government, secured in 1993. Such victories through much of the region were a surprise to many in western Europe, but it has become clear that anti-communism has not been a sufficient force to maintain support for parties and leaders who have overseen what even analysts writing for respectable international bodies now refer to as an 'economic disaster'.[3] Kwasniewski's opponent, former Solidarity leader and Polish President Lech Walesa, tried hard to mobilise support for his campaign by referring to the injustices and oppressions of the communist regime with which Kwasniewski was associated, but clearly, this was not a convincing enough argument for the majority of voters.[4]

---

[1] A.Agh & S.Kurtan, 'The 1990 and 1994 parliamentary elections in Hungary', in Agh & Kurtan, *The First Parliament (1990-1994)*, Hungarian Centre for Democracy Studies, Budapest, 1995, p.24.

[2] L.Andor, 'The Hungarian Socialist Party', in *Labour Focus on Eastern Europe*, 48/1994, p.58.

[3] L.Szamuely, 'Privatisation in a Transforming Central and Eastern Europe', in *Privatisation in the Transition Process*, United Nations, Geneva, 1994, p.25.

[4] A.Robinson & C.Bobinski, 'Future forged in the past', in *Financial Times*, 21 November 1995, p.19.

Significantly, this was not a convincing argument for western observers and analysts either; international financial institutions and western governments seem reasonably confident that their preferred economic policies genuinely prevail within ruling former communist parties in central Europe, and that no return to the previous model is conceivable. As mentioned, both Poland and Hungary have been run by former communist parties since autumn 1993 and summer 1994 respectively, and in both instances these governments have shown serious commitment to privatisation, huge public spending cuts, sweeping reforms of the welfare systems, and eagerness to join the EU and NATO. If anything, the former communists have been more effective in implementing IMF-endorsed policies than their formally more right-wing predecessors.

Far from returning to the past or flagging up some contemporary socialist option, it seems unlikely that these two former communist parties have any intention of introducing even social democratic policies. One could not uniformly take such an approach to other parties originating from similar backgrounds, however. The Communist Party of Bohemia and Moravia, which is the largest opposition party in the Czech Republic, remains explicitly anti-capitalist whilst releasing itself from many of the trappings of the pre-1989 period.

The record in office of the Hungarian Socialist Party is a particularly stark example of the right-ward trend of some of these parties. Gyula Horn, the veteran former communist, led the Hungarian Socialist Party to a spectacular victory in the 1994 elections. During the election campaign, Socialist Party activists 'were overwhelmed by the support for their party and its leader Gyula Horn, not only in the urban centres and working class districts but throughout the countryside too.'[5] Socialist criticisms of the social costs of the HDF's economic programme, and the attitude that they were hard-hearted and uncaring led the electorate in 1994 to think that an HSP government would be most likely to preserve the country's extensive welfare system – hence the Socialists' massive overall majority in those elections.[6] However, contrasting their records one year on, it seems that the HDF government actually made rather slow progress in economic reform, particularly in making significant cuts in social welfare or from proceeding very rapidly with privatisation. The HDF government had actually intended to retain long term majority state ownership of many strategic companies which the Socialists are now proceeding to privatise. As Swain has observed, 'Hungarian conservatism is interventionist, and in the economic sphere it has favoured state control rather than direction.'[7] The Antall government announced its economic policy almost a year after its inauguration, on 7 March 1992 – what became known as the Kupa programme after the then Minister of Finance. However, the Antall government and its successor after Antall's death, the Boross government, tended to focus primarily on political systemic change, rather than economic. In the opinion

---

[5] B.Lomax, 'Elections in Hungary: Back to the Future or Forward to the Past?', *Journal of Communist Studies and Transition Politics*, 10/4, p.93.

[6] *Financial Times*, 'Hungary Survey', 21 November 1995, p.i.

[7] Nigel Swain, 'Hungary', in S.White et al, *Developments in East European Politics*, London, 1993, p.78.

of Attila Agh from the Centre for Democracy Studies in Budapest, privatisation legislation was delayed partly because of the conflict of interests over restitution between the two smaller members of the coalition government sharing power with the Hungarian Democratic Forum: the Smallholders' Party for peasant land, and the Christian Democratic People's Party for Church property, by the summer of 1992, a decision had been made in favour of partial recompensation versus reprivatisation in kind, except for particular church properties.[8] But interestingly, Agh's main criticism of the Antall and Boross governments is that they had an '... ideological commitment to the traditional values of "Hungarianness", to the "Hungarian Golden Age That Never Was". This has led to the dominance of laws of restoration over laws of modernization.'[9]

Agh goes on to state that although the coalition government had a perfectly workable majority it made no clear priorities for an entire programme of systemic change. Furthermore:

> 'The mentality of the coalition government has in its legislative activities, reflected the Hungarian political model of the late 19th century or the interwar period, although it has been confronted with the realities of late 20th century Europe and the urgent tasks of institutional adjustment to it'.[10]

Agh goes on to observe that a swing to the right in the form of the political dominance of the traditionalist-nationalist conservative right has been a common feature in the ECE countries since 1989, and may well be judged to have been a necessity in the early transition period. But he is sure that it has had a very negative impact on the legislation of systemic change, or what he describes as the 'Europeanization of the Central European polities'. In Agh's view this is particularly true of Hungary where there has been very great potential for modernisation and in fact the process had begun very early in terms of parliamentary change. Writing again in 1995 after the HSP victory, Agh reiterated his point:

> 'It can be seen everywhere, but most notably and visibly in the First Parliament, how detrimental this return of the historical political class was for Hungary and why a radical turning point was needed in 1994 to return to the process of mainstream democratization.'[11]

It may perhaps appear ironic, but the type of modernisation sought by Agh is now being brought about by the HSP. The nationalism and traditionalism of the more conservative and interventionist government of 1990-94 was an obstacle to the process of Europeanisation and liberal free-marketisation. Clearly, the electorate did not think that they were voting to reduce the state's social and economic role, when they supported the HSP, but Horn's view is clear as he defends his policies:

---

[8] A.Agh, 'Bumpy Road to Europeanization', in A.Agh, *The First Steps*, Hungarian Centre of Democracy Studies, Budapest, 1994, p.75.
[9] *Ibid.*
[10] *Ibid*, pp.75-6.
[11] Agh, *The First Parliament*, p.254.

'I'm accused of pursuing very right-wing policies. These are not right-wing policies, they are realistic policies. We have to pursue them. If we don't no one will be able to save Hungary. This is the reality, there is no alternative.'[12]

Horn also points out that social and economic reform are not a new approach for Hungary's communists, even prior to 1989, and this is undoubtedly true: from 1980-1 the formation of small-scale semi-private businesses was stimulated; in 1982, Hungary joined the IMF and the World Bank and a small capital market began to emerge as enterprises were allowed to offer interest bearing bonds; in 1988, the Hungarian Socialist Workers' Party government introduced a Law on Foreign Investment allowing 100% foreign ownership and favourable rates for repatriation of profits; stock exchange operations were introduced in January 1989 and from the beginning of the same year, the government began to implement legislation to transform state enterprises into joint stock companies:

'The Companies Act which came into force on 1 January 1989 not only permitted the formation of private joint stock companies, it also allowed for the private ownership of shares in these companies by private citizens – capitalism.'[13]

Parallel steps were also taken in the political field, as noted by Attila Agh:

'The transitional parliament (1985-90) connected the submissive, "rubber stamp" type parliaments of state socialism with the first, active parliament of systemic change. The "old" parliament played a very important role in preparing and managing political change in the period of original crisis ... it did a relatively good job by passing most of the laws of the market economy ... The "old" parliament certainly prepared the way for the new parliament in many ways, and thus continuity in parliamentary affairs in Hungary has been much stronger than in any other ECE country.'[14]

In other words, even before the Hungarian communists had reformed away their leading constitutional role, they had introduced a considerable amount of the legal and institutional framework necessary for the full introduction of capitalism and western-style parliamentary democracy. From 1987, organisations that were really emergent de facto opposition parties began to appear, including the Hungarian Democratic Forum, the Alliance of Young Democrats and the Alliance of Free Democrats. From November 1988, former parties from the pre-communist period reconstituted themselves, like the Smallholders' Party, the Social Democratic Party and the Christian Democratic People's Party and in February 1989 multi-party democracy was formally accepted.

---

[12] *Financial Times*, 'Hungary Survey', p.iv.
[13] Swain, 'Hungary', p.68.
[14] Agh, *The First Steps*, p.72.

Horn's own assessment of the record of his government since election in 1994 is the following: 'To appreciate what we have done you must realise that we have abolished what Hungarians grew up to accept as sacred rights'.[15]

Horn's Finance Minister, Lajos Bokros, who has given his name to March 1995's controversial austerity programme, is very clear about the Party's purpose: 'The historic task of the Socialist government is to roll back the frontiers of the welfare state'.[16]

Bokros' austerity programme was designed to cut government spending and lower interest rates in an attempt to reverse the widening of the trade and current account deficits and reduce the cost of financing enormous levels of domestic and foreign debt. The impact on the average Hungarian, who earns about $300 a month, has been an 11% cut in real wages in 1995 with a planned further 3 to 4% decline in 1996. This cut in living standards has been compounded by further promised radical reforms of the whole social security and health systems to reduce, amongst other things, spending on an old age and disability pension system which accounted for 11% of GDP in 1993. The 1996 budget, conforming to IMF targets, includes a budget deficit set to fall below 4% of GDP, in contrast with 9.5% in 1994.[17]

As Bill Lomax has correctly observed, 'Fears that a socialist victory would mark a communist restoration, or that a landslide would bring into parliament a band of old Stalinist functionaries, can largely be discounted'.[18]

The HSP could well be described as the mass party of the Hungarian working class from a simple reading of the election results, yet in traditional class terms the HSP could hardly be described as acting in the interests of the workers. Laszlo Szarvas, writing in 1994 before the Socialist election victory, observed that 'the left-right scale is extremely restricted in explaining the true relations between parties in today's Hungary'.[19] Szarvas found this description particularly unhelpful because of the weakness of what he described as 'class-based' parties that is, the left. Rather, he preferred to speak of the bi-polar party system in Hungary in terms expressed by G.Markus – 'the party blocks of National Christian versus Liberal- Westernized parties.'

This approach supports Agh's view of the HDF coalition as an obstacle to modernisation. Markus describes the values of the national-christian bloc as populist, culturally and religious ethnically orientated, pro-collectivism, state control of the market and 'authoritarian democracy'. The values of the liberal-westernized bloc are urbanist, economically orientated, secular, pro-individualist, the free market and competitive democracy.[20]

The Hungarian Socialist Party would seem to fit very well into this latter category, and one wonders to what extent Szarvas would still describe them as a class-based party, despite their origins and support.

In Lomax's view, the HSP is not a successor party to the former ruling

---

[15] *Financial Times*, 'Hungary Survey', p.i.
[16] *Ibid*, p.ii.
[17] *Ibid*, p.i.
[18] Lomax, 'Elections in Hungary', p.96.
[19] L.Szarvas, 'European Standards in the Hungarian Parliamentary Party System', in Agh, *The First Steps*, p.128.
[20] *Ibid*, pp.128-9.

HSWP but to the reformist factions within it which brought about its dissolution. He points out that the current leaders are either – like Horn – from the pragmatic wing of the former HSWP or from its democratic reform wing.[21] My slight variation on this assessment is that the HSP is *a* successor party of the HSWP, but not *the* successor party, because different trends existed within the HSWP, and within the Hungarian left prior to 1989 which evolved in different ways after the bureaucratic state socialist system ceased to exist. In addition, one should note that the main leaders of the reform wing, Pozsgay, Nemeth and Nyers, all left the Socialist Party, moving further to the right, and the party is by no means politically homogenous. I would argue that three trends have existed within Hungarian left politics and now find their expression in different ways within contemporary Hungarian political life.

The first trend is that which has emerged as the leading group in the HSP – the group which reformed away the state socialist system, and sought to replace it with the political structures of liberal parliamentary democracy and the economic structures of free market capitalism.

The second trend is the grouping which coalesces around both the Left Platform within the HSP and the Hungarian Left Alternative – an umbrella organisation drawing together a number of groupings and individuals. This trend takes its political framework from the tradition of the workers' councils movement dating from 1956, and defined itself on foundation in 1988 not as a party but as 'a social organization building a democratic society based on workers' property, self-management and self-governmental organizations'.[22]

The third trend is that which has formed the other successor party to the HSWP – the Hungarian Workers' Party. This small party, which secures around 4% of the popular vote and is therefore excluded from parliament by the 5% rule, represents that section of the former ruling party who did not support the restoration of capitalism, but relied on the Soviet bureaucracy for its political orientation. Faced now with charting an anti-capitalist path without its previous material and ideological prop, the Workers' Party is politically more akin to the Communist Party of Bohemia and Moravia than to the HSP or the ruling party in Poland. In other words, when it was no longer possible for the ruling communist parties to continue in the same old way after the demise of state socialism in eastern Europe and the Soviet Union, those parties broke up, with the component parts moving either to the right on a pro-capitalist track, or to the left, trying to redefine an anti-capitalist politics in the new situation.

The most interesting question to be addressed is how the HSP is going to evolve politically: it is currently a pro-capitalist party implementing IMF policies, but its electoral success was built on mass support from the working class which it is currently in the process of alienating through its economic policies. Is it possible for the HSP to consolidate itself as a social democratic party under these circumstances?

If the HSP is to be re-elected at the next General Election, or indeed

---

[21] Lomax, 'Elections in Hungary', p.96.
[22] 'The Activity and History of the Left Alternative', paper published by the Left Alternative, Budapest, 1994, p.1.

remain as a serious political force in Hungarian politics, then it needs to establish a stable electoral base for itself. The emerging capitalist class in Hungary is small and will continue to give its support to the Alliance of Free Democrats, described by one Hungarian economist as 'without exaggeration the political wing of the IMF in Hungary'.[23]

The HSP is currently in voluntary coalition with the Free Democrats, who are effectively able to veto more left-wing or labour movement orientated governmental appointments, such as that of the former trade union leader Sandor Nagy, who Horn tried unsuccessfully to appoint as deputy premier in charge of economic strategy.[24] The Free Democrats are the most stable electoral force, coming in second in both 1990 and 1994.

The HSP built its 1994 electoral victory on its opposition to the hardships of the transition which it has actually exacerbated. Much of its backing came from the organised labour movement, which it could also lose if living standards continue to deteriorate and it pursues its current punitive approach towards the public sector, which provoked strike waves last year; as Anthony Robinson and Virginia Marsh have commented:

> 'Civil servants, teachers, health workers and other public sector workers have seen their incomes fall since the collapse of socialism ... Crucially, it was their votes which brought the socialists back to power in 1994.'[25]

The HSP has no formal relationship with the trade union movement – membership is on an individual rather than collective basis – but a number of cooperation agreements have operated: these ensured that where unions supported the HSP in the elections, their leaders or nominees would secure places on the party's electoral lists. As a result of this arrangement, several union leaders currently sit on the HSP benches in parliament.[26]

It would clearly be in the interests of the HSP leadership if the HSP were to stabilise as a mass social democratic party – a pro-capitalist party with a mass working class electoral base, for without this there is very little chance of the HSP remaining the main party in Hungary. The real question therefore, is whether or not a material basis for this exists. In order to retain its electoral support, the HSP must improve the living standards of ordinary Hungarians, and in order to do this the economy must improve significantly. This is the gamble Horn is currently undertaking: policies are harsh now and people are dissatisfied, leading to growth in support for the right-wing Smallholders Party, but the next elections are not due until 1998.[27] If the economy improves sufficiently in that time as a result of the current policy, then the electorate can reap the benefits before 1998, in time to re-elect a stabilised HSP. If the economy does not improve sufficiently, then the HSP will be ousted and the right-wing and extremist parties will stand to gain.

---

[23] Interview with Laszlo Andor, London, June 1995.
[24] *Eastern Europe*, 9/18, 7 September 1995, p.6.
[25] *Financial Times*, 'Hungary Survey', p.i.
[26] *Eastern Europe*, 10/1, 4 January 1996, p.5.
[27] *Ibid.*

If the material basis for social democracy does not develop from the transition process, then the HSP will either become politically marginalised because it will lose its working class base and will not become the main party of the emerging bourgeoisie, or it will have to adopt a more left programme to retain its working class support. (A cartoon in a recent issue of the Hungarian daily paper *Nepszava* showed Horn leaving a parcel labelled 'Left Values' at a pawn shop, saying 'I will come back for them in 1998'.[28] Whilst there seems to be no likelihood of the latter occurring in the near future, nevertheless the existence of a diversity of political opinions within the HSP, in particular the Left Platform, does make it a possibility.

The organised left within the HSP formed initially within the HSWP as the People's Democracy Platform, opposed to the establishing of a new party on the principles of a market economy. According to Laszlo Andor,

> 'The Reform Alliance, led by political scientist Attila Agh, was determined to form a new party and the People's Democracy Platform, led by historian Tamas Krausz, eventually decided to join it in order to save party unity. In effect, the right and the left opposition of the Kadarists formed a new party together.'[29]

Thus the pattern of the left trends can clearly be seen: the HSP encompasses both the reformist trend who are pro-capitalist and the left opposition who are anti-capitalist but remain within the Socialist Party trying to put it onto a realistic left course; the former ruling Kadarists now in the Workers' Party, remain anti-capitalist. Although the Left Platform is small, it is articulate, well-organised and mounts regular political challenges to the policies of the HSP leadership, putting forward concrete alternatives which take it out of the realms of mere political rhetoric. The most significant step taken recently was its submission of a Declaration of the Platform's Principles for debate at the HSP Congress in November 1995. This document outlined the Platform's position on: the transformation of the world system and the left; the reasons for the collapse of state socialism and the lessons to be learnt; socialist identity; the systemic changes and its consequences; and possible political demands. In this document, two trends in the Hungarian left are defined in the following way:

> 'The Hungarian Socialist Workers Party (the former ruling communist party) later became the Workers Party and this stands for the defence of state property. The Left Platform of the Hungarian Socialist Party (and the Association of Left Alternative) was the only political current which has consistently represented the mixed economy, cooperatives and workers ownership.'[30]

The HSP it describes in the following way:

---

[28] *Nepszava*, 15 December 1995.
[29] L.Andor, 'The Hungarian Socialist Party', p.60.
[30] *Declaration of the Principles of the Left-Wing Platform in the Hungarian Socialist Party*, Budapest, 10 November 1995, p.7.

> 'The HSP is the most characteristic organization of the building up of the bourgeois system, inasmuch as within it one can find the political representatives of almost all the social groups in Hungary (and this can be compared with the old Hungarian Socialist Workers Party). Bank capital, trade unions, workers, entrepreneurs, intellectuals and pensioners – all have their specific position in the HSP. However, bourgeois interests play an overwhelming role.'[31]

The basic economic argument of the Left Platform is that capitalism in Hungary means the domination of multinational capital, and that this could be restricted by the government to the benefit of the Hungarian population, rather than progressing as it is, and constructing a semi-periphery form of capitalism. Essentially arguing for a left social-democratic approach, the document argues that 'within the growing capitalist system the socialist party should first of all, and above all else, represent the interests of workers, the unemployed, small producers, disadvantaged women and young people starting out in life – in short, they should represent 80% of society. Thus the political struggle should extend the representation of the special political interests of the workers in cooperation with the trade unions and other self-organising communities.'[32] The document concludes that unless the HSP expresses the interests of the mass of the people, then it could easily be swept away at the next general election by nationalist populism.

In the debate at the Congress, Bokros received a huge ovation for his economic approach.[33] Tamas Krausz, who put the case for the Left Platform's proposals, is not an MP – the parliamentary leader of the Left Platform is Paul Fillo. Krausz received a fair level of applause, but the Congress was widely seen as a triumph for Horn and Bokros; the membership is not ready to push for a change in approach, although the next opportunity for the party to express its view on the leadership – the spring leadership elections – will probably show trade unionist Sandor Nagy as the strongest challenge to Horn. Nagy is known to favour a long term industrial strategy for Hungary, so this will give an indication of any changes in opinion.

In 1994, Laszlo Andor commented,

> 'The new coalition represents an integration into the transnational capitalist system, while at the same time attempting to build up and maintain a strong bargaining position for domestic Hungarian labour. In the new government the ADF represents the first, and the HSP the second strand of this strategy.'[34]

The fact is, however, that the last year has shown that the HSP has failed to deliver to the labour movement and the vast majority of the Hungarian population, and itself champions integration into the capitalist system on terms that are unfavourable to the working class. Unless the balance is redressed in favour of its working class supporters, the HSP will lose the next election.

---

[31] Ibid.
[32] Ibid, p.8.
[33] Eastern Europe Newsletter, 9/24, p.6.
[34] L.Andor, 'The Hungarian Socialist Party', p.71.

Conceptual Boundaries in the Third World

Lesley McCulloch
University of Aberdeen

'The Misallocation Phenomenon of Defence Spending in South East Asia: A Global Political Dilemma or a Nation's Prerogative?'[1]

Overview

This paper examines the notion of resource 'misallocation' as applied to nations' defence outlays. It is intended to contribute to, and inform, the existing though minimal debate on this theme. It challenges the presumptions of 'misallocation' as a phenomenon calling into question assertions about the inappropriateness of levels of military spending in some countries. A central theme is that the nation-state has the right to determine its own security agenda; and statements alleging 'misallocation' reflect outsiders' judgements about resource use. Such statements typically embody the assumption that resources diverted from other sectors of a country's budget to be concentrated in this specific area, necessarily and inevitably produce an especially damaging negative impact elsewhere. It is in the least developed regions of the world, of which South East Asia is one example, that such 'misallocation' is thought to be particularly widespread.

The second purpose of the essay is to introduce two concepts into the field for debate. These are firstly the notion of the rights of intrusion, to reflect the fact that major powers act as though they have some entitlement to views about how lesser powers should apportion resources and secondly, the norm of convenience; to reflect the fact that major powers invoke the intention of norms, but the specific 'norms' which they cite change from time to time in accordance with their own priorities. These are notions without which major states attitudes and priorities vis-à-vis development cannot be fully understood.

The Current Situation

Global military spending shows a small but steady decline in monetary value since the late 1980s. The general trend is one of diminishing resources being committed to this sector. However, there are countries, and indeed areas of the world where the general trend is upward, notably in the Middle East and South Asia. It is in these geographical areas where much international

---

[1] I am deeply indebted to the Carnegie Trust for their financial assistance to date. Also many thanks to my PhD supervisor David Greenwood, Department of Politics and International Relations at the University of Aberdeen for his advice, support and inspiration, and also to Alasdair McLean for his comments on this paper.

attention is focused with regard to the notion that resources are being 'misallocated'. South East Asia is a region whose countries have shown a steady or increased commitment to military spending, but there appears to be no common rationale for this. Reasons most commonly cited are responses to threats or programmes of modernisation. For many countries in this region, fears of internal or external instability are very real indeed.

The Association of South East Asian Nations (ASEAN), includes some of the most dynamic economies in the world, enjoying substantial economic growth, such as Singapore and Thailand. However, within the region itself are some of the poorest countries in the world, Vietnam, Cambodia, Laos and Myanmar, struggling to survive in the global economic market-place. These countries are among those who find it difficult to provide for growth and social needs. It is these poorer countries who more readily find themselves accused of misallocating their finances, even though they often endure security situations more precarious than their neighbours, their economic plight ensures a level of military spending much less.

Much has been written on the notion that globally an excessive amount is spent on the military. 'In a world spending over $US 600 billion a year on military programs, over 1 billion people lack basic health care, one adult in four is unable to read and write, and one fifth of the worlds population goes hungry every day'.[2] In 1992, the year these figures allude to, about one-fifth of the $US 600 billion was accounted for by the countries of the developing world, in 1994 the proportion was about the same. In that year the countries of South East Asia devoted $US 13.5bn to security spending compared to the $US 456bn of NATO.[3] Concern over this 'diversion' of resources comes in the guise of concern for the economy, stability and growth of poorer countries. Whilst the end of the Cold War has given most major powers a greater sense of security, factors such as poverty, inequality and ethnic discrimination have exacerbated the traditional security concerns of much of the developing world. The states of South East Asia are no exception. These concerns have ensured a continuing upward pressure on the military budgets of some countries whose governments are attempting to ensure the security of their territory and people.

The concept of 'misallocation' comes from the notion that reducing the amount spent on the military in developing countries would 'accelerate the rate of economic growth and social advance of their five billion inhabitants'.[4] A secondary method of distress alleviation is suggested in the form of a 'peace dividend', available from the industrialised world due to their decreasing military spending. This would be given in the form of aid to reinforce the reversal of the 'misallocation' trend within individual countries. The 'rich' appear to have the financial capacity for far-reaching defence modernisation and proliferation projects. Meanwhile increasing international attention is given to the debate on misallocation, primarily focused on the developing world.

---

[2] R.L.Sivard, 'World Military and Social Expenditures, 1993', *World Priorities*, p.5.

[3] International Institute for Strategic Studies, *The Military Balance*, Oxford University Press, 1995.

[4] R.McNamara, 'The Post-Cold war World and Its Implications for Military Expenditure in the Developing Countries', *Internationale Spectator*, 46/11, 1992, p.622.

The underlying concern for this may be suggested as fear of the unknown: fear of the unknown actor, action and weapons acquisition. During the Cold War there were specific supplier/recipient relationships, the system worked to the advantage of the producer states who knew the capabilities of their customers. Despite partial success of the UN Arms Register to enhance transparency, lack of this remains one of the key sources of distrust resulting in the quest for ever-increasing defence capabilities. Indeed, 'the rich are afraid that the arsenals of developing countries now contain some of the world's most advanced weapons'[5] In contrast, the poor continue to fear a widening disparity in North – South and regional defence capabilities.

Resource Misallocation and the Rights of Intrusion

The concept of 'misallocation' has been imposed from outside and is therefore an example of the exercise of a presumed right of intrusion. International institutions and bilateral donors feel that they are entitled to be concerned about supplying finance to those who spend 'excessively' on arms. This notion has been asserted by bilateral donors such as Japan, Canada and Germany, all of whom have criteria for considering a nations' military spending as part of their overseas development assistance decision-making process. Yet the countries of the developed world who subscribe to the 'misallocation' concept, continue to devote billions of dollars to arms acquisitions. These countries are not constrained by outside influences which impacts both on monetary supplies and economic policies. High-income countries rarely find it necessary to borrow from a multilateral institution, thus the prospect of conditionalities being imposed from outside on their budget-making process is minimal. Under the current international economic order the balance of power and spheres of influence are likely to remain.

To the countries of South East Asia as indeed with all nations, military spending is a sensitive issue. This region receives attention as its military spending is not decreasing along with the prevailing trend.[6] To the governments in this sensitive geographical area, the intrusive suggestion that they are 'misallocating' their resources is resented. For them the concept of 'misallocation' is an alien one, based on a set of norms and priorities which bears little or no relation to their own perceived needs. Thus the very existence of misallocation is called into question.

The rationale for this concept is the direct correlation between resources spent on the military and resources denied to other sectors, usually thought to be social spending and investment. Military spending is perceived as non-productive with no direct positive impact on growth.[7] Critics lament what could have been produced with the money, labour and raw materials invested, suggesting that the money absorbed by the military 'could have

---

[5] *The Reallocation of Resources to meet Global Shelter Needs*, Building and Social Housing Foundation, 1994, p.16.
[6] Both the states of ASEAN and Asia show increases in imports of major conventional weapons and in overall security spending. For details and figures see *SIPRI Yearbook*, 1995.
[7] S.George, *The Debt Boomerang*, Pluto press & TNI, 1994.

supported worthier life-enhancing purposes'.[8] Moreover, after the initial weapons purchases, building a suitable infrastructure and continuing maintenance places a further long-term drain on resources.

In assessing the situation, it is suggested that if programmes of military modernisation and proliferation are in line with other policy objectives and development plans,'misallocation' does not exist. The defence studies community could argue that perceived military threat and resources used set against 'real' threat and resources required may provide the basis for a judgement to be made on whether a 'misallocation' is occurring. Moreover, the aid-diversion link, diverting money received as development assistance to the military, can be suggested as a 'misallocation' only when it goes against government policies. This notion, externally-imposed assesses domestic and foreign policy situations from the periphery.

In terms of the military build-up in South East Asia, and indeed in the wider regional context, fear fuels much of the debate on 'misallocation'. This has led to a general agreement that many governments commit excessive amounts of financial resources to their nations' security. However, even a tentative attempt at defining what exactly is an appropriate or excessive level of defence spending has been elusive. It has become generally accepted that military expenditure considerations must, where possible, form part of overseas development assistance decisions. The multilateral donors face problems on this issue. The IMF and World Bank for example, have mandates which are economic, prohibiting them from making lending decisions based on political criteria. Yet both have developed an argument for examining military budgets. The Organisation For Economic Co-operation and Development's (OECD) Development Assistance Committee, has developed linkages between their financial assistance and the military policies of the recipient countries. Furthermore, a working group has been set up by UNDP to identify excessive military spending. These measures constitute interference in the sovereignty of a state as they are concerned with a government's set of priorities, they are thus an example of a perceived 'right of intrusion'.

Most donors however, shy away from outright conditionality as it is seen as confrontational. The most effective method of change is to promote a climate where demand-side constraints are dominant. The answer lies in recognising the damaging consequences of these 'rights of intrusion' which lead to 'norms of convenience'. The existence of these two phenomenon in the international arena prevents trust and true collaborative technology management.

International Norms v. Norms of Convenience

Notwithstanding current debate on the role of the nation-state in International Relations, rejection of the externally-imposed theory of 'misallocation' remains. There is no doubt that the theory and practice of sovereignty are facing challenges. However, with regard to military transfers and spend-

---

[8] Commission on Global Governance, *Our Global Neighbourhood*, Oxford University Press, 1995, p.13.

ing, international norms, customs and conventions are secondary to the notion that a sovereign state has the right to instigate its own security policy initiatives. Thus the nation-state discourse remains outwith the parameters of this paper and is not discussed in legitimising any conclusions reached.

The 'international norms' with regard to sovereignty suggest that the state has supreme authority over all matters that fall within its territorial domain. Apart from this central principle there are three generally accepted 'norms', these are:-

- all sovereign states have equal rights;
- the right to territorial integrity;
- there should be no interference in the domestic affairs of sovereign states.

Moreover, since 'no nation should be denied the legitimate right to self-defence', the assumptions and debate on 'misallocation' are at best misplaced and at worst redundant.[9] Why then do accusations of 'misallocation' occur? The reason lies in the challenge to 'international norms' by the competing rules of the 'norms of convenience'. The military and economic dominance of some states is encroaching on the sovereignty of the weaker. Hence introducing new norms which will either accompany or replace those of the traditional international arena which have been sanctioned by long-standing custom and practice.

The World Bank classifies all states in South East Asia as having low or middle in economies, as such, they are part of the 'developing world'.[10]

It is thus to be expected that these countries, as part of a wide-ranging development plan, will undertake military modernisation programmes. Malaysia, Singapore and Thailand are undertaking such plans, most notably adding to their military capacity advanced aircraft and warships. These countries continue to experience sustained economic growth and are devoting less than $US 3bn each to these programmes. As their economies continue to grow increased military commitment is forecast.

These middle-income countries experience accusations of 'misallocation' in almost the same way as the lower-income nations. The 'norm of convenience' is implicit here, as it appears to be the prerogative of major states to apportion budgetary priorities as they see fit, with little or no interference from external bodies. However, whilst in principle governments of the developing world are free to set their own budgetary priorities, in practice they are often subject to external pressures and influences. The 'norm of

---

[9] J.McCain, 'Controlling Arms Sales to the Third World', *The Washington Quarterly*, Spring, 1991, p.79.
[10]

Table 1
World Bank Classification, 1993 ($US per capita)

Low-Income	Less than 695
Middle-Income	696-8,625
High-Income	8,626 or more

convenience' is a powerful phenomenon becoming increasingly integrated into generally accepted international game-play.

In relation to the international arms trade, one such 'norm' is the restrictive policies imposed by individual producer-states and in the increasing number of supplier cartels. The members of these cartels tend to be the richer states whilst the recipient groups against which these constraints are levied, are in the poor 'South'. It has been suggested that these cartels operate in a discriminatory manner, identifying 'problem' states. [11] Furthermore, they show a lack of trust towards some governments and reinforce normative notions of the rational actor.

The 'norms of convenience' are short-term, short-range missiles. Sort-term because they change as the international political, economic and security arena requires. Short-range as they only skim the surface of the underlying problem which is one of distrust and fear. However, as economies develop and technology spreads, supply controls will become more ineffective. Moreover, these 'strategies centred in the conflicting interests of the major suppliers, are unlikely to succeed', leaving in their wake antagonisms and resentment.[12] The root of conflict between states is still present, thus for many countries there is an upward pressure on military budgets. Indeed in South East Asia all but Singapore have experienced unrest in recent years. These countries continue to rely on their ability to import arms, technology and expertise perceived as necessary to their requirements. Thus to a degree their military capabilities are externally controlled.

This is the prevailing position of the weaker states in the international political and economic arena, whilst the more powerful ensure the continuance of their own dominant position. In February 1995 the United States, who accounted for 55% of deliveries of major conventional weapons in 1994, announced its Conventional Arms Transfer Policy.[13] Among the policy goals are the intention by the United States to maintain technological superiority over potential adversaries, and also to help allies and friendly states deter and defend themselves against aggression. The former breeds inequality and distrust, whilst the latter puts upward pressure on the military spending of the neighbours of the 'privileged' states. Also included in the policy is the intention to promote regional stability in areas critical to United States interests. By arming these strategically important nations, localised instability can be the only outcome. However, this forms part of the rationale for the high priority afforded to arms exports from the United States. Similar political and security motives drive the export policies of most producer states.

Conclusion

The fear and distrust which characterises the international military arena can be overcome only by increased transparency, accountability and tech-

---

[11] See for example K.Subrahmanyam, 'Export Controls and the North-South Controversy', *Washington Quarterly*, 16/Spring, 1993.

[12] D.Mussington, 'Understanding Contemporary International Arms Transfers', *Brassey's UK*, IISS, 291, September 1994, 291, p.5.

[13] *SIPRI Yearbook*, Oxford University Press,1995.

nology exchange. The countries of South East Asia exist in an unstable and volatile environment. Internal unrest poses a more real security threat than external factors. The countries of this region defend most vigorously the sovereign rights which independence afforded them. The externally-imposed concept of 'misallocation' is seen as an unwelcome invasion of their authority and policies. Furthermore, it is an abstract concept if not tied to a definitive measure of excessive military spending. 'Without any agreed standard against which to measure behaviour it is difficult to determine when a state goes beyond maintaining an inventory of equipment which is reasonable and sufficient to defence'.[14]

In a world in which the authority of the nation-state is coming under increasing external pressure, security policies are regarded as the *sine-qua-non* of nation-hood. The countries of South East Asia, indeed of the developing world, continue the defensive against the policies of intrusion, based on the erosion of the well established, universal standards of international norms and the promotion of the 'norms of convenience' by selected states. It should remain the prerogative of the nation-state to chose an appropriate level of security capabilities, whether the state be small or large, rich or poor, weak or powerful. It should be able to do this without excessive external intrusion based on dubious preferences dressed up as 'norms'. It would appear that the 'misallocation phenomenon' is not the uncontroversial fact of international political life that many assert. It is in fact a product of the practice of intrusive behaviour and the imposition of 'norms of convenience', and as such its very existence should be open to debate.

---

[14] *Ibid*, p.633.

Conceptual Boundaries in the Third World

Heather Deegan
Middlesex University

'The Middle East and Africa: An Alternative Development Agenda'[1]

Introduction

As global changes have radically altered the international political scene, so the relationship between the Middle East and sub-Saharan Africa requires re-examination. Traditional approaches to the politics of the region deal only with the West's responses to Africa in the form of World Bank and IMF assistance. This paper argues that an alternative Islamic development agenda for Africa exists which in part mirrors that of the World Bank and the IMF. The Secretary General of Islam in Africa, argues that Africa 'craves for Islam' as a part of its quest for 'cultural freedom' and its search for 'an alternative world view which can stand up to challenge the West'. (Usman Bugaje 1994) Statements by the United Nations Secretary-General Boutros Boutros-Ghali, however, highlight Africa's need for democracy and an informed body of citizens. (UN Focus on the New Agenda for Africa) In a sense, both these interpretations are accurate simply because Western and Islamic influences on the continent have been so profound and are part of Africa's historical and cultural development. However, the significant factor in the case of Africa, a region of the Third World, is that the Middle East, also part of the Third World, had and continues to have an influence over the economic and political direction of a number of states. An increased interest in Islam has been evident in Sub-Saharan Africa in recent years. In the case of Sudan Saudi Arabia exerted pressure on the country to declare a constitution which would enable it to become an Islamic State. (Warburg 1991) For increasingly impoverished Sub Saharan African states external influences or inducements to proclaim themselves Islamic can be significant, and this is where organisations like the Islamic Conference Organisation, the Islamic Development Bank and the Arab Bank for Economic Development (BADEA) in Africa are important.

BADEA was established in November 1973, and funded by the governments of the member states of the League of Arab States. At the end of 1991, the total resources of the Bank amounted to US$1579.4million. (BADEA Annual Report 1991) In 1987 BADEA approved loans and grants to African states amounting to US$828.8million. By the end of 1992 the bank had contributed almost $1.1billion. (BADEA Annual Report 1993 p16) Initiatives were sustained during 1993 with the objective of 'activating Arab-African cooperation and infusing fresh vitality into its structures and organs.' (BADEA 1993 Annual Report) The 1993 OAU Summit called for an 'intensification and coordination of direct contacts between African and Arab institutions such as chambers of commerce, businessmen, and trade unions'. (*Ibid*) Several visits were made to African countries by BADEA

---
[1] This paper is part of a book which will be published by Routledge in August, 1996, entitled *Third Worlds*.

representatives and the Bank participated in a number of meetings both on Arab/Islamic sides, as well as at African and international levels: Arab League Council Sessions, the Higher committee for Coordination between the League of Arab States and the Arab Joint Action Institutions, the Arab Development Finance Institutions, the Arab Fund for Technical Assistance for African Countries, the Board of Governors of the Islamic Development Bank, the OAU Council of Ministers, the African Development Bank, the Association of African Finance Institution, ECOWAS, the World Bank and the agencies of the United Nations. Loans and grants approved in 1993 divide into Project-Aid and Technical Assistance. West Africa received assistance of US$21 million for 4 operations, representing 29% of 1991 lending compared with 8 operations in East Africa, amounting to US$50 million, which represented around 70% of total lending. (Ibidp15) In its lending operations BADEA admit that 'aggravating conditions' confront the economies of countries which receive aid from the bank: accumulating debt and a shrinking volume of external financial flows, all of which contribute to the reduced number of projects which were viable for BADEA's financing. BADEA's lending strategy is affected by similar concerns which confront World Bank and IMF programmes. On 1991 figures, BADEA attributed its decrease in lending to West Africa as being attributable in part to the accumulation of arrears, political instability and economic and financial difficulties. (*Ibid*, p.14)

The Islamic Conference Organisation (ICO) was established in May 1971 with the objective of promoting Islamic solidarity among member states in order to gain mutual assistance in 'economic, scientific, cultural and spiritual fields, inspired by the immortal teachings of Islam.' (Moinuddin p65) ICO member states must proclaim their intention to uphold the objectives of the organisation for which they gain access to the resource allocations of Islamic financial institutions. The majority of member states are from the African continent. The ICO admits that more needs to be done to promote cooperation and understanding among Muslim countries and Muslim peoples. (SWB FE/1673 27 April 1993) However, the ambivalent principles of the ICO outlined in the Articles of its Charter raise difficulties of interpretation. Article 11 (a)6 refers to support of the struggle of Muslim peoples which should be undertaken in order 'to safeguard their dignity, independence and national rights'. (Moinuddin p82) There are Muslim minorities in non-member states of Asia, Africa and Europe and it is unclear whether 'Muslim peoples' should be construed as Moinuddin suggests: Muslim peoples living under colonial rule or military occupation, or Muslim minorities permanently resident in non-Muslim states. (Ibidp83) Any interference in another sovereign territory would contravene the principles of self-determination and non-intervention contained in sub-paragraph 2 of Article 11 (B) which upholds 'respect of the right of self-determination and non-interference in the domestic affairs of Member states'. It would also undermine the principle of sovereignty outlined in Article 11 (B)3 which calls for 'respect of the sovereignty, independence and territorial integrity of each member state'. (*Ibid*, p.87, 92) Equally, the Preamble of the ICO Charter reaffirms the commitment of its members states 'to the United Nations Charter and fundamental Human rights, the purposes and principles of which provide the basis for fruitful cooperation amongst all people.' (*Ibid*, p.74)

Yet, the ICO does operate on a political level. From its inception it called for Arab territories to be restored by Israel, the rights of Palestinians and of the Palestine Liberation Organisation to be recognised and Jerusalem to be returned to Arab rule. In fact, the 1981 Summit conference called for a 'jihad' (holy war) for the liberation of Jerusalem and the occupied territories. The ICO was particularly active in the early 1980s following the Islamic revolution in Iran and was quick to affirm the importance of the Iranian Islamic Republic's sovereignty, territorial integrity and political independence, opposing any foreign pressures which might be exerted against Iran. By 1989 it declared that as Muslims in Africa shared a common colonial heritage there was a need for unity between all Muslims. (Brenner) Its proselytising function was clearly outlined in July 1991, when the ICO's Secretary General visited a number of African states 'in order to promote the organisation of the Islamic movement in the world.' (SWB ME1139 1 August 1991) Continual ICO meetings refer to the 300 million Muslims who live in non- Muslim countries whose rights should be safeguarded and assert that only when there is solidarity between Muslims will the full potential of the Muslim world be realised. (*Ibid*) President Rafsanjani of Iran refers to the 'enormous powers and resources' the Islamic world possesses, which could be employed in the pursuit of its goals.' (SWB ME/1253 12 December 1991) King Hussein of Jordan speaks of the Muslim community's 'distinctive cultural identity' and its need to 'draw up comprehensive plans to spread its message in the world, to achieve solidarity, and to protect its rights'. (King Hussein Jordan Times 1993; Hamid Algabid ICO Secretary-General. SWB ME/1252 E/3 11 December 1991) ICO member states are exhorted to unite and join ranks in order to manage 'Africa's' problems and to 'prepare them for a better future'. (*Ibid*)

Links tween the OAU and the ICO have been steadily increasing as numerous states are members of both organisations. Inevitably, similar problems are debated in both organisations. In fact, some view the two organisations as comparable given their dual emphasis on brotherhood and solidarity 'in a larger unity transcending ethnic and national differences'. (Moinuddin p74) Yet there are differences. Whereas the OAU Charter refers to a compact geographical area, the Charter of the ICO refers to the eligibility of every 'Muslim state', regardless of geographical location, to join the ICO. Eligibility exists when a state, anywhere in the world, expresses its desire and preparedness to adopt the ICO Charter. (*Ibid*) According to the Secretary- General of the OAU, Salim Ahmed Salim, the closeness between the two organisations is the result of the support the 'Middle Eastern states within the ICO extend to many African states in their struggle for economic development' (Salim Ahmed Salim 1995)

Nevertheless, criticism is levelled at the Arabs: 'black Africans respect Arabs more than they respect us.' (Africa Bulletin 1992) Despite the very strong cultural links, it is admitted that 'ill-educated Arabs have disparaged black Africans,' although this tendency is deemed to be slowly changing.

(El-Affendi) Certainly the ICO has been criticised for devoting too much time to Arab issues and ignoring other areas. (SWB ME/1254 13 December 1991) The 1991 ICO Summit, the first of its kind to be held in sub-Saharan Africa, was deeply affected by Iraq's invasion of Kuwait and the subsequent Gulf War. African leaders condemned the Arabs as 'immature' and predicted a worsening of Arab-African relations as a result of the conference. (*Ibid*) Political events in the Middle East and the obvious lack of unity within the Arab world undermined statements concerning the great Muslim community 'umma'. It was quite apparent that the Arab world was as divided and riven with conflict and animosities as were parts of sub-Saharan Africa.

However, with a Muslim population in Africa having increased by an estimated 50% in the past decade to 149 million which according to one interpretation now results in Africa having more Muslims than the Middle East the potential for a closer relationship exists. (Africa Bulletin 1992) For Hasan Turabi, the leader of Sudan's National Islamic Front the ICO is a failure: 'Perhaps the highest disenchantment is that the ICO, a professedly Islamic association, has turned out to be politically impotent and totally unrepresentative of the true spirit of the community that animates Muslim people.' (Turabi.Islamica 1993) An alternative view, however, sees the ICO as having considerable radical potential. Moinuddin maintains that a change of attitude towards the principles enshrined in the ICO Charter could be accelerated and supported by a steady radicalisation of Islamic orders at a national level. This would give an opportunity for radical elements in the Islamic world to pursue a militant course and,'perhaps even translate it collectively, that is, through ICO action.' (Moinuddin p110) The time is now right for such a move according to Turabi on the grounds that the present growth of Islamic revivalism implies a 'deeper experience of the same culture and a stronger urge for united action, nationally and internationally.' (Islamica)

One organisation, set up by the ICO, to 'further augment the financial aspects of co-operation between countries' is the Islamic Development Bank (IDB) which has been judged by one authority to be 'a proven and effective instrument of mutual cooperation.' (H.Moinuddin) Its stated aim is to encourage the economic development and social progress of member countries and of Muslim communities in non-member states. The Bank adheres to the Islamic principle forbidding usury and does not grant loans or credits for interest. Instead, its methods of financing are: provision of interest-free loans (with a service fee) mainly for infrastructural projects which are expected to have a marked impact on long-term socio-economic development; provision of technical assistance, eg for feasibility studies, equity participation in industrial and agricultural projects; and leasing operations. Funds not immediately needed for projects are used for foreign trade financing, particularly for importing commodities to be used in development, such as raw materials and intermediate industrial goods, rather than consumer goods; priority is given to the import of goods from other member countries. In addition, the Special Assistance Account provides emergency aid and other assistance, with particular emphasis on education in Islamic communities in non-member countries. (Islamic Development Bank Annual Report1991-1992)

At the annual meeting of the IDB in Iran in 1992, President Rafsanjani called for a strengthening of the Bank in Islamic and Third World countries'in order to fight against plundering of their national resources by the West.' (SWB ME/WO257 17 November 1992) He pointed out that Islamic countries often needed urgent loans and in obtaining them from the West they were 'ready to give political concessions'. A fact which was 'very detrimental to the Islamic world and highly beneficial to the colonial powers'. (*Ibid*) He warned the IDB not to be manipulated by Western policies. Yet the Bank has forged much closer ties with both multilateral financing institutions and other international instuitions including UNCTAD, UNESCO,UNICEF. It states in its annual reports that it 'continues to hold regular consultation/coordination meetings with the World Bank.' (IDP Annual Report Op cit p57) Equally, when the World Bank announced in 1993 that it had suspended disbursements to Sudan due to the country's arrears of $1.14 bn, the IDB immediately agreed to finance an $8million road building project in the country. (Africa Research Bulletin 1993) Both the World Bank and the IDB have been fully aware of political factors when dealing with Sudan. (Van Eeghen 1994;El Affendi)

The Islamic Development Bank (IDB) and the World Bank link economic progress to the wider issue of development. Interestingly, both institutions identify the same priorities for assistance in their respective member countries: food security, trade among member countries, infrastructure, human resource development and technological advancement. As the World Bank and the International Development Association (IDA) emphasise their continuing commitment to health and education projects, IDB reports also stress their financing of social sector projects such as education and health. Equally, as food security and poverty reduction are highlighted in World Bank literature, the IDB declares its full participation in the achievement of the goals and objectives of the Decade of Food Security for the Islamic Countries. With regard to infrastructure, the IDA declare good roads, ports, water supply, and irrigation to be the 'lifelines of a nation' underpinning production and 'creating the channels vital to bringing goods to domestic and foreign markets'; whilst the IDB pronouce the development of infrastructure to be vital 'in order to stimulate the flow of investments, especially from the private sector, and to make these investments more productive.' (IDA and Infrastructure;IDB Annual Report 1991-1992p33) In essence, parts of a development agenda for poor nations, advanced by organisations which are essentially the aid agencies of the West and Islamic worlds, are virtually identical. Yet, according to Choudhury the emphasis is different: the Islamic formula looks to 'an integrated co-operative socio-economic model of development as opposed to a neo-classical competitive equilibrium model.' (M.Choudhury p88) Islamic economics upholds the market and assumes that the forces of supply and demand will give rise to a just price. (Hardie & Rabooy 1991p53) Equally, whilst monopolies are condemned 'Muslim societies impose little tax upon profits' which might, at first sight, appear to undermine redistributive policies. However, Islamic banks have social welfare duties, such as the payment of 'zaka' on their deposits. The payment of 'zaka' is a religious obligation for Muslims and the money is used to assist the poor and other designated purposes. (*Ibid*, p.62)

The Islamic Development agenda does not detach the countries of the South from the industrialised world but it demands that 'international multilateral resource flows', ie. aid, concessional lending, grants, must be 'untied' from the West's conditionality arrangements. (Choudhury p62) These unconditional resources together with indigenous resources could be mobilised on the basis of shared interests and co-operation. This approach is allegedly different from IMF and World Bank strategies because it overrides the emphasis on the needs and requirements of the nation-state in favour of a 'collective self-reliant integrated development of the South' as a whole. (*Ibid*) OAPEC countries would be expected to contribute more to the poorer areas of Africa. The difficulties with this model is not its economic imprecision nor its predominantly theoretical basis but rather its unwillingness to acknowledge that resources which flow from the Middle East to Africa are also conditional or 'tied' to an Islamic political agenda.

Between 1975 and 1991, the Islamic Development Bank allocated 21.6% of its budget to transport and communication works, and in 1991, it accounted for 28% of total expenditure. (IDB Report pp67/68) The Bank also promotes Intra-Islamic trade on the grounds that it is 'convinced of the role that intra-trade plays in consolidating economic cooperation and integration' (IDB Report p47) Loans are a mode of financing used by the IDB to finance infrastructure projects in member countries, particularly the least developed. They are interest-free but they carry a service fee intended to cover the actual costs of administering them. Normally, the repayment period ranges from 15 to 25 years, including a grace period of 3-5 years. The 'Mudarabah' is a form of partnership where one party provides the funds while the other provides the expertise and management. The latter is referred to as the Mudarib. Any profits accrued are shared between the two parties on a pre- agreed basis, while capital loss is borne by the partner providing the capital. Another Islamic financing technique, the 'Musharakah', adopts 'equity sharing' as a means of financing projects. Thus, it embraces different types of profit/loss sharing partnerships. The partners (entrepreneurs, bankers, etc.) share both capital and management of a project so that profits will be distributed among them according to determined ratios of their equity participation.

Up to the end of 1992, total trade financing commitments have reached around US$8 billion. (*Ibid*) Yet Islamic economic processes have a tendency to stifle trade, in that prices fail to reflect real costs. (Rodney Wilson 1994) Although the IDB is regarded as doing 'good work' it is felt it has not achieved its economic goals. (Al-Affendi) In a sense, the Bank is constricted by the economies of the Arab world which fail to generate high levels of resources over and above oil production. The agricultural sector has traditionally been weak in Arab states with poor levels of irrigation, low degrees of mechanisation or use of fertilisers and pesticides. Equally, industrialisation and technological development has been restricted. According to some economists economic cooperation and integration among Islamic countries has now become urgent largely because of the deficiencies in the economies of individual nation states. (Choudhury p155-157) Yet the ratio of intra-trade between IDB member countries remains low. Also, around 60% of the Bank's subscriptions come from only four countries, Saudi Arabia, Libya, Kuwait and Iran, nations with varied patterns of Islamic political expression.

Attention is now focusing on the role of 'Islamic Investment Companies' (IICs) or 'Islamic Finance Houses' (the translation from Arabic of Sharikat Tawzif Al-Amwal is 'Capital Employment Companies) which are thought to number around 104 in Egypt with an estimated deposit value of US$2.3 billion. (Abdel Monem Said Aly; Zubaida 1990) They are, in fact, closed companies which attract savers either to deposit their savings in exchange for returns (without participation in the decision making) or to own shares and stocks in the company. The companies utilise 'Islamic' forms of investment such as those outlined above: Mudarabah:- capital-labour participation; musharaka:- venture-capital participation, and murabaha:- cost-plus operations. (*Ibid*) These organisations, apart from syphoning money away from other institutions, can convey political overtones: 'The IICs are the economic symbol of rising Islamic tendencies in Egypt. The shift in the ideological makeup of Egyptians toward Islam has made them ready to deposit their money in the IICs. They use nonusurous concepts of economics and Islamic symbols. They open their speeches and their advertisements with Quranic verses.' (Ibidp53) Some IICs are linked to the Muslim Brotherhood but generally religious leaders and personalities are recruited as consultants. Islamic groups have 'propagated the idea of an independent Islamic economy' and these companies play an important role. (*Ibid*) From the perspective of Egypt and other countries with strong Islamic communities, the position is complex; whilst the IMF/World Bank hand down strictures on privatisation and economic liberalisation, Islamic companies are organising alternative forms of economic exchange. When the Egyptian government passed Law 146 in 1988 legalising and regulating Islamic companies, Hasan Al-Gamal,a Muslim Brotherhood member of the People's Assembly condemned Law 146 as representing a 'conspiracy against the Islamic solution and the Islamic movement.' (Ibidp54) At this point it is, perhaps, appropriate not to lose sight of the fact that petro-dollars were invested in Western banks suggesting that the adoption of 'Islamic economics' has not always been entirely obligatory under shariah. Equally, a number of the Islamic investment companies have beem criticised for resorting to 'Islamic rhetoric to legitimise their activity.' (Zubaida)

African and Arab member states of the ICO do not lack the necessary resource base for a better future. They command, as a group 'a rich endowment of natural resources and minerals, a big market of around one billion consumers and a relatively important number of scientists and experts in various disciplines scattered all over the world.' (Zeinelabdin 1993) Their relative underdevelopment resulting from technological backwardness and dependence: 'most of the ICO countries lack the basic technologies that would be essential for the realisation of their industrial revolution.' (*Ibid*) Rafsanjani stated in 1994 that Iran's 'first priority' in foreign policy was to 'develop further our relations with African states and Muslim nations in political and economic spheres.' (Kayhan. Vol.XV.3917 Tehran.21 July 1994) Ayatollah Khamenei of Iran announced in 1993 that Muslims living in other regions should pay attention: 'The Islamic struggle is like a traditional military battle. It is confrontation. You sit, think, show initiative and counter any move of the enemy'. (Kayhan Vol.XV 1993) Accusations that Zambia's United National Independence Party, had formulated a destabilisation plan, funded by Iran were made in 1993, although Iran 'strongly rejected' the allegations. (SWB ME/1633 8 March 1993)

The Interior Minister of the Islamic Republic of Mauritania overtly stated that Islamic groups, especially the Islamic Movement in Mauritania (Hasim) were strongly linked with Islamic organisations in Algeria, Sudan, Kuwait and Saudi Arabia. (SWB AL/2021 14 June 1994) The infiltration of the NGOs was especially condemned: 'They exploit the relief organisations residing in our country in order to obtain the necessary revenues to implement their plans, ignoring the rights of the poor and needy who are more entitled to such assistance.' NGOs would be used as channels through which to funnel monies from overseas. (SWB AL/2111 27 September 1994) Clearly, tensions exist between Islamic groups within Muslim countries who are members of the ICO. These activities sit uneasily with claims made at ICO summit meetings that only in 'non-Muslim countries' are the 'basic human rights of Muslims violated' and their places of worship undermined. (SWB FE/1673 27 April 1993) Splits between Islamists deeply affect the lives of Muslims. Interestingly, the whole of the northern belt countries below North Africa are regarded as 'borderline states' by Sudan because of their close association with the Arab world and the possibility of their integration into the wider Muslim community 'Umma'. The increase in Arab education and the Arabic language is further promoting the possibility of integration and the formal establishment of Islamic statehood. (El-Affendi 1995)

Conclusion

What does an Islamic development agenda mean for sub-Saharan Africa? Initially we must acknowledge that the historicity of African societies contains forms of Muslim leadership. (Constantin 1993 p46) In some instances, Islam completely transformed identities (Thorold 1993p90) The coastal Swahili Muslims see themselves as the 'rightful guardians of the true Islamic heritage in East Africa', with a language based on Arabic whilst Islamists in Sudan claim their policies represent a return to 'Afro-Islamic authenticity.' (Brenner 1993, R.S.O'Fahey p7-9) The degree to which many immigrants from Arabia were assimilated into Swahili society from the 12th Century has been largely underestimated. (Frankl 1993) There is considerable strength and depth to the Islamic heritage of Sub-Saharan Africa and these 'very strong cultural links' are sustained and enhanced by North African influences particularly from countries such as Egypt, Libya and Algeria. (El-Affendi)

The fact that the 'Islam in Africa Organisation' has been established at the behest of the Islamic Conference Organisation with the stated objective of ensuring the appointment of Muslims to strategic posts and the ultimate replacement of western legal systems with the 'sharia' is significant especially as pre-colonial Africa was, in part, Islamic Africa. Nevertheless, whilst sub-Saharan states continue to look to the West for aid and assistance contradictions exist if they are also members of the Islamic Conference Organisation. The ICO requires of its member states support for Muslims and potentially the declaration of Islamic rule if they are to gain access to resources from the Islamic Development Bank and other institutions. The World Bank/IMF conditionality programmes with their emphases on political and economic liberalisation confront the Islamic politico/economic agendas of the Middle East resulting in potential destabilisation and conflict in African states.

Interviews/Meetings

Akbar Ahmed, Royal Institute of International Affairs, London, 10 May 1991.

Professor Sadik Al-Azm, St Antony's College Oxford, 17 May 1995.

M.El-Affendi, former Cultural Attache, Sudan Embassy, 25 January 1995.

Fr.Mark Connolly, Holy Ghost Fathers London 6 June 1994.

W.Van Eeghen, Senior Economist, World Bank, Banz Castle, Germany, 24 February 1994.

Dr.Hamido Hammade, Curator, Aleppo, Syria, 23 November 1993.

Reverend Paul O'Leary, Society of African Missions, London, 2 May 1994.

Dr.Richard Rodgers, Light & Hope for Sudan, 10 April 1995.

Dr.Salim Ahmed Salim, Secretary-General of the Organisation of African Unity, Royal Institute of International Affairs, London, 18 May 1995.

References

Africa Research Bulletin.

Akbar Ahmed & H.Donnan, *Islam, Globalisation and Postmodernity*, Routledge, 1994.

Akbar Ahmed, *Postmodernism & Islam*, Routledge, 1992.

Arab Bank for Economic Development (BADEA), *Reports* 1991, 1992, 1993.

Mohammed Arkoun, *Rethinking Islam*, Westview Press, 1994.

Nazih Ayubi, *Political Islam*, Routledge, 1991.

BBC Summary of World Broadcasts, Various daily reports.

J-F.Bayart, *The State in Africa*, Longman, 1993.

Louis Brenner (ed), *Muslim Identity and Social Change in Sub Saharan Africa*, C.Hurst & Co, 1993.

Usman Bugaje, *Africa Events*, Nigeria, April 1994.

M.Choudhury, *Islamic Economic Cooperation*, Macmillan, 1989.

Heather Deegan, *The Middle East and Problems of Democracy*, Open University Press, 1993.

F.K. Ekechi, 'Colonialism and Christianity in West Africa the Igbo Case', *Journal of African History*, lXX1, 1971.

Raghid El-Solh, 'Islamist Attitudes towards Democracy', *British Journal of Middle Eastern Studies*, 20, 1993.

Ernest Gellner, *Muslim Society*, Cambridge University Press, 1993.

Juan Goytisolo, *El Pais*, 28 March 1994, translated by Peter Bush, 1995.

A.R.Hardie & M.Rabooy, 'Risk, Piety and the Islamic Investor', *British Journal of Middle Eastern Studies*, 18, 1991.

Nigel Harris, *The End of the Third World*, Penguin, 1990.

IDA and Infrastructure, World Bank, Washington B.05.4-93.

Islamic Development Bank, *Annual Reports*, Saudi Arabia, 1991-1992.

T.Ismael, *International Relations of the Contemporary Middle East*, New York, 1986.

Kayhan, XV, 3917, Tehran, 21 July 1994.

Mehran Kamrava, *Politics and Society in the Third World*, Routledge, 1993.

Ephraim C.Mandivenga, 'Resurgence of Islam: Implications for African Spirituality and Dialogue', *Religion in Malawi*, 3, 1991.

Hasan Moinuddin, *The Charter of the Islamic Conference*, Clarendon Press, 1987.

Robert Pinkney, *Democracy in the Third World*, Open University Press, 1993.

Hasan Turabi, *Islamica*, 1993.

Bryan Turner, *Orientalism, Postmodernism & Globalism*, Routledge, 1994.

Sudan Update, 5, 30 April 1994.

United Nations, *Focus on the New Agenda for Africa*, New York, 1993.

John Voll, 'Islamic Fundamentalism', in H.Maull & O.Pick (eds), *The Gulf War*, Pinter, 1989

S.Warburg, 'The Sharia in Sudan', in John Voll (ed), *Sudan, State and Society in Crisis*, Indiana University Press, 1991.

Max Weber, *The Protestant Ethic and the Spirit of Capitalism*, Unwin University Books, 1974.

Rodney Wilson, 'The Middle East after the Gulf War', in H.Jawad, *The Middle East in The New World Order*, Macmillan, 1994.

J.Milton Yinger, *The Scientific Study of Religion*, Macmillan, 1970.

A.Zeinelabdin, 'Technology, Sustainable Development and Environment ICO?UN Cooperation, *Journal of Economic Cooperation Among Islamic Countries*, 14, 1993.

Sami Zubaida, 'The Politics of the Islamic Investment Companies in Egypt, *British Journal of Middle Eastern Studies*, 17, 1990.

Defence and British Politics in the 1980s

Andrew Dorman
Birmingham

'Defence as an Electoral Weapon:
The Case of the Conservative Party in the 1980s'

Introduction

The premiership of Margaret Thatcher witnessed a transformation in the world situation. In 1979 the ebb tide of *détente* was in full flow and in its place the flow tide of the Second Cold War loomed large on the horizon. From the highpoint of the early-1970s, East-West relations appeared to be in a state of terminal decline. Yet by August 1990, the Berlin Wall, so long the symbol of East-West conflict, had been breached and the two superpowers were co-operating with Britain in a wider coalition confronting the Iraqi invasion of Kuwait. Domestically also, the 11 years of Margaret Thatcher's premiership witnessed significant changes. The wide-scale privatisation of state industries, the huge growth in share ownership, trade union reform, changes in taxation and the high level of unemployment were just some of the features associated with the 'Thatcher legacy'.

Within this context of both international upheaval and domestic change British defence policy emerged from its traditional post-war position of relative inconsequence as an election issue to one of the key issues that surrounded both the 1983[1] and 1987 elections. The resurgence of CND, the Trident acquisition, the Falklands War and the Westland saga were just some of the more memorable incidents that surrounded Conservative defence policy.

This paper seeks to demonstrate that defence was not just an important area of inter-party division which the Conservatives exploited to their maximum advantage at election time but that the need to use the 'defence electoral weapon' had an impact upon defence policy itself. More fundamentally this paper illustrates the divisions within the Conservative Party itself over this important area of policy and argues that an overview examination of the Thatcher years which fails to take account of defence policy is flawed. The paper has, therefore, been divided into three parts. The first part examines the internal divisions within the Conservative Party over defence policy and the effects that had within the Ministry of Defence [MoD] and elsewhere. The second part takes an overview of the inter-party debate and shows how the Conservatives targeted defence as an area upon which they could damage their opponents, and this led them to make or avoid certain defence decisions in order not to undermine their own position within the inter-party debate.

---

[1] In 1979 only 2% of the electorate thought defence was a major issue compared to 38% in 1983. M.Heseltine, 'The United Kingdom's strategic interests and priorities', *The RUSI Journal*, 128/4, 12/1983, p.5.

Defence and the divisions within the Conservative Party

Whilst defence has always been a sacred cow to the Conservatives, Margaret Thatcher, with her openly vehement opposition to the Soviet Union, went considerably further in eulogising defence than any of her predecessors. This was somewhat surprising given her background, which had done little to suggest that such a change in emphasis would occur. Yet as early as January 1976, less than a year after becoming leader of the Conservative Party, and three years before she became Prime Minister, she pledged the Conservative Party to 'shaking the British public out of a long sleep' to confront the threat posed by the Soviet Union.[2] This rhetoric, however, remained unchanged and continued, at least for the first half of her time in office, reflecting her emergence from within the 'New Right'. The result was a shift in the balance of government spending between the various departments, with the MoD becoming one of the chief beneficiaries.

Yet one of her other two policy goals, the arrest of Britain's long-term economic decline, led one observer to inappropriately refer to this Jekyll and Hyde character as the 'Thatcher Schizophrenia' in which she could never decide whether she wanted to be remembered in history as the 'Iron Lady' or the 'Iron Chancellor'.[3] This inherent tension was reflected in what Jordan & Richardson have referred to as her 'clear policy *theory*'[4] which reinforced her emphasis upon the reduction in government expenditure, whilst at the same time requiring significant fiscal support for defence. It was, therefore, hardly surprising that the defence budget remained a constant target for her monetarist Treasury team, much to the dismay of her defence team and their supporters on the Conservative Backbench Committee on Defence.

Furthermore, this 'policy *theory*', with its' reduction in public expenditure matched to less regulation and greater entrepeneurship linked into the policies of privatisation of state industries, reducing civil service numbers, management reforms to the civil service, changes in industrial policy and trade union reform. Through all this the MoD 'as both the largest Department in central government and the biggest employer of Civil Service manpower ... was in the forefront of such studies and pressures'[5] and openly became one of the main focuses for the internal conflicts of the Conservative Party.

Mrs Thatcher appointed Francis Pym as her Defence Secretary. It meant a demotion from his Shadow Cabinet position of Shadow Foreign Secretary and a clear attempt by Margaret Thatcher to pass the 'poisoned chalice' of defence to one of her main political rivals within the party. However, it also meant that defence would not be subject to the monetarist zeal faced by other departments since Pym did not share her belief in imposing strict cash controls upon government spending and thought that such a policy was particularly inappropriate in the MoD. Instead he chose to let

---

[2] 'Thatcher warning on Soviet Strength', *The Daily Telegraph*, 20 January 1976.
[3] Quoted by A.Raphael, 'Nott fights regard action in Whitehall whispering war', *The Observer*, 20 June 1982.
[4] Italics in original. A.G.Jordan & J.J.Richardson, *British politics and the policy process: an arena approach*, Allen & Unwin, 1987, pp.105-6.
[5] Sir E.Broadbent, *The Military & Government: from Macmillan to Heseltine*, Macmillan for RUSI, 1988, pp.59-60.

the Service Chiefs take the principal decisions on policy and procurement within his overall guidelines. Thus his first 12 months in office were marked by a revival in defence spending matched by an economic downturn in the country. As a result, his period in office marked a watershed within the Conservative Party as the realisation grew that the pursuit of monetarist policies and increasing defence spending was at best problematic, and at worst incompatible during a recession. This culminated in the division of the Cabinet during the November 1980 public expenditure review, with the monetarist Treasury calling for far greater defence reductions than Pym was prepared to accept. The Treasury climbed down, and Pym was replaced six weeks later.

Pym's successor, John Nott, moved from the Department of Trade and represented Margaret Thatcher's only attempt at putting one of her close circle in a position to try and exert control over this difficult ministry. According to Geoffrey Howe, the then Chancellor of the Exchequer, '[b]oth Margaret and I saw Nott as a trustie, who could be relied upon to get on top of the brass-hats'.[6] They both felt that he would be able to achieve the twin goals of improving the capabilities of Britain's armed forces whilst at the same time making the reductions in the defence budget which they believed were essential if the strains on public expenditure were to be alleviated.

Nevertheless, Nott fundamentally differed from Margaret Thatcher in two important areas of defence policy. First, 'I was a sceptic about the nuclear programme. I had been the only member of the Cabinet who, to the surprise and horror of the Prime Minister, had protested when it was announced to the whole Cabinet that we were going to replace Polaris with Trident I.'[7] The second area of divergence was more problematic since it covered the essential question of where the focus of defence policy should be. In Nott's eyes Britain was a medium-sized power which needed to avoid costly defence commitments, and instead, concentrate upon improving her economic and trading performance. Defence first needed to focus on the home base, and second, on support for the North Atlantic Treaty Organisation [NATO]. Margaret Thatcher, in contrast, still wanted to retain at least a token world presence and to maintain the ability to provide active military support to the United States. She was, therefore, far more inclined towards the Conservative 'east of Suez' tradition rather than the 'New Right' ideas proposed by Nott which involved consolidating Britain's defence efforts.

Nevertheless, Margaret Thatcher backed John Nott in his imposition of the strict monetarist controls on defence spending which she felt were necessary on the MoD if the government was to bring the defence budget into line. Like Nott, and his successor Michael Heseltine, she shared the 'New Right's' view that Britain's defences could be improved without a significant increase in defence spending by far greater managerial efficiency and the targetting of defence spending on the frontline. This led to what John Nott 'elliptically called the defence review programme – less than a full-scale policy review, more than a mere adjustment to the programme'.[8] The final product, *The*

---

[6] G.Howe, *Conflict of Loyalty*, Macmillan, 1990, p.198.

[7] Interview with Sir John Nott. D.Boren, *Britain's 1981 defence review*, PhD thesis, Department of War Studies, King's College, University of London, 1992, p.240.

[8] F.Cooper, 'Ministry of Defence', in J.Gretton & A.Harrison (eds), *Reshaping Central*

United Kingdom Defence Programme: the Way Forward,[9] caused considerable controversy, both within the Conservative Party and in the wider inter-Party arena, and resulted in the sacking of Keith Speed, the junior minister responsible for the navy, prior to its publication. Its conclusions had a considerable impact upon British defence policy and reflected the more managerial functional approach of Nott and the 'New Right' towards defence. Its main conclusion was that there was a need to re-distribute the restricted funds within the defence budget away from NATO's maritime commitment to towards NATO's continental commitment. It thus represented a move away from the traditional Conservative priorities *vis-à-vis* NATO towards the more functional based approach more in tune with the New Right's agenda. The result was a major reduction in the surface fleet, the closure of two out of five Royal Dockyards and a further dockyard suffering a severe curtailment in its operations. These reductions were not without cost to Conservative Party unity, but apart from a few constituency MPs who were particularly adversely affected they were agreed to, only to be toned down following the Falklands War one year later. Of more long-term significance was Nott's moves towards the centralisation of the MoD's decision-making process within as part of the 'New Right's' emphasis upon management reform within Whitehall.

In her search for a successor to John Nott, Margaret Thatcher had two principal requirements. First, the successor needed to be a far more effective communicator than John Nott in order to combat the success that the unilateralist message of CND was having with the general public. Second, John Nott's successor required the ability to carry on implementing a much more business like approach within the MoD than it had hitherto seen. In both these areas she felt that Michael Heseltine would be able to exert his strengths.[10] In particular, she like his management style and had previously arranged for him to present a seminar on his ideas on management systems to his Cabinet colleagues whilst he was at Environment. This 'she saw as an object lesson to those of us who appeared to be interested only in policy'.[11] Like her, he shared the belief that the MoD did not require greater resources. Instead, it could generate the necessary funds for defence improvements through greater efficiency within the MoD.

Nevertheless, her relationship with Michael Heseltine remained distant and his appointment to the post promised to remove a thorn in her side on domestic issues as he concentrated his attentions on defence issues. In his tenure as Environment Secretary Heseltine had, in Margaret Thatcher's eyes, been far more concerned with being 'Minister for Merseyside' than with local authority finance and finding an alternative to the rating system, and had, therefore, been somewhat at odds with government policy.[12] At defence he would be held responsible for the nation's defences and the priorities therein, particularly by the important Conservative Backbench

---

Government, Policy Journals, 1987, p.112.

[9] Cm.8288, HMSO, 1981.

[10] M.Thatcher, *The Downing Street Years*, Harper Collins, 1993, p.424.

[11] N.Lawson, *The View from No.11: memoirs of a Tory radical*, Bantam Press, 1992, p.673.

[12] M.Thatcher, *op cit*, p.424.

Committee on Defence, and this had the potential to significantly reduce his popularity within the Conservative Party if his management reforms failed and he was forced to undertake cutbacks in the armed forces. Thus, through his appointment she had managed to pass the 'poison chalice' of defence to the minister who was most likely to mount a challenge to her leadership.

Although he did not want to go to defence, or expect to remain there for any length of time, Michael Heseltine had little choice but to accept the promotion. He viewed the appointment merely as a stepping stone in his quest to become Prime Minister and made that clear to his immediate advisers within the MoD. He had no previous interest or experience in foreign or security issues, but as a committed European, and with a deep interest in trade and industry, he found three areas in which he could immerse himself. 'Firstly, he was extremely interested and very effective in some of the political issues that the programme represented. Secondly, he was extremely interested in the organisation of the MoD ... The third area in which he became extremely interested in ... was the industrial area, and in particular, the position of British industry and British industrial interests *vis-à-vis* the United States in one area and the Europeans in the other'.[13]

The first area offered him a means of highlighting his communications skills and enabled him to bring his name regularly before party members and the wider electorate as he sought to combat the CND message of unilateralism. The second area allowed him to consolidate his reputation as an administrator and organisational ideas man with the introduction of the Management Information System for Ministers into the MoD. This he followed by the re-organisation of the department itself with the objective of creating a combined defence staff and thus finishing the centralisation of the defence process initiated by Healey but given a new life by Nott.

However, it was in the third area of industrial policy that the intra-Party divisions over defence were most marked. Besides becoming Prime Minister Michael Heseltine's other goal was to become the Secretary of State for Trade and Industry 'and organise what he saw as a Japanese-style industrial policy'.[14] The MoD's close links with industry and the number of nationalised companies involved in the defence field offered him in effect this opportunity. Furthermore, the lure of this apple was enhanced by the fact that Britain had a history of defence collaboration with Europe, forced upon it by economic circumstances, which fitted neatly into Heseltine's pro-European agenda.[15] As a result, whilst Margaret Thatcher emphasised his role in campaigning against unilateralism and management reform, Michael Heseltine also became rapidly aware of his chance to pursue the type of industrial policy that he had long sought but which would inevitably bring him into conflict with the Prime Minister from whose views he fundamentally differed.

For the Conservatives the privatisation process represented one of their major policy flagships during Margaret Thatcher's second term in office.

---

[13] Interview with Sir John Blelloch.
[14] N.Lawson, *op cit*, pp.673-4.
[15] T.Taylor & K.Hayward, *The UK defence industrial base: development and future policy options*, Brassey's for RUSI, 1989, p.19.

The large number of privatisations included a number of defence firms. Here Michael Heseltine and Margaret Thatcher were in agreement that Britain's defence industry needed to be privatised. Such a process required these industries to be able to show significant medium-term order books or at least the prospects of significant orders and here Michael Heseltine was happy to provide MoD top-up orders to achieve this.

Tensions, however, arose within Cabinet over how best to implement the policy of increased competition. To Margaret Thatcher and her supporters the best method was to let market forces have as free a reign as possible with competition for MoD orders being open to domestic suppliers and those from allied states. Michael Heseltine, in contrast, felt that such a policy was inherently dangerous in that the sheer costs of tendering for major weapons systems encouraged industry to amalgamate and eventually lead to monopoly suppliers. Furthermore, he believed that in certain areas Europe's fragmented defence industry would not be able to compete with its American counterparts in the short term who had the large United States market to help reduce their unit costs. Instead Heseltine argued for a more interventionalist policy which sought to protect the defence industrial base on a primarily West European basis. 'His instinct was to emphasise the European dimension because I think he felt that it was only in a European context that British industry could ever operate as a remotely equal partner and, therefore, to fight for their own interests on any sort of business part of the economy.'[16] Heseltine 'had a great vision of Europe for the procurement side and so anything that wasn't a European project was very suspect and tended to be delayed and procrastinated upon because what he wanted was for everything to be built on a European scale.'[17] Consequently, Heseltine took advantage of Cabinet system which gave individual ministers a substantial degree of autonomy to pursue his own goals. In this his pro-European standpoint became particularly noticeable because his period in office coincided with a number of procurement decisions that inevitably had to be examined in a European context as well as the resurgence in a pro-European agenda in other West European countries. Moreover, the Westland crisis, which so heavily interlinked with this subject, resulted in his resignation.

His successor, George Younger, was a loyal stalwart of the Prime Minister yet still remained largely outside the monetarist camp. His seniority and lack of pretentions towards the post of Prime Minister, together with his experience in cabinet and as Shadow Defence Secretary allowed him to partially move defence outside of the intra-party debate. In this he was assisted by the support of Geoffrey Howe and the relative proximity of the next general election. He was thus able to achieve the additional financial support for the ministry that had been denied to Heseltine and take defence beyond the 1987 election outside of the intra-party debate. Post 1987 the reduced importance of defence was clear and became most apparent with the appointment of Tom King as Younger's successor in 1988 to take responsibility for the defence review that became 'Options for Change'.

---

[16] Interview with Sir John Blelloch.
[17] Interview with Field Marshal Lord Bramall.

Defence and inter-party rivalry

The postwar political consensus on defence policy had already begun to fracture from the early-70s onwards, reflecting the effect of the left wing in the Labour Party, and the 'New Right' within the Conservative Party, pulling their parties in opposite directions. Within the Labour Party defence had always been a sensitive issue and as the era of *détente* began to be replaced by that of the Second Cold War, the issue of defence became increasingly fraught within the party as internal support for unilateralism grew. This resurgence culminated in the election of Michael Foot, a noted unilateralist, as leader of the Labour Party ahead of the multilateralist Denis Healey, and the level of support for Tony Benn in the deputy-leaderhip contest.

This schism significantly contributed to the creation of the Social Democratic Party (SDP) which rapidly gained the allegiance of the majority of Labour's experienced defence speakers. Those from the multilateralist right-wing who remained found themselves marginalized as the Shadow defence porfolio was temporarily passing to Tribunite control. The result was a severe weakening of Labour's frontbench defence team. 'The lack of experience of Labour defence spokesmen, certainly post-83, was an extraordinary thing, even some on the Labour side like Bruce George could not understand how these choices had been made for defence spokesmen because they were people who nothing about the subject at all and it showed desperately in the defence debates.'[18]

These divisions within the Labour Party allowed the Conservatives to conclude that this was an area which they could exploit to their own benefit. However, it was not until they witnessed the effect of 'Falklands factor' in restoring their own domestic popularity that they really appreciated the importance that defence could play. Thus the Conservatives sought to make defence the tool by which the general public evaluated the reliability of the different political parties, a phenomenon which the Conservatives used to their full advantage in both the 1983 and 1987 general elections. According to John Cartwright 'they saw it as a crucial issue because it skewered both the opposition parties with one shot. It got Labour who were notoriously unreliable on defence and then you had this funny alliance thing which didn't know what it wanted to be. And I think they used defence not just for itself but for what I used to call the litmus test of the trustworthiness of a political party.'[19] Thus in the 1987 election the Conservatives immediately sought to question the trustworthiness of their opponents and were quick to exploit the slip Neil Kinnock made during an interview by David Frost and the divisions over nuclear weapons within the SDP/Liberal Alliance.

In pursuit of these goals the Conservatives throughout the mid- to late-1980s were acutely aware that they had to avoid making any decisions on defence issues which the other parties could exploit. Thus, whilst the Conservatives ensured that the defence debates invariably focused on the nuclear question where they felt Labour were vulnerable and where they could ridicule SDP suggestions about alternatives to Trident, they sought to maintain that Britain's conventional forces were not adversely affected by the

---

[18] Interview with John Cartwright.
[19] Interview with John Cartwright.

Trident decision.

They therefore avoided a number of decisions on defence programmes that were in trouble until they were forced by circumstance to do so. Thus the mid-1980s witnessed the saga of the failure of the Nimrod AEW aircraft which lasted from 1981-1986 and was only finally cancelled after George Younger replaced Michael Heseltine at the MoD. Problems with the Foxhunter radar led to the initial deployment of Tornado fighter aircraft with concrete ballast in their noses and the Royal Air Force suggesting the use of an alternative United States radar. The collaborative AS-90 howitzer was fundamentally flawed from its initial conception in 1979 but survived until 1987 despite the protestations of the army.

Instead the Conservatives placed emphasis on maintaining frontline numbers and continuing to search for remedies to allow these projects to be completed. The result was the steady rundown in the fighting capacity of the frontline units as the shortage of manpower and lack of the necessary spares worsened. The result was a frontline of units increasingly unable to sustain themselves in combat and which were ever more dependent on untrained Army reserves to make up their numbers in wartime. However, this situation did allow the Conservatives to project themselves as the only party which could adequately provide for the nation's security.

Conclusion

It is clear that defence had an impact far beyond mere electioneering and and was, in fact, one of the central battlegrounds within the Conservative Party between the two wings of the party. As a result, far more emphasis was given by the various factions of the Conservative Party to the management of defence and the procurement decisions within the MoD and far less to a consideration of matching threat assessment with procurement decisions, military doctrine and force deployments. Moreover, the defence post was frequently used by Margaret Thatcher as a means of side-lining her most vociferous opponents within the Cabinet and preventing them organising opposition within the party to her.

On the inter-party front defence proved to be a major electoral card which the Conservatives were able to use to their advantage in both 1983 and 1987. Their success in making defence a litmus test by which the various parties were judged by the public had an adverse effect upon the armed forces themselves as the Conservatives sought to avoid making defence decisions which might be construed as them weakening Britain's conventional forces. Thus, arguments over defence in many ways reflected the intra-party and inter-party debates that existed and help to explain not only the electoral success that the Conservatives had but the evolution of defence policy during the 1980s.

Defence and British Politics in the 1980s

Lucy James
Birmingham

'Defence and British Politics in the 1980s:
The Greenham Alternative'

Introduction

The most prolonged, radical and profound domestic challenge to Britain's nuclear defence policy in the 1980s was posed by the women-only peace camp at Greenham Common. While the Labour party tore itself apart over unilateralism, and the Campaign for Nuclear Disarmament (CND) staged predictable, regular rallies with little effect, the camp at Greenham volubly and visibly opposed the deployment of Cruise in Britain, using an imaginative range of methods from obstruction and civil disobedience to symbolic protests and more conventional political debate. In doing so, the women at the camp not only challenged a particular defence policy, but the gendered construction of the state itself and its dominant power relations. In this paper we will look at the thematic substance of the Greenham protest, in terms of how the camp linked its women-only status with its peace activism and how Greenham developed into a broader challenge not only to the state itself, but also to how defence policy was constructed – Greenham made connections beyond the narrow confines of nuclear strategy to its impact on issues of domestic expenditure, North-South exploitation and, most significantly from a feminist perspective, the personal, subjective realm.

Women's protest groups: an explanation.

In her definitive account of the history of the feminist peace movement in Britain, Jill Liddington identifies several distinct, fairly constant strands of thought which link women with anti-militarism, each gaining a particular predominance at different times. In the early stirrings of the movement, from the 1820s, women extolled the virtues of peace and the vices of war in their capacity as mothers. These maternalist ideas were developed by later writers, such as Olive Schreiner, who argued that as mothers 'pay the first cost of all human life, so they are necessarily instinctively anti-war'. This strand was in evidence at Greenham as well, with women feeling compelled to protest out of a sense of duty to their children.[1]

A second conceptual strand connecting women with peace is identified by Liddington as equal rights feminism, which argues that an end to women's exclusion from the central mechanisms and processes of political power would bring about peace.[2] This thinking was particularly popular during the pre-WWI suffrage campaign, and was later developed by Virginia Woolf, who felt that war would continue for as long as the men in power

---

[1] J.Liddington, *The Long Road to Greenham: Feminism and Anti-Militarism in Britain since 1820*, Virago, 1989, p.6.
[2] *Ibid*, p.7.

excluded 'women's socially constructed traditional values of the private life' from national and international decision-making.[3] Whereas the maternalist strand of thought was essentially emotive, appealing to women as carers and nurturers, and to their fears for their children, this equal-rights approach had a more intellectual appeal, calling on women to become involved as citizens, to work within the existing system, in order to effect change by making the men in power 'see sense'. These two traditions of feminist anti-militarist thought at times conflicted: equal-rights feminists saw maternalist campaigners as reinforcing negative feminine stereotypes of over-emotional nurturers; the more intellectual approach was criticised for lacking force and compromising with a male encoded system and values.

Yet while maternalist arguments appeal to the heart, and equal-rights arguments appeal to the head, the third strand of feminist anti-militarist thought could be said to have gut appeal: this is radical feminism, which stresses essential gender difference and inherent male violence. An early advocate of this analysis was the American, Charlotte Perkins Gilman at the turn of the century;[4] however, this approach had little impact on the more mainstream women's movement until its more radical phase from the 1970s onwards, especially in the writings of Andrea Dworkin (who, in *Pornography*, states that 'violence is male, and the male is the penis') and Robin Morgan (who, in *Going Too Far*, blames men as a whole for 'the evils of sexism, racism, hunger, war and eco-disaster').[5]

While there has been some degree of continuity in terms of themes and institutions in the women's peace movement, these features tend to be cyclical and recurring rather than constant – while small numbers of women kept plugging away at peace issues, women *en masse* tended to get involved for limited periods of time (whether weeks, months or years) before shifting their focus onto other, more immediate issues.[6] To a large extent, this pattern followed national and international events and the fortunes of the peace movement as a whole. Thus, the extent of support for the Greenham peace camp can be seen as reflecting broader opposition to the NATO decision to deploy ground-launched Cruise missiles and Pershing IIs in Europe in 1979 (CND membership grew from 3,000 in Britain in the 1970s to 50,000 in the early 1980s); yet the nature of Greenham, and the form it took, are rooted in the development of the Women's Liberation Movement (WLM) as well. In the early 1970s, there was renewed political activity around women-specific issues – demands for equal educational and job opportunities as well as equal pay, access to free contraception, abortion and childcare – which was largely the result of widespread low-level, grass-roots changes, especially with the spread of Consciousness-Raising (CR) groups using new methods of working (for example, rejecting formal, hierarchical political structures).[7]

At this time, the women's movement seemed to have little time or con-

---

[3] S.Oldfield, *Women Against the Iron Fist – Alternatives to Militarism 1900-1989*, Blackwell, 1989, p.3.
[4] J.Liddington, *op cit*, p.8.
[5] Quoted in Oldfield, *op cit*, p.214.
[6] J.Liddington, *op cit*, p.9.
[7] *Ibid*, p.198.

cern for issues of peace or nuclear weapons, and the Liaison Committee of Women's Peace Groups (the umbrella grouping that held together small, local women's peace groups and guilds) was criticised for its traditional emphasis on maternalist arguments for peace, as these appeared to perpetuate the female stereotype as peaceful and nurturing, and the idea of separate male and female spheres, which the WLM sought to deconstruct.[8] However, while the WLM was focusing on women's personal experiences of domestic and sexual violence, the more radical elements of the peace movement began to recognise the importance of this personal sphere in understanding broader, global issues of violence and war. War Resisters' International began to explore the relevance of feminism to peace issues and, in July 1976, a workshop was held at Les Circauds in France, attracting small groups of women from across Europe to discuss concepts of maternalism in relation to crimes against women, lesbianism and patriarchal religion, with a new emphasis on nonviolent feminism and change based on gender differences.[9] Over the next few years these ideas spread, and developed, to a wider circle of CR and peace groups.

Meanwhile, the anti-nuclear campaign was growing throughout Europe and the United States, boosted by the NATO decision to deploy Cruise and Pershing missiles in Europe. While there remained some feminist opposition to widening the movement's agenda to embrace peace issues, other feminists argued that feminism could not be contained solely in traditional, 'women's issues', and that its analysis extended to the whole of society, to develop an understanding of violence on all levels. They also advocated that women should in fact act more assertively as peace-makers, to overcome the conciliatory/nurturing stereotype. At the same time, traditional maternalist arguments continued to appeal, as many women felt compelled to act because of their traditional roles as mothers and carers, and out of fear for their children; they organised separately to feel comfortable and accepted as mothers, with others who recognised familial ties and constraints on their time.[10]

In Britain, one of the first women-only anti-nuclear networks to demonstrate was Women Against the Nuclear Threat (WONT). WONT was established as a response to the sexism some women encountered within CND. Initially, it sought not to be an alternative group *per se*, but a support group within CND, with different basic ways of organising (for example, allowing each person to speak in turn, listening properly to each other, sharing skills and so on). It also offered space for women to voice their feelings, and who might feel inhibited in a mixed group, lacking men's technical and political knowledge, and hence confidence, to speak and argue.[11] Women often formed these groups seeking empathy in terms of making sense of the nuclear threat: in a Leeds feminist peace group, 'quite a lot of us [were] women with children ... we saw it as an exchange of feelings ... just to say how we all felt. Which was mainly that we all felt scared stiff'.[12] Many women

---

[8] *Ibid*, p.100.
[9] *Ibid*, p.206.
[10] *Ibid*, p.4.
[11] M.Broderick & L.Davison, *Peace News*, 17/4/1981, p.8.
[12] J.Liddington, *op cit*, p.216.

in mixed groups felt used, as they were providing all the servicing, and promoting the group's dynamic in a supportive rather than proactive role. WONT aimed to have an integral approach, so that the issue of nuclear weapons could not be separated out from wider issues of power and male control, and the intellectual response was inextricably intertwined with the emotional.

The origins of Greenham

The most memorable grouping of women peace activists in Britain was at Greenham Common air base. When it was announced that Greenham would be the main proposed site for Cruise missiles from December 1983, Anne Pettit organised a 120-mile march from Cardiff to Newbury; she had heard of a similar march, from Scandinavia to Paris, organised and led by women, and shared its aim to inspire 'women not necessarily in the women's movement, but who were worried, anxious and isolated like myself'.[13] From the very outset, the protest sought to legitimise an emotive response to the nuclear threat, thereby continuing the more instinctive approach, of articulating fear and concern, that had characterised the maternalist strand of the women's peace movement: 'fear is the starting point and, given the dreadful potential of nuclear weapons, it is absolutely reasonable to be afraid'.[14] There were three main justifications for the march being women-led: firstly, to show the prominence and significance of women in the peace movement; secondly, to emphasise the maternalist argument that women often feel a special responsibility for children, and for caring for future generations; and thirdly, the equal-rights argument, protesting against the exclusion of the majority of women from the decision-making process under which social services are cut (hitting women hardest) while resources are spent on potentially devastating nuclear weapons.[15]

Thus, on 27 August 1981, forty women and four men formed the 'Women For Life on Earth' protest march to Newbury, where they arrived on September 6, asking for a televised, public debate on the issue. As this was ignored, four women chained themselves to the fence – echoing suffragette action – to form a 'permanent peace picket', to generate wider publicity.[16] This particular protest caused disagreement within the group of marchers, as some felt it was too militant, and potentially illegal; so, to reach a resolution, everyone in the group took turns in speaking and presenting their view, without interruptions – a style of decision making which was to be used throughout the life of the Greenham camp – until a consensus was reached, and the action went ahead.[17] While some demonstrators returned home, others stayed on, and were gradually joined by more; many women would come for the odd day, or weekend, and some committed themselves to living there full-time.

---

[13] B.Harford & S.Hopkins (eds), *Greenham Common: Women at the Wire*, The Women's Press, 1985, p.9.
[14] A.Cook & B.Kirk, *Greenham Women Everywhere*, Pluto, 1983, p.11.
[15] J.Liddington, *op cit*, p.227.
[16] L.Jones in D.Russell (ed), *Exposing Nuclear Phallacies*, Pergamon, 1989, p.198.
[17] J.Liddington, *op cit*, p.231.

Methods of operation

Non-violent action and civil disobedience were central to Greenham: the women reasoned that as decisions to do with the deployment of Cruise all too often sidestepped Parliamentary and any meaningful public debate, then less traditional, more hands-on and immediate forms of protest and obstruction were appropriate, to express anger non-aggressively, grab public attention, impede the instalment of the weapons and 'directly confront the assumption of military ideology' by opposing and resisting the weapons and the system that created them.[18] Greenham's goals extended beyond creating publicity: some of the women's actions were designed to prevent the base from running effectively, for example with blockades, by removing sections of the fence, occupying an air traffic control tower, and taking documents.[19] Obstructive methods continued throughout the camp's existence – according to a report in Peace News in 1986, almost every Cruise convoy was being stopped by Greenham women or Cruisewatch. Overall, this received little publicity, apart from the odd case; and yet these actions cumulatively cost the Ministries of Defence and Transport, as well as Thames Valley Police, millions of extra pounds expenditure in prevention and reparation, and each High Court order against the women cost £3,000. The government chose not to use its full powers of prosecution, fearing adverse publicity and 'Greenham martyrs'.[20] Yet while there was an aim to obstruct the base's operations, at the core of Greenham was a sense of protest – it was never an attempt to seize power *per se* but, rather, it offered an alternative to the established, hierarchical, demarcated socio-political structure.[21] The demonstrations aimed, essentially, to be lighthearted, and were never part of a planned campaign, or organised response, being more concerned with presenting and living a different lifestyle and set of values.

At the first Embrace the Base action on December 12, 1982, 30,000 women from across Europe encircled the Greenham airbase. This influx of women was fuelled by chain letters, by the strong networks built by the WLM in the 1970s, and by more specific women's peace networks, such as Women's International League for Peace and Freedom, the Co-operative Guilds, WONT and so on. At a grass-roots, largely unnoticed level, the number of women peace activists was growing significantly in the early 1980s, via a loosely structured, flexible, ad hoc means of organisation: there was no one, central body that had absolute authority – instead, small, autonomous, local-level groups were forming links with each other, in a web-like rather than pyramidal power structure.[22]

Some actions were conducted off the base; all were direct and nonviolent, and sought to make contact and connect with people as humans, with feelings, rather than to provoke point-scoring arguments and anger; in this way, they moved beyond the established, active-speaker/passive-audience

---

[18] F.Bradshaw & T.Thornhill, 'Non-violence and Greenham Common – Connections and Contradictions', *Spare Rib*,, 8, 1983, p.62.

[19] L.Jones, *New Statesman*, 30/11/1984, p.8.

[20] J.Liddington, *op cit*, pp.267-268.

[21] J.Marsh, *New Society*, 69, 1984.

[22] J.Liddington, *Sanity*, 8, 1986, p.30.

framework of formal demonstrations, and beyond the narrow issues of security, peace and war, to place the arguments in a broader, systemic context, taking on board the more immediate, low-level and universal issues. These actions also spread the message of Greenham: a central theme of the camp was 'carry Greenham home' – women were encouraged to tell others of their time there, to raise awareness of the nuclear issue and the women's protest. The media also played a role in carrying the message – by covering Greenham's more imaginative and outrageous actions, so the concepts behind the camp, of non-violent, feminist, humorous and persistent opposition to Cruise directly confronted women through their televisions, newspapers and radio, having a radicalising effect.[23]

The concept of security offered by the state was also challenged, when Greenham women were charged for 'breaching the peace'. Many claimed that they were in fact seeking to keep the peace, and refused to plead guilty or pay fines, and so were sent to prison. Often, the women called up expert witnesses to argue for the illegality and immorality of Cruise deployment, giving evidence of the effect of radiation and uranium contamination, thereby using the trials to put across their own arguments.[24] The women used surreal, imaginative methods – humming from the dock, weaving webs of wool, insisting on swearing on the Goddess, and challenging the meaning of the words 'keeping the peace' – to question the authority of the state, and protesting against the perceived hypocrisy of a legal system that allows the deployment of nuclear weapons in rural England, while attempting to outlaw the nonviolent women's camp beside them.[25]

The demonstrations that took place were non-violent and often strongly symbolic: these were qualitatively different from the protests of the traditional Left, oppositional politics, which tend to share certain values, methods and vocabulary with the state; instead, the women were able to define and construct politics and arguments in their own terms, and gained strength and confidence from that.[26] The camp's gates were painted different colours, and were used to represent different issues, such as the food mountains, a nuclear-free pacific and so on, making links. At demonstrations, children's clothes and photos were pinned to the fence, and certain images were often particularly prevalent, such as the web (that the collection of intertwined strands creates strength) and the snake (that it can shed its skin and survive).[27]

'Security' arguments

The camp at Greenham was protesting against more than nuclear weapons alone: the women made links with wider struggles, to do with changing the nature of the society that produced Cruise, 'exposing and ending the economic exploitation on which the arms race depends,' stressing the fundamental links between male violence against women, and the violence of the

---

[23] J.Liddington, *op cit*, p.252.
[24] B.Harford & S.Hopkins (eds), *op cit*, pp.104-105.
[25] J.Liddington, *op cit*, p.238.
[26] *New Statesman*, 17/12/1982, p.3.
[27] C.Blackwood, *On the Perimeter*, Flamingo, 1984, p.21.

arms race that produced nuclear weapons.[28] They also sought to highlight the links between men's dominance over and exploitation of women, and the North's exploitation of the South – that both are based on structural, systemic, hierarchical forms of oppression and violent exploitation, seeking power and profit.[29] As the camp continued, these broader links became increasingly important, with the earlier, mass symbolic action that focused solely on Cruise being replaced by women talking of integrating their political activities into their everyday lives, uniting the personal and political. Thus, the purpose of the camp at Greenham shifted outwards, encouraging many women to take up some of the related issues it raised, and organising links with other campaigns. Moreover, as more Greenham women faced antagonism from the police and the authorities in general, so they were able to identify more strongly with other harassed, oppressed groups, and their endangered civil liberties.[30] The camp challenged established concepts of gender identity, transgressing the public-private divide by showcasing the subjective and presenting the personal cost of nuclear policy in assertive, unconventional ways.[31] Thus, Greenham provided an access point into an awareness of a certain way of thinking and working, a consciousness of women's issues and interlinked systems of oppression, of which Cruise was only a part.[32]

These arguments linking nuclear weapons with a broader, gendered power dynamic were reinforced by incidents of rape at Molesworth, a mixed peace camp – five rapes occurred between September 1985 and July 1986; the women involved felt the rest of the peace movement tried to hush up the incidents. For many women peace activists, the Molesworth rapes made strikingly clear the need for the movement to embrace a broad understanding of violence, as male violence against women structurally undermined any progress towards peace; and that only by bringing the issue of male violence into the open could it be possible 'to unwind the spiral of violence'.[33] Just as the peace movement constitutes part of society, and cannot exist in a vacuum, so it needs to acknowledge undercurrents of violence running through society as a whole, and work from within to bring about fundamental changes. In this way, rape and nuclear weapons are both essentially acts of violence and serve similar functions, to instil fear and assert power.[34] And only by giving the concept of peace a gendered dimension, taking account of this level of personal violence within the broader structure of power, can it become meaningful. In this way, it is more fully formed than a concept that is restricted to narrow, abstract concepts of nation-states and strategic, high politics, ignoring the nature of the structure beneath them.

---

[28] B.Norden, 'Voices of the Non-Aligned', *Spare Rib*, 9/1987, p.45.

[29] J.Green, 'Women: Making the Links', *Peace News*, 16/11/1984, p.10.

[30] J.Freer, *Raging Women – In Reply to Breaching the Peace: a Comment on the WLM and the Common Womyn's Peace Camp at Greenham*, Carole Harwood file CN (iv)), Feminist Archives.

[31] S.Roseneil, *Disarming Patriarchy: Feminism and Political Action at Greenham*, Open University Press, 1995.

[32] B.Harford, 'Greenham: Four Years Later', *Peace News*, 4/10/1985, p.8.

[33] J.Cliff, 'But what's it got to do with peace?', *Sanity*, 3, 1987, p.15.

[34] L.Peirson, 'Mixed Feelings', *Peace News*, 22/8/1986, p.10.

Evaluation/aftermath

The success of the camp in terms of affecting national defence policy cannot really be assessed outside the context of international events, such as Gorbachev's reforms in the Soviet Union and so on. Yet despite Greenham's bad-tempered dissolution, the camp's initial aim was realised with the signing of the INF Treaty in 1987: under this, NATO agreed to scrap Cruise and Pershing in exchange for the Soviet Union getting rid of SS-20s and other, shorter-range missiles in Europe and Asia, as well as introducing strict verification procedures, Soviet withdrawal from Afghanistan and a large unilateral reduction in Soviet conventional troops.[35] Yet the camp itself continued, as a womanspace 'set up on the edge of a military madness ... women came here to challenge the British state and stayed to challenge powerlessness, the heterosexual nuclear family, and the myth of compulsorily mixed action'.[36] In addition, many Greenham women have continued their peace activism elsewhere, using the skills they learnt at Greenham: as well as the obstruction of missile convoy journeys, some women have joined (mixed) peace camps at Faslane (a nuclear base) and Porton Down (a chemical weapons research centre); and at Menwith Hill (a United States intelligence centre) there is a women-only camp, employing similar methods, philosophy and outlook to Greenham. The connections that women made at Greenham, linking the nuclear issue with other concerns, such as the West's food mountains, nuclear power, a nuclear Pacific and so on, meant that many carried on using non-violent direct action in other fields.[37]

In this way, by combining maternalist motivational arguments, such as a sense of heartfelt duty to act against the possibility of nuclear war, with intellectual arguments about the irrationality of such destructive warfare, and the need for more women to be heard, to 'take the toys from the boys', Greenham made connections between different feminist approaches, centred on the issue of nuclear weapons. And yet the protest had more than one focus: just as the different strands of feminist thought were connected, so too were different levels of security and peace – the women's anger at the very existence and cost of nuclear weapons led them to see how the issue related to cutbacks in domestic state expenditure, the international arms trade, the potential environmental threat posed by nuclear waste, and the underlying, hierarchical power structure that controlled the weapons, and which was reflected in other power relations, from the North-South divide to male-female relations. The women made these connections clear through the imagination and persistence of their protest, challenging established political conventions and divides, extending a feminist consciousness to empower individuals and to address new issues. The protest itself gave depth and meaning to the concepts of peace and security, broadening the agenda from the individual to the state and the international.

---

[35] J.Liddington, *op cit*, p.284.
[36] C.Harwood, *Peace News Supplement*, 4/8/1989.
[37] J.Liddington, *op cit*, p.277.

British Politics and Defence in the 1980s

Roger Wicks
University of Birmingham

'The Case for the Defence: The Labour Party, Political Ideas
and Nuclear Disarmament in the 1980s'

Introduction

The changes in the Labour Party's defence policy in the 1980s were crucial to wider developments in British politics. They had particular electoral significance in the 1983 and 1987 general elections, and the defence issue is often cited as a key factor, if not the most important factor, determining their outcome. Defence policy was also of critical importance to the changes that occurred in the Labour Party on the inter-connecting levels of policy and political ideas. This is the predominant issue on which the paper will focus. The move away from unilateralism during the latter years of the decade – though there was also movement on this front in the years between the two elections – represents a dramatic policy reversal and, more importantly, the most significant change in a wider context of political transformation

The Historical Context

An understanding of the divisions and debate over the Labour Party's defence policy in the 1980s necessitates an historical conceptualisation of the different strands in Labour and, more broadly, British socialist history. A wide distinction can be drawn between an orthodox approach to foreign policy, which largely accepts the dominant principles of western defence and foreign policy, leading to what appeared to be a post-1945 consensus; and a radical critique which seeks the opposite: to overturn these very doctrines, which are seen as combining capitalist and nationalistic precepts, in favour of a socialist internationalism. The former orthodox approach is largely held by the right-wing of the Labour Party and has been represented in office by the actions of Labour administrations, as Stuart Croft has reminded us:

> '... it was the Labour Government of Clement Attlee and Ernest Bevin who took the decision to produce an atomic bomb in January 1947 ... Later, it was the Wilson Governments which carried through the decision to purchase the Polaris system and ... the Callaghan Government had taken the decision to pursue the deployment of INF systems – the Ground Launched Cruise Missile in Britain – in order, as it was seen, to strengthen NATO against a developing Soviet challenge.'[1]

A revealing questions asks: who was against this consensus? The radical strand of political ideas, however, which opposes this orthodoxy is marked by less cogency. On the one hand, there is a significant, if politically

---
[1] S.Croft, 'The Labour Party and the nuclear issue', in M.Smith & J.Spear (eds), The Changing Labour Party, Routledge, 1992, pp.201-202.

marginal, pacifist strand which has its roots in certain Christian denominations such as the Quakers and evolved into the Peace Pledge Union.[2] There is also a radical analysis which is strikingly non-pacifist and has its roots in opposition to fascism and Nazism in the 1930s. An analysis of different generations of socialists is revealing here as there appear to be certain formative eras which influence peoples' outlooks. This does not imply a generational homogeneity, as many went off in altogether different directions; rather, that there is a relationship between decisive world events and the predominant political ideas of the era. Hence, pacifism attained a powerful resonance in the Labour Party following the First World War, symbolised by the leadership of the Labour Party by the pacifist George Lansbury. Conversely, the 1930s provoked a divergent analysis, particularly in debate focusing on the position that the European left should take during the Spanish Civil War which began in 1936. It is the socialists who argued that their countries should support the democratic Republican Government against Franco's fascists, some of whom fought and died in Spain as volunteers, which gave birth to a highly significant school of thought. The great significance of this event as a defining moment in any study of political ideas on foreign policy and political history should not be under-played.[3]

This was only one part though of a broader opposition to the policy of appeasement which British and other governments in Europe were pursuing against the fascist dictatorships of Italy and Germany. The classicus locus of this argument was the work *Guilty Men* (1940),[4] one of the most powerful polemics of the century, of which Michael Foot was one of the authors, which blamed the senior Conservatives of the day for the outbreak of war due to the policy of appeasing fascists. For this group also, fascism completely destroyed the pacifist argument of opposing war in any circumstances. It is this anti-fascist, non-pacifist strand that has proved to be the most important opposing thesis to the orthodoxy Labour tended to pursue in office. This analysis could unite with pacifism against much of the Cold War era, from the Keep Left group of Labour Members of Parliament, which criticised the pro-Americanism of the post-war Labour governments, to the campaign against the Vietnam War, to the opposition to nuclear escalation. However, the division between those opposed to war and militarism and those who could countenance the use of military force against aggression, provides the ideological explanation for Labour's support, under the peace campaigner Michael Foot, for the Conservative Government's Falklands campaign in 1982.

---

[2] S.Morrison, *I Renounce War: the Story of the Peace Pledge Union*, Sheppard Press, 1962.
[3] It is completely ignored, for example, by Edward Johnson's study of the influence of ideology on policy, 'Foreign and Defence Policy', in L.Tivey & A.Wright, *Party Ideology in Britain*, Routledge, 1989, pp.165-171.
[4] Cato, *Guilty Men*, Victor Gollancz, 1940.

Michael Foot's recent advocation of western military intervention in support of Bosnia, and the ideal it represented of a pluralist, multi-ethnic society, in the face of the genocidal actions of the Bosnian Serbs is the most recent example and certainly no less important.[5] It is a matter of interest that this has been a minority position in the Labour Party with the Party leadership adopting their historical orthodoxy in foreign affairs and generally adopting the Government's position of caution and the compromise option of humanitarian aid.[6] The war in Bosnia was thus highly indicative of the strands in Labour's political thinking on foreign affairs. The campaigns against US involvement in central America and Vietnam – a key formative experience – imbued an ethos opposed to military intervention and in support of the sanctity of national borders in much of the left, which made any talk of intervention in 'another Spain', as Foot and others saw it, deeply unpopular. For Foot, however, the West had been again engaged in an episode of appeasement against fascist aggression, and the reason for the left's opposition to the Vietnam War had been a concern for human rights and antipathy for unwarranted US aggression, rather than the co-option of pacifism. Labour's interventionists of the 1990s have also had to tackle some of their colleagues' tendency to apologise for the Serbs as 'good socialists' acting to hold together Tito's Yugoslavia.[7]

Biting the Bullet

The Labour Party's adoption, therefore, of a policy of unilateral nuclear disarmament in the early 1980s, coupled with a decision to remove all American military basis from British soil, had crucial historical and political relevance. On the party political level, it stood out in its divergence from the Conservative Government's policy of nuclear defence, indeed expansion of nuclear weaponry, and commitment to the principle of nuclear deterrence. This is significant historically because the British Constitution, although largely unwritten, holds a convention whereby the official Opposition party in the House of Commons is seen as duty bound to support the broad parameters of the government of the day's foreign and defence policy.[8]

The so-called 'post-war consensus', notwithstanding the ambiguous and contentious nature of this term, is usually understood as a socio-economic conception which states the broad responsibilities and roles of the state.[9] But equally there was a consensus shared between Labour and the Con-

---

[5] Michael Foot & Jill Cragie's film, *Two Hours From London*, 1994, is a brilliant and powerful illustration of this position.

[6] It is important to note, however, that Labour MPs who did call for rigorous military intervention came from all wings of the Party; see for example a letter to *The Guardian* signed by seventeen MPs on 17/4/93, and the recent establishment of Labour Friends for Bosnia which received support from seventy Labour MPs.

[7] This writer is also one who has observed with incredulity much of the left's knee-jerk anti-Americanism when President Bill Clinton appeared to be showing resolve in his hostility to ethnic cleansing.

[8] There are of course important exceptions, such as Labour's opposition during the Suez crisis.

[9] D.Kavanagh & P.Morris' concise *Consensus Politics*, Basil Blackwell, 1989, forms a useful introduction to the subject. The critique of the notion of consensus can be found in R.Barker's *Political Ideas in Modern Britain*, Methuen, 1978.

servatives on foreign affairs. This supported the confines of Cold War, East-West polarisation and accepted: the position of the Soviet Union as the main threat; the legitimacy of nuclear deterrence; the North Atlantic Treaty Organisation (NATO); and the relationship this inferred between Britain and the United States (US). Such a paradigm was held by the main political parties and, seemingly, by the majority of public opinion. This was the consensus that was ended not just with the Labour Party conference's support for unilateralism, but due to the general ethos of the Labour left that had risen to predominance in the Party following the frustrations and tribulations of the last Labour Government.[10] There was an altogether different understanding of East-West relations; a move away from the viewpoint, as it was portrayed, which cast the US and its allies as the only possible saviour of all mankind from the 'evil empire', as President Ronald Reagan called the Soviet Union.[11]

The argument that Thatcherism, with its refusal to maintain full employment and intended dismantling of the welfare state, constituted the end of consensus politics, is well documented. But in foreign affairs, the consensus that does appear to have existed between the two major parties was broken, and broken not by Margaret Thatcher's Conservatives, but by the Labour Party. It is true of course that Labour's annual conference had before voted for a unilateralist defence policy, as it had notoriously in 1960 provoking Hugh Gaitskell's 'fight, fight, fight', speech. The critical difference this time was that unilateralism became official party policy and Labour was now under the leadership of the life-long supporter of unilateralism, Michael Foot.

On the other hand, however, there was proposed continuity in Labour's plans, for perhaps remarkably, as Mike Gapes, who was a member of the Labour Party's policy directorate, has written, Labour remained committed to membership of NATO: 'No Labour Party Conference even in the most strongly anti-nuclear years of the 1960s or the 1980s had ever got anywhere near voting for Labour to adopt a policy of British withdrawal from NATO'.[12] The reason is largely historical: it was a Labour government, the first ever majority Labour government of 1945-1950, that first took Britain into NATO. Moreover, the historical antecedent of the following consensus in foreign policy was in many ways the war-time coalition government.

How tenable was it for Labour to now argue that in government they would unilaterally rid the country of its nuclear weaponry while at the same time remaining within NATO? As Dan Keohane has stated, in his informed book on the Labour Party's post-war defence policy, 'Labour's principal defence statement of the 1980s, *Defence and Security for Britain* (1984)' rested upon these two 'potentially incompatible assumptions'.[13] For Keohane: 'the early ejection of United States nuclear arms from the United

---

[10] For an informed account of the rise of the left see D.Kogan & M.Kogan, *The Battle for the Labour Party*, Fontana, 1982.

[11] This position had always been criticised by sections of the left of the Labour Party, starting from the 1940s with the Keep Left group and the analysis of Aneurin Bevan; see M.Foot, *Aneurin Bevan: 1945-1960*, Volume 2, Paladin, 1975.

[12] M.Gapes, 'The Evolution of Labour's Defence and Security Policy', in G.Burt (ed), *Alternative Defence Policy*, Croom Helm, 1988, p.87.

[13] D.Keohane, *Labour Party Defence Policy since 1945*, Leicester University Press, p.126.

Kingdom threatened to sunder a vital alliance relationship and therefore was unsustainable'.[14] On the other hand, an alternative analysis paints a different picture: this points out that most of NATO's member countries were of course non-nuclear, and half have never permitted US nuclear weapons into their countries. Furthermore, some, such as France, Spain and Canada, have actually ordered out the bases. Indeed, as Gapes has pointed out, 'the typical NATO member country is not a nuclear weapon state and it has either no nuclear weapons at all, or far fewer than it used to accept'.[15]

Why then did Labour gradually remove its commitment to unilateralism? Two hypotheses are conventionally offered. The first is essentially electoral: it states that Labour's about-turn was purely concerned with the notion that Labour was 'weak' on defence due to the perception that Labour in government would 'leave the county defenceless'. The second hypothesis attempts to make the considered argument that the change in policy was based on a genuine reappraisal of the changing world. The advent of Gorbachev's leadership of the Soviet Union and then the end of the Cold War itself necessitated a revision of policy.

The 1980s were disastrous years for the Labour Party. A dramatic political upheaval had occurred: the Party had been seriously challenged as one of Britain's main two political parties, and in 1987 Labour suffered its third successive general election defeat. The thinking in the Party which marked the 'soft left' and then the Kinnock leadership can be understood in terms of both these hypotheses: election victory and rethink. Both are equally significant. After three successive defeats, victory was regarded as crucial, and for this reason key policy changes were seen as necessary. Simultaneously however, a genuine reappraisal was regarded as essential in light of wider social, economic and international changes. The reasoning appeared to be that only if the 'changing world' was accepted could values be confidently and realistically re-affirmed.

Perhaps the key point about Labour's approach to the 1992 General Election was the thinking that the Party realised it had to enter the modern world. For critics this meant that Labour abandons its principles and accepts the Thatcher agenda; to advocates of this 'new thinking' it entailed applying Labour's values to a changed and changing world. Moreover, it was argued that to react in a way believing that the social, economic and international environment remains unchanged, reveals a naivety and arrogance of self- opinion. Hence, Roy Hattersley's main theme in 'Choose Freedom' was that socialist values were equality and liberty, and not unilateralism and nationalisation, which was one of the 'means' of an era gone by, not an 'end'.[16] It would be foolish, however, to hold this intellectual analysis aloft and dismiss the electoral factor. The point to make is a fundamental one: the two imperatives, rethink and victory, are inter-connected. The question 'which came first, the reappraisal or the desire for victory?', is neither viable nor helpful. Although the electoral factor provoked the new thinking, the latter has broader foundations – historical and ideological.

---

[14] *Ibid*, p.130.
[15] M.Gapes, *op cit*, p.87.
[16] R.Hattersley, *Choose Freedom*, Penguin, 1987.

Unilateralism had been a Cold War construct: a strategy devised to break the seemingly apocalyptic eye-balling of nuclear escalation. Bertrand Russell, one of the most important of the early unilateralists, and founding member of the Committee of 100 which practised civil disobedience in opposition to nuclear weaponry, himself made this point:

> 'The CND had been working for unilateral disarmament, believing that if Great Britain gave up her part in the nuclear arms race and even demanded the departure of United States bases from her soil, other nations might follow suit.'[17]

Following the 1987 General Election, it became clear to the leadership of the Party that for both electoral reasons and for the sake of genuine policy reappraisal in the light of epoch-making developments in the Soviet Union, unilateralism was no longer tenable and could no longer serve its purpose. As Colin Hughes & Patrick Wintour wrote in their sympathetic and informed work tracing Labour's Policy Review period: 'Both the electoral imperative, and the possibilities for disarmament in the nineties, required change'.[18] Neil Kinnock's move away from unilateralism was based on a genuine reappraisal of the changed and changing world. It may also have been influenced by the realisation that in office, relinquishing nuclear weapons unilaterally may have less impact than was previously thought. At the crucial two day meeting of Labour's National Executive Committee (NEC) on 8th and 9th May 1989, which approved Labour's Policy Review, Kinnock described the difficulties that emerge when ideas are turned into policies which then have to be pursued through international negotiations: 'Many in this room have protested and marched in support of nuclear disarmament. I have done something else: I have gone to the White House, the Kremlin, the Elysee, and argued the line for unilateral nuclear disarmament'; he continued:

> 'I knew they would disagree with the policy. But above that, they were totally uncomprehending that we should want to get rid of nuclear missile systems without getting elimination of nuclear weapons on other sides too ... I argued for the policy because of the integrity of the objective of eliminating nuclear weapons. But I am not going to make that tactical argument for that unilateral abandonment of nuclear weapons without getting anything in return. I will not do it. The majority of the party and the majority of the country don't expect me to do so.'[19]

The argument that the goal of nuclear disarmament can be more fruitfully pursued in a different way is not the same as the abandonment of the ambition of a nuclear-free world. Some commentators completely fail to attempt to make any appreciation of this approach. Richard Hefferman & Mike Marqusee's conspiratorial analysis of this episode, for example, is based on an

---
[17] B.Russell, *The Autobiography of Bertrand Russell*, Volume 111, George Allen & Unwin, 1969, p.104.
[18] C.Hughes & P.Wintour, *Labour Rebuilt: The New Model Party*, Fourth Estate, 1990, p.107.
[19] *Ibid.*

essential confusion between means and ends.[20] Unilateralism is portrayed as synonymous with the goal of nuclear disarmament: 'from the outset one of the primary purposes of the Policy Review was to engineer a change from "unilateralism" to "multilateralism" – that is, from a determination to end British participation in the nuclear arms race to a willingness to retain and even threaten to use the country's nuclear capacity'.[21] If the desired end was a nuclear-free world then this analysis is based on a misconception of the purpose of non-unilateral strategies such as multilateralism. There is no discussion of the potential that came to exist for disarmament on a greater scale than merely Britain's nuclear capability; and was it not the case that unilateral disarmament could be reversed by change of government whereas international agreements hold the prospect of greater durability?

There was though a split among Labour's non-unilateralists, which includes the group who had revised their thinking. There were those who had always been pro-nuclear, who were earlier described as advocates of Labour's orthodox approach to foreign affairs. On the other hand, the revisionists of the 1980s genuinely believed in the principle of a non-nuclear global future. Stuart Croft has made the point that Labour remains ambivalent regarding the concept of deterrence and is committed to negotiating Trident away, and concludes that 'the goal of a non-nuclear world therefore remains'.[22] It is also slightly unclear whether or nor Labour would pursue bilateral negotiations if wider talks failed.[23]

The international context had changed completely. Unilateralism had lost its original purpose for Kinnock: what impact would the unilateral dismantling of one north-west European country's nuclear capacity now have? It would represent nothing but parochialism: just as the phenomenon of 'nuclear-free zones' established by numerous Labour councils symbolised the powerlessness of the British left in the 1980s, perhaps unilateralism would leave the United Kingdom in a similar position on the world stage. Kinnock's Labour Party increasingly believed that tremendous scope existed for disarmament in the Gorbachev age if only the west could be persuaded to take advantage of the opportunity. The internal political problem this caused for Labour was that this was a strategic, or political approach which is ethically neutral – at best – and conflicts with the antipathy towards nuclear weapons that was held by many in the Party and in the leadership itself. This is the medicine that Kinnock himself swallowed before passing the bottle for the Party to do the same.

---

[20] R.Hefferman & M.Marqusee, *Defeat from the Jaws of Victory*, Verso, 1992.
[21] *Ibid*, p.245.
[22] S.Croft, *op cit*, p.212.
[23] C.Hughes & P.Wintour, *op cit*, pp.120-121.

Local Government and the Environment in the 1990s

Stephen Ward
University of Salford

'United Kingdom Local Government and Environmental Agenda Change'

Why Study Local Environmental Agendas

The widespread development of local authority corporate environmental policies over the last few years could be seen as indicative of the growing importance of environmental issues within the local government arena. The new policies appear to represent attempts to create a more coherent and holistic environmental agenda at the local level. This paper examines not only the significance of local corporate environmental policies, but also the applicability of agenda building concepts and issue emergence theories to the study of local environmental agendas.

Given the increasing focus on international and national environmental problems and policies, it is not unreasonable to ask, why concentrate a study of environmental agendas in the 1990s at the local government level?

Firstly, although there has been a number of studies related to environmental agenda building much of the literature has been concentrated at the national level of politics, and many of the major studies have been based on American examples.[1] Thus many of the agenda models and concepts have not been applied to the local arena in the United Kingdom.

Secondly, there appear to be some contradictory developments in the local environmental arena. Traditionally United Kingdom environmental policy has had strong devolved elements, with local government having considerable statutory responsibilities in the fields of planning and environmental health. Since the 1970s though, the context within which local government operates has clearly undergone considerable change. Studies have suggested a considerable weakening of local government environmental responsibility, by central government reforms and the impact of European integration.[2] Moreover, the traditional role of local authority as service provider has been extensively challenged by notions of enabling. Yet in the environmental field, many local authorities have been remarkably active and pioneering, despite the apparently difficult climate created by central government.

Thirdly, the development of local authority environmental plans allows us to compare local agenda building to international and national governmental arenas who were engaged in similar process of developing broad policy responses.

---

[1] See, for example, M.Crenson, *The Unpolitics of Air Pollution*, John Hopkins, 1972; A.Downs, 'Up and Down with Ecology: The Issue Attention Cycle', *Public Interest*, 28, 1972; W.Solesbury, 'The Environmental Agenda', *Public Administration, 54/2 1976*.

[2] N.Haigh, 'Devolved Responsibility and Centralisation: The Effects of EEC Environmental Policy', *Public Administration*, 64/2, 1986.

Agenda Theory and Concepts: A Brief Summary

There is a diversity of agenda building models and limited space does not permit a full discussion of the variety of approaches here.[3] However, it is possible to identify some main areas of concern and concepts which provide a framework for examining the development and change in agendas. In the main, the study of agendas has been dominated by the question of how issues emerge onto governmental agendas or why others remain dormant and fail to make it onto agendas. In the case of the latter, an issue can remain latent unconsciously because it is not recognised, through lack of either knowledge or understanding. Or it may consciously be kept off the agenda by decision makers deciding not to decide (non decision making).

Issue emergence is generally linked with two concepts: attention and legitimacy. Attention refers to the task of problem recognition brought about by triggering events such as disasters and accidents; the promotional activities of pressure groups, policy entrepreneurs and the media; issue visibility; issue particularity, that is whether it affects sizeable or prominent sections of society.

Whilst issues may attract attention, this does not guarantee that they will necessarily be taken on board by policy makers. The issues need to be seen as legitimate areas of concern. Legitimacy depends largely on the value systems of those taking decisions and the power and status of those seeking to force issues onto an agenda.

Two other areas of concern have arisen in agenda building theories, the importance of issue action and the concept of issue fade. In many policy process models, policy action is separated from ideas of agenda building. Once action is being taken, the issue is regarded as clearly on the agenda. In practice though, it is difficult to analyse agendas without looking at policy actions as these can determine future agenda outcomes.

Issue fade looks at the notion of issue disappearance from an agenda. This has generally attracted less interest than emergence. However, issues can attain attention and legitimacy but still fall from the political agenda. The common causes of issue fade include: policy solutions, removing issues from agendas through successful action; the excessive costs and resources of potential action; the breakdown of consensus about the definition of a problem leading to divergent voices and the stalling of action; the overcrowding of governmental agendas; and finally boredom and possible loss of interest in an issue once it is no longer new.

Much of the remainder of this paper looks at the applicability of these concepts as a framework for understanding change within local government environmental agendas.

---

[3] The main ones referred to here include Solesbury, *op cit*; Downs, *op cit*: J.Kingdon, *Agendas, Alternatives and Public Policy*, Little Brown, 1984; R.W.Cobb et al, 'Agenda Building as a Comparative Political Process', *American Political Science Review*, 70/1, 1976; F.L.Cook & W.G.Skogan, 'Agenda Setting and the Fall and Rise of Policy Issues', *Environment and Planning C*, 8/3, 1990; J.Stringer & J.J.Richardson, 'Managing the Political Agenda: Problem Definition and Policy Making in Britain', *Parliamentary Affairs*, 23/1, 1980; B.W.Hogwood, *From Crisis to Complacency: Shaping Public Policy in Britain*, Oxford University Press, 1987.

Local Authority Corporate Environmental Policies

Environmental or green plans are corporate co-ordinating documents which publicise the responses and objectives of councils with regard to a wide range of environmental issues. Such policies have encompassed environmental charters, action plans, audits and latterly Local Agenda 21 strategies. These documents act as:

- awareness raisers both internally within the council and externally in the locality.

- coordinators of individual policy elements to try and avoid overlap and policy contradictions across departmental boundaries.

- signposts for future action and guides for future policy routes and direction.

- information centres, providing benchmark information about the environment from which standards can be set, future targets outlined and evaluated.[4]

The growth of these corporate environmental policies has been swift and extensive. Before 1989 fewer than 5% of authorities in Britain possessed any form of corporate environment policy. By 1993 some 80% of authorities had drawn up such a document or were in the process of doing so. This spanned both different tiers of authority and political complexion, although upper tier urban, Liberal Democrat and Labour councils were generally the most active.[5]

From Pre-problem to Issue Emergence? Or Issue Emergence to Agenda Emergence?

Theories of agenda setting have often concentrated on the movement of issues from a pre-problem phase to one of issue emergence involving the need to gain attention and legitimacy. The first difficulty for agenda theory and local environmental studies is the problem of being able to define a pre-problem period for environmental issues. As environmental plans indicate, some environmental issues have a long history on local agendas, but have fluctuated in importance. This suggests that environmental issues have not necessarily moved on and off agendas but have moved up and down.

Much depends on the definition of the term 'environment'. In most local authorities before the late 1980s it would be difficult to identify a coherent environmental policy in the shape of a single department, document or committee agenda. It was not that many problems were not recognised,

---

[4] S.J.Ward, 'Thinking Global, Acting Local? British Local Authorities and their Environmental Plans', *Environmental Politics*, 2/3, 1993.
[5] J.Raemaekers et al, 'An Index of Local Authority Green Plans', Department of Planning and Housing, Heriot Watt University, 1991; J.Raemaekers, 'Corporate Environmental Management in Local Government: A Review of Action Programmes, Internal Audits and State of the Environment Reports', *Planning, Practice and Research*, 8/3, 1993.

but rather that they were fragmented and considered of low political status. What characterised the traditional environmental health or planning agendas was a failure to make connections between individual issue agendas. The arrival of environmental plans represented, in some authorities, an attempt to create an environmental agenda of previously disparate issues, rather than single issue emergence.

Identification of a pre-problem phase is not easy with a broad term such as the environment, which consists of bundles of issues. Pre-problem phases are easier to identify in cases of single narrowly defined problems which have few linkages to existing agendas.

This still leaves questions as to why authorities decided to create an environmental policy agenda and build corporate policies in the period of the late 1980s. Significant change occurred in some local authorities, where a fundamental redefinition of problems, along with clustering or coalescing of previously separate issues began to form a broad agenda. Essentially this involved making connections on two fronts, issue connections and geographic connections. In the case of the latter this meant adapting the global environmental issues into a local framework to give these issues a legitimacy and relevance to local authority concerns. Issue connection meant that previously disparate issues had to be made part of a common nexus. Moreover, if they could be linked to some fundamental cause such as the environment then each of the specific issues comes to be symptomatic of a broader problem. The increasing emphasis on global problems provided part of the fundamental cause, and thus links between global and local problems also helped to link the issues together locally. Issue salience is therefore partly associated with the task of making connections, particularly if there is a need to persuade policy makers of the requirement to make a major policy initiative.

Establishing a complex nexus of issues does not necessarily enhance the capacity for action. Whilst the profile and salience of the issues may be raised, institutions may feel their capacity for action is overwhelmed by the enormity of the newly connected agenda. This can lead to token placebo policy responses, which is undoubtedly what some corporate environmental policies were designed for.

Triggers and Issue Climate

The process of making these connections is interwoven with the key agenda setting concepts of attention and legitimation. Agenda setting theories have placed considerable emphasis on the role of triggering events and the media in raising attention and framing debates. In local environmental plans, specific triggers are difficult to locate. Undoubtedly there was a ripe issue climate created by increased media attention and national and international governmental activity in the environmental sector in the late 1980s. Much of this ripe issue climate however was centred around national and international environmental problems.

Two events, however, did prove to be something of a catalyst: the Green vote in the 1989 European elections[6] and the production of Friends of the Earth's (FoE) Environmental Charter for Local Government,[7] both sparked a significant increase in interest in environmental plan production.

The importance of the Greens' vote was that it provided political parties and institutions with an immediate political focus. The potency of the Greens' performance had an arguably greater impact at the local level. This is partly because of the increased frequency of local elections, which added to the electoral immediacy. One of the initial reasons for the uptake of environmental plans was that, by claiming the environmental high ground, there were potential votes to be won at local elections.

If the Greens provided the political push, then FoE's Environmental Charter provided the policy push. The document produced a practical concrete policy option at a time when little existing material was available within the local arena.

Legitimacy: Arguments about Definitions

The danger of focusing too heavily on short term factors, like ripe issue climates and triggering events, is that of identifying only symptoms and not the underlying causes of agenda change. Issue legitimacy is correctly regarded as the key to serious agenda consideration, but this is difficult to assess in terms of models or case studies. Many of the processes behind legitimacy involve long term change. Legitimacy and the local government environmental agenda have been bound up in two interrelated definitional debates, one concerning the meaning and definitional boundaries of environment policy, the other concerned with a debate about the role of authorities given the long term shift in their position and powers and their relations with central government.

In the emergence of local environmental policies two competing visions of environmental agendas tended to emerge. Environmental activists within local authorities have defined the environment as a broad agenda, seeing environmental considerations as a prerequisite to all the authorities' activities. They were concerned to make the issues and geographic connections described above, and were keen to promote community ownership and partnership of environmental initiatives. The majority view, however, tended to see a limited agenda where environment was essentially an add on, to be traded against primary economic concerns. This limited agenda based environmental policies on traditional statutory functions and concentrated on local impacts.

The definitional debate has significant effects on environment's agenda position. Overt opposition to the development of environmental policies has been minimal, partly because politicians wanted to appear environmentally concerned, but also because of confusion over what corporate environmental agendas might entail. This meant that some policy actors could define environment in a way which involved little challenge to their fundamental

---

[6]The Greens achieved 14.8% share of the poll, the highest ever achieved by a Green Party in major election.

[7]Friends of the Earth, 1989.

values or institutional culture. The uncertainty over what an environmental policy agenda concerns, allowed some authorities to pay little more than lip service to a vague concept of a green strategy.

Along with the definitional debate about the boundaries of environment policy, there has been an interconnected argument about the role of local government. This debate about a general philosophy and role of an institution has an impact on the way in which the institution organises itself and the sorts of issue it addresses. In the case of local authorities, agendas have been changed, not only by central government reforms, but also by the way in which proactive authorities and the local authority national associations have responded and used the environmental agenda as part of a wider attempt to redefine the role of local authorities. Much of the environmental agenda set out in environmental plan documents is non statutory. Whilst this can mean that environmental plans are not prioritised in the tight financial climate, equally however, authorities are not rigidly tied to statutory functions, allowing them to create a new issue space and work creatively and experimentally.[8]

The changing nature of local government has brought further changes in the mode of policy consultation. A process of mutual legitimacy has arisen through environmental plans, whereby many local authorities are looking to environmental groups to legitimise their policies and give them public credibility. Authorities often seek Friends of the Earth seal of approval on their policies as a means of confirming their sincerity to their local electorate. This points to a decline in the ability of local authorities to control the processes of legitimacy, which now have to be shared with non governmental organisations. This is a reflection in part of the fragmentation of policy making at the local level. Local authorities are no longer the prime controller of policy in a locality.[9] This erosion of the legitimising function of local authorities reflects a wider trend in society concerning environmental policy, namely a long term loss of trust in politicians, civil servants, scientists and authority figures. In contrast environmental pressure groups have gained more credibility and trust with the public over the last decade.[10]

Issue Actions: Corporate Policies as Agenda Setters

Some agenda theory models separate issue action from processes of agenda setting. One of the interesting features of many local authority environmental plan documents is the way in which the policies themselves have been intended to create frameworks for long term agendas and contribute to raising awareness. This adds further weight to the argument that policies should be seen not as the end of the policy process, but merely as one part of a process of agenda change or maintenance over a longer period. Environmental audits are often designed to collect information from which

---

[8] L.Mills, 'Economic development, the environment and Europe: areas of innovation in United Kingdom local government', *Local Government Policy Making*, 20/5, 1994.

[9] Association of Metropolitan Authorities, *Action for the Future: Priorities for the Environment*, AMA, 1989.

[10] S.Yearley, 'Social Movements and Environmental Change', in M.Redclift & T.Benton (eds), *Social Theory and The Global Environment*, Routledge, 1994.

policy priorities can be set.[11] Many environmental policy documents have introduced specific targets and goals, and this is important in routinising some issues onto agendas. Standard setting, for example acts as an important tool in allowing local groups, as well as the local authority, to measure, define and challenge targets and problems on a regular basis.

Issue Fade or Priorities and Differential Progress

Environmental issues have generated less public attention at the local level in the past two or three years. They have not, however, moved off local authority agendas altogether. In some cases they have moved from a high profile political platform to a more routinised agenda management style. Progress has undoubtedly slowed as authorities have tried to set priorities and implement initiatives. Individual environmental issues have made differential progress within the environmental plan framework.[12]

The overall position of environmental policies on local agendas was undoubtedly weakened after 1991, by a combination of recession, lack of available resources, and an erosion of enthusiasm caused by the realisation of an inability to implement policy preferences. The recession helped to submerge environmental concerns beneath the need to try and protect employment and business interests within localities. Despite rhetoric to the contrary, and acknowledgement of the importance of environmental problems, environmental concerns have not been absorbed into the primary economic arena in many authorities.[13] One of the tasks of the current Local Agenda 21 process begun in 1992/3 has been to legitimise fully the connections between environment and economic development agendas.

For some agenda models there are difficulties in understanding what happens to issues when they are acted upon and if they are not removed from the agenda. Issue attention cycles appear to indicate that issues move into a mysterious limbo until the attention cycle starts again.[14] The danger is that because issues begin to lose public attention, it is assumed they have fallen from the agenda. In fact institutions may not necessarily have removed an issue from the agenda but may be in a process of institutionalising or prioritising issues, or simply shifting responsibility in an institution, away from the limelight. Indeed, as environmental plan packages as a whole received less attention, this masked the differential progress of individual environmental issues. Within their environmental plan agendas, authorities have prioritised issues on the basis of familiarity or knowledge, costs and resources, statutory responsibilities, issue popularity and visibility. Thus many authorities concentrated initially on promoting and reforming issues where they had already had programmes prior to the environmental plan policies, notably nature conservation, energy efficiency and recycling poli-

---

[11] See for example Oxfordshire County Council, *An Environmental Audit for Oxfordshire*, 1991.
[12] S.J.Ward, *The Politics of Environmental Agendas: The Case of United Kingdom Local Government*, Unpublished PhD, University of the West of England, 1994.
[13] D.Gibbs, 'Greening the Local Economy', *Local Economy*, 6/3, 1992.
[14] B.W.Hogwood, *Is there an Issue Attention Cycle in Britain?*, Strathclyde Papers in Government and Politics, 89, 1992.

cies. Partly this reflected the placebo elements of some of the documents but it also represented an attempt to buy time to tackle more difficult problems by producing high profile 'successes' which could maintain the momentum of the environmental plan as a whole.

Agenda Management: Changing Environmental Networks

If environmental issues have not disappeared from local agendas then this suggests a process of institutionalisation. One useful concept of examining such a process is agenda management and control through policy networks. The traditional authority, operating autonomous departmental and committee systems to manage issue agendas, would seem to provide fertile ground for deploying a policy community approach, although in the area of local environmental policy it has rarely been examined. The increasing tendency towards the creation of apparently new environmental networks, particularly in the form of institutionalised environmental policy forums, provides an ideal opportunity to analyse key questions about the way policy networks form, change and break down.[15]

Traditionally it has been difficult to identify an environmental policy network at the local authority level since environmental policy was often fragmented throughout authority structures. However, much environmental policy was centred around the Planning and Environmental Health Departments, and studies have implied relatively tight policy communities around planning and wildlife/countryside management issues.[16] The emergence of corporate environmental plan documents has begun to see shifts in these network patterns. Overall, the pattern of networks has become more complex, with at least two levels of environmental policy network operating.

Policy communities still operate, but they have been supplemented by new, looser networks dealing with transport, recycling, energy efficiency policy. Overarching these is a broader issue environmental network, sometimes institutionalised in the form of an environmental forum which acts as a cross sectoral, co-ordinating and consultative network.

Initially, existing policy communities proved unable to deal with the breadth and the weight of issues and the corporate nature of working which environmental plan emergence brought. Local authorities required not only groups who were expert in a particular specialist part of environmental policy, but also policy actors who could tie together environmental issues. This point diverges from some group-government relations literature which stresses that groups gain their recognition from creating a highly specific issue niche.[17] This is evidently important in many policy debates, but where major policy initiatives span a number of areas, government officials seek out groups with the necessary breadth of knowledge. FoE, for example, gained a niche in the environmental plan process not only through their specific

---

[15] D.Marsh & R.A.W.Rhodes, *Policy Networks in British Government*, Oxford University Press, 1992.

[16] P.Lowe & J.Goyder, *Environmental Groups in Politics*, Allen & Unwin, 1983.

[17] See A.G.Jordan et al, 'Insiders, Outsiders and Political Access', British Interest Group Project Working Paper 3, University of Aberdeen, 1992.

knowledge of certain policy areas, but also from their ability to provide a broad holistic framework for policy makers.[18] This suggests that where issues cluster together, or policy actors seek to make connections to issues previously regarded as outside the domain of the existing policy community, such networks can quickly come under strain.

A number of studies have indicated that environmental groups previously regarded as outsiders have gained access through the environmental plan process.[19] This access has often been negotiated through key individuals, who are both environmental group activists and also councillors or local government officials. Through such key individuals local authorities have become more aware of environmentalist agendas and environmental groups more familiar with local government capabilities and deficiencies.

The new networks in the local environmental arena also reflect an interesting new phenomenon. Following the fragmentation of legitimacy and the lack of resources and knowledge, local authorities are becoming increasingly reliant on the voluntary sector. Their co-operation is essential for policy making and for assisting with the implementation of policies which authorities can no longer implement on their own. Practical implementation networks are therefore being created to manage policies previously under the sole control of local authorities.[20]

Two interesting implications for policy network and agenda management theory can be drawn from the local environmental policy framework. In network literature, policy networks and especially policy communities are often viewed as a force for agenda inertia.[21] However, new networks in the local environmental field are paradoxically seen as both radicalising agents and policy protectors, in that they incorporate new groups, increase participation, incorporate new information and act to keep awareness high. Yet the new networks are also about routinising a new generation of relations between groups and local authorities and protecting policies set out in environmental policy documents. Whether this dual purpose can be sustained over time is doubtful. The danger is that environmental groups newly incorporated into networks move from generating ideas to defending pre-existing policy agendas of which they are now part.

The second problem concerns the compatibility of policy communities and holistic environmental solutions. Policy communities are based around heavily sectorised and closed policy making, thus potentially undermining the corporate function of environmental plan policies. Already many environmental forums have broken into sub-forums concentrating on specific environmental issue areas. Consequently holistic environmental policy making will depend on how successful the overarching issue networks institutionalised in environmental forums and corporate environmental policy committees are in co-ordinating and influencing policy.

---

[18] S.J.Ward, 1993, *op cit*.
[19] See, for example, T.P.Atkinson, *Planning Environmental Policy: A Case Study of an Emerging Policy Community in Kent*, Unpublished M.Phil Thesis, University College London, 1992.
[20] G.Stoker & S.Young, *Cities in the 1990s*, Longman, 1993.
[21] Marsh & Rhodes, *op cit*.

Interrelated Agendas: Autonomy or Integration?

Whilst much can be gained from analysing environmental issue emergence at the micro level, to gain a full understanding of local agendas they need to be placed in a wider context, given that environmental agendas are extensively interrelated at local, national and supranational levels. The interdependency of governmental tiers would appear to be an increasingly important factor as authorities attempt to devise local solutions to global problems. As the impact of the international agenda dealing with cross national issues increases it raises important questions about the extent of local agenda autonomy and the impact of and role of authorities in the increasingly globalised arena.

The interrelated nature of institutional agendas can be seen at three levels:

Firstly, in the importance of inter authority learning between local authorities themselves. There is in the local authority world a potential to create a domino effect through agenda transference between authorities. The importance of inter- authority learning means that a momentum of change can be built up. Authorities in the environmental field were, and indeed are, heavily dependent on policy exchange and best practice guides. Inter authority learning is therefore important in two senses: pioneering authorities have the potential to set the boundaries of debate and policy alternatives, but such example setting also acts as peer pressure on authorities to take up issues and contribute to debates.[22]

A second consideration for local agenda theory should be the connections between national and local environmental agendas. Environmental policy has historically been considered as low politics, with local government allowed considerable licence to manage its own environmental policies. Given that much has been written about the erosion of the powers of local authorities over the last two decades,[23] it is initially surprising to find the appearance of a considerable degree of autonomy in environmental agenda setting. Local authorities have placed reliance on their own world, rather than taking any direct lead from the centre in designing their own environmental plans. The attitude of pro-active councils and the local associations has been to view environmental policy as an arena where opportunities exist for local authorities to stake a claim. This was partly a response to lacking a lead from the centre but also because the Thatcher government had eroded local autonomy in other issue areas. Apart from attempts to liberalise the planning system in the early 1980s the environmental field remained relatively un-Thatcherised until much later in the decade, allowing authorities a certain degree of latitude within which to operate.

The third area of institutional agenda relations is the link between the international and the local. The impact of supra national organisations on local environmental agendas has become increasingly apparent, most notably through the advent of the UNCED Agenda 21 programme and also from EC legislation and initiatives. Although the original wave of corporate

---

[22] Ward, 1993, *op cit*.

[23] See, for example, J.A.Chandler, 'Local Autonomy and a Local-National Policy Community: Do they Exist?', PSA Conference Paper, Leicester University, 1992.

policy documents in the late 1980s was not stimulated by these bodies, the requirement to produce Local Agenda 21 plans has given the environmental plan movement a renewed stimulus. In the face of a perceived lack of enthusiasm from national government for environmental action, authorities have tended to see supra-national bodies as allies, having similar environmental aspirations.[24] Consequently, EC programmes such as 'Towards Sustainability' are regarded as methods of legitimising and supporting their own local environmental activities. As a result any study of local authorities' environmental agendas can no longer be restricted to central-local relations but also needs to encompass intergovernmental relations.

Corporate Environmental Policies: The Significance and Development of Local Agendas

Reflecting on the development of environmental plans and environmental policy agendas in local authorities and analysing their significance produces mixed messages. Environmental plans have helped some authorities to think systematically about the environment for the first time, creating an environmental policy agenda. They also produced a greater awareness of environmental issues, a greater range of issues were brought onto environmental agendas and tentative steps were made towards corporate working. Furthermore environmental plans have left a legacy of new organisational structures and new personnel which will act to defend and institutionalise environmental policy agendas.

On the deficit side, however, there is a danger of viewing the progress of local authorities through the activities of a small band of pioneering authorities who claim attention through their unique approaches. In a significant number of authorities, documents have been written, and authority structures reformed, but the impression is of lip service, with environmentalism as a bolt on extra. As Gordon has argued 'the best authorities have shown what can be done within existing constraints. The gap between them and the worst is enormous. Many councils are hardly aware that environment is an issue.'[25]

Studying Local Environmental Agendas: The Problem of the Four S's

Evidence from the local environmental arena supports Hogwood's contention that much agenda setting is more accurately concerned with policy succession and problem redefinition, than with the access of purely new issues to governmental agendas.[26] Local agendas have seen a process of adaptation, merger, clustering and relating new global environmental issues to older issue concerns. In some cases this substantially redefined local authority issue agendas over the course of a number of years, by creating an environmental

---

[24] P.Roberts et al, *Europe: A Handbook for Local Authorities*, Centre for Local Economic Studies, 1993.
[25] J.Gordon, 'Letting the Genie Out: Local Government and UNCED', *Environmental Politics*, 2/4, 1993.
[26] Hogwood, 1987, *op cit*.

agenda, rather than individual issue agendas. In trying to understand local environmental agenda development through existing agenda theory four main faults can be highlighted: problems of singularity, simplicity, short termism and status.

Singularity: Agenda studies have on occasions accentuated their artificiality by assuming the environment to be a coherent homogenous single issue.[27] Alternatively, in treating environmental issues separately they have failed to detail how environmental issues relate to one another. It seems that agenda setting theories work best with tightly packaged single micro issues rather than broad based agendas. In the environmental arena this single issue pattern of emergence is increasingly problematic, as policy actors increasingly stress the necessities of holistic and integrative environmental policy making. As Hogwood has succinctly argued:

> 'Attempting to identify neat self contained issues, each of which are processed through their own policy cycle may present a misleading picture ... issues are not processed in a neat way: they attach themselves or have attached to them a whole set of other issues.'[28]

Simplicity: Agenda setting studies have generally outlined two broad abstract agendas, the institutional and the systemic, and have concentrated on the movement of issues between the two.[29] In fact there is need for more complexity. Despite moves towards building a corporate environmental agenda, fragmentation is still a feature of institutional agendas. It is likely that there will be agendas within agendas. Consequently, as well as considering systemic and institutional agendas it is important to examine both intra and inter institutional agenda relations. Any attempt to understand local authority environmental agendas without reference to national and supra national agendas would be nonsensical. Similarly, within an authority, agenda setting needs to take account of committee, departmental, political agendas.

Short termism: The framework of agenda case studies tends to accentuate short term factors in issue emergence. It is difficult to build in long term organisational, societal, and political change. In the local environmental sector it was difficult to account for the impact changing central-local relations and the role of local authorities.

Status: Agenda setting theories have difficulty locating issues or establishing where issues go once they have been processed or when attention fades. An examination of agenda setting is often taken as a study of how issues arrive on agendas, or move off an agenda. In many instances it is not a straightforward on-off agenda movement that occurs. Examination of agendas needs to give more emphasis to why issues move up and down agendas. The shape of governmental agendas is not always determined by access, but often by redefinition and prioritisation of problems. The shaping

---

[27] For example, Solesbury, *op cit*.
[28] B.W.Hogwood, *From Crisis to Complacency? Shaping Public Policy in Britain*, Oxford University Press.
[29] R.W.Cobb & C.D.Elder, *op cit*.

and building of an agenda does not stop when issues are receiving serious consideration. Agendas are shaped by routines, priorities, non decisions and implementation, as well as by the policies themselves.

In order to understand the environmental response of local authorities, an examination of not only issue emergence was necessary but also the workings of the broader agenda which dealt with the packages of issues. Thus within policy agendas it can be argued that all or some of the following processes can be operating at any one time:

- Agenda setting: encompassing the traditional focus of agenda studies, that is the emergence of new issues and the redefinition of older ones;

- Agenda priorities: concerned with the ranking of issues, policy options and the implementation of choices;

- Agenda management: relating to the organisational operation of agenda(s) and the way in which issues are maintained or kept off agendas, the way in which policy actors negotiate change;

- Agenda fade: involving the termination of issues from agenda(s) completely;

- Agenda relations: providing the contextual emphasis by seeking to understand how agendas relate to one another (a) internally within an institution, (b) with other institutions and (c) with broad public agendas.

?panel

Stephen C. Young
University of Manchester

'Participation Strategies in the Context of Local Agenda 21:
Towards a New Watershed?'

Acknowledgements

The author is grateful for the financial support for this research from Phase Two of the United Kingdom ESRC's Local Governance Initiative – Grant Ref L311253061.

Thanks to all those who agreed to be interviewed, and to those who supplied materials relating to their authority. To save space, primary documents relating to individual authorities are not listed.

The Environmental Context

At the Rio Earth Summit in 1992, governments of the world signed up to Agenda 21 (Grubb et al, 1993). This is the name given to the international action plan to promote sustainable development – and thus to safeguard the environment for future generations – during the 21st century. The main consequence for sub-national governments everywhere is that they have to draw up their own Local Agenda 21 (LA21) strategies showing how they will apply the principles set out in the main Agenda 21 document at the local level (Ward, 1994). The aim of completing LA21s by the end of 1996 has begun to slip.

Participation is central to LA21 for three reasons. First the need to construct broadly based consensus approaches was acknowledged and agreed. Second, Chapter 28 of Agenda 21 specifically mentions the need to involve different interests and minorities in the processes of preparing each document. The nine mentioned are young people, indigenous peoples and those with their own cultural traditions, women (not technically a minority, but referred to as such), non-governmental organisations (NGOs), local authorities, trade unions, business, the scientific and technical community, and farmers. Some British authorities have added to the list by drawing in minorities like the elderly and the disabled. So, in agreeing to Agenda 21, governments accepted the need to involve all groups in society and not just the more articulate, self-presenting groups.

Third, almost all interpretations of sustainable development focus on the notion of equity. The Brundtland Report itself specifically spells out the way the concept is about 'meeting the basic needs of all and extending to all the opportunity to satisfy their aspirations' (WCED, 1987, p 44). Although apparently related to North/South issues and third world poverty, it has also been linked to making opportunities available to marginalised groups in inner city and remote rural areas in industrialised societies. The argument goes that if equity issues are to be addressed, it will be necessary to establish effective participation processes at the policy-making stage.

It is important to stress the consequence of what was agreed at Rio for participation processes in the LA21 context. Producing consensus and involving the minorities promoted participation itself to being an integral part of the whole policy-making process. In the LA21 context it was no longer – as so often in contemporary politics – an optional extra. Rio thus gave participation processes a new status.

The British Local Government Context

By the late 1980s and early 1990s, growing numbers of authorities had began to appreciate the limitations of most of the post-Skeffington approaches to participation (Boaden et al, 1982); and writers were pointing to the limitations on participation in the broader sense of voting and other forms of involvement in the political system (Parry et al, 1992). By the late 1980s, partly as a result of the New Urban Left experiments of the mid-1980s, officers in some authorities were 'rediscovering' participation and community involvement while trying to promote more people-oriented approaches. These ideas were promoted by for example, the Groundwork Trusts in their environmental improvement work; by organisations involved in the community technical aid movement; by bodies trying to promote user group involvement in developing aspects of health and social services; and in the context of tackling the social as well as economic dimensions of regenerating rundown housing estates (Gyford, 1991).

At first these and similar initiatives appeared to be isolated experiments, based very much at the local, neighbourhood level. But some writers began to link them to broader debates about different conceptions of citizenship (Miller, 1995); empowerment (Clarke & Stewart, 1992); and the re-making of local democracy (Stewart, 1995).

The Variety of Approaches in the LA21 Context

In the early, and more especially, the mid-1990s, developments in the wider sphere of participation were linked to the need to promote participation in the environmental field. The result has been a huge variety of innovatory and experimental approaches. In Europe, Britain is perceived as being a world leader in the participation aspects of LA21. The next part of the paper summarises the breadth of what has happened, with examples of authorities given in brackets.

Environment Forums

A primary concern for local authorities has been to forge stronger links with environmental groups, so as to bring their expertise into the policy-making process. Two main approaches have been used. First they have coopted group representatives onto both new and existing committees and working parties (Croydon). But much more common has been the creation of new bodies.

A variety of Green Forums, Environment Forums, and similarly named organisations have been set up. These predate the 1992 Rio Summit. Since then their numbers have mushroomed. With these initiatives authorities have aimed to draw stakeholders together; to attract interest to environmental issues; and to promote discussion. Some authorities have established Forums that relate to specific aspects of the environment – like the countryside and its users for example (Calderdale).

With regard to composition, practice varies enormously. There is no simple model. Authorities usually start with representatives of local environmental, community and other voluntary groups. Some add representatives of national/regional bodies with local interests – like the Royal Society for the Protection of Birds (RSPB). Some welcome interested individuals. Some draw in economic interests – National Farmers Union (NFU), Country Gentleman's Association (CGA), and chambers of commerce for example (Herts CC). Some invite representatives of statutory bodies – like the National Rivers Authority (NRA) (Mendip). Some ask the local parish/community councils to send representatives. Some appoint officers from different departments and/or sections within the authority. Counties usually include officers and/or members from districts – and vice-versa (Lancashire).

On the organisational side, the whole Forum meets only occasionally. Between the formal meetings, it breaks up into groups covering different aspects of LA21 and the environment – transport, waste, energy, wildlife, work and so on. A number follow the BT Environment City model. The arrangements for electing officials vary enormously. Officers provide support, arranging meetings, circulating papers, taking minutes, and so on. Because of the range of members and the complexity, some authorities have appointed steering groups to guide their Forums (Bedfordshire).

The main functions of these bodies are to react to draft council proposals on all manner of environmental issues; to produce draft chapters for the authority's LA21 document; and to discuss draft LA21s. This can get into great detail, by for example, arranging day-long meetings so that the members of each topic group can discuss the draft chapters and recommendations prepared by all of the others. In addition some councils give them their head, letting them identify topics that may be relevant locally, and investigate them (Cardiff, Leeds). They are also used to promote participation, by for example, organising public meetings and getting other groups involved (Woking, Guildford). In some places the Forum is established as an independent charitable trust, thus making it more independent and able to raise external funds (Peterborough and Leicester).

The nature of the link to the council is confused by the fact that some Forums have no councillors (Calderdale), while others have them as Forum members (Mendip). But two main models have emerged. Some Forums are free-standing independent bodies that advise the local authority. What happens here is that officers interpret the views of the Forum and report on them to the relevant committees. Other Forums are formally linked to the council's committee structure, sending their minutes and recommendations to higher committees for consideration by members. There are some variations on these two models. In Sheffield for example, three representatives go from the Forum to the City's Environment Working Party.

Empowering Techniques

This section briefly deals with a range of broad approaches, aimed at drawing stakeholders together and building consensus (DoE, 1995; Wilcox, 1994). They mostly relate to the local neighbourhood level, although some have been used in North America and in Europe at a higher strategic level.

First there is the visioning technique. This is done in groups, getting people to discuss the kind of neighbourhood they would like theirs to be in twenty years time. It is then possible to work backwards, constructing programmes that lead there.

Next there is the citizens juries approach. This relates the jury principle to political decisions. The organisers pick representative citizens as jurors. They then define the questions to be considered; provide information; select witnesses; and bring in a facilitator as moderator. He or she writes the report setting out the jurors' findings. The recommendations are not binding, but are taken seriously by decision-makers (Stewart et al, 1994).

Third there is the 'planning for real' technique which has mainly been developed by the Neighbourhood Initiatives Foundation. Drawing from their experience and training packages, they aim to bring local people together at the neighbourhood level for short intense periods to produce consensus about future development and improvements.

Dividing people up into small discussion groups is used in a variety of circumstances. These range from setting up small groups of people from specific neighbourhoods, to dividing up those attending a meeting. In the relaxed conditions of the informal group, they then discuss what is wrong with their local environment and what they would like to see improved and changed.

Finally here, focus groups have received growing attention in the mid-1990s. They are a specific form of small group discussion. This refers to bringing together selected individuals to meet on a regular basis with a set agenda. Individuals are carefully chosen on the basis of socio-economic criteria to get groups of individuals together from a common background – rural professionals, Asian women, or long-term unemployed men for example (Macnaghten et al, 1995).

The Deployment of More Conventional Techniques

Common approaches include writing to groups on consultation lists asking for comments on draft policies and different options;doing presentations to local groups; setting up series of regular meetings with some groups;and holding public meetings. Similarly the following have been much in evidence – organising static and touring exhibitions for opportunistic use in libraries, shopping centres and so on, and at conferences, green fairs, and agricultural shows; establishing slide and video shows for use at different venues; and publishing leaflets explaining what the council is doing/proposes to do.

Well-tried techniques have been adapted to the LA21 context – distributing to every household either a council newspaper with a LA21 pull-out included, or a LA21 newspaper; exploiting local media opportunities by giving detailed information/articles to journalists, pushing for interviews for committee chairs about council initiatives, and getting environmental coordinators to do radio phone-ins; and developing participation programmes around events like Green Transport Week, International Women's Day, and locally organised community arts events. Also the questionnaire approach has been considerably adapted – as with street surveys, village audits, and interviews – whether aimed county-wide, tailored to schools or neighbourhoods, or aimed at specific sets of shoppers – to gather information and help assess different options, or to encourage local groups to do their own surveys.

A lot of energy has gone into focusing techniques on specific minorities, as with audio-cassettes for the blind, meetings and leaflets in different languages for local ethnic groups, and visits and conferences for youth groups and others. So far it is easier to point to examples of this than to assess its impact.

Also mention needs to be made of environmental education issues. These are primarily aimed at getting people to think about changing their lifestyles. But they also increase people's knowledge, and thus their potential input into participation processes. Of importance here are the demonstration projects like the eco-houses (Bolton); the centres of excellence (Lancashire); and the environment shops (Leicester).

Local Agenda 21 Participation Strategies

One of the most widely discussed distinctions in discussions about participation is the difference between 'top-down' and 'bottom-up' approaches. The top-down approach is a one-way process dominated by the council, whereas the bottom-up approach is a two-way process that develops into a genuine dialogue between the council and the community (LGMB, 1994).

The reality is of course more complex. In the context of LA21 in the 1990s British local authorities have developed four different strategies to promote participation. The main features of each are set out below and summarised in a chart.[1]

The Top-Down Strategy

Here the authority remains firmly in control. It sets up a one-way process. Its attitude is that participation is mainly concerned with passing information about what the council is doing down to the public and interested parties. It sets and controls the agenda during the participation process. It determines the direction of policy proposals and the choice of priorities. It dominates the participation process itself. It ensures there is no real scope for change to its position after the participation process.

This strategy is generally used where an authority wants to publicise what it has been doing, and what it plans to do in the future. The par-

---

[1] For technical reasons the chart accompanying this paper has not be reproduced here. A copy may be obtained from the author at the Conference or by post from the Department of Government, The University, Manchester M13 9PL.

ticipation process helps to legitimise its activities. This strategy is always widely criticised for structuring the participation stage in such a way as to prevent any real input from local communities. In the context of LA21 such approaches undermine attempts to implement the community participation aspects set out in Chapter 28 of Agenda 21.

The Bottom-Up Strategy

This is the polar opposite of the Top-Down Strategy. The authority takes a quite different approach, giving participation contrasting features. It conceives of participation as a genuine two-way dialogue based on a sharing of information. It aims to reach out beyond the groups that were usually involved in participation exercises in the 1970s and 1980s; to give people a real role in shaping council decisions. The authority takes a hands-off, listening and learning stance, and aims to empower people. It leaves the agenda open, to be set by local people. It leaves the direction of policy and the choice of priorities open to discussion. It shares power with the participants: groups and local communities thus *own the participation process*. The authority ensures there is wide scope to change its position after the participation process is over. This strategy developes the ideas at the top of Arnstein's ladder (Gyford, 1991, pp.52-3).

This strategy has been followed in varying degrees by authorities like Mendip, Kirklees, Derbyshire, Leicester, Gloucestershire and others (Environ, 1994; Kirklees Environment Unit, 1995; LGMB, 1995; Church, 1996).

The 'Yes ... But ... ' Strategy

This occurs where the authority has the *rhetoric* that goes with the Bottom-Up Strategy, but finds it difficult to let go of the participation process and carry that Strategy right through. The main problem is that the council is committed to some policies and projects that are widely seen as being environmentally-damaging – like open-cast mining or a big road scheme. So the authority's approach changes. What happens can be summed up as follows: 'Yes let's aim to have a bottom-up strategy, but some issues are too important to compromise on'. The authority thus changes the character of its approach to participation as the participation programme develops. It evolves into a more limited and controlled exercise.

The council establishes a two-way dialogue. It *aims* to open things up and get away from simply passing information out, and to give groups and communities a real role in shaping decisions. It sets much of the agenda, but relinquishes control and welcomes additions. It opens the direction of policy and the choice of priorities up for discussion, but the reality is that it is committed on some issues and cannot compromise. It aims to promote power-sharing, but in fact remains in control. There is scope for change at the end of the participation process, but there are some positions that the authority is committed to, and will not budge from. These may only become apparent after the participation process. The strength of the authority's commitment is such that some inputs from the participation process are vetoed.

This strategy seems to emerge as it develops. What seems to happen is that the environmental co-ordinator and those setting up the participation process present it as a Bottom-Up strategy. However, the reality is that some senior officers and/or committee chairs are strongly committed to broad policies like promoting economic development, or specific projects like a major housing scheme or developing a specific land-fill site. Bolton, Nottinghamshire, and Durham County Council appear to be examples in this category.

Such approaches may be implicit in a draft document published for discussion. Sometimes though, the extent of local authority commitment only becomes clear over time. In the context of Environment Forum discussions for example, the truth about the strength of a council's commitment will only emerge slowly. In practice this undermining of the Bottom-Up Strategy may only become clear during, or even after, the participation process.

The Limited Dialogue Strategy

This strategy arises where an authority is drawn to the Top-Down approach, but sees the problems with it and wants to be more flexible, as in the Cheshire County Council case for example. The authority conceives the dialogue with the public as being a two-way process but within limited parameters. It aims to get beyond pushing information out to the public to get some feedback on what it is proposing – mainly over the details. It sets the agenda. It determines the direction of policy and the choice of priorities.It holds the balance of power and controls the participation process. It is prepared to amend its proposals at the end of the participation process. Although they can affect significant issues, they mostly relate to details.

This is a common strategy, especially in areas that have been relatively unaffected by the new approaches to participation that emerged during the late 1980s. It is also being adopted in places where the council's approach to planning does not lay much emphasis on participation.

Timing the Participation Process

The stage at which the participation process comes is covered in Column 7 in the chart. The timing has an important influence on what can be achieved. With the Top-Down Strategy and the Limited Dialogue Strategy the authority does a lot of data collection and analysis and then publishes its draft proposals. The participation stage comes after that. It is thus *grafted* onto a policy-making process that has already generated both momentum and commitments.

Bottom-Up approaches are partly designed to address this problem. The argument here is that the participation stage should come *at the very beginning of the policy-making process*. Then it becomes possible for the authority to play a hands-off, listening and learning role as it has no position to defend. Meanwhile local people are able to own the participation process, and use it to develop their own agenda.

With the 'Yes ... But ... ' Strategy the timing of the participation stage is more complex. Usually it is grafted onto the policy-making process the authority has already initiated. On some occasions though, councils pursuing the 'Yes ... But ... ' approach try to have it earlier. However, in practice – as shown in Column 6 – there are some issues where the authority is committed and is not prepared to compromise. So even though the participation process has been timed to come early, the reality is that it has been grafted onto the authority's policy-making process.

Building Consensus?

It is too early to assess the extent to which the participation processes that have been established are capable of producing widespread consensus. In particular three issues need to be resolved before conclusions can be reached.

Balancing The Input From Economic Interests

Economic interests in fact account for three of the nine minorities specifically identified in Chapter 28 of Agenda 21 – business, farmers and trade unions. Many of the concerns of a fourth minority – the scientific and technical community – also relate to economic development issues.

Environmental Forums have been seen by some as one means of controlling the influence of economic interests, and of integrating their ideas with those of others. Some authorities have set them up to balance industry's influence. The claim here is that economic interests have their own well-established routes into policy-making processes within the Town Hall. Creating an Environment Forum can provide a Forum where non-economic interests can clearly establish their views.

Other authorities have followed the Round Table principle and included representatives of different parts of industry on their Environment Forums. The argument here is that consensus can only emerge if the interests of farmers, industrialists and major local employers are clearly stated at the same time as those of environmentalists and others. As stakeholders in their own right, they can help produce consensus.

One particular problem has emerged where attempts have been made to involve economic interests in Round Table situations, as through the Lancashire Environment Forum. Representatives from statutory bodies like the NRA and English Nature can speak for their organisations and return to them after a meeting, and try to deliver. By contrast, representatives from the CGA or the NFU cannot commit their members to new courses of action. They can talk about their members' perceptions and worries and likely reactions, but they cannot commit them to – for example – using twenty per cent less fertiliser. Chambers of Commerce face similar problems.

Another common problem is that those attending Forums from manufacturing companies tend to come from big companies and be enthusiasts for the environment. They understand how sustainable development affects firms, and how clean technology and greening industry offers new investment strategies and market opportunities. But the trouble is that they speak only for the sympathetic and converted minority. In particular small firm perspectives get overlooked. The majority of industrialists, with their short-term perspectives, are busy influencing the authority and its senior officers and committee chairs via other channels. The result is that LA21 agendas do not engage with much of industry.

Irreconcilable Views

Despite all the emphasis on the need for consensus there are times when irreconcilable views are unavoidable. Issues like open-cast mining and major road projects polarise views inside and outside the town hall. Here it is useful to distinguish between two levels of policy-making.

First there is the approach that emphasises the very local – the village or the urban neighbourhood. At this level it is often possible to produce consensus especially where the focus is on improving environmental conditions. However, it is more difficult if controversial developments are in the offing, as with a quarry extension, a waste tip, or a housing project.

Second there is the strategic level where the whole of an authority's area, or a wider sub-region, is being considered. This is the level for which the Canadian Round Table approach was developed. This follows the principle of drawing in all the stakeholders on the grounds that generating consensus is then much more likely to be achieved. This problem is closely linked to the issue of drawing the whole range of economic interests in – as discussed above.

Producing an authority-wide LA21 on the basis of consensus will need some kind of combination of the two approaches – especially in areas where pressures for development are strong.

There is also a more general problem – a wider range of views are now being considered. The nature of the debates about environmental issues and sustainable development has changed since the late 1980s, and especially since Rio. It is not just that the conservation-oriented views of the Council for the Protection of Rural England (CPRE) and Linda Snell are now taken more seriously. It is that the more radical green ideas about promoting sustainable development have reached more agendas. Those pushing these ideas have come from the new social movement groups. In the 1980s in Britain they were marginalised. In the 1990s, post-Rio, their views are being considered in the LA21 context because of the need to involve all groups in society in reaching consensus. Radical views have thus been legitimised. Reaching consensus has become harder because a broader range of perspectives have to be considered.

Participation Outputs v. Political Realities

This is the problem of what happens when the outcome of the participation process meets the processes of preparing the budget for the next three years, and revising the authority's statutory plan. There are fears that it will be difficult to relate some of the more idealistic ideas coming from an Environmental Forum to the authority's prevailing view of its priorities and resources. In particular there are concerns that the conclusions likely to emerge from the visioning exercises will not fit easily with existing budgets and the council's likely approach to the updating of the existing statutory plan – be it a structure or local plan, or Unitary Development Plan (UDP).

Transport is an oft-quoted example. Many environmentalists want short-term changes leading to the development of new strategies. They oppose the building of new car parks; the widening of ring roads; and arguments for new roads. They see the issues in terms of the need for new infra-structure investment to promote cycling and public transport. Yet the authority has to prepare next year's budget within existing constraints; try to influence the budgets of other organisations; and update its statutory plan. This is all made more complex by the overwhelmingly pro-road transport views of business interests; and by the wider context of central government's controls and guidance, as through the *Planning Policy Guidance Notes*; and its roads programme.

From the perspective of the authority, environmentalists are over-ambitious and unrealistic. Environmentalists on the other hand argue that the authority is supporting a system that will continue to damage the environment, and is refusing to confront the issues.

One of the ways of addressing this issue is trying to ensure that the Environment Forum is involved in the monitoring and review of the LA21 plan, so that it can be central to the process of resolving the subsequent conflicts.

A second route is to try to marry the participation stage of the LA21 process with other ongoing processes. In Hamilton-Wentworth in Canada for example, those creating the structures to draw the stakeholders together appreciated the way LA21 proposals had complex implications for restructuring budget programmes and introducing new headings. As a result some of the stakeholders involved in preparing the LA21 were party to the subsequent process of discussing how to take the budget to pieces, and then reconstruct it so it related more positively to the promotion of LA21 (Whittaker, 1995).

Extending Empowerment?

Councils promoting the Bottom-Up Strategy appear to be empowering their citizens in new ways. The same is happening in the context of the 'Yes ... But ... ' Strategy in those policy spheres where authorities are not committed to specific views. However, firm conclusions cannot be reached until it is clear that participation processes have had a *strong influence* on the *contents* of LA21s; and that the LA21s have had a strong influence on both statutory plans and the restructuring of budgets.

It is simply too early to assess these complex issues. As of January 1996, only a handful of LA21s have been completed. Meanwhile each of the three issues raised just above will repay further research via case-studies and more ambitious comparative research projects.

What can be said at this stage is that the promotion of the Bottom-Up Strategy is energising local democracy, and getting more people involved. This is not just because of the legitimising of the radicals discussed earlier. People are getting involved from right across the political spectrum.

This fits in with Hill's civic republicanism tradition of citizenship; and with Miller's republican conception (Hill, 1994, pp 24, 27, 238, & 249; Miller, 1995). Such interpretations of citizenship build from a set of rights to emphasise participation and the practice of citizenship, and involvement in debate and decisionmaking. This is moving away from the Right's more liberal interpretations which have been prevalent in the 1980s and early 1990s. They emphasise citizens having more choice as parents, tenants, consumers and so on.

This all relates to the much broader issue of whether the promotion of more participatory local democracy starts to undermine representative democracy. If some of the Environment Forums become very influential, and holistic interpretations of sustainable development take them into increasing areas of local government activity, then they may well be in conflict with majority party opinion within some councils.

Approaching A New Watershed On Participation Issues?

The overall conclusion has to be that it is too early to judge the long-term significance of the participation developments reviewed here. The approaches developed in the context of the Bottom-Up Strategy are a promising and necessary first step – the foundations for a new bridge. But bridges get destroyed by floods and natural catastrophes. Bottom-Up strategies are being developed in the context of the harsh reality of the local government policy-making processes summarised above; and the inability of incremental opportunism to produce radical change.

These strategies are also being developed in the context of wider social change. This is a second constraint on the progress of Bottom-Up approaches. The social context is well summarised in a report by the Centre for the Study of Environmental Change (CSEC) at Lancaster University for Lancashire County Council (Macnaghten et al, 1995). The report highlights the ways in ways in which people are increasingly sceptical of central and local government attempts to improve living conditions. It also shows – despite all Lancashire County Council have done in becoming a world leader on LA21 – how distrustful people are of local government, and fatalistic about their own prospects.

Promoting participation, overcoming apathy and exclusion, and moving towards a new watershed given this wider social context, remains a formidable task. The Sustainability Indicators Research Project report (LGMB, 1995) also emphasises the danger of the LA21 message appearing to come, not from a dynamic, caring, imaginative authority, but 'from them' – that is from a council perceived as being insensitive and out of touch.

Attempts to combat apathy are further constrained by the phenomenon of the 'green ghetto'. Messages about environmental issues are widely perceived amongst the public to be coming from activists with extreme points of view, who are out of touch with the concerns of people in the real world, and the issues they relate to. Even though it is soberly clothed officers conveying the LA21 message, they get tangled up in people's minds with anti-roads protestors and Greenpeace activists. Many members of the public are confused by messages from people they see as extremists, about the need for radical change and everything being a threat to the planet. To many, most of it looks alright. They are pre-occupied with family and friends, with work and money, and with living. As a result, greens are left, lost in a ghetto, talking to each other, and not persuading others to take LA21 seriously.

Two main responses to the situation as analysed by the CSEC Report have emerged. The first is to avoid actually mentioning the environment! The aim here is to try to reach people who are disinterested in environmental issues as they are commonly presented, via other aspects of their lives. Thus people are very concerned about their children, about health issues, and about food for example. These topics are aspects of sustainable development, and of holistic approaches. Some see potential in using discussions about aspects of anti-poverty strategies for example, as a means of drawing people disaffected from 'environmental issues', into thinking about the LA21 agenda.

The other response, despite all the resource problems, is to develop the Bottom-Up Strategy, and to reach down in very specific, targeted ways to the local – to villages and urban neighbourhoods. The argument here is that people relate most positively to the area immediately around where they live. It is only by finding means of engaging with their aspirations there that progress towards the watershed can be made (Young, 1996).

In summary then, there were two contradictory trends developing by the start of 1996 – an infusion of life and energy into participatory programmes in a minority of authorities in the context of LA21 on the one hand; and evidence of apathy and exclusion on the other. It will be several years before it is clear which becomes the predominant trend.

Bibliography

N.Boaden et al, *Public Participation in Local Services*, Longman, 1982.

C.Church, *Towards Local Sustainability: A Review of Current Activity on Local Agenda 21 in UN*, United Nations Association Sustainable Development Unit, London, 1996.

M.Clarke & J.Stewart, 'Empowerment: A Theme for the 1990s', *Local Government Studies*, 18/2, 1992.

Department of the Environment, *Community Involvement in Planning and Development Processes*, HMSO, 1995.

Environ, *Approaches To Community Participation*, Environ, Leicester, 1994.

M.Grubb et al, *The Earth Summit Agreements*, Royal Institute for International Affairs, 1993.

J.Gyford, *Citizens, Consumers and Councils*, Macmillan, 1991.

D.M.Hill, *Citizens and Cities*, Harvester Wheatsheaf, 1994.

Kirklees Council Environment Unit, *Local Agenda 21 and Transport: Processes and Mechanisms For Change*, Kirklees Council, 1995.

Local Government Management Board (LGMB), *Community Participation in LA21*, LGMB, 1994.

LGMB, *Sustainability Indicators Research Project*, LGMB, 1995.

P.Macnaghten et al, *Public Perceptions and Sustainability in Lancashire*, Centre for the Study of Environmental Change, Lancaster University, 1995.

D.Miller, 'Citizenship and Pluralism', *Political Studies*, 43/3, 1995.

G.Parry et al, *Political Participation and Democracy in Britain*, Cambridge University Press, 1992.

J.Stewart, *Innovation In Democratic Practice*, INLOGOV, 1995.

J.Stewart et al, *Citizens Juries*, Institute for Public Policy Research, London, 1994.

S.Ward, 'Thinking Global: Acting Local? British Local Authorities and Their Environmental Plans', *Environmental Politics*, 2/3, 1994.

S.Whittaker (ed), *First Steps: Local Agenda 21 In Practice*, HMSO, 1995.

D.Wilcox, *Guide To Effective Participation*, Joseph Rowntree Foundation, 1994.

World Commission on Environment and Development, *Our Common Future*, Oxford University Press, 1987.

S.C.Young, *Promoting Participation And Community-Based Partnerships In The Context of Local Agenda 21: A Report For Practitioners*, EPRU Paper, Government Department, University of Manchester, 1996.

Fuzzy Boundaries and Policing Futures

Stephen Cope
University of Portsmouth
Sarah Charman
University of Portsmouth
Stephen P Savage
University of Portsmouth
&
Peter Starie
University of Portsmouth

'Redrawing the Boundaries of Police Governance:
Centralisation, the Association of Chief Police Officers
and Policing Futures'

Abstract

This paper examines the role of the Association of Police Officers (ACPO) in shaping the future of policing in Britain. It charts the growing concern with futurology, and investigates futures of governance generally and of policing specifically. The paper, by drawing extensively on findings of a research project examining ACPO and the policing policy process, then assesses the role of ACPO in policing futures. In particular, it examines the widely predicted policing future of centralised policing, and investigates the position of ACPO in shaping this future.[1]

Futures and Futurology

From Thomas More's *Utopia* to George Orwell's *1984*, the past is littered with utopian and dystopian futuristic discourses. Many have believed that by understanding the past, the present can be changed to herald a desired future or to accommodate a not-so-desired future. Much effort, such as the trivial outpourings of Mystic Meg, the actuarial calculations of insurance companies and the increasingly sophisticated economic forecasting techniques employed by governments, has been expended to predict the future. However, the track record of predicting the future is poor (Hutton 1995). Bauman wrote:

> 'All truly decisive departures this century took us ... unawares. Like weather forecasters, we are at our best when prognosticating more of the same; it is the change, the radical change, change in the rules of the game and thus in the game itself, that defies our imagination, shackled as it has been since the beginning of the modern age to continuous time and monotoneity of institutional reproduction' (1995, p.140).

---

[1] A bibliography of references cited in the paper can be provided on request at the Conference or by post from us at the University of Portsmouth.

For example, the collapse of communism in Eastern Europe and the Soviet Union took almost everyone in the West by surprise. Ironically this unpredicted event has spawned considerable anxiety about the future. In examining the new post-communist world Hughes concluded (albeit naïvely):

> 'We cannot know the future ... We can only hope to define our values, identify important leverage points, and thereby increase the likelihood that our choices will achieve our goals. After all, we do have a world order to create' (1993, p.167).

In addition to the end of the Cold War, other factors contributing to the rise of futurology include the turbulence generated by increasing globalisation (Campanella 1993; Dahrendorf 1995), the sirens of postmodernism (Rosenau 1992; Smart 1992), and end-of-millennium musings (Bradbury 1995; Woollacott 1995).

If explaining the past is difficult, then, predicting the future is even more difficult. The two main methods of predicting the future 'are extrapolation (trend projection) and causal analysis (a consideration of cause-and-effect relations)' (Hughes 1993, p.3). Extrapolation requires describing what is happening, and assuming what is presently happening will be more or less what happens in the future. Causal analysis requires explaining what is happening, and theorising what will happen in the future by understanding the past and present. The paper deploys both extrapolation and causal analysis to investigate policing futures. However, there are significant difficulties in predicting the future, most important of which is that social scientists are unable to conduct laboratory-type experiments to ascertain causality. Tilly warned:

> 'Analysts of large-scale political processes frequently invoke invariant models that feature self-contained and self-motivating social units. Few actual processes conform to such models ... Better models rest on plausible ontologies, specify fields of variation for the phenomena in question, reconstruct causal sequences, and concentrate explanation on links within those sequences' (1995, p.1594).

His concern for 'the historically embedded search for deep causes operating in variable combinations, circumstances, and sequences with consequently variable outcomes' is a salutary reminder that futurologists (in whatever guise) should be more modest when building models of the future (Tilly 1995, p.1602). Their work should concern 'not the identification of similarities over whole structures and processes but the explanation of variability among related structures and processes' (Tilly 1995, p.1602). Consequently this paper examines not one but a series of futures for governance generally and policing specifically. By constructing and comparing different, yet relatively simple, models of the future based on present trends it becomes possible to enhance understanding of causal relations between factors shaping the future.

From Government to Governance

States are both restructuring themselves and the societies they govern in order to remain competitive in 'the global marketplace' (Dahrendorf 1995, p.41). Since the mid-1970s the state in Britain has been radically transformed and indeed reinvented (Hogg 1995; Painter 1991; Painter 1994; Ridley 1995). Perhaps the most useful description in capturing this transformation is the term, 'the new governance' (Rhodes 1995). Rhodes wrote:

> '... governance refers to self-organising, interorganisational networks and has the following characteristics.
> - 1. Interdependence between organisations. Governance is broader than government, covering non-state actors. Pushing back the boundaries of the state dissolves the boundaries between public, private and voluntary sectors.
> - 2. Continuing interactions between network members caused by the need to exchange resources and negotiate shared purposes.
> - 3. The interactions are game-like, rooted in trust and regulated by agreed rules of the game.
> - 4. There is no sovereign authority, so networks have a significant degree of autonomy from the state and are not accountable to it. They are self-organising.
> - 5. Networks are a governing structure: an alternative to markets and hierarchies' (1995, p.11).

Similarly Dunsire defined governance as 'a process of co-directing in a network of many separate actors with different and opposing interests and more or less independent positions' (1993, pp.26-27). The Commission on Global Governance stated that governance 'is the sum of the many ways individuals and institutions, public and private, manage their common affairs' (1995, p.2). Whereas government is about imposing order and ruling relatively simple systems, governance is about managing disorder and steering complex systems (embracing not just hierarchies but also markets and networks). Rhodes warned:

> 'The state becomes a collection of interorganisational networks made up of governmental and societal actors ... The challenge for British government is to recognise the constraints on central action imposed by the shift to self-organising networks ... Governance as self-organising networks is a challenge to governability because the networks become autonomous and resist central guidance. They are a prime example of governing without government' (Rhodes 1995, pp.17-18).

According to Rhodes, the British state is being hollowed-out as a result of increasing privatisation, the use of 'alternative service delivery systems' (such as Next Steps agencies), Europeanisation and new public management (1994, pp.138-139). These trends represent highly significant developments weakening the policy-making capacity of the state. However, Rhodes ignored counter-trends that attempt to enhance its policy-making capacity, leading to the filling-in of the state. It is important to assess all major trends affecting the governance of Britain – namely, centralisation, decentralisation, privatisation and Europeanisation – to fully understand its futures.

These four interconnected trends have shaped the contours of governance in Britain (Cope et al 1995, pp.557-560; Savage et al 1994, pp.15-74). First, there is increasing centralisation within British government, whereby successive governments have strengthened the core executive by extending its influence far beyond central government. Second, there is also increasing decentralisation within British government, with a concerted attempt by the core executive to diminish its control over policy delivery while extending its control over policy strategy. Third, there is increasing privatisation within British government, involving the sale of nationalised industries, market-testing and compulsory competitive tendering. Fourth, there is increasing Europeanisation of British government, with the European Union extending its influence in shaping policy.

The thesis that the state is being hollowed-out is supported by the trends towards decentralisation, privatisation and Europeanisation, but not by the trend towards centralisation. Two generalised future scenarios of the British state can be constructed – the hollowed-out state and the filled-in state scenario. The hollowed-out state scenario envisages a withered and disembowelled state increasingly unable to steer society, with policy-making capacity displaced downward by decentralisation, outward by privatisation and upward by Europeanisation (Crook et al 1992, pp.79-105; Dunleavy 1994; Dunleavy & Hood 1994; Jessop 1993; Marquand 1995; Peters 1993; Rhodes 1994; Strange 1995). The filled-in state scenario portrays a restructured and rejuvenated state increasingly able to govern society, with policy-making capacity strengthened inward by centralisation (The *Economist* 1995; The *Economist* 1995-1996; Mulgan 1995). These two scenarios will be applied to policing as a way of examining its futures.

The New Policing Governance

Policing in Britain is characterised by a 'new police governance' comprising a network of state and societal actors operating at different spatial levels (namely, the local, national, European and international level). Its governance includes chief constables, local police authorities, the Home Office, the HM Inspectorate of Constabulary (HMIC), the Audit Commission, the Committee of Local Police Authorities (COLPA), MI5, the European Police Office (Europol), International Criminal Police Commission (Interpol), ACPO, the Police Superintendents' Association, the Police Federation and private security companies (Leishman et al 1995; Leishman et al 1996, pp.17-20).

Following Johnston, 'policing is undertaken by a complex and diverse network of public, private and hybrid agencies' (1996, p.54). Though he added:

'To refer to policing as a "network" does not imply that its components are yet coordinated – in that respect, "patchwork" might be a better term – but it does suggest that the actions and reactions of one part will impact on the others. For that reason, any rigorous analysis of contemporary policing has to focus upon ... its "diverse totality" ' (1996, p.54).

Mclaughlin and Murji argued the Government's police reforms 'will put an end to public policing' (1995, p.125). This extrapolated claim is wide of the mark. It is not the 'end of public policing' but the end of the 'public policing' monopoly that is evident towards the end of the twentieth century. If the dominance of 'public policing' in the nineteenth and twentieth centuries characterised the modern era, then, the emerging 'diverse totality' of policing reflects the so-called postmodern era (Reiner 1992; Sheptycki 1995). However, the case should not be overstated because the 'new policing governance' is arguably an embryonic and transitional outcome of conflicting pressures whose forms are yet to take shape. The 'new policing governance' will be examined with reference to wider trends both furthering and countering centralisation.

Centralising the police

The centralisation of policing has to be understood against the backdrop of increasing centralisation of local government, because, until the Police and Magistrates' Courts Act 1994 (PMCA) was implemented, police authorities (outside London and Northern Ireland) were part of local government. Central government has attempted increasingly to control local authorities, which has resulted in 'a long-term trend of centralisation of the police service' (Loveday 1994, p.221). Jenkins argued the police have become 'yet another nationalized service' (1995, p.109). Police reforms in the 1990s have furthered this process of centralisation (Alderson 1994; Loveday 1995). PMCA empowers the Home Secretary to lay down key national objectives supported by performance indicators for the police, to call for reports from local police authorities ensuring that local policing reflects national policing objectives, to exercise greater patronage powers in appointing members to serve on police authorities, and to amalgamate police forces. Furthermore, the spending of police authorities is subject to 'capping' by central government. PMCA effectively makes the police authority 'an intermediary of central government and the direct agent of the Home Office' despite the nominal retention of the tripartite structure established under the Police Act 1964 (Loveday 1994, p.232). PMCA substantially shifts the balance of power over policing away from local government towards central government.

Not centralising the police

The centralisation of policing is countered by its decentralisation, privatisation and Europeanisation, each of these counter-trends will be examined. First, police restructuring has involved decentralisation, as well as centralisation (Johnston 1992, pp.9-10). The police exercise greater managerial and operational autonomy within an increasingly centralised policy and financial strategy. Following the Sheehy Report and the White Paper, chief constables have greater freedom to manage their police forces (Home Office 1993, pp.9-16; Home Office et al 1993). There is increasing decentralisation within the police as responsibility for making many operational decisions has been devolved downwards, but these devolved powers must be consistent with the strategy determined locally by police authorities with their chief constables, which in turn must be consistent with the broader strategy determined nationally by the Home Secretary.

Second, privatisation is firmly on the policing agenda, with 'load-shedding', compulsory competitive tendering and contracting-out, charging for services, and imitating private sector management styles. 'Load-shedding' is 'a process ... in which services are ceded to commercial or voluntary providers' (Johnston 1992, p.12). There has been a significant expansion of private policing. The Posen Inquiry is likely to lead to increased opportunities for the private sector to undertake policing work (Home Office 1995). The Home Office is keen to extend compulsory competitive tendering and contracting-out in the police (Home Office 1993, p.16; Home Office 1995). Charging for police services is likely to expand given the Government's squeeze on police budgets. Imitating private sector management styles is increasingly prevalent in the way the police are managed. Police reform measures have asserted the chief constable's 'right-to-manage', and imported a raft of management techniques associated with the private sector (such as fixed-term appointments and performance-related pay). Furthermore, PMCA created considerable scope for increasing the number of people drawn from business serving on the new police authorities (Loveday 1994, p.225).

Third, Europeanisation – the increasing integration of the EU – has profound implications for policing. The Maastricht Treaty consolidated and furthered intergovernmental cooperation in the field of justice and home affairs (including policing matters). In particular, it formally established Europol. This move challenges the sovereignty of member states because the police 'are the principal means whereby a state imposes its authority and rule within its own territory' (Benyon 1994, p.515). Consequently, and despite accepting the need for greater police cooperation, member states have been resistant in establishing common policing structures, making closer cooperation 'very difficult and limited in scope' (Guyomarch 1995, p.249). Notwithstanding these significant obstacles, there is a creeping influence of Europeanisation upon policing in Britain.

Policing Futures

Predicting the future of policing has become more prevalent in recent years with the emergence of the 'new policing governance' (Bayley 1994; Butler 1996; Johnston 1996; McLaughlin & Murji 1995). A wide variety of policing futures have been examined to understand relations within 'a diverse network of policing' generated by police restructuring (Johnston 1996, p.66). These (mainly doomsday) scenarios have ranged along a continuum. At one end, the future of policing is characterised by stability with 'public policing' still dominant in a 'new policing order'; and at the other end, the future is characterised by instability with the 'end of public policing' heralding a 'new policing disorder' (Cope et al 1996). The 'end of public policing' scenario comprises a range of policing futures, ranging from the 'return of private policing' future (with possible 'outright corporate domination of policing') to the 'anarchic nightmare' future (with feral vigilantism and militarised private policing) (Johnston 1996, p.66).

These scenarios of policing futures will be discussed with reference to the emergence of the 'new police governance', whose contours are being drawn and re-drawn by wider pressures towards centralisation, decentralisation, privatisation and Europeanisation shaping the governance of Britain. By extrapolating it is possible to construct four future scenarios of policing – namely, centralised, decentralised, privatised and Europeanised policing futures. The centralised policing future equates to the filled-in state scenario, whereby the national state exerts increasing control over policing. This future scenario posits that police restructuring is essentially leading to an increasingly centralised police, and that the processes of decentralisation, privatisation and Europeanisation will be firmly controlled by central government. The decentralised, privatised and Europeanised policing futures are versions of the hollowed-out state scenario, whereby the national state loses control over policing to a fragmented set of policing agencies (such as local police authorities, chief constables, private security companies and Europol). This future scenario suggests that police restructuring is contributing to the hollowing-out of the national state, and that the process of centralisation will be overwhelmed by the processes of decentralisation, privatisation and Europeanisation. These filled-in and hollowed-out scenarios are, of course, generalised and simplistic policing futures, because the conflicting processes of police restructuring take place simultaneously leading to a multi-level and multi-sectoral policing governance in which 'no single entity dominates yet where, despite some conflict, recognisable order prevails' (Johnston 1996, p.66).

Though policing futures can be extrapolated from examining dominant trends in policing, this form of futurology assumes that what is happening today will be essentially what happens tomorrow. This assumption is complacent, especially given the fundamental changes that have taken place in the police governance of Britain. As argued earlier, extrapolation needs to be supplemented by causal analysis in order to construct feasible models of the future. Policing futures – whether of the hollowed-out or filled-in variety – will be investigated by examining the role of ACPO in the centralisation of policing. This case study of a significant policing actor seeks to deepen the causal analysis of policing futures.

ACPO and Policing Futures

This section draws on primary research data collected from interviews with Past Presidents, the Presidential Team, the Secretariat and members of ACPO, plus representatives from a range of other police-related organisations. It focuses specifically upon ACPO and its role in shaping policing futures, particularly its role in the process of policing centralisation. ACPO enjoys dual status in this process, for ACPO is a crucial centralising agency and an agency significantly influencing the capacity of other agencies to centralise policing. It is both a 'shaping agency' and an agency shaping other 'shaping agencies'. The section provides empirical evidence of the impact and pattern of policing centralisation, by examining ACPO members' views of the relative importance of central and local influences over policing policy; but first, it discusses the organisational features of ACPO pivotal to its current status.

The shaping of ACPO

It is impossible to examine the 'shaping' capacity of ACPO without appreciating the processes by which it has been shaped as an agency, for it is only relatively recently that ACPO has become equipped organisationally to operate on the centre-stage in making policing policy.

During the 1980s several commentators observed a threatening accretion of power by senior police officers generally, and ACPO particularly, involving a disproportionate capacity to influence the government machine. Thompson claimed ACPO 'does not attend on governments; governments attend on it' (1980, p.202). Campbell argued:

> 'The feeling that the ACPO tail is wagging the Home Office dog remains hard to dispell [sic]' (1987, p.12).

There is a danger of exaggerating the degree of coherence then existent within ACPO and its consequent ability to operate in the strategic pursuit of its aims. In 1989 the then Home Secretary, Douglas Hurd, expressed concern over the lack of coherence in ACPO as a policy-making body, and encouraged ACPO to develop a more corporate approach (Savage & Charman forthcoming). Furthermore, chief constables questioned the power of ACPO. In his research on chief constables Reiner disclosed:

> 'For all its image as an eminence grise outside police circles, ACPO is perceived by the chiefs themselves as a weak body. Its influence on the government, and the world outside, is seen as limited to its appearance as the voice of senior police opinion. But its capacity to represent this is weakened by its inability to cajole forty-three individuals, schooled to take pride in their own autonomy, into a united front (1989, p.215).

Similar sentiments have been expressed in more recent research (Savage & Charman forthcoming). The relative lack of corporacy within ACPO during the 1980s was referred to by a number of former Presidents of ACPO in the following statements:

> '... there were in my opinion some quite unnecessary divisions ... I detected a certain unwillingness on the part of some members of ACPO to pull together and to view the problems collectively' (P10). '... criticisms had come from various places that [ACPO] couldn't get their act together' (P06).

It is against the backcloth of relative fragmentation that subsequent steps were taken to enhance corporacy within ACPO. Moves towards a more organisationally cohesive approach within ACPO was already apparent at the time of Reiner's research (1991, pp.281-284). Since then ACPO has developed apace towards corporacy (Savage & Charman 1996, pp.52-53). Encouraged by Douglas Hurd's push for stronger policy-making machinery, ACPO initially established a centrally-funded professional secretariat. However, subsequent, though less supportive, political measures were to drive ACPO further. The shock of the Government's police reform plans launched in the early 1990s contributed to the sense of urgency for a fully coordinated ACPO response. The outcome has not just been more reactive but also increasingly proactive (Savage & Charman forthcoming).

The organisational vehicles for ACPO's 'new corporacy', in addition to the creation of its own secretariat, have taken several forms. First, ACPO developed an enhanced committee structure, including the creation of three over-arching 'coordinating committees' – International Affairs, Finance and Quality of Service. There has been the increased use of 'focused seminars', usually 'brainstorming' one-day sessions to address particular issues (eg the reform of police authorities, performance measurement, police funding and criminal justice), sometimes employing outside specialist speakers. Such fora enabled ACPO to develop a collective position on matters of pressing concern, and to marshall research and argument in support of its position. Second, ACPO developed a principle of 'presumption in favour of compliance' underpinning the relationship between agreed ACPO policy and individual police force policy. Consequently once ACPO has agreed a policy, it is presumed that individual chief constables will accept and adopt that policy; those wishing to defer from the policy must indicate in writing an intention to do so and the reasons for departure from agreed policy. This rule has been seen internally as an important mechanism in maintaining a collective stance on policy matters. Third, ACPO has strengthened its public relations/information machinery, both in terms of resources and strategy. As a result ACPO has been able increasingly to present its views on particular police-related matters as the 'police view'; the Police Federation, representing rank-and-file police officers, has had to concede some ground in this respect. Also ACPO's more centralised and coordinated information strategy has meant that public relations units of individual police forces increasingly consult with ACPO headquarters before responding to media requests for comment. ACPO argued:

> 'Such corporacy is essential if forces are not to be "picked off" on issues of the day' (1995a, p.43).

Fourth, the recent decision by ACPO membership to accept the reform of its constitution must also be seen in light of the ACPO strategy to develop a corporate approach. ACPO decided to separate its 'staff association' work, concerned with senior police officers' pay and conditions of service, from its 'professional association' work, concerned with representing the professional opinions of senior police officers on police-related matters. A central rationale for this split was to allow the 'professional association' side of ACPO to concentrate more specifically, and therefore more effectively, on policy-making and advice-giving, not least in terms of its status as perceived by the Home Office and other agencies.

The shaping of ACPO into an increasingly corporate body has been a precondition of its capacity to shape policing policy nationally. The section next considers the relative significance of ACPO in the centralisation of policing.

ACPO, centralising agencies and local policy The thesis of increasingly centralised policing in Britain is well-established. Further research remains to be done, however, on the relative significance of the centralising agencies and relations between these agencies. Valuable work has been undertaken by the Policy Studies Institute, using case studies of specific areas of policing policy, on the interplay of central and local agencies in policy-making (Jones et al 1994). Research underpinning this paper focused upon policy-making at police force level and ACPO members' assessments of the formative influences of agencies influencing policing policy – namely, ACPO, the Home Office, the HMIC, the Audit Commission and local police authorities. Further research is examining the influence of local government (particularly the Association of Metropolitan Authorities and COLPA) on policing policy. A cross-section of ACPO membership, (n=40, selected by rank, gender, years of service and force-size), graded and commented on the relative influence of each agency in shaping policy.

Reiner researched chief constables' views on the influence of central agencies on police force policy-making (1991). On the basis of interviews conducted between 1987 and 1988, he found the Home Office was the most important central influence over decisions made by chief constables, with the HMIC second and ACPO third. It is significant that 30 per cent of respondents classed ACPO's influence over decision-making as 'little' or 'none'. The Audit Commission was not effectively a 'player' at the time of Reiner's research. Our research, at the time of writing, is not complete. However, on the basis of interviews conducted to date (n=33), three general, though tentative, findings have emerged.

First, of the five agencies in question, the local police authorities seem to be the least influential in making police force policy. When asked to rank the five agencies in terms of influence, the local police authorities were cited most frequently as the least influential body. The four central agencies were held to be more influential. This ranking acts as a marker of the perceived balance between central and local sources of influence over police force policy-making. One ACPO member, on the standing of police authorities (in this case a shire police force), remarked:

> 'Local authorities have not had a great deal of influence, not because we've isolated them but in an area like ... they didn't want to know, I've tried to get them involved for years in policing' (M22).

However, though police authorities scored weakly on their relative influence, several ACPO members anticipated a possible change as 'independent' members of the new police authorities settled in. In the words of two respondents:

'Once the Chief Constable was able to manipulate the police authorities in a way that you can't do with the new authorities. The independent members are flexing their muscles' (M02).

'It is already beginning to emerge that ... [independent members] ... are having an increasingly significant contribution to make in management terms' (M44).

Such sentiments serve as a significant qualification to those interpreting the constitution of new police authorities as simply extending the centralisation of policing (Loveday 1994, pp.224-226).

Second, of the four central agencies, the Home Office was most frequently cited as the agency with the greatest influence. In line with Reiner's work, this influence is generally held to be extensive – the majority of those interviewed categorised Home Office influence as 'considerable', and many saw it as increasing. One respondent said:

'If a Home Office Circular or notes from the Minister come then we will not go outside of what is recommended by the Home Office ... The Home Office has become increasingly influential over time. I've got no doubt about that. Home Office Circulars are becoming more directive rather than advisory' (M16).

Third, of the three remaining central agencies, the Audit Commission and ACPO appear to be roughly equal in terms of influence, with the HMIC running behind in fourth place overall. Just under half of respondents described the Audit Commission and ACPO as having 'considerable' influence, whereas about a third graded HMIC influence as 'considerable'.

Generally what seems to be emerging is a recasting of the central agencies in the extent they shape policing policy. Consistent with Reiner's research, the Home Office remains most influential, but more recently we are witnessing the increasing influence of ACPO and the Audit Commission, possibly at the expense of HMIC influence. On comparing the Audit Commission and HMIC, the following comments were expressed:

'I happen to think that the HMI has been overtaken ... as an institution ... by the Audit Commission, by the Audit Commission's professionalism, by the skills, you really have to admire the skills' (MO9).

'HMI has been overshadowed by the Audit Commission ... You could almost take the HMI out of it now you've got the Audit Commission'(M44).

'The Audit Commission have left the Inspectorate behind in the way that they do their job and their methodologies' (M14).

Given that the Audit Commission and HMIC operate with 'auditing' briefs, it is perhaps not surprising that the Audit Commission is held by some to be in competition with the HMIC. The Audit Commission seems to have made a major impact upon policing in a relatively short period of time. Its growing influence stems not just from its formal audit brief but also from its apparently high degree of legitimacy in the eyes of senior police officers. Second, there appears to be within ACPO some scepticism about the work and role of the HMIC. One respondent remarked the HMIC 'are increasingly unhelpful, very subjective in their judgement of things' (M09); another said it is 'totally ineffective and shouldn't exist in my view' (M10). Such comments may indicate a significant shift from the collegiate and supportive relations between the HMIC and senior police officers identified in Reiner's research (1991, pp.277-278), possibly reflecting the HMIC's increasingly Home Office-driven agenda of performance measurement and police performance 'league-tables'.

ACPO has been largely successful in gaining ground as a central source of influence over policing policy. ACPO's 'new corporacy' seems to have reaped benefits, reflected in its capacity both to shape policy of police forces and to influence other 'shaping' agencies and the wider policing environment. ACPO has a vast array of 'off-the-shelf' policies on a wide range of areas of policing which individual police forces increasingly adopt. The following comments were expressed:

> 'I would be surprised if there was any force that was not seriously influenced by what ACPO is saying in terms of policy formation' (PO2).
>
> 'I would be very surprised if knowingly any [police force] would go in the face of policy after appropriate debate through the committee structure onto the Chief Constables' Council' (P04).
>
> 'I can't think of an occasion when we have not followed ACPO policy' (M09).

With the possible exception of the Metropolitan Police, whose relationship with ACPO is more complex than with other police forces, ACPO appears to wield a substantial influence over policing nationally. Though scope always exists for individual police forces to forge their own policy on specific matters, where a policy has already been made within ACPO machinery it tends increasingly to be accepted by police forces. Furthermore, ACPO is increasingly addressing broader strategic issues facing the modern (postmodern?) police, such as privatisation, personnel strategy, income generation potential and performance management. Inevitably such agendas encroach periodically on established territories of other central agencies such as the Audit Commission and HMIC, generating tension in some quarters but involving cooperation and networking in others. ACPO's influence thus extends from local police forces to other central agencies of the 'new policing governance'. Its relations with the Audit Commission and Home Office will be examined.

ACPO developed new forms of relations with the Audit Commission, from one of consultation into one of incorporation and active cooperation. Cooperative ventures between them have emerged (eg the future of criminal investigation (Audit Commission 1993), and police patrol (though controversy broke out in October 1995 when part of the Audit Commission's work on police patrols was 'leaked' to the press).

The fluctuating relationship between ACPO and the Home Office has been most telling. In the late 1980s the Home Office pushed ACPO to develop as a professional association by supporting the case for a centrally-resourced ACPO secretariat. Later, however, ACPO was side-stepped by the then Home Secretary, Kenneth Clarke, with his launch of the Sheehy Inquiry in 1992 and the White Paper on police reform in 1993. As a result ACPO mounted a 'counter-offensive'. Through strategic alliances formed, amongst others, with local authority associations and peers (including former Conservative Home Secretaries) and a well targeted media campaign, ACPO played a key role in stunting the Government's reform agenda (Leishman et al 1995). Since the early 1990s, and following Michael Howard's appointment as Home Secretary, relations between ACPO and the Home Office entered a new phase, with a renewed emphasis upon consultation if not active cooperation. Two ACPO members remarked:

> 'At the moment there is an awareness within Government that ACPO is there to be consulted with and at the moment the Home Secretary is using consultation with ACPO almost as a way of saying that I'm doing my job because I'm consulting with ACPO' (M16).
>
> 'There's a strong influence both ways ... [The Home Office and ACPO] are both influential on each other ... they don't always agree but they do listen to each other and I think there is almost an equal relationship there' (M14).

ACPO seemingly benefits from an enviable degree of old-fashioned 'corporatism' in its dealings with central government. The irony is that ACPO was driven to become a more effective and strategic body partly to resist aspects of Home Office policy. Two respondents stated:

> 'I think ACPO speaking as one voice provides a very powerful vehicle to offset Government pressure' (M13).
>
> '... the more powerful the enemies you confront, the greater the need for corporacy, and ... Sheehy, the Police and Magistrates' Courts Act, probably have been the most significant developments which have caused the police service and the upper echelons of the police service to really become cohesive' (P04).

With a more supportive Home Secretary, the enhanced corporacy was applied to develop a more extensive strategy influencing the wider policing environment. On criminal justice legislation, one respondent said:

> '... in the areas of criminal justice, a lot of ACPO recommendations in terms of things like pre-trial issues, the right of silence, the work on disclosure, ACPO has been quite influential and the Home Secretary does show signs of wanting to listen' (M10).

ACPO published its agenda for criminal justice reform (1995b). Its agenda appears to have found a receptive audience in the Home Secretary and Conservative Party desperate to win back the 'law-and-order prize' partly snatched from it by the opposition (Savage & Nash 1994).

Conclusion

ACPO, with its 'new corporacy', wields significant influence as a central agency shaping policing policy. Whether this influence means that ACPO is itself a centralising agency is debatable. What ACPO has done is not so much further centralisation as extend standardisation. Centralisation is 'top-down' where policy is made by the centre and executed by others lower down the organisational hierarchy. But much policy-making within ACPO is 'bottom-up', because much policy originates from regional or sub-committees and agreed by the main committee, the Chief Constables' Council, which itself is an aggregate committee of all chief constables of local police forces. Furthermore, ACPO extended its influence, through consultation, cooperation and forming strategic alliances, over other central agencies shaping policing. Yet this influence also need not necessarily be seen as centralising. A view often expressed within ACPO is that this influence can be used to counter centralisation (Campbell 1987, p.11). One respondent claimed:

> 'I see it [ACPO] as becoming more influential, not less. I see it as being the only sensible counter to a national police service and I see it as a necessary bulwark against over-centralisation' (M26).

This view was very much in evidence during the campaign against elements of the police reform agenda, and in particular, proposals for increased Home Office controls over local policing. It further complicates the thesis that ACPO is part of the process of centralisation of British policing.

This case study on ACPO and policing centralisation has significant implications for any discussion on policing futures. First, the centralisation of British governance generally and policing particularly is countered by decentralisation, privatisation and Europeanisation. The centralised policing future, reinforcing the filling-in of the state, may be overtaken by decentralised, privatised and Europeanised policing futures, reflecting the hollowing-out of the state. Second, even if the trend towards policing centralisation is dominant, the precise form of the centralised policing future remains unclear. There is no single process of centralisation, and moreover, no single actor centralising the police. There are many competing processes of centralisation sponsored by many central agencies, some of which (such as ACPO) may not be the centralising bodies they appear to be. Third, predicting policing futures is not easy. By extrapolating, several policing futures can be constructed based on the trends towards the centralisation, decentralisation, privatisation and Europeanisation of policing. But the case study of ACPO and policing centralisation revealed that relatively simple extrapolated models of policing futures need to be refined by causal analysis based on empirical research in order to construct more sophisticated and plausible models of policing futures.

Alasdair MacIntyre

Kelvin Knight
University of North London

'Revolutionary Aristotelianism'

Introduction

E.P.Thompson expressed a 'wish that MacIntyre could complete his own thought' about 'emergent socialist consciousness within capitalist society', a consciousness that Thompson perceived in the 'ways in which men and women seem to be more "realized" as rational or moral agents, when acting collectively in conscious rebellion (or resistance) against capitalist process'.[1] Recently, however, it has been claimed that MacIntyre 'locates himself in the Aristotelian tradition, and can be read as a conservative' and, more particularly, that his 'central' concept of a practice is apolitical in that it does not involve an account of 'the exercise of power which calls for justification or critical scrutiny'.[2]

I shall argue that it is profoundly mistaken to 'read' MacIntyre as a conservative and that the political conclusions he draws from the Aristotelian tradition are, on the contrary, revolutionary. More particularly, I shall argue that his theory of practices most certainly does involve subjecting the exercise of power to critical scrutiny, and that it provides sound reasons for opposing the prevailing justifications and forms of power in contemporary society. MacIntyre has, therefore, continued to develop his ideas about conscious resistance to capitalism, as Thompson hoped he would. These ideas constitute MacIntyre's politics, his view of how philosophy should inform collective action.[3]

Practices

The concept of practice is basic to MacIntyre's entire project. 'The concept of a virtue ... always requires for its application the acceptance [of] some prior account of certain features of social and moral life in terms of which it has to be defined and explained'. The primary feature in MacIntyre's novel account is that of a practice.[4]

---

[1] E.P.Thompson, 'An Open Letter to Leszek Kolakowski', in Ralph Miliband & John Saville (eds), *The Socialist Register 1973*, Merlin Press, 1974, pp.58-9.

[2] Elizabeth Frazer & Nicola Lacey, *The Politics of Community: A Feminist Critique of the Liberal-Communitarian Debate*, Harvester Wheatsheaf, 1993, pp.103, 19; Elizabeth Frazer & Nicola Lacey, 'MacIntyre, Feminism and the Concept of Practice', in John Horton & Susan Mendus (eds), *After MacIntyre: Critical Perspectives on the Work of Alasdair MacIntyre*, Polity Press, 1994: pp.267, 271.

[3] A draft of a longer version of this paper defends these claims against other critics of MacIntyre's politics and relates the claims to an account of MacIntyre's theoretical development and broader epistemological and historiographical concerns, as well as to other theorists' uses of the concepts of practice and institution.

[4] Alasdair MacIntyre, *After Virtue: A Study in Moral Theory*, Duckworth, (first edition 1981) second edition 1985, pp.186-7.

This linking of practice to virtue immediately distinguishes MacIntyre's theory from that of most other theorists of social practice who, whether advocates or antagonists of conventional practices, identify morality with their subject in considering morality to comprise individuals' subordination to conventional rules of behaviour. MacIntyre, in contrast, does not reduce morality to convention or rule-following. Instead, he adopts the Aristotelian approach of identifying morality with virtues, or good dispositional qualities, that may be cultivated by persons. Social practices are not constitutive of morality, but they are the schools of the virtues. Such cardinal virtues as justice, courage and truthfulness are cultivated through participation in practices, as practitioners come to find outside of themselves things that may be valued for their own sake and to devote themselves to pursuit of those goods.

What is also immediately distinctive about MacIntyre's conception of social practice is the way that it involves rationality. Every practice has a particular form of reasoning internal to it, enabling practitioners to pursue 'internal goods' that can 'be had *only* by engaging in some particular kind of practice'.[5] This idea of practical rationality differentiates MacIntyre's concept of practice from both conservative conceptions, of practices as subrational, and Foucauldian conceptions, of practices as discourses of power. His basing of reason in practices also, of course, differentiates MacIntyre from what he calls 'the Enlightenment project' of justifying morality with a universalizing reason.

It is 'the concept of the best, of the perfected, [that] provides each of these forms of activity with the good toward which those who participate in it move', its internal good of excellence.[6] As practitioners advance toward that concept the concept is itself further advanced, if the practice is in good order, so that practitioners always have a goal ahead of them. Both practices and human lives should, then, be understood teleologically, the goals of human lives deriving from those of social practices.

In specifying what he means by a practice, MacIntyre differentiates it from a 'technique'. Practices include architecture ('but not bricklaying'), 'the game of football' (but not 'throwing a football with skill'), chess, farming, 'the enquiries of physics, chemistry and biology ... the work of the historian ... painting and music', as well as 'politics in the Aristotelian sense, [and] the making and sustaining of family life'.[7] He continues by discussing the politically trivial cases of chess and painting.[8] When pressed, however, he has acknowledged that certain points that are vital to understanding his idea of practices 'may have been obscured by [his] lack of attention to productive crafts such as farming and fishing, architecture and building'.[9]

As a vital aspect of practices is that pursuit of the good internal to a practice enables a person to give narrative order to her life, they might be thought of as vocations. Nevertheless, practice should not be considered a

---

[5] MacIntyre, *After Virtue*, p.188, MacIntyre's emphasis.
[6] Alasdair MacIntyre, *Whose Justice? Which Rationality?*, Duckworth, 1988, p.31.
[7] MacIntyre, *After Virtue*, pp.187-8, 273.
[8] MacIntyre, *After Virtue*, p.188ff.
[9] Alasdair MacIntyre, 'A Partial Response to my Critics', in Horton & Mendus (eds), *After MacIntyre*, p.284.

synonym of job. Bricklaying is not a distinct practice but a technique, a means to the good internal to building. One might also, of course, engage in practices other than that of which one's job is a part. For example, one might be a professional builder who plays chess. In this case, one is engaging in the same form of practical reasoning as a professional chess grandmaster, but it is more likely that the grandmaster is the one who plays a significant part in advancing its standards of excellence. Conversely, it is master builders who establish and advance standards of excellence in building, and a chess grandmaster who dabbles by building an extension to his house will gain by learning from the techniques and maxims developed by professional builders.

In attempting to achieve a good internal to a practice, a practitioner has 'initially to learn as an apprentice learns' from the standards already established.[10] However, 'the greatest achievements in each area at each stage always exhibit a freedom to violate the present established maxims' by those practitioners who have become expert through such learning.[11] It is in this way that practices and practical rationalities advance. The goods internal to practices are properly regarded as prior to rules within those practices, the purpose of those rules being to subserve pursuit of the goals of the practice.

This, then, is, in part, how MacIntyre furnishes his virtue ethics with an account of social life in terms of which it may be elaborated. However, MacIntyre is not content to elaborate his own moral philosophy. He also argues for its superiority over rivals, and each of these rivals also 'presupposes a sociology' because it supposes that the concepts it employs to describe reasons and actions 'are embodied or at least can be in the real social world'.[12] The most influential rival is that which he characterizes as emotivism, which issued from the failure of the Enlightenment project and anticipates the challenge to that project from Nietzscheanism. Emotivism gains much of its influence from the plausibility of its Humean supposition that sociology must be value-free because 'no valid argument can move from entirely factual premises to any moral or evaluative conclusion'. MacIntyre counters this contention with the idea of 'functional concepts'; 'from the premise " He is a sea-captain", the conclusion may be validly inferred that "He ought to do whatever a sea-captain ought to do" '.[13] The reasoning internal to a practice enables practitioners to judge between right and wrong actions, whilst a more general form of practical reasoning enables people to judge between good and bad practices.

MacIntyre characterizes such general forms of practical reasoning as traditions, and the tradition with which he identifies as that in which Aristotle and Aquinas are the seminal figures. 'It is rival conceptions of practical rationality ... which are in contention' between Aristotelians and others, embodied in 'the life of particular communities which exemplify each specific conception'.[14] 'What Aristotelian theory articulates are in fact the

---

[10] MacIntyre, *After Virtue*, p.258.
[11] MacIntyre, *Whose Justice? Which Rationality?*, p.31.
[12] MacIntyre, *After Virtue*, p.23.
[13] MacIntyre, *After Virtue*, pp.56-8.
[14] Alasdair MacIntyre, 'The Privatization of Good: An Inaugural Lecture', *The Review*

concepts embodied by such modes of practice' as those found 'in some relatively small-scale and local communities – examples range from some kinds of ancient city and some kinds of medieval commune to some kinds of modern farming and fishing enterprises – in which social relationships are informed by a shared allegiance to the goods internal to communal practices'. This contrasts with the mutually 'competing moral idioms' of contemporary liberal and conservative ideology, which have abstracted 'different aspects of the life of practice' from their particular contexts and transformed them into 'a set of rival theories'.[15] Aristotelianism is, then, less a particular (syllogistic) conception of practical rationality than the general rationality of practices as such, in contrast with which all other rationalities may be described as ideologies.

It may be inferred from this that 'the life of practice', in the absence of ideological obfuscation, tends to generate a commonly intelligible morality that facilitates the cultivation of virtue. The Aristotelian tradition of philosophy is that which justifies the life of practice and characterizes itself in terms of higher level reflection upon the reasoning generated by traditional practices. This contrasts with both Enlightenment philosophy, which attempted to transcend practice and tradition, and Nietzscheanism, which shared the Enlightenment aim of liberating people from practice and tradition but denied the epistemological certainty of any means of so doing. Aristotelianism is also, then, the philosophical tradition that maintains the rational validity of tradition and practice against other traditions that attempt to deny it.[16]

Since *After Virtue* MacIntyre's primary concern has been with elaborating and justifying his claim that all of the claims of philosophy can only be properly understood within the context of the historical development of philosophy, that this history can only be properly understood within the wider context of the history of society as a whole and that, thus understood, the proper way in which we should couch philosophical claims is that developed within the Aristotelian tradition. In attempting to persuade his philosophical opponents of the veracity of his case, MacIntyre has been drawn into arguments conducted on a level of theoretical abstraction that is inhospitable to the combination of theory with practice that he is arguing for. This was bound to produce 'a tension between [his] account of what it is to be rational and [his] account of the possibilities of understanding alien, rival traditions'.[17] Whilst he maintains that the Aristotelian tradition is incommensurable with other Western philosophical traditions and that Western culture is incommensurable with other cultures, he nonetheless recognizes that other cultures have philosophical traditions concerned with articulating the practical wisdom of members of their own societies and, therefore, calls for more 'importance ... to be accorded to the study of

---

of *Politics*, 52/2, 1990, p.355.

[15] Alasdair MacIntyre, *Marxism and Christianity*, Duckworth, (first edition 1968) second edition 1995, pp.xxvi-xxviii.

[16] Alasdair MacIntyre, *Three Rival Versions of Moral Enquiry: Encyclopaedia, Genealogy, and Tradition*, Duckworth, 1990.

[17] Alasdair MacIntyre, 'Reply to Roque', *Philosophy and Phenomenological Research*, 51/3, 1991, p.620.

what ... the philosophy and practice of [China] Japan, India, Africa and elsewhere' have 'contributed to virtue ethics'.[18] Aristotelianism is the tradition of the moral theory of practice that has developed in the West, but other civilizations have other such traditions. What is important everywhere is to guard against both the moral stultification of practices legitimated by ideological obfuscation, such as that which occurred in Polynesia with *taboo*[19] and in the West with the Enlightenment, and against the institutional concomitants of such stultification.

Practices versus Institutions

'Debate and conflict as to the best forms of practice have to be debate and conflict between rival institutions and not merely between rival theories'.[20] A concept of institutions is, therefore, vital to MacIntyre's social theory of practices. Whereas other such theories may be vulnerable to the criticism that they cannot explain how such a thing as a practice can be reproduced through the behaviour of different individuals,[21] he explains such transmission as largely conducted through formal organizations and their rules which are, therefore, necessary to the sustenance of practices.

> 'Practices must not be confused with institutions. Chess, physics and medicine are practices; chess clubs, laboratories, universities and hospitals are institutions. Institutions ... are involved in acquiring money and other material goods; they are structured in terms of power and status, and they distribute money, power and status as rewards. Nor could they do otherwise if they are to sustain not only themselves, but also the practices of which they are the bearers ... Indeed so intimate is the relationship of practices to institutions ... that institutions and practices characteristically form a single causal order in which the ideals and the creativity of the practice are always vulnerable to the acquisitiveness of the institution, in which the cooperative care for the common goods of the practice is always vulnerable to the competitiveness of the institution. In this context the essential function of the virtues is clear. Without them, without justice, courage and truthfulness, practices could not resist the corrupting power of institutions.'[22]

Money, power and status are all what MacIntyre calls goods external to practices. Such goods are 'never to be had *only* by engaging in some particular kind of practice'.[23] If our grandmaster were to give up chess for building because he calculated that he could earn more money as a cowboy

---

[18] Alasdair MacIntyre, 'Virtue Ethics', in Lawrence C.Becker (ed), *Encyclopedia of Ethics*, Volume 2, Garland, 1992, p.1281.
[19] MacIntyre, *After Virtue*, pp.111-3.
[20] MacIntyre, 'The Privatization of Good', p.360.
[21] For example, Stephen Turner, *The Social Theory of Practices: Tradition, Tacit Knowledge and Presuppositions*, Polity Press, 1994; Turner does not acknowledge MacIntyre's idea of institutions.
[22] MacIntyre, *After Virtue*, p.194.
[23] MacIntyre, *After Virtue*, p.188, MacIntyre's emphasis.

contractor than as an excellent chess player, then he would be acting in pursuit of goods external to any practice. He would, thereby, be foregoing the opportunity of cultivating the virtues, because he would be pursuing no goal other than that of satisfying his egoistic desires. External goods also differ from those internal to practices in 'that when achieved they are always some individual's property. Moreover, characteristically they are such that the more someone has of them, the less there is for other people'.[24]

Because external goods are necessary to institutions and institutions are necessary to practices, the tension between goods internal and external to practices is ineradicable. MacIntyre is no utopian. Indeed, he identifies the Athenian *polis* of Aristotle's day (towards which he has, misleadingly, been accused of longingly looking backward) as the place where the conflict between these two types of goods became explicit.[25]

The relative importance which people attach to internal and external goods is profoundly affected by the beliefs dominating their society. If practices are not to be corrupted by the goods pursued by institutions those institutions must always be subordinated to the goods internal to practices, which constitute the ends to which institutions should be considered means. Institutions should be structured and run in accordance with the particular practice of which they are the bearer. In the post-Enlightenment world, however, the reverse rationale has increasingly prevailed. Both capitalist corporations and states are structured in the same, bureaucratic way.

Managerial reasoning and action are, MacIntyre claims, an embodiment of emotivist moral philosophy, which 'entails the obliteration of any distinction between manipulative and non-manipulative social relations' by denying the reality of the latter.[26] Managers are obliged to adopt a certain attitude to the world through their work, such that they may be described as 'typical characters' or 'moral representatives' of emotivism. Their power and status are justified by their claims to be cost-effective and impartial means to any given end. Their concern is with organizational 'effectiveness', and therefore with manipulating the behaviour of others, treating others as means rather than ends.[27]

The sociology presupposed by emotivism is that of Weber, who denied that disagreements about ends can be rationally resolved. Both liberals' 'belief in an irreducible plurality of values' and the way in which 'Marxists organize and move toward power' are, for MacIntyre, best accommodated within Weber's sort of political sociology, 'for in our culture we know of no organized movement toward power which is not bureaucratic and managerial in mode and we know of no justifications for authority which are not Weberian in form'.[28] Contemporary authority is legitimated by reference to bureaucratic effectiveness, thereby reducing authority to 'successful power'.[29]

---

[24] MacIntyre, *After Virtue*, p.190.
[25] MacIntyre, *Whose Justice? Which Rationality?*, p.42.
[26] MacIntyre, *After Virtue*, p.23.
[27] MacIntyre, *After Virtue*, pp.25-31, 73-8.
[28] MacIntyre, *After Virtue*, p.109.
[29] MacIntyre, *After Virtue*, p.26.

Weber is right in explaining how the idea of their effectiveness 'is used to sustain and extend the power and authority of managers', and he elevates that idea into an entire theory of modernity. Nevertheless, he is wrong in claiming that social science gives managers veritably predictive knowledge, such that they really can exercise control over society. Instead, MacIntyre asks us to 'consider the following possibility: that what we are oppressed by is not power, but impotence', 'a masquerade of social control'.[30] Bureaucratic institutions affect society, but their effects are less often intended than unintended. Institutions do manage to manipulate people's behaviour, but this does not enable them to achieve the sort of society that their plans envisage. Totalitarianism (MacIntyre himself predicted, in 1981) is, therefore, heading for defeat.[31]

Weber's conception of the iron cage of bureaucratic rationality is, for MacIntyre, a 'moral fiction'.[32] The dominance of bureaucratic rationality is possible only because of the prior discrediting of substantive rationality by the failure of the Enlightenment project. Management is a mere technique, not a practice with goods internal to itself, and therefore putting administrative technique and its goods of effectiveness before the goods of excellence internal to practices is a moral error.

What the intellectual and social dominance of instrumental rationality does achieve is the atomization and demoralization of society. As people come to think of themselves as without moral purpose and as manipulated 'means' to others' arbitrary ends,[33] those people are likely to attempt to retain a sense of themselves as effective actors by becoming manipulative also. In this context, of a society demoralized by bureaucratic manipulation and the failure of the Enlightenment project, we face the alternatives of continued demoralization and manipulation (emotivism, which is not a reasonable option), of substituting will for morality and asserting our will over others (the Nietzschean option), or of enacting our lives as the narrative of a quest for our true good through participation in social practices, thereby finding a teleological justification for morality (the Aristotelian option). The Nietzschean option is that which is effectively taken by those who wield institutional power, in attempting to impose their will over others and, also, upon intractable, social reality.

'Government itself' is, for MacIntyre, 'a hierarchy of bureaucratic managers'.[34] Therefore, although he is bound to agree with the familiar communitarian claim that the liberal state's claim to neutrality is fictitious, given that Weber's claim about the morally neutral instrumentality of bureaucratic rationality is fictitious, MacIntyre is also bound to agree with much of the liberal counter-critique of communitarianism. 'Where liberals have characteristically urged that it is in the activities of subordinate voluntary associations, such as those constituted by religious groups, that shared visions of the good should be articulated, communitarians have insisted that

---

[30] MacIntyre, *After Virtue*, p.75; for an extension of this critique to Critical Theory, see Alasdair MacIntyre, *Marcuse*, Fontana, 1970, pp.70-2.
[31] MacIntyre, *After Virtue*, pp.106-7.
[32] MacIntyre, *After Virtue*, pp.76-7.
[33] MacIntyre, *After Virtue*, pp.23-4.
[34] MacIntyre, *After Virtue*, p.85.

the nation itself through the institutions of the nation-state ought to be constituted to some significant degree as a community', an ideal against which MacIntyre sides with liberals in 'understanding how it generates totalitarian and other evils' and, therefore, in 'resisting'.[35]

Just as in *After Virtue* MacIntyre cites the criticisms of different justifications of rule-constituted morality against each other as demonstrating that incoherence is the inevitable result of attempting to elaborate such a justification, so, since then, he has cited the criticisms of liberal and communitarian legitimations of the state against each other as demonstrating that incoherence is the inevitable result of attempting to elaborate any such legitimation. On the one hand, the state is justified as the guarantor of individuals' rights to pursue their own self-chosen goals. On the other hand, it is justified as the expression of a form of social life for which its subjects may, whenever necessary, be required to risk their lives. There cannot be a rational legitimation of the state that satisfies both of these criteria. As both criteria represent necessary aspects of the state, there cannot be any coherent solution to the modern problem of political obligation.[36] Unfortunately, however, exposing incoherence is far from sufficient to achieve its transcendence.

In going beyond the exposure of rational inconsistency in legitimations of modernity, MacIntyre draws on Marx for a critique of its characteristic institutions. He indicts 'the institutional injustice of capitalism' for the alienation and exploitation of labour. 'It becomes impossible for workers to understand their work as a contribution to the common good of a society which at the economic level no longer has a common good, because of different and conflicting interests of different classes. The needs of capital formation impose upon capitalists and upon those who manage their enterprises a need to extract from the work of their employees a surplus which is at the future disposal of capital and not of labour', so that practitioners are considered dispensable means to the goal of profitability. MacIntyre's classes are, however, different from those of Marx. 'Small producers' are in a similarly unfortunate position to workers, as both are practitioners manipulated by others through 'market relationships'. Conversely, MacIntyre's remarks about capitalism's 'systematic incentives to develop a type of character that has a propensity to injustice', if conjoined with his critique of managers as characters, indicate that management rather than ownership constitutes the opposing interest.[37]

Under capitalism, 'work tends to become separated from everything but the service of biological survival and ... institutionalized acquisitiveness'. Work 'on a production line, for example', has 'been expelled from the realm of practices with goods internal to themselves' and '*pleonexia* ['acquisitive-

---

[35] MacIntyre, 'A Partial Response to my Critics', pp.302-3.

[36] Alasdair MacIntyre, 'Poetry as Political Philosophy: Notes on Burke and Yeats', in Verene Bell & Laurence Lerner (eds), *On Modern Poetry: Essays Presented to Donald Davie*, Vanderbilt University Press, 1988, p.149; Alasdair MacIntyre, 'The Theses on Feuerbach: A Road Not Taken', in Carol C.Gould & Robert S.Cohen (eds), *Artifacts, Representations, and Social Practice: Essays for Marx Wartofsky*, Kluwer Academic, 1994, p.281; Alasdair MacIntyre, 'Is Patriotism a Virtue?', in Ronald Beiner (ed), *Theorizing Citizenship*, State University of New York Press, 1995, *passim*.

[37] MacIntyre, *Marxism and Christianity*, pp.x-xiv.

ness'], a vice in the Aristotelian scheme, is now the driving force of productive work'.[38] His critique of capitalism therefore shares something with R.H.Tawney's influential contrast of 'the acquisitive society' with the socialist or 'functional society', in which work is recognized as a duty to be undertaken for the common good.[39] However, MacIntyre's teleological conception of work enables him to avoid the 'banal earnestness' for which he had earlier dismissed what we might call Tawney's anticipation of deontological communitarianism.[40]

MacIntyre clearly departs from Marxism, also, in rejecting its form of revolutionary politics. He rejects the way that its adherents organize and move toward power, along with any other 'systematic political action of a conventional kind' aimed at achieving power or influence within the state.[41] Marxists may seek to use state power to overthrow capitalism and effect a communist utopia, but all they thereby achieve is harsher imprisonment within the iron cage of instrumental rationality. 'Those who make the conquest of state power their aim are always in the end conquered by it', just as reformist trade unionism inevitably leads to 'the domestication and then the destruction of effective trade union power'.[42] Marx did not perceive the dangers in managerial rationality that Weber theorized and the past century has made evident. Instead, he inherited from Hegel the belief that bureaucratic administration can be transparently rational and, therefore, that it represents the social liberation of humankind. Although he identified the proletariat as the revolutionary class that would put scientific socialism into practice, it remained the bureaucracy that would represent the universal interest in administering an ostensibly classless society.

If his rejection of Marxist politics is a clear change in MacIntyre's stance since the 1950s and '60s (when he moved from the Communist Party to the Socialist Labour League to the International Socialists), he has nevertheless been constant in his wholesale opposition both to dominant institutions and ideologies and to any kind of reformism. He also remains sympathetic to Marxism insofar as it is 'a body of theory designed to inform, direct and provide self-understanding in the practice of working-class and intellectual struggle against capitalism', although he considers that Marxists 'were the agents of our own defeats' in failing to think through the practical bases of reason, and, therefore, that what is to be done now is 'first to understand this and then to start out all over again'.[43]

Politics

MacIntyre's notoriously pessimistic conclusion to *After Virtue* is that 'what matters at this stage is the construction of local forms of community within

---

[38] MacIntyre, *After Virtue*, pp.227, 137.
[39] R.H.Tawney, *The Acquisitive Society*, G.Bell & Sons, 1921.
[40] Alasdair MacIntyre, 'The Socialism of R.H.Tawney', in *Against the Self-Images of the Age: Essays on Ideology and Philosophy*, Duckworth, 1971, p.39.
[41] Alasdair MacIntyre, 'After Virtue and Marxism: A Response to Wartofsky', *Inquiry*, 27/2-3, 1984, p.252.
[42] MacIntyre, *Marxism and Christianity*, pp.xv, xxi.
[43] MacIntyre, *Marxism and Christianity*, p.xxx; MacIntyre, 'The Theses on Feuerbach', p.290.

which civility and the intellectual and moral life can be sustained through the new dark ages which are already upon us', given that 'the barbarians ... have already been governing us for quite some time'.[44] He still persists in his belief that 'the problem is not to reform the dominant order, but to find ways for local communities to survive by sustaining a life of the common good against the disintegrating forces of the nation-state and the market'.[45] He suggests looking for such a way in 'a politics of self-defence for all those local societies that aspire to achieve some relatively self-sufficient and independent form of participatory practice-based community'.[46] In illustration, he cites 'the account given by Edward Thompson in *The Making of the English Working Class* ... of the communal life of the hand-loom weavers of Lancashire and Yorkshire' 200 years ago. 'What the hand-loom weavers hoped to, but failed to sustain "was a community of independent small producers" '. MacIntyre compares them, and their later Chartism, with 'the insurrection of the Silesian weavers of the Eulengebirge in 1844', adding that Marx 'seems not to have understood the form of life from which that militancy arose, and so later failed to understand that while proletarianization makes it necessary for workers to resist, it also tends to deprive workers of those forms of practice through which they can discover conceptions of a good and of virtues adequate to the moral needs of resistance'. The practice of such weavers, in contrast, was 'entitled to be called "revolutionary" ' because 'those engaged in it transform themselves and educate themselves through their own self-transformative activity, coming to understand their good as the good internal to that activity'.[47]

Unfortunately, although workers were often able to collectively 'make' their own way of life in local communities during the formative stages of industrial capitalism, it does not follow that such a possibility still exists. Even those local communities embodying the 'Gaelic oral culture of farmers and fishermen' that engrossed MacIntyre's early imagination have now all but succumbed to the demands of state and market, as MacIntyre acknowledges.[48] He also acknowledges 'that an adequate sense of tradition manifests itself in a grasp of those future possibilities which the past has made available to the present'.[49] Such a sense should, then, manifest itself in identifying other available possibilities for resisting the dominant order, given that 'there are forms of institutionalized community in the modern world other than those of the state, and the preservation of and enhancement of certain at least of such forms of community may set tasks for a less barren politics'.[50]

I suggest that the rationale of MacIntyre's social theory of practices is that the bases of these certain forms of community is not now to be found

---

[44] MacIntyre, *After Virtue*, p.85.

[45] Alasdair MacIntyre, 'The Spectre of Communitarianism', *Radical Philosophy*, 70, 1995, p.35.

[46] MacIntyre, *Marxism and Christianity*, p.xxvi.

[47] MacIntyre, 'The Theses on Feuerbach', pp.287-8.

[48] Alasdair MacIntyre, 'Nietzsche or Aristotle?', in Giovanna Borradori, *The American Philosopher: Conversations with Quine, Davidson, Putnam, Nozick, Danto, Rorty, Cavell, MacIntyre, and Kuhn*, University of Chicago Press, 1994, pp.139-40.

[49] MacIntyre, *After Virtue*, p.223.

[50] MacIntyre, 'Poetry as Political Philosophy', p.157.

in locality but, rather, in particular practices. Accordingly, the tasks for a politics in the Aristotelian tradition are to defend the rationality, ideals, creativity and cooperative care for common goods of practices against institutional corruption and managerial manipulation, and to uphold internal goods of excellence against external goods and claims of effectiveness. The present dominance of institutions over practices, and of bureaucratic technique and procedural rules over practical wisdom, is the embodiment of the dominance of abstract reason and will over tradition, of Kantianism and Nietzscheanism over Aristotelianism. It is, therefore, in collective defence of the goods and rationalities of practices against those of institutions that the bases for a politics in the Aristotelian tradition is now to be found.

MacIntyre indicates how the tasks of such a politics might be undertaken. 'When an institution – a university, say, or a farm, or a hospital – is the bearer of a tradition of practice or practices, its common life will be partly, but in a centrally important way, constituted by a continuous argument as to what a university is and ought to be',[51] affording scope for opposing the goods internal to a practice against those external to it. MacIntyre contends that the 'peculiar and [socially] essential function' of universities is, now, to be 'places where ... the wider society [can] learn how to conduct its own debates ... in a rationally defensible way'.[52]

Exposing the incoherence 'of the rhetoric of official academia' is, of course, far from sufficient to prevent the advance of managerialization because such rhetoric is symptomatic 'of a much deeper disorder',[53] and the same is true regarding farms and hospitals. Nevertheless, given that the 'hierarchical division between managers and managed is ... legitimated by the superior knowledge imputed to themselves' by managers,[54] if that legitimacy is to be challenged it is necessary to theorize a general justification of the priority of practical over instrumental reason, and this is what MacIntyre does in opposing the abstraction of moral and organizational theories from personal virtue and social practice.

This challenge to the legitimacy of the modern age provides bases for a form of class politics. Those who have acquired money, power and status have an interest in maintaining the institutions and ideologies of manipulation. Conversely, 'Aristotelian theory articulates the presuppositions of a range of practices a good deal wider than Aristotle himself was able to recognize', including those of many workers and small producers.[55] Perhaps proletarianization has alienated many from the ends of their activity as workers, rather than from their ends as waged employees. However, proletarianization lacks the universalizing logic that Marx imputed to it. 'A production line' already characterizes work in industrialized countries less than it did when MacIntyre wrote *After Virtue*, and managers are having to find new ways of deskilling or otherwise marginalizing workers. One way is casualization. Another is through the second managerial revolution being carried out in the name of Total Quality Management, the culmination of

---

[51] MacIntyre, *After Virtue*, p.222.
[52] MacIntyre, *Three Rival Versions of Moral Enquiry*, p.222.
[53] MacIntyre, *Three Rival Versions of Moral Enquiry*, p.227.
[54] MacIntyre, 'The Theses on Feuerbach', p.286.
[55] MacIntyre, 'A Partial Response to my Critics', p.301.

which would be the total proceduralization of work. That this is producing massive demoralization and alienation throughout the economy is obvious, but that its victory is a foregone conclusion is no more obvious than was that of Soviet planning. Self-management of practitioners remains a future possibility. What Aristotelian theory may contribute to pursuit of the subordination of institutions to practices is legitimation and coordination, so that previously isolated struggles can be transformed into a new class war of attrition.

MacIntyre offers no blueprint for a society in which institutions are subordinated to practices. Nevertheless, as an Aristotelian practice of politics comprises 'the making and sustaining of forms of human community – and therefore of institutions',[56] this practice must involve some conception of excellence in the making of institutions. The institutions of an entire territorial polity must be 'concerned, as Aristotle says ... with the whole of life, not with this or that good, but with man's good as such'.[57] Such a polity must provide 'an ordering of goods ... to be achieved by excellence within specific and systematic forms of activity, integrated into an overall rank-order by the political activity of [its] citizens'.[58] All may share in the practice of politics if the polity comprises what might be called a community of communities or, even, a functional society.

No hierarchy of practices or of their internal goods is given by either nature, a priori reasoning, or history. MacIntyre rejects any such 'notion of an absolute standpoint, independent of the particularity of all traditions'.[59] He is, instead, a radically political thinker.

He is also a politically radical thinker. His novel juxtaposition of practices to institutions prohibits any susceptibility to the 'deification of the state', 'Institutionalism' and political conservatism with which Critical Theorists[60] and Foucauldians typically charge Aristotelians. It also renders him innocent of 'extreme philosophical idealism'.[61] Rather, his opposition to the Enlightenment's legitimation of capitalism is 'not only [to] a theoretical mistake. It is a mistake embodied in institutionalized social life. And it is therefore a mistake which cannot be corrected merely by better theoretical analysis'.[62]

MacIntyre should, therefore, still be read along with Thompson and Marx, not with either conservatives or conventionally academic philosophers. The philosophers have only *interpreted* the world in rival ways; the point is to *change* it.

---

[56] MacIntyre, *After Virtue*, p.194.
[57] MacIntyre, *After Virtue*, p.156.
[58] MacIntyre, *Whose Justice? Which Rationality?*, p.133.
[59] MacIntyre, 'A Partial Response to my Critics', p.295.
[60] Herbert Schnaedelbach, 'What is Neo-Aristotelianism?', *Praxis International*, 7/3-4, 1987, p.235.
[61] A charge made by Ian Shapiro, believing that MacIntyre implies 'that all we need to do to change our current circumstances is rethink our philosophical commitments', *Political Criticism*, University of California Press, 1990, pp.150-1.
[62] MacIntyre, 'The Theses on Feuerbach', p.284.

Marx and Hegel

Christopher J. Arthur
University of Sussex

'Capital: A Compulsive-Neurotic Subject'

Abstract

Marx's concept of capital is illuminated through comparison with Hegel's two concepts of the infinite.

Joan Robinson, in her *Open Letter to a Marxist* of 1953, asked rhetorically what business had Hegel putting his nose in between her and Ricardo. The answer is that Marx's concepts are different from Ricardo's and it is unlikely that Marx would have been able to rethink such questions as the concept of capital without his background in Hegel's philosophy, albeit that for tactical reasons he tried to diminish the evidence in his published texts.

The whole question of the influence of Hegel on Marx is very complex. It cannot be easily settled by studying such explicit acknowledgements of it as are made by Marx; for these are in general very cryptic. Furthermore there is a problem about the interpretation of Hegel, which also involves the issue of what Marx's interpretation of him was, and whether it was fair.

In the literature we see two tendencies. One, represented most strikingly by Herbert Marcuse, reads Hegel as materialistically as possible so as to claim his ideas may be readily resituated in a Marxian framework. The other, represented best by Lucio Colletti and Louis Althusser, argues that Marx struggled to leave behind this influence because Hegel was idealist through and through and hence could only be a bad influence.

The very same words are interpreted entirely oppositely by such commentators. Hegel says in his *Science of Logic* that finite things must perish and hence give way to the infinite. Marcuse situates this in the context of Marx's historical materialism (*Reason & Revolution*, pp.136ff) whereas Colletti (*Marxism & Hegel*, p.7 and *passim*) finds this is the gateway to idealism.[1]

My own position in this debate is that Hegel's logic can be drawn on in the study of capitalism because capital is a very peculiar object, grounded in a process of real abstraction in exchange in much the same way as Hegel's dissolution and reconstruction of reality is predicated on the abstractive power of thought. On the basis of the equivalences set up by the exchange abstraction I have shown how the value implicit in exchangeable commodities becomes explicit in money, becomes its own aim in capital, and is grounded in production.[2]

---

[1] It may be doubted whether Colletti understood Hegel; for on p.49 he cites as a 'profession of idealism' by Hegel something (from his *Encyclopaedia Logic*, para. 76) which is clearly not his view, and which turns out to be a paraphrase of Descartes and Jacobi.

[2] See my 'Hegel's *Logic* and Marx's *Capital*' in F.Moseley (ed), *Marx's Method in 'Capital'*, Humanities Press, 1993.

In this paper I shall address just one aspect of the concept of capital: Marx's characterisation of it as a 'subject' (*Capital*, Volume 1, Fowkes translation, 1976, p.253); and, even then, mainly in so far as Hegel's two concepts of the infinite throw light on the issue. In my view the term 'subject' need not necessarily involve reference to consciousness, merely that the thing in question has its end within it, rather than just 'being there', or used for some other end. Thus, applying the term 'subject' to capital is not metaphorical; it should be understood literally, although I cannot give the full argument for this here.

The key passages from Marx's chapter on The General Formula for Capital on which I wish to comment are the following:

> 'The repetition or renewal of the act of selling in order to buy finds its measure [*Mass*] and its goal in a final purpose which lies outside it, namely consumption, the satisfaction of definite needs. But in buying in order to sell, on the contrary, the end and the beginning are the same, money or exchange-value, and this very fact makes the movement an endless one. Certainly 100 pounds sterling become 110. But, considered qualitatively, the 100 is the same as the 110, namely money; while from the quantitative point of view, the 110 is, like the 100, a sum of definite and limited [*beschraenkte*] value ... The value of the 110 has the same need for valorization as the value of the 100, for they are both limited expressions of exchange-value, and therefore both have the same vocation, to approach richness simply by quantitative increase.'[3]

Marx goes on to conclude that, since 'the circulation of money as capital is an end in itself', 'the movement of capital is therefore limitless [*masslose*]' (*Capital*, 1, p.253).

He also stresses that accumulation is achieved 'by means of throwing money again and again into circulation' (*Capital*, 1, p.255). And to this last remark he appends an interesting quotation from Galiani: 'Things possess an infinite quality when moving in a circle which they lack when advancing in a straight line.'

To begin our commentary at the end, let us look at this Galiani passage. While from a mathematical point of view a straight line is infinitely long, Galiani intends us to note that at any given moment in the advance the line has a definite finite length: the circular path by contrast, once having been established (like a planetary orbit), has no beginning and no end.

While Marx deliberately chose another economist to lend authority to his argument that the movement of capital accumulation is circular and infinite, he would have done better here to have cited Hegel; for the latter has very interesting, more sophisticated, things to say about infinity, which apply very well to capital. In fact, in the passages from Marx just quoted several terms reminiscent of Hegelian categories are employed: measure,

---

[3] *Capital*, 1, p.252 – translation amended: Fowkes here follows previous translations in wrongly putting 'approach absolute wealth'.

limit,[4] limitless, and infinite. Of great importance is Marx's statement that 'the movement of capital is limitless [*masslose*]'. The term '*masslose*' is a category of Hegel's logic,[5] usually translated 'measureless'.[6] If one followed the Engels edition and said the process C-M-C 'is kept within bounds by the very object it aims at' (*Capital*, FLPH, 1961, p.151) then the contrast could be put by saying the M-C-M movement is boundless. The 'measureless' is linked to the notion of 'infinite progression', treated earlier in the Logic under the head of 'spurious [*schlechte*] infinity' (paras 94 & 95; see also *Science of Logic*, Miller translation, pp.139ff.) Hegel there introduced the notion that there are two kinds of infinity:

> 'But this infinite progression is not the genuine infinite, which consists rather in remaining at home with itself in its other, or (when it is expressed as a progress) in coming to itself in its other.' [7]

This distinction between the bad and the true infinite is widely deployed by Hegel in more concrete contexts. It turns up in his political philosophy in which genuine infinity is said to characterise the free will (*Elements of the Philosophy of Right*, para. 22); and in the Addition to this paragraph he writes in terms of the metaphor we have already come across:

> 'Infinity has rightly been represented by the image of the circle, because a straight line runs on indefinitely and denotes that merely negative and false infinity which, unlike true infinity, does not return to itself'.[8]

Hegel's analysis of unilinear progress is quite subtle; it is both finite (at any given time) and infinite (in tendency) for there is always something beyond the finite. Hence in this alternation it never attains completion. But the circle has no beyond because the movement stays within a set of points defined by it. It is complete in itself. So the movement always returns to itself and abides with itself. It should be said that the bulk of Hegel's discussion of the category of limit appears under 'Quality' and the infinite is thereby also taken in terms of qualitative transformation rather than in terms of quantitative magnitude. More specifically, these terms occur in the discussion of '*Dasein*' (Being There) and it is the self-relation characterised as true infinity that makes possible the transition to 'Being-for-Itself' which, although here simply a 'One', may be taken as a very abstract precursor of the '*Subjekt*'.[9]

---

[4] Hegel uses two terms: '*Grenze*', which may be translated 'limit', and the stronger '*Schranke*', which Miller translates as 'limitation', and Garaets et al – in the new translation of the *Encyclopaedia Logic*– as 'restriction'.

[5] See *Encyclopaedia Logic*, para. 109.

[6] Hence the reference back in the Marx quotation is not to 'limited' but to 'measure'.

[7] *Encyclopaedia Logic*, para. 94, Addition.

[8] Indeed '*schlecht*' – 'false' – can also mean in dialect 'straight', so there may be a pun here.

[9] Thus all subjects introduce difference within themselves and then close it. For example a person might say 'It seems to me that if I study Hegel long enough I might understand him.' In this case we can see that the person saying it is distinct from the person talked about, simply as a matter of the logic of utterance; yet at the same time posited in the 'I' as the very same.

To return to the beginning of Hegel's argument, he introduces first the incontestable notion that 'something only is what it is *within* its limit and by *virtue* of its limit', by which he explains he means qualitative limit (para. 92A). The argument proceeds by developing the 'dialectical' consequence that there is 'something else' beyond the limit, and that 'everything finite is subject to alteration'. It is here that the infinite is evolved as a category: 'Something becomes an other, but the other is itself a something, so it likewise becomes an other, and so on *ad infinitum*'. This is, of course, the 'bad infinite', which needs to be superseded. This occurs when something and other are grasped as phases of the same thing 'and this relation to itself in the passing and in the other is *genuine infinity*'. Also the other is the other of its other hence likewise affirmed via 'the negation of the negation' as Being-for-Itself (para. 95).

It hardly needs pointing out that in the M-C-M circuit money does relate itself to itself; so in this sense capital is on the way to being a free self-determining subject (as defined in Hegel's *Elements of the Philosophy of Right*, para. 23). But Marx has also pointed out here that the movement of capital is constantly renewed because the aim in question, namely valorization, is open-ended; there is no possibility of reaching a conclusion, for at every stage there remains the possibility – indeed the necessity – to go further, while at every stage there is an infinite distance still to travel.

So both Hegelian concepts of infinity are relevant to Marx's discussion. Let us explore them in turn.

Capital, as a subject, appears in one way under the head of the genuine infinite. We saw in the 'Formula' chapter of Volume 1 that the renewal of investment on the basis of the return achieved in the previous cycle presented us with a circular development. At that stage of Marx's exposition this was purely *formular* and the possibility of accumulation likewise merely a formal potential. For Hegel the true subject has its conditions of existence within its power rather than being determined by external conditions. However by the end of the first volume Marx has grounded this movement of accumulation in production, and the exploitation of labour; thus by the start of the second volume we have a concept of capital that does not merely cover its form but which grasps a wealth of content and founds itself on the permanent movement of valorisation.

The circular quality of this process is beautifully developed by Marx in *Capital*, Volume 2, under the head of 'The Metamorphoses of Capital and their Circuit'. In his *Science of Logic* Hegel acutely remarks that faced with the already existing categories the problem was 'to render this material fluid' (Miller, 575). Even more than with logical forms, this is true of the forms of value including the shapes in which capital establishes itself, and it is a great merit of Marx's discussion at the start of Volume 2 that he grasps capital in its fluidity.

I read Marx's analysis of the capital circuit, not as his subjective reflections on it, but rather an account of how capital itself, based as it is in a system of exchange predicated on a 'real abstraction', in its own process achieves the positing of such elements as money and commodities as abstract moments of itself and produces itself by supervening upon them in its movement through them.

With regard to the total process of the capital circuit (wherein money capital – M – purchases factors of production which give rise – P – to a saleable commodity – C – and thus restores its money form again – M) Marx gives the following important summary:

> 'The two forms that the capital value assumes within its circulation stages are those of *money capital* and *commodity capital*; the form pertaining to the production stage is that of *productive capital*. The capital that assumes these forms in the course of its circuit, discards them again and fulfils in each of them its appropriate function, is *industrial* capital – industrial here in the sense that it encompasses every branch of production pursued on a capitalist basis.
>
> Money capital, commodity capital and productive capital thus do not denote independent varieties of capital, whose functions constitute the content of branches of business that are independent and separate from one another. They are simply particular functional forms of industrial capital, which takes on all three forms in turn.'[10]

Marx earlier referred to 'the different forms with which capital clothes itself in its different stages, alternately assuming them and casting them aside' (*Capital*, 2, p.109) Notice the importance of the metaphor of 'clothing' here. It indicates the conceptual character of capital as something that cannot be immediately identified with any of the forms M, P, C. It is rather their unity, a process going on through their connection in a circuit of *transformation* of capital. Already then we can see here the superiority of Marx's conception over empiricist concepts of capital which would reduce it to a single form, for example money, or produced means of production. Marx goes on to explain the point that money, for example, is not *in itself* capital; it is so only in relation to the other elements of the circuit, a whole within which the moments are internally related (*Capital*, 2, p.112).

Marx sums up the nature of the circuit thus:

> 'All premises of the process appear as its result, as premises produced by the process itself. Each moment appears as a point of departure, of transit, and of return.'[11]

The dialectical character of Marx's understanding is obvious here. All moments are purely internally related figures of a given whole of self-positing capital which unifies its own phases and exists in their unity. Hence capital 'can only be grasped as a movement and not as a static thing' (*Capital*, 2, p.185). It is one of the great merits of Marx that he achieved this understanding of capital as a circuit, or, as he says, more properly a spiral. When we say value unifies the circuit as a circuit of capital's self-valorisation it is important to notice that this is not empirically given but a theoretically

---

[10] *Capital*, 2, Fernbach translation, 1978, p.133.
[11] *Capital*, 2, p.180.

established connection. Philosophically, Marx, unlike bourgeois economists, has conceptual depth to his theory.

It is necessary to grasp the inner moments of capital, as well as its own phases of motion, as *internally related* to each other; for in isolation its moments lose this determinate economic meaning, being reduced to determinations characteristic of simple circulation or production in general. Conversely, capital does not appear in its *complete* determinacy in any of its phases but supervenes upon them. The shapes can stand alone and operate as money, commodity etc, but not thereby *as capital*; only in the circuit does this function emerge for them. Only as shapes of capital, its bearers, do they become posited as definite functional forms of capital. Capital itself is an emergent form that cannot be reduced to a particular inner moment or phase of its cycle of activity – just as 'life' itself lies in, yet supervenient upon, the parts of an organism, and its development. In sum, the particular functions of the various phases of capital in the circuit become universal functions of valorising capital 'only through their connection as functional forms which industrial capital has to go through' (*Capital*, 2, p.161).

Incidentally *the capitalist* and his activity are subordinated to the movement of capital, according to Marx; certainly the capitalist is not the subject on whose activity the circuit is grounded. The capitalist is merely 'the conscious bearer of this movement', that is 'capital personified' (*Capital*, 1, p.254); the true '*Subjekt*' is self-valorizing value (*Capital*, 1, p.255, makes this claim three times!).

To summarise: at each stage, in going beyond itself, a given shape of capital is only returning to another of its shapes, and since the whole movement forms a circuit it remains always itself as it traverses every stage in its round; thus capital qualifies as a Hegelian subject at least in so far as in its movement it attains genuine infinity; its circuit allows it to remain always within its own terms of existence, its divisions are internal moments, its relations are only to other parts of itself, hence its advance is not to something beyond itself but only into itself, bringing forth from itself all its potentialities and displaying them to itself.[12] Capital develops a wealth of content for itself, new products, new productive forces, and so forth.[13] Marx even speaks in this context of capital's 'civilising mission'.

Let us now turn to the relevance of Hegel's 'bad infinite'. All this wealth of content just mentioned is *incidental* to the only purpose capital is capable of recognising according to its concept of itself, namely the accumulation of value, a one-dimensional purely quantitative measure of its achievement which negates all content. From this point of view capital is embarked on an infinite progression of reinvestment of its earnings. In every measure of itself it finds its existing limit, which, under the imperative of valorization, is a restriction to be superseded.[14] Capital is so structured that its truth lies not within itself but always beyond itself – a case of Hegel's bad infinite.

It reminds one of compulsive neurotic behaviour, for example of repeated

---

[12] For more on this see my forthcoming paper 'The Fluidity of Capital and the Logic of the Concept'.

[13] But as this reference to its content reminds us, capital, however much it subordinates them to its own aims, depends on its 'internal other' labour and its 'external other' nature.

[14] Compare Hegel's categories of '*Die Schranke und das Sollen*' in *Science of Logic*.

washing of hands.

Locked into this spiral of accumulation, capital does not value its activity and its product in any other terms than those of convertible currency. Interest in the boundlessness of money making goes back to the Greeks of course, as Marx acknowledges, quoting Aristotle on the subject.[15] Aristotle thought that C-M-C was inherently limited but that the M-C-M circuit, being limitless, was an unnatural perversion of it.

Apologists for capitalism will argue that just as Greek culture was built on slavery so Western civilisation is only possible under the spur of the drive for valorization. Marx agrees here with regard to the past, granting that the improvements in productivity, and the creation of an 'industrious' spirit, were premised on the compulsive quest for accumulation. But he argues that with regard to the future the acquisitions of the past may be freed from capital's one-dimensional criterion. Now the social synthesis provided by the alien mediator (the value form) can be superseded, and 'socialised humanity' (*Thesis 10* on *Feuerbach*) develop itself in freedom, knowing itself to be an end-in-itself, not content to remain what it already is, but being always 'in the absolute movement of becoming' (*Collected Works*, 28, p.412). And what is this but the genuine infinity?

The lesson of this study so far is that to understand the concept of capital *both* of Hegel's concepts of the infinite (the true and the spurious) need to be drawn upon. Capital is a subject in so far as in its circuit of motion it is self-referring and relates itself to itself – the true infinite – but at the same time its spiral of development is in the service of purely incremental advances in amount. It can only develop as more of the same. In coming to itself as valorized value it achieves only an abstract identity with itself as a form, the developed wealth of content being degraded to its mere bearer. The liberation of the content may be achieved for us by throwing off this its bourgeois form.

Thus far the discussion has assumed a definition of capital as self-valorizing value. However I would like in this final section to address an issue raised by Terrell Carver, who has drawn attention to links between Marx's discussion of capital in his *Grundrisse* and Hegel's discussion of limit, with its transcendence towards the infinite.[16] How does money become capital, not in the historical sense but on the basis of a claim that there is something about the *concept* of money that ineluctably leads to the concept of capital as embarked on infinite expansion? In his paper Carver relates such a discussion in the *Grundrisse* to Hegelian categories of 'limit' and 'infinite'. His treatment is so brief it is hard to know what he makes of this; in so far as I understand it he thinks that Marx relied on Hegelian procedures and was mistaken just because of that.

---

[15] *Capital*, 1, pp.253-54. Fowkes, 254n, queries Marx's translation of Aristotle. While this is not above criticism, Fowkes bases himself on the absurd supposition that the standard English translation of the *Politics* by Jowett is more exact than Marx. Contrary to Fowkes's insinuation, Marx did not impose the terms 'economics' and 'chrematistics' on the Greek, for these terms are simply transliterations of Greek words; the English translation resorts to paraphrase of them in order to bring out their supposed sense; but the English has itself been subject to criticism, for example by K.Polanyi, by M.I.Finley, and by S.Meikle.

[16] T.Carver, 'Marx – and Hegel's *Logic*', *Political Studies*, 1976.

Let us examine Marx's argument and compare it at relevant points to Hegel's logic. Marx's discussion moves back and forth from money to capital so it is not easy to grasp the distinction between them and the argument from the first to the second. However it is essential to set the context for the discussion by understanding that Marx's interest in money here is not that of money as measure of value, or medium of circulation, but as the general representative of wealth, which it is only by a thoroughgoing abstraction from any particular form of wealth, notably that of commodities.[17]

Marx then argues that, in the sense of money as such, a limited amount of it contradicts its essential character of generality. This is because a finite amount would itself be merely a particularisation of the general, whereas the purely general cannot be further determined, not even by a magnitude. The purely general is then a 'measurelessness' (*Grundrisse*, Nicolaus translation, p.271) Hegel argues that everything is defined by its limit, but money, while a form of value qualitatively different from that of commodities, has no quantitative limit in its character as general representative of wealth. At the same time, as an abstraction from the heterogeneity of commodities, it is always *pure* quantity. This is also why it is exempt from the general principle that quantity turns into quality; it lacks all quality in the first place so no problem arises for it in its expansion.[18]

Marx says that the fact that in reality money always appears in definite amounts 'contradicts' its essential character as measureless (*Grundrisse*, p.270). Now this is a purely conceptual point about its form. This essence does not in itself ground the drive of capital accumulation; it merely prefigures the form this will take. But it does prepare the ground, so to speak, for a further more complex form, namely capital, in which there is an inherent drive for expansion. Money is not by definition expansionary, but its characterization as limitless means that when, with capital, it is set as the *aim* of circulation then its 'vocation' can only be to accumulate *more*. But, again, the conceptual space for this won here requires the presence of further conditions of existence to allow the material possibility of accumulation: Marx goes on in a very complex argument to affirm that this can only occur through the appropriation by capital of productive activity.

We have argued that capital in its concept is expansionary because money is measureless. Another argument can be based on the character of money as pure quantity. If capital is to actualise itself as Being-for-Itself in the M-C-M circuit then, in furthering itself through this, it must become different from itself in this its own otherness as well as identifying itself in it. In the case of money as a pure quantity the only possible difference between two instantiations of this universal is in amount. Conversely there would be no purpose in capital risking itself in circulation in order to return to itself unchanged. Alteration is the superseding of limit, which here must mean a limited amount. One can see the same impulse necessarily re-arises again

---

[17] For the notion of measurelessness arises only then, but *not* when it functions in other ways which can easily be seen to require only finite amounts. Thus when money functions as the circulating medium in C-M-C the amount required is set by the needs of circulation and is thereby limited.

[18] It is this 'insubstantial substantiality' (Marx) of value that makes possible the indefinite creation of 'fictitious capital' through bank credit.

and again.

This iteration is absolutely necessary if the aim of M-C-M is to be the actualisation of value-for-itself, the true infinite, as against the finitude of the world of commodities. For example, a single circuit, M-C-M, could only be undertaken as a purely speculative exploit,[19] in which a particular conjuncture makes contingently possible a large profit on which the speculator could retire to live the life of Riley. The object of his endeavour is in effect still C not M, the latter functioning merely as an intermediary agent. However, 'capital personified' seeks to secure a regular predictable return, and in principle would abhor wasting its substance on riotous living or embarking on incalculable risks.[20]

Capital makes its own self the object of its activity and in this way secures the permanence of value, which otherwise would merely appear ephemerally in the interstices of commodity markets. Only as capital is value 'Being-for-Itself' instead of merely 'Being There'. The autonomy of value is actual only when it both participates in circulation – hence is really money – and yet opposes itself to commodities as representing the general form of wealth, and thereby acquires the form of pure quantity. Paradoxically it is then the inability for this move from Quality to Quantity to be reversed, for quantitative change to bring about a higher quality, that development is boundless in the 'bad infinite' sense. So in the value form the good and bad infinities get all mixed up; because here we have a Being-for-Itself furthering itself through its own otherness; but whose peculiar essence is to be pure abstraction of quality, namely quantity; hence the movement is limitless, it must always go on, for its return to itself always fails to close with itself because its very essence is boundlessness. So a particular capital never measures up to its concept and is compelled to throw itself into ever more twists of the spiral of accumulation.

Before closing, let us consider an attack on Marx's *Grundrisse* by John Mepham.[21] In section VII of his paper he argues against Marx by way of the following analogy:

> 'A similar argument could be used to show that since length always exists as both some particular distance between two points on an object and also as the general measure of two-dimensional distances, therefore all material objects must be constantly striving to get longer and to expand to infinity.'[22]

One sees immediately there is a disanalogy here; for Marx never said that the commodity form of wealth must expand of itself, only the capital form rooted in the measurelessness of money does so. At best Mepham should have restricted the analogy to rulers.[23] In response to this Mepham

---

[19] See Veblen on the distinction between an exploit and regular work.
[20] Weber treated at length the distinction between 'the spirit of capitalism' and pre-capitalist forms of wealth getting and spending.
[21] 'From the *Grundrisse* to *Capital*', in J.Mepham & D-H.Ruben (eds), *Issues in Marxist Philosophy*, Volume One: 'Dialectics and Method', Harvester Press, 1979.
[22] *Op cit*, p.166.
[23] Another interesting disanalogy is that if we are talking of a material object then it could not grow forever without passing beyond its proper limits; for example, because

makes an interesting move; he says 'any material object ... could function as the general form of length ... as a ruler, ... just as any commodity ... could function as money'. (*Ibid*) This is interesting for it shows that for Mepham money is merely a numeraire, no different in essence from a commodity. However, close attention to what Marx says about the form of value shows that such an interpretation is quite wrong, for the practical effectivity of money as a representative of value is what grants commodities a value form in the first place, whereas length is inherent in every extended thing whether or not commensuration goes on. It is indeed precisely this idea of the constitution of value in money as the general form of wealth, which is thereby granted 'immediate exchangeability', that sets off Marx's theory of money from both classical and neo-classical theories, for whom money merely 'veils' the 'true' relations, whether of utilities or labours. In order to deal with Mepham's argument by analogy it is essential to grasp the *peculiar* character of money, which disqualifies all analogies.

Mepham then concedes that, after all, money has the 'formal potentiality' for self-expansion, but this 'cannot be actualised except in conditions which are not contained in the money form itself' (*Ibid*,p.167). But this is not contested: Marx makes the same point in the *Grundrisse* itself. The *key* point is that this 'formal potential' is by no means of negligible importance. It is precisely this point of form that makes capitalism so utterly different from any other mode of production. In all modes of production it would be possible to seek ways of improving the productivity of labour and all exploitative modes rely on some way of 'pumping out' surplus labour. *Only* capital is *in point of form* as such *driven* by this interest as a necessity. This is what the argument in both the *Grundrisse* and *Capital* relies on.

In sum, a full account of valorization requires *both* formal and material explanation.

It is probably true to say that Marx's arguments are not as clear as they might be. But, in the view of this writer, the solution is not to de-Hegelianize Marx, but to take seriously Marx's hint in the second edition of *Capital*, and to refer on all points of form to Hegel's logic.

---

the bulk of the body expands at the power of the cube, and the cross-section of the leg to the power of the square, there is a limit to human giantism beyond which the weight is not self-supporting. But, as we already observed, amounts of money are limitless.

Hegel and Marx

Gary K. Browning
Oxford Brookes University

'Good and Bad Infinites in Hegel and Marx'

Introduction

The focus of the paper will be on Marx's *Grundrisse* and Hegel's *Logic*. Conceptual affinities between these two works will be exhibited by looking at the works in the light of Hegel's notion of good and bad infinites. The argument of the paper will be that the dynamic of concepts in these works of Hegel and Marx turn upon the negative, unsatisfactory character of conceptualisations (bad infinites) which run up against external barriers, whereas the positive pull of progressively more satisfactory conceptualisations (good infinites) is their capacity to treat seemingly external barriers as internal moments of their own specification. In sum the hallmark of a rich and inclusive explanation for Marx, as it is Hegel, is one which leaves nothing merely presuppposed or external, hence it will be reflexive and totalising.

The close conceptual affinity between the theorising of Marx and Hegel in respect of the *Grundrisse* and the *Logic* also intimates a close theoretical linkage between the overall theorising of Hegel and Marx. A focus upon the *Grundrisse*'s reworking of Hegel's notion of good and bad infinites provides a conceptual underpinning to its account of alienation which links it to the account of species-being articulated in the *Economic and Philosophical Manuscripts*, and hence establishes a strong connection between the early and the late Marx.

This paper sees Marx's deployment of arguments concerning good and bad infinites in the *Grundrisse* as constituting strong and multiple links with Hegel. In the *Grundrisse* and elsewhere, it will be argued that Marx, like Hegel in a number of his works, employs the argumentative logic of good and bad infinites to develop synchronic systematic arguments .[1] Moreover the notion of good and bad infinites for both Marx and Hegel by its very drive to be inclusive and remove barriers to free development, entails that evaluative language cannot be divorced from descriptive language.

The course of this paper will follow from what has been set out above. Initially Hegel's notion of good and bad infinites will be explored by explaining its formal characterisation within the *Logic*, thereafter it's deployment in the *Phenomenology of Spirit* and the *Philosophy of Right* will be analyzed. Having set out Hegel's understanding of good and bad infinites and their relationships to conceptual understanding, Marx's overall argumentative strategy in the *Grundrisse* will be shown to reflect Hegel's understanding of both good and bad infinites. Finally, the continuity of the *Grundrisse* and Marx's *Economic and Philosophical Manuscripts* will be explained.

---

[1] Most commentaries on the *Grundrisse* recognise its links with Hegel's *Logic*, for example, Uchida, but do not pick up on its links with other works by Hegel.

Good and Bad Infinites in Hegel

Hegel's *Logic* is a notoriously difficult book to read, but an argumentative guiding thread shedding light on what is going on in the book as a whole is the notion of infinity . This is formally and explicitly addressed at the end of chapter two but it also informs transitions throughout the work. Discussion of the infinite in the *Logic* emerges out of the argumentative impasse arising out of the preceding examination of the nature of Being. Being is the conceptually primitive affirmation of reality commencing the *Logic*. Its very poverty, however, does not decisively distinguish it from nothing, and the uneasy oscillation between Being and Nothing demands a further conceptual specification in terms of determinate being. Determination is however taken to imply limits and finitude and an urge to supersede barriers of the finite. For Hegel, however, it is a mistake to conceive of the finite as distinct from the infinite.'Contrasted with the finite, with the sphere of affirmative determinateness, of realities, the infinite is the indeterminate void, the beyond of the finite, whose being-in-itself is not present in its determinate reality'[2] For Hegel true infinity is not something opposed to or beyond the finite, rather it is a way of conceiving of the finite as in itself infinite, conceptually united and rendered coherent by a totality of conceptual connections. Hegel expresses the contrast between his conceptions of good and bad infinity by likening the true infinite to a circle where a series of determinate concepts meet with one another, whereas the bad, untrue infinite is represented by a straight line which goes on forever, stretching beyond the points at the end of the line. '..the image of true infinity, bent back into itself, becomes the circle, the line which has reached itself, which is closed and wholly present which is beyond beginning and end'.[3]

An important implication of Hegel's notion of infinity is that the subject of his *Logic* cannot be a supra-human 'infinite' subject which is beyond finite human beings. The infinite for Hegel is not opposed to the finite, an infinite subject has no extra-finite powers to propel human history or conceptual development. The *Logic*, on this reading, is not the story of how abstract supra-human thought creates its own logical conditions for a world, but is an examination of categories of human thought by which reality is to be conceptualised in a general way, which are progressively seen as being able to explain themselves, by being inclusive, and hence dealing with all that is implied by them.

Ultimately Hegel argues that a full, self-sufficient categorial explanation of reality must invoke categories which explain the character of conceptual explanation itself, which for Hegel, is produced by categories of the Notion. The concrete representation of the Notion is the ego the dynamic source of human, free thinking. But for Hegel a full explanation of reality must include categories which explain how the freedom, and infinite conceptual power of the ego underlies all reality. Hence the categories of the Idea exemplify the good infinite of developmental categorial thinking in which the free self-development of thought itself is taken as pervading all categories. The Idea of Life takes reality as developing in a self-reproducing way in which

---

[2] G.Hegel, *Hegel's Science of Logic*, Humanities Press, 1976, p.139.
[3] *Ibid*, p.149.

living organisms relate to one another and nature in ways which sustain the species. The death of the individual in the on-going life of the species, however, points up deficiencies in this mode of being; the gap between the individual and the universal is palpable. The category of teleology is important in that Hegel recognises the deficiencies of an external teleology in which there is a gap between ends and means. He invokes the notion of an infinite teleology in which the framing of ends and means are internal to the process of developing ways of thinking and being and there is a circular good infinite in existence. The notion of an infinite teleology leads on to the Absolute Idea, which is seen by Hegel not as an absolute beyond what has gone before but a category which posits that reality is to be understood as a series of categories which successively capture its character as an infinitely self-related series of concepts, which reflexively explains its categorial character. It is absolute because it is reflexive and inclusive. There is nothing external to it which limits its perspective; it registers difference, not as an unknowable, external barrier but as a series of distinct expressions of its own character.

Hegel's notion of the inter-related character of the finite and the infinite entails that his system as a whole does not involve the privileging of thought as an abstract but potent subject which creates nature and the finite, as both Taylor and Michael Rosen have suggested.[4] Hegel's dialectic is not the outcome of the externalisation of a pre-constituted subject but is the presuppositionless investigation of categories and concepts which progressively make sense out of experience.[5]

The worlds of nature and human life are not to be created out of nothing by thought but are involved in the development of categories themselves if those categories are to be genuinely infinite and inclusive. For this reason, the general categories of the *Logic* imply & apply to the more concrete explorations of the natural and human worlds which Hegel undertakes. The categories of the *Logic* invoke modes of subjectivity and objectivity and thereby imply natural and human worlds and hence concrete investigations where Hegel develop these implications. Indeed, the priority for Hegel resides with the concrete, for without an actual natural and human world in which human beings develop ways of acting and thinking which make possible the logical investigations, reality would not be knowable .

The essential interconnectedness of Hegel's philosophical system has two important implications for this study of Hegel and Marx. It means on the one hand that Hegel's important categorial notions of good and bad infinites will inform his other more concrete works, and that Marx's *Grundrisse* , in following the *Logic*'s deployment of notions of good and bad infinites, will also evoke other works of Hegel. Hence Hegel's discussion of utility or profitability in the *Phenomenology of Spirit* exemplifies an endless and bad process of infinity which resembles Marx's account of money. Likewise Hegel's discussion of needs and freedom in the *Philosophy of Right* has affinities on the one hand with the infinite and insatiable expansion of capital

---

[4] See C.Taylor, *Hegel*, Cambridge University Press, 1973 & M.Rosen, *Hegel's Dialectic and its Criticism*, Cambridge University Press, 1982.

[5] see the excellent commentary, A.White, *Absolute Knowledge: Hegel and the Problem of Metaphysics*, Ohio University Press, 1983.

and on the other with the infinite self-mediating character of social labour under communism.

Hegel's *Phenomenology of Spirit* represents an investigation into the conditions whereby consciousness can undertake a philosophical explanation of reality. Its end point is the standpoint of absolute knowledge where the conscious knowing mind sees truth as integral to the object of its consciousness. For Hegel, this standpoint of the Absolute is depicted in a way which evokes the notion of the Good Infinite. 'It is the process of its own becoming, the circle which presupposes its end as its purpose, and has its end for its beginning; it becomes concrete and actual only by being carried out, and by the end it involves'.[6] The absolute of self-consciousness as it is depicted in the *Phenomenology of Spirit* consists in the absolute mediation of finite and infinite.

This meeting point of the finite and infinite is what lies behind the significance of the dialectic of recognition and the master-slave dialectic in *the Phenomenology of Spirit*. The format of the *Phenomenology of Spirit* is for the most part synchronic in its evocation of forms of consciousness which claim to know truth, and during the course of the work Hegel follows the inadequacy of modes of consciousness which invoke richer modes of consciousness. The dialectic of recognition, and the struggle between the master and slave makes clear that consciousness and its claims must be social. An individual consciousness cannot know itself; its determinacy and finiteness only make sense in a wider setting of reciprocal social recognition and the process of social development set in train by the master-servant relationship. Hegel in his discussion of the master servant interaction explicitly recognises that the master servant struggle actually takes place in history, but in the *Phenomenology of Spirit*, he reviews this struggle for recognition conceptually as showing in a general way the necessarily social and developmental aspects of human experience. While the struggle for recognition shows that individual, finite minds are self-mediating the master-servant relation sets up barriers between minds which must be overcome if finite spirits are to see themselves as infinitely self-related.

Thereafter Hegel proceeds to examine a series of historic modes of human interaction, such as Stoicism, scepticism and the unhappy consciousness in which the universal is either affirmed or denied in abstraction from finite concrete phenomena. Hegel in dealing with the estranged world of post-medieval Europe and the dislocation of history and experience expressed in the Enlightenment, sees estrangement in ways which anticipate Marx's focus upon economic and social life . He depicts alienation in terms of a discordant conceptual world, evoking the notion of a bad infinite. For instance state power and wealth are seen as vital aspects of the absolutist states of the early modern world sucking in all human endeavours into an infinite series of supposedly contrasting activities which in fact imply one another, and generate a spiritual critique which admonishes against the vanity of such enterprises.[7]. Again, in his discussion of the truth of the Enlightenment, Hegel fixes on the way the drive for pure insight in Enlightenment

---

[6] G.W.F.Hegel, *The Phenomenology of Mind*, George Allen & Unwin, p.81.
[7] Ibid p.547.

thought focuses upon utility, the idea of the useful and the profitable which posits 'the shifting change -...of the moments of being-in-itself, of being-for another and of being-for itself.'[8]. The notion of utility or profitably thereby relates objects, all finite objects to the infinite process of insightful judgment, but the unsatisfactory way in which the process of insight and its objects are presented is disclosed in an endless infinite specification without adequately reflecting back on the infinite character of thought.'...Thinking this knowledge about finitude as the truth to be the highest knowledge attainable'.[9]

The logic of the *Logic*'s characterisation of thought as setting up good and bad processes of infinite progression also informs the *Philosophy of Right*. While resting upon historical developments which Hegel himself set out in his *Lectures on the Philosophy of History*, the argument of the *Philosophy of Right*, like that of Marx's *Grundrisse*, is presented synchronically in which basic and simple categories of social and political life are seen as insufficient in themselves. They are shown to generate more inclusive, self-sustaining ones. The key foundational concept of the *Philosophy of Right* is the notion of the will which is taken to be coterminous with freedom. The simple notion of freedom is recognised to be infinite, matching the logical category of the notion itself. The pure freedom of the will is exemplified by the will's infinite capacity to abstract from any particular determination. But this infinite potential of the will, is abstract and only invokes a bad infinite of endless repetition in which the form of the will is forever external to particular contents.[10]

The dialectical drive of the argument in the *Philosophy of Right* is to provide an inclusive concept which will incorporate the infinite self-determining power of the ego within a concrete world of social content which expresses this infinity. For Hegel the ultimate answer is the development of a concrete world of social and political life incorporating family life, a range of 'private' activities in civil society and the overarching political laws of the state. Any standpoint short of this encompassing social and political perspective is defective for Hegel as the universal of the will can only be expressed and understood coherently in this setting. The institutions of property and contract for example, can only be fully understood when they are seen as moments of a social and political perspective which explains their logical emergence. Marx in the *Grundrisse* shows that he is aware of the systematic logic of Hegel's argument in relation to property.[11]

Marx, Conceptual Development and Infinity

Marx's *Grundrisse* since its emergence in 1953 has been seen as notable, amongst other things, for its explicit invocation of Hegel and Hegelian modes of argument for its analysis of economic life under capitalism.[12] A notable presentation of this argument is Uchida's in Marx's *Grundrisse* and Hegel's

---

[8] *Ibid*, p.594.
[9] *Ibid*, p.580.
[10] G.Hegel, *Hegel's Philosophy of Right*, Oxford University Press, 1967, p.21.
[11] K.Marx, *Grundrisse*, Penguin, 1974, p.102.
[12] See, for instance, the introduction by Nicholas to the Penguin translation, 1973.

Logic.[13] Uchida quite rightly observes the dependence of the *Grundrisse* upon Hegel's *Logic*. But his work suffers from an insufficiently developed recognition of the overall manner in which Hegel and Marx approach the task of conceptual explanation. A brief summary of Uchida's argument is that the *Grundrisse*'s chapters on money and capital mirror the chapters on Being and Essence in the *Logic*. This explanation is neat and tidy but in itself it doesn't do justice to the, overall, common dialectical form of argument in the two works.

The notion of good and bad infinites helps to explain the dynamics of dialectical development in both Hegel and Marx. Just as for Hegel a bad infinite of finite beings or utilitarian, profit-making calculations does not register the infinitely self-related and self-producing character of categories, so money and capital in distinct ways reduce aspects of social reality to the external, (bad infinite) rhythms of their own circulation. Again, just as social and political freedom, and a philosophical consciousness, for Hegel, register the goals of a good infinite in their capacity to fully explain their own character, so capital, in its capacity to reproduce its own conditions and control all aspects of production, approaches a true infinity of self-mediated, self-production. Moreover underneath the surface of Marx's arguments about money and capital in the *Grundrisse* resides the notion of an explicitly ordered social organisation of social labour as matching the requirements of true infinity.

In the introduction to the *Grundrisse*, Marx makes some general comments on his approach to the study of political economy which make clear his general intellectual, and methodological debts to Hegel. He is concerned to establish a methodological procedure which points in the direction of Hegel, and allows scope for his self-conscious use of Hegelian notions of good and bad infinity to advance his subsequent arguments.

Marx observes that social reality is not a world of discrete things but is relational, which Ollman has justly noted to be foundational for the practice of dialectical argument.[14] The basis of the relational character of reality for Marx lies in its social character which he affirms in his critique of political economists. In the course of the *Grundrisse*, Marx employs an argument against the notion of a private language to confirm conceptually the social, relational character of reality.[15] While Marx in the introduction emphasises that his material reading of reality contrasts sharply with Hegel's idealist reading, he at the same time observes that relations 'can be expressed, of course, only in ideas ...'.[16] The conceptual expression of the thoroughly relational character of reality allows Marx in the *Grundrisse* to conceive of the capitalist political economy in terms of infinitely self-related categories.

Marx also affirms in this introductory chapter that the correct mode of theoretical analysis is one which ascends from a small number of determinant abstract general relations. The reason he gives for this follows Hegel's line of reasoning.'The concrete is the concrete because it is the concretion

---

[13] F.Uchida, *Marx's Grundrisse and Hegel's Logic*, Routledge, 1988.
[14] B.Ollman, *Dialectical Investigations*, Routledge, 1993, p.11.
[15] K.Marx, *Grundrisse*, Penguin, 1973, p.490.
[16] *Ibid*, p.164.

of many determinations, hence unity of the diverse.'[17] Marx's designated procedure here, entails that a developed explanation will have the form of a self-mediated unity in diversity which Hegel sees as the hallmark of the good infinite. Marx explicitly recognises the concordance of his theoretical method with that of Hegel. Marx invokes the *Philosophy of Right* to explain how more abstract categories should be tackled before more complex ones, thereby confirming the relevance of the *Philosophy of Right* for the *Grundrisse* and Marx's recognition of the intimate relationship between the argument of the *Philosophy of Right* and the *Logic*. Marx notes how, in the Philosophy of Right, possession is treated before the concepts of the family, clan or state even though the latter might be historically prior to, and conditional for, possession. What Hegel has rightly alighted upon, for Marx, is an ordering of concepts whereby the more inclusive and explanatory succeed the relatively simpler ones.[18] The succeeding chapters on money and capital exemplify this methodological precept in that the concrete world of a material production is developed out of simple general abstractions, money and capital.

Finally, the introduction to the *Grundrisse* emphasises that a political economy is an interconnected world in which production, distribution, exchange and consumption must be seen as inter-related phenomena. Within this notion of an interconnected set of relations, Marx gives priority to production; the priority is a logical one in that the inter-related conditions of a political economy must be produced in history and it is the conditions of production that produce and reproduce a given mode of production. The chapter on capital makes clear that a capitalist political economy can only be seen as a self-reproducing system within the context of capital constituting the conditions of labour and production. It is capital's capacity to make its own conditions of production and also to determine the patterns of exchange and distribution and consumption which gives capital the form of a good, self-mediating infinite system in which all determinations do not function as external limits but internally related conditions.[19] The inter-related conditions of a productive system are established at the outset of the *Grundrisse* by Marx's critique of Proudonist schemes for credit reform whose partial measures abstract from the totality of inter-related conditions composing a system.

The introductory chapter of the *Grundrisse* sets out an Hegelian conceptual framework, which is exemplified subsequently in the chapters on money and capital. In making sense out of these discursive conceptual investigations, it is important to see the argumentative wood for the terminological trees. Uchida in *Marx's Grundrisse and Hegel's Logic* connects the two works by observing how particular concepts employed by Marx match those deployed in the *Logic*. Overall, however, he does not show how the dynamics of the arguments of both Hegel and Marx display a common pattern. While there are many affinities between the terms and concepts used in the *Grundrisse* and the *Logic*, their shared conceptions of good and bad infinites are

---

[17] *Ibid*, p.101. Arthur and Smith in their articles in F.Mosley (ed), *Marx's Method in Capital*, Humanities Press, 1993, point up the significance of this method.
[18] *Ibid*, p.102.
[19] *Ibid*, p.80.

central in an explanation of the development and logic of their arguments. A concept or category such as money or quantity, capital or measure is at key points shown to require development when it specifies an endless series of instantiations which do not reflect back to explain their conditions. The resulting failure of explanation demands a new form of categorisation. Likewise in both works, a concept is taken to be satisfactory insofar as it is truly infinite in explaining its own conditions and development.

One of the implications of a developmental argumentative procedure as employed by Hegel and Marx is that concepts and levels of argument are not external to one another. Hence, while Hegel's *Logic* concludes by seeing reality as a self-mediating series of thoughts this does not exclude it from having being. Likewise a complex world of social and political practices does not exclude specific acts of freedom. Similarly, Marx's conceptions of the circulation of money and the self-reproduction of capital contain simpler determinations of the conceptions of commodities and exchange value. The linkages which Uchida observes between the *Grundrisse*'s chapter on money and the *Logic*'s chapter on Being, and the *Grundrisse*'s chapter on capital and the *Logic*'s chapter on Essence do obtain, but these connections do not preclude an overall affinity between the dynamics of argument within the two works which takes its bearings from the completely self-mediating, comprehensive categorial explanation exhibited by the good infinity of Hegel's absolute idea.

Certainly Marx's understanding of a commodity in which a commodity's identity is bound up with its relation to another commodity recalls Hegel's notion of determinate being in the *Logic*. Again, Marx's account of circulation does evoke the rhythm of becoming as it is set out in the chapter on Being in Hegel's *Logic*. Marx's account of capital in the *Grundrisse* also evokes Hegel's account of semblance and appearance in his account of Essence. The simple circulation of commodities and money assumes the character of the appearance of money and commodities in distinct phenomenal forms in which the process of appearance has not been explained. Uchida is right to see within Marx's explanation of the increasingly self-reproducing nature of capital intimations of the logic of Hegel's account of essence. The form of capital lies behind its various appearances and acts as their ground. The capitalist political economy in a developed capitalist world does constitute a unified whole composed of distinguishable parts, and the reciprocity of cause and effect.

The chapter on money in the *Grundrisse* does echo Hegel' s logic of being; commodities are determined from one another by endless discrete qualitative use values; money is an endless quantitative measure of exchange value, and exchange value is expressed phenomenally in the 'becoming' of monetary transactions. Similarly, the chapter on capital does resonate with Hegel's account of essence in the *Logic*. Uchida is right to see within Marx's account of the circulation of capital intimations of Hegel's concept of an essential form lying behind phenomenal appearances. A developed capitalist political economy does serve as a unified whole composed of many parts, in which the reciprocity of cause and effect is operative.

Central to the dynamics of Marx's explanation of money and capital in the Grundrisse, however, is the contradictory nature of the bad infinites constituted by the circulation of money and the quasi good infinite, but ultimately flawed infinite described by capital as a self-reproducing system. Insofar as capital and money in one of its circuits exhibit the self-reproducing character of Hegel's category of the notion, then Uchida's understanding of the *Grundrisse* as exhibiting the Hegelian logical categories of Being and Essence is partial.

In the *Grundrisse* the circulation of money comes up against the 'bad infinity' of limits acting as barriers to its own continued production. Marx observes, 'The circulation of money, like that of commodities, begins at an infinity of different points, and to an infinity of different points it returns'.[20] Marx highlights the way in which the circulation is infinite in the sense of being endless but also points to the way this endless process does not explain the conversion of money into and from commodity form. 'At first sight, circulation appears as a simply infinite process. The commodity is exchanged for money, money is exchanged for the commodity, and this is repeated endlessly.'[21] This circuit (CMMC) appears endless and does not produce or explain its own conditions. Likewise the reverse circulation where money is translated into a commodity and commodity translated into money (MCCM) inserts break points in the circle of motion where money might be expended. But, when money is deployed to make money through commodities and then to generate more money to acquire commodities so as to make money to give impetus to the process in an on-going way, then, for Marx, the logical basis of capitalism has arrived.[22]

Insofar as money in circulation generates its own conditions for circulation then it assumes the aspect of a good infinite, but it has not established a rhythmic control of the productive process. Capital expresses the self-mediating character of the good infinite more adequately by acquiring in commodity form fixed and variable capital which it deploys to generate the conditions of its own production. 'The immortality which money strove to achieve by setting itself negatively against circulation, by withdrawing from it, is achieved by capital which preserves itself precisely by abandoning itself to circulation'.[23]

But while Capital has features of the good infinite, it is nonetheless beset by contradictions which undermine its claims to be a good infinite. On the one hand the trajectory of the self-reproducing process of capital constantly promotes the build-up of fixed capital whereas surplus value depends upon the use value of labour power. The logic of the process of capitalism thereby undermines its own process of reproduction, a token of which is the tendency for the rate of profit to fall. The tendency for capital to be infinitely self-reproducing is thereby undermined. Additionally, the kind of infinite self-reproducing system to which capitalism aspires is also one in which the generative, creative conditions of its production and reproduction are not genuinely affirmed. The creative power of social labour which the infinite

---

[20] K.Marx, *Grundrisse*, op cit, p.186.
[21] *Ibid* p.197.
[22] *Ibid*, p.216.
[23] *Ibid*, p.261.

self-reproducing power of capital trades upon is expressed in an alienated form. 'The creative power of his (proletarian) labour establishes itself as an alien power confronting him'.[24] Marx in the *Grundrisse* refers to the master-servant dialectic of recognition in the *Phenomenology of Spirit* in expressing this alienated, limited aspect of capitalism. 'It (the master-servant relation) is represented – in mediated form – in capital, and thus likewise forms a ferment of its dissolution and is an emblem of its limitation'.[25]

The 'bad' limit of the infinity of capital is also exhibited in that in its denial of the social and creative power of labour, it is driven to constantly seek more quantitative profit; an endless and sterile bad infinite. Marx observes that capital functions as Hegel's bad quantitative infinite.

> 'Fixed as wealth, as the general form of wealth, as value which counts as value, it (capital) is therefore the constant drive to go beyond its quantitative limit, an endless process.'[26]

Hegel, in his lectures on the *Philosophy of Right*, had likewise concluded that the multiplication of needs under the spell of those hoping to make a profit exemplified a bad infinite. 'What the English call "comfort" is inexhaustible and illimitable'.[27]

Capital, for Marx, contains the seeds of its own destruction in terms of the kind of self-reproducing infinite system which it generates. It will be superseded by a form of social organisation which exemplifies the self-limiting ideal of ethical life which the Greeks had recognised.[28] Social labour under communism will generate the conditions for social individuals to find fulfilment in productive activity and leisure consequent on a rational organisation of social labour. The social and creative conditions of production will be enhanced and recognised in social development.

The self-sustaining 'infinite' logic of communism had been highlighted in Marx's early writings. In the *Economic and Philosophical Manuscripts* species-being is portrayed in ways which evoke Hegel's good infinite. The species character of man's being resides in a person's universal character; s/he can produce freely and universally, and under communism the free universal character of the individual will be expresseed in a productive system in which the individual marks her universal character by developing a range of powers and needs . The 'infinite' character of species life whereby the species and individual are internally self-related is exhibited in the following quotation.

> 'Man's individual and species-life are not two *distinct things*, however much-and this is necessarily so-the mode of existence of individual life is a more *particular* or a more *general* mode of the

---

[24] *Ibid*, p.307.
[25] *Ibid*, p.501; Arthur in *Dialectics of Labour: Marx and his Relation to Hegel*, Blackwell, 1986, is generally right to underplay the importance of the master-servant figure for Marx's thought, but it does feature in the *Grundrisse*.
[26] *Ibid*, p.270.
[27] G.Hegel, *The Philosophy of Right*, op cit, p.191.
[28] See S.Meikle, 'Was Marx an Economist', in P.Dunleavy & J.Stanyer (eds), *Contemporary Political Studies 1994*, Volume 2, PSA, 1994.

species-life, or a species-life a more particular or more *general* individual life'.[29]

Marx in the *Economic and Philosophical Manuscripts* had shown his awareness of the notion of a good infinite in Hegel, by characterising the relationship between the three parts of Hegel's mature system as an illicit portrayal of a movement from the infinite to the finite and back.[30] The continuity of Marx's interest in and employment of the argumentative logic of Hegel's notion of infinity is also exemplified in *The German Ideology*. I have previously urged in a paper, 'The German Ideology: The Theory of History and the History of Theory', that Marx and Engels in their critique of Stirner's celebration of the particularity of the individual, in conscious reference to Hegel's notion of a good infinite, invoked the universality of the social individual'.[31]

In a breezy, short critical review of Marx's thought, Elster has specifically castigated the Hegelian conceptual dialectic of the *Grundrisse* . He urges, 'Although some of the transitions make sense when seen as historical developments, the purported dialectical connection is unintelligible. Concepts have no "logic of development" independently of the actions that men undertake for purposes of their own'.[32] This paper has been concerned to make Marx's *Grundrisse* intelligible in terms of its use of an Hegelian mode of argument. Moreover, while Elster is right to point to the fact that concepts are not independent of the actions of men, it is also true that individual actions are related to a world of social meanings. Hegel's *Logic*, on my reading is concerned with the inter-relations of concepts involved in man's contact with the world and remains a plausible project. Marx's *Grundrisse* founds its conceptual investigations on the basis of the social nature of men and women. Human activities are seen as social and inter-related and the only way of expressing and understanding these relations is held to be through ideas. The exploration of the inter-relation of ideas in a political economy is intelligible and does not exclude, rather it demands, accompanying human activities. The notion of the good infinite in both Hegel and Marx turns upon a recognition that the activities of men and women are inter-related and that if they are to be free, then a way of grasping and structuring these relations must be found. This is a distinct view of freedom, but it is not a nonsensical one.

---

[29] K.Marx, 'Economic & Philosophical Manuscripts', *Early Writings*, Penguin, 1975, p.350.
[30] *Ibid*, p.382.
[31] G.K.Browning, 'The German Ideology: The Theory of History and the History of Theory', *History of Political Thought*, 14/3, 1993.
[32] J.Elster, *An Introduction to Karl Marx*, Cambridge University Press, 1986.

Multiculturalism, Equality and the Public Sphere

Elizabeth Sperling
Liverpool John Moores University

'Women and Quangos: a Step Backwards in the Progress Towards Equal Representation in Public Service Provision'

Introduction

The issue of the political representativeness of quangos is one that has not been considered beyond notions of numerical equitability of women and ethnic minorities. It is a concept that has tended to be debated, and argued for seriously, by groups that are underrepresented in formal political institutions. Indeed, the work of such groups in putting underrepresentation on the political agenda has met with some success at different levels of the state. The direction in which public policy making and implementation in Britain appears to moving, presents a danger that as the formal state yields more powers to the less transparent quango arena, the advances in representation made by women, in particular, will be reversed.

Women and political representation

In making a case for political representation of specific groups in any decision making forum, an assumption is made that distinct interests can be identified which need direct scrutiny and inclusion in policy decisions. In the case of women, historically they have always been deemed to have separate interests from men, even if these were not 'political'. Modern society can no longer legitimately uphold the 'public-private' divide as a means of denying women access to positions in representative institutions or to representation as consumers of services. In the UK, women constitute nearly 50% of the workforce (EOC, 1995), they are the major consumers of public and private sector goods (Button, 1985, p.32; Ashworth, 1992, p.9), and they have proved their ability at all levels of public service. Moreover, as Ashworth (1992, p.15) notes, most, if not all, policy decisions impact in the private sphere.

The case for women's political representation does not rest on the fact that policy and implementation decisions affect them *per se*. Rather it is the fact that such decisions impact on them differently from men. Women endure a double, and often triple, burden of public sphere duties, private sphere responsibilities and sometimes study or training requirements. This cannot fail to result in policy on, for example, paid employment, economy, education, welfare benefits and services, and transport, affecting women differently to the majority of men who do not have to tolerate the same level or amount of responsibilities. As Dahlerup (1987, p.112) notes, in illustrating differential effects of public policy, ostensibly sex-neutral policy has

> 'different consequences for men and women because of their different social positions'.

For quangos, and other assemblies, the issue of political representation of women is not simply a case of acknowledging that women have interests that need addressing. For, as with any 'group' of individuals, not all women's interests are held in common. While the arguments for group representation require a coherent group identity (Phillips, 1993, p.33) the differences between women also need accommodation.

Women and quangos: we're alright Jacqui

The profile of quango memberships suggests that the representation of women is not really a problem. Following a government initiative to attract women to serve on non-departmental public bodies and NHS trusts (officially acknowledged quangos), female representation on quangos was 30% in 1994 (WNC, 1995, p.ii). This compares favourably with the 25% women elected local councillors and 9.3% women MPs. Women's membership of NHS Trusts is particularly impressive, being 39%, with women holding 31% of Trust Chairs (LGIU, 1994). Of course, the familiar pyramid-shaped, gendered pattern of organisations is present in quangos, with the exception of the NHS Trusts, as senior positions tend to be held by men.

The relatively respectable presence of women on quangos should not be confused with the realisation of political representation. The methods of selecting quango appointees and the lack of procedures and structures to ensure accountability of quangos, wherein direct answerability on gender issues could be required, disregard the potential to achieve genuine inclusiveness. For example, the majority of appointments are made through informal channels of patronage (Wright, 1995; Davis and Skelcher, 1995). While it is obvious that women have benefitted to some extent from this system of recruitment, it is also evident that selection will be from a restricted base. Thus, Wright (1995, p.16) states that the increase in women's presence on quangos has been facilitated by

> 'the recent discovery of wives of Conservative MPs and other prominent Conservative women on public bodies'.

Moreover, the dearth of women in senior positions in political parties and other organisations, from where quango appointees are selected, further limits the broad recruitment base needed to ensure equitable political representation.

In addition to party political and organisational restrictions to women's political representation on quangos, it cannot be assumed that women appointees automatically represent the needs of women consumers of public services. The very diversity of women as a 'group' precludes full representation by a minority of individuals. Of course, not all women are feminists putting issues of gender on the agenda, promoting women's interests or alerting decision making processes to the specific needs of women. Moreover, even feminists in decision making positions represent a geographical or consumer constituency rather than a particular sub-group within this.

Without analysis of what representation really means, arguments and recommendations for increasing the representation of women on quangos run the risk of falling into the trap of so- called post-feminism. It may well be that numbers of women on quangos are increased, even equalised, but that political representation remains the same.

Is there a tide of progress for quangos to abate?

Evidence exists, for example in the EU, Scandinavian assemblies and in British local government, to demonstrate that where enough women committed to improving the situation of women are present in decision making fora, progress can be made. Naturally, this commitment cannot work in isolation from a certain amount of bureaucratic, political and community or grass roots support. However, even in fairly hostile environments, women's interests can be made visible and placed on policy agendas.

The example of women's initiatives in British local government demonstrates these assertions. At a fairly fundamental level, Halford (1989) shows that the presence of women councillors precipitates the establishment of women's initiatives, and that greater percentages of women councillors in local authorities lead to higher status initiatives, such as full Women's Committees.

However, as already mentioned, the presence of women *per se* is not conducive to the establishment of mechanisms to ensure women's political representation. In local government the political complexion and stability of a local authority's leadership, is instrumental to whether a women's initiative is supported. Thus, the majority, although not all, women's initiatives are in metropolitan and marginal Labour authorities (Halford, 1989, p.16). In addition, the support of local government managers and politicians is acknowledged as a prerequisite for the establishment of successful women's initiatives (Button, 1985, p.16; Riley, 1990, p.54). However, such support is often tokenistic, and it is usual for initiatives to face hostility from such groups. Thus, Riley (1990, p.54) shows that local government managers often resent, and resist, intervention by women's initiatives in their work, and Button (1985, p.15) demonstrates that, while councillors may accept the relevance of women's demands, they often resort to methods of covert sexism, such as undermining women committee Chairs and timetabling women's caucus meetings against other important business, to maintain control of policy processes and outcomes. Despite the internal organisational, administrative and political obstacles that women's initiatives have to overcome, both to get established and in their work, they have made considerable progress in addressing the, hitherto neglected, needs of women in policy decisions. For example, the visibility of women's policy and service implementation needs has been strengthened by the initiatives; initiatives have addressed internal employment issues with regard to women's access to, and progress through, local authority hierarchies; they have supported campaigns on issues such as low pay, paternity leave, women's health, job sharing and childcare provision; and they provide discussion fora for women in the local authority, the community and consumer groups as a means to provide detailed policy, implementation and scrutiny recommendations to Councils (Halford, 1989; Riley, 1990).

Women's initiatives in local government not only legitimise gender issues within the policy process, they have also advanced representative methods and working practices in local government, some of which have been adopted by 'mainstream' committees. Thus, co-optees to women's committees represent a diverse range of women's groups and interests in the communities served, and inclusive consultative practices have been pursued, and networks established, to create accessible channels of policy influence within the traditional, exclusionary hierarchy of local government (Halford, 1989).

The restrictive number of decision making positions offered by quangos, together with the relatively 'closed' access to such positions, and the distance of quangos from the more transparent and accountable public sector, endanger the advances that institutions like local government have made in the political representation of women. It is proving difficult enough to achieve diverse representation in large elected, assemblies. Such a task in small, select quangos is likely to prove even more onerous. It is unlikely that, under the existing system of selection, or that recommended by the Nolan Committee on Standards in Public Life, enough women committed to change on behalf of women service consumers will be appointed to quangos. Suggested reform of the appointments system is concerned only with numerical representation of women. Moreover, the mechanisms of scrutiny and accountability that require public sector organisations to demonstrate, at least minimal, commitment to gender inclusiveness and equality do not pertain to quangos.

As many women's initiatives in local government are often supported under sufferance, and as responsibility for local services shifts from local government to quangos, it must be ensured that gender, and other, specifications are incorporated into whatever measures are developed to accrue and maintain democratic control of quangos.

Can the tide be turned?

Various recommendations have been made to reform quangos' appointments procedures and to increase accountability in the quango sector (Nolan, 1995; Stewart et al, 1994). However, while these are relevant, they present a generic perspective which will not address issues of political underrepresentation of women and other 'disadvantaged' groups. Nolan's recommendations that appointees be selected by merit and that the recruitment base from which the patronage system operates should be widened will not undermine entrenched attitudes that exclude 'different', in this case feminist, contributions to policy debate. Similarly, recommendations to local authorities on increasing local democratic control over quangos (LGIU, 1995; Stewart et al, 1994), while acknowledging the significance of gender issues, do not lend emphasis to the requirement to ensure proper political representation of women, or other underrepresented groups.

What is required to diminish the loss of present levels of representation, and to improve on what currently exists, is comprehensive monitoring and evaluation of recruitment to, procedures and performance of quangos. Variables pertaining to gender, race, social and professional backgrounds of quango appointees should be monitored, and all required reports from Ministers of State, the Public Appointments Commissioner (Nolan, 1995), and quangos themselves, should include analyses of quangos' performance and effects of policy implementation on women in the communities they serve. Such analyses must include notification of successes and failures, specifying future developments in those areas. Although the designated, detailed gender aspect of such reports may be new, reporting on the progress of organisational performance, and service delivery, is not a unique requirement on public service providers but is something that local government has been obliged to do for some time. Thus, quangos would not be required to develop new practices but to conform, and improve on, existing ones in the public sector. In addition, where quangos are required to develop Codes of Conduct or practice these must be inclusive of genuine equal opportunities specifications. All reports and documents should be easily available for public scrutiny, and members of quangos should be accessible to interrogation by members of the public. Ministerial and Parliamentary scrutiny of the work of quangos should also specify representative issues, and time be given to consider them adequately.

Local government should also act directly to ensure that the advances it has made in the political representation of women are not sacrificed as control of service policy and implementation moves to quangos. For example, in following the Local Government Information Unit's (1995) advice to scrutinise and offer contributions on quangos' future job specifications for potential appointees, and the development of Codes of Conduct for quango members, local authorities can assert the need for inclusion of comprehensive gender specifications where these are absent or partial. Local government is also in a strategic position to scrutinise the work of quangos and to hold them to account on behalf of women and other groups of consumers in the community. Moreover, as local authorities are encouraged to nominate candidates for selection to quangos, they can ensure that they include women from diverse local community women's groups as well as members and officers from different levels in their organisation.

Ultimately, the number of women on quangos may be irrelevant. The small membership of individual quangos does not lend itself to comprehensive representation in terms of proportionality to the communities they serve. Moreover, numerical proportionality does not guarantee political representation. If proper, inclusive and stringent procedures are established to ensure that the demands and needs of women and other underrepresented consumers are accommodated in the work and output of quangos, then strict proportionality of quango memberships becomes extraneous. However, in the absence of a full and inclusive analysis of political representation as it pertains to the changing profile of policy making in Britain, and its effects on women, and other, service users, the shift of responsibility for public services from the public sector to quangos contains deeper and broader dangers to the democractic function in Britain than the quango debate currently allows.

Bibliography

G.Ashworth, *When Will Democracy Include Women?*, CHANGE Thinkbook VII, Change, 1992.

S.Button, *Women's Committees: A Study of gender and local government policy formulation*, SAUS, 1985.

D.Dahlerup, 'Confusing Concepts - Confusing Reality: a theoretical discussion of the patriarchal state', in A.Showstack-Sassoon, *Women and the State*, Hutchinson, 1987.

H.Davies & C.Skelcher, *Joseph Rowntreee Foundation Synthesis Paper on Quangos*, University of Birmingham, 1995.

Equal Opportunities Commission, *Some Facts about Women*, EOC, 1995.

S.Halford, *Local Authority Women's Initiatives 1982-1988*, University of Sussex, 1989.

Local Government Information Unit, *Quango File*, 5, LGIU, 1994.

Local Government Information Unit, *Quango File*, 10, LGIU, 1995.

Nolan Committee, *Report of the Committee on Standards in Public Life*, HMSO, 1995.

A.Phillips, *Democracy and Difference*, Polity, 1993.

K.Riley, 'Equality for Women - The Role of Local Authorities', *Local Government Studies*, 16/1, 1990.

J.Stewart et al, *The Quango State: An Alternative Approach*, Commission for Local Democracy, 1994.

Women's National Commission, *Public Appointments: A Directory for Women*, WNC, 1995.

T.Wright, *Beyond the Patronage State*, Fabian Pamphlet 569, 1995.

Multiculturalism, Equality and the Public Sphere

Stuart White
Nuffield College, Oxford

'Freedom of Association and the Right to Exclude'

Introduction

Freedom of association is widely considered to be one of the basic liberties constitutive of a free society. With the freedom to associate, however, there comes the freedom to dissociate – the freedom of those who belong to a given association to exclude those with whom they do not wish to associate. Moreover, exclusion of this sort may be morally worrying because of its possible implications for equality of opportunity between citizens and/or because of its possible stigmatizing effect on minority or disadvantaged groups. Categorical exclusion on the basis of (for example) race, ethnicity, gender, or sexuality, will strike many observers as especially worrisome in these respects. In the context of a society which is significantly multiracial and multicultural, the freedom to exclude becomes all the more important as some groups struggle to maintain a distinct cultural identity. But on the other hand, anxieties concerning the right to exclude will increase precisely because of the way certain racial or cultural groups may deploy such a right so as to sustain their superior access to scarce social goods and/or to stigmatize those belonging to other groups.

There is, then, an apparent tension between the value of associational freedom and other values such as equality of opportunity, a tension which may be particularly acute in societies which are significantly multiracial and multicultural (which I take a society like contemporary Britain to be). To get to grips with this apparent conflict of values, we have to confront the following basic question: When is the freedom to exclude essential to meaningful freedom of association and, therefore, something which a state may not legitimately restrict or prohibit, and when may (and should) a state legitimately override this same freedom in the interests of securing other important values such as equality of opportunity and personal dignity? The purpose of this short paper is to explore, and to sketch out a tentative answer to, this question.

We shall proceed as follows. In section 2, I will set out one possible criterion for evaluating the legitimacy of rules of what I shall term 'categorical exclusion', the 'choice principle', advanced by Paul Hirst in his recent book, *Associative Democracy*.[1] I shall argue that this principle is inadequate to the task of sorting out when, and why, categorical exclusion (blanket exclusion on the basis of characteristics such as race, gender, or religious beliefs) is legitimate or illegitimate. In sections 3-4, I then outline an alternative approach to the evaluation of categorical exclusion rules which centers on a context-sensitive balancing of three core interests (so-called 'expressive', 'opportunity', and 'dignity' interests). Section 3 defines and elaborates these

---

[1] See Paul Hirst, *Associative Democracy: New Forms of Economic and Social Governance*, Cambridge, Polity Press, 1994.

three core interests and section 4 then tries to draw out some of the more obvious policy implications which follow from the acknowledgement of their importance. Section 5 briefly summarizes our main conclusions.

The Choice Principle and its Limitations

In this section I will outline and critique one recent proposal for evaluating the legitimacy of categorical exclusion rules. First, however, a few words about what is meant by 'categorical exclusion' from a secondary association. By categorical exclusion I mean the exclusion of individuals from secondary associations, by existing members of these associations, on the basis of some characteristic such as race, gender, sexuality, or religion, that is shared with some community of others. Not all exclusions from membership of secondary associations need be categorical in this sense. One might, for example, be excluded from membership of a given association simply because of the association's resource constraints – on the grounds, say, that the addition of new members would impair existing members' enjoyment of some resource (e.g., a beach) which the association controls. Or one might be excluded on purely personal grounds – 'blackballed', say, because existing members believe one to be a bore or untrustworthy. I will not say anything about exclusions of these kinds here; my focus will be solely on exclusions of the former, so-called categorical kind.

How, then, are we to evaluate the legitimacy of categorical exclusion rules? One possible approach has been suggested by Paul Hirst in his recent book, *Associative Democracy*. Hirst's first rule of 'associationist ethics' says that '... individuals cannot be excluded from associations except on the conditions that they choose to accept or reject.'[2] We may express the essential thought here slightly more formally in terms of a Choice Principle (CP), according to which: A categorical exclusion rule is legitimate if and only if individuals excluded by the rule may reasonably be said to fall under the relevant category of exclusion in virtue of personal choice as to the kind of persons they wish to be, rather than in virtue of forces beyond their control ('fate'). To operationalize the CP we then have to supplement it with some propositions as to what kinds of personal characteristics are a matter of choice and which a matter of fate. Hirst asserts that religion is a matter of choice, while gender and race are not:

> '... subscribing to Catholic doctrine is a choice, one may or may not accept the doctrines of the Church, whereas being black or being female is not a choice, one cannot decide to be white or to be male ...'[3]

It thus follows from the CP that it is never legitimate to exclude on the basis of race or gender, but always legitimate to exclude on the basis of religion.

---

[2] Hirst, *Associative Democracy*, p.58.
[3] Hirst, *Associative Democracy*, p.58.

Now the CP certainly has some attractions as a criterion for evaluating the legitimacy of the categorical exclusion rules which secondary associations can apply. Firstly, if all categorical exclusion rules had to conform to the requirements set by the CP, this would (setting other kinds of exclusion aside) entail that no citizen could ultimately be excluded from membership of an association against his/her will. According to the CP, I can only be legitimately excluded from association A on the basis of categorical characteristic, X, if X is something over which I have control; I must, in principle, then, be able to choose to discard X, and, if I so choose, I will then be eligible to join association A. The unlimited freedom of entry into secondary associations which the CP thus implies seems to cohere with the familiar and intuitively attractive liberal commitment to secure for each citizen the liberty and opportunity to pursue the conception of the good life he/she wishes to pursue (consistent with like liberty and opportunity for others).

Secondly, when we come to apply the CP to evaluate the legitimacy of categorical exclusion rules in certain important 'test-cases', the CP often appears to give intuitively appealing answers. Many people, for example, find the idea of whites-only or men-only sports or business clubs ethically repugnant. And according to the CP, whites/men-only exclusion rules of the kind operated by such clubs are indeed illegitimate because of the fact that race and gender are not personal characteristics over which individuals can be reasonably said to exert any choice. On the other hand, I'm sure that few, if any, of us would want to claim that members of a given religious association or political party may not legitimately exclude from church or party membership individuals who hold conflicting religious or political beliefs. And, once again, according to the CP, the exclusion rules we have in mind here are indeed perfectly legitimate – so long as we assume, following Hirst, that religious and political beliefs are indeed a matter of choice rather than fate.

On further examination, however, we rapidly encounter some serious difficulties with the CP as a criterion for evaluating the legitimacy of categorical exclusion rules. Application of the CP to the evaluation of such rules does not always produce results that are consistent with our intuitions; and even in cases like those considered a moment ago, where the CP does appear to produce results which accord with our intuitions, it is by no means clear that it produces the 'right answers' for the right (that is, morally pertinent) reasons.

A first, and fundamental, problem for the CP is simply that, in some cases, rules excluding individuals from membership of specific secondary associations on the basis of characteristics over which they have no control do not necessarily strike us as morally troublesome. Imagine, for example, that a group of women decide to get together and set up a women-only health and fitness club. This club would exclude about half the population from membership on the basis of a characteristic (being male) that is not reasonably seen as a matter of choice. But do we really find anything so terribly wrong about this in the case of this health and fitness-club? I just do not see this example of categorical exclusion as being morally worrisome in anything like the way that many (including myself) find the example of the whites-only sports club to be. But the CP does not allow us to make any moral distinction between the two cases. It suggests – implausibly, I think – that both instances of categorical exclusion are equally wrong.

A second problem with the CP is that it will legitimate categorical exclusion rules, based on personal characteristics over which individuals can supposedly exert control, that we may in fact have good reason to regard as morally questionable. For example, if we continue to provisionally accept Hirst's characterization of religious identification as a matter of choice, then it is far from clear that the CP will actually prohibit all forms of morally questionable racist exclusion. While it is clearly illegitimate under the CP for a group of racist whites to bar membership of the local cricket club to, say, Asians, on the basis of skin-colour, it is not illegitimate under the CP for them to operate a rule which excluded potential willing cricketers on the basis of holding Hindu, Sikh, or Islamic religious beliefs, and such a rule would, in certain social contexts, be clearly racist in intent and effect.[4]

These are the cases where it is not clear that the CP gives us the right answer when we apply it to evaluate the legitimacy of a given categorical exclusion rule. However, even where the CP does give us what intuitively looks to be the right answer, it is not clear that it always comes up with this answer for the right sort of reason. Let us return to the case of religious associations and political parties which exclude those who hold conflicting religious/political beliefs. Why should, say, the Catholic Church be allowed to exclude Protestants and Buddhists from membership of the Church? I suggest that the answer actually has precious little to do with the supposed fact that a person's religious belief is a matter of choice. The relevant consideration is simply that the Catholic Church would quickly cease to be the *Catholic* Church if it were unable to exclude those with conflicting beliefs. Individuals are hardly free to associate in pursuit of some shared conception of the good life and/or good society unless they are also free to exclude from this specific association those who do not share their distinctive beliefs. The pertinent consideration is that of protecting the integrity of such an association as a community of shared belief (what we may call an 'expressive community'), and not the supposed voluntariness of religious belief. The voluntariness of religious belief is a quite irrelevant consideration. Whether one is a Protestant by choice or not, it is perfectly legitimate for Catholics to exclude you from membership of their Church because this is patently necessary to maintain the integrity of their Church as a distinct expressive community.

---

[4] There is clear point of connection here with Tariq Modood's observation that racism in societies like contemporary Britain may be proximately based on considerations of cultural difference, rather than biological characteristics. See Tariq Modood, 'Racial Equality and Multiculturalism in Britain: The Progressivist Bias Against Some Minorities', in this set of conference proceedings.

Three Core Interests at Stake in Exclusion Controversies

For the reasons just outlined, the CP fails to offer a credible criterion for evaluating the legitimacy of categorical exclusion rules. I doubt, in fact, that there is any one single principle which can be used to evaluate their legitimacy. A more credible approach consists, I believe, in considering in more detail just what morally significant interests are centrally at stake in controversies about the legitimacy of categorical exclusion rules, and in attempting to draw out a number of principles for policy guidance from a consideration of what is necessary to protect these key interests. In this section, I will attempt to draw out the interests that I think are fundamentally at stake in exclusion rule controversies, before turning to attendant principles and policy implications in section 4.

Our discussion of religious and political associations in section 2 has already alerted us to one of the interests which is centrally at stake in considering the legitimacy of various categorical exclusion rules. This is the *expressive interest* of the individual in being able to associate with others in pursuit of shared beliefs about the good life and/or good society. Individuals come to possess beliefs on questions of fundamental value and meaning, and to frame life-projects in the light of these beliefs. Often they need to associate with others who have similar beliefs or life-projects in order to further these beliefs and projects. Freedom of association is, from this point of view, absolutely essential to the expression (not to mention, prior development) of the individual's ethical personality. Individuals may also come to hold beliefs about the appropriate structure of their society and polity, and will also need to come together with others of like opinion to pursue these beliefs in the political domain. In this way, freedom of association is also essential to meaningful political liberty, to effective participation in collective self-government. To put the point in Rawlsian terms, freedom of association is essential both to the development and expression of the two moral powers of the democratic citizen: the power to frame, revise and pursue a conception of the good (which power might be manifested, for example, through participation in a religious association), and the power to deliberate and act in accordance with a sense of justice (which power might be manifested, for example, through participation in a political party or campaigning issue-group).[5]

To be able to develop and exercise such moral powers, however, democratic citizens must also have access to resources, to the various goods needed to pursue their life-projects, and for democratic participation. Justice (as the liberal egalitarian conceives it) requires, roughly speaking, that citizens have equal access to certain key, strategic goods, such as income and wealth.[6] Now associations of one kind or another may play an important role in mediating access to such goods. Liberal justice would thus appear

---

[5] On the two moral powers, see John Rawls, *Political Liberalism*, Columbia University Press, 1993, pp.19, 81. Rawls explicitly lists freedom of association as a 'basic liberty' – a liberty essential to the adequate development and exercise of these two powers – at p.335.

[6] By equal access I mean, roughly speaking, that individuals should not suffer disadvantage in access to such goods in virtue of discrimination or differential brute luck.

to require that citizens have equal access to these 'goods-conferring associations'. We are thus able to formulate the second of our core interests as the *opportunity interest* of the individual in having (equal) access to those associations the membership of which confers significant instrumental advantages in the acquisition of strategic goods (such as income and wealth). When, for example, women or disadvantaged minorities claim a right of access to business associations in which lucrative networking takes place, or to trade unions currently operating discriminatory membership policies, it is precisely this opportunity interest which is being appealed to in support of this rights claim.

One's effective freedom to pursue a conception of the good and/or capacity for political participation can be impaired, however, not only by inadequate access to resources, but by social practices of stigmatization which serve to diminish one's sense of self-worth. And the blanket exclusion from membership of secondary associations on the basis of one's race, gender, sexuality, or religion, provide one pertinent example of a type of social practice which may be stigmatizing in this way. We are thus able to identify our third core interest as the *dignity interest* of the individual in not being denied access to associations on grounds that, given the prevailing social context, are stigmatizing, and thus potentially detrimental to his/her sense of self-worth.

These, then, are the three core interests which would appear to be at stake in considering the justice of various categorical exclusion rules.[7] These interests have in common that they all derive from the fundamental interests of the citizen in being able to freely pursue a conception of the good and to participate substantively in the political domain (and, in this way, to develop and exercise Rawls' two moral powers). In order to evaluate the legitimacy of a given categorical exclusion rule, or type of categorical exclusion rule, we must therefore consider how this rule/type of rule affects these three core interests. More specifically, we can use our account of the three interests to derive some broad principles of policy guidance which we can then apply to particular cases. The elaboration of these principles is the concern of the next section.

Policy Implications

In formulating public policy towards the categorical exclusion rules operated by various secondary associations, our central aim should be that of protecting the three core interests outlined in section 3. To this end, public policy must be guided by three basic principles. The principles may be seen as providing an outline for legislation, and for subsequent judicial interpretation of whether the relevant legislation has or has not been conformed to in specific instances.

---

[7] The importance of the opportunity and dignity interests to the evaluation of categorical exclusion rules is also clearly implicit, I think, in a recent brief discussion of the subject by Brian Barry. See Brian Barry, *Justice as Impartiality*, Oxford University Press, 1995, pp.15-17.

The first of these may be termed the expressive exclusion principle. According to this principle, secondary associations which are clearly expressive communities, constituted by a shared commitment to a particular conception of the good life and/or good society, have the right to exclude individuals from association membership on the grounds that they hold incompatible religious or philosophical beliefs or any other characteristic that makes it impossible to hold the association's expressive goals with sincerity. It is on the basis of such a principle, for example, that Catholics may legitimately exclude Protestants from joining their Church, and members of a traditional left-wing political party may legitimately exclude someone of conservative beliefs from joining their party. Expressive associationism is, as we noted in section 3, vital to the development and expression of the individual's ethical personality, and to effective political participation. And the right to exclude secured by the expressive exclusion principle is, as we saw in section 2, essential to maintain the integrity of expressive associations in the face of those with conflicting beliefs who may wish to join them to subvert the goals of their original members.

The expressive exclusion principle permits secondary associations with strong expressive commitments, that is, whose goals are centrally defined by commitment to a particular doctrine of the good life and/or good society, to exclude from association membership those individuals who have expressive commitments at odds with those of the association. An association lacking a strong expressive orientation cannot, therefore, appeal to the principle to justify excluding people from association membership on the grounds that they lack, or possess, some specific expressive commitment. Thus, while the principle allows Catholics to ban Protestants from membership of their Church, it does not legitimate (or, at least, does not clearly legitimate) the aforementioned racist whites who wish to ban Asians from their local cricket club by introducing a membership rule excluding Hindus, Sikhs, or Muslims. Note also, however, that the expressive exclusion principle doesn't only legitimate categorical exclusion rules which make reference to persons' beliefs; where this is relevant to the maintenance of the integrity of the expressive association, it can also legitimate exclusion on the basis of such characteristics as race and gender. Take the hypothetical case of an association called the White Patriarchalist Party, whose members are dedicated to the proposition that white males are inherently superior to other human beings, and therefore deserving of more resources and power. The White Patriarchalists might plausibly claim that being a woman, or being non-white, is incompatible with being a sincere supporter of the association's values and goals, and, under the expressive exclusion principle, they may therefore legitimately exclude women and non-whites from full membership of the association. This is, it may be noted, an example of a case of categorical exclusion which is illegitimate from the standpoint of Hirst's CP, but which would be perfectly legitimate from the standpoint of our expressive exclusion principle.

The second of our principles for policy guidance is the equal opportunity principle, according to which: Secondary associations which are significant in conferring access to strategic goods (such as income and wealth) must have maximally open admissions rules, that is, there is, in the case of such goods-conferring associations, a strong presumption against the legitimacy of any categorical exclusion rules. This principle follows from the underlying liberal egalitarian view that citizens should have equal access to strategic goods and, therefore, to those associations which are important in providing access to these goods. Thus, it would be illegitimate under this principle for associations whose primary aim is to facilitate networking amongst businessmen to operate categorical exclusion rules based on such things as race, gender, or religion. A sports or social club would also be prohibited from operating such rules under this principle if/when it can be established that these associations in fact perform a similar social function. It can be argued that it would also be illegitimate under this principle for associations like trade unions to operate discriminatory membership policies.

There may, of course, be some conflict in practice between the expressive exclusion principle and the equal opportunity principle. Such conflict will occur in the case of an association which is significantly expressive and also to some degree goods-conferring. The appropriate response, I think, is to consider the relative importance of the association's expressive and goods-conferring functions to its typical members, and to give priority to one or other of the two principles on this basis. Courts would have to evaluate which principle properly has priority on a case-by-case basis, as legal challenges are brought in specific instances of categorical exclusion. This, in essence, is how the scope of the right to exclude has been gradually elaborated in the US context, through a succession of Supreme Court and lower court decisions which have made more or less explicit reference to the three core interests distinguished in section 3.[8]

In order to appreciate the importance of our third principle of policy guidance, it may help if we first consider the following example. Imagine two fitness clubs, call them simply club X and club Y, one of which, X, is strictly women-only, and the other of which, Y, is strictly whites-only. Neither club X nor Y is significantly goods-conferring. Nor is either association strongly expressive in kind – for the essential goals of the clubs have to do with the attainment of physical fitness, a goal which in itself hardly amounts to a distinct conception of the good, but is rather an objective that may fit into a wide range of otherwise different and conflicting conceptions of the good. In these cases, then, it is hard to see how an expressive defence, or an opportunity-based critique, of the clubs' categorical exclusion rules can be given. But our third principle, which represents the dignity interest distinguished in section 3, might enable us to say something about the respective legitimacy of these clubs' rules. This is the non-stigmatization principle, according to which: Categorical exclusion rules that are not clearly required

---

[8] See especially Justice Brennan's opinion in *Roberts v. United States Jaycees*, in which the Supreme Court denied that the Jaycees organization (a business association) had a constitutionally protected right, grounded in the freedom of association guaranteed by the First Amendment, to exclude women from full membership. Brennan argues that the equal opportunity (and dignity) interests of the women excluded by the Jaycees' membership rules are weightier than any expressive interest of the existing male members which might be slightly infringed by forcing the Jaycees to admit women as full members. See Roberts v. United States Jaycees, 468 U.S. 609 (1984).

to protect significant expressive interests are illegitimate when exclusion on the basis of the relevant characteristic(s) is likely, in the prevailing social context, to be read as signalling the supposed inferiority of the excluded group, and thereby, to potentially damage the sense of self-worth of those belonging to this group.

This principle helps us to make an important, and intuitively compelling, moral discrimination between the exclusion rules operated by clubs X and Y. In the context of countries like contemporary Britain, a women-only exclusion rule of the kind operated by club X is (on the whole) unlikely to be perceived as stigmatizing to men, and it is hard to imagine many men experiencing any diminished sense of self-worth as a result of this rule's operation. But in this same social context a reasonable case could be made for saying that the whites-only exclusion rule operated by club Y is stigmatizing to non-whites, and that this categorical exclusion rule is thus illegitimate. It will be recalled that using Hirst's CP we were quite unable to draw any moral distinction between two such cases; the non-stigmatization principle enables us to draw, and to rationally defend, this intuitively compelling distinction.

Conclusion

In this short paper I have tried to set out the elements of an answer to the question of when, and on what grounds, secondary associations may or may not legitimately engage in the categorical exclusion of individuals from association membership – a question which is, I suggest, especially pressing in the context of a society which, like contemporary Britain, is becoming significantly multiracial and multicultural. I have argued that the Choice Principle recently advanced by Paul Hirst fails to provide a plausible criterion for evaluating the legitimacy of categorical exclusion rules. A more plausible approach, I have argued, consists in applying a range of principles, each of which represents one of the morally significant interests – the expressive, opportunity, and dignity interests – which may be centrally at stake in specific exclusion controversies.

Associational life is often presented as, or simply assumed to be, a part of the 'private sphere' of a liberal society, and, thus, as being beyond the legitimate purview and regulation of the liberal state. But the core interests approach to the evaluation of categorical exclusion rules sketched here challenges this view. This approach has as its corollary a reconceptualization of the 'public-private dichotomy', in which the liberal state is seen as having the right, if not the duty, to regulate the membership policies of secondary associations in various ways in order to protect and promote equal opportunity and personal dignity (while still giving appropriate respect to citizens' expressive commitments). It is especially important to emphasize this in a multicultural society like our own in which more privileged ethnic groups may frequently try to shelter behind a supposed right to exclude in their efforts to maintain their (unjustly) advantaged position.

The Politics of Health

Peter K. Falconer
Glasgow Caledonian University

'To Charge or Not to Charge: the Politics of Health Charges in Britain'[1]

Quotation

'Much of the current advocacy of charges rests on the proposition that the services in question should not be in the public non-market sector, indeed often that they should not be in the public sector at all ... Many socialists and social administrators, stung by this attack on the fabric of the welfare state, are tempted to respond by claiming that all charges are bad and all taxes good ... (thus giving rise to a) prevalence of crude pro- and anti-charging views ... What emerges clearly from the evidence on the structure and scope of charges within the welfare state is the complete absence of any coherent philosophy about their role.' (Heald, 1983, p.305).

Introduction

Since the establishment of the National Health Service (NHS), the issue of health charges has been the subject of regular debate between the political parties. This paper considers the nature of charging policies pursued by successive Labour and Conservative governments from the inception of the NHS to the present, a fifty-year period which has seen 12 general elections, 10 Prime Ministers, six changes in party control of government and 16 successive years of Conservative endeavours to 'roll back' the welfare state.

A central problem facing policymakers surrounds the task of reconciling the conflict between the absolute values which politicians expound and the highly constrained actions of government for which they are responsible. As such, compromises are required on the part of policymakers between the political principles they hold and the practical realities of government. This distinction, of course, leaves open important questions concerning which values are important to whom and which constraints have the most influence on political action. The paper examines this central problem as it applies to the question of charging for health care in Britain. It considers the rationale for, and the politics surrounding, the use of charges in the National Health Service (NHS), and contends that decisions on whether or not to levy charges for health services are based less on questions of political principle and more on pragmatic concerns, given that income from charges can represent an important source of revenue.

---

[1] This paper provides an analysis of the central themes and issues underlying the politics of charging for health care in Britain. Supporting statistical material will be provided to panel attendees at the conference, or can be obtained from Dr Peter Falconer, Department of Law and Public Administration, Glasgow Caledonian University, City Campus, Cowcaddens Road, Glasgow, G4 OBA (Tel. 0141 331 3434; FAX 0141 331 3798).

The Scope of Health Charges

Health charges currently account for around 5 percent of NHS revenue (Bruce & Bailey, 1993, p.2). There is no shortage of values, either political, social or economic, justifying the use of charges in health care delivery. Similarly, there is no shortage of values suggesting that public services should be provided free of charge (see Walsh, 1995, pp.85-89). Nevertheless, despite the fact that the conclusions of these value positions point in opposite directions, they share one common theme: both lay down absolute principles for action which governments are expected to follow. In the NHS, the use of charges has been a growing phenomenon, and the financial difficulties faced by the health service, together with the many reforms which have swept through the organisation since the mid-1980s, have encouraged a stronger emphasis on the use of charges as a means of income generation. Although, as Walsh (1995, p.98) states, 'the value of charges lies largely at the margin of services rather than as a central mechanism for the introduction of market forces', by the early 1990s charging for health services had become an important theme within government thinking toward public spending on health care. Indeed, today, we have a wide range of health services for which charges are imposed: prescriptions; dental and ophthalmic appliances; dental and eye examinations; 'hotel' charges in hospitals; and charges for certain appliances. Given that some 95 percent of hospitals have moved to Trust status, these autonomous units are making more and more use of charges for non-medical services in order to raise much-needed revenue. A summary of a number of specific income generation schemes currently operating in the NHS is provided in Table 1 below.

Of course, the idea of charging for health care is not new. The NHS Act of 1946 contained provisions for charges under Part 1 (2), which stated that health services would be provided free of charge 'except where any provision of this Act expressly provides for the making and recovery of a charge'. Under Part 44 (1) and (2) of the Act, the provision was made for charges for dental and ophthalmic appliances. The 1946 Act made no mention of prescription charges, provision for which was introduced under Section 16 of the 1949 Health (Amendment) Act. Justifying the legislation for prescription charges in the House of Commons, Prime Minister Clement Atlee stated that the charge was intended to

> 'reduce excessive and, in some cases, unnecessary resort to doctors and chemists of which there is evidence which has for some time troubled the Minister of Health ... The resultant saving will contribute about £10 billion, although this is not the primary purpose of the charge.' (Hansard, 24th October 1949, col.1019).

In November 1949, Minister of health Aneurin Bevan, in a classic statement in support of prescription charges, declared, 'I shudder to think of the ceaseless cascade of medicine which is pouring down British throats' (quoted, *The Campaign Guide*, Conservative Central Office, 1970, p.443). Charges themselves were not introduced until 1951, when the Labour Government, in its final months in office, introduced charges for ophthalmic services only. This charging policy was justified on two main grounds: first, that the charge was economically necessary to help provide finance for the NHS; and second, that it would help prevent the abuse which might arise from a completely free service. This policy was not universally accepted within Labour ranks. In a manner which was to set the tone for future Labour back-bench/front-bench exchanges on health charges, the Government was subjected to a wave of back-bench criticism. Health charges represented a thoroughly miserable measure'; 'a tax on the poor'; and 'a breach of a great socialist principle' (*Hansard*, 24th April 1951, cols.289-290).

Table 1
Income Generation Schemes

services to patients	*services to staff and visitors*	*services to the private sector*
Sale of baby clothes	Restaurants	Health screening for employers
Private TV/video	*additional menu choice* Laundry/dry cleaning Newsagents	Laundry/dry cleaning Occupational health
Baby photography	Florists Nursery products Pharmacies Financial services	Fitness testing Pathology Incineration Vehicle servicing Training Catering for functions Supplies to nursing homes Property leasing Printing

Source: Bruce & Bailey, 1993, p.30.

The 1945-51 Labour Government did not introduce charges for dental appliances or prescriptions. These were brought in by the Conservative Government under the National Health Service (Charges for Drugs and Appliances) Regulations of 1952. Again, these charges were justified on grounds of economic necessity, though prescription charges were introduced partly to reduce the demands on doctors for low-priced medicines which patients might reasonably be expected to buy for themselves.

Between 1952 and 1986, the policy of charging for dental and ophthalmic services remained fairly stable, with a cross-party consensus in favour of these charges. Up to 1986, the only development in charging policy was the 1974-1979 Labour Government's introduction of charges for dental treatment in 1977 (with no significant opposition to the legislation). In 1986 and 1989, the Thatcher Government introduced more sweeping changes in these areas. In 1986, a voucher scheme was introduced in relation to ophthalmic services, and in 1989 charges were introduced for both dental and eye examinations.

Under the 1986 voucher scheme, people on low income could obtain assistance toward the cost of glasses or contact lenses. this assistance came in the form a voucher supplied by the Department of Social Security. Where an individual chose a pair of glasses or contact lenses which cost more than the value of the voucher, he or she paid the difference. The introduction of charges for dental and eye tests in 1989 was a more politically problematic issue. The Government argued that these charges were consistent with long-established charging policies - that people should be expected to make a contribution (over and above their taxes) to the cost of health services. Objections to these charges came from both sides of the House an for different reasons. The Labour benches, as expected, opposed these charges on grounds of principle. Opposition from the Government benches was grounded in the view that, while charges were perfectly reasonable for curative medicine, they were less desirable in the case of preventative medicine. This case was argued most vociferously in regard to eye tests which have an important diagnostic role in regard to such conditions as glaucoma and hyper-tension. Charges were undesirable, it was argued, because they would deter people from having their eyes examined. Consequently, such medical conditions might not be diagnosed. As it transpired, the strength of Mrs Thatcher's majority at that time won the day for the government. Interestingly, despite the fervour of Labour opposition to these charges at the time, the present Labour Party has given no indication that it would repeal these charges in office.

The one aspect of health charges which has been a constant focus of attention over the years has been prescription charges. First introduced, as stated above, In 1952, prescription charges were abolished by a Labour Government in 1965. At that time, the Government also promised to abolish dental and ophthalmic charges in due course. However, later in 1965, Chancellor of the Exchequer James Callaghan announced in the House of Commons that it would not be possible to remove charges for dental and ophthalmic services due to 'economic realities'. Moreover, in 1968, prescription charges were reintroduced by the same Labour Government, and at a higher rate. Again, this 'U-turn' was explained by the Government by the need to obtain additional revenue to help fund 'higher social priorities', such as hospital construction and care for the elderly and mentally ill. Labour Minister of Health Kenneth Robinson's statement to the House explaining the reintroduction of prescription charges serves as a clear demonstration of the victory of pragmatism over principle:

> 'it is not the view of this Government, as it appears to be of the party opposite, that prescription charges are a good thing in themselves ... The Government regard their reintroduction as a regrettable necessity, and it is primarily on the grounds of economic necessity that (they are reintroduced) ... Ideally, the NHS should be free to everyone. I can tell the House that (the choice we have made), however distasteful ... was the one which did the least damage to the health service and its patients.'

(*Hansard*, 30th May 1968, columns 2254-2258).

Following their reintroduction, the prescription charge remained at 12.5p per item until 1971 when, under the Heath Government, it was increase to 20p at which level it remained until 1979. Under post-1979 governments, the prescription charge has escalated to its present level of £5.25 per item. This dramatic increase has been justified on two grounds: first, that it is right that people who can afford to pay toward the cost of prescriptions should do so; and second, that rising costs have necessitated the increased charge which still remains small in relation to the average cost of prescription items.

Overall, as regards the rationale for health charges in the post-1979 period, these are advocated on a variety of grounds and from different political perspectives:

• They help to "bridge the gap" between the spending needs of the NHS and the income received from government.'

• They serve as a signal of demand. It is assumed that the payment of a charge provides a signal as to what people who make use of a service are willing to pay in order to receive that service.

• Charges are 'fair', in the sense that people who use the service are paying toward the cost of the benefit they receive.

• Charges serve as a means of reducing public spending since people are paying directly for a service which otherwise would be financed through taxation.

• Charges improve efficiency in the provision of services since the use of charges introduces the discipline of the marketplace into the allocation of services.

• Charges are educative and thus recommended as a way of informing members of the public as to the cost of public service provision. The idea here is that the best way of 'bringing home to people' how much a service actually costs to provide is to charge for it.

Of course, a central problem with charging for services lies in the view that ability to pay should not determine access to service, particularly since many people who use local government services lack the financial capacity to pay for them. Consequently, in the real world of NHS finance, exemptions exist as an inevitable corollary of charges. Within the welfare state,

> 'exemptions from charges serve as a pragmatic political compromise between the conflicting pro-charge and anti-charge value positions. Exempting certain people from a charge satisfies the argument that particular groups of people, such as the low-paid, are unable to afford to pay for a service. On the other hand, imposing charges upon some people acknowledges that certain people who receive a public service are in fact able to pay toward its cost.' (Bailey et al, 1993, p.39).

For Birch (1986, p.163), health charges represent a government policy aimed at 'requiring all except exempt groups to pay an increasing proportion of the cost of their own treatment'. As such, for Birch, the increased use of patient charges gives rise to something of a two-tier system of health funding, consisting of 'exempt patients, for whom the cost of the service is met entirely by the taxpayer, and non-exempt patients, for whom a decreasing proportion of the cost of the service is met out of central government finance' (Birch, 1986, p.163).

Exemptions from Charges

To quote Walsh (1995, p.96), 'it is common to try to take account of distributional issues in the setting of charges by varying them in relation to income or other factors'. Although generally in the public sector, objectives in charging policy have become more transparent in recent years, due in some part to the development of a 'consumerist ethos' in public service delivery and to the financial problems facing public service delivery agencies, there remains

> 'a fairly unconsidered process of cross-subsidy, often inherited from past practice, so that the impact of the public services on distributional equity is as much accident as design. The issue of whether services should be provided on a universal or selective basis is particularly muddled, with an ideology of universality existing alongside widespread, but unsystematic means testing and de facto rationing.' (Walsh, 1995, pp.96-97)

In the particular case of the NHS, exemptions from charges tend to be on universal grounds, whereby exemptions from charges are enjoyed by people who belong to a particular societal group or category. Exemptions from prescription charges, dental charges and charges for eye tests are enjoyed by the following categories:

<u>prescription charges</u>

people aged 60 and over; everyone under the age of 16; pregnant women and mothers of children under 12 months of age; people who hold an exemption certificate because they suffer from a medical condition which requires continuous medication for long periods; war pensioners, in respect of the treatment of war disabilities; people on low income (that is, in receipt of certain social security benefits such as income support or family credit).

There are also special arrangements for people who require frequent medicines but who are not eligible for a complete exemption. These arrangements come in the form of 'season tickets', whereby the patient can purchase either a six-monthly or 12-monthly prepayment certificate which covers the charge for all prescriptions dispensed within that period. The saving enjoyed by the patient will depend on the number of prescription items dispensed.

<u>dental charges</u>

everyone under the age of 16; students engaged in full-time education, aged under 19; pregnant women and nursing mothers; people on low income (that is, in receipt of certain social security benefits such as income support or family credit).

eye examinations

people who are registered blind or are partially sighted; diagnosed diabetics of glaucoma patients; people over 40 years of age who are the parent, brother, sister or child of a person with diagnosed glaucoma; people on low income (that is, in receipt of certain social security benefits such as income support or family credit).

In the case of dental and ophthalmic charges, unlike prescription charges, the elderly are not exempt from charges unless they qualify under a 'low income' category (that is, if their only income is the national insurance pension.

An important question on the subject of exemptions concerns whether the financial pressures on the welfare state will lead future governments to reconsider the feasibility of universal exemptions. Given the increasing difficulties associated with financing the welfare state in general, and the NHS in particular, it is an important question as to whether the country can afford to continue exempting people from health charges who are well able to afford to pay a charge. At present, over 80 percent of prescriptions are provided free of charge to patients, many of whom are financially able to make a contribution toward their cost. It is a matter of debate as to how long governments can avoid the shift toward more selective exemptions, a move which will have significant political ramifications given public perceptions toward the NHS and its funding.

The Politics of Charging

Do political parties make a difference in charging policy? It is a commonly held view among politicians that parties can and should make a difference in the way the nation is governed and in the policies pursued to that end. In Britain, the two main parties - Conservative and Labour - have represented more or less mutually exclusive ideologies with very different prescriptions for government. In regard to the question of charging for services, disagreements between the parties tend to reflect these conflicting political values and ideologies. The 'conventional wisdom' is that Conservative governments favour the use of charges, whereas Labour governments eschew their imposition. Undoubtedly, there exists a clear ideological divide between the two major parties on this question. Evidence of Conservative support for, and Labour opposition to, charges can be found in a variety of sources, such as election manifestos, policy documents and records of Parliamentary debates. The 'parties matter' literature (see, for example, Castles, 1982; Sharpe & Newton, 1984) contends that, in the policymaking arena, it should matter whether we have a Conservative or a Labour government. However, in the study of charging policy, we must differentiate between rhetoric and action and between principle and practice. The simple truth is that, while it is relatively easy to enunciate absolute values in support for, or opposition to, a particular charging policy, the practical realities of government impose constraints on political decision makers who are required to act in accordance with economic necessity rather than principle. Moreover, given that the politics of charges tends to be concerned with questions of the level of, incremental adjustments to, and conditions of exemption from, a charge, do real conflicts of principle arise? The study of charging practice demonstrates that identifiable differences in charging for health care between Labour and Conservative governments tend to be differences in degree, not principle. As such, the politics of charges is governed by a number of constraints to which politicians are subjected.

Charging Practice and the Politics of Constraints

The politics of charging advises us that parties may differ in what they articulate, but not in what they do in office. Public policies are effected through public institutions, and the institutions of government possess properties which can represent 'something stronger than parties' (see Rose, 1984, pp.142-162). As such, any attempt to understand charging practice must be grounded in an appreciation of the practical realities of government and the constraints which limit the actions of politicians and the implementation of values. the inheritance of past programmes, the practicalities of Treasury control and collective responsibility, and the parliamentary divide between front-bench and back-bench MPs each represent powerful constraints which leave politicians with limited scope for putting values into practice in regard to charging for services.

1. Inherited programmes

Following an election, an incoming administration inherits a 'policy legacy' from its predecessor comprising a wide range of programmes, together with the public expectation that the great majority of these programmes will be maintained. It also inherits a large administrative apparatus, consisting of the institutions, personnel and procedures through which the day-to-day responsibilities of government are exercised (Rose, 1990a, 1995; Rose & Davies, 1994). As such, politicians spend less time deliberating on what they would ideally wish to do, and more time deciding on what selective interventions that can make to modify the legacy they have inherited. As a consequence, most programmes, either with or without charges, tend to continue by routine.

Any changes in policy, therefore, tend to comprise incremental adjustments to the level of charges, rather than the abolition of current charges or the introduction of new charges. For example, despite their ideological predilection for charges, post-1979 Conservative governments have been restrained in bringing to the House of Commons legislation introducing new health charges. Such legislation would be important, since Acts of Parliament are central to the ongoing process of inheritance. Unlike the white papers and speeches of previous governments, they have binding authority, unless and until repealed. Statutes are also fundamental in determining whether particular health services are or are not subject to charges. Moreover, statutes constrain both Conservative and Labour governments.

For example, given her political principles, it is improbable that Margaret Thatcher would have chosen a health service in which most medical treatment and hospital services are free of charge. yet, having inherited a health service in which the scope of charges was limited, the Thatcher administration was constrained to maintain it on this basis. In Klein's (1995, p.162) words, the Thatcher Government's approach to health charges involved 'a process of cautious incrementalism, gradually ratcheting up the level of charges, rather than a sudden rush of ideological blood to the head'. Moreover, no attempt was made to limit the scope of exemptions from health charges.

2. The collective acceptance of Treasury control

Under the British system of government, the Secretary of State for Health cannot pursue an aggressive departmental policy concerning charges and spending, for he or she is constrained by the doctrine of collective responsibility. The Treasury must endorse any change in expenditure, including changes arising from an increase or reduction in charges. The Treasury will normally resist seemingly small increases in net expenditure on the grounds that they may subsequently become large commitments.

The history of the NHS offers a clear example of the power of the Treasury. Successive Labour Chancellors, contrary to party values and electoral commitments, have made NHS charges a necessary part of their budget packages, even when the sums involved were so small that they could have been obtained in other ways. As such, Labour Chancellors have compelled colleagues to accept policy measures which directly oppose party principles as a means of demonstrating publicly that Labour governments are committed to an ethic of fiscal responsibility, even in the face of strongly held absolute values. Moreover, because charges are a form of revenue, the Treasury also determines whether or not the agency levying the charge can retain the money as additional revenue. Because of its institutional fear of losing revenue, the Treasury will always have a preference that money collected should be pooled as part of general revenues, rather than retained by the collecting agency. To the extent that charges serve as a means of reducing net expenditure, the Treasury may cut its funding of programmes as revenue rises from charges. In the case of the NHS, health care officials are thus left in the 'front line', having to bear the brunt of objections to charges by patients and the added administrative burden, with no additional funds. The central point here is that Treasury control can be a disincentive for the NHS to make increased use of charges, since any money raised could give rise to a commensurate reduction in the government subsidy to the NHS. Ministers may promise that this will not happen, but no current minister can bind his or her successor, never mind the Treasury.

3. The Parliamentary divide between front-bench and back-bench

The House of Commons not only institutionalises a division between the governing party and the Opposition, but also an equally important divide between members of the front-benches and back-benches. A back-bench MP, regardless of party is usually free to say whatever he or she thinks, since the views expressed are deemed to be those of an individual. In contrast, a front-bench MP, either of the governing or opposing parties, is subject to a collective constraint, an ethic of responsibility, which negates the 'freedom of speech' enjoyed by back-bench colleagues. When a minister speaks, what is said is immediately regarded as a statement of departmental policy, committing the Cabinet as a whole. Consequently, a minister cannot announce a change in charging policy without the approval of Cabinet colleagues who will be principally concerned with the wider political implications of any such change for their own departments and for the Government as a whole.

A shadow minister enjoys a little more freedom, because his or her words are not immediately acted upon. Nevertheless, a shadow minister will try to avoid making statements which could be interpreted as commitments to act should the Opposition move into Government. While Labour back-benchers, for example, have long decried the imposition of charges for health care, Labour front-benchers have been more cautious, promising at best to reduce or remove charges as quickly as possible. Two MPs, both of whom are frontbenchers, will often have more in common with each other regardless of parry affiliation, than are two MPs who occupy contrasting parliamentary positions within their own party, because the former are bound by an ethic of responsibility whereas the latter are free to enunciate absolute values.

For example, the debate on prescription charges has produced a greater division between the front- and back-benches of the Labour Party than between Labour and Conservative parties. Over time, the Labour front-bench has both supported and even introduced health charges, and tends to be concerned with the level of charges, not their removal. Labour back-benchers, on the other hand, have remained fiercely opposed to health charges in any form. Since the establishment of the NHS, the Labour Party has been clearly divided on principle versus pragmatism, with Labour governments retaining health charges, against the party's value position, on grounds of economic necessity.

Conclusion

It is clear that health charges will continue to be both a subject of political debate and a feature of NHS revenue. The demand for health care continues to place growing financial pressure on a service which must look increasingly to sources of finance over and above that received from the Treasury. It seems reasonable to suggest that, under Conservative governments, charging policies will continue to grow on an incremental basis, with further increases in the level of prescription charges and an increased variety of hospital charges for such items as private rooms, other hotel services, certain forms of treatment not universally available, and appointments made within a specific time period. All of these options, of course, entail different implications for principles of equity sand choice. Under a future Labour Government, it appears equally certain that charging policies will persist in the NHS. As history tells us, both Conservative and Labour governments accept both the principle and necessity of charging for certain areas of health care. Where difference do arise, these will tend to be in the level of charges. We should not expect a future Labour Government to abolish those charges currently in force, though we may expect charges to increase at a slower rate. As such, the central debates on health charges will continue to revolve mainly around the question of degree rather than principle. Consequently, it may be that 'to charge or not to charge' is not the question!

References

J.Appleby, *Financing Health Care in the 1990s*, Open University Press, 1992.

S.Bailey et al, *Local Government Charges: Policy and Practice*, Longman, 1993.

S.Birch, 'Increasing Patient Charges in the National Health Service', *Journal of Social Policy*, 15/2, 1986.

A.Bruce & S.J.Bailey, *Funding the NHS*, Policy Analysis Research Unit Discussion Paper 21, Glasgow Caledonian University, 1993.

M.Calnan et al, *Going Private: Why People Pay for Their Health Care*, Buckingham, Open University Press, 1992.

F.G.Castles, *The Impact of Parties*, Sage, 1982.

B.Davies, *Universality, Selectivity and Effectiveness in Social Policy*, Heinemann, 1978.

D.Heald, *Public Expenditure*, Martin Robertson, 1983.

K.Judge & J.Matthews, *Charging for Social Care*, Allen & Unwin, 1980.

R.Klein, *The New Politics of the NHS*, third edition, Longman, 1995.

R.Rose, *Do Parties Make a Difference?*, Macmillan, 1984.

R.Rose, 'Inheritance Before Choice in Public Policy', *Journal of Theoretical Politics*, 2, 1990a.

R.Rose, 'Charging for Public Services', *Public Administration*, 68/2, 1990b.

R.Rose, 'States of Inertia: Are Governments Slaves to History?', *Demos*, 7, 1995.

R.Rose & P.L.Davies, *Inheritance in Public Policy: Change Without Choice in Britain*, Yale University Press, 1994.

M.Sculpher & B.J.O'Brien, 'Do Patient Charge Increases Reduce the Use of Prescription Medicines? An Economic Perspective', *Public Money and Management*, 11/2, 1991.

L.J.Sharpe & K.Newton, *Does Politics Matter: The Determinants of Public Policy*, Oxford University Press, 1984.

J.Straw, *Parental Contributions to the Cost of School Activities*, House of Commons, 1987.

E.Wagner, *Charging for Government: User Charges and Earmarked Taxes in Principle and Practice*, Routledge, 1991.

K.Walsh, *Public Services and Market Mechanisms*, Macmillan, 1995.

Ideology, Hegemony and Political Subjectivity

David Howarth
Staffordshire University

'Theorising Hegemony'

Introduction

It has been recognised by numerous political scientists that the concept of hegemony constitutes an invaluable tool of analysis for understanding and explaining a wide range of empirical phenomena. However, despite this centrality, rigorous theorisation of the concept has not been forthcoming. In comparison to a range of 'family resemblance' concepts such as power, domination, leadership, and force (not to mention other key concepts of political theory such as freedom, obligation, social class and the state), theoretical labour on hegemony has remained underdeveloped. One recent exception to this generalisation is the work of Ernesto Laclau and Chantal Mouffe. They have drawn on post-structuralist and post-modernist themes to articulate a novel conception of hegemony (See Mouffe, 1979; Laclau & Mouffe, 1985; Laclau, 1990). Though this theorisation has attracted a good deal of commentary – both positive and negative – the discussion has tended to be of a typically 'either/or' variety: either their work has resolved all the problems associated with the concept, and requires very little further investigation, or it has no relevance at all in advancing theory in this field, and should be immediately abandoned. In the too rapid desire to praise or condemn, usually for short-term political advantage, much of the richness of Laclau & Mouffe's problematic has been lost, while careful analysis of its sources, and the unanswered questions it raises, foreclosed. In this paper, I shall situate and contextualise their innovative theorisation of the concept of hegemony, while at the same time pointing out a series of difficulties and weaknesses which still need to be clarified if their approach is to be theoretically coherent and empirically applicable.

The Classical Precursors

The emergence of the concept of hegemony in the Marxist tradition can be traced back to debates in Russian social democracy from the late 1890s to 1917 (Anderson, 1976). Nevertheless, echoes of the problem which generated the concept, can be found in Marx and Engels. The question of politics in Marx and Engels' writings generally concerns the role of the state and ideology in the maintenance of class domination, in which the state is understood principally as an agent of coercion, and ideology as the inculcation of 'false consciousness'. There are, however, at least two important supplementary dimensions to their theorisation. In the first place, the working class must transcend its own particular interests to become a universal class in any succesful social revolution; second, the organisation of class rule involves more than narrow state coercion and ideological deception but the creation of an ideal, though illusory, community to justify its particular mode of existence, and a set of state institutions designed to supervise, regulate and enmesh the private lives of individuals (See Marx, 1977, pp.169, 316).

Despite these supplementary additions to the class domination theory of politics and ideology, it was left to later Marxist thinkers to elaborate upon the complexities of class rule and the strategic prerequisites of succesful political class struggle. Foremost amongst these was Gramsci. Most commentators have emphasised the central role of hegemony in his political thought, though this concept has a number of different and at times contradictory meanings (Anderson, 1976; Femia, 1981; Hoffman, 1984; Mouffe, 1979). In brief, there are at least four dimensions of hegemony in Gramsci's writings. Firstly, in contradistinction to a Leninist conception of 'class alliances', it designates a particular type of political practice in which a social class endeavours to 'become hegemonic' by winning the consent of forces external to it and in so doing exercising leadership over them (Gramsci, 1971, pp.180-185). Secondly, it represents a type of political form in which supremacy is characterised by the predominance of consent and leadership over force and domination (Gramsci, 1971, p.55 n.5). Thirdly, it refers to the liberal democratic historical bloc which is structured by the 'normal exercise of hegemony', that is, hegemony is equated with a historical bloc in which there is a proper balance between consent and coercion (Gramsci, 1971, p.80 n.49). Finally, and this is paramount to many Leninist readings of Gramsci, hegemony is made equivalent to class supremacy as such, in which all political rule comprises a combination of the exercise of leadership over allies, and the domination of enemies (See Buci-Glucksman, 1980, pp.47-68).

This explication of the concept must be seen against the backdrop of Gramsci's rethinking of Marxist political theory more generally. This consists in Gramsci's twofold expansion of the category of political society (or the state) to include those aspects which Hegel had bracketed under the name of civil society, on the one hand, and his transformation of the functions of class domination (especially evident in the institutions of civil society) to encompass the manufacture of consent, and the exercise of 'leadership' through 'ethico-political' and 'intellectual and moral' means. Both of these developments were predicated on a sharp separation between 'the East', where 'the State was everything, [and] civil society was primordial and gelatanious', and the West, where 'there was a proper balance between State and civil society', a division which meant that in the West there ought to be a prioritisation of the 'war of position' over the 'war of movement' as the most appropriate political strategy for advancing socialism by the working classes (Gramsci, 1971, pp.229-238).

Laclau & Mouffe's Critique of the Marxist Tradition

While Laclau & Mouffe presuppose and build upon Gramsci's theory of hegemony (See Laclau, 1977; Mouffe, 1979), they are critical of the Marxist ontology and epistemology underpinning it. In short, there are two fundamental assumptions which they criticise. These are Gramsci's commitment to a fundamental social class – in capitalist societies the working class – bringing about important social change, as well as the centrality of a 'decisive economic nucleus' as the object of political struggle and the ultimate determinant of the character of the political and ideological superstructures. Both of these assumptions require the Marxist notions of a unified and expressive social totality with a set of predetermined laws of motion and development. In this sense, Gramsci's innovative theorisation of hegemony, and his introduction of concepts such as a historical bloc mediating between, and condensing, the different moments of a social formation, remains constrained by a linear theory of history (Laclau & Mouffe, 1985, pp.65-71).

This critique of Gramsci is symptomatic of Laclau & Mouffe's overall deconstruction of the Marxist tradition. In this respect, they posit an ineradicable tension between what they call the 'logic of necessity' and the 'logic of contingency' (Laclau & Mouffe, 1985). These two logics are traced back to the writings of Marx and Engels, and are manifested, according to Laclau & Mouffe, in two competing theories of historical change: one, epitomised in the 1959 'Preface' to *The Contribution to Political Economy*, , in which social change is determined by the contradiction between the forces and relations of production, and the other, manifest in *The Communist Manifesto*, in which there is the primacy of class struggles in the production of historical transformation (Laclau, 1990). While, according to Laclau & Mouffe, both logics are present in Marxist theory they do not have an equal status. Instead of a mutual co-existence and contamination of the two logics, Marxist theoreticians have posited a sharp separation between them, and have prioritised the logic of necessity. (Though structurally undecidable, to use Derridean terminology, Marxist discourse subordinates contingency to necesssity, making it a supplement of the latter.) Hence, the logic of contingency – which, according to Laclau & Mouffe, is synonymous with questions of political subjectivity, strategy, the role of the state and ideological efffects (in short, the political *par excellence*) – has a restricted field of application, which is both theoretically indeterminate, in that it is beyond rigorous and scientific analysis, and ultimately reducible to the necessary laws of economic development (Laclau & Mouffe, 1985, pp.47-48).

Laclau & Mouffe's Post-Marxist Alternative

Laclau & Mouffe's post-Marxist alternative and their retheorisation of the concept of hegemony is predicated on an ontology of the social in which there is an interweaving of the logics of necessity and contingency, rather than a prioritising of the former over the latter. To do so, they introduce a theory of discourse where there is no ontological separation between an extra- discursive and objective reality, on the one hand, and the particular discourses which constitute the social meaning of reality on the other. They also refuse a sharp distinction between a realm of ideological practices, on the one hand, which can be counterposed to other practices, such as those pertaining to the economy on the other, while also rejecting any attempt to concede an *a priori* primacy to any particular set of practices.

In addition, and importantly, Laclau & Mouffe stress the contingency of identity, insofar as any particular discursive formation is always limited by the existence of other discourses. In this sense, discourses are never completely able to domesticate a particular field of meaning (sometimes referred to as the 'field of discursivity'), such that any particular discursive identity is 'surrounded' by what they call a 'surplus of meaning', which prevents its full closure. The structural inability of a discourse to dominate meaning means that social identities are never determined by an underlying logic of historical development, but are always precarious historical and political constructions, vulnerable to the destabilising effects of discourses external to them (Laclau & Mouffe, 1985, pp.110-114).

This theory of discourse draws upon Derrida's deconstruction of structuralist linguistics (and Western metaphysics more generally). That is to say, though Laclau & Mouffe accept Saussure's relational conception of linguistic value, they weaken his view that there is a rigid fixity between signifier and signified, which is itself the product of the total linguistic system. Instead, following Derrida, they argue that the production of identity always involves the deferring of certain differences. This dual process of differing/deferring both stabilises identity, while exposing it to the effects of exclusion. According to Derrida, this is consequent upon the nature of the linguistic sign which must, in principle, always be repeatable in different linguistic contexts (or systems of signification), if it is to perform the function of a linguistic sign (Derrida, 1971).

According to Laclau & Mouffe, the contingency of social identity is shown in the experience of antagonism. Antagonisms represent the political moment *par excellence*, namely, the moments of struggle, decision and subjectivity. In this capacity, they are both constitutive of social relations, while revelatory of the impossibility of any total closure of identity upon itself. What are social antagonisms in Laclau & Mouffe's perspective? In opposition to traditional conceptions of social conflict, which represent antagonism as the clash of social agents with fully constituted identities (such that the task of the political analyist is to describe the causes, conditions and resolution of conflict), Laclau & Mouffe insist that social antagonisms occur because of the failure or inability of a social agent to attain its identity, in which case the task of the analyst is to explore the different forms of this impossibility, and the mechanisms by which the blockage of identity is constructed as antagonistic by social agents. As they put it:

> '[I]n the case of antagonism, we are confronted with a different situation: the presence of the "Other" prevents me from being totally myself. The relation arises not from full totalities, but from the impossibility of their constitution ... Insofar as there is antagonism, I cannot be a full presence for myself. But nor is the force that antagonizes me such a presence: its objective being is a symbol of my non-being and, in this way, it is overflowed by a plurality of meanings which prevent it being fixed as full positivity (Laclau & Mouffe, 1985, p.125).

In this sense, antagonisms are witness to the finitude of identity in that they show the limits of any social objectivity. Furthermore, antagonisms are also essential for stemming the relational flow of differences which make up the social field. They thus actively form identity by requiring the institution of political frontiers which divide social agents into opposed camps and discursive formations. In the latter sense, they perform an ontological role, that is, they are vital for the very constitution of identity, while paradoxically showing the limits and precariousness of identity (Laclau & Mouffe, 1985, p.125).

This brief contextualisation of Laclau & Mouffe's social ontology enables us to make sense of their conceptualisation of hegemony. There are two different models of hegemony at work in their writings. Let us examine each in turn.

Model 1

In *Hegemony and Socialist Strategy*, Laclau & Mouffe present the concept of hegemony as a particular type of articulatory practice – a 'political type of relation' or 'form of politics' as they put it. It is made possible in a very specific set of conditions: firstly, the existence of 'antagonistic forces' and, secondly, a social field in which there is the 'presence of a vast area of floating elements', that is to say, the availability of a proliferation of meanings not stabilised into a system of differences, which can be articulated into opposed hegemonic projects (Laclau & Mouffe, 1985, pp.135-136). Given this situation, hegemonic articulations consist in the practice of partially condensing and stabilising social meaning around privileged signifiers, which Laclau & Mouffe call nodal points. Alongside the ontological openness of social identities, which makes the hegemonic practice possible, is the abandonment of any privileged social agent peforming the function of the hegemonic subject. Contra the Marxist positing of the working class as the universal agent of progressive historical change, Laclau & Mouffe argue that any social agent can assume this role depending on specific historical circumstances. Similarly, they argue that hegemonic practices always involve a dislocation between hegemonic tasks and the social actors supposed to carry them out. In other words, hegemonic operations require there to be no necessary link between a social class and its 'natural' tasks; this implies that hegemony has a metonymical form involving the displacement of actions from a certain shere to another.

Model 2

In *New Reflections on the Revolution of Our Time*, Laclau presents a purported 'radicalisation' of the concept of hegemony (Laclau, 1990, pp.28-31). This corresponds to three levels of the necessity/contingency relationship. In the first level of radicalisation, and this is the model presented in *Hegemony and Socialist Strategy*, Laclau & Mouffe stress the contingency of the elements which make up the social, arguing that in times of organic crisis, these signifiers take on a floating character, and become the objects of contestation amongst competing hegemonic projects. The difficulty with this model, according to Laclau, is the transparency of those projects which attempt to hegemonise the available floating signifiers. A second level of theorisation recognises the incomplete and contingent character of the projects which endeavours to hegemonise a field of signifiers. Though, according to Laclau, this movement deepens the degree of contingency in political analysis (and simultaneously begins to weaken the duality of structure and agency), it remains trapped within a perspective dominated by the notion of equivocity – that is, following Aristotle, the idea that terms can be used differently in separate situations – rather than authentic ambiguity, such that 'the ideal of a pure contextual transparency is not placed in question' (Laclau, 1990, p.29). Laclau's solution is to move to a third level of radicalization in which ambiguity operates within structures themselves. Drawing again on Derrida, Laclau argues that structures are necessarily undecidable in their formal constitution, with the result that hegemonic operations always involve 'acts of radical construction', actualising possibilities inherent in formal structures. In this case, hegemonic practices always involve the emergence of political subjects whose task is to reconstitute structures in new forms (Laclau, 1990, pp.30-32).

Theorising Hegemony

Before I turn to a critical evaluation of Laclau & Mouffe's concept of hegemony, it is important to clarify what is in need of theorisation. It is possible, I think, to isolate three important senses of the concept. First, hegemony is a kind of political practice involving the drive to break down and reconstruct historically constituted social and political forms. Second, hegemony refers to a substantive political and social formation; that is, it refers to a particular political project which at any particular time has succesfully 'become hegemonic'. Third, hegemony designates a practice and form of political rule which involves more than the simple exercise of force or domination. This is to say that hegemony always has a normative dimension in that it implies a politics which goes beyond the imposition of one force over another, and requires the construction of consent, and the exercise of leadership and authority by one group over another. (As Gramsci suggests, hegemony thus operates on the terrain of civil society, as opposed to political society, and crucially involves the cultural dimension of social life.) Each of these dimensions of the concept raises a precise set of theoretical questions in need of further investigation. Let us consider to what extent Laclau & Mouffe's theorisation of hegemony resolves each of them.

(a) Hegemony as a form of political practice

With respect to the first dimension, Laclau & Mouffe present hegemony as a practice of disarticulation and rearticulation, a practice which is only possible given the availability of a proliferation of floating signifiers, and a social field criss-crossed by the existence of social antagonisms. This is the strongest and most convincing aspect of their theorisation, though it is not without some difficulties. It is predicated on their controversial theory of discourse in which all social identity is structurally incomplete and unfixed, that is, penetrated by contingency.

My main question in this regard centres around Laclau & Mouffe's theorisation of structural incompleteness: What do they mean by the concept of structure here? And when do structures become incomplete? On a general historical level, Laclau & Mouffe's answer to the latter question is to assert that the unsutured nature of identity, and with it the centrality of hegemonic politics, only becomes dominant 'at the beginning of modern times, when the reproduction of the different social areas takes place in permanently changing conditions which constantly require the construction of new systems of differences ... Thus the conditions and the possibility of a pure fixing of differences recede; every identity becomes the meeting point for a multiplicity of articulatory practices, many of them antagonistic' (Laclau & Mouffe, 1985, p.138). However, apart from their devastating attacks on the Marxist notion of structure, they provide no positive account of structure other than it being synonymous with their theorisation of discourse. The suspicion is that Laclau & Mouffe's conception of a generalised structural incompleteness (or unsuturedness) remains too abstract and formal to be used unproblematically in concrete social and political analysis.

This criticism can be amplified if we consider Laclau's radicalisation of the concept of hegemony in Model 2. In *New Reflections*, Laclau introduces the concept of structural undecidability by presenting an example of rule following 'inspired by Wittgenstein':

> 'If I begin the counting the numerical series, 1, 2, 3, 4 and ask someone to continue, the spontaneous answer would be 5, 6, 7, etc. But I can adduce that this is wrong, since the series I have in mind is 1, 2, 3, 4; 9, 10, 11, 12; 17, 18, 19, 20; etc. But if my interlocuter believes that s/he has now understood the rule and tries to follow it by continuing the series in the stated way, I can still adduce that s/he is wrong, since the series I have in mind was merely a fragment of a different series – for example, one comprising the numbers 1 to 20, 40 to 60, and 80 to 100 etc. And obviously, *I can always change the series in a different way* [my emphasis]. As can be seen, the problem here is not that the coherence of a rule can never be fully realized in empirical reality, but that the rule itself is undecidable and can be transformed by each new addition. Everything depends, as Lewis Carroll would say, on who is in command. It is a question of hegemony in the strictest sense of the term. But in this case, *if the series is undecidable in terms of its very formal structure* [my emphasis], the hegemonic act will not be the realization of a rationality precedeing it, but an act of construction (Laclau, 1990, p.29).

There are, it seems to me, a number of problems with this formulation. First of all, it is not clear whether or not the example constitutes an instance of undecidability (at least in the Derridean sense); the issue raised by the example is not the ambiguity of the rule as such, but the inability of the interlocuter to grasp what the rule really is, as the rule is being constantly altered by the person in power. In this sense, for the interlocuter, the game becomes one of attempting to determine which rule is being employed, that is, instead of a structural ambiguity, there is an increasing complexification of the rules which are being formulated. As it stands, the example seems to confer to Laclau the power to determine at will what the rule shall be, whereas presumably in a hegemonic struggle both parties will be attempting to fix the precise form and meaning of the rule. (Besides, if every rule was as structurally undecidable as Laclau suggests, it would seem to undermine the very idea of a rule, in that it would be impossible to determine in any particular case whether or not a particular act was in accord with a rule, and without this minimal normativity, it would be impossible to rule out instances of incorrect rule following.)

Further, it is not clear what it means to say that a social structure is undecidable. There are two aspects to this problem, which relate to the extension of the concept of undecidability to social and political systems, and the question of political subjectivity respectively. Let us examine each in turn.

Aspect 1

Here, the concept of undecidability has two related meanings: on the one hand, it is a function of an antagonistic relation, that is, it is the revelatory moment when the 'outside' which both forms and threatens introduces contingency or undecidability into social objectvity; on the other hand, as we have seen in the rule following example given above, it is a property of social structures themselves. In what sense are these two aspects undecidable? To answer this question, we need first to remember that for Derrida (to whom Laclau explicitly refers) undecidability refers to those infrastructural concepts such as differance or the supplement which resist, baffle and weaken the preordained decisions and oppositions of metaphysical thought. Hence they open philosophy to its own constitutive exclusions without closure or decision, and in this sense embody an ethical refusal to decide. As Derrida remarks in Positions, to call conceptual 'infrastructures' undecidable is to stress that they are

> 'unities of simulacrum, [of] "false" verbal properties (nominal or semantic) that can no longer be included within philosophical opposition, resisting and disorganising it, without ever constituting a third term, without ever leaving room for a solution in the form of speculative dialectics (Derrida, 1971, p.43).

In what sense is this commensurate with Laclau's usages of undecidability for political theory? With respect to Laclau & Mouffe's theorisation of antagonism, we have seen how in this relation identity is shown to be dependent on an other for its consitution. This opens the purity of identity to that which is external, but it is not clear why this relation is necessarily undecidable. Undecidability in this context requires, it seems to me, something additional: the positing of an ethical relation between self and other, that is, an opening of self to other. It is is not clear why this is so in the case of an antagonistic relationship.

What then of the case in which social structures themselves are deemed to be undecidable? While Laclau & Mouffe's argument against social structures having an essence is plausible, and results in a relational and contextualised conception of social relations, it is not clear why and how undecidability is an inherent possibility (or necesssary possibility) of the structure? It cannot mean, simply, that social structures are vulnerable to social historical change, or that they are internally contradictory, for this is the Marxist conception of structure which Laclau & Mouffe have severely criticised. Instead, structures are made analogous to instances of intrinsically ambiguous rule following. This idea of rule following captures, a la Winch, the idea of structures as institutionalised social habits and customs, but as we have seen it is not clear why they are inherently ambiguous, nor why this model of undecidability is generally applicable to social relations and structures as such. As it stands, the idea is too formal to capture the intricate network of constraints and facilitations (to borrow from Giddens) which operate in particular kinds of historically specific social structures. In short, as against Laclau & Mouffe's too thin and abstract conception of structure which is universally applicable to all societies, we need (following Ryle and Geertz) a 'thicker' conception of the structure, which allows for a fuller contextualization and historicization.

Aspect 2

An essential correlate of Laclau's concept of undecidability is his rethinking of political subjectivity. Here he argues that the dislocatory logics of modern societies continuously disrupt social structures, thereby revealing their essential undecidability. These dislocatory effects open up the possibility of political agency as subjects attempt to reconstitute dislocated social structures. As these subjectivities cannot be derived from the previously dislocated forms, new political subjectivities are seen to emerge in the space between the dislocated structure and the decisions of agents (Laclau, 1990; Laclau & Zac, 1994). In this sense, all social structures are political constructs in that they are ultimately the product of 'founding' acts or decisions which involve the exercise of power. This claim adds further weight to the idea that all structures are in the final analysis undecidable. That is to say, if social forms are constituted by irreducible choices, and these decisions are not algorithmic, then there must be a plurality of options from which to choose.

This reasoning proposes an interesting resolution to the so-called structure/agency debate without apparently privileging either a determining social structure or an autonomous, self-determining subject, but it is not without some difficulties. The major question mark surrounds the decisionist and voluntarist connotations of Laclau's theorisation of the subject. As it has been suggested, Laclau distinguishes between subjects positioned within a discursive structure, and political subjects which actively produce structures. Apart from the problem of assuming a unified and homogenous subjectivity with clearly articulated intentions, the difficulty with the latter conception is the positing of an unconditional subjectivity which is literally able to 'create' meaningful structures out of itself. This latter view is seemingly appropriate for what we may call extreme or 'limit' situations such as revolutionary conjunctures (or the total breakdown of social and political orders) when a thorough restructuring of social relations is possible, but even this must be qualified if we accept that the most revolutionary movements and subjectivities are conditioned by previously existing ideological traditions and organisational infrastructures. (This qualification is implicitly acknowledged by Laclau when he introduces the concepts of 'availability' and 'credibility' to explain the discursive raw materials which movements and subjectivites rely upon in order to attempt to construct new social orders (Laclau, 1990, pp.65-67).

A second difficulty concerns the question of taking a decision itself. In this regard, Laclau establishes an equivalence between taking a decision, the emergence of a strong political subjectivity, and the creation of a new social order. This is, however, to collapse the distinction between different kinds of decisionmaking. A distinction needs to be made between decisions taken *within* a structure and decisions taken *about* a structure. With respect to the former, it is evident, I think, that consumers in free markets, or politicians in parliaments, are continuously taking decisions without ever questioning or creating new structural contexts in which those choices are made. The latter sense of taking a decision covers the kinds of cases in which structures fail and new structural forms emerge. With the kind of qualifications noted above, these are the situations in which Laclau's novel theorisation of structure and agency becomes applicable. What this means is that rather than a general theory of a radical political subjectivity, we need to remain sensitive to the specific historical contexts in which different kinds of subjectivity come into play. The criterion for this analysis is dependent on the kinds of decision which get taken, and the circumstances in which these decision are taken.

(b) The formation of hegemony

Having examined hegemony as a type of political practice, we need now to consider the substantive dimensions of hegemony, that is, hegemony as an 'achievement' of political projects. Two issues are raised here: the process of hegemonic consolidation or institutionalization, and the site in which hegemony is contested and consolidated. While Laclau & Mouffe do not explicitly address the former question, they provide important hints for its analysis. This emerges when they assert that hegemonic practices are basically metonymical in nature in that they occur when social forces in one sphere (for example trade unions in the economic realm) begin to address issues in another sphere (for example community and housing issues in the social sphere), thereby extending their domain of activity (Laclau & Mouffe, 1985, pp.141-142). To develop this important insight, we can draw on Derrida's concept of iterability to show how every repetition of a linguistic sign results in some alteration of its meaning. Without exploring the idea in sufficent detail here, it is possible using this concept to account more adequately for the process by which projects attempt to hegemonise different forces, while consolidating their particular discourses in different institutions (See Howarth, 1995).

The second issue concerns the key political spaces in which hegemony is exercised. For the classical precursors in the Marxist and non-Marxist traditions, hegemony was seen to be exercised within the limits of the nation state (or was even considered to be synonymous with the nation state). According to Gramsci, for instance, the achievement of hegemony by the working classes was akin to their 'becoming state'. In *Hegemony and Socialist Strategy*, however, there is a double movement. On the one hand, the nation state is presented (albeit implicitly) as a key site for hegemonic politics while, on the other hand, Laclau & Mouffe make it clear that a discursive formation does not overlap with an empirical social formation (in the Marxist sense). On an abstract level, as they put it, a discursive formation is characterised as any formation which signifies itself by drawing political frontiers separating it from others (Laclau & Mouffe, 1985, pp.143-144). While this is suggestive, it leaves many important theoretical questions unresolved. Without exploring them in depth, it is worth pointing out that a fuller theorisation of hegemonic formations needs to take into consideration the different types and forms of state, as well as the emergence of new political forms (at the global and local levels for instance) which go beyond the state form as we know it. These issues (contra Laclau & Mouffe) cannot be resolved on a purely formal and analytical plane, but must be examined in specific historical conjunctures, and if this is the case then appropriate concepts must be developed for that analysis. This brings us to the third and final dimension of hegemony.

(c) Hegemony as a type of political rule

Apart from its analytical and descriptive usages, the concept of hegemony in the Marxist tradition also implies a normative and critical perspective. Hegemony suggests something more than the succesful imposition and consolidation of one political project over others; it entails the winning of consent and the construction of authority. The difficulty with Laclau & Mouffe's position is the weakening of this normative aspect of the concept. This is not to say that there is a complete disappearance of normativity. Laclau & Mouffe distinguish between a democratic and authoritarian practice of hegemonic politics in their critique of Leninist discourses, arguing that the latter conception, which they clearly oppose, is integral to a theoretical perspective which retains an ontological and epistemological privilege for certain classes and organisations (Laclau & Mouffe, 1985, pp.58-59). This critique of different types of hegemonic practice, however, is not extended to an analysis and evaluation of different forms of political rule.

The point is also taken up by Laclau in *New Reflections*. Considering the relation between consent and coercion, he argues that

> 'the opposition between consent and coercion must not be conceived of as an exclusive polarity. Consent and coercion are, rather, ideal limitative situations. What would be, in effect, a type of consent which excluded any coercion? An identity so perfectly formed that it would leave no space for any *identification* in the Freudian sense of the term. But this is exactly the

possibility which our entire critique of the objectivist conception of social relations excludes ... [T]he mere choosing of possible courses of action and the exclusion of others implies, in itself, a form of violence.' (Laclau, 1990, p.171)

Again, at a formal level, this provides us with a convincing rethinking of the relationship between consent and coercion; a rethinking which is adequate for all possible systems of power or political formations. At a more concrete level, however, it is still important to retain a distinction between coercion and consent in order to evaluate and criticise different types of political rule. That is to say, we need to be in a position to explore the variable balances of coercion and consent in particular political systems. This would enable the analyst, for instance, to examine the degree to which regimes and states rely on the exercise of coercion to sustain themselves. In this way, borrowing from Gramsci and Poulantzas, it might be possible (and useful both critically and descriptively) to construct a typology of different forms of political rule depending on their degree of organicity or inorganicity. This would depend, following Gramsci's theorisation of the state and civil society in the East and West (or Poulantzas' analysis of fascism and dictatorship), on the organisation and circulation of consent in different states and forms of regime.

Conclusion

Laclau & Mouffe's deployment of post-structuralist and post-modernist themes has opened up new possibilities for theorizing the concept of hegemony. While this paper agrees with many of their assumptions and substantive arguments, in the limited space available it has endeavoured to point out certain deficiencies in Laclau & Mouffe's approach, while also pointing to possible ways in which their approach might be extended and deepened. Three areas were singled out in this regard. First, the need to rethink the theorisation of social structure and its relationship to political subjectivity. Second, the need to concentrate on hegemony as a substantive political formation. Third, the need to explore the normative dimension of hegemony, and its implications both for critically evaluating and analysing concrete hegemonic forms of political rule.

Bibliography

P.Anderson, 'The Antinomies of Antonio Gramsci', *New Left Review*, 100, 1976.

C.Buci-Glucksman, *Gramsci and the State*, Lawrence & Wishart, 1980.

J.Derrida, *Positions*, University of Chicago Press, 1981.

J.Femia, *Gramsci's Political Thought*, Clarendon, 1981.

A.Gramsci, *Selections from the Prison Notebooks*, Lawrence & Wishart, 1971.

J.Hoffman, *The Gramscian Challenge*, Blackwell, 1984.

D.Howarth, *The Discursive Construction and Character of Black Consciousness in Apartheid South Africa*, Essex Papers in Politics and Government, 8, 1995.

E.Laclau, *Politics and Ideology in Marxist Theory*, Verso, 1977.

E.Laclau & C.Mouffe, *Hegemony and Socialist Strategy*, Verso, 1985.

E.Laclau, *New Reflections on the Revolution of Our Time*, Verso, 1990.

E.Laclau & L.Zac, 'Minding the Gap: The Subject of Politics', in E.Laclau (ed), *The Making of Political Identities*, Verso, 1994.

K.Marx, *Karl Marx Selected Writings*, Oxford, 1977.

C.Mouffe, 'Hegemony and Ideology in Marxist Theory', in C.Mouffe (ed), *Gramsci and Marxist Theory*, Routledge, 1979.

Local Governance

William A.Maloney
University of Aberdeen

'Regulating the Privatised Water Industry:
Complexity, Conflict and Compromise'

'New policies create new politics.'[1]

Introduction

The privatisation of the water industry in England and Wales in 1989 transformed the sector from a quiet 'backwater' of a largely technical nature, characterised by extremely low political salience, to a highly politicised policy area, characterised by extremely high political salience. The political salience of the sector has been fuelled by several other factors: the furore over executive pay and share options; droughts and water shortages (and leakage control); domestic disconnections; and a general perception that the industry was sold-off *too cheaply*.[2] Privatisation also brought with it a new and extremely complex regulatory regime, involving a large number of actors (some of which are 'new') with various regulatory responsibilities.

Increased political salience and the complex regulatory structure have lead to a considerable degree of conflict within the policy sub-system between (predictably) the companies and the regulatory authorities, and the regulatory authorities themselves principally the National Rivers Authority (NRA) and the Office of Water Services (OFWAT). Yet it would be a misleading to suggest that the system is besieged by conflict. There are instances of more private bargaining (policy community-type arrangements) within the sector. Thus regulatory politics is played out as a two-level game. On the one hand it can be characterised by bargaining and negotiation, operating along the lines of the preferred British policy style. While on the other, there is conflict, with in some instances the threat (and use) of legal sanction to ensure compliance with relevant legislation.

Regulation Under Public Ownership

Under public ownership the regulatory regime was much less rigorous and less complex than current arrangements. The industry was involved in an arms length relationship with government predicated on what one civil servant described as a basis of trust in the industry to do a good (and legal!) job: *public* organisations were trusted to operate in the *public interest* (Interview). This *public service ethic* was thought to be a more efficient regulatory tool than any set of formal institutional rules or laws. Effectively it

---
[1] E.E.Schattschneider, *The Semi-Sovereign People*, 1960.
[2] The companies were sold for £6.5bn, with £5bn in debt written-off, they now have a market value over £12bn and have paid out over £2bn in dividends to shareholders since privatisation.

was self-regulation with increasingly tight financial regulation from the Department of the Environment (DoE). As Sir Gordon Jones, the chairperson of Yorkshire Water plc stated:

> '... the degree of Government interference in the water industry was quite low ... we were left on a fairly loose rein subject only to severe financial constraints on how much we could borrow. There were, of course, second order targets, such as reductions in operating costs, numbers employed, disposal of assets and the like, but they were fairly minimal: in addition, there were nudges about charges, but no explicit directives.' (private correspondence)

Insofar as there was serious conflict it was within government, particularly between the industry's lead department – the DoE – and its financier – the Treasury. On occasions, they appeared to have divergent interests with the DoE generally pressing for more resources to enable the industry to meet it environmental obligations (for example, European Community [EC] directives), while the Treasury framed its stance in terms of investment levels and charging policy on the basis of macro-economic requirements (for example, public sector borrowing requirement).

Regulation Under Private Ownership

While the 'new' regulatory system is quite complex there are two broad areas of regulation: economic and environmental.[3] There are essentially two economic regulators the Monopolies and Mergers Commission (MMC) and OFWAT (headed by the Director General of Water Services [DGWS]). The main economic regulatory mechanisms are the Water Acts 1989, 1990, 1991, and the Competition and Service (Utilities) Act 1992; the instrument of appointment which is the licence under which the companies are permitted to operate; and a basic pricing formula for their products and services RPI+K within which K may be negative, positive or zero. This mechanism was designed to ensure that the companies are under constant pressure to cut costs and improve efficiency, by permitting them to increase their prices by the level of inflation minus/or plus a factor of K per cent. The companies' licenses also includes provision for 'Interim Determinations' a cost pass-through mechanism which '... seeks to ensure that cost changes that are genuinely exogenous (for example, European Community directives) and outside management control do not alter the wealth of shareholders' (Armstrong et al, 1994, p.337).

The MMC now has an important role in the water sector, particularly in relation to licensing conditions, and mergers and take-overs. The MMC's approval is required in setting licensing conditions and changes thereto. The MMC acts as a final court of appeal for both the DGWS and the water companies, for example, companies can appeal to the MMC against DGWS decision on the K factor in the periodic review. (Does the reduction in the

---

[3]This paper concentrates largely on the relationship between the two main regulators the NRA and OFWAT.

number of water companies reduce the DGWS's ability to make meaningful comparisons with regard to comparative competition?)

These legislative requirements provoked the MMC's early involvement in the sector. Since privatisation there have been several proposed mergers between water only companies, three of which have been referred to the Commission. The MMC has proved to be an important actor in the post-privatised water sector, and is likely to remain so. It is the *regulatory backstop and the ultimate court of appeal*. Thus it appears that it's recommendations may prove to have a major impact on the future structure, that is, the number of competitors, and their ownership.

OFWAT is a non-ministerial government department headed by DGWS (Ian Byatt) who stated that his primary duty '... is to ensure that the 39 water companies ('Appointees') carry out their functions properly and can finance them. Subject to that I must protect customers, facilitate competition and promote economy and efficiency ... (Through) 'arms length' regulation ('Water Industry Watchdog Sets Out His Stall', 8 August 1989). Through the instrument of appointment the DGWS regulates restrictions on charging, customer interface, levels of service and service targets, conditions on maintenance of assets and disposal of protected land. In his first Annual Report, he stated that the style of regulation would be an open and consultative one: 'I shall aim to stimulate debate and explain the reasons behind my decisions' as well as working with the industry in developing regulatory information' (OFWAT, 1991, p.10).

An environmental regulator was imposed on the industry partly because of: the European Community's insistence on a public body being the *competent authority*; the deluge of opposition to the Government's initial (1986) proposal to privatise the Regional Water Authorities (RWAs) with their regulatory functions intact; and the then Secretary of State for the Environment, Nicholas Ridley's belief that the gamekeeper/poacher role could not continue after privatisation. However, the European Community requirement for a competent authority was probably the most significant factor. It requires each member state to nominate 'competent authorities' to monitor and enforce the implementation of European Community legislation. The British Government intended to nominate the privatised water companies as such bodies. However, the Commission stated that competent authorities must be public bodies, and consequently the Government established the NRA (see Maloney & Richardson, 1995, for a full account of the competent authority issue).

The NRA's main duties and responsibilities include: river quality and the quality of inland coastal waters; land drainage and flood control; management of water resources; fisheries; recreation and conservation; navigation; licensing and abstraction of water; independently monitoring river quality and discharges from sewage treatment plants; enforcement of water quality objectives to be determined by the Secretary of State. The NRA is the 'competent authority' for England and Wales monitoring the implementation of the relevant European Community water directives; it issues discharge-consents to polluters (ensuring that discharges do not have a significantly detrimental effect on the receiving waters); acts as a governmental adviser (for example, the Government drew upon the NRA's recommendations in formulating its own Water Quality Objective recommendations); licenses abstractions of water; and has executive, as well as regulatory, functions in flood defence, conservation and navigation.

Lord Crickhowell, the NRA Chairperson, stated that the Authority's key objective is to *protect and improve* the water environment, and that it would be a:

> '... national body with national policies to improve all aspects of the nation's aquatic environment ... No-one should be in any doubt whatsoever about the willingness of the NRA to prosecute cases of serious or persistent abuse'. ('The National Rivers Authority – A Powerful Watchdog New Environmental Watchdog, 10 July 1989)

The Regulatory Game

Following privatisation regulation of some kind was inevitable, because of: the (technical) nature of the industry itself; the high political salience of privatisation; and the implementation of European Union law. The post-privatisation water sector is interesting because the *policy settlement* has not returned the sector to the *private management of public business*. If industry professionals had the franchise before privatisation they have not completely regained it post-privatisation. In policy areas where values are contested, such as the water sector currently, the area becomes more open to both public scrutiny and more fluid patterns of participation. These contested values have manifest themselves most clearly in the cleavage between the two main regulators the NRA and OFWAT over the costs and pace of environmental improvements.

The NRA and OFWAT illustrate the old adage, where you stand depends on where you sit. Each agency has begun to act autonomously from government and has emerged as a key actor in its own right so much so that a considerable degree of initiative has slipped away from the DoE. Consequently many water companies have appealed to the Government to take action to simplify the system of control. On the appointment of Michael Heseltine as Secretary of State for the Environment in 1990, North West Water called on him to 'narrow the gap between the objectives of the privatised industry's principal regulators'. While Northumbrian water claimed it was a 'pig in the middle', caught between the NRA's calls for rapid anti-pollution improvements, and the Office of Water Services' strict economic regulation (*The Financial Times*, 29 November, 1990).

Partly as a result of discrete regulatory objectives, broadly different regulatory styles are being pursued. The former Secretary of the Water Services Association (WSA) Michael Carney has argued, there are two broad regulatory models operating in the water sector:

- 1. *The policing (or enforcement compliance* approach 'which checks scrupulously on infringements of standards and requires large resources of staff as inspectors and analysts'.

- 2. *The improvement (or negotiated compliance)* approach 'which identifies what has to be done in order to maintain or improve standards and then secures enforceable undertakings to make sure that the promised action is taken' (Carney, 1992; see also Hunter & Waterman, 1992).[4]

While the approaches may not contrast quite as sharply as Carney outlines, evidence from the formative years suggests that the NRA has tended to adopt an *enforcement compliance* approach, and OFWAT has tended to follow the *negotiated compliance* approach. For example, in its maiden year, the NRA brought 389 prosecutions for pollution incidents, which represented a 20 per cent increase on 1988 when the water authorities brought actions.[5] Whereas OFWAT has, generally been less aggressive, operating closer to a negotiated compliance approach (see below). Diverging regulatory objectives and regulatory styles has led to regulatory conflict between the two main regulators. One constant theme in the water debate is the argument about striking the right balance between the need for environmental improvement and the cost. The central questions are: How much improvement?, At what cost?; and Who pays? In it's 1993 report Mr Byatt stated that, 'I believe that customers want prices to rise no faster than inflation ... The challenge facing all the regulators ... is to achieve prices which reflect the right trade off between quality and price' (OFWAT, 1993a, p.4). The differing stances of the NRA and OFWAT reflect the unavoidable conflict of organizational and philosophical goals.

Thus there has been several very public and acrimonious disputes. For example, in an open letter to the Secretary of State for the Environment, Michael Howard, Lord Crickhowell stated that:

> 'The statement by Ian Byatt ... "the principle factor driving up customers" bills is legislation requiring further increases in quality standards for drinking water, inland watercourses and bathing and coastal waters" is highly misleading. I am concerned that we are beginning to see the creation of a myth and this needs to be firmly rebutted ... a very substantial part of the increased charges arise not from an increase in quality standards, but from a long overdue drive to achieve the standards set many years ago and which were for too long ignored. (*Water Bulletin*, 16 April 1993, number 553)

---

[4] Hunter & Waterman (1992, pp.408-410) found that the Water Office of the Environmental Protection Agency in the United States was operating two regulatory models: an *enforcement compliance* approach in which agency personnel employed strict sanctions such as fines and penalties, and a *negotiated compliance* approach in which agency personnel used enforcement mechanisms that allowed them to *communicate and bargain* with the regulated industry' (emphasis added). They noted that approximately 70 per cent the Office's actions were of an informal nature (for example, warning letters, phone calls, etc) associated with a *negotiated compliance* approach, and 30 per cent were on a more formal basis (for example, administrative orders, consent decrees, etc) associated with *enforcement compliance*.

[5] The number of prosecutions brought by the has NRA declined since 1990. For example, in 1990 there were 5,811 pollution incidents recorded and 92 successful prosecutions, the figures for 1992 were 6,134 and 44 (*ENDS Report 230*, March 1994).

The NRA has been very anxious to resist any diminished standards, or to see a significant slowing-down in the drive towards higher standards. It believes that improvements can be achieved through more efficient management practices, not solely greater investment. Lord Crickhowell maintains that increases in costs may not be as sharp as the industry, or indeed, OFWAT claim:

> '... the WSA place the highest possible estimates on all proposed obligations. However, as soon as these obligations are imposed, the Finance Directors of the water companies soon find the cheapest way of meeting the requirements ... Mr Byatt sees it as his role to talk anxiously about the costs to the consumer, *but his job is not to regulate a fellow regulator. The NRA is not in the business of giving OFWAT an easy time.*' (Interview)

Conversely, OFWAT sees its role as the guardian of consumer interests, claims that the NRA's disregard of the cost implications is unreasonable and against water customers interests.[6] OFWAT perceives some of the legislative requirements as excessively burdensome and argues for the slowing down of the *price escalator*.

Such *publicly* acrimonious disputes between public bodies is truly exceptional in British terms, as the negotiative process between such actors normally involves a closed and secret exchange of views within policy community-type arrangements.

New Configurations of Actors in Regulatory Arenas

Regulatory conflict and the continued high political salience of water has encouraged wider participation from a more diverse range of groups,[7] and has thrown up new configurations of actors. Sabatier (1993, p.26) argues that most policy subsystems contain between two to four important advocacy coalitions. In the water sector regulatory politics had witnessed the formation of two main advocacy coalitions/*constituencies of interests* – a *cost constituency* and an *environmental constituency*. These coalitions have distinct (and largely competitive) value systems. The cost value system effectively requires a cost-benefit analysis of environmental and health based improvements: are the scientific and health benefits commensurate with the funds required to secure them? There is also a greater emphasis on more self-regulation, and a strong rejection of recourse to legal sanction in the regulatory game; it is seen as a last resort activity or indeed a failing. The environmental constituency accepts that cost is important, but argues that it is not the economic regulator, nor the water companies place to decide where the balance lies, it is a political decision. Consumers do not simply benefit from water supplied as cheaply as possible, they also benefit from water of high quality. There a stronger emphasis on the use of a sanctioning

---

[6]The NRA had been subject to bitter criticism from the industry in 1990 for its report, *Discharge Consent Compliance: A Blueprint for the Future*, which contained no cost estimates.

[7]For example, Dr Barnado's Homes, *Surfers Against Sewage* [SAS], the British Medical Association [BMA].

approach to regulation: compliance will be secured through legal means if necessary.

The main regulators have been cultivating (competing) constituencies of interests as heavy supporting firepower. OFWAT established the OFWAT National Customer Council (ONCC)[8] which is composed of the ten chairpersons of the Customer Service Committees (CSCs). The Council 'will provide a new forum for the development of a voice for water customers' views ... [aiming] to present an 'independent' view on what customers thought were the important issues' (*Water Bulletin*, 2 April 1993, number 551). OFWAT also maintains close contact with other consumer bodies (not just those it creates) – such as the Consumers' Association, the National Consumers' Council and the Public Access Forum which represents the interests of customers disadvantaged by low income or poor health. These bodies can be useful to OFWAT by adding weight (albeit pounds or ounces) to its public stance on consumer issues. For example, the ONCC condemned the price increases suggested in the market plans published by the companies in 1993 claiming that such rises could produce annual water bills of £450 in some areas. It therefore, pledged itself to 'put pressure on the Director General of Water Services and the British Government to keep prices down and on the European Community to limit obligations on companies which are drawing up bills faster than customers are willing to pay' (ONCC press release, 5 July 1993). At certain times the NRA has been criticised by members of its home constituency. Groups such as Greenpeace and FoE have, at certain times, initiated or fuelled critical media reports alleging regulatory inadequacies or regulatory capture.

However, these criticisms are not necessarily dysfunctional to the regulatory agencies' goals. The NRA and OFWAT benefit from vociferous coalitions. Being able to point to the external pressure that one is under (even if it is ill informed) is often a very useful bargaining chip in the private negotiations which follow these public debates. They attract media attention to issues and provide a source of pressure which the regulators can point to in its negotiations with the DoE and other interested parties. Thus while the NRA may be irritated and embarrassed by a FoE press release giving the NRA a twenty- one day deadline concerning pollution from a particular chemical works in Castleford – Prosecute or We Will! ('Friends of the Earth Gives 21 Deadline to NRA', FoE press release 29 April 1993). Lord Crickhowell has, nevertheless conceded that, in general, 'noisy environmental organisations, while being hysterical in some of their claims, do perform a useful role for my organisation' (Interview). Thus, it appears that, if organisations like FoE or the ONCC did not exist then the regulators would probably try to create them as OFWAT has done with the ONCC.

These coalitions are far from harmonious. For example, on the consumers side OFWAT advocates the introduction of universal metering on an equity

---

[8] These groups do not appear to be 'sham' consultative bodies on the old nationalised industry model. For example, the chairmen of the CSCs were closely involved in the price setting process in the summer of 1993. They saw the confidential reports which OFWAT sent to the companies and saw the companies' representatives and attended the meetings with 'their' companies.

basis: consumers pay for what they use. The National Consumer Council has opposed metering seeing the costs of metering as being under-estimated by OFWAT and the companies, and as a diversion of resources which would be better spent elsewhere (for example, leakage control) (*Water Bulletin*, 10 July 1993, number 516). It has argued for a fixed licence fee. We find environmental groups such as the Council for the Protection of Rural England (CPRE), overlapping with the (main body of the) consumer constituency, as it shares OFWAT's enthusiasm for universal metering. The CPRE's water policy officer says that 'Efficiency is our key consideration' (*Water Bulletin*, 12 March 1993, number 548). The group is lobbying for selective metering and better leakage control. While other environmental groups such as FoE have come out against metering (*Water Bulletin*, 13 November 1993, number 533).

Regulatory Conflict: A Two Level Game

Water regulation in the post-privatised era appears analogous with Putnam's (1988) concept of a two-level game used to describe the behaviour of nation-states in international negotiations. In this game, there is public conflict over the differing goals of the various actors – essentially between the 'quadripartite group' of DoE, NRA, OFWAT and WSA – accompanied and/or followed by the usual process of private bargaining in order to reach acceptable and workable outcomes. As in international negotiations, some of the key players are responding to, and to a degree articulating, the interests of their 'home' constituencies of groups. Each player, therefore, has particular obligations (often statutory) and objectives, and can mobilise the support of its own network of groups and organisations.

A spectacular example of the two-level game and conflict between the regulators – over the actual cost of implementing the 1991 European Community Urban Wastewater Treatment Directive (which came into force on 30 November 1994). In its (1993) paper, *Paying for Quality: The Political Perspective*, OFWAT argued that 'the cost of cleaning up Britain's water has become unacceptable, and it is up to the government to reduce it by renegotiating or relaxing water quality standards' (OFWAT, 1993b). OFWAT claimed that full compliance with the European Community directive would cost approximately £12 billion, when the original estimate was £2 billion. The DGWS stated that: I don't believe that increases of that kind are what people want or what they are prepared to pay' (*The Financial Times*, 14 July 1993). The NRA said that the OFWAT document 'exaggerated the problem and provided misleading analyses of the issues' (*The Financial Times*, 14 July 1993). Its Chief Scientist, Jan Pentreath, said that it is the Government's responsibility to ensure that environmental improvements flow from privatisation: 'When the industry was privatised Government said that we would get cleaner beaches and rivers. The public haven't got that short a memory' (*Water and Environmental Management*, September 1993).

In this public game OFWAT won governmental backing. At the European Community finance ministers meeting in November 1993, the Chancellor of the Exchequer Kenneth Clarke called for a delay in complying with the Municipal Wastewater Directive on the ground that the costs of compliance within the current time limits were 'unacceptable' (*The Financial Times*, 23 November 1993). Mr Clarke accepted OFWAT's figures, as did the Secretary of State for the Environment, Mr Gummer. In response to a written question on safety and environmental standards, Mr Gummer said that 'we must strike the right balance between the pace of quality improvements and costs, so that people do not face excessive bills in the short term' (House of Commons Debates, 19 October 1993), and that he intended to 'sound out European Community partners to see if the urban waste water directive could be modified' (*The Financial Times*, 5 November 1993). Predictably, environmental groups said they were disappointed that the minister had followed the general OFWAT line. Guy Linley-Adams, a water campaigner at Friends of the Earth (FoE) argued that the Government was 'allowing Ian Byatt to dictate policy' (*Water Bulletin*, 29 October 1993, number 580).

The public exchanges represented the phoney war and initial bargaining positions of the belligerents. The conflict was eventually resolved in the traditional way - in private. Throughout the summer the quadripartite group of DoE (and Drinking Water Inspectorate) NRA, OFWAT and WSA eventually had to resolve the question of cash estimates and did so by treating it as an essentially technical and bargainable matter. The conflict itself forced a close examination of the problem by those who have to run the industry. As Lord Crickhowell noted, one consequence of the vigorous public debate over costs was that 'much valuable new information has been revealed and increasingly we are finding common ground' (Crickhowell, 1993). In the event OFWAT reduced its cost estimates significantly from the £12 billion projection. In February 1994 after a number of meetings with the DoE, NRA and WSA, OFWAT announced that the actual capital cost would be £6.8 billion (ENDS Report 229, February 1994).[9]

Following this exercise, work continued on a more detailed level, company by company, producing cost estimates that were broadly agreed by all participants. Effectively, the game shifted from the public to the private level, at which point some kind of policy community, in the old model, emerged, consisting of only four or five key actors.

A similar process took place in the case of OFWAT's negotiations with the companies over the first Periodic Review (setting the 'new' K factors) – the results of which were announced in July 1994. Again, contrasting images can be presented. On the one hand, the DGWS is at great pains to deny that the consultative style is a common feature of OFWAT's approach. While on the other, the evidence suggests otherwise (The finance Director of Welsh Water, Paul Twamley, said that 'Everyone knows this is a negotiation' [*The Financial Times*, 29 July 1994]). Detailed discussions were held with each company prior to publication of OFWAT's decisions. In almost every case the draft K factors distributed to the companies in May 1994, were revised

---

[9] The European Community Commission said that extensive discussion had been undertaken with United Kingdom officials during 1989 and there had been an agreement that the cost would fall somewhere between £7-8 billion (*ENDS Report 228*, January 1994). OFWAT subsequently conceded that it had got its figures wrong and that its estimate was some 50 per cent above the likely cost.

upwards at the final announcement in July. It has been suggests that several companies negotiated better Ks at that late stage in timetable in order to *steered* them away from MMC referrals.[10] Generally, the companies (or more accurately 9 of the 10) perceived the periodic review as yet another good deal, and the DGWS received a bad press for the outcome of the Review, the argument being that his approach to the companies had been too cosy and consensual. Even *The Financial Times* (29 July 1994) was critical, describing it as 'Watered Down Regulation'. OFWAT was also attacked by many in its home constituency (consumers) for the annual price rises. While somewhat tellingly, the City reaction was described as one of satisfaction (*The Financial Times*, 29 July 1994).

Thus the regulatory game presents a confusing, and at times, contradictory image. On the surface, there is open and public conflict between the two main regulators, and conflict between the regulators and the regulated industry. However, if we scratch beneath the facade there is a considerable degree of co-operation, co-operative problem solving, and even consensual decision-making. The regulators have not found themselves 'locked' into one regulatory model: the demands of *realpolitik* dictate that they pursue their objectives via a mixed regulatory style – being tough (enforcing), or flexible (negotiating) which ever is deemed appropriate. Thus irrespective of the DGWS's protestations that OFWAT is not involved in a negotiation process, the United Kingdom style of regulation remains best understood 'as operating in the shadow of the law' and 'as a complex interaction between politicians, civil servants, industry, consumers, interest groups and regulatory bodies' (Veljanovski, 1991, p.13).

An Uncertain Future?

The regulatory process in the water sector has moved towards a more confrontational phase – as it has in the other utility sectors. This has occurred for two main reasons: first, privatisation focused attention on the quality versus cost issue; and secondly, because OFWAT and, to a greater extent the NRA, believed that the water industry achieved a very advantageous deal at the time of privatisation. The 'generous deal' view is shared (somewhat reluctantly in public) by the water companies. For example, a Finance Director of one water company conceded to Sawkins (1993, p.230) that, 'They (the Ks) were too generous. *The companies pulled the wool over the DoE's eyes by throwing the kitchen sink into the book of numbers'* (emphasis added).

Accordingly, OFWAT has set itself the objective of creating a level playing field (for consumers who were excluded from the privatisation negotiations) than that which had been conceded to the companies and potential investors at the flotation. As Kay (1993, p.2) points out, initially the companies felt that such a regulatory objective was not totally unreasonable, and decided that it could 'give way' on a number of issues. However, '...

---

[10] In setting the K factors the DGWS attempted to perform a difficult balancing act. As one water company director pointed out, 'If everybody goes (to the MMC) then Byatt will be seen to have failed ... If nobody goes then he will be attacked for being too generous' (*The Financial Times*, 20 May 1994).

there comes a point at which the ground has been won back, the fat has been trimmed away. At that point, stiffer resistance from the industry is ... expected'.

The NRA, perceives its main regulatory task as ensuring that privatisation delivers the environmental improvement government promised. It sees itself as a regulatory (counter-)balance to the economicism of consumer interests – consumers may have been poorly represented during the privatisation negotiations, but they are not entitled to a monopoly position in the regulatory aftermath.

The conflict has also heightened because of the Government's *downgrading* of water. The Government somewhat naively believed that it was privatising it water problems when it privatised the water industry. However, the reality of the post-privatisation era has been that many water 'problems' have come firmly back onto the desks of government ministers. This naive 'mind-set' had significant 'practical' ramifications. For example, Peter Hall, the former Deputy Director of the WSA, noted that following privatisation many experienced civil servants within the DoE were transferred to other areas, and this, according to Mr Hall had a significant effect on the drafting of policy 'the good fixers within the civil service were moved away from water, and this transferral was reflected in the drafts of proposals' (Interview). This downgrading also had significant policy implications as Ministers attention turned to other areas. The policy making function was partly taken over by the NRA and OFWAT.

In addition to this, privatisation has not removed political interference in the sector. Arguably, the private companies are more *heavily* regulated in the private sector than they ever were in the public sector. As argued above, the regulatory authorities have 'interfered' in the activities of the privatised industry more than the sponsoring departments did under the public ownership model. Thus the state's role has been recast as the protector of the consumer and the environment. As far as the water industry is concerned: *There is nothing quite so public as being private.* Thus, there appears to have been a further erosion of the strict public/private divide following privatisation. The transfer of ownership involved in privatisation does not alter the fact that the water companies continue to have a significant impact on the economy and public health. Thus, it is likely that governments of whatever political complexion, are likely to take a keen interest in the companies' behaviour irrespective of ownership status. In fact, Veljanovski (1991, p.4) has argued that the greatest threat to the companies' independence is not '... the prospect of renationalisation but the tightening of the regulatory corset'.

The regulatory process in the water sector is best characterised as a two-level game. Thus, even though the sector has been characterised by conflict and instability there is consensus and stability, and while the water companies argue that some regulatory demands are *excessive or unreasonable*, there is also evidence that many of the regulatory authorities' requirements are perceived as *moderate and just*: as the former head of HM Inspectorate of Pollution, David Slater, has commented *'We're not in the business of putting business out of business'* (*The Financial Times*, 11 August 1993) (emphasis added). While regulatory politics is likely to continue on an unpredictable and conflictual basis for the foreseeable future because of the reasons outlined above (see introductory paragraph) and the *privatisation* mess. The traditional British approach of *bargained regulation* is still *alive and kicking* in the water sector.

References

M.Armstrong et al, *Regulatory Reform: Economic Analysis and British Experience*, MIT Press, 1994.

M.Bishop et al (eds), *The Regulatory Challenge*, Oxford University Press, 1995.

M.Carney, 'The Costs of Compliance with Ever Higher Quality Standards', in T.Gilland (ed), *The Changing Water Business*, London, CRI, 1992.

Lord Crickhowell, 'Water Service Quality and Water Bills', paper presented to *The Economist* Water Conference, London, 1993.

S.Hunter & R.W.Waterman, 'Determining an Agency's Regulatory Style: How Does the EPA Water Office Enforce the Law?', *The Western Political Quarterly*, 45/2, 1992.

J.Kay, 'The Economic and Financial Background', a paper presented at the Institution of Water and Environmental Management, Annual Conference Water Industry Regulation Three Years On, Harrogate, 1993.

W.A.Maloney & J.J.Richardson, *Managing Policy Change in Britain: The Politics of Water*, Edinburgh University Press, 1995.

OFWAT (1991), *Annual Report, 1990*, OFWAT, 1991.

OFWAT, *Paying for Quality: The Political Perspective*, OFWAT, 1993a.

OFWAT, *Paying for Growth: A Consultation Paper on the Framework of Relecting the Costs of Providing for Growth in Charges*, OFWAT, 1993b.

R.Putnam, 'Diplomacy and Domestic Politics: the logic of two level games', *International Politics*, 42/3, 1988.

P.A.Sabatier, 'Policy Change Over a Decade or More', in P.A.Sabatier & H.C.Jenkins-Smith (eds), *Policy Change and Learning: An Advocacy Coalition Approach*, Westview Press, 1993.

J.W.Sawkins, *Can Yardstick Competition Work? A Study of the Water and Sewerage Industry in England and Wales*, PhD Thesis, University of Edinburgh, 1993.

E.E.Schattschneider, *The Semi-Sovereign People: A Realist's View of Democracy in America*, Holt, Rinehart & Winston, 1960.

C.Veljanovski (ed), *The Regulation Game*, IEA, 1991.

Comparative Think Tanks
Donald E. Abelson
University of Western Ontario
&
Christine M. Carberry
University of Western Ontario

'In Search of Policy Advice:
Why Presidential Nominees Turn to Think Tanks'[1]

Introduction

Throughout the 1996 presidential campaign, nominees will draw on the advice of academics, party members, former government officials, pollsters, political consultants, business leaders, and union and interest group representatives. However, if the past is any indication of the future, they will likely also rely on scholars from think tanks or policy research institutions to identify, develop, shape and at times implement policy ideas. Attracted to think tanks because of their ability to produce timely and policy relevant, though not always empirically sound research, presidential nominees are likely to become even more voracious consumers of information and ideas generated by policy research institutions in the coming months. Indeed, even a year before the 1996 presidential election, close ties have been established between several presidential nominees and a handful of think tanks. Pat Buchanan's long-time association with the Illinois-based Rockford Institute, Alan Keyes' personal and professional relationship with the American Enterprise Institute (AEI) and Bob Dole's and Phil Gramm's ongoing interaction with a number of Washington-based think tanks including, though by no means limited to AEI and the Heritage Foundation, suggests at the very least, that a number of presidential nominees will be turning to think tanks for policy advice.

The purpose of this study however is not to predict which think tanks will likely capture the attention of presidential nominees during the 1996 campaign, nor is it to speculate on the various think tank scholars who might receive high-level appointments in a Dole, Gramm or perhaps even Clinton administration. It is far too premature to predict the outcome of the November 1996 election. Rather, the purpose of this paper is to explain why and under what conditions presidential nominees have and will likely continue to actively solicit the advice of think tanks.

The growing dependence of presidential nominees on think tanks can have profound consequences for the future direction of American politics. At the very least, it will facilitate the efforts of dozens of think tanks committed to imposing their particular ideological and political agenda on the electorate. Unlike think tanks such as the Russell Sage Foundation (1907), the Carnegie Endowment for International Peace (1910) and the Brookings

---

[1] For technical reasons it was not possible to print this paper's footnotes. Those wishing to have copy should approach the authors at the Conference.

Institution (1926) which were created to improve governmental decision-making by applying scientific expertise to public policy issues, the policy making community has become inundated in recent decades by so called advocacy think tanks committed to influencing the content and outcome of major political debates. Recognizing the overtly political positions taken by think tanks, despite their obligation under the Internal Revenue Code to remain non-partisan, several presidential nominees as well as members of Congress and the Executive have established close and lasting ties to many of these institutions. Among other things, policy-makers realize the benefits that can be derived by receiving the endorsement of dozens of recognized policy experts. By taking a closer look at the relationship between presidential nominees and think tanks, it is possible to provide observers of American politics with greater insight into the various organizations that will likely be called upon to help shape the direction of American politics. Such an examination will also enable scholars to debate the potential consequences of providing additional channels for ideologically driven think tanks to rely on to advance their goals.

In the first section of this study, we will explain the various functions think tanks perform and why some presidential nominees are drawn to them. It will become apparent that while some presidential nominees have relied extensively on these institutions to help define, mould and reinforce their policy platforms and administration goals, others have been less than enthusiastic about surrounding themselves with think tank scholars. The uneven patterns of think tank recruitment by presidential nominees, despite the growth in think tank influence and activity in American politics, leads to the following question: why do some presidential nominees rely on thinks tanks more than others?

In the second section of this paper, we will address this question by proposing several conditions under which presidential hopefuls are likely to actively solicit the advice and support of think tanks. By constructing this analytical model, it is possible to explain why for instance Jimmy Carter and Ronald Reagan relied extensively on think tanks during their campaigns and why conversely George Bush, a longtime member of the Council on Foreign Relations, did not draw heavily on the talent pool of scholars available at some of America's leading policy research institutions. To test the conditions under which presidential nominees are likely to use think tanks, this section will draw on empirical evidence from several recent presidential campaigns.

The relationship between presidential nominees and think tanks is a relatively recent development. Nonetheless, the dramatic growth in the number of think tanks in the policymaking community and the concomitant willingness of several presidential nominees to enlist their support, warrants closer consideration. In short, by explaining why and under what conditions nominees employ think tanks, scholars can better understand the potential impact policy experts can have in presidential politics.

Why Presidential Nominees Turn to Think Tanks

As noted, contemporary think tanks, regardless of their mandate, policy resources and ideological leanings seek to become actively involved in presidential campaigns. What needs to be addressed is why some presidential nominees are more inclined to solicit their advice than others. This examination must begin by identifying some of the principal services and functions performed by think tanks.

The most obvious service think tanks can offer to presidential nominees is policy expertise on a number of critical domestic and foreign policy issues. Although the types of issues examined by think tanks and the quality of their research varies considerably, many are able to attract the attention of nominees in part because they can assemble a group of experts capable of transmitting and packaging a set of manageable policy ideas. This in fact is a key feature of think tanks. Rather than generating new and provocative policy ideas, many think tanks do little more than package issues for nominees in an easily digestible form. What is critical for think tanks and nominees is to share information on timely and policy relevant political issues. The ability of policy-oriented think tank scholars to identify and respond to emerging policy questions distinguishes them from many mainstream academics who are less constrained by political timetables.

The attractiveness of think tanks to nominees is further enhanced by the composition of their staff. Since many think tanks, including the American Enterprise Institute, the Center for Strategic and International Studies, the Brookings Institution and the Heritage Foundation, house former high-level policy-makers and government officials who have considerable experience in Washington politics, nominees can take advantage of their knowledge as well as their extensive professional contacts. This service is provided by think tanks through their frequent use of seminars and conferences which bring together corporate leaders, journalists, academics and policy-makers.

The ability of think tanks to educate and to inform presidential nominees is vital. What is equally important however, is the validation function think tanks perform. In other words, advocacy think tanks, whose mandates are ideologically driven, can offer nominees sharing similar values and beliefs an important forum within which to establish and expand upon their political platform. More specifically, given the presence of former high-level policy-makers and recognized policy experts, think tanks can help reinforce the preconceived ideological beliefs of nominees by making some of their policy ideas more credible. As the Heritage Foundation's involvement in the 1980 presidential campaign illustrated, think tanks can also create blueprints for nominees who are prepared to usher in a new ideological revolution.

A Model of Think Tank Recruitment

Despite the many services think tanks can offer, several recent elections have demonstrated that some presidential nominees rely more heavily on these institutions than others. Indeed, the types of think tanks nominees are drawn to has also varied considerably. What factors may account for this uneven pattern of think tank recruitment? A useful point of departure is to focus on some key characteristics of presidential nominees. More specifically, how does their level of national policy-making experience influence their decision to tap into the think tank network? Secondly, how might the strength of their ideological views, as evaluated by the public and reflected in voter election studies, persuade or dissuade them from seeking the advice of think tanks? These two characteristics have been selected for a number of reasons. In the first place, it provides a useful mechanism to distinguish between nominees who may require greater insights about the policy-making process in Washington and those who, as a result of their prior experience in federal politics, are less inclined to recruit think tanks for policy expertise. Assessing the ideological intensity of a candidate's views also helps to explain why some nominees are more likely to turn to advocacy think tanks, as opposed to traditional policy research institutions for advice. As we have previously noted, nominees with a strong ideological mandate may require, or at the very least, could benefit from the validation function performed by advocacy think tanks.

Table 1
Functions of Think Tanks Required by Presidential Nominees
(Based Upon Candidate Characteristics)

	Washington Insider	*Washington Outsider*
Weak Ideologue	Little need for policy expertise <u>or</u> ideological validation	Need policy expertise, but little ideological validation
Strong Ideologue	Need ideological validation, but little policy expertise	Need policy expertise <u>and</u> ideological validation

Based on these characteristics, it is possible to construct a typology to explain the ideal conditions under which presidential nominees will enlist the support of think tanks. Before we do this however, it is necessary to define what is meant by a Washington insider and outsider and how the concept of ideological intensity can be evaluated. The distinction between Washington insider and outsider is based on the last elected position held by the candidate immediately prior to securing the party nomination. For example, a candidate who had previously served in the United States House or Senate, or had held a post in a presidential administration would be considered a Washington insider. This is premised on the notion that this level of federal experience provides nominees with considerable exposure to the inner workings of the policy-making process. Such experience also affords nominees an opportunity to create professional networks that are vital to launching a presidential bid. Conversely, a candidate who did not hold a federally elected position, but instead gained prominence at the state level would be considered a Washington outsider. This is not to suggest that serving as a governor, as many presidents have, would prevent nominees from interacting with federal policy-makers, but that this exposure tends to pale in comparison to the opportunities available to federal politicians. This distinction in the levels of policy experience in federal politics may influence the propensity of nominees to turn to think tanks for information and advice. It may also help to explain why some nominees rely on think tanks to educate them about the intricacies of Washington politics. The concept of ideological intensity of nominees is more difficult to operationalize, but is nonetheless vital to explaining the types of think tanks they are drawn to. Ideological intensity does not refer to differences between political parties, but to where nominees in each political party are located along the ideological continuum. For instance, in the 1996 Republican presidential race, it is well known that Senator Phil Gramm of Texas as well as Pat Buchanan and Alan Keyes are considered to be to the right of former Education Secretary Lamar Alexander and Pennsylvania Senator Arlen Specter. The public's perception of where nominees are located along this continuum helps to substantiate this categorization of nominees' relative ideological stance. We have relied on data from the National Election Studies focusing on the public's perception of the ideological views of presidential nominees to measure this concept.

Employing these two characteristics, we are now able to construct four types of think tank recruitment by presidential nominees. This was summarized above in Table 1.

A Summary of the Four Categories

Washington Outsider, Strong Ideologue

Nominees possessing these characteristics are inclined to rely on think tanks for two main reasons. Washington outsiders need to solicit policy expertise offered by think tanks not only to become better acquainted with key domestic and foreign policy issues, but to acquire a more informed understanding of the inner workings of federal politics. Think tanks inside the Beltway are often well positioned to comment on the dynamics of congressional-executive relations and on key political figures. Therefore, they may be more attractive to Washington outsiders than those institutions located outside the nation's capital. However, as Ronald Reagan's campaign for the presidency in 1980 illustrated, think tanks such as the Hoover Institution in California can also play a key role in assisting nominees obtain information and advice. Washington outsiders not only require policy expertise, but depending on the strength of their ideological views, may also benefit from the validation function think tanks perform. Nominees requiring this service will likely be attracted to advocacy think tanks as opposed to traditional policy research institutions which are not as well suited or prepared to engage in political advocacy. Well known advocacy think tanks such as the conservative Heritage Foundation and the left leaning Institute for Policy Studies have research programs designed to meet these particular needs.

Washington Insider, Strong Ideologue

Washington insiders may look to think tanks to be kept apprised of current policy debates, but unlike outsiders do not need to be advised on how Washington works. Rather, they are attracted to think tanks which can develop or at the very least reinforce their ideological mandate. Here again the validation function think tanks provide helps to explain why seasoned politicians with strong ideological views interact with advocacy think tanks.

Washington Outsider, Weak Ideologue

This category is similar to that of Washington insider, strong ideologue in that these nominees tend to rely on think tanks for one of the two major functions they provide. One critical difference however, is that nominees falling into this category are less inclined to approach advocacy think tanks since they are not seeking validation. Nonetheless, they will likely seek policy expertise from traditional policy research institutions or university-based think tanks who regard themselves as policy experts, not political advocates.

Washington Insider, Weak Ideologue

Nominees meeting these criteria are the least likely to rely on think tanks. They require little policy expertise regarding the Washington establishment and are not inclined to search for institutions to market their ideological positions. They may occasionally attend conferences and seminars sponsored by think tanks and may also read some of their reports. However, these individuals are unlikely to heavily recruit members from think tanks to serve in their campaigns or in their administrations.

Testing the Recruitment Model

The involvement of think tanks in presidential campaigns is a fairly recent phenomenon. Policy experts have advised presidential nominees throughout American history, yet only recently have groups of policy specialists assembled at various think tanks provided formal institutional support to presidential hopefuls. Furthermore, while think tanks have played an integral role in advising policymakers in the United States since the early 1900s, their overt desire to participate in the political arena appeared to coincide with the emergence and proliferation of advocacy think tanks in the early 1970s. As a result, the data that we use to test our hypothesis is drawn primarily from recent presidential elections. In particular, we focus on the relationship between presidential nominees and think tanks since the 1976 election. To test our model, the Democratic and Republican presidential nominee for each election (1976- 1992) was assigned to one of the four cells corresponding to think tank recruitment. These assignments were based upon the nominee's status as a Washington insider or Washington outsider given the criteria outlined above. For ideological strength, nominees were coded as either weak-strong, using data from the National Election Studies (NES). Ideological scores were compiled using the NES seven point liberal-conservative scale. Respondents were asked to rate the nominees according to this scale which ranges from one (extremely liberal) to seven (extremely conservative). In addition, respondents were also asked to rank their own ideological placement along this scale from one to seven. To code nominees as strong or weak ideologues, we calculated the mean respondent self-placement (for each election year) as well as the mean placement for each candidate. For each election year, the absolute difference between the mean respondent self-placement and each candidate's score on this scale was determined. For the time period of our study (1976-1992), the mean absolute difference between mean respondent self-placement and mean candidate score was difference score greater than .86 were designated as strong ideologues, while those with absolute difference scores less than .86 were denoted as weak ideologues.

The placement of each candidate into one of the four categories described above is illustrated in Table 2.

Table 2
Presidential Nominees, 1976-1992

	Washington Insider	Washington Outsider
Weak Ideologue	Ford ('76) Reagan ('84) Carter ('80) Bush ('88) Mondale ('84) Bush ('92)	
Strong Ideologue		Carter ('76) Dukakis ('88) Reagan ('80) Clinton ('92)

Evaluating the Evidence

Drawing on evidence from recent presidential campaigns, it is now possible to assess the accuracy of the think tank recruitment model.

1976: Jimmy Carter and Gerald Ford

The efforts of Governor Jimmy Carter to solicit the advice and support of several prestigious think tanks is well documented. By accepting David Rockefeller's invitation to become a member of the New York-based Trilateral Commission, an organization created to establish closer links between policy-makers and business leaders from Japan, North America and Europe, Carter was introduced to several Trilateral members including Zbigniew Brzezinski and Harold Brown who advised him on a wide range of foreign policy issues. Indeed, after his election victory, Carter invited well over two dozen officials from the Trilateral Commission to serve in his administration. To further establish links to some of the nation's most prestigious policy research institutions, Carter also attended several seminars sponsored by the Council on Foreign Relations and the Brookings Institution. These activities were intended to provide Governor Carter with an opportunity to listen to the ideas of policy experts and to engage in meaningful dialogue with them.

The close ties Carter had to these and other think tanks during his 1976 bid for the presidency confirms our stated hypothesis that Washington outsiders who possess little expertise in federal politics have an incentive to rely on think tanks for policy advice as well as access to political contacts. Since Carter was a relatively unknown one-term governor from Georgia, it is not surprising that he relied on these institutions to enhance his national exposure. Carter's decision to solicit the assistance and advice of these particular institutions also appears to conform to the second condition of our hypothesis. His status as a 'strong ideologue' would in part explain why he not only relied on more mainstream academically oriented think tanks, but also according to some, welcomed the advice of ideologically-driven left leaning organizations such as the Institute for Policy Studies.

Jimmy Carter's opponent in the 1976 presidential election, incumbent Gerald Ford, apparently did not believe he could significantly benefit by tapping into the Washington think tank community. In fact, there is little evidence to suggest that Ford went beyond his close circle of policy advisors and friends for policy advice. Even those policymakers whom Ford could rely on during his short time in office did not appear to be completely committed to his re-election efforts. According to Robert Wood,

> '[A]cademic involvement in Ford policy-making was limited not only by the short duration of the administration and the considerable disarray in the White House. Experts were also withdrawing of their own accord.'

Ford's decision not to seek the assistance of think tanks conforms to the characteristic traits of a Washington insider. In addition, Ford registers as a weak ideologue, which would explain in part why he would not turn to think tanks for ideological validation.

1980: Jimmy Carter and Ronald Reagan

Having established himself as a Washington insider during his term in office, there was little need for Jimmy Carter to conduct an extensive search for think tank support during his 1980 presidential campaign. However, his status as a strong ideologue had changed by 1980. Indeed, according to our data, Carter was perceived four years later as a weak ideologue, and therefore did not require the ideological validation function advocacy think tanks provide.

Conversely, his opponent, the former California governor Ronald Reagan, was an ideal candidate for think tank recruitment. As a Washington outsider, Reagan depended heavily on several traditional policy research institutions for intellectual support and guidance. The Hoover Institution at Stanford University became, largely as a result of Reagan's close ties to its director W. Glenn Campbell and senior fellow Martin Anderson, his primary regional think tank. In addition, Reagan's status as a strong conservative ideologue also helps to explain why he was drawn to the Heritage Foundation, the Committee on the Present Danger and the American Enterprise

Institute, organizations that were well suited and equipped to market Reagan's political and economic agenda. It also helps to explain why Reagan invited dozens of members from these particular organizations to serve in his administration.

1984: Ronald Reagan and Walter Mondale

Despite the fact that the mean ideological score of respondents from the National Election Surveys declined from 4.39 in 1980 to 4.24 in 1984, Ronald Reagan could still rely on American voters to mount a landslide victory. What is interesting to note however, is that although Reagan was regarded as a strong conservative ideologue in 1980, by 1984, he ranks as a weak ideologue based on our measures from the NES. Notwithstanding this ranking, it is clear that Reagan maintained his commitment to conservative ideals and values. Moreover, despite becoming a Washington insider, it appears that Reagan continued to rely on several think tanks for political guidance and ideological reinforcement. Reagan's second term affiliation with a handful of traditional policy research institutions such as the Hoover Institution and the Center for Strategic and International Studies does not conform to our hypothesis for Washington Insiders, Weak Ideologues.

Reagan's challenger in 1984, former Vice-President Walter Mondale had little success in marketing his ideas during the campaign. Indeed, with the exception of capturing his native Minnesota, Mondale lost every other American state. During his presidential bid, Mondale clearly demonstrated the characteristic traits of a Washington insider and weak ideologue. He did not turn to Washington-based think tanks for advice on the policy-making process, nor did he appear to embrace the views of liberal think tanks. While Mondale received policy advice from academics at some prestigious American universities, his affiliation with the policy research community was limited.

1988: George Bush and Michael Dukakis

It is difficult to find any other presidential nominee in our study more deserving of the title Washington insider than George Bush. A United States Congressman, Ambassador to the United Nations, former director of the CIA and Vice-President, George Bush required little insight from think tanks on how Washington worked. Moreover, since Bush registered as a weak ideologue, his need for ideological validation from advocacy think tanks was limited. In fact, there is little evidence to suggest that Bush welcomed the advice of think tank scholars. Unlike his predecessor, Bush did not invite dozens of academics from think tanks to join his administration, nor did he look to these institutions as a possible retirement home after leaving public office.

As a Washington outsider, Michael Dukakis clearly demonstrated the need to tap into the wealth of information and knowledge available at America's leading think tanks. Yet, instead of relying heavily on such traditional policy research institutions as the Brookings Institution as Jimmy Carter had done, Dukakis looked to university-based think tanks in the Northeastern part of the United States for policy advice. Having been educated in that part of the country as well as serving as Governor of Massachussetts, Dukakis had already established a network of policy experts that he could draw on for political guidance.

Dukakis registered as a strong ideologue which seems somewhat surprising given his lack of interest in ideologically-based think tanks. However, the public perception of Dukakis formed by his opposition to the death penalty and his association with the ACLU, may help explain his extreme liberal score. Although the public's image of Dukakis may have been that of a strong ideologue, he did not manifest this characteristic trait in his association with think tanks.

1992: George Bush and Bill Clinton

Four years after George Bush assumed the presidency, little had changed that would have inspired him to turn to think tanks. His knowledge of the mechanics of government had, if anything increased, and therefore he did not require think tanks to assist him in this regard. Furthermore, Bush remained a weak ideologue, which as we have stated, suggests that he would not require advocacy think tanks to aggressively market his ideas.

However, for Bill Clinton, the five-term Governor of Arkansas, think tanks provided a wealth of policy expertise and professional networks. Despite having served as an intern on the Senate Foreign Relations Committee and attending Georgetown University as an undergraduate, Bill Clinton was according to most accounts, a Washington outsider. As a founding member and later chair of the Democratic Leadership Council (DLC), it was only natural for Clinton to turn to the organization's policy arm, the Progressive Policy Institute (PPI) for advice during the 1992 election. Clinton did far more than just carry some of PPI's policy ideas into the campaign. Once in office, he tried to translate several of the institute's suggestions into concrete public policies. Indeed, several administration policies including reforming America's health care system, linking student aid to national service, helping communities cope more effectively with crime, demanding that welfare recipients perform a variety of community services, and injecting an entrepreneurial spirit into the federal government, are among the many program initiatives that bear a striking resemblance to the recommendations made by various contributors to the PPI study, Mandate for Change. Although some of these ideas have been advocated by other individuals and organizations, few institutions in the 1992 campaign offered a more comprehensive guide to reforming government than PPI.

The DLC and the PPI provided Clinton with more than a blueprint on how to govern. Both institutions, through their extensive lobbying efforts offered Clinton the ideological support and reinforcement he required to bolster his election platform. As a strong ideologue, Clinton's association with these organizations should not be surprising.

Conclusion

The model of think tank recruitment outlined in this study provides scholars with an opportunity to predict and explain why certain presidential nominees are more inclined to rely on think tanks than others. Given the changing role of think tanks from policy research institutions to political advocates, how and under what circumstances nominees draw on them can have profound consequences for the development and refinement of policy issues. Although little research has been conducted on the involvement of think tanks in presidential campaigns, this study has revealed some of the benefits that can be derived by exploring this avenue of scholarly inquiry. As think tanks begin to occupy an even more influential position in the political arena, the relationship nominees establish with them warrants closer scrutiny. By examining presidential nominees from 1976 to 1992, we have found that two characteristics (Washington insider vs. outsider and strong or weak ideologue) serve as useful barometers to measure the nominees' inclination to recruit think tanks. With few exceptions (Reagan 1984 and Dukakis 1988), our model helps to explain the think tank recruitment patterns of presidential nominees. Although we have only drawn on a limited number of case studies here, our model may be applied to future presidential elections. One final note regarding the findings of the 1984 presidential bid by Ronald Reagan is in order. As a weak ideologue and a Washington insider, our model predicted that Reagan would not have turned to think tanks for policy advice and ideological validation. However, Reagan's association with several think tanks continued well into the 1984 campaign. This leads us to consider the possibility that think tank recruitment patterns may change when presidents seek re-election. In other words, although Reagan may have required and indeed benefited from receiving the ideological support of the Heritage Foundation and other advocacy think tanks during the 1980 campaign, by 1984, he had to depend on think tanks less for ideological validation and more for policy expertise. This may in turn explain why the Heritage Foundation denounced Reagan for many of the policy positions he adopted during his second term. In the future, this incumbency effect may become clearer when a larger body of campaign data is available.

Boundaries and Identities in Post-Cold War Africa

Christopher Clapham
University of Lancaster

'Territoriality and Statehood in Tropical Africa'

Introduction

The states of sub-Saharan Africa have often been classed as the most 'artificial' in the world. All states, of course, are artificial, in that they are the product of conscious human contrivance: there is no such thing as a 'natural' state. State boundaries across the whole of the world have likewise generally been demarcated as a result of military conquests or diplomatic settlements which paid little if any attention to the wishes of the people who were allocated to the states on one side or the other. The idea that such people had the right to choose which state they wished to belong to has been admitted only in exceptional circumstances, such as the allocation of certain districts of the former German and Austro-Hungarian empires after the First World War.

African states are, however, distinctive in that their existence commonly resulted from the imposition of externally defined boundaries, and of the statist structures needed to control the territories within those boundaries, on peoples to whom – initially, at least – they had little meaning. This set them apart even from other regions of the 'third world' affected by European colonialism, where the newly created states were usually either – as in the Americas – controlled and mostly populated by immigrants who, as it were, brought their statehood with them; or else – as in much of Asia – broadly corresponded to the territories of indigenous peoples who had in many cases already developed pre-colonial statist political systems of their own. As a group of states whose statehood was imposed on indigenous peoples by outside powers, those of sub-Saharan Africa are unique. They are therefore potentially especially at risk from the challenge to state structures which, arising in its broadest form from the universal processes of social, economic and political change that have conveniently been summarised as 'globalisation', has been made more explicit and intense by the changes in the international system that have followed from the collapse of the Soviet Union.

The concept of territoriality provides only one of a number of possible entries to the analysis of the problems of African statehood, and the threats facing African states in the aftermath of the end of the Cold War. It is however one which has been relatively little explored, and which seems to be worth examining, especially in the context of a conference which has taken the role of spatial relationships in politics as its guiding theme. What follows is therefore a 'conference paper' in the purest sense of the word: an attempt to outline a number of very general points in a speculative and uncommitted way, in the hope that this will promote discussion and an exchange of ideas which may help to take the subject further.

Territoriality and Statehood in Tropical Africa

The starting point for this discussion must be the striking difference between the conceptions of territoriality implicit in most of pre-colonial Africa, and those imported by colonial statehood. Bayart's work has emphasised the continued importance of 'governmentalities', or attitudes to questions of authority and government, which are deeply embedded within the cultures and historical experiences of African (as indeed of all other) peoples.[1] A preliminary survey of such attitudes suggests that several widespread features of pre-colonial African society served in most cases to weaken the relationship between territoriality and political authority.

The first of these was that most Africans have defined their identities not by territory at all but by descent, and specifically by descent through one or other parental line, either paternal or maternal. Societies defined in this way are commonly described as 'tribes', and though the term has often been frowned on in modern African political discourse, not least as a result of the attempt to impose territorialist conceptions of political identity derived from post-colonial statehood, it remains useful. Though the mobilisation of descent as an explicit source of political support dates largely from the second half of the twentieth century, the idea of descent through a single line as a source of personal identity is much older, and its ramifications are pervasive. The tension between territory and descent as alternative principles of political identity remains at the core of the dilemma of African statehood.

The role of territoriality has further been weakened by longstanding traditions of population movement. Many if not most African peoples retain a folk memory of migration, into their current area of occupation from somewhere else. In some cases, as with the Somali expansion into the area south-west of the Tana river, or the Ndebele migration northward into what is now Zimbabwe, this movement took place in recent and recorded historical times. In a sparsely inhabited continent, political protest or demands for 'independence' have until very recently been expressed by 'exit' from existing polities, and the establishment of new ones elsewhere.[2] Even though the opportunities for such migration have been severely restricted by the imposition of territorial statehood, as well as by population growth and the depletion of resources, Africans retain an exceptional propensity to move. That Africa has by far the largest percentage of its population as refugees of any major land area certainly reflects the often intolerable political conditions from which many Africans have suffered; but it can also be related to a readiness to up sticks which descends from the African past. Africa also has a very large number of 'economic migrants', whose movements certainly reflect the extremely uneven patterns of economic development resulting from the impact of externally-oriented structures of production and exchange, but likewise indicate a willingness (or indeed a need) to move to wherever the prospects are best.

Much of Africa, thirdly, is endowed with resources too sparse to sustain permanent cultivation, and movement (usually within a fairly circumscribed area) is essential to subsistence. Pastoralist peoples, to take the most obvi-

---
[1] See Bayart, *The State in Africa*.
[2] See Herbst, 'Migration, the Politics of Protest, and State Consolidation in Africa'.

ous example, necessarily acquire different conceptions of territoriality from settled agriculturalists. Wealth and authority depend on control over flocks and herds, not on control over land, and the boundaries that demarcate land are at best irrelevant, at worst obstructive. Many African peoples practice 'mixed' agro-pastoralist forms of subsistence, while much agriculture depends on temporary 'slash and burn' cultivation by people who have to move on every few years, as fragile soils are exhausted. In all of these ways, the idea of a fixed relationship between territoriality and political structures culminating in statehood has been blurred.

Fourth, even in those relatively densely populated parts of the continent where statist political systems were formed in the pre-colonial era, such as the Ethiopian highlands, the Great Lakes region, and parts of the West African forest belt, these rarely possessed fixed boundaries, but expanded from a core area into progressively less manageable hinterlands during periods of military and economic strength, contracting again in times of weakness. They were likewise subject, as already noted, to what would in modern terms be described as 'secessionist' movements by regional rulers seeking to establish their own independence, or by dissidents who emigrated to set up new states of their own.

Like all such grand generalisations, these ones are subject to a certain amount of qualification. One area in particular, the northern highlands of Ethiopia, combined a dense agricultural population with an absence of descent-based social structures, a well-established statist political system and a physical topography which emphasised territorial divisions, to create concepts of territoriality expressed through precisely defined boundaries which had more in common with Western Europe than with most of the rest of Africa.[3] So, save for the persistence of a patrilineal descent system which helped to maintain the demarcation between Tutsi and Hutu, did Rwanda and Burundi. Zones of relatively rich resources and consequently dense population were evidently more likely to engender attachments to particular territories than zones that were poorly resourced and sparsely inhabited. On the whole, nonetheless, conceptions of territoriality derived not just from some faintly discerned African past, but from features of African social and economic life which continue into the present, differ very markedly from the sedentary, territorial, and for the most part non-tribal societies of, say, Western Europe or much of south and east Asia.

The contrast with the political structures established by colonialism is consequently acute. For European rulers, the exercise of political authority was virtually inconceivable without the prior demarcation of territorial entities within which states could be created. The colonial 'partition' of Africa, as the word implies, was centrally concerned with the definition of territorial boundaries, a task so immediately undertaken that by 1914 – when the administrative structures of African statehood were still at the most rudimentary stage, and a great many Africans had never even seen a European – the frontiers of the African states which were to emerge at independence in the 1960s had already been laid down on European maps.

---

[3] See Peter Woodward's paper for this panel; I have also examined the peculiar structure of territoriality in the Horn in 'Boundary and Territory in the Horn of Africa'.

The central problem in conceptualising the territoriality of present-day African politics thus lies in articulating the relationship between the weakness of the territorial principle in pre-colonial African political life, and the European structures imposed from the late nineteenth century onwards, with their fixed territories and sharply demarcated boundaries – not only at national level but in their subdivisions into regions and districts. As has often been noted, this demarcation usually paid little if any attention to existing ecological zones or population groups, the main exceptions being in cases, such as the present-day Lesotho, Swaziland, Burundi and Rwanda, where colonialism involved the takeover of existing African political units.

Initially, at least, a broad distinction could often be identified between descent as the basis for political mobilisation and territorial statehood as the basis for the exercise of political power. Or in other words, the state provided the prize which political leaders sought to attain, and descent – often organised in very different ways in different colonial and post-colonial territories – provided the means through which they sought to attain it. In the process, a concept of 'foreignness' was established which had hitherto been alien to African societies: only those people who originated within the territory had the right to compete for control of its state. This most notably affected the political status of recent immigrants: due to the operation of the descent principle, these could not become 'naturalised' into the society to which they had moved, but remained associated with their peoples of origin; due to the operation of the territorial principle, on the other hand, they could not participate in the politics of states to which they did not 'belong'. They were therefore politically marginalised, and were vulnerable to exploitation and potential expulsion, as happened with the expulsions of 'foreigners', many of whom had been born within the states concerned, by Ghana in 1969 and Nigeria in 1983. Where internal territorial divisions within states acquired political significance, as for instance in Nigeria, these too defined regional citizenships with their corresponding rights and vulnerabilities.

There was thus virtually no dissent from the assumption that colonial territories, no matter how arbitrarily created, should be converted into the newly independent states that succeeded the colonial empires from the later 1950s onwards. The sole significant exception was the case of the Somalis, where the complete absence of territorial concepts in Somali pastoralist culture combined with a frontier demarcation which left large numbers of ethnic Somalis outside the boundaries of the Somali Republic to produce the Somali irredentist movement. The popular definition of the boundaries of the Somali political space, 'wherever the camel goes, that is Somalia', provides the classic expression of a non-territorial political culture. In no other case did pastoralist peoples control the apparatus of an independent state, and other trans-frontier pastoralists such as the Maasai, the Afar or the Touareg were politically marginalised. Other separatist or irredentist movements, as in Eritrea or the Togoland area of western Ghana, sought to re-establish former colonial territories which had lost their status as a result of European wars.

The ready adoption of the territorial principle by the leaders of African independence movements can evidently be ascribed to their central goal of taking over (and greatly expanding) the state apparatuses created by colonialism. Their common commitment to this goal in turn enabled the Organisation of African Unity to formulate the principle that all of its members should be pledged to uphold the frontiers inherited on their accession to national independence. Touval identified only four states – Ghana, Morocco, the Somali Republic and Togo – as challengers to this principle.[4] Nkrumah's Ghana was the most quixotic, since the legitimacy of its boundaries was in this case denied in the name of a Pan-Africanism which would sweep them away, and establish a continental 'union government' in their place; there was however no suggestion that this principle might justify any challenge to Nkrumah's own control over Ghana's territory, and with his demise the idea was forgotten, and Ghana reverted to the normal conventions of African statehood. The 'idea' of Morocco derived from the alleged boundaries of the pre-colonial Moroccan kingdom, and was used by King Hassan II in order to associate his own monarchy with a historic Moroccan mission which could be used to claim territory allocated under colonial rule to Algeria, Mauritania, and Spanish Sahara. The Somali claim was explicitly nationalist, and sought to bring all of the Somali peoples within a single state through a union of Italian Somalia, British Somaliland, and the Somali-inhabited areas of Djibouti, Ethiopia and Kenya. The Togolese unionist movement sought to restore the former German colony of Togo, divided in 1919 between France and Britain, and in the process to unite the Ewe people who were thus split between Togo and what became Ghana.

Despite these few exceptions, the very high level of agreement between the rulers of newly independent African states meant that they did not suffer from the boundary conflicts that might well have been expected to result from the fact that the boundaries concerned had been both recently and externally imposed. One could indeed put it the other way round, and suggest that it was precisely because African state boundaries were so artificial that it was essential to maintain them. On the one hand, the raison d'être of the post-colonial governments was to rule the territories established by colonialism; since the boundaries of these territories established their right to existence, they could not be challenged without calling into question the existence of the states which they defined. There only was a state called Chad or Zambia because the colonial regimes had drawn those boundaries rather than others; in the process, the fortuitous activities of late nineteenth or early twentieth century colonial officials became central to the claims to power of late twentieth century African bureaucrats and politicians. On the other hand, no African state had any legitimate basis on which it could make claims against the territory of any other African state, except for the very limited number of cases in which such claims could be derived from ambiguities in the colonial settlement. Even the Somalis, whose irredentist demands fundamentally derived from the assertion of ethnic identity as the basis for nationhood, sought desperately to make a 'legal' case by questioning the validity of the boundary settlement between

---

[4] Touval, *The Boundary Politics of Independent Africa*.

British Somaliland and imperial Ethiopia, or the demarcation of the line between Ethiopia and Italian Somalia. The governments of Dahomey (now Benin) and Niger squabbled over the ownership of an island in the River Niger which, hidden by flood waters when the French had demarcated the boundary, reappeared during the dry season.

This broad consensus was of enormous value in enabling African states to achieve independence without simultaneously unleashing a mass of territorial conflicts which they were completely unequipped to deal with, and also placed them comfortably within an international political structure which placed great emphasis on the unviolability of state boundaries. In the process, it reinforced the position of domestic state élites, and helped to insulate ethnic conflicts arising within states against spreading across their frontiers. It rendered illegitimate the assumptions – so important to the definition of European statehood – that peoples with a common language, culture and historical identity were entitled to be governed as part of a single state, and that international frontiers should be demarcated in order to allow for this. Even where ethnicity in practice provided much of the impetus behind demands for a separate political status – as for example in Togoland, Biafra, or indeed the secession of Somaliland (the former British Somaliland) from the united Somali Republic – the territorial principle prevailed.

Given this striking lack of congruity between a notably weak conception of territoriality in most indigenous African societies, and the intense commitment to the territorial principle in the definition of post-colonial African states, this convenient solution to the problem of territoriality in post-colonial African states could not however be expected to last. It was called into question most basically by the failures of African statehood in the decades after independence: by a record of political decay which was most strikingly indicated by gross human rights violations, and by resistance movements which arose to a considerable extent in response to them; and by an often precipitous process of economic decline. Subsequently, and especially after the end of the Cold War, the external support which African states had received was drastically undercut by the loss of whatever strategic value they had previously possessed in the eyes of the major powers, and by the explicit limitation of their economic powers (for example, over their currencies) imposed by external institutions as their price for economic rescue. The benefits of statehood in providing a prize, which in turn imposed at least a nominal respect for certain rules of political competition on those who competed for that prize, have been drastically reduced; and if states do not provide much by way of money or power for those who nominally control them, a very important part of the rationale for their existence has been removed.

At this point, it may be helpful to introduce a very broad distinction between territories that are determined by their states, and states that are determined by their territories. In the first case, which has been the common experience not merely of the major European states, but equally of parts of Asia such as Iran, Thailand, Cambodia or Vietnam, a state is first created through the establishment of the appropriate instruments of domination, whether these be derived from autocratic power, the shared beliefs of a group of people, or something in between. Where the jurisdiction of this state comes up against the jurisdiction of other states which control adjacent territories and peoples, a frontier is formed and the territorial definition of the state is established. These frontiers may be moved in one direction or the other, without basically affecting the identities of the states which lie within them: the German state, for example, remains a recognisable entity, despite the dramatic changes in its frontiers over the last century.

In the second case, which has been the common (though not universal) experience of modern African states, the boundaries came first, and the state was then established within them. The Congolese or Kenyan state is the organisation which has been created in order to govern a territory already defined as Congo or Kenya. In this second case, the frontiers were more 'artificial' than in the first, but they were for that reason more, and not less, central to the identity of the state that lay within them. There was, to put in another way, no conception of Congo or Kenya which preceded its frontiers and which could therefore be used to challenge them.

Not all African states, however, depended on their boundaries for their identities. Some of them embodied an idea of the state which made it possible to conceive of the state in terms separate from its boundaries, and thus potentially questioned those boundaries. Apart from Somalia, where as already noted the idea of statehood depended directly on descent, both Rwanda and Burundi in central Africa, and Lesotho and Swaziland in southern Africa, had conceptions of statehood which preceded the demarcation of their colonial boundaries, but either because they were broadly satisfied with these boundaries, or else because they recognised the imprudence of challenging neighbours much more powerful than themselves, their frontiers were not seriously contested. Two other states, Ethiopia and Sudan, were guided by an idea of the state which implicitly ascribed a dominating role to some people within it at the expense of others, and which consequently legitimated the control of 'peripheral' territories by governments based on the core area – in Ethiopia by Christian Amharic-speaking people, especially from the central region of Shoa; in Sudan by Arabic-speaking Moslems, especially from the Nile valleys around Khartoum. A further state, in a sense pre-colonial, which rested on the assumed right of an ethnically distinguishable governing élite to maintain control over other peoples, was the Republic of Liberia.

The mere listing of those states with a pre-colonial element in their identities draws attention to a remarkable paradox: that such states have had a very high propensity to degenerate into an appalling level of internal conflict and bloodshed. They are certainly matched by a number of states which are pure colonial inventions, including Angola, Chad, Mozambique, Uganda and Zaire. But given the very small number of sub-Saharan states which can claim any pre-colonial identity, their prevalence in any list of Africa's collapsed states is striking. Among them all, indeed, only the small southern African monarchies of Botswana, Lesotho and Swaziland have avoided breakdown.

This certainly gives us some cause to question the common belief that the colonial imposition of artificial territories is at the base of the problem of African statehood, and that some more 'natural' process of state formation would have created more peaceful, stable and viable political units.[5] One could more plausibly argue, on the basis of the evidence, that stability is more easily attained when states are entirely artificial, and no group therefore benefits or loses from the 'premise of inequality' which in the pre-colonial system gave one of them a privileged position over others. Even in colonial states such as Chad or Uganda, or pre-civil war Nigeria, the determination of a particular ethnic group to establish ownership of the state, and deny access to it to others, was a major precipitant of rebellion and breakdown.

The question as to whether there is any longer any economic and political base on which to maintain the system of territorial statehood inherited from colonialism now certainly needs to be raised. A significant number of African states can no longer exercise even the most nominal control over the territories formally ascribed to them. The idea that states are permanent entities that can be relied on to go on for ever is a peculiar ahistorical aberration, born of the brief period of relative stability that resulted from the Cold War, and the institutional inertia that carried post-colonial institutions into the era of independence. In recent years, states have fallen apart not only in Africa, but in parts of Europe and Asia as well. The list of collapsed states in Africa extends across the continent from Sierra Leone and Liberia in West Africa to Chad and the Horn, and down through Uganda, Rwanda and Zaire to Angola and Mozambique.[6]

It is now also possible to detect the emergence of alternative forms of political organisation which have in several areas displaced the territorial state, and which provide some guidance as to what a non-state or post-state Africa might look like. In some cases, relatively long-lived 'quasi-states' have made their appearance, as the territories ruled by insurgent movements or 'warlords'. The most notable of these, Charles Taylor's 'Greater Liberia', extended across the borders of Liberia into Sierra Leone; it has now formally been superseded as a result of Taylor's incorporation into the still fragile 1995 Liberian peace settlement. Others have included the territories of insurgent groups such as the EPLF and TPLF in Eritrea and Ethiopia (both of which captured formal state power in 1991), the SPLA in Sudan, and UNITA in Angola, as well as the fiefdoms of the various Somali warlords. These 'quasi-states' gain their political power from a combination (varying in its details very widely from case to case) of brute military force and a measure of popular legitimacy that usually derives largely from descent-based identities. They gain their economic base from control of informal trading networks in commodities that may include narcotics (such as *chat* in Somalia), wildlife products (such as ivory and rhino horn), minerals (such as diamonds in both Angola and Sierra Leone), and anything else that can be sold for ready cash. They can also profit, not only from the covert economic

---

[5] See, for example, Davidson, *The Black Man's Burden*, for an expression of this view.
[6] For a recently published volume on state collapse in Africa, see Zartman, *Collapsed States*.

and even military support of external governments and corporations, but also from control over relief aid provided by humanitarian organisations. In classic precolonial African fashion, they have no fixed territories, and the areas under their control both fluctuate and fade out into borderlands where political authority is uncertain.[7]

In no case, save for the areas of Eritrea under EPLF control before the capture of Asmara in May 1991, have such quasi-states provided any viable alternative to territorial statehood, in terms either of administrative efficiency or of moral legitimacy. A strong case can be made for the assertion that the territorial state is essential in order both to assure a reasonable degree of security to those who live under its protection, and in order to provide the conditions necessary for economic development. The collapse of a significant number of African states can be ascribed to their failure to achieve either of these legitimating functions. New regimes, once these have attained power, have sought to reconstruct the institutions of territorial statehood, as for example in Ghana, Uganda and Chad. In Ethiopia, though not elsewhere, this reconstruction has involved the explicit recognition of ethnic identities through the creation of a federal system based on 'nationalities', which in turn have been accorded a constitutional right to secession.

As noted in the introduction, this is a highly provisional discussion paper, and any firm conclusions lie well beyond its scope. It suggests that an examination of the territoriality of post-colonial African states raises worrying questions about the ability of such states to maintain themselves, given the weakness of territorial concepts in pre-colonial Africa, and the dependence of African states both on the institutional residue of colonialism, and on their ability to provide a diminishing level of patronage, not only to the populations which have to tolerate them, but even to the élites who seek to control them. The threat to states has been most marked in those cases where there is some pre-colonial basis, not only for state formation, but also for resistance. It has also been notably greater in the former colonies of weak colonial powers – notably Belgium and Portugal – which have been much less successful that Britain and France in bequeathing viable post colonial institutional and political structures. On the other hand, African states have had a greatly varying level of success in creating a sense of national identity, and the former colonial state still remains the primary focus for political identity in the majority of cases. Even in cases where such states have broken down, there has still – even, remarkably, in Chad – been a residue of nationalism which could be used as a basis for reconstruction.[8] It may well be that territorial statehood will reimpose itself on Africa, as the result of a learning process which suggests that there is no viable alternative. That learning process, if such it proves to be, has however already proved an extremely costly one, in terms of death, disablement and refugee flight, and there is no real sign that it has ended.

---

[7] Published material on these 'quasi-states' is still fragmentary, but see Richards, 'Rebellion in Liberia and Sierra Leone'; Reno, 'Foreign Firms and the Financing of Charles Taylor's NPFL'; Ellis, 'Liberia 1989-1994'.

[8] See William J. Foltz, 'Reconstructing the State of Chad', in Zartman, op.cit.

Bibliography

J.-F.Bayart, *The State in Africa: The Politics of the Belly*, London 1993.

C.Clapham, 'Boundary and Territory in the Horn of Africa', in P.Nugent & A.I.Asiwaju (eds), *African Boundaries: barriers, conduits and opportunities*, Pinter, 1996.

B.Davidson, *The Black Man's Burden: Africa and the Curse of the Nation-State*, Currey 1992.

Stephen Ellis, 'Liberia 1989-1994', *African Affairs*, 94/375, 1995.

J.Herbst, 'Migration, the Politics of Protest, and State Consolidation in Africa', *African Affairs*, 89/355, 1990.

W.Reno, 'Foreign Firms and the Financing of Charles Taylor's NPFL', *Liberian Studies Journal*, 18/2, 1993.

P.Richards, 'Rebellion in Liberia and Sierra Leone', in O.Furley (ed), *Conflict in Africa*, I.B.Tauris, 1995.

S.Touval, *The Boundary Politics of Independent Africa*, Harvard, 1972.

I.W.Zartman (ed), *Collapsed States: The Disintegration and Restoration of Legitimate Authority*, Rienner, 1995.

Territoriality and the State in Africa

Peter Woodward
University of Reading

'Borders and Conflict in North-East Africa'

Introduction

Having started this paper with the bald injunction that it should be on 'Territoriality and the State' in Africa, I felt that a liberal interpretation was in order. The most obvious interpretation is the state's own definition of territory, and the extent to which that has been contested with neighbouring states, leading inevitably into the realms of international relations. But the independence of Africa's newest state, Eritrea, in 1993, was a reminder that the issue of territory, in the form of secessionism, has also been a feature of the domestic politics of contemporary Africa, though not elsewhere with Eritrea's success. However borders have not only been the subjects of conflict in Africa, whether between states or within them, they have also been facilitators of conflict, especially for opposition movements that can take refuge in neighbouring states. Such a situation often involves the opposition's new host state in the conflict, however unintentionally. And it is not only neighbouring states that may be thus involved, but other international actors with an interest in the original conflict itself, and with some political weight in the opposition's host country. Thus the issue of territoriality as a source of dispute between and within states does not stop at border issues, but becomes part of broader international relations.

This is not the place to rehearse the causes of conflict in Africa once more, on which there have been numerous publications over many years.[1] Northeast Africa does however provide not only many examples of conflict for a wide variety of reasons, it also includes a number of cases of all the above dimensions of conflict and territoriality. For while there are essentially local disputes between and within states, there is also a regional dimension to north-east Africa. In recent history this has had two main and overlapping dimensions. One is the position of north-east Africa as an area on the edge of Middle Eastern politics (indeed Somalia and Sudan, as well as Egypt and Libya are members of the Arab League). Its position on the fringe of such a major area of volatility has drawn most of the major players in the Middle East into the region in support of both regimes and opposition movements. In addition, the superpowers became involved, not only for Middle Eastern reasons, but also for broader strategic reasons, sometimes perceived as part of their global competition. Such involvement was in turn to become a dimension of the unfolding local issues of state and territoriality.[2]

---

[1] O.Furley (ed), *Conflict in Africa*, I.B.Tauris, 1995.
[2] Southern Africa is the other region similarly affected.

Territorial disputes between states

The major territorial disputes between states in the region have focussed, unsurprisingly, on the old colonial borders. It is frequently remarked how much African states have accepted their colonial boundary inheritance; and especially the way in which the Organisation of African Unity (OAU) made a fetish of the independence borders. But in north-east Africa this has not been the case, with the majority of states becoming involved in a territorial dispute.

Most attention has been drawn to Somalia's borders with all three of its neighbours, Ethiopia, Kenya, and Djibouti. This was in origin a straightforward case of irredentism. British, Ethiopian, French and Italian ambitions and competition in the late nineteenth century had left a large minority of Somalis outside the colonial territories of British and Italian Somaliland which together formed the Somali republic in 1960. The new Somali constitution (and national flag) both explicitly challenged the inherited borders. Somalis in the Ogaden region of Ethiopia, and the Northern Frontier District of Kenya were armed by the Somali government, though both those states soon showed their intransigence, and from 1967 Somalia desisted from actively pursuing its claim. However, ten years later it was hard for Somalia's military ruler, Siad Barre, to resist the opportunity to seize the Ogaden which was apparently afforded by the upheavals brought about in Ethiopia by the revolution which had begun in 1974. Western Somali guerrillas aided by regular soldiers out of uniform were making headway, and the Somali army was keen to exploit the opportunity. The 1977-78 war was the largest conventional war fought in Africa since the Second World War, but Somalia's initial success was reversed when the Soviet Union switched from supporting Somalia (which it had advised not to attack) to a shift of allegiance to Ethiopia, bringing massive arms' shipment together with Cuban troops. Somalia was forced to retire to its old borders and had little capacity to attack thereafter. In 1988 the increasingly beleaguered leaders of the two countries agreed to sign a cooperation agreement. From Somalia's standpoint the 1977-78 war has been seen as of long term importance in the decline of the regime, with the 1988 agreement with Ethiopia of major short term significance. From the perspective of Ethiopia's military regime, led by Mengistu Haile Mariam, the intention of freeing sufficient forces from the south-east to crush northern resistance was equally unsuccessful, and the two dictators fell almost simultaneously in 1991.[3]

Given the oft-cited uniqueness of Somalia's irredentist impulse, it is unsurprising that other territorial disputes attracted rather less attention. However, the dispute between Libya and Chad over the strip of land between the two countries known as the Aouzou strip proved both long running and bloody. Its origins lay in disagreement over the border inherited from an agreement between France and Italy in 1935, but which was never formally ratified. As a slice of the middle of the Sahara with a small population with limited attachment to either state, it seemed hardly worthy of conflict.

---

[3] Recent works on Somalia include I.M.Lewis, *Understanding Somalia*, HAAN, 1993; on Ethiopia see C.Clapham, *Transformation and Continuity in Revolutionary Ethiopia*, Cambridge University Press, 1988.

However speculation grew concerning the mineral potential of the region, while Libya's claim to it was also seen as something of a barometer of its involvement in Chad from Colonel Qaddafi's seizure of power in 1969. By the early 1980s Libya's forces were effectively occupying half of Chad, and kept at bay by French rather than Chadian resistance. However the then president of Chad, Hissein Habre, had long been an opponent of Libya, and in 1986-87 Chadian troops made dramatic and highly mobile attacks on the apparently well armed Libyan defences and pushed the northern intruders back. The conflict did not have the dramatic repercussions for either regime that occurred in Ethiopia and Somalia (though Libya did later help Idris Deby prepare to overthrow Habre in 1990). Subsequently there was agreement to take the dispute to the International Court of Justice which ruled in favour of Chad, and with some reluctance Libya withdrew its remaining forces from the strip.[4]

The dispute between Egypt and Sudan over a part of their common border area east of the Nile, known as Halayeb, has a similar colonial history to the Aouzou strip. The 1899 Anglo-Egyptian Treaty set the border between the two countries on the 22nd parallel. However for convenience Halayeb was to be administered from Sudan even though north of the parallel. It seemed of little account when Britain dominated Egypt; Egypt regarded Sudan as her territory anyway; and Sudan was officially an Anglo-Egyptian condominium. On Sudan's independence in 1956 it continued to administer Halayeb, and internationally it was thought of generally as Sudanese. But in 1958 Nasser, smarting at Sudan's independence and with rising pan-Arab aspirations, laid claim to Halayeb. The tension between the two countries contributed to the air of political uncertainty in Sudan which resulted in General Abboud's military coup in the same year. Subsequently the two military rulers put the issue on ice as they agreed instead a package which resulted in the building of the Aswan High Dam and the consequent inundation of much of Sudanese Nubia.[5]

In 1992 the Halayeb dispute surfaced once more. As in Aouzou, it appeared that prospecting for minerals on- and off-shore played a part in triggering the Egyptian decision to send forces to occupy the region; but similarly too, the claim came at a time of great general strain in Egyptian-Sudanese relations. The seizure of power in 1989 by a regime in Sudan that soon became identified with militant Islam led to charges by Egypt that its own violent Islamist opposition was being actively encouraged by Sudan. Ever since 1992 Egypt has remained in control of Halayeb, but the situation remains far from accepted by the regime in Sudan which has sought unsuccessfully to stage a mass march on Halayeb as well as wishing to take the dispute to some form of international arbitration. Thus, unlike the former cases, the Halayeb dispute lingers on, and the wider context of Egyptian-Sudanese relations appears unpromising as far as an agreed solution is concerned.

When compared with the three cases above, other border issues in the

---

[4] R.Lemarchand (ed), *The Green and the Black: Qadhafi's policies in Africa*, Indiana University Press, 1988.

[5] B.Korany & A.Dessouki (eds), *The Foreign Policies of Arab States*, Westview, 1991.

region appear comparatively minor. The Sudan-Ethiopia and Kenya-Sudan borders have both been subject to some 'rationalisation' developments, but they have not been of comparable political or military significance. And though Idi Amin appeared to have delusions of grandeur in laying claim to swathes of the territories of his neighbours it was of no major importance. (However, it was a cross-border incursion into Tanzania in 1979 which provided President Nyerere with the casus belli to invade Uganda and overthrow the tyrant.)

Opposition movements and borders

One opposition movement in the region which had the aim of changing borders has already been mentioned. It appears that the Western Somali Liberation Front (WSLF) represented genuine aspirations of many Ogadenis to be united with their fellow Somalis to the east. Yet while being clear from the outset, it also ended in failure – though there is still some unrest amongst Somalis in the system of ethnic-federalism introduced in Ethiopia after the downfall of Mengistu. Some other Somalis were more successful than the Ogadenis. In the wake of the collapse of the regime of Siad Barre and the final disintegration of the state in Somalia, the Issaq-based Somali National Movement (SNM) declared a separate independent state of Somaliland (in the territory of the former British Somaliland). In spite of some problems it has maintained a rudimentary state in the region since that date, but it has not been accorded international recognition. There were doubts about the potential stability and unity of Somaliland; while both Somali leaders in the south, and the international community, hoped that in some future reconstruction of Somalia north and south might still be in a common state, however loosely connected. However Somaliland's sheer survival may in time win it a recognition of which there are already some unofficial indications.

In contrast to the failure in the Ogaden and the uncertainty over Somaliland, the independence of Eritrea appears to show what can be achieved by great determination and effort on the part of a small minority against one of Africa's largest states, and with a big army backed by a superpower. The Eritrean movement, whether led first by the Eritrean Liberation Front (ELF) or later by the Eritrean People's Liberation Front (EPLF) was always determined to seek the independence of Eritrea, claiming the illegality of the manner of the incorporation of the former Italian colony and later UN Trust Territory into what was supposed to be federal Ethiopia in 1952, let alone opposing Ethiopia's subsequent complete incorporation of the territory. What was even more remarkable was that the Eritreans had little indigenous unity. They were a mosaic of different ethnic and religious identities, and yet the determination of the Chinese-trained and formerly Marxist leadership of the EPLF in particular was maintained across decades of the vicissitudes of warfare. And once the war was won with the collapse of Mengistu's regime in 1991, Eritrea was not to be deflected from holding its almost unanimous self-determination exercise two years later. In this it was helped by being in the unusual situation of having a new government in the country from which Eritrea sought to become independent that was willing to accept the loss of sovereignty as previously claimed by Ethiopia. (There were too historic links between the two leaderships who took power in Eritrea and Ethiopia respectively.) The strength of Eritrea under the former EPLF leadership, coupled with the attitude of Ethiopia, ensured international recognition of the new state.[6]

The independence of Eritrea, coupled with the policy of ethnic federalism, could lead to renewal of opposition movements in Ethiopia with claims for self-determination and further changes in the present boundaries of the state. It appears that such an assertion may be constitutionally possible in the future, and at least some amongst the Ogadenis, Oromos and Afars in particular may seek to exercise such a right.

Another major conflict within a north-east African state in which territorial borders have been questioned has been in southern Sudan. Here there is not the same colonial experience as in Eritrea and Somaliland, for though administered somewhat differently from the north, southern Sudan was never formally a separate territory. Ethnically the south is at least as diverse as Eritrea, but for decades it has asserted the racial differences of African southerners and Arab northerners, as well as consequent exploitation (for which there is certainly evidence). In addition there has been a rising awareness of religious differences with the growth of Christianity in the south contrasting with the Muslim north, and especially since the growing Islamization of successive Sudanese governments began in 1983. On territory, the arguments of the southern movements have varied since independence. Before the onset of the first civil war concern was mainly with federalism, but as open warfare developed secessionist sentiments began to flower. However in 1972 the civil war appeared to be settled by the negotiation of the Addis Ababa agreement. Under it Southern Sudan became a special region distinct from the rest of the country and largely self-governing. Various factors gave rise to the collapse of this agreement by 1983, and the re-opening of civil war. The Sudan People's Liberation Army (SPLA), which has maintained the civil war ever since, saw the answer to the country's problems not in terms of separation, but rather the pursuit of a 'New Sudan' which would involve the overthrow of the northern Arab dominance of central government and justice for all backward and exploited peoples and regions. However, such a view is now changing. It appears that the SPLA is ever more disillusioned with all northern politicians, and sees a greater acceptance internationally of claims for self-determination. There are suggestions that this could be pursued through a new military offensive which will win it a *de facto* position that will be recognised eventually, rather along the lines of the experience of Eritrea, and the hopes of Somaliland.[7]

By no means all the opposition movements in north-east Africa seek to challenge the existing state as territorially defined. Chad suffered years of civil war in which there were factions with clear territorial and ethnic identities, but which struggled for control of the state of Chad (or what was

---

[6] R.Iyob, *The Eritrean Struggle for Independence*, Cambridge University Press, 1995.

[7] P.Woodward & M.Forsyth (eds), *Conflict and Peace in the Horn of Africa*, Dartmouth, 1994.

left of it) rather than its dismemberment. Likewise the numerous factions of former Italian Somalia continue their power struggles, but do not seek complete separation in efforts to re-constitute that collapsed state. And while Buganda contemplated independence from Uganda in the decolonising process, the recent restoration of the monarchy scarcely poses a threat to the country's unity.

Opposition movements and exploitation of borders

Whether or not opposition movements themselves have been concerned to re-draw borders, it has certainly been the case in practice that having a cross-border base in a neighbouring country has been important for success. The major opposition movements in the region have all made use of bases beyond their country of origin in order to enjoy the relative safety of respect for territorial sovereignty of neighbours (though there are occasional accusations of opposition movements being pursued across borders by national armies). As well as bases, neighbouring states have been used as sources of supplies, and as centres for communicating with the outside world.

Probably the most sophistcated opposition movements in this regard have been the Eritreans, especially the EPLF; and their example was later taken up by the Tigrean People's Liberation Front (TPLF). While making much of their self-reliance, and especially their rehabilitation of captured Ethiopian supplies, in reality they used Sudanese territory in all of the ways mentioned. An efficient supply route was set up from Port Sudan; and the effective relief organisations, the Eritrean Relief Association (ERA) and the Relief Society of Tigre (REST), both brought supplies, and sometimes people, across the border. Some of the refugee camps in eastern Sudan were effectively operated by and for the fronts. While Khartoum was an important communications centre with the outside world, including links with diplomats, journalists and even academics. It is impossible to estimate the overall importance of cross-border links for the EPLF and the TPLF, but they were clearly an integral part of both their organisations.

The southern Sudanese likewise made use of cross-border facilities. In the first civil war these were with Uganda and to a lesser extent Ethiopia. The importance of a cross-border base was shown even more clearly in the second war. From the outset of the conflict in 1983 the SPLA operated from Ethiopia, and when the Mengistu regime fell in 1991 the SPLA had to make a hurried exit. Its subsequent weakness was due in part to the confusion of establishing relatively reliable routes for the new sources of arms, and as Uganda has provided opportunities so the SPLA's performance in the field has improved. At the same time Nairobi has been an important diplomatic and communications centre for southern Sudanese.

The Somali opposition movements were a later development, taking shape in the 1980s after the Somali-Ethiopian war. They too found sanctuary across a border, even though it meant operating from the territory of the arch-enemy Ethiopia. In terms of the long run conflict in Somalia, Ethiopia was clearly an important base for a number of factions; and while the Siad-

Mengistu pact of 1988 was supposed to stop such cross-border activities, it served only to launch the SDM attack and raise the whole level of conflict down to Siad's overthrow and beyond.

But perhaps the most dramatic example of the value of a cross-border shelter comes from Chad. In the factional fighting of the early 1980s, Hissein Habre was forced to retreat to western Sudan. But there he was able to rehabilitate his forces and in 1982 he launched an attack that brought the downfall of the existing government and his installation in the presidency. In 1990 history repeated itself. Idris Deby, a forrner lieutenant of Habre, failed in a coup attempt, retreated to Sudan, and staged a successful invasion, installing himself in the presidency in turn.

Thus across the region, lack of acceptable opportunities for opposition movements to participate in the domestic political systems of their own countries led many of them to operate from the territory of one or more neighbouring state. This widespread experience made such neighbouring states extra-territorial arenas for a part of the politics of the state in which the conflict had arisen.

Neighbour states and conflict

The value of a refuge for an opposition movement in a neighbouring state is obvious; what is less clear is why neighbouring states themselves should permit such activities, especially since they are highly likely to be damaging to relations between states.

Part of the answer may lie in the limited capacities of states themselves, especially if opposition movements are utilising remote areas near borders. The state's own capacity to control such activities may be limited, for Africa's borders often seem beyond the capacity for effective policing and control.[8] Furthermore, opposition movements may have their own roots in local communities on which to draw, and which governments do not wish to offend. Muslim Eritreans of the Beni Amer in particular enjoyed such a position in eastern Sudan in the halcyon days of the ELF; Somali opposition movements in the 1980s benefited from cross-border clan support in the Ogaden; and Deby's Zaghawa background was of importance to him during his retreat from Chad into western Sudan. As well as permitting or being unable to prevent such activities, government's might even use such situations. Mengistu's regime effectively left local security in part of western Ethiopia to the SPLA.

There was also a refugee situation which made the position more complex. In recent decades Africa has had the fastest growing number of refugees, and within the continent southern Africa and the Horn have been the regions most affected. Hundreds of thousands of refugees have crossed borders in almost all directions, and mainly driven by conflicts. As political refugees they can claim an internationally recognised status, and receive assistance from UNHCR, host governments and other agencies. In reality it is difficult to draw a hard and fast line between legitimate refugees and the activities of opposition movements, even if UNHCR and host governments may

---

[8] I.Zartman (ed), *Collapsed States*, Lynne Rienner, 1995.

claim so to do.[9] It was a situation which the more sophisticated opposition movements, such as the EPLF and TPLF, became adept at using to their advantage both within the politics of host countries and more widely in the international environment.[10]

There was also the possibility of a genuine degree of sympathy in host government circles for the opposition movements. Support for the ELF was found not only in eastern Sudan, but in ruling circles as well. Sudan's wish to assert its Arab credentials included identifying the ELF with the Arab interest in Ethiopia which centred on challenging the Coptic Christian state with its links with Israel. The corollary of this view was Ethiopia's sympathy for southern Sudanese in both civil wars. Sudan also regarded Habre's activities from western Sudan as a challenge to the ambition of Sudan's enemy, Libya, to gain dominance in Chad. More recently Sudan's militant Islamic regime has denounced the failure of the nation state in the Muslim world, speaking instead of the long term unification of the *umma*. To this end it has declared itself in support of Islamist movements in neighbouring states (notably in Egypt, Eritrea, Ethiopia, Kenya, Somalia and Uganda), and those states in turn have become more united in isolating Sudan and supporting the Sudanese opposition.

In spite of the strictures of the OAU, sympathy for movements in neighbouring states may go as far as supporting a change of borders. The secessionism of the Eritreans did not deter Sudan from aiding their movement. While since the independence of Eritrea, Sudan's neighbours have increasingly accepted the possibility of secession. Indeed the neighbours involved in the mediatory efforts of the Intergovernmental Authority for Drought and Development (IGADD) in the second Sudan civil war, have accepted the idea of self-determination for the southern Sudan.[11] It was a short step from sympathy for opposition movements to straight forward tit-for-tat support. There has been an element of this for decades in Ethiopia-Sudanese relations, and it was even clearer between Ethiopia and Somalia in the 1980s. Somalia's defeat in 1978 did not stop low level guerrilla activities in the Ogaden, and Somalia also sent supplies to Eritrea: in response Ethiopia supported Somali opposition factions. In the 1990s Uganda has been more helpful to the SPLA, while Sudan has apparently encouraged rebel elements in northern Uganda; and Egypt and Eritrea have responded to Sudan's Islamic pretensions by hosting Sudanese opposition groups. (In 1995 Eritrea broke diplomatic relations with Sudan and called publicly for the overthrow of the current regime in Sudan.) It appears obvious also that tit-for-tat support for opposition could be replaced by agreement between the governments of two neighbouring states to agree to restrict such activities, but here

---

[9] The moral maze thus created has been seen even more starkly as a result of developments in and around Rwanda.

[10] G.Loescher, *Refugee Movements and International Security*, Adelphi Papers, 268, 1992.

[11] In contrast, in Mengistu's time the SPLA had a clear prudential reason for advancing the cause of 'New Sudan' rather than possible secession. On Somaliland, however the position of neighbours has been more ambiguous with little willingness to recognise the territory's claim. (With the exception of the Addis Ababa agreement, mediation, whether by neighbours or others has been of limited success for reasons that go beyond the scope of this paper.)

the origins of conflict in domestic politics may come into play. The Addis Ababa agreement of 1972 which ended Sudan's civil war had an Ethiopian dimension. In return for Haile Selassie's backing for the agreement there was an understanding that Sudan would restrict the activities of the Eritreans. For a while this was done, but Sudan also thought that its own negotiated peace for the Southern Region would be followed by Ethiopia for Eritrea, which proved to be far from the Emperor's thinking. In any case the Ethiopian revolution soon erased any understanding between the two governments. As already mentioned, the increasingly beleaguered rulers of Ethiopia and Somalia made an even more explicit deal in 1988, though it proved too late to save either of them. It was particularly hard for Siad Barre and meant that he, like the opposition before him, was supping with the devil (critics at the time likened it to the Hitler-Stalin pact).

Other international actors

Armed conflict may be tragic, but it also provides opportunities. With cross-border dimensions of importance to opposition movements, they also provide opportunities for other international actors to pursue their interests, especially if they have the agreement of the government(s) of the state(s) giving refuge. Reference has already been made to Arab identity with the cause of the Eritreans; and Arab states other than Sudan used the latter's territory to supply various factions of the Eritreans. In the era of radical pan-Arabism in the 1960s, Syria was a prominent supplier of the ELF, and after Qadaffi's seizure of power in Libya in 1969 his regime supplied the EPLF (though later after the Ethiopian revolution it changed sides). From the mid-1970s Saudi Arabia and the smaller Gulf states sought to become more assertive and aided the Eritreans. In response to this Arab activity, Israel not only aided Ethiopia, but played an important part via Ethiopia and Uganda in arming and uniting the southern Sudanese in the first civil war (ironically that new unity helped make negotiated peace possible).[12] As well as opposition movements in the region being influenced by developments in Middle Eastern politics, the superpowers had a part to play. Increasingly states became identified with one or other of the superpowers, and indeed Egypt, Sudan, Somalia and Ethiopia all changed superpower partners between 1972 and 1978, with the former three becoming closely associated with the United States, and the latter with the former Soviet Union. By the time of the Second Cold War in the 1980s, north-east Africa was a significant part of the 'arc of crisis' which extended from Libya around the Gulf and up to Afghanistan. The implications of this for cross-border support for opposition were mixed. The most obvious involvement was that of the supply of Soviet weapons and Cuban training to the SPLA in southern Sudan (though the movement itself was not explicitly Marxist). The US (and Egypt) had a clear success in backing Habre's attack on the Libyan-supported (and therefore Soviet-armed) regime in Chad in 1982. American attempts to support non-Marxist opposition elements in northern Ethiopia in the 1980s were less successful. And the Cold War was over by the time

---

[12]B.Korany, *op cit.*

America decided to ride the winds of change as represented by the EPLF and TPLF shortly before Mengistu's downfall. In Somalia the US actually used its influence to inhibit cross-border activity by Siad's regime, and welcomed the agreement with Ethiopia in 1988. Overall the superpowers contribution lay in supporting regimes far more than opposition movements, and the arms that were provided to them encouraged policies of repression which increased conflicts but ultimately saw more regimes overthrown than survived.[13]

Conclusion

Borders have clearly been a factor in conflict in north-east Africa, and in a variety of ways but there have also been a number of conflicts in which border issues have not played a part (though cross-border facilities may still have been of use). The combination of struggles over border and non-border issues across much of the region makes it difficult to surmise just how significant border issues are in relation to other sources of conflict. Border changes may reduce conflict, but they are certainly no guarantee of peace. There is also the question of defining more viable borders. The region has been seen as an Afro-Arab frontier, and this is relevant to conflict, but any implication of a split along such a line does not reflect any indications towards unity on the part of either the Arabs or the Africans on either side of it. Nor are there old historic guidelines for new borders. There are long traditions of state formation in highland Ethiopia and in central Sudan, but these have no clear boundaries, and are surrounded by peoples whose traditions are largely stateless. If one looks instead to the claims of political opposition for border changes, then the irony of it is that they largely represent the *de jure* or *de facto* divisions of most of the imperial period: Eritrea as an Italian colony; Somaliland as a British colony; and southern Sudan as a distinct administrative and cultural area. It appears that the nationalist political awakening took place within these borders, and most post-independence political experience concerned with the loss of that identity and resistance to another 'national' identity which has been perceived as partial and discriminatory. With Eritrea already independent, Somaliland a *de facto* state, and southern Sudan pressing for self determination, these may be the most dramatic changes to the map of north east Africa. They would certainly be more substantial than the border changes from interstate disputes. Furthermore, although neighbours and other international actors have played and will continue to play a part, the outcome will be determined more by developments within the states than the forces acting from outside.

---

[13] J.Lefebrve, *Arms for the Horn*, Pittsburgh University Press, 1991; R.Patman, *The Soviet Union in the Horn of Africa*, Cambridge University Press, 1984.

The European Union in International Perspective

Andrew Geddes
University of Liverpool

'Immigration and Asylum as Political Issues in the European Union'

Introduction

The significance of immigration and asylum issues within the European Union has increased since the Treaty on European Union's (TEU) provision for an intergovernmental 'pillar' dealing with Justice and Home Affairs (JHA). Given this increased issue salience how are we to understand the development of European Union immigration policy?

In this paper I argue that member state immigration, asylum, nationality and citizenship policies provide a crucial context for understanding European Union policy. In particular, exclusion of many third-country nationals and people of immigrant or ethnic minority origin from the political process (at national and supranational level) illustrates the importance of considering participatory constraints when assessing both the development and effects of supranational policy. One consequence of exclusion is that European Union may not reflect the interests of Europe's immigrant and ethnic minorities.

This paper outlines recent policy developments and assesses the domestic participatory constraints which contribute to the narrow, security-related conceptualisation of immigration and asylum issues.

The development of European Union immigration and asylum policy

Even the most cursory analysis of the recent history of European integration would point to the significance of the single market programme and its anticipated and unanticipated effects. The programme's importance went far beyond what, at first sight, were seen by some as rather technical measures designed to complete the market integration initially envisaged by the Treaty of Rome. There are, for example, close links between the single market programme and a 'paradox of liberalisation' whereby freer movement of Member States' nationals (since the TEU, Europe's citizens) within the single market is accompanied by tighter control of external frontiers.

Analyses of European Union immigration and asylum policy must take account of the central role played by single market liberalisation in impelling policy development. Following this impetus the nature of policy cooperation has been influenced by the reluctance of Member States to cede sovereignty in an area of 'high politics'. Particularly when national governments feel vulnerable to anti-immigration/immigrant political pressure at domestic level from the extreme right, or are keen to be seen as 'tough' on immigration/asylum for domestic political reasons (although these two factors are often linked). One result is that European Union immigration and asylum policy is narrowly conceived as 'security'-related. Domestic political factors play an important part in European Union immigration policy development and help illustrate the contrast between a relatively 'positive ideology' of 'Europeanness' and a 'negative ideology' of immigration.[1]

Two streams of migration-related policy have developed in the European Union. First, provisions flowing from Articles 48 to 51 of the Treaty of Rome provided for free movement of workers within the common market for labour, established in 1968. The EC sought to protect the rights of intra-EC migrant workers; particularly regarding employment, social security and education. However, the Treaty's provisions did not extend to movement by nationals of 'third-countries'.

Second, there are the immigration- and asylum-related provisions arising from the single market programme. During its 1986 Council Presidency, the British government instigated informal methods of intergovernmental cooperation by establishing the Ad Hoc Group on Immigration to promote co-operation on immigration and asylum policies. In 1988 the Rhodes Group of free movement co-ordinators was created (named after the location of one of that year's European summits). It brought forward the Palma Programme – a series of measures seen as essential if free movement of people within the internal market was to be fully realised. This 'informal intergovernmentalism' was supplanted by the TEU's provision for a JHA 'pillar'. These arrangements have been described as 'improved intergovernmentalism'[2], although it has been pointed out that the term 'intergovernmental' may not be an entirely accurate way of characterising European Union policy cooperation. First, because the idea that governments seek to protect and advance 'national interests' may conceal a more complex reality where other institutions and organisations also seek to influence relations between Member States and the European Union. Second, because it may not be easy to demarcate a clear boundary between 'home' and 'abroad' because officials carry both national and Community affiliations making them subject to pressures from both levels which blur the boundaries.[3]

The TEU created a JHA 'pillar', Title VI, dealing with immigration and asylum policy. Article K.1 of the JHA pillar outlines nine areas of 'common interest', three of which relate to immigration and asylum policy. The Council acts by unaminity when deciding on immigration and asylum policy. Indeed, there is a 'double-lock' mechanism whereby decisions made in the Council to establish conventions in international law (as opposed to supranational law regulated by European Union institutions) must also be ratified by national parliaments. It has been argued that the JHA pillar accentuates the European Union's 'democratic deficit'.[4] For ex-

---

[1] M.Livi-Bacci, 'South-north migration: a comparative approach to North American and European experiences', in *The Changing Course of International Migration*, OECD, 1993.

[2] J.Cloos et al, *Le Traité de Maastricht. Genèse, Analyse, Commentaires*, Editions Bruylant, 1993.

[3] F.Hayes-Renshaw & H.Wallace, 'Executive power in the European Union: the functions and limits of the Council of Ministers, *Journal of European Public Policy*, 2/4, 1995.

[4] See A.Geddes, 'Immigrant and Ethnic Minorities and the European Union's 'democratic deficit", *Journal of Common Market Studies*, 32/2, 1995.

ample, the Council's endemic secrecy means that most immigration- and asylum-related discussions are beyond the purview of elected bodies at either national or supranational level. Supranational institutions have little involvement in JHA decisions. The Commission has watered-down powers of initiative which it shares with Member States (Article K.3.2); although it does have powers under Article 100c of the European Union Treaty (added by the TEU) to determine a list of countries whose nationals require a visa to enter the European Union. The European Parliament has only the right to be informed about discussions covered by the JHA provisions (Article K.6). The European Court of Justice is given authority to review decisions and adjudicate in disputes only if the JHA Council decides by unanimity to extend such powers (Article K.3.2). There is a potential 'bridge' from the JHA pillar to the Community as Article K.9 provides that Article 100c of the European Union Treaty (already covering visa policy) could be extended to cover other immigration and asylum issues, provided all Member States agree. However, the Commission acknowledged that even though bringing immigration and asylum into the Community pillar did offer advantages, it was too soon after TEU ratification to propose such action.[5]

Domestic political institutions and the 'two-level game' of European Union decision-making

The Single European Act (SEA, 1986) impelled European Union immigration and asylum policy (as it did other policies). The resurgence of integration prompted some revival in neo-functionalist accounts of European integration, which attribute a central role to Commission activism.[6] However, other analysts have preferred intergovernmental interpretations of the integrative rélance. For example, Moravcsik develops a 'liberal intergovernmentalist' model which rests on the assumption that 'state behaviour reflects the rational actions of governments constrained at home by domestic societal pressures and abroad by their strategic environment'.[7] An implication of Moravcsik's analysis is that existing approaches to the study of international relations serve as adequate accounts of European integration. Thus, the European Union does not need a sui generis theory.

Moravcsik's analysis builds on the work of Putnam who analysed interactions between diplomacy and domestic politics as a 'two-level game'; although in fledgling areas of imperfect integration such as JHA the 'games' can be as much about the nature of cooperation as they are about specific policy decisions.[8] 'Two level' analyses seek to build on the 'partial equilibriums' of 'second image' and 'second-image reversed' approaches by constructing a 'general equilibrium' theory. Putnam notes that it is fruitless to ask whether it is domestic politics that affects international negotiations, or whether it is the other way around, because the answer is 'both,

---

[5] Commission of the European Union, *Communication to the Council and European Parliament on Immigration and Asylum Policies*, COM (94) 23, OOPEU, 1994.

[6] For example, M.Holland, *European Community Integration*, Pinter, 1992.

[7] A.Moravcsik, 'Preferences and power in the EC: a liberal intergovernmentalist approach'. *Journal of Common Market Studies*, 31/4, 1993.

[8] F.Hayes-Renshaw & H.Wallace, *op cit.*

sometimes';[9]

Putnam and Moravcsik seek to open the 'black box' of domestic politics to enhance understanding of societal pressures on governments in international negotiations. Their analyses of domestic politics are predicated upon liberal assumptions. For example, Moravcsik writes that '(g)roups articulate preferences, governments aggregate them.[10] These liberal assumptions can be questioned when analysing European Union immigration and asylum policy because evidence suggests that substantial numbers of people of immigrant and ethnic minority origin are excluded from formal political processes in European Union Member States. This means that governmental aggregation of societal preferences is likely to be imperfect. This can result from exclusive citizenship laws (for example, in Germany); or from situations where, even if citizenship laws are more inclusive, exclusion from the political process remains (for example, because of racism). Participatory constraints challenge the liberal paradigm and draws attention away from 'who gets what, when and how?' towards the necessary prior question of 'who participates?'. This is especially pertinent when analysing immigration and asylum policy development, because the effects of policy need to be assessed in the context of thirteen million people resident in European Union Member States who are third country nationals, plus Member State nationals of immigrant or ethnic minority origin. Any attempt to strengthen the ramparts of 'fortress Europe' has effects on the position of many third country nationals and people of immigrant and ethnic minority origin who live in European Union Member States and become part of the 'problem' (as defined by the narrowly conceived policy framework).

The conceptualisation of international negotiations as a 'game' played out on two levels – the domestic and the international – draws attention to the importance of the effects of domestic politics on international negotiations. Bulmer's analysis of the relation between domestic politics and European integration focused on domestic policy-making *structures* and *attitudes* held within the member states to the EC and their effects on European integration.[11] This was in line with empirical analyses of EC policy-making which drew attention to differing national 'policy styles' and their effects on supranational policy-making. Bulmer argues that '(t)he methodological implication of this is that EC policy-making should be examined in the same way as domestic politics'.[12] A difference between 'domestic politics' and 'liberal intergovernmentalist' approaches is that the latter is more explicitly played out on two levels and combines a liberal theory of comparative politics with concepts derived from analysis of international relations.

Recent work – labelled 'new institutionalism' – has highlighted the importance of political institutions as mediating structures in decision-making

---

[9] On 'second-image' see K.Waltz, *Man, the State and War*, Columbia University Press, 1959; on 'second-image reversed see P.Gourevitch, 'The second-image reversed: the international sources of domestic politics', *International Organization*, 32/3, 1978; on 'two-level' approaches see R.Putnam, 'Diplomacy and domestic politics: the logic of two-level games', *International Organization*, 42/3, 1988.

[10] Moravcsik, *op cit*, p.483.

[11] S.Bulmer, 'Domestic politics and European Community policy-making', *Journal of Common Market Studies*, 21/4, 1984) original emphasis.

[12] Bulmer, *ibid*, p.351.

processes. One implication of the focus on political institutions as mediating structures in the decision-making process is that 'correlational thinking', whereby systemic 'inputs' (such as societal pressures) and 'outputs' (legislation) are 'measured' to understand the policy-making process, is avoided.[13] The rise of 'new' institutionalism also implies that there was an 'older' variant of institutionally-oriented analysis which, amongst other things, was seen as too static and as over-emphasising national historical particularities at the expense of potential cross-national insights.[14]

For the initial progenitors of 'new institutionalism' the definition of what actually constitutes an institution was very wide, covering: 'rules of behaviour, norms, roles, physical arrangements, buildings, and archives that are relatively invariant in the face of turnover of individuals and relatively resilient to the idiosyncratic preferences and expectations of individuals'.[15] For another 'new institutionalist' writer, the concept of institutions refers to 'formal rules, compliance procedures, and customary practices that structure the relationship between individuals in the polity and the economy'.[16] Ikenberry makes a threefold distinction between levels of the institutional structure: the specific characteristics of government institutions; the overarching structures of the state, for example, the centralisation and dispersion of power; and the nations's normative social order.[17] Critics of the 'new institutionalism' contend that its definition of institutions is too broad, that it is not actually very new, and that a more reliable approach to analysis of the decision-making process is derived from 'policy community realism' rather than 'new institutionalist ambiguity'.[18]

Political opportunity and the domestic context

Recent analyses of European integration which utilise institutional perspectives – whether they are 'new' or not – can facilitate analysis of immigration as a political issue in the European Union. However, the focus on institutions and structures conceals other important aspects of the political process. In particular, insights derived from social movement theorising and notions of political opportunity draw attention to the importance of analysing participation.

Political opportunity perspectives highlight the relevance of domestic institutional factors such as access to institutional participation and the strength of electoral alignments. They also demonstrate how these factors affect 'the dimensions of the political environment that provide incentives for people to undertake collective action by affecting their expectations of

---

[13] E.Immergut, 'The rules of the game: the logic of health policy-making in France, Switzerland and Sweden', in S.Steinmo et al (eds), *Structuring Politics: Historical Institutionalism in Comparative Perspective*, Cambridge University Press, 1992.

[14] On 'new institutionalism' see, for example, J.March & J.Olsen, *Rediscovering Institutions*, Free Press, 1989.

[15] March & Olsen, *op cit*, p.741.

[16] P.Hall, *Governing the Economy*, Polity, 1992.

[17] G.Ikenberry, 'Conclusions: an institutional approach to American economic foreign policy', *International Organization*, 42/1, 1988.

[18] G.Jordan, 'Policy community realism versus 'new' institutionalist ambiguity', *Political Studies*, 38/3, 1990.

success or failure'.[19] An implication of this is that governments may not always be tightly constrained by domestic political interests and thus may have a measure of autonomy when interstate bargaining occurs. However, this could be because some voices are not heard (or not listened to) rather than because societal interests are not always 'sharply defined'.[20]

Political opportunity structures are conceptualised as a set of independent variables serving to explain social movement mobilisation, strategic choices and success and are typically seen as having four main variables: the degree of openness/closure of the formal political process; the degree of stability/instability of political alignments; the availability and strategy of potential alliance partners; and, the level of conflict between elites.[21] This model was refined by Kriesi who distinguished between three broad sets of properties of a political system: its formal institutional structure (including the electoral system); informal procedures and strategies with regards to challengers; and, the configuration of power in the political system. The first two provide the general setting and act as a constraint on the configuration of power.[22]

Analyses of political opportunity structures have been criticised for placing excessive focus on structural and institutional factors. Gamson and Meyer stress the importance of 'culture' and 'context'.[23] They locate political opportunity along two continua. The first focuses on institutional structure and related levels of stability and volatility which 'frame' political action. The second broadens the analysis by considering how 'culture' and 'context' – by which they mean factors such as national belief systems, class consciousness and the prevailing national mood – are also important. For example, if the 'prevailing national mood' is hostile to full incorporation of immigrant and ethnic minorities then governments are unlikely to effectively articulate national preferences in the two-level game of European Union policy-making. The implication of this is that participatory constraints at domestic level, linked to unequal political opportunity, provide fuller contextualisation for analyses of European Union policy-making than approaches that lay emphasis on the importance of domestic politics.

Two national examples illustrate how participatory constraints can structure immigration and asylum policy and contextualise the institutional 'playing field'. In Britain, where most post-war immigrants came as citizens of the Empire/Commonwealth, policy responses to immigration have been predicated around the notion of 'race relations', developed in the 1960s. A central aspect of this policy response was that the two main political parties decentralised responsibility for management of 'race-related' issues to local institutions and organisations in order to reduce the potentially

---

[19]S.Tarrow, 'The Europeanization of conflict: reflections from a social movement perspective, *West European Politics*, 18(2), 1994, p.85.
[20]Moravcsik, *op cit*, p.484.
[21]K.Beckwith, *The Opportunity in Political Opportunity Theory: A Review of the Social Movements Literature*, unpublished Paper, 1995.
[22]H-P Kriesi, *The Political Opportunity Structure of New Social Movements*, WZB (Berlin), Working Paper.
[23]W.Gamson & D.Meyer, 'Framing political opportunity', in D.McAdam et al (eds), *Opportunities, Mobilizing Structures and Framing: Comparative Applications of Contemporary Social Movement Theory*, Cambridge University Press, 1994.

damaging electoral effects of anti-immigration sentiment on two-party competition at national level (the Labour Party was particularly fearful of its effects). One consequence of 'race relations' policy was the rendering of immigrants and their children as 'objects of' policy rather than 'actors in' the political process.[24] This perspective helps explain under-representation of ethnic minorities in the United Kingdom's formal institutions of representative politics, although the interlinked effects of social inequality and racism are also important.

In Germany, both the Völkisch conception of nationhood and lack of recognition in German official discourse make it extremely difficult for gastarbeiters and their descendants to acquire German nationality and political rights.[25] Policy is based on Ausländerpolitik, where the reference to 'foreigners' makes a clear distinction between, on the one hand, 'Germans' and, on the other, people whose presence is seen as temporary; despite evidence to the contrary provided by de facto permanent settlement by gastarbeiters and their children. German Ausländerpolitik was thrown into renewed crisis after the end of the Cold War and the vast movements of people that followed in its wake. The 'asylum crisis' has been a major concern for the German government and, in July 1993, new legislation tightened the relatively liberal asylum provisions of the 1949 Basic Law.

Similar patterns of exclusion are evident in other European Union Member States and demonstrate the importance of carefully considering the framework for analysis of domestic political factors and their effects on European Union immigration and asylum policy. It is significant to consider formal political institutions and structures and the ways in which they mediate decision-making; but it is also important to consider political opportunity and 'who participates?' because this question frames domestic interest aggregation processes and affects interstate bargaining.

Conclusion

The single market programme and the ensuing integrative rélance underscored European Union immigration and asylum policy development. A focus on the mediating capacities of national and supranational political institutions facilitates analysis of the conceptualisation and development of European Union immigration and asylum policy. However, 'cultural' and 'contextual', as distinct from 'structural' and 'institutional', factors also play important roles in configuring national settings and contribute to both issue formation and the under-nourished European Union conceptualisation of the immigration issue as being one of 'security'. To understand why this is the case the domestic management of immigration-related issues and exclusion of many people of immigrant and ethnic origin from the formal political process in the countries in which they either reside or are citizens should be considered.

---

[24] J.Crowley, 'Paradoxes in the politicisation of race: a comparison of the United Kingdom and France', *New Community*, 19/4, 1993.

[25] D.Cinar, 'From aliens to citizens. A comparative analysis of rules of transition', in R.Bauböck (ed), *From Aliens to Citizens: Redefining the Status of Immigrants in Europe*, Avebury, 1995.

The European Union in International Perspective

Lee Miles
University of Humberside

'The 1995 Swedish European Parliamentary Election:
Is Sweden Turning its Back on the European Union?'

Acknowledgements

The author would like to thank Anders Widfeldt, Department of Political Science, Göteborg University, for his comments on earlier drafts of this paper.

Introduction

On 18 September 1995, Sweden held its first European Parliamentary election since becoming a full member of the European Union in January 1995. This paper briefly assesses the results of this election. It argues that the Swedish public has, albeit to a limited extent, become quickly disillusioned with full membership and that this is a net result of exaggerated expectations (before joining) of the economic benefits of being a full European Union member.

The Legacy of Pre-Accession

To some extent, the Swedish European Parliamentary election has to be placed in the context of the public's expectations regarding the benefits of full membership. Although difficult to quantify, the general impression amongst the Swedish public was that full membership would help to deal with some of Sweden's pressing economic problems in the 1990s. This impression was, at least partially supported by the leading pro-European Union political élites and the 'yes' camp during the November 1994 referendum campaign. Economic issues, such as increasing economic growth, greater inward investment, rising international trade, support for the government's liberalisation of the Swedish economy and ultimately, tackling unemployment and deteriorating public finances in Sweden were seen as the key aspects of the 'Swedish Impact Assessment' and the pro-European Union campaign.[1] In practice, Swedish full membership was not going to immediately, nor single-handedly, solve these problems. Thus, in psychological terms, Swedish membership initially suffered from the problem of rising domestic expectations and has been set an artificially high target to fulfil by the Swedish population.

---

[1] These points are more extensively developed in L.Miles, 'Enlargement of the European Union and the Nordic Model', *Journal of European Integration*, 19/1, 1996.

The Symbolism of the Swedish European Parliamentary Election

In many ways, the Swedish European Parliamentary election was also symbolic for both Sweden and the European Union. From the Swedish perspective, it was the first direct election to the European Parliament to take place in Sweden since accession in January 1995 and thus, provided an early official test of Swedish public opinion regarding membership since accession, and to a lesser extent, Swedish awareness of the role of the European Parliament itself. To a limited degree, the election also attracted interest as Sweden had only narrowly approved full European Union membership in its referendum (13 November 1994) by 52.2 per cent. It was hoped by the pro-European Union forces that there would be a significant increase in support for the European Union now that the country was a full member.

The election represented the first national election in which a new electoral procedure had been comprehensively used in Sweden and acted as a de facto constitutional test-bed. Finally, this election was being conducted almost exactly twelve months after Ingvar Carlsson's minority Social Democratic government had been elected to power in September 1994 and provided a timely opportunity for the Swedish people to voice their opinions on the performance of the Social Democratic government and their austerity programme.

For the European Union, the Swedish election was also of significance. In one sense, the election was unusual in that it did not take place simultaneously with European parliamentary elections in other member states. The European Parliament had already been through its five-yearly cycle of direct elections in June 1994 before Sweden had joined the European Union. For the political scientist, the Swedish election could provide a useful occasion to consider the potential for 'opinion transfers' between member states and whether, there are any implications for public opinion formation due to external influences of direct elections in other member states.[2]

In addition, the election also represented the first of the three direct elections to take place in the new member states since the enlargement of the Union to fifteen. It was argued that these elections may provide some rather tentative indicators of the success of full membership and to a lesser extent, the European Parliament in these new member states. From this perspective, the Swedish example seemed to be very relevant given that public opinion had been consistently the least enthusiastic about the merits of full membership and had according to opinion polls, turned solidly against membership since the referendum in November 1994. In theory then, the Swedish direct election should have attracted substantial interest from within Sweden and from outside observers.

Certainly, for the Swedes, the European direct election was the first time that a personal vote system had been used in Sweden. The new electoral system had, to a limited extent, been tried previously in the 1994 local elections and would, if successful this time, be used for the general election

---

[2] For example, whether the 1995 Swedish result will influence the voting patterns in the forthcoming Finnish direct election on 20 October, 1996.

in 1998. The electoral procedure used was, in fact, based largely upon the party list system which had traditionally operated in Sweden. However, Swedish voters were permitted in this election to also express a preference for specific candidates on the party list on their voting forms. The electoral rules stipulated that if any candidates gained a 'personal vote' of more than five per cent of that party's overall national vote, then they would rank above all those on the national party lists. They would also rank in descending order of popularity according to the share of their personal vote.

This new electoral procedure did introduce some interesting and at least for the Swedes, new aspects to elections. Personal as well as party campaigns became more apparent as candidates sought to raise public awareness of their personal attributes in order to differentiate themselves more from other party candidates. For example, Cecilia Mälmstrom, a liberal ran a personal campaign in Göteborg. Indeed, this new option seemed to be popular with Swedish voters as 55 per cent of those who voted in the election indicated a preference for individual candidates, even though this was not compulsory. However, at the same time, the new procedure may have also deterred some voters, although this remains still to be proven.

However, despite all the symbolism associated with these Swedish elections, the actual event was rather low-key. It can be argued, albeit to a limited degree, that Swedish voters were suffering from the dual problem of electoral fatigue and rising disillusionment with the issue of the European Union. The Swedish government only completed the long process of negotiating and ratifying accession a year earlier and, for the most part, full membership had been a dominant political issue in Sweden for most of 1994. The November 1994 referendum had proved to be the culmination of a divisive debate on the merits of full membership and had only narrowly approved accession. Furthermore, public opinion polls during 1995 had already indicated rising disillusionment with the European Union. In July 1995, for instance, 61 per cent of Swedes stated that they would vote against membership, if the referendum on approving Swedish accession had been conducted then.[3]

To the Swedish public, there seemed to have been few apparent benefits related to full membership during January-September 1995. Sweden's food prices, for instance, have not dramatically fallen (as they have done in Finland) as her agriculture was more closely adjusted before accession, while unemployment still remained steady at around eight per cent and interest rates remained stubbornly high. Indeed, the Swedish public perceived that the severe austerity packages of the Social Democratic government were in part, forced upon them because of the government's desire to eventually participate in Economic and Monetary Union (EMU).

The party campaigns during the election were rather lack-lustre. The campaigns can be roughly split into two types – those of the pro and anti-European Union membership parties. For the most part, the pro-European Union parties concentrated on themes which centred on how they intended to influence the future development of Europe. One of the main campaign slogans of the Social Democrats was 'Sätt Europa i arbete' (Put Europe

---

[3] 'Nordic States March to Different EU Tunes', *The Financial Times*, 5 July 1995, p.3.

to Work), while the Liberal's (People's Party) main party slogan was 'Se mojligheterna' (See the Opportunities). However, the pro-European Union parties did not refrain from criticising each other's positions even though they all followed a pro-European Union membership line. The Moderates, for example, led their campaign with the slogan 'Man maste veta vad man vill' (One Must Know What One Wants), which was targeted at the governing Social Democrats and alluded to both their limited success in revitalising Swedish public finances and took a swipe at their internal party division over full membership.

In contrast, the two main anti-European Union parties, the Greens and the Left party emphasised that they were pro-Europe, but against Swedish European Union membership. In particular, the Greens focused on the theme of 'Mot Europa' (which in Swedish is actually a pun as 'Mot' can mean 'against', yet also 'towards'). The Left Party also tended to follow this line and with the Greens, stressed the threats of European Union membership to Swedish social and environmental policy, women's rights, the welfare state and Swedish democracy under the banner 'Mer demokrati – mindre union' (More Democracy-Less Union).

However, the campaign that attracted the most attention and criticism came from the Swedish Centre Party. The Centre Party based its campaign around the slogan, 'Nja till Europa' (which actually translates in English as both 'Yes' and 'No' to Europe at the same time) and argued that they provided the most honest campaign of all the Swedish parties by taking a moderate stand. In theory, the Centre Party claimed that there were both positive and negative benefits to Europe and that this should be seen as the most pragmatic and realistic approach. However, in practice, this campaign was tailored to cater for intra-party opposition, especially within the rural heartland of Sweden where the Party is especially popular and for the most part, the Centre Party was criticised as being indecisive and vague.

The results of the Swedish European parliamentary election were striking. In general, the pro-European Union parties did badly and the anti-European Union parties benefited. The Social Democratic Party (SAP) was the main loser, having gained only 28.1 per cent of the votes, compared to 45.3 per cent in the 1994 general election some twelve months earlier. However, this disastrous result for the Social Democrats cannot be entirely attributed to their pro-European Union stance and did in fact, also reflect their open division on the issue. In addition, they are presently in government and following unpopular austerity policies – hardly likely to be vote-winners.

Although the pro-European Union Liberals also suffered (their share of the vote fell to 4.8 per cent in 1995 from 7.2 per cent in 1994), the Moderate party of the former Prime Minister Carl Bildt (widely regarded as the most solidly pro-European Union party in Swedish politics) slightly improved its share of the vote to 23.1 per cent in 1995 from 22.4 per cent in 1994.

However, in contrast, the clearly anti-European Union parties, the Greens and Left Party did exceedingly well. The Greens, for instance, more than trebled their share of the votes (17.2 per cent compared to 5 per cent in 1994), while the Left Party also doubled its share (12.9 per cent instead of 6.2 per cent). In sum, the results indicate that the Swedish electorate is not enthusiastic about full membership nor the role of the European Parliament.

Indeed, probably the most indicative variable in the Swedish election result was not the levels of party support, but the very poor turnout amongst Swedish voters. The overall turnout, including invalid votes amounted to a mere 41.63 per cent and thus represented less than half of the entire Swedish electorate. For Sweden, this turnout figure was unusual as she has a tradition of very high turnouts in elections; for instance, the turnout for the previous September 1994 general election was 83.3 per cent.

Thus, in many ways, the first Swedish European parliamentary election displayed similar characteristics to those in other member states. The fact that this was a secondary election to a mostly unpopular European institution in Sweden had a dual effect. On the one hand, the electorate was suffering from the problems of electoral fatigue and growing disillusionment regarding the membership issue. Moreover, the fact that a new electoral procedure was also introduced could have also deterred voters. On the other hand, the election also provided a chance for the electorate to register a 'protest' vote at the progress of the minority Social Democratic government, especially as the government had introduced numerous cost-saving reforms aimed at cutting the large budgetary deficit and national debt. To some extent, the very poor performance of the Social Democrats was exaggerated by the fact that they were in government, cutting back public expenditure and trimming welfare state provision, which were all unpopular among their traditional voters.

Similarly, the exceedingly good performance of the Left Party and the Greens can in part, be explained by the transfer of disillusioned Social Democratic voters to these parties. Yet, the success of the Greens and the Left Party must also be due to the fact that these two parties were the two main anti-European Union parties. In particular, as the Social Democrats were internally divided on the issue, these parties acted not only as a reservoir for disillusioned voters, protesting at the national performance of the Social Democratic government, but also for voters across the political spectrum who vehemently oppose full membership. In sum, the Greens and the Left party benefited from both 'protest' votes aimed at the national government and from those focused at European Union membership.

Nevertheless, the outcome of the Swedish direct election does have ramifications for both the Swedish political scene and the European Parliament. As regards Swedish politics, both the Left Party and the Greens were quick to call for a national referendum on whether Sweden should stay in the European Union and for the wider principle of using referenda to approve any further extensions of European Union competencies. Although the former demand is unlikely to succeed and Sweden will continue to remain a full member, the principle of using further referenda to approve any future TEU-based reforms will be more difficult to ignore.

The result of the election will also have implications for the composition of the European Parliament. Prior to the September 1995 election, all of the Swedish MEPs were appointed by the Riksdag, based on the proportion of seats each party held in the national legislature. However, since the direct election, Swedish Social Democratic representation in the Parliament has been reduced from eleven to only seven MEPs, which will severely inhibit its influence on the Socialist Group. In particular, Pauline Green, leader of the Parliament's Socialist Group, claimed the poor Social Democratic performance in Sweden illustrates that

> 'Europe has to deal with issues that affect people's lives. We need to take action on issues, like the Employment Union which the Swedish Social Democrats have been trying to pursue in the Council of Ministers. When the Swedish people see the result of that sort of policy, they will reassess the way they vote.'[4]

The Moderates retained their five seats in the European Parliament, the Centre Party its two and the Liberals their single seat, although the Christian Democrats lost their only seat as a result of a fall in their vote to below the 4 per cent threshold for seats (their vote fell from 4.1 per cent in 1994 to 3.9 per cent in 1995). All these parties will retain their limited influence on their various party groups in the European Parliament.

Nevertheless, whereas the Left Party only had one Euro-MP (and the Greens none) before the election, the Left Party now has three and the Greens four. This will have two effects. First, roughly half of the twenty-two Swedish MEPs have been elected on anti-European Union platforms and could be seen as comparable to Danish 'anti-marketeers'. Secondly, the inclusion of four anti-European Union Swedish Greens will create some tension with the Parliament's Green Group as the Swedish Greens will be joining a Group that is by no means anti-European.

Conclusion

In general then, the 1995 Swedish direct election resulted in resounding victory for the anti-European Union forces. Overall, they (the Greens and Left Party) captured 30.1 per cent of overall vote. In comparison, the pro-European Union forces seemed in disarray. The Social Democrats were divided; even to the point of offering two lists of candidates – one headed by a pro-European Union campaigner and another by an anti-European Union figure. Consequently, their party took just 28.1 per cent; their worst electoral result since 1911.

None the less, despite the up-turn in the Swedish economy, reaching nearly 4 per cent growth in 1995, this has not been equated with the benefits of full membership as the government continues to stress the need for further belt-tightening within the Swedish economy as part of drive towards EMU. Rather the psychological legacy of the pre-accession campaigns led the Swedish public to expect relatively immediate benefits from full membership – something that was always going to be unlikely. Hence, despite the symbolism of the 1995 direct election in Sweden, the country is far from being reconciled with its new role as a full member. The Swedish public are only just beginning to realise that the benefits of European Union membership are more political and considerably more long-term.

---

[4] *Agence Europe*, 19/9/1995, p.3.

The European Union in International Perspective
Richard Whitman
University of Westminster
'The European Union's Southern Flank:
Euro-Mediterranean Partnership or new-found pacifier?'

Introduction

This paper uses the European Union's proposal for a Euro-Mediterranean Partnership (EMP), with the proposal for a Euro-Mediterranean Economic Area (EMEA) as its centrepiece, as a basis from which to illustrate the Union's definition of its security interests in the region. The paper suggests that the EMEA, driven by the declared Union aim of seeking a zone of stability and peace in the region, is the outcome of a set of sources of influence identifiable both from within and without the Union.

The EMP proposal is the latest manifestation of long-standing relationship that was initiated with the signing of Association Agreement's with Greece (1961) and Turkey (1963). Subsequently, the Community policy towards the region has undergone successive revisions. The Commission's own assessment of policy undertaken in recent years is mixed noting that dependence upon Community agricultural exports remained, co-operation among the partners had not substantively increased and that aid from the Community budget only represented an average of 3% of the total aid to the region between 1989 and 1992.[1]

The Corfu European Council meeting in June 1994 mandated the Council, together with the Commission, to evaluate 'the global policy of the European Union in the Mediterranean region and possible initiatives to strengthen this policy in the short and medium term, bearing in mind the possibility of convening a conference attended by the European Union and its Mediterranean partners'.[2] The Commission's response was a proposal for a new EMP launched by the Commission in a communication to the Council in October 1994.[3] Interestingly, in introducing its proposal the Commission drew its rationale from the CFSP annex of the Lisbon European Council conclusions reiterating; 'the Southern and Eastern shores of the Mediterranean as well as the Middle East are geographical areas in relation to which the Union has strong interests both in terms of security and social stability'.

The Commission Communication explicitly excluded a focus upon the countries of the former Yugoslavia. Its primary focus was upon relations with countries of the Maghreb (Morocco, Algeria, Libya and Tunisia)[4],

---

[1] Commission of the European Communities, *Strengthening the Mediterranean Policy of the European Union: Establishing a Euro-Mediterranean Partnership*, COM (94) 427 final Brussels, 19.10.1994.

[2] *Presidency Conclusions*, 24-25 June 1994, European Council at Corfu, Commission of the European Communities, London, SN150/94.

[3] *Strengthening*.

[4] Mauritania was not included with the Maghreb states as it is already covered by the Lome Convention.

Mashreq (Egypt, Lebanon, Jordan and Syria) and Israel and noting the existent relations with Turkey, Malta and Cyprus. The EMP was intended to encompass all of these states of the Mediterranean basin and the European Union. The approach proposed by the Commission was for a strategy of variable geometry progressively updating the existing agreements with the states of the region but also creating sustained support through a programme comparable to PHARE replacing eleven independent financial protocols and costing the Union 5,500 million ecu between 1995-1999.

The notion of a EMP was intended to be an objective, rather than immediately attainable. The process of achieving such a partnership was to come through a twin-track approach of the progressive development of a free trade relationship alongside the increased, and enhanced, provision of financial aid. Through this twin-track approach, accompanied by enhanced political co-operation, there would be a move 'towards a close association, the content of which will be defined at a later stage.'

The EMP was intended to meld a close political dialogue, extending to security issues, with an enhanced economic relationship. In particular, the provision of Community aid was to be furnished for the purposes of structural adjustment and economic restructuring. The economic dimension of the Partnership was to result in the long-term in a EMEA providing for a free-trade area that encompasses the Member States of the Union, the Mediterranean non-Members and any Central and Eastern European country that had not, at that time, acceded to the Union. The free-trade area would provide for reciprocal free-trade in manufactured products and preferential and reciprocal access for agricultural products 'of interest to both sides'. The co-operation was also intended to extend beyond free trade to encompass areas including energy, the environment, drug-trafficking and illegal immigration.

The Commission envisages creating a series of Euro-Mediterranean Agreements with Egypt, Israel, Morocco, Tunisia, Jordan and Lebanon as soon as possible – association agreements to replace the existing co-operation agreements in place.[5] In the near term, five objectives were detailed; the conclusion of, then, current negotiations with Israel, Morocco, Tunisia and Turkey; an increase in technical and financial assistance, in particular through the creation of a MED aid programme; the encouragement of private investment; an 'economic policy dialogue' under the auspices of the Association Agreements; and measures to promote regional co-operation amongst the Mediterranean states.

The Commission defined two primary challenges to the potential to peace and stability in the region to be faced by the Union:

> '– to support political reform, respect for human rights and freedom of expression as a means to contain extremism; – to promote economic reform, leading to sustained growth and improved living standards, a consequent diminution of violence and an easing of migratory pressures'.

---

[5] 'Strengthening the Mediterranean Policy of the European Union: Proposals for Implementing a Euro-Mediterranean Partnership', COM (95) 72 Final.

The Commission also acknowledged the interdependent relationship between the Union and the other states of the region detailed above through the environment, energy supply, migration, trade and investment and the production and smuggling of narcotics. The European Council meeting in Essen approved the recommendation of the Council supporting the EMP and endorsed the proposal for a Euro-Mediterranean Ministerial Conference in the latter half of 1995[6]

The Euro-Mediterranean conference in Barcelona between 27-28 November 1995 brought together the European Union and twelve Mediterranean countries. Libya remained uninvited. The Union's position at the conference was somewhat contrastive to the other states of the region who lack a collective common position. As a Jordanian diplomat noted prior to the conference, 'Barcelona will be the European Union facing 12 countries, each with its own agenda and not listening to the others'.[7] The two-day Barcelona conference was the first occasion in which Israel, Syria and the Lebanon will have attended the same multilateral forum. The conference illustrated differences between the European Union and the Mediterranean non-Members with the non-Members preferring a greater stress on the economic rather than the political and Tunisia and Algeria favouring Libya's participation.

For its part the Union proposed two main elements to form the basis of the partnership established through the conference.[8] Firstly, a political and security partnership described as establishing a common area of peace and stability and founded upon the adoption of a declaration of principles by all the partners setting objectives for internal and external security in two broad areas human rights, democracy and the rule of law and stability, security and good-neighbourly relations. Secondly, an economic and financial partnership, building a zone of shared prosperity, through the trade and aid relationship detailed above.

The launching of the new EMP in Barcelona can be read as the outcome of individual European Union Member States as sources of influence upon the European Union policy-making process. The Barcelona Conference represented the centrepiece of the Spanish Presidency of the Union and the Italian government has signalled its commitment to pursue the Partnership as one of the priorities of its Presidency. In attempts to create the EMP France pressed Germany, during the latter's Presidency, to ensure that the Mediterranean was given priority.[9] Likewise, Spain and Italy sought to jointly prepare their positions for the Euro-Mediterranean conference by bringing together their respective ambassadors from sixteen Mediterranean countries in preparatory work.[10] The Union has also committed itself to enhancing its Mediterranean profile through accession. The

---

[6] *Presidency Conclusions*, 9-10 December 1994 Essen, Commission of the European Communities, Annex Council report for the European Council in Essen concerning the future Mediterranean Policy.

[7] 'Barcelona Euro-Med conference to be a turning point', *Reuters Euro Community Report*, Aug 9, 1995.

[8] 'Conclusions of Cannes June 26-27 Summit', *Reuters' Euro Community Report*, 28 June 1995.

[9] 'Terror threat tops Union agenda', *The European*, 5-11 August 1994, p.1.

[10] *Agence Europe*, 11 May 1995, p.11.

Union has embarked upon a structured dialogue and a pre-accession strategy with Cyprus and Malta prior to the opening of membership negotiations within six months of the completion of the 1996 Intergovernmental Conference. The decision to set a date for the negotiations was a quid pro quo required by Greece for the conclusion of the Turkey customs union agreement.[11]

The process of ratification of the Customs Union agreement with Turkey demonstrated the European Parliament's (EP) interest in the policy towards the region and its willingness to influence Union policy through the means at its disposal. The EP has used the assent procedure to demonstrate its displeasure of the domestic policies of third parties since it first exercised the power of assent on international agreements in September 1987. In December 1987 the Parliament postponed voting on two protocols under the Association Agreement with Turkey in protest at the arrest of a number of politicians in Turkey and in March 1988 the EP refused to assent to three agreements with Israel. The Parliament has frozen protocols containing aid provisions for Morocco, because of failure to implement UN resolutions on the Western Sahara, and aid to Syria because of human rights concerns.

Defining the Union's security interests

In a wide-ranging survey on the security aspects of European integration in 1991, Jacques Delors defined the Community's 'Southern flank', encompassing the Maghreb, the Mashreq and the Middle East, and the requirement for economic development by the states of the region as a pre-requisite for the peace and stability of the region.[12] The re-emergence of a concern with trans-Mediterranean threats, alongside a newly-defined agenda for intra-European security was a part of the re-formulation of the European security order in the aftermath of the Cold and Gulf Wars.

In focusing upon the potential security threats that impact upon the Member States of the Union from the Mediterranean region commentators have noted the interdependent relationship that exists with the region. The suggestion is that the primary threats to European security in the region are not derived from the malevolent use of state power directed against European Union Member States but rather from the partial, or full, collapse of the existing political authorities.[13] Interrelated sources of instability that have been identified encompass economic performance and energy supply; demographic change and population movements; Islamic rivalism and cultural difference; terrorism; drugs trafficking; conventional and unconventional weapons proliferation. At their most acute elements are brought together in the conflagration of Algeria.

---

[11] *The European*, 28 July-3 August 1995, p.4.

[12] J.Delors, 'European integration and security', *Survival*, XXIII, 2 1991 pp.99-109.

[13] E.Mortimer, 'Europe and the Mediterranean: The Security Dimension', in P.Ludlow (ed), *Europe and the Mediterranean*, Brassey's for CEPS, 1994.

Economy and energy

The economic contrast between the European Union member states and the Med countries can be noted by the contrasting figures of average GDP per head with a figure of $19,242 for the Union and $1,589 for Southern and Eastern Mediterranean countries.[14] The Mediterranean countries provide 24% of the total European Union energy imports, 32% of the imports of natural gas and 27% of oil imports. However, there is a disproportion between the European Union Member States who are reliant upon the producers of the southern and eastern Mediterranean; Spain, France, Italy, Greece and Portugal derive 24% of their oil supplies from the region; Spain, France, Italy, and soon Portugal and Greece derive 42% of their gas supplies from the region.[15]

The European Union is physically linked to supply from the region via the Transmed pipeline carrying Algerian gas to Italy, via Tunisia, and the Maghreb-Europe pipeline, under construction, to carry Algerian gas via Morocco to Spain and Portugal. An electricity interconnection is also intended to come on stream between Morocco and Spain in 1996. The volume of future energy exports from the region to the European Union, and their relative share of total European Union energy imports, is dependent upon the increase of the Med countries population and economic growth and consequent enhanced domestic energy demand together with the ability to attract sufficient investment to enhance production and distribution infrastructure. The Commission has sought enhance the energy relationship through the SYNERGY programme promoting energy co-operation. Representatives from both government and private industry from both the Med states and the European Union Member States energy sectors adopted the Tunis Declaration as an input into the Barcelona Conference.[16]

Demographic change and population movements

Projected global population growth and its impact upon both the natural environment and human societies has been noted as a future determinant of global affairs.[17] The European Union abuts onto a region that is projected to have considerable population growth in contrast to its own projected population decline. European Union population is projected to fall to peak in 2000 and to decline to 300 million by 2100.

World Bank projections suggest a 58% increase in population across the Partnership countries between 1990 and 2010, even with a doubling of GDP by 2010 the wealth gap between the European Union and the Maghreb and Mashreq countries would increase from the present one to ten to a level of one to twenty.[18] However, considerable differences exist in population

---

[14] 'Europe and the Mediterranean', Background Report Commission of the European Communities, December 1994, ISEC/B21. The figures exclude Cyprus and Malta.

[15] 'The Mediterranean Region in 2020 and its role in the European Energy Network', Commission of the European Communities MEMO/95/52.

[16] 'European Union and the Mediterranean Countries put their energy act together in Tunis', Commission of the European Communities IP/95/283 27/03/95.

[17] P.Kennedy, *Preparing for the Twenty-First Century*, Harper Collins, 1993.

[18] 'Economic and Social Development in the Middle East and North Africa', Discussion

growth across the region with Algeria, Morocco and Tunisia with declining rates of population growth.[19]

The Member States are home to 4.6 million immigrants from the Mediterranean non-members and the distribution of these immigrants across the Union has generated a stronger concern for a Mediterranean policy in some quarters than in others.[20]

Terrorism

The concern of the Member States with the location of terrorism in Western Europe as an emergent common threat to security was reflected in the creation of the Trevi group in 1976 and the burgeoning intergovernmental infrastructure that was codified in Title VI of the Treaty on European Union. With Western Europe as the location for eighty-eight international terrorist incidents in 1994, second in volume only to the Middle East, the concern of the Member States to combat terrorism represents a perennial security concern.[21]

In particular, the operations of groups originating in the Mediterranean and directing violence against the citizens or property of the Member States in 1994 encompassed Hizballah in the Lebanon, the Turkish-based left-wing group Devrimci Sol (Dev Sol) and the Kurdish Workers' Party (PKK), the Algerian-based Armed Islamic Group (AIG) and the Egyptian-based Islamic Group (IG).

Islamic rivalism and difference

Samuel Huntington delineated the Mediterranean as one of the faultlines of the new era of the clash of civilisations intended to take the place of the Cold War with Western and Islamic civilisations opposed to one another.[22] Drawing the inference that Islamic rivalism has political implications for the Union does not equate with an acceptance of the Clash of Civilisations hypothesis. Rather, from the perspective of the security of the Union three elements would appear pertinent; the uncertainty generated by Islamic rivalist movements and their challenges to existing regimes; the compatibility of Islam to modernity, and in particular capitalism; and the extent to which Islamicist regimes would represent a direct threat to the Union. However, 'coming to terms with political Islam' has been adopted as a strategic policy

---

paper series 3, October 1992.

[19] Annual population growth in Algeria and Morocco has moved downwards, respectively, from the 3.14% and 2.45% recorded in 1975-1980 to the 2.27% and 2.06% of current estimations. The current figure for Tunisia is 2.3% projected to decline to 1.19% between 2010 and 2020. 'Politics mask N.African population successes', *Financial Times*, 15 February 1995 p.5.

[20] For a discussion of the emigrant communities and as a composed across the Union see Y.Courbage, 'Demographic Transition among the Maghreb Peoples of North Africa and in the Emigrant Community Abroad', in P.Ludlow, *Europe and the Mediterranean*, Brassey's for CEPS, 1994.

[21] *Patterns of Global Terrorism*, 1994.

[22] S.Huntington, 'The Clash of Civilizations?', *Foreign Affairs*, Summer 1993, pp.22-49.

issue.[23] The notion that the South represents the most serious contemporary threat to Europe is particularly evident in France.[24]

Conclusion

The Union has embarked upon a new strategic partnership for the Mediterranean as a counterpoint to its strategy towards central and eastern Europe. However, in contrast to Europe the Mediterranean region lacks the proliferation of institutions that can be identified in Europe. The Conference on Security and Co-operation in the Mediterranean (CSCM) proposed by Italy and Spain in September 1990 that would extend beyond the Mediterranean basin to encompass the Middle East has not been realised. The assertion of this paper is that, in the absence of such a multilateral structure the EMP represents an attempt by the Union to play the leading role in the pacification of sources of potential instability in the region.

---

[23] See, for example *Strategic Survey 1993-1994*, IISS, 1994.
[24] M.Blunden, 'Insecurity on Europe's Southern Flank' *Survival*, 36/2, 1994, pp.134-148.

The European Union in International Perspective

Andreas Kintis
University of Hull

'Two Years of CFSP: A Review'

Introduction

The demise of the bipolar Cold War international system forced the European Union to contemplate its future following its elevation into the position of 'a superpower in the making'. It also generated debate concerning the role of the European Union in the international and regional milieux as a prosperous and mature representative of the Western block of advanced capitalist democratic states, particularly after the inclination of the United States towards the ceding of its leading role to Europe opting instead for an equal partnership with her. In this situation the Treaty on European Union (TEU) transformed European Political Cooperation (EPC) into Common Foreign and Security Policy (CFSP).

CFSP Provisions

Title V of the Treaty on European Union contains the main provisions governing the CFSP.[1]

Title V, like Title III of the Single European Act (SEA), remains strictly intergovernmental escaping the ECJ's control (Article L). Article C of the Common Provisions of the TEU requests for consistency between action under the CFSP and under the Community Treaties in the context of the Union's 'external relations, security, economic and development policies'. The Council and the Commission have a shared responsibility to ensure such a consistency. Article C provides for a single institutional framework to serve the European Union. However, it should be noted that Article E confined the power conferred on the Community's institutions to the provisions of Title V by stipulating that their operation is governed by different rules in the Community Treaties on the one hand and the CFSP on the other.

The objectives of the CFSP are laid down in Article J.1.2. These objectives are to be realised through 'systematic cooperation' (Article J.2) and 'joint action' (Article J.3). Article J.2 constitutes basically a continuation of the EPC. However, it modestly enhances Article 30.2 of the SEA by being couched in a mandatory form. Article J.3 represents a significant and important expansion of the EPC's level of commitment and range of policy instruments. Under Article J.3.1 the Council on the basis of general guidelines from the European Council decides unanimously whether a foreign policy issue should be the subject of joint action, its specific scope, the Union's general and specific objectives in carrying out such action, its duration and

---

[1] See Andreas Kintis, 'The EU's CFSP: transition to a single foreign policy?', in J.Lovenduski & J.Stanyer (eds), *Contemporary Political Studies 1995*, PSA, Volume III, 1995.

its means, procedures and conditions for its implementation. However, it is the following proviso (Article J.3.2) that breached new grounds by providing for the possibility of qualified majority voting every time the specific details for implementing joint action has to be taken. Once a joint action is adopted it commits the member states in the positions they adopt and in the conduct of their activity (Article J.3.4).

Article J.4 constitutes a major breakthrough in the taboo area of defence by extending Article 30.6 of the SEA to 'include all questions related to the security of the Union, including the eventual framing of a common defence policy, which might in time lead to a common defence' (Article J.4.1). The new CFSP provisions call for the Western European Union (WEU) 'which is an integral part of the development of the Union, to elaborate and implement decisions and actions of the Union which have defence implications'. With respect to the inclusion for the first time of a defence dimension, three points have to be made. First, defence issues are not subject to qualified majority voting (Article J.4.3). Secondly, CFSP must respect any existing obligations on member states in the NATO framework (Article J.4.4). Thirdly, CFSP should not impede the development of bilateral defence cooperation within the WEU or NATO (Article J.4.5).

The remaining Articles of Title V endorse marginal adjustments of the EPC's practice. Maastricht provides for a rejuvenated Council; the Commission is granted a non-exclusive right of initiative (Article J.8.3); the EPC Secretariat is merged with the Council's General Secretariat; the role of the Presidency is confirmed while the Troika procedure is formally recognised; and the 48-hour emergency procedure is modified. Finally, CFSP's administrative expenditure is financed from the Community's budget whereas operational expenditure is to be charged either on the Community budget or to the member states in accordance with a scale to be decided (Article J.11.2).

CFSP in practice

Since the entry into force of the Treaty on European Union in November 1993 and until September 1995, the Council has adopted nineteen joint actions. These concerned:

Humanitarian aid to Bosnia-Herzegovina and the EU Administration of Mostar[2]

In the first CFSP joint action, the Council decided after having received the European Council's general guidelines (29 October), to increase its contribution towards the resources placed at the disposal of the Office of the United Nations High Commissioner for refugees and support the convoying of international aid, in particular through the identification, restoration and preservation of priority routes.

In seven subsequent renewals and extensions, the Council: (i) set a budget of ECU 48.3 million to finance the convoying of humanitarian aid, and

---

[2] Council Decision 93/603/CFSP of 8 November.

decided that half of the amount would be borne by the Community budget; (ii) extended the application of Decision 93/603 until 30 September 1994; (iii) amended its Decision of November 1993 so as to allocate ECU 32 million, from the budget of ECU 48.3 million to finance the administration of Mostar. The Council decided that the administrator would assess the requirements and the means necessary to finance them and, in the light of this information, the Presidency, assisted by an advisory working party composed of representatives of the Member States and in association with the Commission, would issue guidelines and determine what measures were needed to meet the requirements, and decide to release the necessary sums in instalments. The administrator would carry out the measures and report regularly to the Presidency. The Member StatesU shares of the ECU 24.15 million to be contributed by them in accordance with the Decision was determined by means of the GNP scale. The Decision extended the application of Decision 93/603/CFSP, as amended, until 31 December 1994; (iv) established the procedure for disbursing a sum of ECU 7.15 million as part of the Member StatesU contributions to the joint action to support humanitarian aid convoys in Bosnia-Herzegovina; (v) further extended the application of Decision 93/603 until 31 December 1995; (vi) ensured continued financing of the joint action in Mostar for 1995; (vii) set the total budget corresponding to the requirements for European Union administration of the town of Mostar at a maximum of ECU 80 million.

Dispatch of a team of observers for the parliamentary elections in the Russian Federation[3]

On the basis of the general guidelines established by the European Council meeting in Brussels, the Council sent a team of observers to cover the December 1993 parliamentary elections, and also the election campaign, in accordance with the wishes of the Russian authorities. The European Union was to coordinate its efforts in conjunction with the international organizations concerned, including the Council of Europe and the then Conference on Security and Cooperation in Europe (CSCE). To these ends a Special Coordination and Reception Unit was set up, with which the Commission was fully associated.

Support for the transition towards a democratic and multiracial South Africa[4]

On the basis of the general guidelines issued by the European Council meeting in Brussels in October the Council approved the implementation of a coordinated programme of assistance for preparing and monitoring the April 1994 elections in South Africa. The programme comprised the provision of advisory services, technical assistance and training, and also the provision of a number of European observers forming a 'European Electoral Unit' acting in the framework of an overall international effort coordinated by the United Nations.

---

[3] Council Decision 93/604/CFSP of 9 November.
[4] Council Decision 93/678/CFSP of 6 December.

Stability pact in Europe[5]

On the basis of the general guidelines established by the meetings of the European Council in Brussels in October and December the Council convened in Paris in May 1994 a conference on a pact on stability in Europe. The conference put into effect preventive diplomacy aimed at fostering good neighbourly relations and encouraging countries, in particular through the conclusion of appropriate agreements, to consolidate their borders and to resolve the problems of national minorities which arise. On 14 June 1994 the Council decided to continue the joint action on the stability pact.

Support for the Middle East peace process[6]

On the basis of the general guidelines issued by the European Council meetings in Brussels in October and December 1993 the Council decided to participate in international arrangements agreed by the parties to guarantee peace, use its influence to encourage all the parties to support the peace process unconditionally and work for the strengthening of democracy and respect for human rights, and consider additional ways in which it might contribute towards the development of the region. In addition, the European Union was to continue its contacts with a view to obtaining an end to the boycott of Israel by the Arab states, follow closely the future of Israeli settlements throughout the Occupied Territories, pursue the confidence-building measures which it had submitted to the parties, provide assistance for the creation of a Palestinian police force by releasing as a matter of urgency ECU 10 million from the Community budget, participate in the protection of the Palestinian people through a temporary international presence in the Occupied Territories, and assist in preparing for and observing the elections to be held in the Occupied Territories.

Non-proliferation of nuclear weapons[7]

The objective of the joint action was to strengthen the international nuclear non-proliferation system by promoting the universality of the Non-Proliferation Treaty (NPT) and by extending it indefinitely and unconditionally. It included approaches to non-Community countries not yet party to the NPT, and the possibility of assisting them with a view to accession and establishing the procedures necessary for meeting obligations under the Treaty, if possible before the 1995 Conference of Signatories to the NPT. The European Union was also to try to help build a consensus around its approach to nuclear non-proliferation with an eye to the conference.

Dual-use goods[8]

The Decision provided for the establishment of a common system for the control of exports of dual-use goods to non-EU countries. Council Decision

---

[5] Council Decision 93/728/CFSP of 20 December.
[6] Council Decision 94/276/CFSP of 19 April.
[7] Council Decision 94/509/CFSP of 25 July.
[8] Council Decision 94/942/CFSP of 19 December.

95/127/CFSP postponed the entry into force of Decision 94/942/CFSP until 1 July 1995.

Anti-personnel mines[9]

The aim of this joint action was to help combat the indiscriminate use and spread of anti-personnel land mines which are very dangerous for civilian populations. The action aimed at increasing the chances of success of the Conference to Review the Convention on Prohibitions or Restrictions on the Use of Certain Conventional Weapons which may be deemed to be excessively injurious or to have indiscriminate effects. The joint action entailed a common moratorium on exports of anti-personnel mines, active preparation of the 1980 Convention Review Conference, and a contribution by the European Union to international mine clearance.

Pursuant to Article J.2 the Council also decided to take seventeen common positions. These are the following:

- *Libya*: Council Decision 93/614/CFSP with regard to the reduction of relations with Libya;

- *Sudan*: Council Decision 94/165/CFSP concerning the imposition of an embargo on arms, munitions and military equipment on Sudan;

- *Haiti*: Council Decision 94/315/CFSP regarding the reduction of economic relations with Haiti. Council Decision 94/681/CFSP regarding the termination of the reduction of economic relations with Haiti;

- *Former Yugoslavia*: Council Decision 94/366/CFSP concerning prohibition of the satisfaction of the claims referred to in paragraph 9 of United Nation's Security Council Resolution 757. Council Decision 94/672/CFSP concerning the reduction of economic and financial relations with those parts of the territory of the Republic of Bosnia-Herzegovina under the control of the Bosnian Serb forces. Council Decision 94/673/CFSP regarding the suspension of certain restrictions on trade with the Federal Republic of Yugoslavia (Serbia and Montenegro). Council Decision 95/11/CFSP regarding the extension of the suspension of certain restrictions on trade with the Federal Republic of Yugoslavia. Common position 95/150/CFSP regarding the extension of the suspension of certain restrictions on trade with the Federal Republic of Yugoslavia. Common position 95/213/CFSP on the suspension of certain restrictions on trade with the Federal Republic of Yugoslavia. Common position 95/254/CFSP regarding the extension of the suspension of certain restrictions on trade with the Federal Republic of Yugoslavia. Common position 95/378/CFSP regarding the extension of the suspension of certain restrictions on trade with the Federal Republic of Yugoslavia;

---

[9]Council Decision 95/170/CFSP of 12 May.

- *Rwanda*: Council Decision 94/697/CFSP on the objectives and priorities of the European Union vis-a-vis Rwanda;
- *Ukraine*: Council Decision 94/779/CFSP on the objectives and priorities of the European Union towards Ukraine;
- *Burundi*: Common Position 95/91/CFSP with regard to Burundi. Council Decision 95/206/CFSP with regard to Burundi;
- Common position 95/379/CFSP concerning blinding lasers.

The results produced by the CFSP are not limited to defining common positions and adopting joint actions but encompass, in addition to a large number of declarations which express an EU concern about the situation in a particular country or with regard to an international issue, the many contacts and approaches which are an integral part of conducting foreign policy.

A brief assessment

It is not easy to assess the initial performance of the CFSP. Considering the results described above, the immediate question that arises is whether this new machinery is adequate to cope with the new challenges for the Union's external dimension. Opinions differ:

> 'Some point to not inconsiderable results, not only in terms of quantity, but also of quality, and consider that a 'running-in' period is normal in an area which is at the heart of national sovereignty. Others, on the other hand, referring in particular to former Yugoslavia, say they are disappointed by the results obtained so far, which they regard as falling short of initial ambitions, and question the effectiveness of the means offered by the Treaty.'[10]

No doubt CFSP has its shortcomings, which are of various kinds. Some are real structural weaknesses such as the confusion about the role of joint actions and common positions or the financing of CFSP. Other inadequacies are the result of the failure to apply the Treaty. These have nothing to do with the Treaty itself, which has potential that has not been exploited. For instance, the possibility which exists of taking decisions by qualified majority voting has only been used once in the joint action concerning anti-personnel mines. In addition some of the limitations of the foreign and security policy emanate from the existence of separate pillars for the conduct of the European Union's external activities.

Whatever the reasons for the difficulties inherent in the Treaty's CFSP design, it is becoming increasingly apparent that 'the provisions of the Treaty cannot alone provide ready-made solutions to problems, but only the means to tackle them. The political will to act is a determining factor in the proper use of the instruments of the Treaty'.[11] As Nuttall observed:

---

[10] *Report of the Council on the functioning of the Treaty on European Union*, p.25.
[11] *Report of the Council on the functioning of the Treaty on European Union*, p.25.

> 'The question is not whether the Community succeeded or failed [in former Yugoslavia], but whether it had the means of fulfilling its ambitions, and if not, whether it prefers to give itself the means or abandon its ambitions.'[12]

However, that requires political vision. Because 'where there is no vision, the people perish'. This is the spirit which should prevail in the 1996 Intergovernmental Conference.

---

[12] Simon Nuttall, 'The EC and Yugoslavia – Deus ex Machina or Machina sine Deo', *Journal of Common Market Studies*, 32, 1994, p.25.

European Citizenship and
European Union Justice and Home Affairs

Jörg Monar
University of Leicester

'European Union Justice and Home Affairs:
the deficits and reform possibilities of a policy area
of major concern to European citizens'

Introduction

The final report produced by the Reflection Group preparing the European Union Intergovernmental Conference of 1996 shows that the Group had considerable difficulties to agree unanimously on concrete receommendations for the reform of the European Union. One of the few points on which there emerged a clear consensus within the Group was that a key element for the success of the Conference would be 'to place the citizen at the centre of the European venture by endeavouring to meet his expectations and concerns, that is to say, to make Europe the affair of the citizen'.[1] To any reform effort leading into that direction the development of the Citizenship of the Union is obviously central.[2] However, there are also a number of policy fields of the European Union which will certainly have a major impact on the Union's eventual success or failure to 'to make Europe the affair of the citizen'. One of these policy areas is a rather new one: 'cooperation in the fields of justice and home affairs' established by Title VI of the Union Treaty, commonly referred to as the 'Third Pillar'. So far the Third Pillar has attracted comparatively little attention, being still considered a subject for 'specialists' rather than one of general interest. Yet the political importance of cooperation in the fields of justice and home affairs for the relations between the Union and its citizens as well as for the Union's development in general is enormous, and this for two reasons.

First, the policy areas covered by the Third Pillar are of direct relevance to some of the major concerns of the citizens of the European Union. It seems hardly exaggerated to say that issues like internal security, the combat against drug addiction and organized crime and the problems of immigration are much closer to immediate interests of the citizens than, for example, the question of a common currency or of a more efficient common foreign and security policy. The major role the topics of immigration and internal security played in the 1995 Presidential elections in France is just one example for the importance European citizens attach to these issues and of the political importance they have acquired at the national level. As a result, the 'Third Pillar' represents both a chance and a danger for the European Union: A chance because the development at the Union level of

---

[1] *Report of the Reflection Group*, SN 520/95 (REFLEX 21), Brussels 5th December 1995, paragraph 29.
[2] Dr.Siofra O'Leary's and dr.Antje Wiener's contributionson European Citizenship to this panel could not be finished in time for the publication of these proceedings. They will be published elsewhere.

comprehensive policies and effective measures in these fields could greatly help to increase the citizens' confidence in the Union and to restore some of the legitimacy the integration process has lost during the last years. But a danger as well because a failure of the Union in these policy fields will inevitably be seen by the Union's citizens as another major proof for the Union's incapacity to address effectively issues which really matter for them.

Second, it is precisely within the domain of the Third Pillar that the European Union will have to face one of the biggest challenges of many years, perhaps even decades, to come: the challenge of international migration. Although none of the Member States of the Union considers itself to be a country of immigration the increasing flows of international migration and abuses of their asylum systems have already transformed some of them into de facto countries of immigration, a development which is connected with enormous political, social and economic problems. The increasing migration pressure and the abolition of internal borders inside of the Union make it impossible for the Member States to find adequate responses to this major challenge on an individual basis. A common response at the Union level appears to be more and more urgent. In a similar way this is also true for other fields covered by the Third Pillar such as the combat against international organized crime and drug addiction.

The purpose of this contribution is to examine the present functioning of the Third Pillar and possibilities of its reform and further development by the Intergovernmental Conference of 1996.

The origins of the Third Pillar and its place in the Union Treaty

Any assessment of cooperation in the fields of justice and home affairs since the entry into force of the Union Treaty in November 1993 has to take into account the recent origins of the Third Pillar. When introduced in the Union Treaty cooperation in the fields of justice and home affairs did not have any political and legal basis comparable to those of the other two pillars: There was neither an 'acquis communautaire' grown over almost 40 years nor twenty years of continuously developed procedures and experience with intergovernmental cooperation in the sphere of EPC.

As a primarily economic treaty the EEC Treaty of 1957 had made no direct reference to matters related to justice and home affairs. It was only in the mid-1970s that the Member States gradually started to engage in cooperation on an a number of internal security issues such as the combat against terrorism and international drug trafficking in the intergovernmental 'TREVI' framework of European Political Cooperation. This first effort, however, did not go beyond more or less regular meetings of Member State representatives and an increased level of mutual information.

It needed a number of new driving factors in the 1980s to make the Member States look for more progress in the area of justice and home affairs. These were the successful political relaunch of the European integration process from 1984 on, the growing awareness of the importance of freedom of movement for all persons reflected in the 1985 Adonnino Report on a

'Europe of the citizens', the signing in 1985 of the Schengen Agreement on the abolition of internal border controls by the Benelux countries, France and Germany, the progressive removal of barriers at internal frontiers after the Single European Act (1987) and the increasing problems of immigration and of international crime since the mid-1980s. As a result of these various factors an increasing number of groups dealing with compensatory measures for the removal of internal border controls were set up which covered central fields of justice and home affairs such as asylum, immigration, visa policy and external border controls. However, what emerged was an increasingly non-transparent and confusing set of bodies and cooperation frameworks in which decision-making was extremely slow, fragmentated and in most cases of a non-binding nature. Being particularly concerned by the increased influx of migrants from Central and Eastern Europe since 1989 and the increasingly unstable situation in this part of Europe it was mainly the Federal Republic of Germany which at the Luxembourg European Council in 1991 put justice and home affairs as a central issue on the agenda of the Intergovernmental Conference on Political Union, with Chancellor Kohl insisting upon the need to take initiatives regarding the fields of asylum policy and immigration policy as well as of the creation of a European police authority. Before and still during the Intergovernmental Conference several Member States, the United Kingdom in particular,[3] were rather reluctant to engage in any form of common policy-making in the fields of justice and home affairs. In the end a compromise emerged: Justice and home affairs were included in the Union Treaty but not within the Community pillar and its supranational method of decision-making as the European Parliament and some of the Member States had wished. Instead a separate part – Title VI of the Treaty – was introduced which put cooperation in the fields of justice and home affairs on an intergovernmental basis rather similar to that of the Common Foreign and Security Policy (former European Political Cooperation).

Taking into account the previous situation the introduction of justice and home affairs in the framework of the Union Treaty was clearly a pioneer deed, and this in at least four respects:

First, the Treaty defines – in Article K.1 – an ambitious set of areas of common interest ranging from asylum and immigration policy over the combat against all major forms of international crime to judicial, customs and police cooperation. It seems not exaggerated to speak about a real revolution of the formerly limited and fragmentated fields of cooperation.

Second, the Treaty provides for a single institutional framework for all these areas of cooperation, putting an end to the multiplication and fragmentation of bodies and procedures which had taken place previously.

Third, the Treaty defines a number of specific legal instruments for cooperation in the fields of justice and home affairs, that is, 'joint positions', 'joint actions' and 'conventions' (Article K.3.2).[4]

---

[3] The British attitude is well described in Kenneth Baker (Home Secretary 1991-92), *The Turbulent Years*, 1993, pp.439-444.

[4] Article K.5 provides also for 'common positions' which the Member States shall defend within international organizations and at international conferences. It is not clear whether or no this refers to 'joint positions' as mentioned in Article K.3.2.

Fourth, the Treaty brings intergovernmental cooperation in justice and home affairs closer to the integrated community structure than ever before. Although still essentially an intergovernmental framework of cooperation the Third Pillar is closely linked to the first by

- the roles given to the Community institutions by, in particular, the right of initiative of the Commission (Article K.3.2) and its full association (Article K.4.2), the central decision-making authority of the Council (Article K.3.2), the involvement of the European Parliament (Article K.6);

- the inclusion of certain Community features such as the possibility of qualified majority voting on certain measures of implementation (Article K.3.2(b)) and the use of the Community budget (Article K.8.2);

- the 'passerelle' of Article K.9 which allows to apply Article 100c of the European Community Treaty and its 'Community method' of decision-making to action in areas referred to in Article K.1(1) to (6).

Taken together all this can certainly be regarded as a first major breakthrough, from a political, a constitutional and an institutional point of view.

The Third Pillar two and a half years after its establishment: a critical assessment

While there can be no doubt about the substantial breakthrough achieved in the Union Treaty the picture is clearly less positive if one comes to the question what concrete progress has been made on the basis of the new provisions after the entry into force of the Union Treaty in November 1993.

An analysis of the decisions taken by the Council shows that the use of the new legal instruments provided for by Article K.3.2 has been very limited: Only two 'joint actions' of a rather limited scope [5] and four 'conventions',[6] have been adopted until now (January 1996). Even those have been arrived at only after difficult and protracted negotiations although the matters covered by these acts had been under discussion already well before the entry

---

[5] Decision 94-795/JAI on a joint action adopted by the Council on the basis of Article K.3.2(b) of the Treaty on European Union concerning travel facilities for school pupils from third countries resident in a Member State (OJ No L 327, 19.12.1994) and Joint action concerning the Europol Drugs Unit on the basis of Article K.3(2)(b) of the Treaty on European Union (OJ No L 62, 20.3.1995).

[6] The Convention on the simplified extradition procedure between the Member States of the European Union (OJ No L 78, 30.3.1995) the Convention on the establishment of Europol, the Convention on the use of information technology for customs purposes (CIS) and the Convention on the protection of the Community's financial interests. The last three conventions have only been signed on 26 July 1995, following to a political 'package deal' on the controversial question of the possible jurisdiction attributed to the Court of Justice of the European Community which was agreed on at the Cannes European Council of 26/27 June. These conventions still have to be ratified, and the question of the role of the Court under the Europol Convention is still not definitely settled. The Heads of State and Government have decided to do so at the latest at their meeting in June 1996.

into force of the Union Treaty. One also has to note that the Member States have until know failed to adopt a single 'joint position'.

On the other hand there are several other conventions (such as the Draft Convention on the crossing of external frontiers) under discussion, and since the entry into force of the Union Treaty the Council has adopted roughly sixty non-binding texts such as resolutions, recommendations or conclusions. One also has to note that there has been a considerable quantitative increase in meetings of the various bodies involved in justice and home affairs since the entry into force of the Union Treaty.[7]

The huge discrepancy between, on one hand, the few legal acts adopted and, on the other hand, the many legal acts under discussion, the many non-binding measures adopted and the considerable increase in meetings since the TEU has entered into force clearly shows that there is a major 'blocage' in the Third Pillar. It is not very difficult to identify the reasons for this 'blocage' stemming from 'inside' the Third Pillar.

(1) A particularly cumbersome multi-level structure of decision-making

Title VI has introduced a co-ordinating committee for justice and home affairs consisting of the senior officials responsible for this area of policy-making. Yet this committee, commonly called 'K.4 Committee', has not replaced the COREPER in its role as central preparatory body for the decisions of the ministers in the Council. As a result a five-level structure of decision-making has emerged which consists of

(a) the Working Parties;

(b) the Steering Groups;

(c) the K.4 Committee;

(d) the COREPER;

(e) the Justice and Home Affairs Council.

This means that there are two more levels of decision-making in the Third Pillar – the Steering Groups and the K.4 Committee – than in the already heavy-going Community structure. In addition, the division of tasks between the K.4 Committee and the COREPER has not yet been fully clarified. By all this the decision-making process is considerably slowed down and subject to frictions between the various bodies involved.

(2) The predominance of the unanimity rule

Practice has shown that the requirement of unanimity for the adoption of joint actions, joint positions, conventions as well as the use of the 'passerelle' of Article K.9 leads in most cases to a compromise with far less than optimal results. A good example is the Convention on the simplified extradition

---

[7] According to Commissioner Anita Gradin over 250 meetings took place within the framework of Title VI until mid-May 1995 (speech given at the Europäisches Forum in Bonn, 11 May 1995).

procedures between the Member States of the European Union, which, because of the need to arrive at a consensus in the end became a much less comprehensive instrument than originally intended. The 'lowest common denominator effect' can be clearly seen at work in all areas covered by the Third Pillar. In addition, decisions on major issues can even be totally blocked due to difficulties of a small minority. The blocking of the Convention on Controls of Persons Crossing External Frontiers of the Member States because of the dispute between the United Kingdom and Spain over the status of Gibraltar provides the most well-known example in this respect.

(3) The limited role of initiative played until now by the Commission

Partly for tactical reasons (because it wanted to avoid counterproductive conflicts with the Member States in an area almost exclusively of their competence), partly because of its relatively weak position (by virtue of Article K.3.2 the Commission has only a non-exclusive right of initiative which is, in addition, limited to six out of nine of the areas defined in Article K.9) the Commission has not developed a very active role within the Third Pillar area. Although it has taken a few initiatives of major importance such as the proposals of December 1993 of a draft external frontiers convention and a draft visa regulation, it cannot at present be regarded as a driving force in the Third Pillar.

(4) The difficulties as regards the division of competences between the European Community and the intergovernmental sphere

The European Community Treaty provides for a number of competences of the European Community which are of central relevance for justice and home affairs. The most important of these are the European Community competences for the free movement of persons (Article 7a European Community Treaty), visa policy (Article 100c European Community Treaty), Customs Union (Articles 9-29 European Community Treaty), public health (Article 129 European Community Treaty), and measures countering fraud against the financial interests of the Community (Article 209a European Community Treaty). In a number of cases this has led to confusion on the legal basis to be chosen and controversies around overlapping competences. Decision-making has been further complicated and slowed down.

(5) The uncertainties as regards the nature and the scope of the legal instruments of Title VI

Title VI does not give a clear definition of the legal instruments it provides for. Although there are now two examples of 'joint actions', their legal nature and scope are still far from clear. They can clearly not simply be equated to 'joint actions' within the Common Foreign and Security Policy from which this term has obviously been taken over by the drafters of the

Union Treaty. Even less clear is what a 'joint position' should entail. Controversies have emerged among the Member States about the legal binding force of such 'positions'. The same has happened with the 'common positions' provided for by Article K.5. As a result of these uncertainties some Member States have been rather reluctant to use these new instruments. The basic problem here is that justice and home affairs constitute an area of policy-making in which decisions should normally take the form of binding legal acts and not of co-ordinated political 'positions' like the terminology taken over from the Common Foreign and Security Policy suggests.

(6) The lack of specific provisions on cooperation with third countries and international organizations

Title VI provides for a wide range of possible activities but not for cooperation of the Union with third countries. This tends to reduce the effectiveness of measures because in most of the areas covered by Article K.1 effective action can only be taken in cooperation with third countries or international organizations. The Union has hardly shown any external activity in the area covered by the Third Pillar. The 'Berlin Declaration' of 8 September 1994 on cooperation with the countries of Central and Eastern Europe in certain fields of justice and home affairs is a notable exception but it is legally non-binding and does not fall under one of the acts provided for by Article K.3.2. This poor record is the more striking because since 1993 a considerable number of third countries, among the these all the associated countries of Central and Eastern Europe, the United States and Canada have clearly expressed their interest in close cooperation and even the conclusion of agreements with the Union in the fields covered by Title VI.

To these 'intrinsic' reasons one has to add the 'extrinsic' factors which make progress inside of the Third Pillar difficult.

(7) The highly different political and legal traditions of the Member States in respect to certain of the areas of 'common interest'

Several fields of justice and home affairs such asylum and immigration policy or police cooperation touch core areas of national sovereignty in which different political and legal traditions are still powerful points of reference. The particular French position in respect to immigration from its former African colonies, the very liberal Dutch drug policy and the restrictive interpretation of free movement of persons according to Article 7a European Community Treaty by the United Kingdom are only three examples in this respect. The sometimes enormous differences between these traditional national positions cause serious obstacles to the adoption of substantial joint actions and positions.

(8) The existence of a separate framework of cooperation, the Schengen framework

Although frequently presented as a 'precursor' for the Union, the Schengen system allows for the time being those Member States wanting to make progress in respect to the abolition of internal border controls and to compensatory measures to by-pass both Title VI and the Community institutions. This reduces the pressure on reluctant Member States within the Union framework and represents a political weakening of cooperation under Title VI. It means in practice that the Union is divided into two areas, one in which the free movement of persons is achieved, and another in which this is not the case. It also means that there is a danger that intergovernmental cooperation outside the Union framework may appear more promising to some Member States than the development of justice and home affairs inside the Union framework.[8]

(9) The political sensitiveness of certain areas of 'common interest in the national context

Several of the fields covered by the Third Pillar are 'burning' issues on the national political agenda of some if not most of the Member States. Asylum and immigration issues as well as internal security are the most prominent examples in this respect. Practice has shown that it is quite difficult for these Member States to compromise with other European partners on such sensitive issues, particularly in pre- election times. The rather poor record of the French Presidency in the second half of 1994, which can be to a considerable extent be attributed to the approaching presidential elections, is a case in point.

(10) Difficulties between individual Member States

In the consensus-based decision-making system of the Third Pillar well-entrenched national positions can sometimes lead to controversies among individual Member States which effectively block any progress on central issues. The Anglo-Spanish controversy over Gibraltar or the almost total breakdown of Franco-German cooperation in the Third Pillar area during 1994 are good examples in this respect.

With these points the list of negative factors affecting justice and home affairs cooperation is not yet exhausted. One has to add two more which are not part of the causes for the limited results achieved so far under Title VI but which nevertheless affect the political legitimacy and legal coherence of cooperation in the fields of justice and home affairs:

(11) The democracy deficit

The 'powers' (if one can call them so at all) of control and scrutiny of the European Parliament provided for by Article K.6 are limited to a vaguely defined obligation for Council and Commission to inform the Parliament of discussions in the fields covered by Title VI and a still more vague obligation for the Presidency to consult Parliament on 'principal aspects' of activities

---

[8] See on this point K.-P.Nanz, 'The Schengen Agreement: Preparing the Free Movement of Persons in the European Union', in R.Bieber & J.Monar (eds), *Justice and Home Affairs in the European Union*, Brussels, 1995, p.46.

under the Third Pillar and to take Parliament's views 'duly' into consideration. Practice has shown that the Council understands its information duty in a rather restrictive sense and that the Parliament is, if at all, consulted only after decisions have already been taken.[9] For two reasons this lack of effective democratic scrutiny at the Union level is not fully compensated by national parliamentary scrutiny: The first is that also some of the national parliaments (the French and Italian, for example) have rather limited possibilities for effective scrutiny, receiving only limited information by their governments and being only rarely asked to approve decisions taken under Title VI. The second is that most of the collective element of the decision-making process under Title VI escapes parliamentary control at the national level. There is, therefore, a clear democracy deficit in the Third Pillar area which is going to be widened with every further increase of intergovernmental activity under Title VI.

(12) The lack of judicial control

By virtue of Article L the Third Pillar is exempted from the jurisdiction of the European Court of Justice. There is only one exception: Article K.3.2(c) provides that conventions concluded under Title VI may stipulate that the Court of Justice shall have jurisdiction to interpret their provisions and to rule on disputes regarding their application. This provision, however, has caused lengthy controversies among the Member States which – by way of compromise – led to rather restrictive definitions of the role of the Court under the conventions signed until now. As a result of Article L and the Member States practice judicial review is virtually non-existent in Title VI. The Court has rightly emphasized that the deficit of judicial control is particularly serious as regards the judicial protection of individuals who might be particularly affected by measures taken in the fields of justice and home affairs.[10] Having regard to the already mentioned problems regarding the division of competences between the European Community and the intergovernmental sphere the exemption of the Third Pillar from the jurisdiction of the Court appears also appears problematic in terms of the coherence of the legal order. Both of these deficits must be regarded as major constitutional weaknesses not only of the Third Pillar but of the Union structure as a whole.

---

[9] See on this the European Parliament's resolution of 15 July 1993 on cooperation in the fields of justice and home affairs (OJ C 255, 20.9.1993) and its Report on the functioning of the Treaty on European Union with a view to the 1996 Intergovernmental Conference – Implementation and development of the Union, Part II, Opinion of the Committee on Civil Liberties and Internal Affairs (A4-0102/95/Part II, pp. 121-122 and 129).

[10] Cour de justice des Communautés européennes: *Rapport de la Cour de Justice sur certains aspects de l'application du Traité sur l'Union européenne*, Luxembourg, May 1995.

Reforming the Third Pillar: A strategy for the 1996 Intergovernmental Conference

It should obviously be the task of the Intergovernmental Conference of 1996 to introduce reforms which can effectively counter or even lift the negative factors mentioned above. The question is, however, what would be a realistic strategy and catalogue for reforming the Third Pillar. As usual a maximalist strategy will have its supporters. Such a strategy would consist of aiming at the creation of a Community legislative competence for most or all areas mentioned in Article K.1, qualified majority decision in the Council, an exclusive right of initiative of the Commission, a legislative role for the European Parliament and full judicial control of the Court over all acts adopted in the sphere of justice and home affairs. However, it does not need a deep analysis to come to the conclusion that, taking into account

- the still very much diverging positions of the Member States on key issues of justice and home affairs,
- the problems of constitutional law and national sovereignty resulting from a full communitarization of Title VI (as regards police affairs, for instance), and
- the still persisting rather negative 'post-Maastricht' climate, such a maximalist approach would not only have no chance of success but could even prove to be rather counterproductive.

This was confirmed by the Reflection Group's Report of December 1995 according to which a 'large majority' of the Member States regarded part of the provisions of Title VI 'inadequate and clearly deficient in operation'.[11] However, even this majority was not proposing to abolish the Third Pillar altogether in favour of full communitarization, and some Member States even clearly stated that they regard the separate position of justice and home affairs within the Union structure as essential in order to respect intergovernmental management of matters so closely linked with national sovereignty.

It seems, therefore, that the most realistic strategy in view of the Intergovernmental Conference would be to maintain the Third Pillar as a separate decision-making system while trying at the same time to arrive at more efficiency and effectiveness and even at a higher degree of integration by way of a number of changes in the areas of decision-making procedures and competences.

As regards the first group of the above mentioned 'intrinsic' negative factors (1 to 6) the following changes should clearly figure on the list of necessary reforms:

(A) Rationalization of the decision-making structure

Since the K.4 Committee regroups the senior officials responsible for justice and home affairs in the national administrations it should be clearly established as the central preparatory body for Council decisions under Title VI;

---

[11] *Report of the Reflection Group*, SN 520/95 (REFLEX 21), Brussels 5th December 1995, para. 47.

the role of the COREPER should be limited to check measures elaborated by the K.4 Committee regarding their compatibility with measures in the European Community framework or in the CFSP. It may also be worthwhile to consider an abolishment of the Steering Groups. The question arises, however, whether – due to the many different policy fields covered by Title VI – some intermediate coordinating bodies are not necessary for the smooth functioning of the Third Pillar.

(B) Extension of majority voting in the area of implementing measures

Whereas until now majority voting on implementing measures is only possible after a previous unanimous decision to that effect majority voting in the implementation of joint positions, joint actions and conventions adopted pursuant to Article K.3 should become a rule laid down in the Treaty. This could increase efficiency in the decision- making process and help the Member States to get used to the 'culture' of majority voting in the Third Pillar.

(C) Extension of the Commission's right of initiative to the areas referred to in Article K.1(7) to (9)

The Commission should have a right of initiative in all areas covered by Title VI because it could clearly contribute something in the areas it has been excluded from until now (particularly in the area of customs affairs where it has already a competence in the European Community framework). It could also help the Commission to develop in general a more central role in the Third Pillar.

(D) Application of Article 100c of the European Community Treaty to particular areas[12]

In all these areas Community competences already exist (Article 100c European Community Treaty: visa policy; Article 129 European Community Treaty: public health; Article 209a European Community Treaty: measures countering fraud against the financial interests of the Community). Communitarization of these areas would prevent further difficulties as regards the division of competences and contribute to more efficiency. According to Reflection Group's Report a majority of the Member States would be willing to bring immigration policy, asylum and external border controls within the Community sphere.[13] However, it is highly unlikely that consensus could be reached on that (the United Kingdom is particularly opposed to any move in that direction), and one may also ask whether at this stage national policies and public feelings in the Member States on these issues are not still too much differing from each other to secure sufficient acceptance of such a major move. It would not help the Union to have another

---

[12] Specifically to the areas of Articles K.1(2) (rules governing external border crossing), K.1(4) (combat against drug addiction) and K.1(5) (combat against fraud on an international scale).

[13] *Op cit*, paragraph 49.

debate about sovereignty in some Member States fueled by majority voting on these issues during the ratification process of the next IGC's results. However, the Member States could still agree on a timetable for proceeding to the communitarization of these or other areas covered by Article K.1.

(E) Clarification of the scope and legal nature of joint positions and joint actions according to Article K.3(a) and (b)

A clear distinction between the two instruments should be established and it should be stipulated that they commit the Member States in the positions they adopt and in the conduct of their activity. Alternately, the two terms should be replaced by new ones which would better reflect the need of cooperation in justice and home affairs to arrive at binding legal decisions rather than common political positions only.

(F) Introduction of a specific provision on cooperation with third countries and international organizations

This provision should explicitly enable the Member States to conclude within the framework of Title VI conventions and other types of agreements on behalf of the Union with third countries and international organizations. The Union could also be enabled to conclude such agreements itself, but this would require the major reform of granting legal personality to the Union which at present it has not.

As regards the 'extrinsic' negative factors (7 – 10) most of them depend on the internal context and political positions of the Member States which obviously cannot be remedied by a treaty revision. As regards the problem of the Schengen and Dublin Conventions, however, the following would make sense:

(G) Transfer of the Schengen Convention into the Union framework[14]

This arrangement of variable geometry inside the Union structure would improve the coherence of policy-making and strengthen the cooperation framework under Title VI.

(H) Consultation of the European Parliament on all joint actions and conventions[15]

In respect to the deficits in terms of democracy and judicial control the following reforms could be envisaged and, upon the proposal of a Member State or the Commission, the Council should be enabled to decide by qualified majority to adopt such an act only after the assent of the European Parliament has been obtained. Such a provision would considerably strengthen the position of the Parliament as regards both its demand for adequate information and its political impact within the Third Pillar but at the same time it would still leave a large margin of discretion to the Member States as regards compliance with the Parliament's views.

---

[14] This would be on the basis of Article K.3(c) while giving those Member States not being party to the Schengen Convention an 'opting out' (or, depending on the form of integration chosen, an 'opting in') possibility.

[15] Adopted under Article K.3.2(b) and (c).

(I) Jurisdiction of the Court of Justice

The jurisdiction of the Court of Justice In respect of the interpretation of the provisions of conventions and other legally binding acts adopted under Title VI and rulings on any disputes regarding their application should be made compulsory. Such a provision would be necessary to ensure adequate legal guarantees under the Third Pillar and to settle disputes of the division of competences between the Third Pillar and the other two pillars of the Union.

All these elements of reform would still keep essential parts of the intergovernmental nature of the Third Pillar intact which for the time being some Member States are clearly not willing to give up. But at the same time they would constitute real improvements in respect to efficiency, democratic scrutiny and judicial control in areas which are of increasing concern to the Union's citizens. Since this concern is a major political and social fact it might also be worthwhile to look for possibilities to create within the Union Treaty an explicit link between the provisions on the Citizenship of the Union and the Third Pillar. This could be done, for instance, by formally acknowledging within the chapter on Citizenship the right of the citizens of the Union to a more effective guarantee of their internal security at the Union level and by referring to Title VI as the main instrument to that effect.

European Citizenship and European
Union Justice and Home Affairs

John Benyon
University of Leicester

'Building Police Co-operation:
The European Construction Site around the Third Pillar'

Delving into the European Internal Security Field

It is arguable that Title VI of the Treaty on European Union, on 'Co-operation in the Fields of Justice and Home Affairs', includes some of the Treaty's most significant provisions for the long-term development of the European Union. Title VI, more often known as the 'third pillar' of the European Union, also has the potential to have far-reaching effects on the member states and on the citizens of the Union.

The third pillar is concerned with immigration, international crime, the administration of justice, policing and related matters. Together these constitute the gamut of issues of what Bigo has termed the 'European internal security field' and he has pointed out that this 'directly concerns citizens' rights, state-citizen relations, and group relations of Europeans among themselves and towards third countries'.[1]

Co-operation in this field has tended to take place on an intergovernmental basis, beyond the competence of the European Commission and European Parliament. The Maastricht Treaty has continued this arrangement to a large extent, although visa policy has been brought within the European Community pillar and the Commission and Parliament have each been given a formal role under Title VI. This pillar gives the impression of something of a compromise between the wish to collaborate against perceived threats and a decided aversion (particularly by some states) to surrender any sovereignty. As such, Title VI has an impermanent feel and attempts to amend it seem likely at the 1996 Intergovernmental Conference.

Nonetheless, there are good reasons to believe that the Maastricht Treaty marks a watershed in the development of co-operation on policing and related matters in the European Union. Although by early 1996 it was generally agreed that progress had been slow, the third pillar provides a framework within which a great deal of collaboration is possible. This paper[2] mentions some of the developments which are occurring and proposals which have been made, some of which raise fundamental questions

---

[1] D.Bigo, 'The European Internal Security Field: Stakes and Rivalries in a Newly Developing Area of Police Intervention', in M.Anderson & M.den Boer (eds), *Policing Across National Boundaries*, Pinter Publishers, 1994, p.164.

[2] The paper draws on the findings from the *Police, Crime and Justice in Europe* project which has been undertaken at the Centre for the Study of Public Order at the University of Leicester since 1989. The author wishes to acknowledge and thank staff who have been involved in the project, especially Adrian Beck, Pamela Davies, Michael King, Arianit Koci, Sheridan Morris, Matthew Toye, Lynne Turnbull, Andrew Willis and Rachel Woodward. Publications resulting from the project are available from Robert Pugsley at the Scarman Centre for the Study of Public Order, University of Leicester, 6, Salisbury Road, Leicester, LE1 7QR (Tel: 0116.252.5704; Fax: 0116.252.3944).

about the sovereignty of member states, citizenship rights, accountability and legitimacy, and police efficiency and effectiveness.

One of the features of co-operation in the European Union in the fields of justice and home affairs is the number of structures and organisations which have been established. In addition to those brought together under the third pillar, and their precursors under the Trevi Group, and excluding those, such as the Pompidou Group, set up under the Council of Europe, there are Interpol and the Schengen Group, and an array of informal, semi-official, usually specialist, networks to promote co-operation in particular fields of law enforcement. The position is unclear and confusing – and it would appear that a great many police officers in Europe, let alone politicians and the public, are suitably mystified.[3]

The developing institutions in the European internal security field are characterised by lack of parliamentary and judicial scrutiny at the European level. This lack of accountability raises questions of legitimacy and of citizenship rights. Policing powers, immigration control, the development of sophisticated databases to hold information on millions of people, and other activities by these groups and institutions, raise obvious questions about citizens' rights, civil liberties and the redress of grievances.

Such anxieties are unlikely to be allayed by the provisions in the Maastricht Treaty on 'Citizenship of the Union'. Article 8 of the Treaty Establishing the European Community makes all nationals of member states citizens of the European Union and bestows upon them the right to move freely, to petition the European Parliament and to stand and vote in municipal and European elections. Beyond this, there is no mention of the civil, political, social or human rights, or of the obligations, which one might expect to be ascribed to citizenship. Even the view that 'the European citizen of Maastricht is a skeletal creature'[4] seems something of an overstatement – the European citizen created by the Maastricht Treaty is a phantasm as yet lacking substance. The lack of the European citizen's rights and powers is nowhere more evident than in the developing agreements, institutions, procedures and other forms of co-operation in the fields of justice, home affairs and policing.

In order to delve more deeply into the European internal security field, some consideration of the arguments for European police co-operation is necessary to understand recent debates and developments. The next section briefly assesses the demands for greater co-operation against cross-border crime and to combat illegal immigration. The paper then outlines three levels of police co-operation and applies these to an assessment of the various arrangements which exist for facilitating cross-border law enforcement collaboration. The paper concludes with a brief evaluation of the momentum

---

[3] This became evident during the collection of data for the Leicester CSPO *Police, Crime and Justice in Europe* project, during which researchers visited all European Union countries: see J.Benyon et al, *Police Co-operation in Europe: an Investigation*, Leicester: CSPO, 1993. For further evidence see various issues of *Police Review* and *Police* and House of Commons, *Practical Police Co-operation in the European Community: Seventh Report from the Home Affairs Committee, Session 1989-90, Volume II, Memoranda of Evidence, Minutes and Appendices*, HC 363-II, HMSO, 1990.

[4] A.Duff, 'The Main Reforms', in A.Duff et al (eds), *Maastricht and Beyond*, Routledge, 1994, p.30.

and obstacles for further developments.

Demands for European Co-operation in the Fields of Justice and Home Affairs

Cross-Border Crime

One argument for increased co-operation in justice and home affairs in the European Union is that the removal of frontier controls is likely to be accompanied by an increase in cross-border crime. However, the principal concerns of governments are with threats to national security and social and political stability – matters which fall within Brodeur's category of 'high policing'.[5] Terrorism is a major concern and the Trevi Group was founded in 1975 to promote co-operation in this field. Drug trafficking has also come to be seen as a serious threat, principally to social stability because of the organised crime and violence associated with it.

At a lower level, in terms of the perceived threat to the security of the state, there is the numerically much larger class of less serious crimes. This includes offences against property – which, of course, account for the vast majority of recorded crime in European Union states. There is some (although inconclusive) evidence that the free movement of people and goods may result in an increase in certain types of crime, such as thefts, burglaries and robberies committed by mobile offenders. These types of criminal victimisation are much more likely to impinge directly on the lives of European citizens – there is an inverse correlation between the seriousness and the incidence of victimisation.

The abolition of internal frontiers may also lead to a rise in crime involving the theft of high-value property, such as motor vehicles, construction plant and art and antiques, and its movement to other European Union countries or out of the European Union area. Two-thirds of lorries stolen in Britain are never recovered. A significant proportion of car thefts, especially of more expensive cars, appears to be exported for sale in other European Union countries or further afield.[6]

A field of crime that has not received the attention that it merits is fraud. This is characterised by relative invisibility, complexity and a lack of publicity, but the data which do exist indicate its enormous extent. Most fraud occurs within individual countries, but cross-border fraud of various kinds, including cheque-book and credit-card fraud, appears to be growing.[7] Fraud

---

[5] J.-P.Brodeur, 'High Policing and Low Policing: Remarks about the Policing of Political Activities', *Social Problems*, 30/5, 1983.

[6] M.Levi, 'The Extent of Cross-Border Crime in Europe', *European Journal on Criminal Policy and Research*, 1/3, 1993; House of Commons, *Practical Police Co-operation in the European Community: Volume II, Memoranda of Evidence, Minutes of Evidence and Appendices*, p.25; R.Hadfield, 'Crime in Europe: The Role of the Police', paper presented to CSPO conference on *Crime in Europe: Patterns and Prospects for the 1990s*, Leicester University, 1993.

[7] House of Commons, *Practical Police Co-operation in the European Community: Volume II, Memoranda of Evidence, Minutes of Evidence and Appendices*, pp.27-29: A.Collier, *The Problems of Measuring International Cross-Frontier Crime and their Relationship to Decision Making on Police Resource Allocation*, Bramshill Police Staff College Fellowship Paper, 1993; M.Levi, *Regulating Fraud: White-Collar Crime and the*

against the European Union itself is also a serious problem, as highlighted quite regularly by the reports of the European Court of Auditors.[8] There is also evidence of smuggling within the European Union and the extensive evasion of VAT and excise duty.[9]

Police officers and politicians have also raised other issues about free movement in Europe, including the control of pornography and firearms, standards of motor vehicle safety, and the prevention of the spread of plant and animal diseases.[10] The role of customs officers is important as revealed, for example, by British data for 1993-1994 which showed that HM Customs and Excise seized 1,043 live animals and birds and 4,950 plants, all from endangered species, over 37,014 obscene or indecent items, and 2,944 guns. Most of these seizures were the result of information received and surveillance operations, and so could presumably have occurred anywhere in the country, not necessarily at the borders.

Immigration

Since the Single European Act of 1986 many have argued that the abolition of internal controls requires a strengthening of the external borders to create a 'hard outer shell'. The central issue is fear of an influx of immigrants and associated crime. Anxiety about rising levels of illegal immigration has become a significant political factor in many European Union countries and some perceive it to be a fundamental threat to social and political stability within the Union. Issues such as refugees and political asylum have become bound up with the question of 'illegal immigrants', despite the clear differences between them.[11]

There have been warnings at least since 1990 of an imminent 'flood' of immigrants from the east and south.[12] Although no one knows how many

---

Criminal Process, Tavistock, 1987; Levi, 'The Extent of Cross-Border Crime in Europe'.

[8] Commission of the European Communities, *Report on the Fight Against Fraud: Report on 1992 and the Action Programme for 1993*, Brussels: Commission of the European Communities, 1993; D.Ruimchotel, 'Ambiguities Between Criminal Policy and Scientific Research: The Case of Fraud Against the EC', *European Journal on Criminal Policy and Research*, 1/3, 1993.

[9] P.C.van Duyne, 'Organised Crime Markets in a Turbulent Europe', *European Journal on Criminal Policy and Research*, 1/3, 1993.

[10] See, for example, S.Edwards, 'Sex and the Single Market', *Police Review*, 97, 8th September 1989; Surrey Constabulary, *Surrey Sans Frontieres: The Implications of the Single European State on the Policing of Surrey*, Surrey Constabulary, 1992; Commission of the European Communities, 'Road Safety Background Report', *The Week in Europe*, 17th August 1993; ACPO/Metropolitan Police European Unit, *Briefing Note: Rabies*, Metropolitan Police, 1989.

[11] M.King, 'Policing Refugees and Asylum-Seekers in Greater Europe: Towards a Reconceptualisation of Control', in M.Anderson & M.den Boer (eds), *Policing Across National Boundaries*, Pinter Publishers, 1994; M.den Boer, *Immigration, Internal Security and Policing in Europe*, Working Paper 8, University of Edinburgh, Politics Department, 1993.

[12] House of Lords, *Report of the Select Committee on the European Communities 1992: Border Control of People*, HMSO, 1989; Lord Bethell, 'Crime Knows No Frontiers', *Police*, 22/6, 1990; P.Range, 'Europe Faces an Immigrant Tide', *National Geographic*, 183/5, 1993; see also the views of P.van Reenen, then Director of the Police Academy in Apeldoorn, quoted in J.Benyon et al, *Police Co-operation in Europe: A Preliminary Investigation*, CSPO, 1990, p.47.

clandestine immigrants have entered European Union countries, the best estimates vary between 3.5 and 5.5 million.[13] Some senior police officers now regard 'fighting clandestine immigration' as the principal reason for increased European police co-operation.[14]

A central feature of the 'ring of steel' around the European Union is the development of a common visa policy. This is being introduced under the 1990 Schengen Implementing Convention for the ten countries so far involved and will be extended to all 15 European Union states under Article 100c of the Treaty Establishing the European Community. The common European Union visa seems likely eventually to apply to the great majority of countries – the most recent Schengen list included 129 countries. On 25th September 1995 the Justice and Home Affairs Council of the European Union agreed a list of 101 countries. The criteria raise the prospect of growing injustice in the allocation of visas, the continued separation of families and also the danger of bribery and corruption as visas to gain entry to the European Union become increasingly difficult to obtain.

The position of people seeking asylum is particularly acute and yet their need to be afforded protection may be the greatest. Data from the United Nations High Commissioner for Refugees revealed that the number of people seeking asylum in European Union countries rose from 420,000 in 1991 to 570,000 in 1992, with an estimated 400,000 in the first half of 1993, but the average acceptance rate was only some 9 per cent.[15]

Immigration appears to have displaced terrorism and drug trafficking as the principal 'internal security threat' perceived by the countries of the European Union, although it is often linked to terrorism, serious crimes and public disorder. Immigration is seen as posing a threat to social and political stability and around this lurks the spectre of right-wing extremism. During the last few years, the language of many politicians has become more uncompromising towards asylum seekers and immigrants, reflecting the increased political salience of these issues.[16]

Levels of Co-operation on Justice and Home Affairs

In order to examine the existing structures, and further possibilities, it may be helpful to consider three inter-related levels of police co-operation

---

[13] Council of Europe, *Report on the New Countries of Immigration*, Document 6211, Strasbourg, Council of Europe, 1990; Range, 'Europe Faces an Immigrant Tide', p.100; *Guardian*, 14th February 1995.

[14] F.Diederich, 'Police Co-operation', paper presented at EIPA conference on *Schengen: A First Assessment after the Opening of the Frontiers*, Luxembourg, 14-15th October 1993; M.den Boer, 'The Quest for European Policing: Rhetoric and Justification in a Disorderly Debate', in Anderson & M.den Boer (eds), *Policing Across National Boundaries*.

[15] L.Druke, 'Asylum Seekers and Refugees in the Turmoil after the Opening (or Closing) of the Frontiers', paper presented at EIPA conference on *Schengen: A First Assessment after the Opening of the Frontiers*, Luxembourg, 14-15th October 1993.

[16] Bigo, 'The European Internal Security Field'; M.King, 'Conceptualising "Fortress Europe": A Consideration of the Processes of Inclusion and Exclusion', paper presented to ECPR workshop on *Police and Immigration: Towards a Europe of Internal Security*, Madrid, 17th-22nd April 1994; den Boer, 'The Quest for European Policing'.

in Europe.[17] The *macro level* is that which entails constitutional and international legal agreements and the harmonisation of national laws and regulations. The *meso level* is concerned with the operational structures, practices and procedures of the police and other law enforcement agencies. The *micro level* involves the investigation of specific offences and the prevention and control of particular forms of crime.

The macro level is the level of government ministers at which fundamental questions are resolved and major decisions are taken on issues such as extradition procedures, common asylum policy and visa harmonisation. Co-operative arrangements on these fundamental questions of rights of entry and rules of exit to sovereign states entail treaties and conventions, and parliamentary ratification. Also requiring decisions at the macro level are legal issues concerning operational powers across borders, especially relating to investigation and surveillance, arrest, detention and interrogation.

Co-operation at the meso level is concerned with the structural and procedural frameworks within which operational law enforcement occurs. Developments at the meso level include the establishment of new specialist organisations to enable police, customs and other experts in particular fields, such as counterfeiting or environmental crime, to collaborate. An important feature of meso-level co-operation is face-to-face contact between middle-ranking officers from different countries who share common, professional, interests in specific criminal investigations.

One important meso-level dimension is communications, including information systems, common databases, and co-ordination and access to information such as criminal intelligence. Another aspect of enhanced European police communications is language. Besides the obvious need to speak a common language, when necessary, there are also problems of technical language and terminologies which vary between countries and to overcome this the 'Policespeak' language has been developed in France and the United Kingdom.[18]

Unlike developments at the macro level, meso-level co-operative arrangements do not need intergovernmental agreements and parliamentary ratification, although they may occur as the result of political initiatives. More frequently, meso-level co-operation takes place between different law enforcement organisations, often without the knowledge or sanction of governments.

Police activity at the micro level involves the investigation of specific offences and the prevention and control of particular sorts of crime. To take one example, problems of public disorder tend to vary between different countries and regions in Europe. Micro-level co-operation can be effective in certain circumstances as occurred, for example, during the World Cup in Italy in 1990 when police from different European countries offered information and assistance to their Italian counterparts. Similar co-operation has

---

[17] For further discussion see J.Benyon et al, 'Police Co-operation, Security and Public Order Management and Crime Prevention in Europe', in House of Commons, *Practical Police Co-operation in the European Community: Volume II, Memoranda of Evidence, Minutes of Evidence and Appendices*, HC 363-II, HMSO, 1990, pp. 181-185.

[18] PoliceSpeak, *Police Communications and Language and the Channel Tunnel: Report*, Cambridge: PoliceSpeak Publications, 1993.

taken place on a large number of subsequent occasions and is occurring for the European Football Championships to be held in England in the summer of 1996.

Liaison officers who are seconded from one country to work with their counterparts in another country, especially in the fields of terrorism, drugs, football hooliganism, and organised crime, may participate in micro-level co-operation. Many micro-level initiatives occur through the various formal, and particularly the informal, police networks which exist between officers of different countries. But successful networks themselves tend to be established at the meso level, and indeed many micro-level instances of co-operation depend on effective meso-level arrangements. ***

Arrangements for European Police Co-operation

The main formal arrangements for promoting European police co-operation have been Interpol, the Schengen Group, the Trevi Group, and the new European Union structures, including the K4 Committee and the Europol Drugs Unit/Europol. Each merits brief consideration.

Interpol

The International Criminal Police Organisation, better known as Interpol, is the oldest structure for assisting police co-operation in Europe. It developed from a meeting in 1923 and was given its present name in 1956. Interpol currently has 176 member countries and the European region includes 46 separate states which account for 80 per cent of all the messages which pass through the organisation each year.

Interpol operates as a global conduit for communication. This is restricted to micro-level information exchange on a case-by-case basis and thus its capacity to promote greater police co-operation in Europe is limited. It is also constrained by its international role for the primary obligations of Interpol are world-wide and these may be considered as incompatible with a much enhanced role in Europe. The argument for the 'regionalisation' of Interpol, or the development of an inner-circle of European Union members, would surely be against the spirit of Interpol's constitution and might lead to impoverished international crime control and co-operation.

The organisation has developed some meso-level activities, such as specialist European conferences on subjects such as fraud and drug trafficking, and promotes discussion and analysis of crime trends. However, these meso-level developments are necessarily limited and Interpol is unable to facilitate co-operation at the macro level.[19]

---

[19] For a more detailed discussion of these points see Benyon et al, *Police Co-operation in Europe: An Investigation*, pp.121-133, 222-228 & 266-268; see also M.Anderson, *Policing the World*, Clarendon Press, 1989.

The Schengen Group

The forms of co-operation which are being developed under the Schengen agreements are the most ambitious attempts to formalise police co-operation between European countries and are intended to operate at each of the three levels of police co-operation and criminal justice. At the macro level, the Schengen treaties are concerned with constitutional and legal questions, such as allowing police to pursue criminals across borders. At the meso level, operational police structures, practices and procedures, including a sophisticated information system, have been established. The arrangements are designed to facilitate the micro-level investigation of specific offences.

The original Schengen Agreement was signed on 14th June 1985 by Belgium, France, Germany, Luxembourg and the Netherlands and in June 1990 the Schengen Implementing Convention was agreed, which included measures on visa regime harmonisation, hot pursuit and the establishment of a computerised data exchange system – the Schengen Information System (SIS). On 27th November 1990 Italy joined the Schengen group, Portugal and Spain followed on 25th June 1991 and Greece joined in November 1992. Austria signed the Schengen Conventions on 28th April 1995, but by February 1996 was still in the process of ratifying them. Denmark has observer status and both Sweden and Finland have applied. The meeting of the Executive Committee on 24th October 1995 agreed to negotiations on the admission of Norway and Iceland as associate members of Schengen. Ireland and the United Kingdom are not members of the group, as they have expressed their wish to maintain passport controls at their internal European Union borders.

The Schengen structure reflects the three levels of police co-operation, with macro-level supervision conducted by the Executive Committee of ministers, the inaugural meeting of which took place on 18th October 1993. The meso-level Central Group usually meets about once a month to oversee implementation of Executive Committee decisions and to supervise the work of the micro-level working groups. In early 1996 there were working groups on police and security, free movement of people, judicial co-operation and external relations, with sub-groups on a range of matters including asylum, visas, firearms, drugs, telecommunications, and external and internal frontiers and airports.

Also reporting to the Central Group is ORSIS, the Steering Committee responsible for the Schengen Information System (SIS). This is an ambitious project which consists of a central computer (CSIS) in Strasbourg linked to a national computer in each country (NSIS). When data are entered into a national databank, the CSIS copies them into each of the NSIS computers. The Schengen Information System is thus designed to be a unique common database shared by the participating countries, each of which may add new entries, with a capacity of 8 million personal records and 7 million records on objects. It seems possible that the proposed European Information System (EIS) will be based on the SIS. By September 1995, there were 30,000 entry points to the Schengen Information System, of which 9,000 were in Germany. Out of 3.4 million entries on the SIS, 2.3 million had been provided by Germany.

The SIS is regarded by the ten Schengen countries as a critical compensatory measure for the removal of all frontier checks and as such is intended to facilitate controls at external borders and increase police co-operation in apprehending wanted people. It enables police and other agencies in all the Schengen countries to have access to identical information on wanted persons, 'undesirable aliens', asylum seekers, persons to be expelled or extradited, persons under surveillance, and stolen goods. A separate electronic mail system, known as the Supplementary Information Request at the National Entry (SIRENE), is designed to enable the rapid transfer of additional information – for example, extradition details and fingerprints. At the meeting of the Schengen Executive Committee on 28th April 1995 it was agreed to develop a SIRENE Phase II because of the rapid growth in demand. The Schengen countries have introduced common arrangements for handling asylum and visa applications and to facilitate this they have established another shared information system, known as the Visa Inquiry System In an Open-border Network (VISION).[20]

The Schengen group has forged macro-level agreements, created meso-level structures and facilitated micro-level mechanisms for operational police co-operation. These achievements reflect a high degree of political determination, which has continued despite setbacks. The target date for removing all border controls slipped on at least six occasions and finally came into force on 26th March 1995, for France, Germany, Spain, Portugal and the Benelux countries. Austria will implement the Conventions after ratification is complete. France announced a three-month suspension on full implementation of the agreement, and this was subsequently extended until 1st April 1996. Greece and Italy have announced their intention to follow suit as soon as practicable.

There continue to be criticisms voiced about the mechanisms for accountability and scrutiny of the new arrangements, especially the SIS. The provisions of the Schengen Agreements are subject to each country's own legal and judicial arrangements and so aggrieved citizens could, presumably, bring cases to ensure judicial review, although such a course may not be open to those denied asylum or a visa. The absence of any effective parliamentary scrutiny is a continuing matter of concern.

The complexity of the arrangements necessarily entails some loss of sovereignty by each of the member countries, but this may be taken as evidence of the high levels of commitment and resolve, with the possible exception of the present French government. The loss of some sovereignty is apparently regarded by Schengen states as a price worth paying to produce an enhanced capability to combat crime, limit clandestine immigration and enable internal border controls to be removed, although at the meeting of the Executive Committee on 24th October 1995, the Schengen states agreed to permit 'mobile patrols' to operate at 'mobile frontiers', reflecting the continuing concern of some states about the effectiveness of the controls at the external borders.

---

[20] The Schengen Information System is considered in detail in Benyon et al, *Police Co-operation in Europe: An Investigation*, pp.228-237 & 289-291.

The Trevi Group

The first meeting of the Trevi Group took place in Luxembourg in June 1976. Its initial objective was to foster greater European co-operative efforts against terrorism. In 1985 drugs and serious organised international crime were added to its remit and this subsequently broadened to include equipment, public order and the implications of the Single European Market. All 12 European Community countries were members of the Trevi Group, which in late 1993 was absorbed into the structure set up under Title VI of the Treaty on European Union.[21]

Like the Schengen group, Trevi operated at three identifiable levels. The macro-level Ministerial Group met every six months, hosted by the country holding the European Presidency, and were serviced by the meso-level Group of Senior Officials which prepared the agenda and reports, and monitored progress by the micro-level working groups.

Working Group I, set up in 1977, established a secure rapid communications network, undertook regular analyses of known and suspected terrorist groups, promoted joint work on terrorist funding, and circulated information on other matters. Working Group II had responsibility for promoting co-operation on training, equipment, forensic science and other technical matters, public order and football hooliganism. Working Group III was set up in 1985 to co-ordinate activities against serious crime, especially drug trafficking. Its remit grew to include organised crime, computer crime, environmental crime, vehicle crime, trafficking in stolen antiques and works of art, and money laundering. The group was instrumental in setting up the network of Drugs Liaison Officers and promoted international initiatives against money laundering. Working Group IV, also known as Trevi '92, was concerned with an array of issues related to the policing and security implications of the reduction of internal border controls. It was responsible for drafting the *Programme of Action*, agreed at the Trevi ministerial meeting in Dublin in June 1990, which outlined a number of priorities for improved co-operation to combat terrorism, drug trafficking, organised crime, and illegal immigration.

In addition to the Trevi working groups, four ad hoc groups were set up to promote co-operation in related fields. The Ad Hoc Working Group on Europol was established in August 1991 to develop the idea of a European Criminal Police Office, although it was soon agreed that this should initially be a more modest Europol Drugs Unit. The other three ad hoc working groups were not formally constituted as part of the Trevi structure, although they reported to the same ministers and followed the same cycle of meetings. The Ad Hoc Working Group on International Organised Crime was set up following the murders of the Italian anti-Mafia judges Giovanni Falcone and Paolo Borsellino during the summer of 1992. The Ad Hoc Group on Immigration was established in 1986 and assisted in drafting the Dublin Convention on Asylum and the Convention on External Borders. It was divided into six sub-groups on admission and expulsion, visas, false docu-

---

[21] A detailed account of the development and activities of the Trevi Group is given in Benyon et al, *Police Co-operation in Europe: An Investigation*, pp.152-168, 237-242 & 270-273.

ments, asylum, external borders, and refugees. The Group was involved in the establishment of the Centre for Information, Reflection and Exchange on Asylum (CIREA) and the Centre for Information, Reflection and Exchange on Frontiers and Immigration (CIREFI). Their tasks are to monitor immigration flows and asylum applications, forged documents, illegal immigration and related issues, and to promote the exchange of information and intelligence. The Judicial Co-operation Working Group on Criminal Matters was the forum for the discussion of issues such as extradition, legislation against terrorist funding and fraud, and the mutual recognition of court decisions, such as driving disqualifications.

There can be little doubt that the Trevi Group, and the associated ad hoc groups, assisted in building trust and confidence in sensitive security fields, such as action against terrorism and organised crime, and facilitated progress in more mundane areas of police and judicial co-operation. Particularly from the late 1980s, the activities of Trevi were generally characterised by political commitment at the macro level of ministerial meetings and consequent progress with agreements, conventions and statements of intent. Meso-level structures and procedures were also promoted, including liaison networks and methods for the exchange of information.

Police criticisms of the effectiveness of Trevi tended to focus on the perceived lack of impact at the micro level of operational policing. However, inevitably much of the work was focused on specialist policing areas, which are not the everyday concerns of most European police officers, and, furthermore, it could be argued that the working groups were engaged on mid to long-term developments to establish European Union-wide, meso-level structures and procedures which would in the future facilitate micro-level police co-operation. Criticisms by civil libertarians concerned the secrecy and lack of parliamentary and public accountability. This 'democratic deficit' led to suggestions, in the European Parliament and elsewhere, that Trevi and the ad hoc groups were not legitimate structures for policy making.[22]

The 'Third Pillar' of the European Union

The Trevi Group metamorphosed into part of the new European Union structure as soon as the Treaty on European Union came into force on 1st November 1993. Among the areas which Title VI (Article K) of the Treaty identifies as matters of common concern are: asylum; controls at external borders; immigration; combating drugs and fraud; judicial co-operation; customs co-operation; and police co-operation, including establishing a European Police Office (Europol).

Article K4 states that the Commission 'shall be fully associated' with this work and it established a Committee to co-ordinate activities and to advise the Council of Interior and Justice Ministers. This structure has subsumed not only the Trevi Group but also the Ad Hoc Group on Immigration, the Judicial Co-operation Working Group, the Mutual Assistance Group

---

[22] L. van Outrive, *Report of the Committee on Civil Liberties and Internal Affairs of the European Parliament on Police Co-operation*, European Parliament, 1992.

for customs co-operation, and the Co-ordinators' Group, set up after the December 1988 Rhodes Council to oversee the implementation of the Palma Document.

The K4 Committee consists of senior representatives from the relevant ministries of the member states and an observer from the European Commission. Since its inception the K4 Committee has met about once a month. It has a secretariat in Brussels and, following the standard procedure, its advice and reports are fed through the Committee of Permanent Representatives (COREPER) to the Council of Justice and Home Affairs Ministers. The K4 Committee has three steering groups, each of which has a number of working groups. Steering Group I on Immigration and Asylum has working groups on migration (including CIREFI), asylum (including CIREA), visas, external frontiers, and forged documents. Steering Group II on policing and security matters has working groups on terrorism, police co-operation, drugs and organised crime, customs co-operation, training, scientific matters, crime analysis, combating environmental crime, public disorder and Europol. Steering Group III on Judicial Co-operation has working groups on extradition, international organised crime, criminal and European Community law, mutual recognition, the Brussels Convention, and the transfer of documents. It also handles the legal dimensions of attempts to combat terrorist funding and fraud against the Community.

Although most of the provisions on home affairs and police co-operation in the Maastricht Treaty are dealt with in Article K (Title VI), and are thus intergovernmental matters outside the new European Community Treaty, there is one important exception. This is co-operation on visas, which is provided for in Article 100c of the Treaty Establishing the European Community and is thus an European Community rather than an intergovernmental matter. The Commission is empowered to play a central role in initiating proposals and issuing directives and the European Parliament must be consulted. Article K6 of the Treaty on European Union also provides a role for the Parliament.

Article 100c of the European Community Treaty is linked to Article K in the Treaty on European Union in two ways. First, the *passerelle* ('bridge') Article K9 enables the member states to bring certain areas within the ambit of the European Community Treaty. In this way, asylum policy and other aspects of immigration policy, and action to combat drug addiction and international fraud, may be brought within the European Community structure under Article 100c. Secondly, the K4 Committee contributes to the preparation of proceedings under Article 100c on visa policy. Thus, the same group of officials assists the European Community institutions under Article 100c and advises and oversees intergovernmental activities under Title Vl.

The Maastricht Treaty established a new framework for the further development of co-operation on policing and related matters in the European Union. However, by early 1996 progress under Title VI was generally regarded as disappointing. The Deputy Coordinator of the Europol Drugs Unit spoke of 'teething problems',[23] while Adrian Fortescue, Director at

---

[23] W.Bruggeman, 'Europol and the Europol Drugs Unit', in R.Bieber & J.Monar (eds),

the General Secretariat of the European Commission with particular responsibilities for Title VI, was more forthright: 'It would not be honest to conceal that public and parliamentary expectations, and indeed the Commission's own hopes, have been disappointed in terms of concrete results so far'.[24]

Various reasons for this lack of progress can be identified, not the least important being the lack of political commitment from some of the interior ministers of the member states. Another factor is that the structure of the third pillar is cumbersome with five different layers of decision making – the Justice and Home Affairs Council, COREPER, K4 Committee, steering groups and working parties. Difficult decisions tend to be referred upwards and are then sometimes referred downwards again, causing delay and congestion. There are problems of interpretation of the wording of Title VI and of the demarcation between the first and the third pillars. Different actors in the processes have conflicting views about how to proceed – for example, the views of the Parliament have differed sharply on some matters from those of the Council and those of particular member states, and there have reportedly been differences between the K4 Committee, composed of civil servants from national governments, and COREPER, the members of which are diplomats based in Brussels.

A central issue has been whether the European Court of Justice should be involved in the interpretation of Title VI and in the supervision of new institutions, agreements and conventions agreed under the third pillar. The United Kingdom has remained implacably opposed to such a move, which is favoured by other member states and by the European Parliament. The unanimity required for many decisions under Title VI means one member state is able to block proposals and the Commission has limited powers of initiation.

Although progress has been slow, with as yet limited tangible results, the bodies established under the third pillar have been far from inactive. During 1994 the K4 Committee met on 10 occasions, with Steering Group I holding 7 meetings and Steering Groups II and III each meeting on five occasions. There were 120 meetings of working parties, giving a total of 147 meetings for the K4 Committee structure. The Justice and Home Affairs Council has issued a stream of resolutions, recommendations, decisions, statements, declarations, conclusions and other documents. A small number of conventions has been agreed, on subjects such as extradition, matrimonial matters, insolvency proceedings, the Customs Information System, the protection of the Communities' financial interests, and Europol.

The large output of documents from the Council contrasts with the slow progress in establishing new methods and institutions for real law enforcement co-operation. By the beginning of 1996, no common position had been adopted and only four joint actions had been agreed. Although six conventions had been signed the ratification procedures are lengthy, as illustrated

---

Justice and Home Affairs in the European Union, European Interuniversity Press, 1995, p.219.

[24] J.A.Fortescue, 'First Experiences with the Implementation of the Third Pillar Provisions', in Bieber & Monar (eds), *Justice and Home Affairs in the European Union*, p.25.

by the Dublin Convention on Asylum which was signed in June 1990, but had been ratified by only 10 states by January 1996.

Title VI of the Treaty on European Union is a macro-level agreement designed to create a comprehensive framework for the development of meso-level co-operation on judicial and home affairs, including policing and related issues. Progress has been fitful for various reasons, of which the multi-layered structure of decision making is clearly important. This seems certain to be raised at the forthcoming 1996 Intergovernmental Conference, but given the views of certain member states, notably the United Kingdom, radical overhaul of the procedures seems unlikely.

The Europol Drugs Unit and Europol

One tangible development has been the establishment of the Europol Drugs Unit. Proposals for a European Police Office were evident at least 20 years ago,[25] but it was not until the European Council meeting in Luxembourg on 28-29th June 1991 that the idea received official backing. Chancellor Kohl tabled a motion for the creation of a European Criminal Police Office which would combat international and European crime, especially drug trafficking. Despite the surprise of the other ministers, the proposal was accepted by most of them, with only the British dissenting. The idea fitted neatly with a proposal from Trevi Working Group III that national drugs intelligence units should be established in every European Community member state to facilitate the exchange of information on drug traffickers.[26]

In December 1991, Article K1 of the Maastricht Treaty referred to 'the organisation of a union-wide system of exchanging information within a European Police Office (Europol)'. As the first step, progress was made on the establishment of a Europol Drugs Unit (EDU) and in Copenhagen in June 1993 Trevi ministers agreed its functions, staffing, accountability and finance. At the October 1993 Council meeting it was agreed that the EDU would be based in The Hague.

The Europol Drugs Unit became operational on 16th February 1994 with the task of collecting and analysing information on drug trafficking, money laundering and the criminal organisations involved, and of facilitating the exchange of intelligence between law enforcement agencies in the member states. Initially it had just 18 staff, but by late 1995 this had risen to 86, and its budget for 1995 was just over £3 million. At its meeting on 10th March 1995, the Justice and Home Affairs Council signed a joint action on the EDU which extended its functions to cover smuggling of nuclear materials, illegal immigration networks and illicit trafficking of stolen vehicles.

During the first half of 1994 the EDU responded to 146 requests for information from European Union police forces and this more than trebled in the second half of the year. In the first six months of 1995 there were 660

---

[25] Fijnaut reports that the possibility of a European policing office was discussed at a meeting of the *Bund Deutscher Kriminalbeamter* in 1974: see C.Fijnaut, 'The Internationalisation of Criminal Investigation in Western Europe', in C.Fijnaut & R.H.Hermans (eds), *Police Co-operation in Europe*, Lochem: van den Brink, 1987.

[26] R.Woodward, 'Establishing Europol', *European Journal on Criminal Policy and Research*, 1/4, 1993.

requests. The EDU is accountable through the K4 Committee structure to the Justice and Home Affairs Council. Data protection is subject to each country's own legislation.

Although member states pressed ahead with the establishment of the EDU, the creation of the European Police Office (Europol), referred to in the Article K1 of the Maastricht Treaty, has required agreement on a convention. After much delay and redrafting, the Europol Convention was eventually signed on 26th July 1995. It must now be ratified by all fifteen member states and although the United Kingdom completed its ratification in early 1996 it is likely to take a number of years for all the European Union countries to do this.

The major point of disagreement on the Europol Convention has been whether the European Court of Justice should be given a role in settling disputes. The position of the Benelux countries has been that the activities of Europol should be overseen by the Court, and this would include disputes between the new police office and individual citizens. At the other extreme, the United Kingdom remains implacably opposed to any role at all for the European Court of Justice.

Throughout late 1994 and the first half of 1995 it seemed that this issue was likely to block the Europol Convention indefinitely. However, at the Cannes European Council meeting in June 1995, a compromise was agreed which meant the Convention could be signed whilst postponing a decision on the Court's role until June 1996, thus allowing the process of ratification to begin. It is possible that this disagreement will continue to obstruct the actual establishment of Europol although it seems more likely that a solution will be found, perhaps allowing the United Kingdom to opt-out of the Court's jurisdiction.

When the idea for Europol was first raised in 1991 many were highly sceptical about whether such an initiative could really be developed in the foreseeable future. From this perspective, the establishment of a functioning Europol Drugs Unit, and the subsequent extension of its powers, and the recent agreement on the Europol Convention, show remarkable progress.

The EDU/Europol has come about as a result of a macro-level initiative consolidated in the Maastricht Treaty. Meso-level co-operation in sharing and analysing information is taking place and this is set to increase. Assuming the macro-level Europol Convention is ratified and implemented, meso-level co-operation will be extended after two years to include terrorism and could be further extended to include other forms of crime, including murder, kidnapping, racism and xenophobia, counterfeiting, fraud and robbery.

Other Structures for Co-operation on European Law Enforcement

In addition to the macro-level arrangements, there is a wide array of less formal, meso-level, arrangements for promoting police co-operation in Europe. The number of these law enforcement networks, groups and agreements is large and together they form a complicated, sometimes interconnecting, mesh of structures and arrangements, serviced by a range of information systems.[27]

One example is the Police Working Group on Terrorism (PWGOT), which was established in 1979, and now includes the anti-terrorist specialist groups in all the European Union member states plus Norway and Switzerland. The group holds meetings twice a year, but also facilitates the exchange of intelligence, promotes the secondment of officers to different countries and organises specialist seminars. It also functions on an informal basis and enables specialist officers to gain answers to specific queries. A United Kingdom anti-terrorist officer underlined its value and effectiveness as follows: 'We know these people – they are our personal friends ... It has become a very solid group of working colleagues. We trust each other implicitly and pass information to each other without question'.[28]

There are other meso-level networks which promote the exchange of information in areas as diverse as football hooliganism, traffic management, and technical and forensic matters. The European Association of Airport and Seaport Police exists to promote co-operation between port police and COLPOFER facilitates collaboration and information exchange between railway police in Europe.

Co-operation between different customs organisations is well-developed. International liaison takes place through the World Customs Organisation (WCO), which seeks to work towards harmonisation of procedures, to develop professional techniques and to exchange operational intelligence. In Europe, the Mutual Assistance Group (MAG) was set up in 1989 to address customs issues which arose as a result of the Single European Market. Discussions focused on computerised information systems, drugs enforcement, technical and scientific aids and joint operations. With the abolition of the MAG, its activities were subsumed by the K4 Committee, principally Steering Group II and the Customs Working Group.

In May 1992, European customs authorities signed the Harrogate Declaration which outlined mutual assistance arrangements, including the exchange of liaison officers and information, collaborative training, operational assistance and the development of anti-smuggling techniques. Exchanges and training have been promoted by the European Community Matthaeus initiative. Of particular importance has been the development of the Customs Information System (CIS), which is designed to enable customs officers at external borders and ports to pass information to each other. The Convention which will enable the CIS to be implemented was signed by the European Union member states on 26th July 1995 and it includes 'rolling ratification' which means the CIS may begin once two states have ratified it. Customs co-operation appears to be developing in an effective and organised way at the meso level and this is enabling real micro-level collaboration on investigations and operations, including joint surveillance.

There are also various bilateral and multilateral arrangements for fostering police co-operation between neighbouring European states including, for

---

[27] For a more detailed discussion of these meso-level networks see Benyon et al, *Police Co-operation in Europe: An Investigation*, pp.187-217.
[28] F.Bresler, *Interpol*, Sinclair Stevenson, 1992, p.162.

example, those between the Garda Siochana and the Royal Ulster Constabulary, at the Irish/United Kingdom border, and those between the French and Italian police at their common borders. Co-operative arrangements are particularly well-established between Kent Constabulary and police forces in France and Belgium. These have been helped by the activities of the Cross Channel Intelligence Conference, established in 1968, and have developed considerably with the advent of the Channel Tunnel. Memoranda of Understanding have been agreed by the British and French forces and these meso-level agreements provide a framework within which officers can undertake micro-level co-operation. Information, documentation and intelligence are exchanged on daily basis.

There are various other networks which foster co-operation between European police officers in different ways. For example, the *Union Internationale des Syndicats de Police* (UISP), based in Germany, seeks to represent the interests of police officers and analyses the potential impact on police work of developments in Europe. The European Network for Policewomen, based in the Netherlands, aims to promote equal opportunities in police work and it publishes a regular newsletter and undertakes other activities. Other groups include the Star Group and the Pompidou Group, both of which are concerned with illegal drugs, and the Vienna Group and the Berlin Group, which deal with immigration. Two secret networks, Kilowatt and the Bern Club, are anti-terrorist groups.

There is, thus, a complex patchwork of meso-level institutions, agencies and networks which aim to promote different forms of police co-operation in Europe. There seems to have been a noticeable increase in the number of such networks since the late 1980s, reflecting increased interest and concern about cross-border movements and international crime. The most successful arrangements involve high-status specialist police in politically visible fields, such as terrorism and drug trafficking. These meso-level structures have received some encouragement from macro-level groups, such as the Trevi Group and its successor European Union structures. Under the umbrella of the meso-level arrangements, micro-level co-operation on specific investigations takes place.

Momentum for and Obstacles to Further Developments

Despite delays and setbacks, in recent years there have been notable developments in structures and procedures to facilitate co-operation in law enforcement in the European Union. There is considerable impetus for continued progress, but there are also important factors which militate against further developments and jeopardise a coherent approach.

Impetus

The momentum for further progress in promoting co-operation in justice and home affairs in Europe, particularly in policing, can be divided into macro-level *political impetus* and meso-level *practitioner demands*. The former results, on the one hand, from a coincidence of member states' interests in co-operating to deal with particular problems, which may be termed the *mutual interest impetus*, and on the other hand from a political wish to construct further supranational (federal?) structures to promote European integration, which might be called the *unionist impetus*.

The mutual interest impetus accords with neo-realist explanations of sovereign states seeking to advance their own interests and on occasions establishing co-operative arrangements to this end.[29] The unionist impetus finds its most unambiguous expression in proposals for the development of a federal union, with federal laws and institutions in the fields of justice and home affairs as in other areas: 'the question at issue is whether the powers are to be exercised in common by an intergovernmental system, which is both inefficient and undemocratic, or by an effective system which respects the principles of democratic government, with the rule of law based on fundamental rights and with properly representative government under which representatives of the people – together with, in federal systems, representatives of the states – enact laws and control the executive'.[30]

There are also two types of practitioner demands. The first are *functional demands*, which arise as the result of perceived law-enforcement requirements, and the second are *specialist demands*, which result from the collective interests of particular expert groups of law-enforcement officers. Practitioner demands provide impetus for policy-shaping decisions at the meso level, although they may, of course, affect the perceived problems and needs which influence macro-level mutual interest impetus. Policy networks function at the meso level and the frequent meetings of high-level officials and experts from different countries may lead to a common approach: 'cross-national alliances of actors representing similar functional agencies seek to shape policies against the wishes of other agencies in their own national administrations'.[31] The officials involved at the meso level in the major arrangements which have developed to promote co-operation in law enforcement, notably the Schengen Central Group and the K4 Committee of the third pillar, appear to constitute policy communities, with relatively stable memberships, high levels of insularity and common agendas and understanding.

It is possible to identify two sorts of groups of actors who seek to influence the meso-level policy communities. Functional practitioner demands tend to be promoted by 'advocacy coalitions'[32] on the basis of perceived law enforcement problems. Specialist demands may be couched in similar terms, but are advanced by 'epistemic communities' which are 'networks of professionals with recognised expertise and competence in a particular domain'.[33]

---

[29] See, for example, D.Cameron, 'The 1992 Initiative: Causes and Consequences', in A.Sbragia (ed), *Euro-Politics: Institutions and Policymaking in the 'New' European Community*, Brookings Institution, 1992.

[30] J.Pinder, 'Building the Union: Policy, Reform, Constitution', in Duff et al (eds), *Maastricht and Beyond*, p.283.

[31] J.Peterson, 'Decision-making in the European Union: Towards a Framework for Analysis', *Journal of European Public Policy*, 2/1, 1995, p.78.

[32] P.A.Sabatier & H.C.Jenkins-Smith (eds), *Policy Change and Learning: An Advocacy Coalition Approach*, Westview Press, 1993.

[33] P.M.Haas, 'Epistemic Communities and International Policy Coordination', *International Organisation*, 46, 1992, p.3; for further discussion see Peterson, 'Decision-Making

Political impetus has been evident in some of the most visible and significant developments. The Trevi Group was established as a result of the mutual interest of member states in working together to combat terrorism and the mutual interest impetus was also evident in the establishment of the Schengen arrangements, the provisions in Title Vl of the Treaty on European Union and the creation of the Europol Drugs Unit/Europol.

There is also evidence that the unionist impetus has been important in these developments. In making his proposal in 1991 for a European Criminal Police Office, Chancellor Kohl seems to have been partly motivated by a wish to promote further European political integration through another supranational institution.[34] The Schengen accord, too, while undoubtedly based on mutual interest, also resulted from political belief in the need to create real cross-national police co-operation to facilitate European progress on removing internal frontier controls. It seems evident that in addition to mutual interests, some of the political momentum arises from an idealistic belief in constructing and consolidating institutions of the European 'state'.

Practitioner demands have also been important in providing impetus for increased police co-operation in Europe. The functional demands have arisen as a consequence of needs articulated by law enforcement agencies. These include claims that organised crime is increasingly transnational and action against it requires a concerted trans-European policing effort. These demands may contribute to the mutual interest impetus at the macro level, but may also lead to meso-level structures, of which politicians and others remain unaware.

Specialist practitioner demands also provide momentum for co-operative networks and initiatives. There is a trend of centralising certain specialist policing functions in organisations such as the *Bundeskriminalamt* (BKA) in Germany, the *Centrale Recherche Informatiedienst* (CRI) in the Netherlands, and the United Kingdom's National Criminal Intelligence Service (NCIS). These police experts form an epistemic community, liaising with their counterparts in the other countries and together promoting their own interests through specialist groups and structures. The professionalisation of policing, and the concomitant growth in specialist units, help to explain the proliferation of meso-level networks and groups.

As a result of these different dynamics, quite surprising developments have occurred such as the limited 'hot pursuit' permitted under the Schengen Convention. In September 1995 a German government spokesperson expressed the view that this should be extended so that police from one state were able to pursue criminals into neighbouring territory and make arrests without limitation. There are also suggestions that Europol should be given operational powers.[35]. It thus seems possible that there may be a gradual evolution of some specialist forms of European police units with limited cross-border operational capabilities.

The different types of impetus also resulted in the Declaration on Police

---

in the European Union'.

[34] See Woodward, 'Establishing Europol', pp.12-13.

[35] Woodward, 'Establishing Europol', pp.13-14 & 30-31; Benyon et al, *Police Co-operation in Europe: An Investigation*, pp.306-307; Sir R.Birch, 'Policing Europe in 1992', *Police Review*, 97, 5010, 5 May 1989.

Co-operation, which is one of the 33 declarations annexed to the Maastricht Treaty. This shows strong political commitment to promote further practical measures in the exchange of information and experience, including co-ordination of criminal investigations and search operations, creation of databases, central analysis and assessment of information, and co-operation on training, research, forensic matters and criminal records.

Impediments

There are, however, various countervailing factors which may work against further, coherent, developments.

Policing is, of course, closely related to the issue of political sovereignty of individual nation states, for the police are the principal means whereby a state imposes its authority and rule within its territory. It is therefore not surprising that some states, such as the United Kingdom, have been resistant to moves to develop common policing structures throughout the European Community institutional framework. Where they perceive a common interest, such states are prepared to work together on crime prevention, police co-operation and state security, but they are, for example, opposed to any development of common police units with operational powers across national borders. Arguments about national sovereignty may, therefore, impede various European developments in the field of policing.

There are also serious issues of legitimacy and accountability which, if not satisfactorily addressed, may jeopardise public acceptance of new forms of European police co-operation. There are, for example, criticisms about the lack of accountability of the meso-level policing networks. They are rarely held answerable for their activities and few parliamentarians, journalists or others seem to be aware of their existence. And yet, information about individuals is being exchanged without the possibility of redress. Furthermore, the data may be of commercial value and it is not clear what mechanisms, if any, exist to prevent the improper use of intelligence or information.

Whether accountability is through the courts, Parliament or the media, institutions in a democratic polity should be answerable for their policies and activities. The arrangements for police co-operation in the European Union do not appear to be sufficiently accountable in any of these respects. The absence of transparency and accountability may endanger the legitimacy of the arrangements and structures. So, too, may the increasing emphasis on 'fortress Europe' and the consequent concern about infringement of minority rights.[36] Criminal and terrorist activities have been linked with immigration and refugees to form an 'internal security continuum', which has fed xenophobia in parts of the European Union. There are some signs of growing opposition to police co-operation against refugees, asylum seekers and clandestine immigrants. If the legitimacy of police co-operation is questioned there may be rising resistance to new structures.

---

[36] A startling illustration of the development of fortress Europe came with the announcement in November 1995 that the European Commission and the Spanish government had agreed to finance a 8.5 kilometre wall around the Spanish enclave of Ceuta in North Africa, at a reported cost of some £20 million.

Another impediment to effective structures is the basic lack of knowledge and understanding about the types and extent of cross-border crime. A better understanding is necessary for a strategic approach to the continued and coherent development of police co-operation. Policing arrangements within and between the countries of the European Union are characterised by diversity and complexity and these factors may also hinder enhanced police co-operation. Different traditions and cultures have affected the ways in which European Union countries organise and undertake law enforcement. The legal and judicial systems of member states also vary considerably.

There are also problems of defining what is meant by 'police'. Many European countries have special police organisations, often operating outside the mainstream policing structures. Examples of such police include railway police, ports and airports police, forestry police and a range of tax and revenue police. Excluding agencies with primary responsibilities in such fields, there are over 120 separate police forces in the fifteen countries of the European Union, and they include over 1.3 million police officers. On average, there is one police officer for every 280 people in the European Justice, but there is considerable variation between member states.[37]

European Union policing is thus complex – a large number of highly-differentiated forces with different structures and a variety of roles. A high level of effective co-operation is often difficult to achieve even between forces operating in the *same* country – it is on occasions difficult to achieve within the same *force*. Lack of information and communication, rivalries and jealousies between and within agencies, and different approaches and perceptions, are factors which may cause inefficiency and ineffectiveness in any organisation and policing is no exception. It may be difficult to secure co-operation between police agencies operating in different countries, with diverse cultures and traditions, incompatible communications and procedures, and often quite different legal systems and organisational structures.

A final possible impediment to effective police co-operation in Europe arises from the proliferation of different agencies, structures and institutions at the macro and meso levels. There is a real danger of confusion, duplication and competition between these institutions.

Building Police Co-operation in the European Union

The Treaty on European Union proclaimed at the outset that the member states were 'resolved to mark a new stage in the process of European integration'. The objectives of the European Union are to promote economic and social progress and cohesion, to implement a common foreign and security policy, to introduce citizenship of the Union, and to develop close co-operation on justice and home affairs. On this last objective, there appear to be quite high levels of commitment amongst many member states and there are indications of a real attempt to develop a more coherent approach. Such an attempt certainly seems necessary, given the proliferation of arrangements for co-operation in this field in recent years, and the conse-

---

[37] J.Benyon et al, *Police Forces in the New European Union: A Conspectus*, CSPO, 1995.

quent problems of duplication and competition, but there are, as yet, only mixed signs of a successful outcome in developing an effective and clear division of responsibilities.

Progress has been variable, but step-by-step a series of structures for co-operation on policing and related matters is being built in the European Union, with the third pillar at its centre. The nascent internal security field is a 'European work site'[38] and raises fascinating political questions with the potential to make a considerable impact on the future of the European Union and on the rights of European citizens.

The matters with which Title VI deals are those which states invariably regard as of central importance. Given that 'the state is a human community that (successfully) claims the monopoly of the legitimate use of physical force within a given territory',[39] control of policing by the state is essential as 'the police are the specialist repository domestically of the state's monopoly of legitimate force'.[40] States also seek to control who enters their territory, and are concerned with threats to order posed by organised crime and particularly by terrorism.

The police are the principal means, short of the armed forces, whereby a state imposes its authority within its own territory. Unsurprisingly, states wish to maintain control of the police and this is closely bound up with notions of sovereignty of individual nation states. However, in the European Union and further afield, the various threats, perceived or real, touched on in Section II of this paper, may persuade states to work together on crime prevention, policing activities and internal security. There is, of course, something of an irony in that some of the major threats, such as terrorism and subversion, against which inter-state co-operation may have the greatest impact, are particularly sensitive areas in which individual states are least likely to be prepared to surrender any sovereignty and control.

Among the impediments to the continuing construction of a successful system for police co-operation, the problem of the 'democratic deficit' is a serious one. Police co-operation in Europe is developing at various levels – some of it 'top down', more of it 'bottom up' – but, whether the initiatives are inspired by ministers or generated by officials and police officers, there appears to be a widespread neglect of mechanisms to ensure political and social accountability. These are necessary in order to secure legitimacy and public consent, which are vital for effective policing in open, democratic societies. There is a delicate balance to be struck between granting and restraining police powers, and of providing the effective oversight which is necessary in order to generate the confidence and support which underpins democratic, consensual, policing.

Effective police co-operation at the European level – as at any level – depends on information and assistance received from members of the public. It is time for citizens to be involved in the construction site around the third pillar for ultimately the fight against crime must be waged by both the police *and* the citizens of Europe.

---

[38] Bigo, 'The European Internal Security Field', p.161.

[39] M.Weber, 'Politics as a Vocation', in H.Gerth & C.Wright Mills (eds), *From Max Weber: Essays in Sociology*, Routledge & Kegan Paul, 1948, p.78.

[40] R.Reiner, *The Politics of the Police*, Harvester Wheatsheaf, 1992, pp.268-69.

Political Theory and the Foundations of Value

Mark Evans
University of Wales, Swansea

'Foundationless Liberalism: Coming To Terms With Contingency'

Considering their philosophical outlooks and value commitments, it is hardly surprising that so many liberals have proven to be acutely sensitive to the crisis of confidence engendered by the varieties of scepticism surfacing in the wake of the Enlightenment. For if one combines, as they typically profess to do, a principle to respect individual autonomy with an acknowledgement of the rich diversity in forms of life and society that different people(s) have developed or could otherwise choose, it is not difficult to appreciate how one can come to doubt the rectitude or superiority of that principle, or any others. The sheer variety of human perspectives and experiences with which the liberal consciousness is disposed to identify can even undermine confidence that disputants over values can agree upon the means to settle their conflict authoritatively, let alone reach a satisfactory conclusion.

This problem crystallises in the issue of political justification. For even if a liberal holds fast to her beliefs as personal commitments – and the threat of nihilism posed by the aforementioned crisis suggests this would be no mean achievement – her respect for autonomy and sensitivity to diversity may prompt her to recognise that the reasons she gives to herself in support of her beliefs ('why am I a liberal?') may not be appropriate if invoked to justify the exercise of power to enforce liberal principles within a political community.[1] The value-commitment which prompts the notion of the specifically political justification requires the reasons offered in the latte to be acceptable in some substantive way to all over whom power is to be exercised. Finding plausible candidates for these reasons has become a key preoccupation for much modern liberal thought – but its own values and sensitivities always threaten to undermine this goal and, with it, confidence in liberalism as a political project.

Liberal thinkers have become increasingly creative and sophisticated in their desire (and perhaps accelerating desperation) to square this apparent circle. Among their major representatives are John Rawls, Richard Rorty and John Gray, the differences between them attesting to a certain vitality in the project.[2] In explaining why liberal principles as they define them could be acceptable to members of a free political community, these three profess to avoid 'foundationalist' justifications, which purport to identify essentially self-evident or self-justifying principles (a liberal realism which held that there was some fact, or set of facts, in the world that by itself

---

[1] 'Political justification', as distinct from the personal, has been most extensively employed recently in Rawls's work, but the possibility of the distinction as a characteristic of liberalism in general can, of course, be located in the venerable tradition which insists that subjects' consent is what legitimises political power.

[2] John Gray, *Post-Liberalism*, Routledge 1993, though note how Gray moves further away from liberalism in *Enlightenment's Wake*, Routledge 1995, especially chapter 9; John Rawls, *Political Liberalism*, Columbia University Press, 1993; Richard Rorty, *Contingency, Irony and Solidarity*, Cambridge University Press, 1989.

established liberalism's universal rectitude – such as a natural rights doctrine – is a good example of this species of theory).[3] Yet their alternative approaches still display the problem described here, in generating what I have elsewhere dubbed 'inoffensive' liberalisms.[4] By this, I mean that they appear to localise the applicability of liberal principles to what are already putatively liberal contexts, characterise citizens as being, despite their differences, the kind of people who would find liberalism reasonable and/or restructure the doctrine itself – all to maximise the *theoretical* chances of liberal politics beingently inoffensive and unobjectionable to its subjects as to be capable of passing the political justification test.

Central to the critique of inoffensive liberalisms, which will be asserted without defence here, is the claim that, ultimately, they fail to avoid deeply contestable values and beliefs – or unjustifiably mask this controversiality with unwarranted assumptions about the kinds of principles which could be endorsed by any citizen of a pluralistic liberal democracy. The respect for autonomy and sensitivity to diversity which helped to produce this type of doctrine now conspire to sweep it away for pretending to a potential consensus upon liberalism's claims that simply isn't available.

No doubt the liberalism industry will continue to attract those unprepared to give up on this type of approach. But if one deems that liberalism's tenets ought to be treated as inherently controversial even within societies where its traditions are firmly embedded, is it necessary to conclude that liberalism fails by setting itself aspirations it cannot hope to achieve?

This paper will hereafter outline an altogether more positive conclusion from this premiss, but one which requires a transformation in certain liberal attitudes. Specifically, it challenges the consensus-seeking drive in political justification that bears much responsibility for the doctrine's theoretical travails. I argue that liberalism does not cease to be liberalism if it concedes that there may be no plausible way of rendering its principles freely acceptable to all who may nevertheless be justifiably rendered subject to them. Hence I propose to equip the doctrine with the means to go on the offensive against its foes, abandoning the localisation of its concerns to 'constitutional democracies' or whatever and restoring what was, after all, its historically venerated character as a political possibility for all humanity.

So, using 'the liberal' to refer hereafter to the supporter of this particular variant of the ideology, I begin by proposing a three-fold division of the liberal's concerns into: (i) conceptions of the good life; (ii) specific institutional recommendations for social, economic and political structures; (iii) the fundamental principles of human conduct.

All three are potentially political concerns for the liberal, although anti-perfectionists profess to abjure interference in (i) (I leave aside the con-

---

[3] 'Foundationalism' is loosely used in liberal debate and requires further clarification, which I here leave aside; my 'snappy' definition is drawn from David Brink, *Moral Realism and the Foundations of Ethics*, Cambridge University Press, 1989, chapter 5. It is, of course, hotly disputed as to whether the aforementioned authors do avoid foundationalist appeals.

[4] For a brief presentation of this notion, see my 'Anti-Perfectionism and the Liberalism of Inoffensiveness', *Politics*, 15/3, 1995. The present paper, the first part of a book project, aims to sketch how the 'emboldened' or 'offensive' liberalism promised in the article's conclusion might be delivered.

troversy over whether liberal politics can have perfectionist commitments here). Certainly, no liberal would advocate the imposition of comprehensive, specifically defined ideals at this level. In (ii) the liberal may commend the use of political power to create and/or maintain the central institutions and practices which constitute liberal society, though, I suggest that the sensitivity to diversity renders the liberal alive to the inappropriateness of some, if not all, of the proposals for certain human communities. She could recognise, for example, that parliamentary democracy – which she wishs to uphold in her western society – is not viable for a tribal, traditionalistic culture. Consequently, she would condemn the forcible imposition of that form of regime. She might even be suspicious of purely persuasive strategies to promote it.

Level (iii) is what concerns us most here, for it isolates those principles which the liberal believes are so important that they demand respect in *any* form of society. I propose that a certain set of human rights (to life, basic liberties and just treatment) will fall into this category.[5] The liberal will argue that this set frames the boundaries for toleration and, crucially, does not render the justification for any action in support of its promotion dependent upon the consent of those whom whom respect for rights is required.

Now, the liberal-as-human-rights-activist in political life today does not typically display anything like the inoffensiveness characteristic of many of her philosophical counterparts, because the value and the appeal of the principles in question is so strong as to outweigh or push aside the theoretical dispositions which produced the localised or relativised versions of liberal doctrine. No doubt many such activists are moral realists, in the sense that they believe there to be some fact, or set of facts, independent of their thoughts and feelings which could establish the truth or falsehood of their values. Realist moral commitment is a form of *factual* commitment.

Yet central to some of the trends which nurtured inoffensive liberalism is a powerful scepticism over moral realism: whether we can agree upon moral facts or the methods to identify them, or whether there are any such facts at all. The briefest acquaintance with modern Western philosophy's continuing struggles with these issues would, one might think, dent the confidence of any realist who thinks he has concluded the debate and is operating with The Correct Answers. Richard Rorty argues that, because philosophical searches for truth have been so inconclusive and contested, they are of no real use in the advancement of moral causes and are therefore best abandoned by moral activists.[6] A realist rights-activist who agrees that the philosophical support for his view remains inconclusive might persist in his commitment, acting accordingly, and maintain that the search for truth has simply yet to be completed successfully. But this seems to embody a non-realist *faith* that the relevant truths are indeed awaiting demonstration, yielding a point that is critical to my proposed offensive liberalism: purely

---

[5] Obviously, a proper presentation of this theory would have to explain more precisely the nature of these rights and elaborate upon their centrality for the liberal. This task, though, can be treated as incidental to the necessarily narrower purposes of this paper.

[6] 'Human Rights, Rationality, and Sentimentality', in S.Shute & S.Hurley (eds), *On Human Rights*, Basic Books, 1993.

evaluative, non-factual commitment play a vital role in our typical moral experience. The realist rights-activist will generally promote human rights not just, or even primarily, because he thinks rights are 'the fact of the matter' but because he admires and supports the values they embody. He believes the facts will ultimately support him, too, but he is not usually the sort of person to let doubts over these deflect him from his *evaluative* conviction: he thinks his values are too important for that. He (and, by extension, those on whose behalf he campaigns) is ill-served by those inoffensive liberalisms which take the philosophical worries more to heart.

Offensive liberalism therefore runs with the notion of evaluative conviction and will rely in part upon the claim that it is true to the experience of moralists for its support. As we have noted, Rorty's pragmatist approach disperses with the meta-ethical dimensions to moral inquiry. He does, however, draw a provisional anti-realist conclusion: since our moral development seems to owe nothing to increased moral knowledge as there is very little upon which we agree, he claims, there probably is no knowledge to discover.[7] Indeed, his theory of how to effect moral changes and conversions rests upon familiar anti-realist strategies of 'playing' with people's sentiments, as values are reducible to feelings.

Offensive liberalism taps into many Rortyan themes, but among the points of departure is a more forthright support for meta-ethical anti-realism. Apart from its claim that the latter makes the best sense of morality's nature, which I will not go into any further here, I think it is important to appreciate the contingencies of values entailed by anti-realism. For one ought not to neglect the widespread unease, among philosophers and non-philosophers alike, with the idea that our values are ultimately (only) products of how we feel. Against Rorty, I doubt whether such worries can be assuaged simply by the pragmatist's 'setting-aside' of the meta-ethical issues; using anti-realist methods in moral activity is likely to exacerbate these concerns. Some indication of the challenge faced by the liberal on this score will be glimpsed later on.

Setting out the main meta-ethical claims of offensive liberalism in summary, we have:

1: the world is 'disenchanted', bereft of intrinsic moral meaning. Values rest only on certain kinds of human sentiment though, because at least some of our values are typically acquired through forms of socialisation which impart a pseudo-objectivist character to them, this point is difficult to grasp. Anti-realism in meta-ethics insists, however, that even if morality generally confronts us as a structure of social norms into which we are inducted, the authority of that morality, or anything with which the inherited ethics might be replaced, is rooted in the desirability we feel in its strictures.[8]

2: Moral argument is, therefore, going to be question-begging at some

---

[7] *Ibid*, p.119.

[8] Obviously, much more will have to be said about the precise nature of the doctrine being proposed here. In the space allowed, I am mainly concerned to distinguish offensive liberalism's view not only from the classical metaphysical-realist views, such as natural rights theory, but from the Hegelian- or Wittgenstein-inspired communitarian views which tend to struggle with the problem of how to challenge legitimately the moral authority claimed by 'the community'.

level, in the sense that, in order to accept any moral claim, one will have to share the relevant desires underpinning it. There is nothing else, outside of the desires, by which one could authoritatively adjudicate between rival claims. Given that whatever force and authority morality has for us depends upon how we feel, this view requires us to reconcile ourselves to the fundamental contingency of moral commitments but urges, nevertheless, that we can take them no less seriously than do realists who think their values stand regardless of their contingent attitudes to them.

3: The awareness of the contingency of one's values is further enhanced in the offensive liberal view by the sensitivity to diversity: the liberal reality recognises that there is no uniformity and/or permanence in moral desires amongst all people and we cannot construct a morality with universalist pretensions by ignoring the plurality of moral sentiments and pretending that we all, at heart, desire much the same morals. We might wish that everyone did share them, but this would be the outcome of actual moral conversion and not its presupposition. Put another way, this view proposes that there are a number of desire-generated moral perspectives upon the world, which may be radically at odds with each other and certainly ought not to be theorised at the outset as immediately capable of reconciliation in a universal morality.

4: This pluralist anti-realism does not, however, rule out the usage of realist-*seeming* language in expressing moral commitments, a facility which I believe the liberal would be well advised to employ. Offensive liberalism as I see it ought to borrow heavily from Simon Blackburn's 'projectivism', a recent and rigorous development of this thought. Baldly put, this view suggests that the values of one's moral perspective are projected upon the world and that realist-seeking language is an entirely appropriate way of describing the way the world looks from that perspective. Plenty of other wholly mind-dependent features are referred to in such terms, as objects perceived, even though they are purely theoretical entities. If we grant that there is nothing wrong with the preservation of such language (which would no longer be 'pseudo'-objectivist as it isn't actually pretending to a mind-independent reality), we can also appreciate the way such phrasing of moral commitment also helps to convey its sincerity and depth.

To illustrate how the offensive liberal proceeds with this in support of human rights: the latter, which embodies certain desires as to how people should live and be treated by their fellows, are projected in the liberal perspective upon each person. 'The human' is conceptualised as 'rights-bearer' and the liberal is able to talk of rights as if people 'really' possessed them because this is the way things look from her perspective. One needs to adopt a rights-projecting perspective (and therefore possess the requisite desires) in order to attribute human rights to people and there is nothing outside of the various moral perspectives to demonstrate which of them is superior. All such evaluations require one already to have adopted one such perspective; once again, our desires are our guides here. Crucially (and this is a point to which I shall return) this applies above all to the relativist judgement that is often thought to be entailed by an outlook like this: to conclude that each perspective is as good as any other is obviously to make an evaluation which is as perspective-dependent as any other. As such, it is perfectly coherent but there is nothing that extra-perspectivally necessitates it. Further, one of the most critical claims in offensive liberalism is that it is not necessitated by every combination of values permissible within a liberal perspective. This is what permits the holding of level (iii) commitments such as human rights.[9]

5: For a projectivist, the point of moral argument is to shape and reshape people's morality -generating desires. Critics of anti-realism sometimes suggest that it actually undermines the point of arguing about morality, as if 'proper' arguments could only ever be over factual matters. However, arguments over the purely evaluative are familiar in everyday life as disputants describe and redescribe people, objects or situations to try to alter each other's opinions about them. This is not to say facts have no place in such arguments, of course; one might change an evaluative judgement on X when informed that the initial opinion was based upon incorrect or incomplete information. But plenty of such argument remains fundamentally subjective – and no less pertinent for that.

6: Whether or not we adopt the argumentative strategy, or something altogether more coercive in moral conversion (or, indeed, whether we attempt the latter in any way at all) is a value-judgement which, like all others in this view, is perspective-dependent and can only be defended question-beggingly. There is nothing like an 'ideal-speech situation' for 'free and rational' agents to settle their moral conflicts, for all such solutions rest upon the acceptance of values which are only held or present within certain perspectives.

Much Western moral thinking has had the grand ambition of finding some values and methods upon which we can all agree as a prelude to the resolution of the other outstanding moral conflicts. For all their sensitivities to the implausibilities and inadequacies of their predecessors on this score, inoffensive liberalisms have simply tried to carry this project forward. Once the controversiality of these initial commitments is admitted, these theories begin to unravel and their defence of their values suffers accordingly. Offensive liberalism's meta-ethic attempts to avoid this problem by conceding the initial, deep-seated plurality and controversiality of the most basic principles affirmed by people in all times and places. It urges that this need not undermine the point or the strength of our particular commitments – and specifically need not relativise them. Nor does it deprive its practitioners of all access to the strategies of moral conversion favoured, say, by realists. Bearing in mind the remarks above concerning the underlying non-factual convictions which may persist in a realist's outlook, the offensive liberal can claim that she is merely proposing openly what the realist usually ends up surreptitiously doing.

Let us look more specifically at what the liberal is capable of advocating

---

[9] Blackburn explains and defends his projectivism in *Essays in Quasi-Realism*, Oxford University Press, 1993, especially chapters 8 & 9. A summary of criticisms of projectivism, drawn in large part from the work of John McDowell, is provided in David McNaughton, *Moral Vision*, 1988, especially chapters 6 & 12. Offensive liberalism's use of projectivism is not intended to be utterly faithful to Blackburn; I am currently preparing a detailed, two-paper presentation of these ideas under the general title 'Projecting Human Rights'.

here. It remains reasonable, I think, to assume that an offensive liberal's values are going to leave her biased in favour of purely persuasive strategies in the project of moral conversion. The dialogical examples above can consequently be seen as paradigmatically liberal. Certainly with respect to level (i) issues, which refer to personal ideals of life, no liberal is going to be anything other than extremely cautious in using political power to displace pure persuasion with elements of coercion. Facilitating autonomy and diversity will make liberal perfectionism piecemeal at best, to be applied carefully, sensitively and receptive to the demands of people to do their own thing. If the liberal has strong, comprehensive views on how people should live, she may use the dialogical strategy to shape others' sentiments – but this ceases to be a specifically political matter.

Level (ii), the realm of specific institutional structures, is also very amenable to persuasive strategies for liberals as they debate, among themselves and with others, what are the most appropriate forms of political regime, socio-economic relationships and so on ('how best to translate desired moral values into practice' is a central theme at this level). As mentioned earlier, I believe it is consistent and proper for a liberal also to advocate the use of political power at this level, too. After all, it is a traditional liberal tenet that permits a state's use of power in this area as long as its citizens have consented to its general authority. There are many deep problems here, of course ('can a newly-established liberal state legitimately use its power to consolidate its institutions when a majority of citizens don't yet, or are not ready to, accept it?' and 'can a well-established liberal state use its power to defend itself when the allegiances of a majority of its citizens are shifting markedly towards illiberal, authoritarian allegiances?' are two highly pertinent questions that figure at this level). Over such issues, the liberal clearly has much thinking to do – and let us be clear exactly what the liberal equipped with the meta-ethic above will be doing in such reflection. For, having no alternative but to work within her own perspective of values, the liberal tackles issues such as these simply by working out what kind of answers can be yielded which are consistent with those values and, more demandingly, which answer best expresses her commitments. It is a matter of articulating and re-articulating, honing and refashioning the beliefs within the perspective, rather than seeking answers to such problems which are logically independent of them.[10]

The crisis of confidence, the emergence of inoffensive liberalisms and the other developments which I suggest have come to plague liberal thought are all products of a perceived mis-match within the liberal perspective between its fundamental values and those situations in which the latter are fundamentally opposed. In one way or another, many liberals have screened out of their political concerns these situations in order to preserve the integrity of their perspective. And surely, for those of a liberal disposition who wish to celebrate human freedom and diversity, the use of political power to instantiate specific types of behaviour is generally going to be something of

---

[10]This is not to deny that such reflection might force a wholesale change of perspective, if one's existing outlook comes to appear unsatisfactory in the face of challenges one believes must be taken seriously.

which to be wary. Hence the problematic nature of the issues raised at level (ii).

The argument of this paper, though, is that this angst need not affect level (iii) in anything like the same way. The schema of human rights posited here are as fundamental as universal principles to the offensive liberal as is the relativising interpretation of the respect for authority to the inoffensive liberal. Rather than make all of what is enforceable by a liberal political authority dependent in some way upon the consent of its subjects, level (iii) matters are given moral *and* political primacy regardless. The offensive liberal could claim with perfect consistency that the human rights at level (iii) guarantee the conditions under which humans can be free. But her sensitivity to diversity makes her aware that arguments like this depend upon a very partial view of what it means to be free. There is no one universally grounded conception of 'freedom', or 'agency', or whatever, that could be accepted by all and could provide the foundations for liberal human rights. As we have characterised it here, offensive liberalism doesn't wish away such thoroughgoing conflict but accepts it as unavoidable and proceeds nevertheless to advocate action upon its evaluative convictions.

Now for a lot of people – and perhaps not only those imbued with the ethos of inoffensive liberalism – the conclusions drawn by the offensive liberal that (to use a phrase heard at the last P.S.A. conference) it's all right to go on some kind of liberal 'jihad' looks paradoxically illiberal and unacceptable, especially in the light of her pluralistic anti-realism over the nature of values. I have already suggested how one might deflect criticisms of the doctrine with the example of the realist moral activist but, before moving on to further remarks designed to ease its acceptance as a political position, it is worth stressing that even an offensive liberal doesn't immediately *have* to take up the cudgels for human rights.

To illustrate, let us think of an offensive-liberal state confronting an illiberal neighbour, governed by a regime and an ideology that aims systematically to undermine human rights. The liberal state deems this state of affairs to be wrong (in its purely evaluative sense, remember) and wishes to promote a rights-respecting culture in its place. Despite all that has been said about offensive liberalism, it would not be inconsistent or inappropriate for the liberal state to deploy persuasive strategies of moral conversion in the first instance. Rorty's recent work has highlighted some important themes in this area; to use his rather playful words (though the light-heartedness of the liberal ironist is significantly absent when he deals with such matters) the telling of 'sad' and 'sentimental stories' of human suffering can profoundly shape people's feelings, alter their moral desires and hence transform their evaluative perspectives. He is definitely on to something important in his claim that the violation of human rights is often 'excused' by its perpetrators via the casting of their victims as non- or sub-human.[11] Hence, a critical part of the persuasive strategy is to extend the identifications and the sympathies of such people to generate a conception of humanity and its attendant rights which does not cease to apply at particular social, religious or sexual boundaries. Dialogue, images, litera-

---

[11] Rorty, 'Human Rights', especially pp.112-5, 133-4.

ture: the various media of communication become vital moral tools in this project.

The offensive liberal state likes to think that it 'lives in the real world', though; it hardly expects persuasive strategies to achieve their goals to any great extent. Rights-violators are not usually the sort of people to listen to 'long, sad, sentimental' stories. Hence, the state turns to contemplate coercion. Again, being liberal, its outlook remains infused with ideas of reasonableness and moderation; these values can govern the types and degrees of coercion it decides to employ.

Sanctions, of course, are a form of coercion even though the intervention in the affairs of their object state is indirect. Obviously, they usually require the 'sanctioning' state to coerce its own citizens to prevent them dealing with the 'sanctioned' state. Inoffensive liberalisms might profitably detain themselves at this point to consider whether they have sufficiently sturdy theoretical tools to defend this type of policy adequately when those forced to join a state's sanctions policy fundamentally oppose its aims. This has hardly been an unfamiliar feature in the behaviour of actually-existing liberalism and I would suggest that the offensive liberal has potentially useful ammunition here again to argue that sanctions-supporting liberals have, in effect, been acting in an offensive-liberal manner.

The boldest assertion of offensive liberalism is that human rights are valued so highly that it would be consistent to advocate direct intervention in the illiberal state to prevent further violations. No other principle within the liberal perspective is sufficiently outweighing to rule this move out of court. One has to characterise liberalism as a doctrine which is not so deeply devoted to rights in order to wring a preclusion of this possible policy out of it. Many liberals today, intentionally or not, do seem to end up affirming this in effect, which is why liberalism has come to seem so inoffensive and non-combative. In denying that liberal values have to be construed thus, though, the offensive liberal can point not only to those earlier, foundationist liberalisms which did embody this missionary universalism but also – more powerfully – to the human-rights activists around the world who actually carry forward the agenda she has proposed.

It must be stressed that direct intervention is being advocated as a theoretically consistent possibility. The offensive liberal does not have to believe it is morally mandatory. There may, for example, be pragmatic objections: estimations of the likelihood of success might be sufficiently discouraging to prompt liberals to pass up the possibility, for one thing. Further, admitting the consistency of such a policy does not preclude acknowledgement that there may be instances (which could occur frequently) when it is outweighed by other values within the liberal perspective; all that offensive liberalism has to claim is that it is not always ruled out. Both the remaining pragmatic and moral possibilities militating against intervention are going to be determined by a number of variables: how severe are the rights violations? Will the attempt to eradicate them be worth the lives of the military personnel assigned the task? These are just two of the questions that offensive liberalism may pose during its moral calculations.

But the central claim remains: there is nothing wrong with these calculations leading to the advocacy of the forcible imposition of human rights upon any society. The evaluative convictions of the liberal who thinks that, whatever particular form it takes, no society is decent and tolerable unless it respects rights can be legitimately translated into action. Given the activities of human-rights activists and the myriad instances in the world today of the causes of their concerns, this is a crucial result – and one which avoids the embarrassments of inoffensive liberalism which shies away from this task.

For some critics of the position sketched here, this conclusion is reached far too swiftly, boiling moral argument right down to a case of 'this is how I feel people should be treated and anything that isn't inconsistent with my feelings is justified. To be frank, though this is not the most charitable way of characterising it, one must honestly admit that this is not a fundamentally misleading description of the offensive liberal view. Anti-realism in ethics is hardly a novel feature, but teasing the implications out in this way is still shocking enough to make many insist that 'there must be something more solid to morality than this'. Hence the offensive liberal's stress on the need to 'come to terms with contingency': the contingency of our values upon certain kinds of sentiment that we need not necessarily possess and which many people indeed lack, and the consequent fact that moral justifications can only ever work question-beggingly, if we happen to possess the appropriate desires. In the space remaining, I will raise a few points that the offensive liberal can marshal in support of her perturbing standpoint.

First, the feeling that there must be more to morality than contingently-held desires could be explained by the way people have been generally socialised into viewing it as realist, something constituted independently of our desires and drawing its force and authority from that independent basis. It is this that realists seek to identify – but the offensive liberal will claim that they are simply trying to force metaphysics into grounding something that isn't there. What she argues is that the realist misconception of morality profoundly distorts views of the kind of foundation and justification for morality and moral action many people are disposed to treat as adequate. It is no wonder, therefore, that her doctrine is deemed unsatisfactory. Therefore, it wouuld seem to be crucial to offensive liberalism that the description of the world as, in itself, morally neutral or meaningless is prosecuted with much vigour in order to comfort the realists' concerns and seek converts to its outlook.[12]

Part of the critics' worries is that the anti-realist view deployed by the offensive liberal reduces one to taking morality very lightly, chopping and changing commitments as one pleases. Further, despite protestations to the contrary, it teeters towards relativism in the sense that what one deems as good now depends upon a certain set of desires which, were it to change,

---

[12] As already suggested, this provides a major reason why the Rortyean pragmatist approach is rejected here. Though Rorty inclines towards anti-realism, he excuses himself from having to address meta-ethical questions in depth on the grounds that such inquiries are not of much use in moral activity. My argument is that, on the contrary, they have a critical role to play in unshackling people from the moral-realist assumptions which make their holders deeply unsympathetic to this kind of approach.

would lead us to regard something different (and possibly quite the opposite) as good.[13]

In response to the first problem, the offensive liberal will hope that being freed of realist expectations about morality's status will help us to see that purely evaluative convictions need not be any less deeply affirmed than others. The fact that our moral outlook arises from a set of desires we could very well have lacked, or could hereafter change, does not necessarily mean it isn't serious. Many other profoundly important features in typical lives are based upon similarly contingent happenstanc: my love and intended life-long commitment to my wife is not undermined by my recognition that I was not predestined to meet her and that a host of 'accidents' brought us together, that one of our previous, failed relationships with different people could easily have worked instead and forestalled our present commitment ... and so on.

Really, the offensive liberal can return to the point that it is not the origin, foundation or status of the values that matter; it is the values themselves which grip us. Think again of the realist human-rights activist whose convictions remain firm even when metaphysical philosophy stubbornly refuses to yield a satisfactory realist justification for them. It is this strength of commitment that helps to combat the second problem; indeed, it is the only way to resist the creeping onset of relativist sentiments. True, it is a consequence of the offensive liberal view that if our current rights-ascribing perspective shifts to a rights-rejecting one we would have no reason within the latter to say rights-violations are wrong. From our present perspective we reject the prescriptions of this changed outlook and that is, ultimately, all we can say here. Yet the strength of our current feelings about the features of life protected by rights could – or so we must hope – overcome any sapping of conviction that recognition of such contingency might generate.

Moreover, we ought not to neglect the point that the offensive liberal is not trying to defend a set of values that she has just made up. In a sense, she is the inheritor of a perspective created, moulded and reshaped by many people and societies over time, which has wide appeal and continues to be deemed extremely desirable. That she is not alone in her convictions promises to provide another powerful barrier to the relativising, confidence-draining dangers that contingency's recognition is generally prone to create.

All this is not lazily to assume that the holding of values in this manner is always going to be easy; offensive liberalism poses a challenge to moral agents which is not resolvable on paper but requires the actual fostering of the appropriate characteristics. Unswerving faith is not the only alternative to nihilistic inaction for the offensive liberal in the face of contingency and moral pluralism. For, being a *liberal* view, this perspective will be conscious of its own potential for incremental improvement. The justified charges of cultural imperialism levelled against some of its predecessors, which helped to heighten the sensitivity to diversity in liberal thinking, can dispose this

---

[13] Hence it is not a relativism between different people's perspectives at the same time that is the problem; it was suggested earlier that this value need have no place in the offensive-liberal perspective. Rather, it is a relativism between the changing states of the same perspective over time that is the problem being raised here.

perspective towards learning from other cultures, tolerating other ways of respecting human dignity, thus refining its own sensibilities.

Certain forms of society and human behaviour will always remain beyond the pale for the offensive liberals, though. This paper has sketched the outline of a theory which could be developed to satisfy them that they can have a philosophy which justifies political action against what they regard as assaults on human dignity but which does not lapse into the kind of foundationalist outlook their own sensibilities increasingly lead them to reject. The theory promises a fundamental re-estimation – and downgrading – of what one might hope philosophy can achieve for us in moral and political justification. For, when their core commitments to human rights are at stake in a world where so many flagrantly reject them, do liberals really want to delay action until a 'better' philosophy is found?

Political Theory and the Foundations of Value

Martyn Oliver
University of Westminster

'Rorty on Rawls: The Question of Contingency'

Introduction

What does it mean for political theorists to be mindful of 'contingency'? Does a heightened sensitivity to contingency restrict political theorists to the resources available to them from the dominant political culture? If so, what is meant by the dominant political culture? Does the dominant political culture provide a sufficiently radical set of concepts and ideas from which a significantly more egalitarian and democratic polity, than that provided by contemporary liberal democracy, could be constructed? Or is any notion of radicalism at odds with a 'sensitivity to contingency'? These are enormous questions and are currently defining the self-image of political theory. However, not only is it impossible to provide comprehensive answers to them in the short space below, it is also not possible to provide anything approaching absolute answers to them. This is a point that should not be ignored as some banal relativist logic. Nor as one that can be accounted for by minimal lip service to contextualism via a gloss of historicism and cosmopolitanism. Once accepted in principle, there are no limits to its pervasiveness. For Richard Rorty, the idea that there can be no absolute answers to such questions (or any questions relating to the acquisition and use of human knowledge) works as the starting point for the answers he gives to them. Moreover, contextuality is neither merely a consideration in Rorty's thinking, nor is it an impediment to giving strength to his convictions. For this reason Rorty's treatment of the questions posed above is uniquely important, and will be treated as such in the following discussion.

Understanding Rorty as providing a unique approach to the subject of contingency within political theory, must entail the adoption of a more constructive approach to his work. One that avoids the now exhausted attempt to seek out the familiar self-referential contradictions of the relativist hidden by Rorty's clever rhetorical tropes. First, there is little to be gained by such an approach and second if a more positive attempt is needed within political theory to account for the recent resurgence of anti-foundationalism then overcoming the urge to seek out the performative contradiction will be necessary. That is, ultimately there can be no eternal reproach to the anti-relativist charge of performative contradiction, though this should not be viewed as a reason for abandoning anti-foundationalism. In any case, Rorty would not have risen to the status of one of the most influential and widely discussed philosophers in the past 15-20 years had his claims simply amounted to a pure vulgar relativism. My constructive approach to Rorty will therefore be grounded in the hope that Rorty has provided the most effective method anti-foundationalists are likely to find in their attempts to overcome the pitfalls of relativism. For this reason, the following analysis will be restricted to an attempt to prove, minimally, that Rorty's work cannot so easily be dismissed as a confused and inconsequential relativism.

The answers Rorty does provide to the questions posed at the outset are found in their most acute and controversial form in an article entitled 'The priority of democracy to philosophy'.[1] In it Rorty tackles head on the question of contingency within political theory by addressing the work of John Rawls. He suggests that Rawls 'priority of the right over the good' must be both the guiding logic of our democratic hopes and the position that best accommodates a critique of foundationalism. Although for Rorty such a critique will not be necessary as support for the idea that justice must come before any commitment to particular common goods. To arrive at this claim, Rorty embarks on an interpretation of Rawls that transforms him from a neo-Kantian rationalist committed to a solidly individualist libertarianism, to a pragmatic anti-foundationalist at home with Hegel as much as Kant and unthreatened by a more fragmented and historicised understanding of the self.[2] Despite widespread objections to Rorty's 'strong misreading' of Rawls, the following interpretation will explain how Rorty is entitled, without fear of a serious contradiction with his underlying anti-foundationalism, to embrace Rawls as an anti-foundational pragmatist. However, this is not to suggest that Rorty is right to imply that Rawlsian libertarianism must be the 'final vocabulary' of the anti-foundational political theorist. In this sense Rorty's conservatism is an unnecessary consequence of his commitment to contingency.

Rorty's anti-foundationalism

The entire basis of Rorty's thinking consists of a critique of the pursuit of certainty, a pursuit that for Rorty, is found in its most acute from in philosophy but expressed in less obvious forms within other disciplines. According to Rorty, foundationalism and realism are merely different variations of the persuit of certainty. Consequently, he understands foundationalism, in contrast to the traditional understanding of the term, to mean any attempt to ascertain priviledged access to knowledge:

> 'Philosophy can be foundational in respect to the rest of culture because culture is the assemblage of claims to knowledge, and philosophy adjudicates such claims. It can do so because it understands the foundations of knowledge, and it finds these foundations in the study of man-as-knower, of the "mental processes" or the "activity of representation" which make knowledge possible'.[3]

The broadness of Rorty's critique of foundationalism means that his anti-foundationalism simply amounts to the claim that '... the world does not provide us with any criterion of choice between alternative metaphors, that we can only compare language or metaphors with one another, not with

---

[1] R.Rorty, 'The priority of democracy to philosophy', in *Objectivity, Relativism and Truth. Philosophical papers*, Volume 1. Cambridge University Press, 1991.

[2] This is, of course, not to suggest that Rorty intends to strip Rawls of his libertarianism. Rorty's pragmatist gloss on Rawls actually serves to re-inforce Rawls libertarianism.

[3] R.Rorty, *Philosophy and the Mirror of Nature*, Blackwell, 1980.

something beyond language.'[4] To arrive at this claim, Rorty ties together Wittgensteins holistic view of language with Dewey's emphasis on success and agreement as the synthetic criteria of progress. He uses the Wittgensteinian claim (which is updated through Sellars and Quine) that sentences and words gain their meaning entirely from other sentences and words, to suggest that the concepts and sentences we find favorable, the ones that seem to work, will be the ones that match up best with the vocabulary of our social and political hopes and private desires. Fnding the best sentences, distinctions, dichotomies and metaphors will invariably be a matter of agreement rather than correspondence. For example, the value of the public/private distinction ought not be judged merely on its correspondence to reality, but on its value in relation to our broader democratic hopes. In other words, we would be forced to drop the distinction only if in most contexts the distinction seems to subvert our other wider democratic hopes.

One of the most recent critiques of Rorty, Norman Geras' *Solidarity in the Conversation of Humankind*,[5] takes up a fairly typical position in opposition to Rorty. In the book, Geras makes the following claim:

> 'If there is no truth, there is no injustice. Stated less simplistically, if truth is wholly relativized or internalized to particular discourses or language games or social practices, there is no injustice. The victims and protestors of any putative injustice are deprived of their last and often best weapon, that of telling what really happened. They can only tell their story, which is something else. Morally and politically, therefore, anything goes.'[6]

Geras substantiates this claim by explaining how, in particular, our view of the truthfullness of the accounts of survivors of Nazi concentration camps would be equivicle if we adopted Rorty's understanding of truth. However, and despite his tendency to positively encourage such reactions, Rorty is not suggesting that abandoning a representationalist view of language will mean that the truth of a statement will always be irrelevant, and he is not suggesting that as anti-foundationalists we ought to be sceptical of viewing the descriptions of the concentration camp survivor as truthful . He is simply suggesting that our only criteria for truth will be that provided by our existing social practices and conventions. Those practices and conventions will always contain rules for deciding upon the value of statements and our grasp on the truthfulness of those practices will always depend upon agreement about the different descriptions we have of them. This does not mean that we ought to be any more equivicle about the statements of the concentration camp survivor than we were when we may have held a representationalist view of language.

Our view of whether Rorty is simply employing some rhetorical tropes to disguise his relativism will largely depend on the expectations one has of philosophical inquiry. That is, if one beleives that it is important to

---

[4] R.Rorty, *Contingency, Irony and Solidarity*, Cambridge University Press, 1989, p.20.
[5] N.Geras, *Solidarity in the Conversation of Humankind: The Ungroundable Liberalism of Richard Rorty*, Verso, 1995.
[6] Geras, *Solidarity in the Conversation of Humankind*, p.107.

arrive at a precise and antecedent understanding of the rules guiding the plausibility of truth claims, then one will not be happy with Rorty's claim to have found a non-relativist but contextual conception of truth. If however, one is sceptical that a 'final vocabulary' will be found which will forever resolve the search for an antecedent meaning of truth in whatever form, then one may be looking for some philosophical therapy that would releive one of the temptation to pursue such a goal. If one understands Rorty's approach as an attempt to convince us with some philosophical therapy, that we need not ask questions such as 'what can I know with certainty' then one will be less inclined to tell Rorty that he is caught in a performative contradiction or that he is an 'anything goes relativist'. One will hope that Rorty's philosophical therapy is as convincing form of therapy that one is likely to receive to 'change the conversation to the subject of which ideas best suit our hopes'.

Rorty on Rawls

Paradoxically, even though Rorty's critique of foundationalism works as the starting point for his reading of Rawls, it does not, by his own admission, provide him with any philosophical arguments to justify Rawls libertarianism. Indeed, Rorty's anti-foundationalism probably provides just as much ammunition to reject Rawls, especially considering Rawls apparent neo-Kantianism. There are three issues here: first, Rorty's 'peculiar' approach to the redescription of his contemporaries and ancestors, through which his claims are grounded; second, Rorty's claim that Rawls position, and subsequently liberal democracy itself, does not need philosophical justification; third, Rorty's rejection of communitarianism. None of these issues can be analysed sufficiently in the space below, and I will merely suggest that Rorty is not as weak at these points as may appear to be the case.

Rorty's 'conversations' with thinkers past and present are not guided by the extent to which those thinkers have accurately represented 'the way things are, out there'. An approach which has been hard to accept for many of his contemporaries and critics. Both in the sense that Rorty's redescriptions of other thinkers tend to be purposely idiosyncratic and thus distorted, and that Rorty cannot vigorously defend such redescriptions without producing 'arguments' for his defence of them. However, critics who suggest that Rorty simply has not understood Dewey or Rawls, risk becoming victims of one of Rorty's playful traps. Allowing Rorty to respond by claiming that there is no one way to interpret Dewey and Rawls. Such a response seems closed to rational critique if one also accepts that there can be no permanent criteria for assessing the extent to which one authors interpretation of another is distorted. Once again, as has already been suggested, ones reading of Rorty will be determined by both the expectations one has of philosophy's attempt to be the arbiter of disputes within the rest of culture , and ones committment to anti-foundationalism. A point that would actually seem rather unecessary and banal if it were not for the extent of criticism of Rorty from critics who otherwise share such expectations and committments.

Nonetheless, this is not to imply that Rorty must be let of the hook. It simply entails asking different questions about his 'misreadings'. That is, what do they offer to the re-invention of vocabularies that might strenghten our democratic hopes. So critics who merely hope for one incontrovertable interpretation of the authors in question simply to miss the point. For Rorty, the point of the interpretation of our ancestors and contemporaries is to keep the conversations we have with them alive. To keep alive our private idiosyncracies as philosophers alive, or to hope that these conversations may contribute to our social and political hopes. But for Rorty, realising our hopes will not be decided by 'correspondence' but to what a particular community can agree on, which will invariably be the result of tradition and local prejudice rather than closeness to reality or sufficient philosophical support. As iluustrated by the following passage Rorty's use of Rawls is guided by this pragmatist sentiment.

> '... if we swing to the pragmatist side and consider talk of "rights" an attempt to enjoy the benifits of metaphysics without assuming te appropriate responsibilities, we shall still need something to distinguish the sort of individual we conscience we respect from the sort we condemn as "fanatical". This can only be something relatively local and ethnocentric – the tradition of a particular community, the consensus of a particular culture. According to this view, what counts as rational or as fanatical is relative to the group which we think it neccessary to justify ourselves – to the body of shared belief that determines the reference of the word "we".'[7]

According to Rorty's anti-foundationalist logic therefore, he can only choose to favour Rawls above others, ultimately for political rather than philosophical reasons. He can only do so because for Rorty, Rawls political principles neither have nor need to have philosophical justification. Rorty's motivation for making such a claim is not, as Bernstein suggests, simply to prove that philosophical justification that purports to be unassailable is futile.[8] Bernstein is right to argue that very few political theorists either claim to have provided or to be searching for unassailable philosophical justification. It is also to suggest that critiques of liberal democracy that are based on a deconstruction of its philosophical foundations are unlikely to provide grounds for a radical reconstruction of liberal democracy. This is because liberal democracy is not held up by certain philosophical positions. Those positions are merely variations on the vocabularies produced by 'conversations' between philosophers. In many ways this answer is insufficient. It does not seem to appreciate the way in which philosophical assumptions about the nature of the self for example, can be found quite explicitly in the most widely used forms of political discourse. However, trying to prove Rorty wrong on this point is futile because one cannot begin to do so without playing the language games that Rorty thinks are largely exclusive to a rather parochial form of discourse.

---

[7] Rorty, 'The priority of democracy to philosophy', p.176.
[8] R.Bernstein, 'One step forward two steps backward: Richard Rorty on Liberal Democracy and Philosophy', *Political Theory*, 15/4, 1987, p.546.

So Rorty's position is more than the claim that absolute philosophical justification is impossible, which can be further illustrated by considering in more depth Rorty's response to the communitarian objection to Rawls supposed ssumption of a rationalist/individualist conception of the self. Sandel, MacIntyre, Taylor and others claim that Rawls 'priority of the right over the good' is founded upon an atomistic conception of the individual which fails to understand the way in which the individual is consituitive of the community. Consequently for the Communitarians, once constituitive communual frameworks are no longer present, morality simply can't be considered rationally. However, this claim is both obvious and unhelpful. Obvious because all forms of morality must in some sense refer to a persons relationship to others within a particular community. But so what? This is the same as saying that an individuals moral identity is shaped most decisively by socialisation, which is a fairly banal point. It is also unhelpful, because the idea that an individual is constitutive of his or her community has no bearing upon a given set of institutional arragements. In other words, as Chantal Mouffe argues, there 'is no need ... to reject pluralism and the priority of justice in order to adopt a communitarian approach stressing the character of man as a political and social being whose identity is created within a community of language, meanings and practices.[9]

Rorty is not concerned that a distinction between justice and a particular common goods cannot be absolute. For Rorty, the idea that this distinction cannot be absolute is a reason for thinking about the distinction differently. Moreover, it is a reason for changing the subject and to ask instead: 'are there any alternatives to it, and does it suit our hopes?' This kind of attitude may appear to be dangerous for some. Dangerous because it appears to be the kind of logic that helped Heidegger provide philosophical support for the Nazis. In other words, if we abandon the 'rules of correspondence' then anything goes. However, for Rorty there are no alternatives to this kind of logic. There is no alternative to drawing upon tradition and local prejudices for justification.

In this sense, Rorty actually illustrates the deficiences of the whole communitarian/libertarian debate. First, in the sense that the opposition between 'community' and 'procedural democracy' is a non-sarter. The idea that somehow 'procedural democracy' is exclusive of 'community' seems to ignore the way in which, as Rorty himself illustrates, a procedural democracy where justice is prioritised must surely be understood as the hopes of a particular community within a particularly small epoch. For Rorty, the idea that one can step outside ones 'community' is an athema. But this should not be viewed as grounds for rejecting procedural democracy. Indeed, for Rorty, Taylors conception of the historicised, fragmented and socialised self is indeed the kind of conception of the self one would probably support if such support were needed. The second way in which Rorty's work illustrates the shortcominings of the debate is that it highlights the futility of discussions about human nature or questions relating to substantive sociological grounding for the construction or development of political systems.

However, Rorty does go too far when he suggests that discussion about

---

[9]C.Mouffe, *The Return of the Political*, Verso, 1993, p.47.

the self and indeed about truth is simply irrelevant to politics. Rorty claims that 'For purposes of social theory, we can put aside such topics as an ahistorical human nature, the nature of selfhood, the motive of moral behaviour, and the meaning of human life. We treat these as irrelevant to politics as Jefferson thought questions about the Trinity and about transubstantiation'.[10] Rorty may want to argue that such subjects ought to be irrelevant, and indeed a post-foundational political theory would also have such a hope. Nonetheless, the idea that religion is irrelevant to politics for example, seems to fly in the face of, in particular, the emerging character of contemporary politcs, particularily in America. It is one thing to say that we must change the subject or that we don't have to argue on the same terms as our interculator, and another thing to suggest that the vocabulary that we want to be rid of is irrelevant to politics.

Rorty's unnecessary conservatism

Another unfortunate conclusion drawn by Rorty is his implied claim that Rawlsian libertarianism is virtually all that is on offer for political theorists willing to embrace an anti-foundationalist sensitivity to contingency. As swift et al argue the 'fact that the notion of universal agreement is a chimera in political theory (as well as elsewhere in philosophy) gives Rorty no basis for ignoring or dismissing all anti-liberal critiques in advance, and so no basis for restricting political discourse to the resources of the dominant contemporary culture.[11] In other words, accepting contingency (that we cannot step outside our history, community or language) may require us to accept liberal democracy as the starting point for any attempt to radically strengthen democracy, but it doesn't require us to be content with conservative piecemeal adjustments. Just as there can be no fixed limits or conditions for rational commensurability, there can be no fixed limits for when a critique of current political practices moves beyond the political resources of the dominant political culture.

Conclusion

Despite these very important failings, Rorty's pragmatism offers a great deal to political theorists struggling to come to terms with the consequences of anti-foundationalism for political theory. For, one defining feature of the questions and issues raised by anti-foundationalism is that they are infinite, ultimately irresolvable by definition and can often force political theorists further away from the tasks of imagining institutional procedures that would strengthen our troubled democratic inheritance. So if one is both concerned about the consequences of anti-foundationalism and their relationship to our democratic hopes then Rorty does indeed offer some useful advice. If one hopes that anti-foundationalism, or indeed other philosophical vocabularies, can offer some new philosophical support for a new democratic pluralism or communitarianism, then Rorty's advice will appear to be misguided and

---

[10] Rorty, 'The priority of democracy to philosophy', p.180.
[11] S.Mullhall & A.Swift, *Liberals and Communitarians*, Blackwell, 1992, p.239.

unhelpful. If one is merely concerned with the coherence of Rorty's antifoundationalism and his reading of Rawls, then hopefully my brief redescription of the two has made a modest contribution to the idea that attempting to argue with Rorty at these points is futile.

Models of Community

Andrew Reeve
University of Warwick

'Community, Industrial Society, and Contemporary Debate'[1]

Introduction

This paper is admittedly speculative. In view of the title of the panel, it asks what models of community were offered as a response to the emergence of industrial society, and whether they have present-day descendants. The suggestion will be that both contemporary and 'industrial' models of community can be linked in ways that complement, if not challenge, the classification of models of community associated with the major political ideologies.

Modern communitarianism can be characterised in a number of ways, and it is not unusual to see some acknowledgement of the obvious fact that a concern with community in political thought is not itself novel. It is of some interest to consider the relationship between the contemporary communitarian critique of liberalism, and the historical episode of another critique: the concern with (what were often seen as) the undesirable consequences, or essential components, of industrial society. The contrast between 'society' and 'community' was, of course, elaborated by F.Tönnies, an author to whose essay many today concerned with the character of 'community' refer[2]. In this brief paper I want to look at some typologies of community, and to consider the present incarnations of such models of community restored, or community re-asserted, which were articulated in response to the emergence of industrial society.

The antithesis between 'society' and 'community' constitutes, according to Nisbet[3], one of the main conceptual building blocks of the history of modern thought, and of sociology in particular. I try merely to pull together some ideas to be found in the literature on this topic; to do so, I organize the discussion in four parts. First, I look at the community:society distinction in relation to some other typologies. Secondly, I look at the concept of community as defined by particular authors, and try to draw out some of its implications. Thirdly, I return to Tönnies's discussion of Gemeinschaft and Gesellschaft, the two terms conventionally (but not uncontroversially) translated as 'community' and 'society', and look at an argument provided by Raymond Plant[4], which tries to bring together historical approaches to community with contemporary political theorising. Finally, I propose a classification of models of community offered in response to the emergence of industrial society, and tentatively suggest that some of the major debates

---

[1] I am grateful for discussion to J.Lively, A.Ware, C.Woodard and A.Williams.

[2] Ferdinand Tönnies, *Community and Association: Community and Conflict in Western Thought*, translated by Charles P.Loomis, Routledge & Kegan Paul, 1955, first published 1887.

[3] R.Nisbet, *The Social Philosophers*, Paladine Frogmore, St Albans, 1976, p.11.

[4] R.Plant, 'Community: Concept, Conception and Ideology', *Politics and Society*, 8, 1978, 79-107.

in modern political theory may be seen as continuing their themes outside the narrow confines of the communitarian:liberal debate.

Community and Society; and other typologies

There were naturally many attempts to provide a periodisation of history advanced by those living at the time of great social change which might be described as 'the emergence of industrial society'. Adam Smith's fourfold stadial thesis, Saint-Simon's distinction between military and industrial society, Marx's theorisation of the emergence of capitalism, Spencer's discussion of industrial society, Comte's concern with nascent scientific society – all these are attempts to locate features of a new world within the trajectory of historical experience. Most of these writers thought that the 'new' society was in its infancy, or at least its childhood: they did not think they were looking at the mature version of the society the novelty of which they were concerned to emphasize. Indeed, in their different ways, they had prescriptions to hasten the maturation of the social forms they tried to delineate. So Adam Smith had proposals for legislative reform to unencumber commercial society, Auguste Comte had proposals to institutionalize government by *savants*, and Saint-Simon wished to hasten the progress of *les industriels* in the management of society's affairs. Many of these authors shared the feeling memorably encapsulated by Carlyle's phrase – that they were living 'between two worlds, one not yet dead and one struggling to be born.'

Despite the diversity of description of the nascent society, as 'commercial', 'industrial', 'scientific', 'capitalist', many of the features intended to be so described were common. In particular, the emphasis was placed on an extensive division of labour and an accompanying wage-labour market, on the ubiquity of exchange relations, and the application of knowledge to production. Whether the movement was seen as from agrarian to commercial, from military to industrial, from feudal to capitalist or from metaphysical to scientific, whether the cause of change was seen in the ideological or in the material sphere, there was at least that much agreement about the elements of 'industrial' society.

At the most general level, many writers looking back at the emergence of industrial society have emphasized the notion of a lost world, even if there has been little agreement about when exactly it went missing. The title of Peter Laslett's book, after all, is *The World We Have Lost*[5] which, again not uncontroversially, depicts a society with different social bonds, different rhythms and different commitments to the one which emerged in the late eighteenth century and after. As one commentator has summarized Laslett's thesis:

> 'The coming of the factory system brought new relationships, characterized by distance, impersonality, and lack of emotional solidarity ... It is in this change that we find the shift from

---
[5] Methuen, 1971, first edition 1965.

organic community to individualism.'[6]

At this level of generality, we might also include Hannah Arendt's work, *Between Past and Future*,[7] which is a melancholy reflection on the conditions of mass society, again insisting that the central feature of the contemporary human predicament is a sense of loss, or indeed not just a sense of loss but a justifiable and explicable experience of loss. She put it this way:

> 'This twofold loss of the world – the loss of nature and the loss of human artifice in the widest sense, which would include all history – has left behind it a society of men who, without a common world which could at once relate and separate them, either live in desperate lonely separation or are pressed together into a mass. For a mass-society is nothing more than that kind of organized living which automatically establishes itself among human beings who are still related to one another but have lost the world once common to all of them.'[8]

This loss of a common world (and, again, the sense of being between two worlds) is, of course, simply a general version of more specific doubts and uncertainties encountered in the historical periodisations already mentioned – and others. Marx's theory of alienation, Hegel's discussion of estrangement, Smith's concern with the likely decline of public spiritedness, Rousseau's remarks about Civil Religion, Comte's Religion of Humanity and Saint-Simon's New Christianity, as well as Hegel's Universal State, might all be seen as attempts to (re-)establish that common world. Clearly the debate about community and society, in which attempts are made to locate such a commonality or to find new bases for it, forms part of that wider picture.

There is a second context, however, in which we can look at Gemeinshaft and Gesellschaft. It is provided by modern debates between so-called communitarians and so-called liberals. These hesitant descriptions are required by the increasing uncertainty about what is at stake between these schools, if that be the right word. 'Communitarianism' seems to be deployed, in its widest senses, to cover, with more or less precision, a number of positions.

First, it is used to describe the general view that life in a community is a good thing, that communities should be fostered and encouraged. This applies both to theorising and to ways of life. Hence New Age Travellers are said to constitute a community. Secondly, the term is used to cover the view that the self is socially situated and socially constituted – as a protest against the model of atomised and abstract individualism allegedly embodied in much liberal political thought. And thirdly, it is used as a covenient shorthand to lump together a number of critics of liberalism who may not have much in common beyond some adherence to the first two positions. As the editors of a recent study summarize:

---

[6] W.Stafford, *Socialism, Radicalism and Nostalgia: Social Criticism in Britain, 1775-1830*, Cambridge University Press, 1987, p.18.

[7] H.Arendt, *Between Past and Future*, Faber, 1961.

[8] *Between Past and Future*, pp.89-90.

> 'Indeed, the term 'community' as used in contemporary political thought is a normative concept, in the sense that it desribes a desired level of human relationships. The community, as a body with some common values, norms, and goals, in which each member regards the common goals as her own, is a good in itself. Communitarians argue that it is morally good that the self be constituted by communal ties.'[9]

But as the same editors acknowledge, these concerns are not new today. The notion of community has a long history. If earlier discussions did not explicitly articulate the notion of a socially constituted self, they certainly did not eschew a normative view of community. What in particular unites the present-day discussion with an historical concern is the ambivalent, uncertain but certainly disputed relationship between liberalism and a commitment to community. As David Miller asks of the contemporary debate, has communitarianism come to fulfil liberalism or to bury it?[10] Or, as Raymond Plant stresses about the historical developments we are largely concerned with:

> 'The liberal tradition had its very origins in a critique of communitarian conceptions and institutions. Many theorists, particularly of the seventeenth and eighteenth centuries, tried to come to terms with the new social developments, such as the development of market society, industrialization, increasing division of labour and urbanization, and attempted to provide an understanding of man and society that would help to explain and justify the loss of the old communities.'[11]

For Plant, there is an unsolved (and perhaps insuperable) difficulty in liberalism's problem with community: liberals – and here the exemplar is T.H.Green – are simultaneously committed to the moral value of community and to the importance of the individual.[12] The liberal attachment to diversity, to plurality, vitiates the possibility of a total community – community is possible only at a 'sub-total' level where particularity is unifying.[13]

So we have specific historical typologies; we have a general sense of a lost world; we have an alleged antithesis (or, at least, unresolved tension) between liberalism and communitarianism. Other contrasts have been seen as relevant, as well: Sir Henry Maine's distinction between status and contract as the basis of socio-legal arangements – his view being, of course, that there had been a movements from the former to the latter as the foundation of

---

[9] S.Avineri & A.de-Shalit (eds), *Communitarianism and Individualism*, Oxford University Press, 1992, pp.6-7.

[10] D.Miller, 'In What Sense Must Socialism be Communitarian?', *Social Philosophy & Policy*, 6, 1988/9, p.51, n.2.

[11] 'Community: Concept, Conception and Ideology', p.99.

[12] *Ibid*, p.106. Jack Lively has suggested to me that the model of a community for T.H.Green – combining diversity with shared values – might well have been the University. If so, the present day destruction of the academic community by university society would provide one more example of Tönnies' thesis.

[13] *Ibid*, pp.100 & 104. Of course, participatory theorists of liberal democracy recognized this in their insistence on the important of local government; but participatory theorists are particularly aware of the relation between 'membership' and 'the common good'.

rights and duties. Similarly, C.B. Macpherson's discussion of possessive individualism might be seen as an attempt to expose precisely those tensions (or, more strongly, contradictions) to which Plant refers.

The notion of community

Tönnies' distinction between community and society, or community and association (as it is sometimes rendered), is yet another attempt to characterize historical change and at the same time to point to contrasting forms of social organization or relationship which can co-exist (just as is implied by Carlyle's remark). Before we come to it, it is worth looking at some elements of the concept of community as used by others – others, informed, of course, by reading Tönnies.

We should immediately acknowledge two points widely made. First, the notion of community is deployed both descriptively and prescriptively. Secondly, the notion is at least value-laden and frequently ideologically asserted. There is little prospect of an agreed definition, and what is of interest is rather the elements of particular accounts of community.

Three such accounts provide the basis for discussion. First, Clark tries to provide an ecumenical definition. This has a certain formal appeal, but until it is fleshed out it lacks substance – and once given that substance it loses its ecumenical appeal. Justice may well require *suum cuique*, and freedom may well refer to the freedom of x from y to do (become, etc.) z: and community, as Clark says, may well provide 'a sense of solidarity and significance' in a social structure; but as soon as some specification is given of what is said to be capable of providing that sense of solidarity or significance, or indeed of what constitutes it, then controversy is inevitable.[14] Morgan, in *The Small Community*, is more specific:

> 'A community is an association of individuals and families that, out of inclination, habit, custom and mutual interest, act in concert as a unit in meeting their needs ... Because of variations of degree the term "community" cannot be closely defined. To whatever extent common group needs are met by unified action in a spirit of common acquaintance and responsibility, to that extent a community exists.'[15]

Such an account, taken as it stands, is open-ended about two issues: about whether market society could be a community, and about the level of self-conscious membership required. The third account comes from Nisbet, in *The Social Philosophers*. Community, he says, refers to

> 'relationships among individuals that are characterized by a high degree of personal intimacy, of social cohesion or moral commitment, and of continuity in time.'[16]

---

[14] This point forms the point of departure for Plant, who quotes Clark and then invokes the concept/conception distinction, *op cit*, pp.81-900.

[15] A.Morgan, *The Small Community: Foundation of Democratic Life. What it is and how to achieve it*, Harper & Brothers, 1942, p.20.

[16] R.Nisbet, *The Social Philosophers*, Paladine Frogmore, St Albans, 1976, p.11.

What problems does this sort of more specific characterization of community pose for those concerned with the emergence of industrial society, who nevertheless valued community? A high degree of personal intimacy requires some sort of 'face to face' society, but the emphasis here is not so much on merely knowing a neighbour but on the quality of the relationship. It must be close, sharing, and based on mutual understanding. It must be empathetic and personal. Continuity in time might be provided by the Burkean family, and its political analogue culture, history or tradition. But the central issue is the basis of the social cohesion or moral commitment. Those who responded to the loss of community in industrial society had various prescriptions here, which we shall enumerate later. Nisbet's helpful characterization emphasizes three freatures: the type of relationships between persons, and the quality of them; the idea of persistence; and the idea of shared ends, commitments, purposes, morality or identity.

Such accounts equally stimulate reflection on the problems: could a shared commitment to self-interest qualify as cohering? For most writers, of course, a general disposition towards the pursuit of self-interest was precisely the corrosive agent which had to be neutralized or subjugated by a fuller or richer mutual engagement. The common world of market relations was insufficient. A second problem concerns the persistence of community side by side with societal change, especially when that change is perceived as both rapid and uncontrolled: what exactly persists? Thirdly, how inclusive or exclusive a community is envisaged (or, to repeat Plant's point, is community possible in any overarching, as opposed to pluralistic sub-group, way?). On the face of it, any notion of a common world, and certainly any notion of a common good, stands in a necessary relation to the specification of its members, a point obvious enough in democratic theory but somewhat laboured or even unwelcome in discussions of community. Another problem concerns the depth of the shared commitment: Is it sufficient for the shared life of the community that there be a common commitment to procedures, or is something much more substantive required? Finally, one might ask about the origin of the sharing: is it to be somehow natural, incompatible with any manufactured or inculcated source of social cohesion, or are the origins a matter of indifference? These questions could each be posed of the forms of community Nisbet examined in his impressive historical sweep. He classified six: the military, political, religious, revolutionary, ecological and plural variants. For some of the writers responding to the emergence of industrial society, one or more of these variants would be ruled out by their theories of history (as Saint-Simon, for example, saw the passing of the military principle); for others, perhaps, an attempt was made to combine them (as Comte buttressed the acceptance of governance by the savants with the Religion of Humanity); while other proposals might be seen as specific suggestions within this classification (as the democratic community is of the political).

Community, society and the 'ideological' typology

Tönnies' own essay summarizes the distinction between community and society in the claim that Gemeinschaft contains an essential unity in spite of separation, whereas Gesellschaft contains an essential separation despite unity.[17] This rather gnomic view hides the richness of the essay, which suggests a great many ways of locating the elements of the primary distinction. But with the aid of Tönnies' translator [18], it is possible to draw out a number of points. First, the distinction is clearly intended (like so many others, notably the military-industrial distinction in Saint-Simon) to be applied both to two co-existing social forms and to an historical movement. Secondly, an overarching distinction exists between rational will and natural will. Rational will concerns the calculation of means to achieve ends, the instrumental rather than expressive rationality of modern choice theory. Natural will is an unclear notion, except when seen in contrast to rational will: it refers to the ability, willingess or disposition to see others empathetically, rather than as means to one's own ends. Thirdly, this unifying distinction is applied in a number of different domains of social experience, of which four seem especially important. Gemeinschaft is associated with natural will, and Gesellschaft with rational will, so activities or social locations are distinguished between the two, and so are age and gender. Again, types of relationship within social life are distinguished according to their motivating force or character, so that contract and self-interest are contrasted with friendship and familial ties. Next, the principles by which relationships are regulated are divided between legislation (rational positive law) and custom or common law. Finally, values recognized in society are examined to see what gives them force. The bases of the unity of Gemeinschaft which are mentioned are, of course, only contingently overlapping: blood ties, friendship, neighbourhood, place, kinship.These are allegedly relations in which concord is produced by persons who understand each other, live together and arrange their common affairs accordingly, in contrast to Gesellschaft which is regulated by convention, in which everyone is to some degree a merchant, and which is bougeois society (interestingly described as taking its supreme rule in politeness).[19] It is part of this picture that capitalism is the product of the loss of community, rather than the other way about.[20]

If Tönnies provides one dichotomy, one way of enriching Clark's general formula, and if Nisbet provides an overview of the historical forms of community, Plant's essay provides a three-fold ideological division: between conservative, Marxist and liberal models. He summarizes the conservative vision thus:

> 'is usually backward looking, its appeal connoting a return to a Gemeinschaft type of order, and thus support attempts to resist change and to buttress the existing power and author-

---

[17] *Community and Association*, pp.74ff.
[18] I draw heavily here on the introduction to the edition cited previously, which gives the clearest account I have seen of the complexity of the distinction.
[19] *Community and Association*, p.87.
[20] This point is noticed by C.Bell & H.Newby, *Community Studies*, Allen & Unwin, 1971, p.25.

ity structure. Community then is characterized by hierarchy, place, and mutual obligation between groups in different positions within the hierarchy.'[21]

This defence of hierarchy is also, it appears, a defence of a status society, and Plant specifies the rejection of that hierarchy as the cornerstone of the Marxist vision of future community, in which 'the claims of autonomy and community will be reconciled' [22] without the exploitation which accompanies the appearance of cohesion in pre-industrial societies. The third model is that of the liberal-social democrat, whose dilemmas we encountered in Plant's reference to T.H.Green. One model looks back to hierarchy; another puts the establishment (and not necessarily the recovery) of community in the future; and another suffers from internal tensions, valuing plurality and diversity but at the same time shared commitments.

Community, Industrial Society and contemporary debate

This framework places conceptions of community within those traditions of thought sufficiently developed to qualify as ideologies. But if we ask what models of community were advanced in response to the perception that industrial society possessed novel features, we could perhaps offer a rather different classification, that does not so neatly fit into such a framework. The 'versions' might be identified as the traditional (Coleridge, Southey, Carlyle), the socialist (Bray, perhaps Hodgskin, Ruskin, Morris), the scientific (Comte), the democratic (Tocqueville, J.S. Mill, G.D.H. Cole), and the national [23] – leaving aside Hegel's case for the universal state. It might be tentatively claimed that many recent debates have more to do with components of that classification than with a confrontation between communitarians and liberals, or between rival ideological models of community.

The 'socialist' vision of community, as advanced by Ruskin and Morris, rests upon a shared commitment to worthwhile work in a world which has been aesthetically renewed. Each is happy to devote his or her labours to the satisfaction of others' needs in the absence of capitalist exploitation. There are these days few proposals for the elimination of markets, but several for the eradication of capitalist injustice. Models of market socialism as put forward by Miller and sceptically explored by Pierson, on the one side, and the theory of universal basic income as an answer to the question 'What, if anything, can justify capitalism?' proposed by van Parijs seem to be the contemporary versions of this orientation.[24]

---

[21] 'Community: Concept, Conception and Ideology', p.95.

[22] *Ibid*, p.92.

[23] The complexities here are well explored by Richard Bellamy, *Liberalism and Modern Society*, Pennsylvania State University Press, 1992.

[24] D.Miller, *Market, State and Community: Theoretical Foundations of Market Socialism*, Clarendon Press, 1990; C.Pierson, *Socialism After Communism: The New Market Socialism*, Polity Press, 1995; P.van Parijs, *Real Freedom For All: What (if Anything) Can Justify Capitalism?*, Clarendon Press, 1995. It is also, perhaps, possible to include this last work in the 'scientific' category, below.

The idea of a democratic community, advanced by Tocqueville as an antidote to problems associated with social equality, by J.S.Mill as a catallyst and channel for public spiritedness, and by Cole as a mechanism to produce economic and political harmony, has of course exemplified precisely the problem identified by Plant in relation to liberal theory in general: how to reconcile a commitment to plurality (if that be of interests) with the identification and acceptance of some common good. Mill's ethical voter may be too rare; Cole never managed to harmonize the interests of consumer and producer in a convincing way. Dunn's survey of democracy's unfinished journey still raises the issue of whether an overarching democratic community of sub-communities is possible.[25]

Comte's scientific community rested on a shared commitment to the force of scientific knowledge, to rationality in action. His vision is thus most vulnerable to all the arguments about the limits of rationality, the epistemological uncertainties of scientific knowledge, the anti-universality with which we are now familiar. But if we allow a shared commitment to be procedural, in an enlarged sense, then some recent work on justice might be seen as following in the same tradition. Of course, this does not mean that contemporary writers advocate government by scientists. But the attempt to locate regulative principles of justice which recognize a diversity of conceptions of the good yet can command common adherence from reasonable or rational actors may be seen as an attempt to find that common world in a shared moral commitment – or, at least, to tell us what we are committed to if we share it.[26]

The idea of a national community, and the idea of a benign nationalism to be contrasted with its dangerous variant(s), has certainly enjoyed a theoretical revival. Ignatieff, Kristeva and Habermas have all advanced claims for the national community, and Miller has recently published a full-length study which defends the idea of nationality as the basis of one form of community amongst others.[27] It is an interesting question how far his characterisation of national identity is a characterisation of community more generally – a matter of the weighting of the elements in the accounts of 'community' mentioned earlier:

> 'These five elements together – a community (1) constituted by shared belief and mutual commitment, (2) extended in history, (3) active in character, (4) connected to a particular territory, and (5) marked off from other communities by its distinct public culture – serve to distinguish nationality from other col-

---

[25] J.Dunn (ed), *Democracy – the Unfinished Journey 508 BC to AD 1993*, Oxford University Press, 1993 edition, p.264; A.Reeve, 'Democracy: Past, Present ... and Future? (Part II), *Democratization*, 2, 1995, pp.198-207.

[26] Comte's own appreciation of the limits of rational conviction, of course, was reflected in his advocacy of the Religion of Humanity. Both B.Barry, *Justice as Impartiality: A Treatise on Social Justice*, Volume II, Clarendon Press, 1995, and H.Steiner, *An Essay on Rights*, Blackwell, 1994, undertake to tell us what justice requires, but not why we should be just.

[27] The proposals of the first three authors are critically considered by B.Fine, 'The 'New Nationalism' and Democracy: A Critique of Pro Patria', *Democratization*, 1, 1994; D.Miller, *On Nationality*, Clarendon Press, 1995.

lective sources of personal identity.'[28]

The value of traditional community, as asserted by Coleridge, Southey and Carlyle, undoubtedly rests on the sort of hierarchy to which Plant draws attention. It was based on mutual, if differential, rights and obligations. It was also based on national institutions, especially the Church; and if it wanted to restore what was taken to have been lost, its nostalgia might be combined with a certain novelty, as in Coleridge's preference for a clerisy. The contemporary version of these concerns is possibly with culture, but there seems to be some unwillingness to describe the institutional embodiment of the shared life: or unhappiness about the extent to which it has a cultural embodiment.

To classify 'models of community' in a way which reflects the first blush of concern with its loss or absence, in early reactions to industrial society, challenges ideological typologies. And this is broadly true today: Miller defends both market socialism and nationality as bases for community. Miller and Pierson, who is finally sceptical about market socialism, are also advocates of empowering democracy, more radically asserted by Bachrach and Botwinick.[29] Van Parijs contemplates the justice of capitalism (which may include in its characterisation market socialism) if there is a guaranteed basic income. Barry and Steiner are both to some degree uncertain about the labelling of their positions.[30] Democracy, associated labour, the nation, rational conviction, and tradition remain the contested bases for community, but in ways which begin to challenge ideological classification.

---

[28] Miller, *On Nationality*, p.27.

[29] P.Bachrach & A.Botwinick, *Power and Empowerment: A Radical Theory of Participatory Democracy*, Temple University Press, Philadelphia, 1992.

[30] See B.Barry's response to his critics, forthcoming in *Political Studies*, June 1995; and H.Steiner's reflections in *An Essay on Rights*, pp.280-282.

The Political Science of British Politics

Jim Bulpitt
University of Warwick

'Historical Politics: Leaders, Statecraft
and Regime in Britain at the Accession of Eliabeth II'

Introduction

The aims are three. First, to restate the case for the development of a systematic Historical Politics approach within the political science of British politics. Secondly, to suggest a methodological framework within which this approach might be usefully pursued. Thirdly, to provide a case study illustrating the problems, opportunities and benefits associated with Historical Politics. This final aspect of the exercise identifies and examines the operations of a governing regime in Britain, a regime which emerged in the early 1920s and was sustained after the Second World War through to the early 1960s. This notion of governing continuity between pre and postwar Britain signals both revisionist history and political science. The 'accession of Elizabeth II' (in February 1952) represents a symbolic affirmation of that continuity and revisionism. The general argument is that this regime, Britain's long-delayed ancien regime, is crucial to understanding twentieth century political developments: it brings the interwar period back in from the cold, significantly amends the postwar consensus thesis, furthers our understanding of 'Thatcherism', and allows us to impose some intellectual order on the 'ditherings' of the 1990s.

Historical Politics

Why should political science, more particularly the 'normal' political science of British politics, seek to develop a serious, systematic, Historical Politics research (and teaching) community? Consider, first, the old adage – 'History without politics is like a tree without fruit, politics without history is like a tree without roots.' Typically, the message is ambiguous: a degree of disciplinary interdependence is suggested but, seemingly, within an operational structure allowing considerable duality and autonomy. Whatever the original prescription, contemporary practice, especially in Britain, imposes a considerable separation of functions, organisation, and personnel on the two disciplines. Political history which, apart from biography, is in decline, pays little attention to political science concepts and 'theory'. Political science, on the other hand, either ignores the past or 'rents' its data and explanations for ad hoc purposes. The operational convention appears to be that whilst historians concentrate on the past (defined by the availability of the relevant 'papers'), they may, where appropriate, speculate about contemporary affairs, political scientists should operate in the undefined present and only in exceptional circumstances go back to the past. Political science seems to accept this division of labour on the grounds that since the territorial scope of its interests is now global politics it has more than enough on its plate in terms of teaching and research programmes. The exceptions to this 'presentist' obsession are two. The traditional, and continuing, licensed mavericks are the historians of political thought. Their analytical priorities, however, lie with ideas, rather than political behaviour. Unfortunately, it is not ideas themselves that are interesting for most political scientists, but the circumstances in which they are picked up, used, and abused, by politicians, particularly those in office. The other exception to presentism is what is quaintly called the political development approach. This began and ended in the United States for reasons which I have detailed elsewhere. In any case it made very little impact in Britain, above all in the political science of British politics.

What is wrong with these history and politics conventions? We should note first that they favour the historians. They are allowed to speculate, even encroach in ways they regard as serious, on contemporary political analysis. Political science, however, is squeezed into the restricted temporal parameters of the present. A global scope, which history possesses as well, is not a sufficient recompense for this temporal limitation. Significantly, this particular package deal is not accepted by other social sciences: economics, sociology and geography have all developed organised research and teaching communities to engage seriously and continuously with the past. Presumably, they have done this because they neither accept that their subject matter is confined to the present, nor, though there are some doubts about this, that the past is only interesting because it leads to the present. This raises the key issue, the issue which above all, favours the development of Historical Politics as a serious *fraktion* in political science. How can any discipline which claims to understand and explain political behaviour justify that claim when it confines its attentions to the contemporary era? Is the only political behaviour worthy of its study that which encompasses industrialising, industrial, and postindustrial politics at the end of the twentieth century? Is past politics safely left to historians and, increasingly, historical sociologists? The answer has to be a negative. Note that the message here is not simply that political science needs to understand the past to better explain the present. The message is that past politics is worthy of study by political scientists for its own sake. In other words, we should be interested in all kinds of political milieu, all styles of political behaviour in the past – the 1190s are as interesting and important as the 1990s, the sixteenth century as interesting and important as the twentieth century.

To that basic argument for Historical Politics can be added two others. First, it would enormously 'enrich' the research programme base of political science. If handled properly it would rid the discipline of the stiffling and unproductive impact of its present dominant paradigm, policy analysis. Moreover, it would hopefully bridge the great divide between the history of political thought community and whatever it is the rest of us do. Secondly, the pursuit of Historical Politics would have a beneficial impact on the methodology of present politics analysis. In an important sense 'doing' present politics is too easy: significant problems of analysis can be sidelined by data swamping, interviews with practitioners, and key actors, or, simply by telling stories. Exercises in Historical Politics would have to confront these problems, the 'Once Upon a Time' option would not be available. Interestingly, the most methodologically advanced sections of empirical political science are international relations and voting behaviour analysis both of which cover subject matter which enforces both an awareness of analytical problems and the necessity to discover ways to confront them. It follows that our next port of call must be with the methodology of Historical Politics.

Methodology

Let me start with two negatives. This is not an exercise designed to assist collaboration with history or other social sciences. What follows is designed to promote the political science 'interest' in the subject. Nor does it follow the fashionable path of comparative analysis. This is a single country production and the country is Britain. These limitations stem from a recognition that methodology-building in this area is liable to be difficult and disputed. The major difficulty has been the necessity to construct a framework of analysis which is timeless, or time-consistent, in its application. Any attempt to seriously pursue Historical Politics has to accept this brutal logic. That said, four key items in the methodology must be considered.

(i) The MITGRA Perspective

Clearly there are a variety of ways the subject could be tackled. The one adopted here, and previewed last year, is labelled MITGRA, macro, in-time, governing, regime analysis. MITGRA generates two things. The first consists of the broad analytical domains of the exercise. It is concerned with those macro manifestations of governing which persist over particular time periods. In short, the focus is on past governing regimes. In turn, this generates the research programme, namely the identification, analysis, and assessment of such regimes for their own sake. 'Great Arch' speculations about the links between past developments and the present are not prioritised, at least over very long periods. The case study below will speculate about connections between the 1930s and governing Britain after 1970, but such speculations will be the froth on the beer, not the beer itself. Secondly, all macro exercises require an analytical focus: macro analysis is not synonymous with total politics. This particular perspective on Historical Politics makes that focus the governing process, which is what political science should be about anyway. Governing, however, especially governing in the past, is a slippery thing to study. The rest of this section considers some of the problems it poses and the assumptions we have to make to reduce that characteristic to manageable proportions.

(ii) The Structure-Agent Problem

For an increasing number of social scientists this is regarded as the most difficult problem confronting analysts. It concerns the extent to which the behaviour of political actors, (a better, because more neutral term, than agents) is influenced/determined by the structure or context within which they are forced to operate. Two initial, and different, responses to this problem are (a) that it is unresolvable and, consequently, will always be an essentially contested issue or (b) that it is otiose, because no purely structuralist explanation of political behaviour is either possible or on offer. Where micro, presentist, analyses are concerned both these stances provide plausible escape routes from the problem. For the MITGRA perspective, however, the problem remains, if only because one of the costs (or benefits?) of macro analysis is that some explicit positions must be taken on the extent to which its designated principal actors are affected by, and respond to, structural phenomena.

In an important sense the problem is one of the definition and scope of the structure. Structure is an ambiguous term. Moreover, the scope of structural phenomena depends on the actors designated for analysis: the more inclusive the actor, the more restricted the range of the structure within which they operate. Two options are open to us. One obvious ploy is to 'unpack' structure into its various general components. So, we can start with a basic distinction between deep and shallow structure, the former indicating long term environmental matters, the latter shorter term forces which may or may not become part of the deep structure. We can also accept that structural phenomena can be located in both the domestic and external dimensions of the polity. In addition, we can suggest that the structural environment will generate both constraints and opportunities for political actors. Similarly, structural forces will yield both shocks and gifts. All this would represent an improvement on much existing comment on the problem. Unfortunately, although it provides us a list of things to look for, it provides no ready and easy general stance on the problem. An increasingly popular response to that difficulty is to assume a relative autonomy for political actors from their broad structural context. Again, this is useful, but ambiguous. What is required is some more specific notion of the link between the structure and actors' behaviour.

This can be done if we make the following two initial, 'as if', assumption. First, structure, as unpacked above, will, in any period, grind out or deliver, a natural rate of governability (NRG). It is this natural rate which will confront political actors and their relative autonomy will consist of the degree to which they can choose which aspects of the NRG they will prioritise (their preoccupations). Secondly, we assume that the NRG will not be static: in some periods it will be lower than others. It follows that we must assess the behaviour of political actors not simply in terms of the extent to which they reach their publicised goals, but the degree to which they effectively confront the varying levels of the natural rate of governability delivered by the structure in different time periods.

(iii) Principal Actor Designation

The issue here is whose governing are we studying? As indicated above actor choice will determine the scope of the structural context. MITGRA also demands that several more specific conditions have to be fulfilled. That means we must not only search for, and then assume, a macro oriented, unitary, rational-capable, high politics, actor, which is difficult enough. We must also discover a temporal constant actor, namely one that is present in every past period. This last condition is very difficult to satisfy, at least in terms of the popular options available.

One possibility is to designate a single individual as the principal actor focus. There are obvious, though not insurmountable problems, here with the temporal constant condition. The real difficulties on this count lie with those general to the Great Person approach to politics, whatever happens, happens because of the character, ideas and prejudices of one person. Inevitably, this obstructs inter temporal (and spatial) analysis. Moreover, it also assumes that the meaningful historical norm is a governing process dominated by one individual. Most of the other actor options fail one or more of the conditions listed above, especially those of time consistency and the unitary requirement. Examples are the state, the political élite, the government or cabinet, the political administrative community, or the core executive. This leaves three somewhat unsatisfactory candidates – key state/élite managers, leadership cliques, or the Court. The vote goes to the Court simply because it reflects neatly the English/British power situation over time. Courts are forced to adopt macro, whole polity, orientations. Courts have the capacity to be unitary – through fear, greed, ambition or party pressures. Courts deal with both the external and domestic dimensions of high politics. Finally, Courts are, or can be, rational capable, at least in the weak sense of bounded rationality and 'satisficing' when confronting the natural rate of governability. The problem, of course, is that Courts, in terms of personnel, will be fluid. The best that can be offered is that they will be composed of the operational chief executive plus friends and key collaborators. This is ambiguous and may pose problems. Principal actor designation, then, is a possible major weakness in the MITGRA approach. Who governs is a problem, not a blueprint.

(iv) Statecraft

In the context of the MITGRA approach to Historical Politics statecraft is the key linkage and operational concept. It links the broad analytical domains of macro, in-time, governing regimes with the actual analysis of the process of governing. It also puts some necessary operational substance into the assumption of rational behaviour to achieve actors' preferences and their response to the natural rate of governability. In turn these responses may alter that natural rate. Statecraft, then, is the politics of governing. It is more than mere 'pub admin' or policy provision. Although the concept has been employed before, its treatment here incorporates some significant additions to previous notions. A major amendment suggests that if we are to fully understand the statecraft of Courts then we must recognise its three interlinked dimensions. These are: (a) the governing objectives; (b) the governing code – a set of relatively coherent principles or rules underlying policies and policy related behaviour and (c) polity management – a set of political support mechanisms designed to protect and promote the code and objectives. The problem is that these statecraft dimensions can only be usefully employed if we make explicit some fundamental assumptions concerning how, initially, we expect them to operate. These will appear to be 'unreal'. Their utility, however, depends less on their so-called realism than on their ability to provide parsimonious and fruitful accounts of the politics of governing in the past. These key assumptions run as follows.

- (a) The basic objectives of Courts will be self-serving, subsistence level, and time consistent. In sequence, that means Courts will pursue their own interests, they will attempt to achieve a sufficient governing competence to avoid hassle and stay in business, and these basic objectives will not change over time.

- (b) The governing intelligence and morality of Courts will also be time consistent, or only vary within a narrow range. In plain English there is no point, analytically, blaming Courts for being more than normally stupid or immoral, a common feature of media (and academic) comment. Such normative 'crap' must be excluded.

- (c) The primary field of play for the governing code is political economy, or the politics of economic management. The instruments of that management are the rules underlying this element of statecraft, not detailed policy analysis. And those rules, in the modern period at least, apply primarily to inflation control.

- (d) In addition to state management and political argument hegemony, polity management will include foreign policy. The assumption here is that the primacy of domestic politics will be the norm.

- (e) It follows that the only changing aspects of statecraft are the governing code and polity management. These will reflect the Courts' preoccupations with the N.R.G.

- (f) Governing regimes will change when these two dimensions of statecraft change. In short, regimes are statecraft, not structurally, driven.

Case Study: Governing Britain 1922-1964

In this section the Historical Politics approach, as detailed above, is applied to one particular period in British political development. Specifically, it identifies, analyses, and assesses the governing regime which it suggests operated in the period 1922 to 1964. The discussion runs as follows. First, the circumstances which led to the emergence of the regime in the years 1918-1922 are considered. Secondly, the classic period of the regime's operations, in the 1920s and above all the 1930s, is examined. Thirdly, the case for the continuity of that regime into the postwar period is outlined.

(i) Birth of a Regime, 1918-1922

Traditional historiography for this period stressed its twofold squalid nature: its failure to deliver on the promise that the Great War had been fought to produce a better Britain and a better world; and the corruption or sleaze associated with the behaviour of the governing Court, the Lloyd George coalition. More recent scholarship, on the other hand, tends to stress the considerable continuities between pre and postwar British government and politics. The case outlined here is somewhat different. It emphasises the crucial importance of this period on three counts. It witnessed the emergence of the basic structural problems of British politics which were to plague successive Courts for the rest of the century. It provided, in the coalition, the first statecraft response to those problems. It produced, in the autumn of 1922, an anti Court party coup which gave birth to an alternative statecraft, one which, because it persisted through to the early 1960s, assumed regime form. Each of these points requires some brief comment.

Electoral democracy, via the 1918 Representation of the People Act, arrived late and rapidly in Britain. Its impact was to create a climate of uncertainty and unrest amongst an increasingly professional political élite, an élite concerned that it would produce a permanent decline in the natural rate of governability. The party leaders who feared the future most were the Conservatives. They had been divided over tarif reform, welfare and constitutional issues since 1903, and out of office between 1906 and 1915. In the very flexible political climate of the postwar period the constant danger was that the Conservative Party would be reduced to a natural minority group squeezed between the Liberals under Lloyd George and the rapidly developing Labour Party. The new political economy had three awkward dimensions. It demanded an acceptance by politicians in office that they had some responsibility for the effective macro workings of the economy. It posed constant problems on the inflation front. It revealed the profoundly uncompetitive nature of the manufacturing sector, a state of affairs resulting from the dominance of small scale enterprises, inefficient management, and a highly inflexible labour market. Finally, there had emerged an alarming gap between public and élite perceptions of Britain's external security situation. The former considered we had won the war, defeated Germany, and expanded the empire. The latter saw instability in central Europe, the threat of communism from the Soviet Union, United States hostility to Britain's interests, new nationalism in the White Dominions and, in general terms, a marked asymmetry between Britain's external commitments and the resources available to meet them.

The Lloyd George Coalition of National Unity was the first governing response to these problems. At the time, in 1918 and through most of 1922, it seemed the natural political formula for governing Britain, at least to those outside the Labour Party and the Liberal rump under Asquith. It had a history, the wartime coalition under Lloyd George, and the ad hoc attempts to avoid the costs of single party government in the prewar period. It had specific projects, domestic reconstruction, the Peace settlements, countering the threat from Labour, and appeasing middle class discontent. It served the interests of both Lloyd George and the Conservative leaders. It included almost all the first XI of the British party élite. Moreover, it engineered several notable successes. It resolved the Irish Question. It reconstructed Western Europe. It demobilised the armed services. It, eventually, got on top of inflation and made plans for the return to the Gold Standard. It defeated militant trade unionism. Yet, in October 1922, Conservative parliamentarians decided to drop this particular governing formula. Why?

There were three interlinked reasons, each of which had important implications for the future of governing Britain. The first concerns the polity management dimension of the Coalition's statecraft. Governing without party proved difficult. National unity was the slogan but hardly a basis for effective political management. In practice the Coalition, and especially its leader, Lloyd George, developed a number of techniques which proved to be unpopular with those who believed politics and morality should be permanently united. What developed resembled Giolitti's 'system' in pre-1914 Italy: *trasformismo*, a willingness to accept political support from most groups; *clientelismo*, the politics of political notables; and constant attempts to produce a corporate (and appeasement) bias structure in key areas of political economy. The second reason highlights a paradox of the Coalition formula: designed to avoid the costs of party politics it ended by politicising the governing code dimension of statecraft. Instead of the fixed and public rules thought necessary at the time for sound and consistent economic management, there was uncertainty and unsoundness particularly as regards public expenditure and inflation control. In a sense Lloyd George was never forgiven for the great inflation of 1919/1920. In this vital sphere of governing he could not be trusted. Moreover, this weakness was compounded by his adventures in foreign policy. Playing policeman to the world, especially in the Middle East, was not something which supported a prudent political economy. The final reason provided the actual trigger for the Coalition's downfall, namely the fears amongst Conservative constituency interests, backbench MPs, and junior ministers, that the party's links with Lloyd George would eventually lead to its demise as a major component of British politics. The Carlton Club decision in October 1922, which endorsed that mood, was an extraordinary high stakes party strategy. It meant that future Conservative leaders would have to face the Labour Party on their own, without the benefits of the Lloyd George connection, a proportional representation electoral system, or a strong constitution in terms of the protection of property rights. Never has the difference between the interests of capital and the interests of the Conservative Party been made more clear.

(ii) The New Regime 1922-1939

The internal Conservative coup of October 1922 was legitimised in November when the party won the subsequent general election, the first time it had achieved a victory at the polls without the assistance of another party since 1880. With two short breaks of minority Labour governments in 1923/1924 and 1929-1931 the Conservatives were to hold office for the rest of the interwar period. This was the classic period of the new governing regime, a regime whose statecraft reflected the broad precepts of the post 1918 Treasury View.

This line of argument requires several explanatory comments. First, in the present context the interwar Treasury View is not viewed as a twentieth century expression of laisser faire economic theory, even less a doctrinal cover for finance capital hegemony. It is taken to represent a broad governing strategy, a 'flexible friend' for politicians in office, suitable for managing a fragile political economy operating in 'Hard Times'. Secondly, this Treasury View statecraft was not a minority view, supported only by Treasury mandarins and the right wing of the Conservative Party. It was supported by most members of the political élite, including a majority of senior Labour ministers in the two minority governments. The only serious organised opposition came from the CPGB, the B.U.F. and the friends of Mr.Keynes (which included political oddballs like Lloyd George and Harold Macmillan). Churchill's dissent emerged only in the 1930s and even then was centred on the foreign policy implications of an economic strategy he had supported in the 1920s. Thirdly, in economic policy terms the 1920s and the 1930s look quite different; the former espoused the Gold Standard and free trade, the latter a managed floating currency and protectionism. In statecraft terms, however, they exhibited considerable continuity in relation to the broad strategy adopted and the rules designed to activate that strategy. Finally, the emphasis in this paper will be on the 1930s, if only because the nature of a statecraft becomes clearer when it has to deal with serious economic and security problems.

That said the three dimensions of this new statecraft will be examined – governing objectives, the governing code and polity management.

The basic subsistence level, time consistent, governing objectives remained, namely achieving a sufficient governing competence to remain in business. What was new was the absence of the flexibility and 'can do' culture of the Lloyd George coalition. Britain was now recognised to be a difficult polity to govern effectively, the natural rate of governability had declined in the 1920s and was to decline even more in the 1930s. Hence the new emphasis was a 'safety first', 'limited liability' government, and the avoidance of adventures and adventurers. These were the objectives of pessimistic, even frightened, politicians, conscious of Britain's new external fragility and obsessed with avoiding open defeats. In the 1920s the objective was to return to pre 1914 normalcy. In the 1930s they were to manage the Depression, maintain peace, and hope there was light at the end of the tunnel.

To the governing code was assigned the task of confronting the NRG in its political economy dimension. The components of the code were its preoccupations, its operational rules, and its strategic objectives. The principal preoccupations, even in the midst of the Depression, were the constant fear of inflation and the necessity to maintain foreign confidence in the management of the British economy and sterling. To these were added an awareness that since the private sector of the economy was dominant there was little that governments could do to positively manage the economy. Moreover, given that the basic British economic problem was the lack of competitiveness, significant improvements could not be achieved rapidly. 'Cunctation', wait and see, was the supplyside order of the day. The operational rules were three: a preference for balanced budgets, scepticism about public works, and the necessity to depoliticise economic management. Balanced budgets were the golden rule of any sound money ethic. In theory that meant public expenditure was to be strictly controlled. In practice, it meant that governments should be seen to be serious about spending controls, and balanced budgets should be the target of economic management, if not always the reality. Similarly, opposition to public works schemes to confront unemployment was usually couched in theoretical terms in open debates on the subject. There was a fixed amount of investment capital available and government sponsored schemes would only reduce private investment. In fact, the rule here was political and administrative in character. To achieve any serious reduction in the unemployment figures the money devoted to public works schemes would have to be far in excess of that suggested by proponents of such schemes. Moreover, most schemes would be the responsibility of local authorities who could not be forced to accept them.

The most important rule however was that concerning depoliticised economic management. Depolitisation meant removing important economic decisions as far as possible from politicians. This was why rules were required, this was why the gold standard was so attractive; it was in a famous phrase 'knave proof'. In the 1930s both currency management and tariff policy were regarded as delicate matters for precisely this reason. Rules, then, were the logic of economic management in conditions of electoral democracy. Left to themselves politicians would compete for votes and sound money management would vanish. Note that the difference between the gold standard (an external rule) and a managed currency (a domestic monetary rule) was not seen in terms of national sovereignty. The gold standard was an impersonal, abstract automatic instrument. The difference was seen in terms of the degree to which domestic politicians could interfere in their operation.

Finally, the strategic objectives of economic management can be neatly summed up in terms of the 4 Cs – *credible* policies would produce *confidence* in British economic management, which, in turn, would allow Courts some *'credit'*, for any failures to follow the rules, and 'credit' would go far to sustaining a governing *competence*.

The third dimension of the interwar Treasury View concerns polity management, that is the 'tricks' of the political trade designed to protect and promote the interests of the Courts and disadvantage the interests of the opposition. The relevant questions, then, are what needed to be manipulated and controlled and how was this to be accomplished? The answers run as follows.

(a) Foreign Policy

For the Treasury View foreign policy (or, better, external affairs) was regarded as an instrument of domestic political management. In short, it accepted the doctrine of *primat der innenpolitik*. This meant two things. The public discourse was that of great power politics. The private, élite, discourse stressed the fragility, even hopelessness, of Britain's position and the absolute necessity to subordinate foreign policy to sound economic management. The result, in the 1930s, was appeasement allied to cautious, slow, rearmament. Any rapid, comprehensive increase in defence spending was viewed as a recipe for labour unrest and inflation.

(b) Public Opinion

To be effective the Treasury View needed to achieve political argument hegemony, or the control of commonsense. In the interwar period this meant paying considerable attention to the management of news and information. The press, radio, and the film industry were all viewed as instruments of explicit or implicit 'state', control. All this was useful, but not crucial. As Louis Macneice put it – 'Most are acceptors, born and bred to harness, and take things as they come.'

(c) Party Management

Political parties, even the Conservative Party, were seen as potential sources of opposition to Court objectives. A two party dominant system was preferred. Hence the opposition to changing the electoral system. Otherwise every effort was made to centralise internal party power structures by the process of Westminsterising party politics and the often brutal use of the whips against dissident MPs. Both the Labour and Conservative leadership groups played this game.

(d) The State Machine

The courts operated on the basis of judicial restraint. Within Whitehall this was the great age of 'Treasury control'. Where local government agencies were concerned, the strategy was to create a Dual Polity – leaving local issues to local governors within strict financial limits and ensuring that local interests did not penetrate the high politics concerns of the Courts. This, then, was very much a Court and Country power structure.

(e) Pressure Groups

The only continuously well-organised groups were those representing business, labour, and the professions. Here successive Courts pursued a twofold management strategy: leave these organisations to run their own affairs (even the trade unions) and appease them when awkward conflicts threatened. It was this limited liability, self-regulating, approach which effectively ensured that the competitiveness of the British economy never improved.

(iii) Governing Britain, 1945-1964: The Continuity Thesis

Both the historiography and political science of twentieth century British politics are dominated by one big idea, namely that the business of governing Britain after 1945 was conducted on lines very different from the interwar period. The Second World War, Labour's victory in 1945, and the Conservatives' conversion to social democracy in the late 1940s, all produced, so the argument runs, a governing style and content which rejected, even damned, the experience of 1918 to 1939. In other words, whilst the interwar years represented an unsuccessful, even immoral, aberration, post

1945 saw a return to its normal, nice, moderate, reasonably effective governing traditions. It is time this thesis, surely the last instalment of Whig history, was subjected to some criticism. The argument sketched below provides the outline of an alternative thesis, one which suggests that the notion of governing continuity between pre and postwar needs to be taken seriously. It is presented in four versions of increasing strength. Smokers will recognise the provenance of the labels affixed to each version.

(a) The Extra Mild Version

On this count, continuity stems from the incrementalism rooted in the 'Hard Times' of normalcy, that is peacetime. The interwar Treasury View was designed to cope with a fragile open political economy with awkward security problems. If that situation, that N.R.G., persisted after the War, then the 'official mind' of British Courts would be tempted to return to what had served them so well in 1939. Where the Treasury View scored was its realism; it understood the weaknesses of British governors and drew the appropriate conclusions about what they couldn't or shouldn't do in governing terms. Specifically, that meant no foreign adventures, no supplyside resolution, and a constant preoccupation with sterling, inflation and foreign confidence.

(b) The Low Tar Version

Here the case for continuity stems from the impact, or lack of it, of the Second World War. Rather than viewing the War as a great watershed in British political development, it is more plausible to approach it either as an enigma, or, better, a mere interregnum. The general argument is that democracies which win wars are unlikely to suffer radical change, if only because victory is seen to confirm the utility of traditional values and practices. Moreover, the more we learn about the war, the more the received notions of social togetherness, industrial efficiency, and military competence, are revealed as suspect or downright myths. The 1945 election result may have been less a vote in favour of Labour, and against the Conservative Party, as a rejection of Churchill as a peacetime leader.

(c) The Medium Strength Version

This is the structural argument for continuity. It has two principal themes. The first suggests that most of the principal components of the prewar domestic structure survived the war. That would apply to the mass political culture, the party system and the industrial sector. The second argues that although the external structural environment changed, it did so in ways which, paradoxically, sustained prewar governing operations. Examples would be U.S. hegemony and the Cold War: the former provided the external zimmerframe which Britain had lacked in the 1930s, the latter increased the country's status and, in the process, sustained the great power pretensions of successive postwar Courts, pretensions regarded as essential to maintaining domestic tranquillity. On the other hand, the Bretton Woods international monetary system by imposing the norm of a fixed exchange rate parity with the dollar generated constraints similar to those operating before the War.

(d) The Full Strength Version

This is the statecraft argument for continuity. Once again it can be presented in more than one form. The first simply notes the qualified nature of many of the so-called radical changes in governing after 1945. This would apply to the Keynesian revolution thesis, nationalisation, decolonisation, and the patchwork provision associated with the welfare 'state'. It would even apply to full employment, in so far as its achievement is difficult to relate to government policy. The second suggests that given the structural constraints noted above, the economic revolution was similar to 'a car being driven with the handbrake on'. The third notes that Labour had no well-prepared macro economic strategy in 1945 and that the Conservative Courts in the 1950s did attempt significant, if not always successful, changes in the political economy governing code, changes which reflected the 1930s rules. In combination, these three arguments produce a plausible thesis for the continuity of the Treasury View statecraft of the interwar period, albeit without the 'conviction politics' surrounding the earlier form.

Conclusions

(i) A reasonable response to the analysis above would be that it explains why the Historical Politics approach has not developed earlier. It is too complex, abstract, and pretentious to survive. The response to that is that although political science can often resemble historical analysis in the present, there is no point in doing so for the past. Perhaps the present is wrong too.

(ii) There is no necessary link between the methodology and the case study messages. True, but orthodox political science methodology has failed to produce these messages.

(iii) The approach does identify the 'real' watershed in post 1922 British politics, namely the period 1958 to 1964, when a Conservative Court led by an anti-Treasury View *fraktion* and frightened by developments in the EEC, turned to a new statecraft combining neo-corporatism and Community membership.

Bibliography

The items listed below have contributed to, although they have not always positively supported, the arguments presented in this paper.

P.Abrams, *Historical Sociology*, 1982.

N.Annan, *Our Age*, 1990.

M.Archer, 'Structuration versus morphogenesis', *British Journal of Sociology*, 1982.

C.Barnett, *The Audit of War*, 1986.

A.Booth 'Britain in the 1930s: A Managed Economy', *Economic History Review*, 1987.

R.Brent, 'Tories: High Politics and the Writing of Modern British Political History', *Historical Journal*, 1989.

S.Brittan, *The Treasury Under the Tories*, 1964.

J.Bulpitt, 'Historical Politics: Macro In-Time Governing Regime Analysis', in J.Lovenduski & J.Stanyer (eds), *Contemporary Political Studies*, Volume 2, 1995.

P.Cain & A Hopkins British Imperialism, 1919-1990, 1993.

A.Cairncross, *Years of Recovery*, 1985.

W.Carlsnaes 'The Agency-Structure Problem in Foreign Policy Analysis', *International Studies Quarterly*, 1992.

P.Clarke, *The Keynesian Revolution in the Making*, 1988.

M.Cowling, *The Impact of Labour*, 1971.

M.Cowling, *The Impact of Hitler*, 1975.

C.Emsley et al, *War, Peace and Social Change in Twentieth Century Europe*, 1989.

J.Gallagher, *The Decline, Revival and Fall of the British Empire*, 1982.

P.Gourevitch, *Politics in Hard Times*, 1986.

R.Holland, *The Pursuit of Greatness*, 1991.

R.Lane 'Concrete Theory: An Emerging Political Method', *American Political Science Review*, 1990.

R.Matthews, 'Why Has Britain Had Full Employment Since the War?' *Economic Journal*, 1968.

A.Marwick (ed), *Total War and Social Change*, 1988.

R.Middleton, *Towards the Managed Economy*, 1985.

R.Parker, *Chamberlain and Appeasement*, 1993.

D.Reynolds, *Britannia Overruled*, 1991.

H.Smith (ed), *War and Social Change*, 1986.

J.Tomlinson, *Public Policy and the Economy Since 1900*, 1990.

The Political Science of British Politics

Fred Nash

University of Southampton

'Political Science and the study of British Government and Politics:
"una storia che mai finisce" '[1]

Introduction

The theme of this joint panel is the political science of British politics, and it was, originally, intended to be a forum in which to discuss follow-up papers to those presented at the York Conference, last year.[2] That objective will be achieved somewhat indirectly.

Reading three related papers[3] proved to be a painful experience, mostly because of the poverty and the naiveti of the underlying view of political science that informs them. One paper is published in a refereed journal, and the mark of 'approval' thus stamped upon it has added to the gravity of the problem.

Politicians 'use' words, even when their meaning is less than clear, but political scientists cannot: it is incumbent upon us to speak academic 'sense' to a world of experience out there which is not always coherent.

In section 1, an abstract account of the nature of our discipline is given, which will remind us of some basic truths about what we do. In section 2 (a, b, and c), the gist of the three papers as an example of the type will be critically examined. Clearing away the dead-weight of ideological and methodological debris of many decades, the way will be open for a focused single government study of the British system. Out of these arguments will emerge the contours of a meta-analytic, by definition meta-theoretical, approach to the study of British government and politics, discussed in section 3 b.

1

If political scientists have ever agreed on anything, it is that they disagree about their discipline. Evidently, apart from the name, or so it would appear, we have naught else in common.

Now, it may be in our gift to disagree about the nature of our discipline, but the idea that what we do is a science imports into the argument

---

[1] This paper is published in *PSD*, 1996 [http://www.soton.ac.uk/ psd/].

[2] Jim Bulpitt, 'Historical Politics : Macro, In-Time, Governing Regime Analysis', in *PSD*, 1995, [http://www.soton.ac.uk/ psd/], also printed in J.Lovenduski & J.Stanyer (eds), *Contemporary Political Studies 1995*, PSA, 1995; and Fred Nash, 'Political Science, History, and Contemporary History' in *PSD*, 1995, [http://www.soton.ac.uk/ psd/].

[3] All three are by David Marsh. They are: 'Thatcherism and the Post-War Consensus', unpublished paper, delivered at the Institute of Contemporary History Conference, Queen Mary & Westfield College, London, July 1995 [henceforth ICBH95]; 'Explaining "Thatcherite" Policies: Beyond Uni-dimensional explanations', in *Political Studies*, 43/4, 1995 [henceforth *Political Studies* 95]; and 'Explaining Thatcherism: Beyond Uni-Dimensional Explanation' in *Contemporary Political Studies 1994*, PSA, 1994 [henceforth PSA94].

something external, over which we exercise but little control. For the claim to being a 'science' raises the legitimate expectation that, even if our proclaimed disagreement is true, we still share a concern, duty even, in common, namely to understand and offer recognisably 'political' explanations. This is, of course, a confused state of affairs, but only because we begin with the nonsensical view that the subject-matter of the discipline is not clear to us. In fact this confusion is an unnecessary one. Not only do we share the core objective of explaining, we also seek to explain that which is recognisably political. True, there are competing views concerned with exclusions, but all agree on a broad range of inclusions: 'the political' is always concerned with the fortunes of a collectivity of a people as a collectivity, constituted such that it can pretend a whole in which all the parts recognisably belong. And while this says nothing worth saying about 'politics', it does, for all that, indicate the broader ambit of political science. Here we seek to explain how that collectivity *qua* a collectivity is constituted, what its powers for collective action are, whence they arise and in what manner. We are also concerned to show how such powers are transformed into authority, now, of the 'state', and legitimately exercised by its chosen personnel. Naturally, we also have something to say about the manner in which such personnel are selected, and authorised to act in the name of the collectivity, and, thereby, even if only by implication, examine claims to obedience. Now, the idea of 'acting in the name of the collectivity' naturally takes us into the realm of purpose, practice, policy and 'political behaviour', and the manner thereof. The addition to these abstract principles of a time-continuum raises other fascinating issues, especially on claims to its continued legitimacy through the generations.[4]

Now, if this abstract sketch is correct, it must follow that in political science our essential concern is with government, and only then with the politics of a given collectivity. The fact of this sequence is important. For thereby we argue against the meaningfulness of the claim that it is possible to address politics when we lack a detailed understanding of government, governing procedures and the structure of 'constituted powers' of a given people.[5] That some actually concentrate on politics, even recommend it as a good thing to do, does not make it any more meaningful, nor does the fact make the outcome a political science explanation. They may be good accounts in contemporary history, history and, of course, economics, or deal with ideologies, politicians and their foibles, *et cetera*, but none of these, even when they are read together, can amount to a political science account. Nor, for that matter, is a text book describing the working system always an exercise in political science, neither is it an explanation of the system. In a sense, though this is a slightly different point, political science as such is not a subject taught at any University: the coming together of a limited number of related subject-matters gives rise to political science understanding. It is,

---

[4] Revising this paper, it struck me that, firstly, I have not distinguished between political theory and the study of government, and, secondly, that there is no need to do so!

[5] For a similar argument about the study of the European Union, see my 'The UK and the EU; Reflections on the Problem of Explanation', *PSD*, 1995 [http://www.soton.ac.uk/ psd/].

in truth, only a culmination, recognised when understanding is achieved: it deals with re-constituted politics; it is, strictly, *talk* amongst the *cognoscenti*, concerned with the conceptual structure of a meaningful sentence in politics.

We must ask: how is it done? and what is the character of a political science explanation? For some these questions are readily translated into simple issues of concept and method. But an infantile concern with concept and method in the abstract does not lead anywhere, other than to concept and method. In this we differ fundamentally from the 'hard' sciences in which, for good reason, focus is on method (for example, experimental procedures) which its practitioners must learn *qua* technique. On the other hand, it is hardly helpful to say that in political science we 'read, examine, reflect and judge, then state a view'. Such an account, influenced as it is by a certain view of the hard sciences, causes special problems for us. Firstly, it privileges the analyst: science is often seen as what scientists do. But because we do not have 'objective' – for us, non-linguistics – procedures, and because we also lack a clearly understood and accepted framework indicating the necessary and minimum (training) requirements for a knowing mind to prepare it to function at an inter-subjective level, we are likely to tend to solipsism – culminating in conversation with the self – and, in the event, displacing inter-subjective conceptions by opinion, threatening a proclivity to intellectual relativism. The inevitable tendency to emphasise a few big names, when associated with the obvious absence of a body of recognised theorems upon which all reflect, drains the exercise of any academic and intellectual relevance. But, secondly, and more importantly, it privileges one special view of the subject which focuses on accounting for 'what is'. While we can all look and examine a 'something', be it a worm wriggling on the ground, the glorious beauty of Concorde in flight, or the planets in the sky, and say something about it, neither the zoologist, nor the physicist, will recognise our account as a contribution to the science in question, whereas they are, both, likely to accept that our utterances may be correct to the extent that they reflect common or general knowledge 'explanations' about the matter in question. Similarly, the 'average' citizen has views about the government of the day and opinions about individual members of it, and will, readily, judge this or that policy. That too is a part of common knowledge. And while we may be impressed by the evident sagacity and obvious accuracy of such views, it is almost certainly the case that their albeit 'correct' views are not conclusions issuing from 'serious' (that is, academic) study.[6]

---

[6] A distinction has to be drawn between this and the rather more complicated, and, as I would argue, not altogether meaningful claim that in a parliamentary democracy, the electorate is expected to, and actually does, examine the political record of a government over a number of years, and passes judgement upon it. Sounds good to say, but it is incapable of unproblematical academic construction. If it works, it is also a mystery such that, so far, no theoretical explanation of it makes any sense. In fact, it does not work, and the theory which so explains the situation is more accurate. We must be careful not to be misled by a kind of 'naturalism' in this: it is possible to argue that whatever works in the 'objective' world has an explanation, even if we do not as yet know it. But this cannot be said of volitional human actions. The socio-political system is, when all is said and done, only a convention and, as such, a human construction. Its rules and explanations are not part of what Hegel would have delighted in calling 'reason', but have

In all cases, determining the subject is the *sine qua non* of any discipline. In this, too, we are different. Whereas, broadly, science seeks to explain what is, and the 'what is' of the sciences is actually there, for us it is a construction, so much so that even to assume 'government' and 'politics' is both to make a political statement and to present a problem: government and politics are essentially contingent matters, and have to be understood as such. For us, determining the subject is not an innocent matter at all, for, crucially, the very manner in which the subject is determined is open to argument.[7] This also means that, without *some* epistemology we will be unable to deal with the construction of 'what is', without which there can be no discipline; and without a discipline, the idea of knowing and explaining can have no meaning, for they, both, but especially explaining, derive their meaning and significance from the epistemological limitations of the discipline. We recognise an account to be an explanation in political science precisely to the extent that it falls within the discipline.

In short, we 'shoot at a moving target from a shifting base', and this causes particular difficulties for us. Politics is[8] ubiquitous – for some it is so to such a degree that even the historically significant public/private distinction is thereby destroyed – and because there is a great deal of common knowledge, wisdom, and above all, informed and 'gut-feeling' type opinion about every aspect of it, explanation in political science is in special need of clear understanding and defence. Not every account that touches politics and, for that matter, government, is a political science account, and for that reason also not a political science explanation.[9]

2 a

Rejecting existing explanations Marsh indicates the 'route forward' to a 'new' and preferred type of explanation. I must confess that I, for one, find it increasingly more difficult to cope with infantile – indeed political *qua* intended to persuade – use of language,[10] especially from experienced professionals training the next generation of political scientists. Of course,

---

to be understood in terms of positive statements that both offer a satisfactory account of how it works, and why we should do it.

[7] See Michael Oakeshott, 'Political Discourse' first published in his *Rationalism in Politics, and other essays*, Liberty Press, 1991, pp.70-71.

[8] Politics 'is' or 'are' is itself a serious question, not a mere linguistic play: the choice says something significant about the meaning of the word.

[9] My favourite is the manner in which the Liberal party, in pursuit of their electoral interests, looked at the irrelevant national compilation of figures – which have no place and role in the electoral process of this country – and shouted 'foul'. They coined the idea – it is not a concept – of 'wasted votes', which has become such a major 'concept', especially in arguments about electoral reform. The fact is that this so-called 'concept' is only meaningful in a system designed to give expression to every vote cast. It cannot possibly have any relevance in a system in which voting is the expression of a preference for one person to stand for a defined territorial unit. We must beware the complications that arise from confounding explanation – that is, political science – with what Michael Oakeshott has called 'diagnostic and prognostic interpretations' – that is, politics. Michael Oakeshott, 'Political Discourse', in his *Rationalism in Politics, and other essays*, Liberty Press, 1991, p.71.

[10] See the Appendix to my 'The UK and the EU: Reflections on the Problem of Explanation' in *PSD*, 1995, [http://www.soton.ac.uk/ psd/].

'route forward' makes sense when we know the object destination: knowing the destination, we would have *the* benchmark against which to examine explanations. But, it must be said, if we knew the destination claims to 'knowing' the 'route forward' would be redundant.

A major problem of explanation in political science is precisely that we do not have any such benchmark. We know in general what a political science explanation will look like, but we cannot know what the explanation for a given topic will actually look like, not until we have done it, and shown that it works. Marsh claims that a proper explanation of the 1980s will be inclusive of three (economic, political and ideological) factors, without privileging any one factor (for example, *Political Studies* 95, p. 824) – else we shall have 'subject imperialism'![11] – but we do not know what he has in mind, nor has he produced a 'theory' which rectifies the problem of 'insufficiently theorise[d] relationship, or articulation, between these factors'.[12] For all intents and purposes, the bench-mark is still lacking, and the 'route forward' is only a dream and a desideratum. Furthermore, since political science explanation is relevant only to a subject which has, in some significant sense, already become historical [13] we are, always, faced with the fundamental problem of defining and examining a subject which is already 'there'. Because we cannot begin with *tabula rasa*, the construction of 'what is' becomes even more crucial in and for our analysis, but this is not a free for all process, and not all desirable theories can be forced on the 'facts'. Our subject is, by definition, always historically defined. Therefore, our very close relationship with history and contemporary history are crucially important:[14] these related disciplines ought not to be taken for granted, nor their outputs taken at face value.

The trick is to learn the basic 'science' element of political science and then seek to give an account of a specific subject area in a language and a form that is recognisable to other practising political scientists. In the process we may have to defend the position that there is need to modify the requirements of explanation for reasons esoteric to the subject, but it is simply incomprehensible to begin with the view that the subject is esoteric! Our first and most complicated difficulty is already clear: we must use ordinary words and mean extraordinary meaning by them.[15] And only those who know the words in this way can use them in a meaningful and precise sense; the less rigorous one's command of the language, the more is one likely to speak in clichés and linguistic, rather than disciplined, gener-

---

[11] The desired explanation is freely referred to in the PSA94 paper, and also the *Political Studies* 95 paper, but it is never stated. The odd notion of 'subject imperialism', which is hardly an academic argument, appears in *Political Studies* 95 paper, p.611.

[12] This is a criticism levelled against the existing inclusive explanations, especially that of Andrew Gamble and Jessop et al. This point is made in both PSA94 and *Political Studies* 95.

[13] Given that there is no 'now' as such, but only a past or an extended present which is continuously becoming a past, then all cases that we examine are, by definition, a case of a past, always understood in either historical or contemporary history terms.

[14] See my 'Political Science, History, and Contemporary History' in *PSD*, 1995, [http://www.soton.ac.uk/ psd/].

[15] J.C.Banks once remarked, so many years ago, that in an undergraduate course in Government one only learns the language of political science.

alisations. To the *nescient* linguistic generalisations – always *maxims* – are part of the manner of talk, whereas the *cognoscenti* will recognise specific generalisations – *theorems*, and possibly, *axioms* – as essential components of the apparatus of explanation. Political science is not merely better history, or more complicated contemporary history, in that, using big words, it addresses many dimensions of the issues involved; it is a philosophically sophisticated, theoretical study. As such, its *theorems* and *axioms* are constantly subject to research and re-thinking.

2 b

In all his three pieces, Marsh offers a critique of existing explanations, and seeks to contribute to the process of explaining the Conservative phenomenon of 1980s, identified with the name of the then Prime Minister. To that measure, therefore, all three papers have a *prima facie* claim to being not only pieces in political science, but contributions to the political science of British politics. But there are problems and arguments. His position may be summarised thus:

• The character of his ICBH95 paper is not transparent: on reflection, it may be seen as a cunning piece of 'politicking', for without engaging with any of the arguments, it prepares the ground for a move to the desideratum of a more 'holistic' account, and reveals the fact that no such account is, as yet, available. This despite the claim that he has attempted to do so in *Political Studies* 95 and PSA94.

• PSA94 and *Political Studies* 95 contain brief and selective reviews of a few 'uni-dimensional' and 'inadequate inclusive' accounts. The uni-dimensional accounts are rejected outright, while Andrew Gamble's work is praised ('consistently interesting', PSA94, p.809, and 'interesting and useful starting point', *Political Studies* 95, p.612) then criticised for failing to correctly theorise the relationship between the important factors, and, therefore, it, too, is rejected. All the while, Jessop's argument remains the bête noire of the scenario: it is seen to be potentially fruitful, but in need of modification. Meanwhile, it emerges that any inclusive explanation for any single case has to take into account the political (read electoral) dimension: Jim Bulpitt's 'uni-dimensional' view, already rejected, is right, but he has ignored too much. Meanwhile, in ICBH95 (pp. 9-10) two other accounts are identified as 'consistently interesting'.

• In ICBH95, but not in *Political Studies* 95 and PSA94, Marsh calls for comparative analyses as the necessary approach to a meaningful explanation of the topic under discussion. Moreover, he also calls for 'theoretically-informed thorough empirical research'. Neither of these claims are straightforward, and will be discussed in some detail in section 2c, below.

• In ICBH95 Marsh more directly rejects the so-called exceptionalism 'thesis' and emphasises the need for comparative research. However, words and wished-for thoughts are not deeds, and in between the two lie the innocence or, more to the point, the guilt of the analyst.

It is asserted that the problem begins with a 'partial, in both senses, reading of history' (ICBH95, pp. 1-2), specifically that of 'consensus politics'. It is not simple casuistry to say that this assertion is pregnant with an unspecified claim that it may be possible to have a non-partial reading of history. Indeed, even within the limits of Marsh's own terms, this claim runs into difficulty. This for two reasons: firstly, he betrays a problematical view when, quoting Pimlott, he warns against the danger of reading history backwards. There is, of course, serious danger in viewing any past from the perspective of a present interest, even if that perspective is itself a theoretical one. To be sure, explanations of British (in fact always English) government and politics, at any rate since the end of the seventeenth century, have suffered from the fact that the Whig interpretation has dominated its associated historical perspective. And even though this interpretation has been discredited for some time now, its influence lives on, at any rate to the extent that it influenced and determined Bagehot's and, especially, Dicey's understanding whose accounts are still central to any serious examination of the British working system. To that extent – but also in other ways[16] – we have not yet managed to free ourselves from the influence of the Whig interpretation. But this is not all that can be said.

'Reading history backwards' is only an indirect way of raising the issue of criterion of relevance: history is always a special story, not just an 'account' of events on a cosmic scale. Are we to reduce political science to history, such that a 'full' historical account is the best that we can possibly hope for? How is a full account to be constructed if, purposefully, we ignore the outcome, the 'now' as we understand it? If history is to be independent of our (that is, political science) interests and concerns, what sort of relationship between that kind of history and political science can we envisage?

Wide claims about history, or treating it as a self-enclosed subject to be accessed when necessary, betray an ill-understanding of its nature and role. We do not have anything other than problematical history, and, specially, contemporary history accounts. Research and explanation in political science must also address the issue of the historical context and its meaning. Indeed, though banal but in the circumstances it must be said that, even to select a period for research is to impose a supposed view upon the course of events. Besides, to select a period one must 'know' more than the period thus selected, for to periodise is to judge a number of events as 'somehow' related and, therefore, meaningfully connected. But this cannot be done without knowing the course of events, that is to say *another* account. Our problem in political science is that we have no starting point independent of the subject we wish to examine. And associated with this is the ever-present danger that our efforts might simply collapse into 'diagnostic and prognostic' interpretations, rather than explanatory accounts: too many accounts purporting to belong to political science are clearly partial pieces *in* politics.

---

[16] One is reminded of Leo Strauss's stricture that those who fail to understand Machiavelli's evil do so only because they are his heirs, or are corrupted by him. L.Strauss, *Thoughts on Machiavelli*, University of Washington Press, 1958, p.12.

But the position as understood from the three papers under discussion is more complicated than this may suggest. One suspects that the nature of historical explanation and its generalisations are also of special concern. For, all said and done, Marsh has an ideological agenda which imposes its own view of what the historical account, and, in the longer run, also the political science explanation of the events ought to look like. This view of his position and wished-for outcome dwarfs his criticism that others offer and work with 'heroic generalisations'! We shall re-visit exceptionalism below.

- To be sure, greater detail disposes of generalisations: that is obviously so. But a detailed historical account, better displaying the minutia of the course of events requires to be pruned and abstracted so that its character may be revealed. In fact, no account in history is devoid of generalisations; far from it, every account is based on some generalisation, else no intelligible account can ever be produced. To rely on generalisation in and from history is to occlude political science altogether, while seeking to avoid generalisation in political science, if such were possible, would emasculate it as a discipline.

Marsh enjoins us to go from case study – the empirical – to the theoretical, and this, we are told, can be achieved if we focus on specific accounts (not general explanations), and proceed to generate broader explanations at higher levels of generalisation. This prognosis also enjoins that we incorporate structure[17] and agency, as well as the economic, social and the political dimensions into our analysis. And it is expected that this process will lead to a different wished-for outcome which, for all that, will also be in terms of general explanations.

Now, in so enjoining Marsh may appear, as it were, to be going the wrong way up a one way street, while all the traffic is coming at him. But there is, so to say, no pile up because Marsh is travelling in a ghost car: it passes through solid objects without leaving a trace. He fails to see, or chooses to ignore, the crucial fact that in social sciences in general, and in political science in particular, there are no empirical accounts except in view of some general, theoretical understanding which enables an account to be constructed, and which imparts to occurrences and events the character of being facts, thus making it possible for them to belong to a 'period'. More than that, and to repeat a point, such a 'period', too, is theoretically defined. It is curious that Marsh does not see this point, especially so in view of the fact that approvingly he reports the accepted notion that there was no such thing as 'Butskellism' until *The Economist* invented the word in 1954, nor, for that matter, 'consensus' until Paul Addison[18] 'conceptualised' it. Indeed, examining not just the fortunes of the Conservative party

---

[17] I take this to mean 'government', but this is not strictly what Marsh means. He equates it with 'constraint', from the international capitalist system to trade unions (*Political Studies* 95, p. 609), or, as in Jessop's view, with any accumulation regime (PSA94, p. 818). Structure seen exclusively as 'constraints' is a problem: as will be argued below (section 3), it could, more importantly, also mean capability and power.

[18] *The Road to 1945*, Jonathan Cape, 1975. Incidentally this claim is not strictly true; inexplicably, neither Addison nor Marsh mention P.H.Partridge, *Consent and Consensus*, London, 1971. At any rate, after the general elections of 1964, we were already talking about the end of the Butskellite consensus.

in the 1980s, but also that of the Labour party, some are moved to theorise the meaning of consensus,[19] while commentators express the desirability of another such period. The point is that in much the same way that the agenda of the 1950s was, at least in large part, determined by post-war necessity and the reforms of the Attlee government, it is expected that the next Labour government will, *mutatis mutandis*, accept the agenda of politics as set by the effects of Globalisation and the reforms of the Conservative governments of the 1980s. Neither the 'adversary' nor the 'consensus' conception has an exclusive or dominant hold on the British approach. They are both theoretical reflections upon the character of specific periods, and both are in the tradition of British politics. They are political science attempts at making sense of otherwise diverse historical periods. In short, far from going from the empirical to the theoretical, we can only go from one theoretical to another theoretical.

Only when we read his three papers, as it were, together, does it become clear that he does not mean to say that we should – whether he means we could is a different matter – seek to generate theories and generalisations from empirical accounts, but that we should focus upon specific empirical cases and explain them by reference to a wished-for holistic grand theory. He is arguing from a theoretical position. But this leaves us wondering what role he wishes to assign to comparison in all this? And why specify (in both PSA94 and *Political Studies* 95) that we must go 'from case study to theory' when its full meaning is not meant?

- Finally, but only to the extent that 'structure' includes 'government', there is a positive point to be made. For too long the study of British *government* has been overshadowed by an almost exclusive interest in British *politics*. And just as ignoring grammar at schools has produced generations of the linguistically illiterate, focus on British politics to the exclusion of government has increasingly politicised the study of British government. In claiming that there is too much emphasis on agency at the expense of *structure*, Marsh is simply recognising the danger that awaits anyone who focuses on politics. This is a belated but, nevertheless, a welcome recognition. But two points must be accepted. Firstly, that some never made the transition, and have doggedly continued to concentrate on government and politics. Secondly, if Marsh really wishes to bring government into what has heretofore been the study of politics, he must accept that the focus of his work can no longer be public policy, and that he must engage with the existing literature on British government, not seek to invent it.

Three points stand out. Firstly, Marsh harbours a desired outcome, even though the shape of it is not made clear to us. The proper – inclusive, but different – explanation is, so to say, defined negatively, by what it is not meant to be – which, incidentally, is a criticism that Marsh approvingly quotes against Jessop's view of the state (PSA94, p.812). Secondly, ignoring a few minor differences between the PSA94 and *Political Studies* 95 papers,[20] he seeks to undermine the possibility of British exceptionalism,

---

[19] A.Gamble, *The Free Economy and the Strong State*, Macmillan, 1988, pp.209, 219, 221.

[20] This is an incidental point, and the differences may due to constraints of space:

and, in a connected sense, thirdly, he calls for comparisons and more detailed analysis, including incorporating 'structure' into the analysis. Since the second and the third are instrumentally necessary to achieve his desideratum, we ought to examine their promises and limitations in some detail.

2 c

We are enjoined to study the phenomenon of the 1980s on a comparative basis, across time and space. And the claim is that the first will reveal the extent to, and the manner in which, it differs from previous periods, while the second will reveal the extent to, and the manner in which, it is different from – in this case, similar to – experiences elsewhere. We shall then know the truth and the possible extent, or absence, of exceptionalism, in both its dimensions. An examination of comparison will be followed by a brief account of exceptionalism.

Comparison

There is an inescapable crudeness about comparing, which is also an essential part of its charm. And it is this: our natural mental process of understanding is, plainly, comparative. Our world of experience is a world of cognition, recognition, identification, classification, and internalisation. We naturally think in this manner, even though we are not self-aware of the processes, and cannot offer a detailed account of how the mind works. And this process of understanding is simply a feature of our being in the world. There is no extrinsic purpose attached to such a process of understanding, except that, evidently, it is something we cannot avoid. We may do it well, or badly, but we do it all the same. Put differently, this is not a method we have chosen because of its features, its advantages, or wished-for outcomes.

Now, there is no gainsaying this except to make one point: each personal experience is created against the background of everything that is in us, our whole store of experiences is instantaneously brought to bear on the 'new' – else the 'new' cannot be so identified – and is relevant to the process whereby the new, too, becomes an 'experience'. Not only can we not get away from this in our world of experiences, but we cannot divest ourselves of it when we are self-consciously in a sophisticated – that is, academic – world of 'experiences'. However, whereas ordinarily 'what we are' is the bench-mark of our own understanding,[21] and it cannot be otherwise, in the world of academic judgement, the bench-mark, though still the person, is significantly modified in that the personal store of experiences is no longer the store of ideas against which to judge. Here we must invoke a different,

---

Political Studies 95 is shorter than PSA94. But that cannot justify the change from Gamble (1988) and Jessop (1988 to 1990) 'were constrained by considerations of space and because Auerbach's analysis (1991) was published later' (PSA94, p.812) to 'they were constrained by considerations of space and could not utilise Auerbach's work' (*Political Studies* 95, p.598).

[21] See my 'In search of the Archimedean point: Editorial Gate-Keeping revisited' in *PSD*, 1995 [http://www.soton.ac.uk/ psd/], also published in *Contemporary Political Studies 1995*, PSA, 1995.

now self-consciously created and understood, sets of ideas and understandings. At this level of analysis, 'natural' comparison is no longer the means of dealing with the world, and, for that reason, 'methodological comparison' must be theorised and examined. We can only recommend it and resort to it if we are reasonably clear that it will be not only efficient but also epistemologically coherent. Else we will not be in a position to defend its conclusions.

To compare, it is necessary to have a base and a target subject, which are in some significant sense similar, though possibly in certain respects not so.[22] It is common knowledge, and a simple rule of thought, that only like and like can be related to one another, like and unlike are, analytically, in different categories. This is the most rudimentary point that can be made; yet all the arguments against the meaningfulness of methodological comparison can be deduced from it. A brief explication will suffice.

It is clear that the base account cannot be known comparatively, but must be known before it is 'designated' as base for purposes of comparison. This is naturally the account we tend to be most familiar with; in our case inevitably that of Britain. But this is not an innocent matter, for the actual condition of this account is crucially important. Not withstanding the arguments to be given in section 3 below, the accuracy of our base account – itself a function both of its evidential and theoretical aspects – is subject to further research and theoretical challenge. Given that every account is always tentative, any inaccuracy or theoretical problem built into it will needs also be built into any subsequent comparison, and will, to that measure, determine the 'correctness' of our understanding of the target account. Therefore, it is not safe to assume that such an account can offer a firm foundation and base from which to launch a comparison and against which to evaluate.

However, our target subject must also be identified before a comparison can be set up. That is to say, we must know in advance that the target is, in fact, in the same category as the base argument. And since this is a logical necessity – analytically required before a comparison can be set up – it is clear that we must accept it. Meanwhile, the short answer to the question 'how was the 'knowledge' about the target subject obtained?' is 'not by a process of comparison.'

Furthermore, to judge that the base and the target accounts are, in fact, in the same group, category or class, it is necessary that we have categories, which are strictly theoretical statements. Our next question – and this is where the subject begins to become interesting – is how do we come by these categories? They must be relevant to the base and the target subjects, which for us are always historical accounts, else they can have no relevance to the categorisation of the subjects in question. And if we are told that they are categories that historians have used in the making of their stories, we must ask: 'where did they get them from?'[23] It is an important truism

---

[22] For comments on the 'comparative politics' study of the European Union, see my 'The UK and the EU; Reflections on the Problem of Explanation', *PSD*, 1995 [http://www.soton.ac.uk/ psd/].

[23] There is a simple (that is, weak) answer to this, namely that, as a matter of fact, we do not start with *tabula rasa*, but that we continue from where we are, and, therefore,

that the character of a given historical episode is the result not of, so-called, the 'facts' that the historian creates, but of the generalisations which the historian brings to bear on the 'evidence'. To speak of facts is already to flag a problem: there are only occurrences and events. It is the historian, who, by eliciting and drawing meaning and relevance from occurrences and events, will, in the light of some broader concept, invest them with the quality of being 'facts': there are no eventualities as such other than in the story that the story-teller puts together. But this is not a permanent identification and categorisation: further research, or, more importantly, a different theoretical orientation will question the validity of the judgement of a previous account, and may create further facts from occurrences and events previously not so identified, or previously not invested with significance.[24]

It is clear that comparison in the social sciences, but particularly in political science, is far from the primary and essential tool of analysis. The 'science' in 'political science' cannot derive from its supposed comparative orientation;[25] we must look elsewhere for its origin and import, but that is a somewhat different question. Yet methodological comparison is talked about – even argued against! – and taught in University courses, while numerous books and articles purport to offer comparisons, or present the startling fruits of some comparative research.

For many, comparison in political science is important for the rather simple reason that we do not have any other means of testing ideas. True, but it is not clear that methodological comparison is a substitute. Knowing about the experiences of other peoples may enlarge our store of examined ideas – that is, understanding – but it is by no means clear that 'systematic' comparison is necessary or even relevant to it. And since both the base and the target subjects must be known in advance, the process of obtaining the prior knowledge of the two cases is far more important than the rather contrived process of comparing them. Emphasis on the comparing, which derives from comparative history of the late nineteenth century, is directly related to the problem of induction, and also to the fact that in political science we do not have 'eternal' laws. It also betrays a desire for authoritative answers. The fact that our science is of a certain logical type does not justify methodological comparison, nor indicate its relevance. Besides, that something is seemingly done, does not make it actually meaningful to do. The point is that methodological comparison cannot deliver what its proponents desire, and the 'conclusions' that apparently emerge out of some supposed comparison are not due to methodological comparison at all: rather, the 'comparison' is no more than a familiar façade, an integument, hiding the true manner in which they were derived or arrived at. It is, just as easily, no more than a legitimating integument, for the appellation

---

from accumulated knowledge and experience. This is, in a general and obvious sense, true. The problem is not that we do not, or ought not, to do so, but that the fact has to be understood, and its implications exposed. 'Where we are' is an understanding and may, as such, be part of the problem.

[24] An interesting example, and a case in point, would be the intellectual impact of 'race' and 'feminism' upon 'white' and 'male' dominated political science!

[25] pace S.E.Finer, 'The Vocabulary of Political Science, in *Political Studies*, 23/2-3, especially p.244.

'comparative' bestows an evident air of being 'scientific'.

For some, methodological comparison is a process of theory building. But the poverty of such a claim is made abundantly clear by the foregone discussion of comparison. Here, too, comparison is only an integument. At best a given theory is 'examined' in conjunction with more than one historical account and shown to have some explanatory validity in relation to each.

However, if methodological comparison has no analytical value,[26] the comparative approach has an important didactic value: it is a useful, though very limited, teaching tool.

The didactic use of comparison is relatively self-evident. In fact, we make rather regular use of it in the teaching of the social sciences. It requires that the teacher should know the base and the target subject, while the students must, in the least, know the base argument: features of the known case are used to introduce and define features of another case not known to the recipient. Here, comparison is a bridging process, not one of reasoning, or theory building. Theory and the concepts used in such a didactic process are logically and actually prior to the whole enterprise: they cannot arise out of any comparison.

The point is simply this: comparison is not, for by its nature it cannot be, the primary process of analysis. At best it can be made to apply if and when we already know a great deal in advance. If so, then the relative value of this essentially secondary process of analysis is no more than a means of organising and presenting findings obtained elsewhere. Its true value is a strictly didactic one, whereas habitual and loose references to 'the comparative method' mask the reality that the nature of political science is not of this kind.

An informed analyst – one whose sensitive and extensive understanding of the becoming of this polity is associated with the fruits of political philosophy and the history of ideas – will not be moved by invitations to 'comparative' examination of any given episode. Such a rejection is informed by the recognition of the primacy of specialist accounts, and the well understood futility and conceptual poverty of methodological comparison. More than that, they also recognise that enlarging the ambit changes the nature of the question under examination.

In view of the foregone, then, a call for 'systematic' comparisons assumes a distinctly hollow sound. Frankly, when we are poised at the point of a self-consciously structured comparison, our analysis is already complete. There can be no scientific value in a supposedly systematic comparison in

---

[26] On the other hand, argument by analogy, which is a weaker form of comparison, can, sometimes, be useful. Here it is necessary to have at least two cases both equally well-known to parties to the argument. In such a case contrasting one case against another is used as a device to illuminate points in the process of argumentation, seeking to convince one's opponent of the relative worth of one view as opposed to another. It is recognised that argument by analogy can, at best, illuminate understanding, but cannot lead to discovery, or to new understanding. But then, analogy is only a process of argumentation, not of scientific analysis. There are no critiques of the comparative method that one wishes to recommend or refer to. However, G.E.R.Lloyd's *Polarity and Analogy. Two types of argumentation in early Greek thought*, Cambridge University Press, 1971, is an excellent study, even though its focus is historical rather than conceptual.

the human and social sciences. In view of this, it is not only intellectually abhorrent but also misleading to claim that 'we compare because we wish to explain.'[27] Knowing that methodological comparison is no more than a façade, as academics, we should face and proclaim the fact, and desist from an 'eristical' use of it.

Moreover, arguments about the necessary conditions of an 'account' are, readily, translated into a bemused reaction to a call for 'theoretically-informed accounts of [the] post-war'. Though facile, it must be said that such a call betrays a belief – for it cannot be an understanding – in the possibility that there may be 'theoretically-*un*informed' accounts. It is not possible – for its construction is an analytical impossibility – to have an account of 'pure' facts. On the contrary, any historical account – indeed any account written in any ordinary language – is, in virtue of the fact, theoretically-informed. The supposed criticism that an account may be theoretically uninformed is no more than a Quixotic engaging with windmills: the real engagement – whether the analyst knows it or not – is with the theory underpinning the account, not with the supposed absence of it.[28] To be sure, displacing existing theories is central to the project that Marsh has elliptically depicted in his three papers. Here a call for 'theoretically-informed' means consistently informed by desired theories: indeed, the view that Jessop's 'substantive and empirical work is not consistently informed by his more abstract theory' was expressed as a damning criticism. (PSA94, p. 812).

It may not be too far fetched to say that a concern with the larger 'comparative', international, at any rate the holistically inclined perspective is characteristically informed and validated by problematical views issuing from the Enlightenment, including the (implicit?) assumption that perfect government is possible. While the poverty of theory informing such a view is simply breathtaking, the orientation of such an approach is to systems, rather than to 'Being', 'life' and 'being there'. On the other hand, when our approach is informed by these latter preoccupations, we soon realise that there is no need for any systematic and self-conscious comparison. This view is informed by the rather fundamental point that even if our experiences turn out to be better than most, or far worse than that of some, the fact is that we do not live in a comparative, or cosmological, time-space continuum, but in a strictly local one, in a hard here and now sense: and this view recognises that 'while the grass grows, the horse may starve'! The global dimension is all very well, but the local is more immediately urgent.

Exceptionalism

Some might understand that Rudyard Kipling in saying:

> 'And what should they know of England who only England know.'[29]

---

[27] Block 5, Units 15/16; *Theory and methodology in Comparative Politics*, The Open University, 1979, p.8. Italic in the original.

[28] One has a lingering memory of extended hilarity which met the call for 'theoretically-informed accounts' during the discussion of Marsh's unpublished paper at the Institute of Contemporary British History conference in July 1995.

[29] 'The English Flag', 1891.

meant that we should examine 'England' within a wider perspective. Of course, Kipling, so to say, looked beyond 'Dover Beach', not to Europe, but out to the Empire, in order to proclaim the importance of England to the Empire, and of the Empire to England. For contemporary 'comparatists', 'Dover Beach' is a problem of a different sort. Marsh approvingly quotes a 'kindred' soul, Richard Rose, in criticism of claims to British 'uniqueness through false particularisation', and in defence of the notion that we suffer from the absence of a comparative perspective. But here 'comparative' can only be understood in a looser, non-methodological sense. And when used in this sense, it is analogous to the idea that if the philosophical underpinnings of the British system stop on 'Dover Beach', we may simply lack the wider 'universal' foundation against which to judge the British way. This is, of course, an expression of the fear that stopping at 'Dover Beach' will mean the possibility of an insular relativism,[30] albeit on a national, so to speak, 'Ukanian' State, basis. For Marsh, this means the necessity to discover whether the British experience of the 1980s was the expression of a phenomenon unique to Britain, or was it part of a wider world-spatial perspective. Moreover, and irrespective of whether it is part of wider world experience, for some the question 'to what extent was it exceptional in British history' – the 'Home-Time' dimension – also remains valid.

'World-spatial' Dimension

Comparative statements are of a 'more' or 'less' type. And examining Britain in 1980s within a wider context – subject to everything that has been said about the possibility of comparison, and the limitations thereof – might yield one of, say, three answers:

- Yes, the British experience was unique;
- No, it was not; or, more likely,
- while it was not unique, it exhibited peculiarly British characteristics.

Of course, it is not methodological comparison that establishes the outcome, but a 'judgement' between two or more known cases. And this is a judgement concerned with similarity and difference.

Exception is a rather special case of difference. It depicts uniqueness and exclusion, and, thereby, implies a qualitative deviation. This requires more than a judgement of a more or less type, and is logically predicated on having a *norm*, about which questions arise. What privileges this norm? Is the *exception* a deviation to the better or the worse? Moreover, an exception in respect of what? Answers to these questions are not obvious, nor are they unproblematically in the literature.

That much said, why should we bother with the 'World' dimension at all? What are the likely outcomes of such a study?

While conceptually, and on a cosmic scale, we may appear to live in a time and space continuum, as a matter of fact, we must and can only live

---

[30]See Raymond Plant, *Modern Political Thought*, Blackwell, 1991, pp.321-323.

locally in both time and space. Relativising the conditions also relativises the outcome: to suggest that the British experience of the 1980s is part of a larger phenomenon pleases politicians who wish to suggest that the outcome in our local time and space has not been of their making. Of course we cannot isolate Britain, and its geographical island character is no longer the all important argument it once was thought to be. Equally true, the so-called process of Globalisation has been destructive of the nature and the fact of constituted sovereign power. We may be in some sort of transition and, for that reason, the shape of the world is not clear. But, in the meantime, the outside world cannot be the explanation of every British failure and success. This is not to say that we can, or should, ignore all that lies beyond 'Dover Beach', but rather to suggest that we must, in the first instance, address conditions, successes and failures understood within our local time and space, and take into account relevant extraneous circumstances. This locates the focus of interest of political science of British Government clearly and resolutely within the confines of this political unit: single government study becomes the focus of analysis;[31] the larger – which for some inevitably means the 'comparative', and also the inter-state and the international – perspective is relevant, but once removed. As Jim Bulpitt argues, foreign policy, too, is a domestic politics issue.[32]

So, 'exceptional' or not, one must ask whether it is/was good for this people, or not? And our judgement ought not to be on the basis of what others may or may not have done, but on that of ideas about the good and the bad – essentially theoretical criteria – against which to evaluate our political system. Spurious, specious even, 'comparisons' are not necessary in the making of that kind of evaluation. Of course, this kind of understanding runs contrary to the hubris-ridden world view of those who hide their failure to love their fellows here and now by pretending to love humanity in the abstract.

For some this may be a dangerous relativising of the world of ideas on a national 'Ukanian' state level. It is not. It suggests that in the absence of truly universal concepts, and in order to determine a practical course of action we are, in duty, bound to examine our own conceptions, while not forgetting the wider world out there, nor the fact that aspects of the contemporary concern with that wider world, for example, human rights, have actually issued from 'local' European views. While supremely important, such ideas are not universal realities, and even the least abstract are not homeless concepts floating in the extra-linguistic hyperreality of 'forms'. That is to say, the point is not to privilege our own, but, given that all Universals are cultural products, and that we cannot live ideas, we must develop a 'national' self-consciousness about the way we organise ourselves,

---

[31] Even S.E.Finer cannot avoid but must accept that comparison 'is in a sense, *parasitic*' on the work of the specialist. 'The Vocabulary of Political Science', *Political Studies*, 23/2-3, p.245.

[32] Jim Bulpitt, 'The Ever Present Outsider: *Primat Der Innenpolitik* and the International Relations *Fraktion*', paper presented at the BISA Annual Conference, University of Southampton, 1995, published on *PSD*, 1995 [http://www.soton.ac.uk/ psd/].

and the manner in which we ought to behave towards others.[33] But this can only be done successfully – that is, avoid relativising on a self-inclusive basis – if and when our thinking is deeply informed by 'Being', 'life' and 'being there', moderated only by a necessary self-consciousness that even these notions thus characterised are not true universals.

On the other hand, showing that the British experience was not an exception pleases academics who wish to explain the period in terms of the more holistic world capitalism and related theories. Rejecting the world-spatial exceptionalism is, therefore, absolutely central to the project of re-defining the problem so as to make it amenable to the type of explanation that Marsh prefers.

'Home-Time' dimension

In view of all that has been said against the meaningfulness of the methodological comparison, it needs but little argument to show that, because a meaningful examination of the continuous present is always against some understanding and account of its – distant or immediate – past, then all understanding of the present, which is always a judgement (determining its character, identifying its policy achievements and failures, *et cetera*), will be in relation to an understanding of its becoming. We do it any way, and we cannot do any other. There is no understanding in a vacuum of time: where there is little or insubstantial historical background, there can only be facile familiarity.

In an important sense, therefore, whether the 1980s was, as an 'episode', 'exceptional' or not is an implicit part of our individual understanding of that period. It is, therefore, not clear what is hoped to be achieved when we are invited to engage in a systematic comparison over time. But let us suppose that we should.

Given that we must be clear about the category 'exceptional' and what it may stand for, we can expect one of two answers, for, all said and done, an 'episode' under examination may fall

- within the latitude of difference tolerated by the structure of power; or
- outside this latitude.

But here we run into something of a quandary. If the supposed 'exception' should fall within the range of tolerance of the system, then it can be no problem. In other words, that there is no *normal* in British politics, but only a notion of *bounded normality*, defined by the continued functionality of the structure of power. Put differently, in all cases, whatever falls within the range of tolerance of the structure of power is by definition un-exceptional, and, in virtue of the fact, normal politics.[34] Therefore, an act or episode

---

[33] In some areas of concern, such as in feminism or race studies, the idea of the 'other' is a serious problem, leading to 'exclusionary politics', division, *et cetera*. These ideas are seen to be problematical, and associated with 'modernity'. Alas, critics have no practical alternatives to offer. While conceptually not having an exclusionary 'other' is very attractive, in practice, division and difference are political issues to be solved.

[34] See D.Kavanagh & P.Morris, *Consensus Politics from Attlee to Thatcher*, ICBH, Blackwell, 1989, pp.2-3.

is only exceptional if, and to the degree to which, it results in a change in the structure of power. This shifts the focus of our attention to the true nature of the structure of power; it becomes imperative that we know it. Furthermore, it becomes immediately important for us to determine ways in which reform and change are distinguished.

The upshot is simply this: exceptionalism presages serious conceptual problems with the idea of normal politics. This does not mean that we cannot judge a given episode, but that we cannot do so meaningfully in terms of exception and exceptionalism. On the other hand, each government will be different in style, the policy objectives its members privilege and favour, and also the electoral and extraneous circumstances in which it finds itself and within which it must function. We are faced with a multiplicity of variables interfering with the categories of the 'normal' and the 'exceptional', and judgements in the light of these notions are fraught with endless complications. That said, there is, of course, nothing to occlude a political view of a given episode, only that it cannot be a political science judgement.

It is clear that Marsh must reject (British, presumably all) exceptionalism, for the altogether obvious reason that an exception cannot be explained in terms of a holistic all-in-one theory, containing the three desired factors in an undifferentiated (no 'subject imperialism'!), yet fully theorised conception. It is possible to arrive at the view that the 1980s was an exception on the Home-Time dimension, while not so on the world-space dimension. But this will mean that other periods in British history cannot be explained by the kind of grand theory that explains everything on a global scale. It is imperative for Marsh's project that the 1980s should not be an exception at all.[35]

3 a

One argument has been that not every wished-for account is an explanation in political science for the rather simple but important reason that the nature of our subject and the manner in which we can justify an account as an explanation imposes limitations and creates exclusions. This is a limitation of and in political science, not in politics. And to the extent that political science is concerned with re-constituted, not practical, politics this distinction is reflected in the difference between 'the structure of a sentence in politics' and 'the conceptual structure of a meaningfuless sentence in politics'. In the world of practice many words are used in everyday talk in politics – for example, the mandate, sovereignty, parliamentary democracy, *et cetera* – which to us are complicated and intensely interesting, though also immensely problematical concepts. And, whereas the politician ought not to be taken to task for talking in these terms, nor the commentator for describing events with reference to such 'concepts', we ought to use these words with extreme care. The undeniable fact that these 'concepts' *qua* maxims are in everyday use is less important than their meaning and their

---

[35] On the other hand, Andrew Gamble has no problem with identifying the Thatcher period as new, different, and exceptional. *The Free Economy and the Strong State*, 1988, especially chapter 1.

actual import: it is no good seeking to explain in terms of the so-called theory of the mandate if that theory is vacuous, though we must recognise that in the world of politics, appeal is daily made to it.[36] This creates interesting difficulties for us: for instance, because 'democracy' is an impossibility in theory, what stands for 'a democratic regime' out there is, simply, a certain kind of relations of power, for which the appellation 'democracy' is a legitimating integument.[37] Now politicians and commentators may have no difficulty in using this word, and even believe what they might think it means, but we cannot. We must examine and declare its meaning, but still go into the polling station next time round and cast our vote.

A further argument has been that challenging an explanation, as a matter of fact, challenges and re-defines the 'what is' of the explanation. But this is not a simple game of words. Command of the language of political science is central to this notion; as a string of words, we can say almost anything, just as Parliament in the United Kingdom is supposedly in a position to legislate what it will in the manner it wishes: but in both cases, the outcome will be only a string of words, unless we can also show the conceptual meaningfulness of the claim, or the relevance of the legislation and the effectiveness of its enforcement. Thus, seeking to predetermine the requirements of an explanation, whatever the impetus for so doing, can produce nothing more than a string of words. This is, plainly, the wrong way of going about the business. Put differently, political science must start with, and sharply focus on the subject in hand, which, *mutatis mutandis*, takes it in the direction of single government studies, seeking to explain the necessary 'what is' of the manner in which a people is governed from within the perspective of that manner of life, while self-consciously bringing to bear upon it theoretical arguments relevant to it. And since such a 'what is' is always a historical argument, it follows that our starting point cannot be some ideological or theoretical desideratum, but that the conceptions and the theoretical arguments we shall need are, firstly, in the totality of what distinguishes that people, and only then, secondly, in extraneous circumstances.[38]

---

[36] The nauseating frequency of references to a 'five year mandate' for this government in the wake of two recent 'defections' from the Conservative party is a case in point.

[37] This is a point I shall discuss at length in a separate study. While other commentators have not gone this far, there is a growing recognition that representative democracy is not all that it may seem. To accept that representative democracy is not about power, nor is it about demos as 'actor', but demos as voter, job-holder *et cetera* is a good starting point. See Sheldon Wolin in *PS: 'Political Science and Politics'*, 26/3, September 1993, especially p.475. On the other hand, to proceed as though the concepts under analysis – such as accountability, effectiveness, also citizenship – are in fact possible and that we need to reform our system accordingly, as does Dawn Oliver, *Government in the United Kingdom. The Search for Accountability, Effectiveness and Citizenship*, The Open University Press, 1991, produces, in the least, a disappointing textbook. But it is also misleading: and we ought to ask questions about the social responsibility of social scientists.

[38] Clearly this is an 'ordinarily speaking' kind of statement. Focusing on the extraneous circumstances raises the issue of appropriate response to it. For instance, Andrew Gamble's argument is informed by the thought that the issues to which Thatcherism was a British response were indeed international, and, therefore, extraneous. But, it is not clear that a response to a global problem can be a national one. It may be thought that Gamble is only concerned to show how the response is to re-adjust and re-structure the domestic setting so as to enable the consequences of the extraneous global problem to be

This leads us to make explicit another, so far implicit, line of argument. An explanation can only be judged when it is complete. And a significant principle of judgement has to do with the question 'does the *explanans* deal with the issues and the problems'. But this, naturally, depends upon the manner in which the *explanandum*, our account of 'what is', has been identified. And not being in a position to pre-determine the contents of the *explanans*, we must accept two points: positively, that in any given case the emphasis must be on what is required, and, negatively, that it is intellectually abhorrent *prima facie* to exclude any one concept or type of account. This is, of course, another way of rejecting the claim that an *explanans* must be of a certain type, say, multi-dimensional – whatever that may mean. But labels are irrelevant: an explanation either satisfies, or fails to do so. What is important in either case is the reasons for our judgement.

It is clearly infantile to argue the relevance of an explanation in advance of it. That said, however, it is imperative to know the minimum requirement of an explanation before we can recognise it as a political science account. It was argued earlier that, in a broad sense, our initial criterion of recognition is in terms of the requirements of science in political science; we must now add to that criterion of recognition by shifting the emphasis to the politics in political science.

3 b

For long the political science of British politics has been made to concentrate upon policy. Clearly policy is important in politics, but, it is debatable whether an exclusive, even a major, concentration upon it is justified without prior and connected focus upon other, indeed primary, aspects. Following, broadly, the sense of the argument associated with Keith Middlemas that we should seek to identify an essential 'bias' which remains, at least relatively, invariant, Bulpitt focuses on 'party Statecraft', and shows that, no matter how the issue is initially understood, a limited number of requirements remain constant. I have followed a similar kind of approach in my study of the Imperialism in which I focus not upon policy of Empire or Imperialist policy, but upon an essential meaning and implication which remains constant no matter who pursues the policy, and where. This enabled my analysis to be extended to so-called 'Communist' countries which were, supposedly, and for some by definition, incapable of such policies. However, in the case in point, it is not clear that a focus on 'party Statecraft', vitally important though it is, will suffice. This is not a criticism of Jim Bulpitt's conception,[39] about which he is characteristically, though unnecessarily, modest. It is rather to say that explanations which account for

---

managed on a national basis. But I have not seen that argument articulated anywhere.

[39] Three publications are relevant: *Territory and Power in the United Kingdom*, Manchester University Press, 1983; 'Continuity, Autonomy and Peripheralisation: the Autonomy of the Centre's Race Statecraft in Britain', *Government and Policy*, 2, 1985; 'The Discipline of New Democracy: Mrs.Thatcher's Domestic Statecraft', *Political Studies*, 34/1. And to the extent that it modifies his 'Statecraft' idea, to this list must be added his 'Historical Politics: Leaders, Statecraft and Regime in Britain at the accession of Elizabeth II' in *PSD*, 1996, and in the present volume.

parts of the system are in need of a broader, more important constant without which their meaning and relevance will not be recognised. Jim Bulpitt recognises the supreme importance of the electoral cycle, and accepts that the essential desideratum of 'party Statecraft' is to ensure relative autonomy in 'high politics' for the centre,[40] which, from the perspective of any party, can only mean the desideratum of one party majority government. Equally importantly he always speaks of 'Conservative', not just 'party'. In other words, the temporally restricted relevance of 'party Statecraft' is also spatially confined. This means that we must develop another explanatory tool for Labour party in this respect. More than that, it is also silent on the nature and the powers of the office which is the highest prize for both parties, and, in a serious sense, also the *sine qua non* of their existence and activity. In all cases, the more general picture is missing. Nor is this rectified by the fruits of Historical Politics.

For this reason, amongst others, I focus not on winning access to the centre, but upon the nature of the real prize, which is exclusive access to the power only available at the centre. More than that, this approach also argues that the achievement of relative autonomy, which Jim Bulpitt suggests is the desired outcome of 'party Statecraft', is, in fact, a contingently possible feature of power at the centre. In other words, I accept the relevance of Conservative 'party Statecraft' and Historical Politics, but find it difficult to accept that we can leave the nature of the prize out of the picture. It may well be that a focus on the nature of the prize will entail a revision and modification of other approaches, but, in all cases, to understand any aspect of British politics we must understand the nature of power at the centre, and with it the idea of defence of the centre.[41] More than that, to explain policy we need to know and accept institutions – broadly, structures – not as limitation or constraint, but as the framework within which power necessary to initiate change and create policy is 'defined' and located.[42] Besides, without such power, exclusive access to which is the electoral object of party activity, Bulpitt's governing competence objective can have no chance of being achieved. Put differently, if power to pursue the effective implementation of policy is not there, and if Bulpitt's important 'political argument hegemony' and Andrew Gamble's closely related 'hegemony' has not been achieved, the study of political behaviour or policy will be cut loose from any proper political science moorings.

---

[40] The further additions and elucidation that Jim Bulpitt introduces into the idea of 'Statecraft' ('Historical Politics: Leaders, Statecraft and Regime in Britain at the accession of Elizabeth II' in *PSD*, 1996, and in the present volume) more sharply define its ambit. They shift the emphasis to 'style of behaviour', and identifies it as the 'politics of governing'. Moreover, 'Regime' is said to be 'Statecraft' – hence political behaviour – not structure, driven. Along with this, he also seeks to attach greater importance to structure than heretofore. In this sense, the gap between our two perspectives is being reduced. However, he tends to identify 'structure' with 'structuralist' and suggests that it cannot explain behaviour. But structure of power is not a 'structuralist' argument, and the continuity of the regime cannot escape the essential relevance of the continuing structure of power as its elemental constant.

[41] See my *The UK and 'Union': the problem of explanation*, Strathclyde Papers in Government and Politics, 99, September 1994.

[42] This is not to be confused with 'state machinery' and arguments about institutional failure.

The central concern in explaining British government and politics cannot be policies or behaviour, nor can it be the ideas and ideology of those now in power, but must be the powers they seek to get their hands on without which all their policy ideas will not be worth a hoot. The tragedy of the Liberal Democrats is, as it has been for so long, that their hope of power is not even a pipe dream: it matters but a hoot that they may, or may not, have wonderful policy and constitutional reform ideas, for they can dream on while the two major parties in real competition for real power play their own games.

The approach outlined here requires a sharp focus on the relations of power, not only relational, hegemonic, economic, *et cetera*, but especially constitutional and institutional. And though it is now *passé* to proclaim the renewed relevance of the constitution, constitutionalism and with it essential relations of power, their over-riding importance never diminished but was overlooked.

The argument has been that an essential problem of the political science of British Government is that the 'what is' accounts of it are misleading and in need of re-definition. We need a general theory of British Government, which can act as the larger organising framework imparting relevance and significance to explanations of the various parts, be it the behaviour of political parties, economic or industrial policy, *et cetera*. The existing general theoretical accounts are inadquate.

For this reason, even the better attempts seeking to deal with the question of the nature of power at the centre actually miss the point. In part, this is because they begin in a historical vein, and appeal to the likes of Bagehot and Dicey, treating their offering as important concepts which both inform and explain the system. The failure of such attempts is fore-ordained by the refusal to treat Bagehot and Dicey as problems to understand. We have no account of their role in determining the kind of explanation of the system that we seem always to get. We have been insufficiently critical of the relevance and meaning of their theories. I say this with full cognisance of the fact that the experience of the 1970s provoked both theories of 'overload', 'ungovernability', and 'elective dictatorship', while the manner in which power was used in the 1980s invited attempts at the synthesis and periodisation, exceptionalism, concern with 'British presidency' and with the powers of the Prime Minister. Academic lawyers became concerned with the problem of rule of law and the role and place of the Judiciary. Some even attempted to re-evaluate the relevance of Dicey to the problem of rule of law.[43] But conspicuous by its absence has been any attempt critically to re-examine the theory of British constitution by political scientist, while current accounts of it have stayed close to the problematic account so dominated by the legacy of Dicey. Incidentally, this is a larger issue that may at first appear in that the lawyer's understanding of the British constitution has dominated the views of successive governments and Members of Parliament. Thus, even though the Monarchy has been in the news for too long and has been examined from almost every lurid angle possible, we have not had any analysis of

---

[43] I.Harden & N.Lewis, *The Noble Lie. The British constitution and the rule of law*, Hutchinson, 1986.

the role and the place of that hugely important institution in the creation and the continued legitimation of power at the centre. All references to the Monarchy in the more serious literature, and, in part, in the debate about the future of that institution, have tended to see its irrelevance to practical politics and emphasise its social importance, but not its central relevance to British constitutional theory. The only full-scale study of the Monarchy in the recent decades has proved to be a disappointment. I refer to Vernon Bogdanor's *The Monarchy and the Constitution*. It is a history of what Bogdanor with evident relish calls 'constitutional monarchy', which in effect means he does not have to look beyond the facile features of 'reigning but not ruling'.[44] It focuses on the so-called 'declining powers' of the Monarch, and is a rather general history of the incremental change in the balance between the Monarch *qua* ruler and the institutional constraints that have gradually circumscribed the remaining 'political' powers that the Monarch may exercise.

Meanwhile, since the end of 1950s and especially in the 1980s we have had an on-going 'debate' about the powers of the Prime Minister. And while every textbook has something to say about the powers of the Prime Minister, they often miss the point and list the functions of the office, and what given incumbents have or have not done. A recent and interesting example is that of Peter Hennessy, who contrasts an up-dated list of Attlee's functions (based on primary sources) as Prime Minister with an imagined one for John Major. But he, too, lists functions, not powers, and seeks to explain the increments in terms of the metaphor of a stately home acquiring additions and alterations with each succeeding generation.[45] But, alas, none of the additional functions, save the matter of security services, has any legislative basis: how have the additions been made? This question does not admit of an adequate historical answer, and can only be examined in terms of British constitutional theory.

Now, there is always human agency in any and all political situations. But in all cases, especially in political systems marked by specified rules, there is also a heavy constraint of structure, in the form of a constitution or fundamental laws, or of institutions: even a military dictator needs the armed forces! Of course, over here, we are lucky not to be held back by such constraints. This evident absence has enabled some to concentrate on agency, to the exclusion, more or less, of all else. And the culmination of this view appears in the quintessential truism of British Government which – in the now infamous words of Sir William Harcourt, quoted by, and famously associated with the name of, Earl of Asquith and Oxford – states that the office is what the holder chooses and is able to make of it. But, as with all truisms, this, too, is devoid of essential meaning, and

---

[44] Oxford, 1995. The account is not any better in Peter Hennessy's *The Hidden Wiring. Unearthing the British Constitution*, Victor Gollancz, 1995. On the other hand, Tom Nairn's *The Enchanted Glass, Britain and its Monarchy*, Radius, 1988, though a difficult and annoying book to read, touches aspects of the issue but it is not a sustained academic analysis, its focus is not constitutional issues and powers, and, in the event, leaves a great deal to be desired.

[45] Peter Hennessy, *The Hidden Wiring. Unearthing the British Constitution*, Victor Gollancz, 1995, pp.86-90, 83.

is, in that sense, profoundly elliptical. Agency is relevant only in relation to the framework of some structure, normally a conjunction of institutions, whereby it is invested with meaning. Like freedom, its meaning is dependent upon a set of constraints. Put differently, only one appointed into the office may act in the name of the office, and it is only then that the idea of agency can be invoked. Without the vestment of the powers of the office, agency has no relevance whatever. Given this, calls for a consciousness of structures is refreshing, but also bemusing. What is it that they wish to incorporate into the analysis? The strcuture of power in the United Kingdom or the constraints of the global economy? They do not say. Yet, without a doubt, examining the exceptionalism or otherwise of the 1980s, it is clearly important to examine the office which enables, not just the office holder who acts. If there is a meaningful issue of exceptionalism one must have at least one constant in common between the different variables in all the historical periods under examination else the extent to which agency has played a decisive role cannot be determined. And that constant is that which has continued: the main offices of the state, in short the structure of power, but crucially that of the office of the Prime Minister.

On this view, we have a huge gaping hole in our understanding of British Government for the rather simple reason that we have allowed the 'what is' and, therefrom, the agenda of what is to be examined, to be defined historically, and have, inexplicably, avoided facing the necessity of examining the concepts that are employed for the purpose. Associated with this claim is the contention that without a clear understanding of the basic principles informing the system, attempts at explanation of its parts, or its policy outputs, *et cetera*, will remain tentative, not only in the inevitable sense of being subject to further empirical evidence, but, more significantly, in theoretical terms.

Incidentally, the problem is not a dearth of historical studies; perhaps, in an odd sense, we already have too much of it. Be that how it may, our problem is, in part, that we have not taken a political science view of the matter. History for its own sake is well understood by historians, even if it is not transparent to others. Historical politics for its own sake, too, is important. But in the absence of a clear and definite starting point – such as a defined constitutional basis – we must begin with history, but, now, from a political science perspective. And this we must do becuase the constitutional principles of the United Kingdom system are historically determined. But even a brief examination of this notion reveals its problematical nature. It is here that the concept of meta-analysis comes into its own. It is a process of interrogating the longest possible span of history – not just historical episodes or specific periods – in the light of a limited number of questions we have conceptually formulated. Importantly, this is not history from the perspective of the present, for the questions are not about the present. But as these questions are about the character and the underlying concepts of the system, they are timeless. And it is this timelessness that makes a few concepts the constant which has tended to survive almost irrespective of the reforms and changes in the working arrangements which have given it a different appearance in different periods. Though self-evident it bears pointing out that such a process will not provide a final definitive account. There are no final and defintive accounts for political regimes. And this is so irrespective of whether the system is based upon a codified constitution or not: constitutions do not end the arguments about the meaning of the regime, they provide a firm starting point.

The British system of Government is characterised by an obvious sense of continuity. Often it is thought that because of the many, on the face of it, revolutionary changes that have taken place since the seventeenth century, that continuity has really been only in form: this is the 'new wine and old bottle idea' in which the appearance continues, but the substance has changed and can be changed again when it suits. My contention is that this is not so; that which has continued is not the empty form, but the actual substance. And this reality has been buttressed by a series of insubstantial changes, affecting the manner of action. Furthermore, I would argue that this constant is the whole of the executive powers of the Crown – never defined or delimited – which has simply been re-located in the office of the Prime Minister. The façade of the working system, with its conceptual and historical paraphernalia, including the role and the place of the Monarch in the system, hides the essential truth of the system. And while our attention was focused on evidently important shorter term reforms and changes, specifically in the so-called process of democratisation, the system simply reverted back to historical type, albeit with a difference.

To put it more boldly, the potential of the Revolution Settlement has been undermined in, what I have called, the 'Second Revolution', itself a counter-revolution, which began more or less in the middle of the eighteenth century, and came into its own in the latter part of the nineteenth century. This process of change was marked by a brief interregnum, famously, 'The Golden Age of Parliament'. Even though it is only now that we are beginning to see the nature and the importance of this revolution, its effects were conceptually available and, in part, understood by a few even at the time, except that the two most prominent myth-makers of late nineteenth century – Bagehot and Dicey – never saw it. But, importantly, their myth-making served the purposes of that counter-revolution, and thereby of the system: the myth enabled the true nature of the system to be obfuscated. There is poetic justice in the fact that Bagehot, who was so clear about the 'efficient' and the 'dignified', and Dicey who ingeniously distinguished between the legal and the political and so elegantly accounted for 'Sovereignty of Parliament' – thinking all the while that they were describing the system as it actually worked – should, together, have created a most elaborate and powerful integument which has served so well and for so long to hide the efficient secret of the structure of power in this country. But then, that integument has also been a most important feature of, and a key to, the evident stability of the system: by hiding it, the myth has served to keep intact the basic structure of power, thereby allowing and enabling certain types of reform and change in the working system. And to the extent that this relationship holds, nothing done is exceptional, albeit that each period and episode is, necessarily, different – not just in policy but also shifts in 'apparently' important organising principles, say, from 'having a stake in the land' to being a member of 'a stakeholder society'. This overall continuity makes pragmatism – not 'muddling through' – the relevant description: *qua* 'dealing with practice' it hides the reality that an evidently important change is, in fact, far more apparent than it is real. On this account, a concern with the relative decline of power of Parliament to control the executive is simply a waste of time. On the other hand, the European Union is the first really serious threat to the substance of British power. But that is a different story.

Politics and Health

Maggie Mort
University of Leeds
Stephen Harrison
University of Leeds
&
Gerald Wistow
University of Leeds

'The User Card: Picking through the Organisational Undergrowth in Health and Social Care'

Introduction

The restructuring of public services which has been taking place over the last fifteen years has been accompanied by much language about consulting users and empowering the consumer. Those who have their dustbins emptied, those who travel on trains, those who receive health care have been constructed as consumers, and as such, allocated an homogenised identity. This identification of patient, passenger and resident as consumer has formed an underlying rationale for sweeping structural and ideological change in the welfare state and local government.

In particular, the NHS 'reforms', such as the construction of the purchaser/provider split and new configurations of social care provision brought about by the NHS and Community Care Act, have been accompanied by Government exhortations to management to consult with users of services. One feature of this can be seen to be about legitimation of the management of services following the removal from health authorities of local authority (elected) representatives. In such an analysis the user voice would be sought in order to minimise a perceived 'democratic deficit'. However, this official sanctioning of the user voice, it should be said, has little to do with the autonomous growth in the user movement itself, where increased confidence and militancy has sprung more from a history of being marginalised than being included.

Drawing on interview material, this paper attempts to describe the organisational complexity now encountered in health and social care, and to indicate some of the pathways which certain actors are creating through that complexity. The context in which the empirical material in this paper has been gathered was part of the ESRC programme on Changing Local Governance (award No L311 25 3025). Our team has focused on the growth of user influence in health and social care services, principally the formation and activities of organised user groups. The term 'user' was chosen, rather reluctantly, as the least ideologically loaded term, over the possible 'patient', 'client', 'customer' etc, but it too has its problems.[1] Our overall

---

[1] It has been pointed out that 'user' implies volition, that welfare services are taken up by individuals wishing to use them, and that this omits a sense of extended user, ie relatives or user groups. J.Clarke, 'Capturing the Consumer: consumerism and social welfare', paper given at ESRC seminar, *Conceptualising Consumption Issues*, University

aim has been to discover how six locally based user groups, three active in mental health and three in physical disability, have sought to influence the shape and content of local services and how this fits in with the groups' wider campaigns about access, self determination and civil rights. Part of the research team has worked with the user groups, while others sought the responses of local 'officials', (our term for those who provide, purchase or manage a multiplicity of services). During the course of this research, one important 'finding' has emerged about the way in which both user groups and managers now have to orientate and re-orientate around constant organisational change. It seems that there is so much change that this may be strongly influencing, even partly constructing, the nature of user and user group involvement taking place within a locality. The focus in this paper will be on certain strategies adopted by 'officials' both towards users and between agencies, where there is a climate of organisational change.

Fragmentation and Uncertainty

Since the early 1990s, the United Kingdom systems of health care and social services have undergone large scale changes. To illustrate this point from our research, the extract below is given in full. It is an unbroken answer to the question, 'Can you describe your job?', from a health authority manager whose official title was Corporate Planner (Community Care):

> 'When I came we were the *Health Project* working on behalf of *five health authorities* that were about to merge. So I came in May 1992. In April 1992, all five health authorities, *former health authorities*, had split into *whole-district Trusts*. So that *providers* had a start on the *purchaser* side and it was expected that we would become an authority in May 1992, but that coincided with the General Election. Out of all that it took until December 1992 for it to become *one health authority* so we were a year behind provider structures in terms of trying to negotiate contracts and things like that. So a lot of the *contracting* had been done one authority to one whole district Trust, which meant that a lot of the contingencies had disappeared into the Trust side rather than into the purchaser side, so there was quite a lot of struggling to retrieve the financial position. And still going on trying to balance up things across XXXshire, or balance down unfortunately in some cases, by trying to get equity out of five quite different health authorities. So that is part of the re-structuring.
>
> Since then the first *chief executive* moved on and we got a second one who was appointed *jointly as chief executive of the health authority and the FHSA* and since then there has been a lot of effort to merge in all but legal reality. So we've got the *joint finance director*, the *joint planning department*, the *public health* serving both sides, so that's been quite a strand of re-organisation. And we've had planning in public health and then

---

of Lancaster, 1994.

planning taken out of public health which it now is. So it is now *corporate planning* which is trying to pull things together across the business side as well as relate to *other agencies*. We've had contracting in with finance but now contracting is separated out, and a new director of what is now called *performance management*. And he has been grappling with how to get a structure which reflects current needs but also future requirements in this, what we were saying before about the *primary care-led NHS*, and how much purchasing will we be doing compared with what will *fundholders* be doing and how do you, what does the *accountability framework* mean. Will we be able to say to fundholders "you will do this". Which would be very nice because we'd dearly like you to do this, or well, you do your own thing anyway – and so the balance has to be ... There would also have to be close working with all of that but we don't know what the structures and what the power of that will be.

So I came as *assistant director of planning for community care* and there was another *assistant director of planning for acute care*, and there was the rough idea that I would relate to the eastern half, ** and ** and ** in geographical terms, but do the community care guidance across the whole of XXXshire, but would geographically relate to the eastern half, to ** and **. In practice there was too much of a community care agenda with the *community care reforms and Act* working through, so we've never really cracked the bit about how the *community care guidelines* got fed through to the *acute person* in ** or ** or vice versa and it's ended up with me doing community care more or less across the whole of XXXshire.'

This extract is given in full in order to draw out the convoluted nature and sense of 'permanence' of the organisational change which has been occurring. This quote relates primarily to the NHS, yet within this particular location, the principal city was also in the process of becoming a unitary authority, and this was giving rise to a further wave of highly complex changes later referred to by this interviewee.

From the above extract it is possible to identify a large number of newly constructed actors/entities which are helping to realise and shape this changing landscape.[2] Some are largely organisational entities such as 'fundholders', others are operational entities such as 'corporate planning', then there are policy goals such as 'primary care-led NHS'. Admittedly some of this identification is rather arbitrary – we have picked out 'accountability framework' yet did not highlight 'equity'. But the intention is merely to convey a sense of the sheer number of actors, agencies or concepts with which the user, the patient, the employee, (or the researcher), has to grapple. Interestingly, the interviewee, though he carefully describes mutation, and is skilled in his grasp of how new structures are emerging, yet refers to an element of muddling through at the end of the extract.

---

[2] These have been picked out in italics.

Within such an overarching context of change, questions about user involvement are sometimes, as in this case, answered by officials futuristically, ie what we *intend* to be doing when we've got the new structures in place. Organisational change becomes seen as unending, a sort of 'permanent revolution', one promoted from within the Establishment. Uncertainty becomes part of the working landscape in which chaos should be embraced.[3] But in effect, this often leads to a heightened sense of workplace insecurity and uncertainty; in the construction of a unitary authority for instance, few jobs are 'ring fenced' and officials are often not able to reassure users that services will continue:

> 'I wrote him (a deaf resident) a letter telling him in as clear and simple way as I could what the local government review meant, that it meant that at the moment services are split and now they are going to be put together and we are going to be responsible for a wider area. And I just left it like that. And I had a minicom call with him and he said, "what will happen about deaf social workers?" you see, and I said, "well I don't know, well I'm sure there will be a deaf social worker". And I put the 'phone down and I thought, well actually I don't know. I actually don't know. That sort of anxiety ...'

We asked officials about the possible effect of legislative/organisational change upon the opportunities for involving users. Some believed that although they personally were being traumatised by change, users wouldn't notice much difference in the delivery of services, in fact some believed it was their duty to make the changes invisible to users (contrary to the meta-rationale of the changes mentioned above). Others believed that users were feeling confused and alienated, particularly by lack of continuity where people in post were frequently being transferred or made redundant. Another response to our question raised the possibility that user *groups* might be able to take advantage of the fluid situation and become more skilled at lobbying for their own needs, perhaps benefiting from organisational uncertainty.

Confused or Empowered?

So, does organisational turbulence help or hinder user influence in health and social care? Does chaos, promote or inhibit dialogue? There have been instances during the fieldwork for this research project when localities appeared to be experiencing change as a disabling vortex. On occasion simply finding the hospital or health authority offices has been hugely difficult. If local police on the street, shopkeepers, and even taxidrivers have been confounded when asked for the local Trust or health authority/commission, how are other citizens to gain access? The following is an illustrative episode experienced during the fieldwork:

---

[3] The appropriateness of Tom Peters' philosophy of *Thriving of Chaos* in an NHS context is examined in S.Harrison et al, 'The Wrong Kind of Chaos? The Early Days of an NHS Trust', *Public Money & Management*, January-March 1994.

'In one large town where there had been several waves of NHS closures and reconfigurations, the local community Trust was not featured on the new town map. Stopping and asking people brought only blank looks or wild guesses, so after three circuits of the town centre, I decided to stop next time I passed a building marked 'hospital' or 'health centre', of which there seemed to be many, where I reasoned that reception staff would at least have heard of my destination. Not so. Incredibly, (or is it?), at the health authority headquarters, (itself located temporarily in part of an old long-stay hospital), I could get no directions to or information about the Trust, which later turned out to be situated less than a mile away.'

Part of this ongoing confusion seems to be that Trust names do not usually tell people what is being provided. Since the health service has been fragmented, provider and even purchaser names have become bland and unspecific, as if there is an unwillingness to be too closely associated with actual services, which are themselves seen as transient. However, there are indications that managers and possibly certain user groups are using the present climate of uncertainty, the fragmentation of agencies and multiplicity of actors to their possible advantage.

The User Card

'But very obviously I am, in one's official capacity, one of the cards that you have to play all the time is user need, user preference and user view on something, and whether I am negotiating with other people inside this building, arguing with the provider Trust, negotiating with the Social Services department, arguing about how we ought to spend joint finance, no matter what I'm doing, you do in effect play the user card.'

This notion of 'user card' has often been described by those interviewees who are reflexive about their roles. It is widely recognised that consultation with users can mean almost anything from a chat in the corridor to full scale committee representation or membership of a service management committee, but it is the recent rhetorical legitimation of users as actors which enables them to be 'played' in the sort of strategic game referred to above. If the manager can show or claim to have user support for a position, then that position is strengthened in negotiations with other agencies.

This form of legitimacy has been conferred following vague references to consultation with users in Government policy documents and ministerial speeches.[4] Similarly, patients' and citizens' charters advocate consultation but do not say how this is to be carried out.[5] This vagueness leaves managers free to take what they want from the guidance whilst deriving credibility from 'having the users on board'.

---

[4] For example, *Working For Patients* and *Caring for People*, both HMSO, 1989.
[5] Also, as has often been observed, charters in particular emphasise the role of the individual user, rather than encouraging the collective voice.

We have accordingly found a range of practice, from serious attempts at democratising a service, to the sort of strategic userism described above. Some managers committed to user involvement have described being enabled by the legislative rhetoric to take initiatives, such as including users on staff interview panels, which might otherwise have been considered too radical. Some managers express their frustration at the lack of militancy amongst local user groups, because more activism would help them use the rhetoric to push for better resources. But many admit that user feedback is easily manipulated:

> 'I think as professionals, this is what I feel happens: that we make a decision that is what we want to happen, and then we find the users who want that to happen to support it.'

Perhaps this sort of strategy is nothing new, managers have always had to seek allies and construct supportive networks to carry out their plans.

> 'I do certain things for them to try to help them get funding, you know what I mean, ease their way into networks to get them a place at the table for this, that or the other. They play the same game backing me when they know I need to play the user card ... it is that sort of reciprocal relationship ... but I think there is also some element of dishonesty in it.'

What is perhaps worthy of more research here is whether the number of actors/agencies is affecting the types of alliances being made. While the most visible loci of negotiation include the *purchaser/health commission with the Trust/provider* or between the *NHS and the local authority/social services department*, there are some other interesting arenas where alliances involve the *medical versus the social model of disability/health*:

> 'My perception is that the health services have planned these community services rather than a (residential) centre which is a big step for them and difficult because it goes against what powerful consultants want, medical consultants, and still want, and still lobby for. It also fitted a lot of other people's agendas. I mean I'm a therapist and it has led to more therapy-led services ... '

While this interviewee is describing one effect of NHS and community care legislation, locally the issue she refers to is the case of a powerful county-wide user group which successfully opposed the development of a residential disabled unit which had been proposed by the local health service. This led to the setting up of a large integrated living centre where the independence of adults with disabilities is fostered. User power in this locality was also identified by other manager/official interviewees with the wider struggle between medical and social models of disability and also between general management and clinical management, (who runs the hospital?). This identification was not restricted to our case studies in physical disability. In mental health services, one provider clinician manager (interestingly from a nursing background) described forming alliances with purchaser (health authority) managers in order to promote/legitimate a new user-run patient advocacy project, in the face of opposition from consultant psychiatrists.

Users can also 'oil the wheels' of bureaucracy. By providing radical, independent critiques of the system, they can cut through red tape:

> 'It livens the game up a bit, and it does actually open up opportunities for everybody because if you've only got two stakeholders, purchaser and provider; or the NHS and the Social Services department, if they get sort of horns locked there is then no move and things stagnate for years. The user movement is like a new card in the pack which enables things to shift about a bit that I find quite useful myself ... several years ago people used to imagine that if you had user representatives sitting on committees that it would slow things down and we wouldn't be able to talk about X, Y and Z while the users were here, or we'd have to use simple language and we couldn't go too fast ... now it is almost the other way round. I think they positively oil the wheels in lots of ways. They are allowed to play cards that we are not allowed to play ...'

This health authority manager's view was echoed by the co-ordinator of large non-profit care provider in another location. Here the county social services had withdrawn from a contract with the carers on grounds of cost. The local user group was contacted by the families concerned who wanted to continue having the same carer coming to their homes. In this case the user group could campaign, could 'play cards that we are not allowed to play', with the result that the contract was restored.

But we have more often heard views about the 'game' benefiting managers, than about user groups being able to exploit their potentially powerful situation. The user card, as one consultant psychiatrist commented, is not often played by users. Consultation can sometimes be an elaborate showpiece, an end in itself, serving the strategic needs of officials and politicians with no tangible outcome for users:

> 'It is like, "oh well we've done our bit, we've consulted" ... I think it is all this, you know, saying that they were consulting people ... they wanted the innovative approach to things, people coming up with all these ideas and they were saying "No". I mean I'm involved with advocacy and we were strong. We had a great big meeting with social services in XX, for an advocacy alliance, a lot of money spent on that, were told "You must put in a bid, a realistic bid for a worker and we really must see this get off the ground". March came. "You can have £2,500 to cover admin costs". They can put it in the Community Care Plan, it is in, "We are supporting an advocacy alliance", they fail to mention £2,500, that it is just to cover admin, perhaps getting a directory together, that is all it will cover, it is a token gesture.'

Consultation can be a very useful tool in management as this social services Head of Adult Disability Services explained:

> 'I suppose we all do it in a way, you do a user survey and pick out what you want to hear in a way, a bit of that goes on. I feel that people use, you know, consulting users, as a way of getting what they wanted through anyway ... you kind of don't take too much notice in case you don't agree, but if it happens to say what you want it to say, you say "Well the users say this ..." '

Concluding Remarks

In theory users can occupy territory between health purchasers and health providers, between NHS and local government social services, between different professional groups such as nurses and psychiatrists, between clinicians and managers. There is negotiating space within agencies, such as between purchaser and provider wings of one social services department, between different service arms such as housing and highways. There is other space between the unitary authority and the rump county authority, where one locality's user group can press for parity of resources with groups situated within the new authority or vice versa. And within community care there are now a host of providers, opening up space for user campaigning between the voluntary sector and public purchasers.

The problem is that it takes a highly skilled, politicised user group to exploit this potential. Alliances are crucial. The ground is restless and shifting and the 'game' can be exhausting for anyone with a disability or mental health problem. An independent, radical user group, which can avoid being overmanaged and institutionalised by the agencies, could have much to gain in these turbulent times. Unfortunately, most of the political gains emerging from this upheaval may benefit 'officials', while many user groups, weakened by funding cuts and alienated by fragmentation, will not have comparable opportunities to learn the skills of playing 'the user card.'

Many of the organisational changes have left managers of public services torn between the conflicting demands of providing both high quality and value for money. Other political pressures include removal of legitimacy following fragmentation of services and a perceived denigration of public service itself by means of privatisations and compulsory competitive tendering. Through all this, one unassailable source of legitimacy can be the user. Locally, the politics of involving users and user groups in decisions can be extremely complex, but in terms of credibility more globally, in decision making and in self justification, playing the user card can provide a safe route through uncertain territory.

Politics and Health

Christopher Nottingham
Glasgow Caledonian University
&
Fiona O'Neill
University of Birmingham

'In Care of the European Union? Problems and Possibilities in the Development of a European Health Care Regime'

Quotation

'There is no danger there will ever be a Europe-wide health system. That would be even more controversial than a European currency.'[1]

Introduction

Under the Maastricht Treaty on European Union (TEU) the European Union has assumed a new responsibility for the health of its citizens. Article 129 states:

> 'The Community shall contribute towards ensuring a high level of human health protection by encouraging cooperation between the Member States and, if necessary, lending support to their actions.'

The commitment is defined in a way which indicates a sensitivity to current trends in health discussions:

> 'Community action shall be directed towards the prevention of diseases, ... by promoting research into their causes and their transmission, as well as health information and education.'

The Chapter also demonstrated an appropriate sensitivity to political trends in that the new powers at the centre are softened by doses of transparency and subsidiarity:

> 'Member States shall, in liaison with the Commission, coordinate among themselves their policies and programmes ... The Commission may, in close contact with the Member States, take any useful initiative to promote such coordination.'

While it is clear that the European Union will play a larger part in the health politics of member states than it has done, the depth and nature of that involvement is difficult to estimate. The purpose of this paper is to evaluate whether Article 129 should be regarded as a qualitative step towards a european health care regime. To this end we shall look at steps

---

[1] Hans Stein, Health Policy Officer, German Ministry of Health, 1995.

which have already been taken before examining the pressures making for convergence and those tending towards the preservation of national regimes. The TEU, we believe, raises questions about health politics which are both complex and fundamental and the evaluation of its probable effects offers an opportunity for examining some of the special factors involved.

Present Outlook

From the United Kingdom it is all too easy to underestimate the extent of the day to day engagement of British organisations with the European Union. Perhaps it is not surprising that a public debate which has as yet shown scant attention to the Inter Governmental Conference of 1996 should fail to acknowledge the increasing volume of undramatic interaction which is slowly adjusting the parameters within which political choices can be made. If anything, the gulf is widening between 'Europe' as experienced by those who are engaged in activities which fall within its effective influence, and 'Europe' as an issue in the domestic political debate. In the former sense Europe might be seen as the new efficient secret, part of the obligatory *outillage mental* for those who wish to exercise influence in private or public organisations.

For the main groups concerned with health care in Britain the European dimension has become almost routine. Since 1992/3 the British Medical Association has maintained an office in Brussels. The Royal College of Nursing plans to open one but has had a European Officer for some years past. The Standing Committee of Nurses of the European Union and the Advisory Committee on Training in Nursing have both in operation since the 1970's. Doctors have similar representation through the Standing Committee of Doctors of the European Union and the Advisory Committee on Medical Education. There are numerous working groups dedicated to specialist areas which channel their efforts through these formal committees. There are in addition numerous Europe wide organisations representing doctors. In fact the number of specialist groups is becoming problematical. Richards comments 'if the number of committees representing doctors in Europe bore a direct relationship to the effectiveness of that representation, British doctors and their European counterparts could rest easy in their beds'.[2] Nurses have also established a number of speciality groups. The European Oncology Nursing Society for example has achieved recognition from the Commission and has attracted European Union funds for its training and research programmes.[3] Other groups are also organising European links; the European Healthcare Management Association for instance reports a 40% growth in numbers in recent months.[4]

Raw evidence of group consultation must always be treated with caution. Government agencies will often have in mind the need to neutralise opposition, gain information, or assemble support for a pre-determined course of action and some consultations may be no more than symbolic for one

---

[2] T.Richards, '1992 and all that', *British Medical Journal*, 303, 1991.
[3] Information from Phylip Pritchard, Chief Administrator of the European Federation of Cancer Societies.
[4] 'EHMA Reports a 40% Rise 1994-5', *Health Service Journal*, 13 July, 1995.

or both sides. In spite of formal representation a case can be made that the medical profession has been particularly resistant to the development of European links.[5] It should also be remembered that negotiations between groups and the Commission are different from those between groups and national governments in certain significant respects. Given that for most purposes the effective power of the Commission depends upon its being able to work with and through the governments of the member states, and that nurses and doctors rely on the same organisations for their day to day bread and butter, it is inevitable that european level negotiations are heavily influenced by domestic political considerations. Certainly it would appear to be the case that British professional groups have warmed to the european dimension with the disruption of the national policy community over the *Working for Patients* reforms. For the nursing élite Europe is an attractive forum to advance their notions of health care and redefine a professional status, both of which have been challenged by post-1989 changes.

It is not at all difficult to find examples of decisions in Brussels exercising an influence over health politics in the member states. For example, a current controversy in the United Kingdom surrounds a European Directive which is affecting the training of junior doctors. Directives on Health & Safety in the workplace have also had their effect. Those aspects of health most closely involved with the development of the Single Market are likely to continue to have the most immediate effect. Taylor, for instance has argued that the single market in pharmaceuticals has 'the potential to bring about considerable changes in the differing medical cultures of the European Community's member states'.[6] The creation of the new European Medicines Agency will also exercise an increasing influence over the licensing of drugs across Europe. The special campaigns such as Europe Against Cancer and Europe Against Aids will have a significant impact. While domestic public health policies concerned with smoking, environmental pollution, consumer protection against dangerous products, and standards of hygiene and labelling of food products are already heavily europeanised. In the field of medical research there is the 4 year BIOMED programme which looked at a number of target areas. One must also take into account the reciprocal agreements for the provision of acute medical care for Union citizens. Another area of significant, and developing cooperation is over the mutual recognition of diplomas and the harmonisation of professional training.

So it is not difficult to identify a range of activity in health related issues at the European level, but it must be remembered that there is not always a high level of compliance with European regulations, and that budgets at the European level are small. The European Union may have defined a new role for itself but there is no sign that it is nearer securing an appropriate rise in expenditure. The overall budget for the Action Programme for Public Health Promotion, Information, Education and Training arising out of the

---

[5] See for example Stacey, who highlights the reluctance of the medical profession to give recognition to the medical qualifications of refugees from Nazi Germany. M.Stacey, 'The British General Medical Council', in T.Johnson et al (eds), *Health Professions and the State in Europe*, Routledge, 1995, p.126.

[6] D.Taylor, 'Prescribing in Europe – forces for change', *British Medical Journal*, 304, 1992.

TEU was only £25m. The total health budget which included money to be spent on the major programmes such as Europe against Aids was originally £147m, but this was cut by £9.3m in ministerial horse trading.[7] The same holds true for medical research; BIOMED for example was allocated £93m in the period between 1990 and 1994, but this should be set against the £942m spent on information technology research in the same period.[8] Such figures must also be seen in the context of domestic health care budgets.

Prospects

This picture of activity at a European level does not then dispose of the original question. It is still not clear whether Chapter 129 will herald a qualitative change in the European dimension of health care. At the moment there is no indication that the Commission could attract funds and powers for more ambitious activities on its own account, or has the ability to mobilise member governments to act on its behalf.

Nonetheless there are pressures making for greater cohesion. Firstly there is the nature of the health field itself. In the medical professions the philosophy of caring is an important part of individual self regard and the bedrock of collective definitions of purpose. Caring as a philosophy does not recognise national frontiers. These attitudes have found expression and reinforcement through international organisations such as the Red Cross, Medicins Sans Frontiers and WHO and are supported by popular sentiment. One must also take into account the recent convergence in health politics debates with national political communities. The perspectives of policy makers from Sweden to Spain are increasingly defined by anxieties about how demographic changes, technological advances and rising public expectations are likely to affect health care expenditure. There is a widespread feeling that it is vital to contain rates of increase in order to preserve the competitive position. In recent years factors such as these have produced signs of convergence. Dutch health and welfare politics are in many respects at the opposite end of the spectrum to those in Britain yet in the mid 80s, just after Roy Griffiths had been brought from Sainsburys to examine the NHS the Dutch Minister of Health appointed Wiesse Dekker from Philips to do a similar job. Dekker also came up with recommendations to limit the extent to which health care was driven and defined by public demand, to restrict professional autonomy, to introduce a more powerful managerial stratum, and to restructure healthcare in a way which introduced an element of competition between the component parts.

Some commentators set such developments within the context of the postfordist debate. The pressures to cost control in health and welfare systems are seen as responses to the movements within the international political economy. Just as the commodity sector and commercial and industrial production have been subjected to pressures for restructuring within the domestic and international economy, so too it is argued the public sector

---

[7]'The Health of the Union', *Health Service Journal*, 105, 1995, p.17.

[8]R.Smith, 'European research: back to pre-eminence?', *British Medical Journal*, 4, 1992.

has undergone a similar transition. There is certainly evidence to support this view. Recent efficiency audits in NHS Trust hospitals have produced demands for a breakdown of the traditional division of responsibility and labour between health care professionals. Throughout Europe there is a debate about whether nurses should be allowed to undertake procedures which were previously reserved for doctors. Some consultants have come under pressure to work shifts. Sceptics, however, have stressed that the structural transformations in healthcare systems have not proceeded automatically or evenly. Impulses to change may be similar but outcomes may still be different. As Claus Offe put it:

> 'In a medicalised society, health has become politicised, and will continue to be an area for ideological and social conflicts ... we have to understand the internal structures of control in health systems, and their relationship to wider struggles over citizenship, markets and welfare, as they are expressed in state policy.'[9]

The fact that in Western European polities it has proved easier to reduce or diminish state responsibilities in areas other than health strengthens Offe's case. It may be the case that as states discard other responsibilities health becomes the residual focus for debates about the relative responsibilities of state, family and individual. This makes it even less likely that rationally inspired reforms can be effected.

The case for convergence does not rest on post-Fordism alone. Some commentators suggest that one source of pressure may arise from the greater mobility resulting from the single market.[10] Not only will this test the strength of the Community's procedures for dealing with the health care of citizens of one state who work or live in another,but it could also lead to demands for the convergence in the provision of services. It seems reasonable to suppose that increasing mobility will expose areas of national relative deprivation and produce political pressures to conformity, but there are number of necessary qualifications. Firstly are the people who travel most within the Europe likely to be the ones who make demands on the health systems of the host country? Holiday makers will continue to carry temporary private insurance, many business travellers will have personal or company insurance policies and even those who retire abroad will be unlikely to rely on the public services of their new country, even where they are permitted to do so. Secondly it must be remembered that mobility is by no means as commonplace as is sometimes assumed. Movement among health professionals is minuscule. In spite of elaborate arrangements now in place the number of application to practice in the United Kingdom from nurses in the European Union, apart from the Irish Republic, can be reckoned in tens rather than hundreds.[11]

---

[9] C.Offe, *Contradictions of the Welfare State*, 1984, p.198.
[10] See K.Schaapveld et al, 'The European Health Potential: what we can learn from each other?', *Health Policy*, 33, 1995.
[11] United Kingdom Central Council figures.

There is also the question of whether citizens will make the appropriate connections. British citizens clearly resent being denied treatments available in other parts of the country, but the sense of relative deprivation does not yet stretch to other European states. Allowance must always be made for the deep cultural divisions over healthcare which exist in Western Europe. There is a considerable literature which examines such divisions: the German obsession with the heart, the French obsession with the liver, which lead to considerable differences in diagnostic and prescribing procedures.[12] Differences are clearly of less importance with new than familiar health problems. AIDS, for example has always been easier to deal with at an international and European level. Drug abuse is a public health issue where there is a recognition that national programmes are liable to be ineffective and which lends itself to cooperation.[13]

Conclusion

The question of whether a substantial move towards a common European health policy is a possibility in any foreseeable future is a complex one. Where the role of any single factor is unlikely to prove decisive, we would suggest that it may be useful to consider the matter in the light of the well developed debates on the development of health regimes. What was it for instance that prompted the development of public health regimes in Western European states during the Nineteenth Century? Historical evidence does not seem to us to negate the role of individual campaigners or reduce the importance of either the rational/scientific or ethical/humanitarian arguments by which they advanced their case. It does however suggest patterns of interests and circumstances which predisposed others to listen at some times rather than others. The public health campaigners in the 19th Century demonstrated how the involuntary interdependencies of the new urban environment might be sanitised at an acceptable cost. Their hand was periodically strengthened by particular crises: cholera, the great leveller, accelerated the pace of conversion, by persuading the more fortunate to recognise a commonality of interest with the poor, and helping to still their distaste for higher taxes or subjection to new state regulations.[14]

Elite concerns about international competition seem to have been the predominant force in the creation of the first modern healthcare and welfare systems in many countries of Western Europe at the turn of the century. The threat of military defeat or economic eclipse, reinforced by perceptions of Bismark's new German state, gave added weight to those advocating an extension of state responsibility. The debates surrounding the development of the new health regimes in the middle of the 20th Century involved all the old motivating factors but added new ones. For example, the creation of the NHS in Britain owed a good deal less to the ideology of the Labour party than it did to the need to respond to the deeper and more inclusive

---

[12] See L.Payer, *Medicine and Culture: Notions of health & sickness in Britain, USA, France and Germany*, Victor Gollancz, 1989.

[13] See S.Grüsser & S.White, 'Free Movement and Welfare Entitlement: European Union Drug Users in Berlin', *Journal of European Social Policy*, 5/1, 1995, pp.13-28.

[14] See A.De Swann, *In Care of the State*, 1992.

notion of citizenship which had been necessitated by the demands of war. It was also of importance that the NHS promised to deliver patients to doctors on terms which were both financially acceptable and professionally advantageous to the latter.

Such a summary helps to suggest a number of factors which might be considered in estimating the possibility of the transference of responsibilities from national to European healthcare regimes. On the basis of the above we would suggest that any linear progression along rational lines towards a European healthcare regime is unlikely. Arguments rooted in rationality will have, and indeed have had their place in promoting and shaping developments but they will only operate in coincidence with other factors. Functional factors will assume a larger role than idealistic ones though neither could operate in isolation. Health regimes have tended to come about for what in the 19th century health reformers referred to as police functions; as responses to a requirement for order rather than accommodation of stated need. Public opinion will continue to operate as a conservative force in all but the most extreme circumstances. Historically public opinion had rarely proved an overriding factor in the instigation of health and welfare reform, but once measures are in place and have become embedded in the network of expectation and the reality of day to day life it becomes exceptionally difficult for politicians to remove or even adjust them. Nonetheless dramatic changes in circumstance can produce unexpected demands and opportunities for innovation.

There is a final factor which perhaps more than any other illustrates the nature and scale of the problem. There is a continuous debate in the field of health politics which concerns the grounds on which health care is provided to individuals. In rough terms there is an argument, propagated most actively by WHO but with resonance at every level, which presents health care as a natural right, open to individuals by reason of their humanity. The contrary argument presents health care as something to which individuals become entitled by right of the membership of a political community. While it would be impossible to dismiss either argument it would seem that the second one predominates in most cases and at most times. In practical terms access to health and welfare benefits is at the heart of modern citizenship. The extent of the relationship can be illustrated by the relative decline of the franchise factor. This latter debate served in the 19th Century as the vehicle for discussing what citizenship was and who was or was not entitled to its benefits. If we look at the more heated debates of late 20th Century Europe over the rights of immigrants it is striking how little importance has been attached to voting rights as compared to rights to benefits. Welfare, and health in particular has become part of a relationship which defines and reinforces community. Equally it is welfare which defines and legitimates the modern state. Social welfare systems might one day come to be seen as the skeletal remains, in both a practical and a political sense, that is the last collective ties to the state. Both states and their citizens have a vital interest in the matter. Realistic analysis demands that we look at the political qualities of our existing systems.

There has been a tendency to dismiss the nation state too readily. Healthcare states must be seen in terms of their achievements. They represent complicated political bargains whereby difficult issues have found some practical resolution. Moreover they have a good record of delivery: the bargains they represent are, for most citizens in most circumstances, much more mobilisable than those struck elsewhere. The fact that we may feel that healthcare states are not as good as they should or might be, or even that they may be getting worse, should not blind us to the fact that they are still rightly seen as only available instrument for allocating resources and providing final guarantees.

This element should not however be treated as a final insurmountable barrier to developments at the European Union level. We do after all inhabit a world in which all forms of interdependency are broadening and deepening. Cholera may no longer be around to reinforce the lesson but Ebola, AIDS, and drug related public health crises are abroad. There were rumours recently of black rats coming off an East European ship in London. Any such disaster might rapidly alter the received wisdom as to the limits of the healthcare state. The need to protect and defend ones own health might quickly require a new geographical shape. The nation state may come to seem an inadequate guarantor of acceptable levels of security for individual citizens. Those hitherto excluded from the community might find themselves as subjects of a new order. On a day to day basis there will be a steady decline of national peculiarities over health and healthcare, a gradual erosion of cultural difference stimulated by the introduction of new drugs and treatments, and increased and intensified contacts both among professionals and individual citizens. On its own this might produce a measure of change, but in conjunction with one or more of the more dramatic factors, it could produce a great deal.

There exists then a special and intense relationship between health and politics. In one sense it might be seen as the only area which stands against the post-modern tide and where there still exists a live, continuous, and comprehensive discussion of the respective roles of the individual and the state, of the rights and obligations of citizenship, and of the respective responsibilities of families, professionals and government agencies. Health can certainly be seen as one of the policies which the proponents of the European dimension might develop as a means of building a new political community, but the tendrils of the health debate are so numerous and the passions it arouses so intense that it might be more realistic to say that a full European health policy could not come about before such a community was created.

Barriers to Full Employment

Susanne Blancke
Ruhr-University Bochum

'Proclaimed Goals but Little Consequence:
Trade Unions and Employment Policy in Germany'

Introduction

Due to the employment crisis in the German labour market, job protection and the creation of new jobs are at the top of every union's agenda. Recently, Dieter Schulte, head of the German Trade Union Federation (*Deutscher Gewerkschaftsbund*, DGB), stressed once again that his organisation will dedicate itself to the goal of full-employment and will contribute to its achievement (Schulte 1995, p.37), primarily by helping adjust the German system of industrial relations.

After being subject to criticism in the 1970s, both in Germany and abroad, the 'German model' of industrial relations with its three pillars (the dual system of representation, powerful trade unions and strong employers' associations), has subsequently been regarded favourably, due to its contribution to the German economy and the success of co-determination. In terms of wages and its relatively low level of income polarisation, Germany was at the top of the international league, at least until the 1990s. While other unions in western economies suffered losses of membership, in Germany, unions have been able to retain their bargaining power even during economic crises. This has elevated the German system to the status of a 'model' for unions and social democrats, both at home and abroad (Schmidt & Trinczek 1991; Crouch 1992).

However, in reality, not only has the model failed to act as an exemplar for other systems – due to institutional incompatibility and the consequent problems of imitation – but its efficiency in the German context has been hard to verify (Addison et al 1995). Moreover, recently the model has come under intense criticism in Germany. Recent changes – including the globalisation of markets, the consequent increase in competitive pressures, the immensely high burden of the unification of Germany, and the changes in the structures of production that have accompanied the end of Fordism and Taylorism – have all placed new demands on the system and have revealed its weaknesses. As revealed by the high level of long-term unemployment in Germany, the partners to collective bargaining have been unable to respond successfully to the problems of the labour market. Of course, employment policy has not been a primary task of collective bargaining in the past. However, through their campaign of working time reduction, German trade unions did try hard during the 1980s and 1990s to adjust the supply of work to its demand, in order to effect a redistribution of employment to the advantage of the unemployed.[1]

---

[1] The effects of collective working time reductions are controversial, especially in the case of full wage compensation. These reductions seem to compensate mainly for the effects of rationalisation (Hinrichs/Wiesenthal 1987; see also Seifert 1989; for a detailed

Hypothetically, it can be assumed that the potential for conducting employment policy via bargaining, and thereby reaching significant results, is highest if powerful trade unions and employers' associations compromise on relatively inflexible collective agreements, while, at the same time, actors at the firm level comply with these agreements (Figure 1, box 4). Such positive effects would decrease, however, as the level of social closure at the company level increased; that is, if the implementation of such measures was not supported but undermined by the actors at that level – which is likely to occur especially in a situation of high unemployment (Figure 1, box 2; also Hohn 1987). This latter scenario was effectively that of late 1980s Germany when collectively bargained employment policy reduced the effects of a general working time reduction (Hinrichs/Wiesenthal 1987). With the increasing flexibilisation of collective agreements – as has occurred especially in recent times (to be further discussed in section 2) – a decentralisation of collective bargaining takes place and it can be expected that the effects of social closure will be strengthened. Again, this occurs especially under circumstances of high unemployment (Figure 1, box 1). In such a situation it seems only possible to achieve a medium degree of success with employment policy under collective bargaining if, at the same time, binding requirements on the creation of jobs are agreed upon and if the effects of social closure can thereby be absorbed (Figure 1, box 4). However, the preconditions for this are a relatively closed system of industrial relations without exit options for employers (for example, a shift to lower-wage countries) and powerful bargaining partners with a relatively high homogeneity of interests and economic strength amongst their members.

Figure 1
The Potential for Effective Employment Policy via Collective Bargaining

		collective bargaining agreements	
		flexible	inflexible
social closure	high	1 bad	2 medium
	low	3 medium	4 good

The central argument in this paper is that the state of industrial relations in Germany today corresponds increasingly to the third situation mentioned (Figure 1, box 1) and that an effective employment policy based on collective bargaining has become increasingly unlikely. A tendency towards the extended flexibilisation of collective agreements and an increasing decentralisation of the collective bargaining structure exacerbates the trend towards social closure; and this makes the implementation of a collectively bargained

---

economic analysis of collective working time reductions see Hüpen 1994). However, they are still considered a full success by the trade unions (for example by Riester 1995, and Schulte 1995).

employment policy at the firm level extremely difficult. Furthermore, a crisis of employers' associations can be discerned in which heterogeneous economic capacities and heterogeneous positions of interest have weakened their aggregative function, their capacity to compromise and to oblige their members to follow the collective will, as manifest in the phenomenon of withdrawals ('freebooting'). Under such circumstances the ability of employers' associations to bind their members within a pact for job creation has been immensely diminished. The absence of a strong partner on the employers' side means that, being in a rather defensive situation themselves, the trade unions are able to contribute even less to their proclaimed goal of full employment today than in the 1980s. As is discussed in detail below, this context is hardly conducive for the achievement of collective goals or the ambitious *'Bündis für Arbeit'*(pact for employment) which was recently proposed by the metal workers' union, IG-Metall (section 3).

1. The German System of Industrial Relations

As already mentioned, the pillars of the 'German model' are powerful trade unions and employers' associations as well as the dual system of representation (often referred to as 'co-determination'). Until now, the German model has been marked by a high degree of centralisation (although it can not be compared to Scandinavian centralism). After the second World War, the rebuilding of the unions was carried out according to the principles of the single industrial union (*Einheitsgewerkschaft*) and those of central employers' associations, which together pushed particularist concerns (company, job category, ideology) into the background (Keller 1989, p.136).

Collective bargaining takes place at the regional branch level, where the collective actors – that is, the representatives of regional union and employers' associations – primarily negotiate on matters such as wages, working time arrangements, and formal work regulations etc (Streeck 1991; Müller-Jentsch 1995). Despite its regional character, collective bargaining is mainly coordinated by the central, peak associations. Thus 'pilot decisions' in key branches and, usually, in economically strong regions serve as a 'pattern', with the consequence that inter-industrial income differences are relatively low and other job requirements are mostly standardized.

In the 1970s, a change of paradigm from quantity-oriented to more quality-oriented agreements took place. The traditionally dominant wages policy lost ground and, with only small financial concessions possible, only minimal gains in real income could be accomplished. Instead, protection against rationalisation moved to centre stage in negotiations. In the 1980s, against the background of a dramatic increase in unemployment, more and more working time arrangements were negotiated, the aim of the unions being a 35 hour week (gained by the metal industry in 1995). A flexibilisation of working time arrangements was implemented; but at the same time, the officially established principles of collective bargaining (*Tarifautonomie*) were upheld by both unions and employers (Keller 1989, p.139).

At the company level, employee interests are represented by the works council (*Betriebsrat*). In contrast to the general understanding of works-councils, the German *Betriebsrat* is not a joint body composed of management and labour representatives, but is restricted entirely to employees. The role of the German works councils differs in several respects from that of joint consultative bodies in other countries (Schregle 1989). The German works councils have advisory functions as well as bargaining ones such as grievance handling, bargaining with management or veto rights in personal matters. But they are not allowed to negotiate matters that are usually bargained at branch level by trade unions and employers' associations; and the bargaining rights of the *Betriebsräte* do not extend to the right to strike. On the contrary, according to the *Betriebsverfassungsgesetz* (BVG; Works Constitution Act; the law of company establishment) of 1972, works councils are obliged to use their mandate in mutual trust with management to the benefit of the company.

Since the representatives are elected by all the employees – who have the right to vote whether they are members of a union or not – the works councils have their own legitimation, which is independent from that of the trade unions. It is true, however, that 80% of the members of the works councils are elected from union lists (Streeck 1991, p.55). In this way, unions and works councils are closely connected: the works councils provide a large proportion of the active members of the unions (Schmidt/Trinczek 1991).

The principles of the system of co-determination remove from representation at the bargaining level an aspect that would otherwise cause a great deal of conflict – wages policy. Under this system, the works councils take an intermediate position; they represent the concerns of the employee on the one hand but on the other keep a keen eye on the economic goals and performance of the company (Müller-Jentsch 1995). In a comparison with the British and Scandinavian systems of industrial relations, Crouch (1992) concludes the German model has proven itself superior in its responsiveness to the demands for flexibility coming from changes in work organization and new production concepts. Looking at the gain in importance of *plant* level collective agreements, he expects that German employers will in future prove to be cooperative towards the works councils since the latter have always been collaborative partners. In contrast, the British system shows a stronger tendency to reduce the influence of unions at plant level (Crouch 1992, p.14). At the same time, the Scandinavian model – which has often been regarded as an ideal to aspire to – will prove to be inferior to the German model because its high level of centralisation and the strong role of the peak union organizations are inappropriate and ill-equipped for representing concerns at the company level. The duality of the German industrial relations, with its combination of central collective bargaining and flexible, firm-level, representation is supposed to be conducive to the expression of company (union and management) interests and concerns.

2. Problems and Recent Developments in German Industrial Relations

But what appears to be an advantage from the point of view of employees at the company level, would also seem to imply a further weakening of the representation of the interests of the unemployed. Though plant-level industrial relations do play an important role in the area of job protection[2], this level of bargaining is clearly inappropriate for representing the unemployed. Thus, during the 1980s, management and works councils increasingly displayed a trend towards social closure to the disadvantage of the unemployed; and it can be assumed that the most recent developments in German industrial relations that increase the importance of company-level agreements will further exacerbate this problem. Furthermore, as mentioned above, the other two pillars of the German model – the strength of trade unions and especially employers' associations – are being steadily undermined.

Social Closure

Since the 1980s, as mass unemployment and long term unemployment have become severe problems in Germany, the duration of employment with a firm has become an important criterion of employment security alongside the level of qualification. Those employees that have made their way into the internal (core) labour market seem to be relatively protected from the competition of the external labour market. In addition, labour offices have rarely been used for encouraging new employment (Hohn 1989, pp.9ff). Although the reduction of working time in the 1980s was designed to be an answer to mass unemployment, it led rather to a flexibilisation of working time and, moreover, distributed it to save the jobs of existing employees rather than create new ones (Hinrichs/Wiesenthal 1987).

In a detailed analysis, Hohn (1989) asks what interest the actors involved – employers and works councils – would have in such social closure. Regarding the various responsibilities of the macro- and micro-level of representation, Hohn argues that in the situation of sustained mass unemployment prevailing in the 1980s, quantitative job- and status-protection concerns (negotiated at the plant level) replaced quantitative income concerns (bargained by trade unions and employers' associations at the regional-sectoral level) and shifted the emphasis in policy bargaining from the central to the company level. Here, management and works councils – especially in the companies of those industrial sectors subject to a high level of market competition – have developed a strategy of social closure against the low qualified and passive minority in the labour market (Hohn 1988, p.15). In contrast to recent assumptions about the rationality of employers that foresee the reactivation of an 'industrial reserve army', it seems rather that the new employers' strategy is to integrate the organised sections of the *employed* labour force into cooperative arrangements and to divorce the internal labour market from the external one. With respect to the potential for implementing employment policy at company level, the fact that the works councils supported the strategy of the employers and preferred to represent their clientele's interests rather than the collective concerns of the external labour market is of particular importance (Hinrichs/Wiesenthal 1987; Widmaier/Blancke 1996).

---

[2] The example *par excellence* is the VW model, which provides a guarantee for jobs in return for a reduction of working time without wage compensation in the form of a firm-level collective agreement.

Decentralisation

According to Hohn these effects were the result of mass unemployment in the 1980s. In the 1990s, aspects of social closure seem to gain even greater weight due to the increasing significance of firm-level agreements. There are three explanantions for this increase in the importance of the company level as an arena for collective bargaining: the transformation of structures of production since the demise of Fordism and Taylorism (Kern/Schuhmann 1984, Piore/Sabel 1989); the flexibilisation of working time since the 1980s; and the growing criticism, especially on the part of medium-sized enterprises, of industry-wide collective agreements.

Along with the decline of the production principles of Taylorism and Fordism and globalisation – that is, the emergence of international networks of communications, production, and market processes and increased competition (Henderson 1989; Smart 1994) – new demands are being made on the structure of work and significant problems have been created for the established system of German industrial relations. The new requirements placed on industrial production (a smaller number of components, a technical and organisational capacity for innovation, a flexible reaction to the differentiated needs of customers, a rapid adjustment to changes in the market etc) have led increasingly, albeit highly unevenly, to new strategies of rationalisation and changes in traditional conceptions of production. Different processes of production are connected in order to increase the potential of flexibilisation; and the division of labour and specialisation are being replaced by principles of integration and totality (Kern & Schuhmann 1984; Kern & Sabel 1990; Dörr & Naschold 1992; Seitz 1993). These developments have not been without their consequences for the system of industrial relations and these are manifested primarily in tendencies towards decentralisation. Collective agreements with generally binding standards can no longer meet the differentiated requirements in the representation of employers' and employees' interests. Today, a noticeable tendency is for firms to implement collective agreements differentially and to shift this implementation from the sectoral to the company level (Traxler 1989; Streeck 1986).

Even more than this change – which, although becoming more important, is still in its early stages – such decentralisation tendencies were also encouraged by the policy of working time reduction in the 1980s and the early 1990s. As a move was made away from the 40 hour working week, the need to divorce working time from operating time became clear (Bispinck 1995; Keller 1989); and employers demanded greater flexibility in collective agreements in order to adjust to the needs of the company. Their aim was to counter the aging of equipment and short production cycles through longer running periods for machinery, thereby achieving an amortisation of capital which was used for new technology.

Another problem for the system of collective bargaining is the minimum wage character of collective agreements. Increasingly, these have produced conflicts of interest between large companies and smaller distributers. The latter feel less-well represented by employers' associations and complain about agreements on high wages. Such negotiations have been dominated by large companies that agree to high wages and pass the consequent costs onto the distributers (Schnabel 1995, p.59). In this context, an incomes policy that is more flexible, more decentralised and more closely connected to the company has been demanded. Although such demands have not been met, the issue has gained greater significance in discussions on wages, general flexibilisation and decentralisation (Müller-Jentsch 1993; Schnabel 1995).

Altogether these new developments show a clear shift in industrial relations towards the company level, management and works councils whereby tendencies towards social closure also gain in importance.

Developments among Employers' Associations and Trade Unions

Within this context a partial weakening of the aggregative functions of trade unions and employers' associations can be discerned. Employers' associations are especially confronted with the danger that the heterogeneous concerns of their members can no longer allow for compromise, leading to major problems of organisation.

Such difficulties in securing the loyalty and recruitment of members are not new and, indeed, have always been one of the fundamental problems for employers' associations. Referring back to Mancur Olson's *The Logic of Collective Action*, Traxler (1989; 1991) gives three explanations for this: interest representation is not the exclusive preserve of employers' associations, but wages etc can also be bargained by individual management; companies have sufficient means of power of their own to drastically change industrial relations; the concerns of the members are not congruent and differ by company, branch and region. Companies are clearly aware of their own competitive interests and orientate themselves closely to them. It is often easier for them to realise their own objectives and pursue their own, individual interests, without the support or control of their associations. The capacity of employers' associations to organise and control depends on their ability to conform to the concerns of their members (ability to compromise) and to secure their loyalty (ability to oblige); and this capacity is diminished the more heterogeneous the interests of the members are and the more closely the latter adhere to their own concerns (Traxler 1989, p.60).

However, apart from building a strong force against trade unions, there are two main positive incentives for employers to organise and provide collective representation. First, they gain – even if only in the long term – greater security in a context of market risk (Traxler 1989, p.64). Second, uniform earnings, especially in branches that are pay-intensive, take the wage factor out of competition and shift fundamental bargaining conflicts from companies onto the macro-level (Müller-Jentsch 1993).

But recent economic, political and social developments have put in question the function of employers' associations. First, the demands for flexibilisation and decentralisation stemming from working time reduction and changes in production structures lead to a high degree of heterogeneity in employers'/companies' interests and weaken the aggregative function of the associations. Second, problems of interest heterogeneity (especially concerning wages) also exist between the large and medium-sized companies.

Third, much more so than in the western part of Germany, there are important differences in productivity within the same branches in the eastern parts of the country. There, companies with modern capital equipment and large assets confront those with dated machines and high debts; and the latter are in no position to pay high minimum wages.

All of this undermines the capacity of employers' associations for compromise and their ability to discipline their members.

Although it is not officially quantified[3] there is an increasing tendency for companies to withdraw from employers' associations (especially in East Germany), while the recruitment of new members has also declined. As a consequence of massive withdrawals that took place in 1992 and 1993 in East Germany, the collective agreement for the East German metal industry, which was still in place, was abandoned by the employers' association *Gesamtmetall* (for further details see Henneberger 1994). Furthermore, in the new eastern *Bundesländer*, only a third of all the industry is organised in employers' associations whilst the western part of Germany the level of membership is still 75%. Just to mention three spectacular cases, in the Autumn of 1995, the West-German company Drägerwerk AG decided, at least for some of its production divisions, not to bargain collectively under metal industry arrangments; IBM has already done the same; and even Tyll Necker, president of the Federal Association of the German Industry (BDI) – which is not active in collective bargaining – left the employers' associations with all of his companies. As far as collective agreements are concerned, of the 4500 agreements that were valid in 1993 in East Germany, almost half were plant-level agreements, and in the Western part of Germany just over a quarter; while of the newest agreements about a third were bargained on the company level (Schnabel 1995).

Associations of medium-sized companies such as the *Arbeitsgemeinschaft Selbständiger Unternehmer* (Association of Self-Employed Enterprises) and the *Berufsvereinigung Junger Unternehmer* (Association of Young Employers) argued that companies without an industry-wide collective agreement should still have the possibility of becoming members of employers' associations in order to make use of the various services these organisations can provide (Müller-Jentsch 1993).

Following these developments it has become necessary for both employers' associations and trade unions to create a more flexible structure for collective agreements and connect it to a policy of collective bargaining that is closer to the company. For the employers' associations, this has become an imperative to prevent the further erosion of their interest representation and aggregation functions and membership (Müller-Jentsch 1995).

But the unions too are showing traces of erosion. Altogether, the DGB unions lost 5.15% of their members in 1993-1994 (in both eastern and western Germany) and 10.9% alone in the eastern part of the country, where a further decline in membership can be expected. Klaus Armingeon (1991) has argued that the (still widely spread) positive view of the situation of German trade unions can no longer be supported; and that they will be

---

[3]It is interesting that the Federal Association of German Employers, BDA, does not publish any statistics on this matter.

unable to solve their structural problems. The reasons for this can be found in the changing social structural composition of the unions, especially the long-term increase in the proportion of the work force in white collar jobs – which have always proven particularly difficult to organize. Over the longer-term, German trade unions will face a crisis of membership, the first signs of which can already be found in their shrinking organisations (Schmid/Blancke 1995).

3. Full Employment – A Rhetorical Goal Without Consequence?

Under these circumstances, what are the options for the trade unions in contributing to the goal of full employment, and what are the prospects for success? It should be pointed out that there is union consensus that collective bargaining would be overburdened were it assumes complete responsibility for future labour market policy. However, the trade unions still claim to follow a policy that can be effective in the labour market and reduce unemployment. A new venture has recently been launched by the unions, begun by IG-Metall, which supports a *'Bündnis für Arbeit'* (pact for employment), to be discussed further below.

Whatever form this policy eventually takes, it will mainly take place in the field of industrial relations and is therefore dependent on future developments in this system. The unions still have a certain capacity to shape employment policy, but their bargaining power and therefore their strategic ability has been greatly limited in recent times. They have been put on the defensive precisely by those developments already discussed above – the present situation of mass unemployment, the probability of further dismissals, the flexibilisation that has already taken place, further demands for flexibilisation and the erosion of employers' associations.

Out of a self-interest in legitimation, stability and survival they are compelled to improve the quantitative and qualitative conditions of their own clientele in employment; and this leaves only limited space for an effective representation of the unemployed. Within this context, the policy of working time reduction has disappeared entirely from their agenda; a continuation of this policy would only be possible with massive wage concessions. That might occasionally be possible at firm level (for example, the Volkswagen model); but with regard to regional and branch level collective agreements, the tolerance of employees for sacrifices has been exhausted (Offe 1995). Especially now that cuts in payment would not only mean a severe loss of income but would also have effects on benefits in case of a possible unemployment and, later, on social security. Furthermore, the tendencies of decentralisation in collective bargaining and the increase in social closure already noted make the implementation of employment policy increasingly difficult.

The erosion of employers' associations creates new and additional constraints on the ability to the unions to act. If they do not comply with demands for more flexibilisation, a further erosion of employers' associations can be expected – something which is unacceptable to the unions which require a reliable partner for collective bargaining.

Klaus Zwickel, the head of IG-Metall, recently suggested further adjustments to demands for flexibilisation in the 1997 collective agreement. The agreement is supposed to create a 'menu' (especially in working time) that should be made more concrete at the firm level, and here the IG-Metal insists on the participation of the works councils. These options may contribute to job protection. But it can be also assumed, however, that such a decentralisation is more than inappropriate for the creation of new jobs since it will compound already existing problems of social closure.

Zwickel must have considered this when his offer was accompanied by a proposal for a 'pact for employment'. He demanded the creation of 330,000 new jobs (110,000 of which as early as 1996) in return for abandoning claims for an increase in real income. The representatives of the metal industry's employers' association (*Gesamtmetall*) reacted rather cautiously to this suggestion. On the one hand they expect to cut 100,000 jobs in 1996. But more than that, they do not have the institutional instruments to implement such a policy, since the principles of collective bargaining do not provide the employers' associations with powers to revoke dismissals and oblige employers to create hundreds of thousands of jobs (Mundorf 1995). Furthermore, the current crisis of employers' associations does not allow them to burden their members with further interventions into individual company plans and thereby provoke further withdrawals – especially since individual employers are currently demanding still more flexibility and autonomy.

Gesamtmetall and the trade unions are only left with the option of creating positive incentives for new job creation and job protection in the form of (flexible) collective agreements; thus opening clauses would create the framework within which new jobs or job protection could be agreed to in return for cuts in income. However, such a policy is unlikely to contribute significantly to the creation of new jobs; once again, it is more likely that job *protection* would receive greater attention. Such flexible regulations might also mean that the economically more prosperous companies would create new jobs (that might be needed anyway) and could secure the windfall gains of a wage reduction, while weaker firms would have to carry the burden of high wages. Due to the problems faced by employers' associations in securing the loyalty of their members, such a policy would produce a dilemma in which employers' association (but also trade unions) would have to consider carefully the danger of a further loss of employers from their organisatior.

4. Conclusions

This paper began by arguing that with a flexibilisation of collective agreements, effective labour market policy at the level of collective bargaining is only possible when the prerequisites of powerful trade unions and employers' associations are fulfilled. It could be demonstrated that these requirements are increasingly unmet in German industrial relations. On the contrary, a greater heterogeneity of interests, especially among employers, undermines the aggregative functions of their associations, leads to withdrawals and reduces the possibilities for both trade unions and employers' associations to carry out an effective employment policy. As a consequence of the weakness especially of the employers' associations, the most probable future scenario is the flexibilisation of collective agreements, a further decentralisation of collective bargaining and a higher degree of social closure. In spite of all the efforts of German trade unions to fight unemployment with a 'pact for employment', the most recent developments in industrial relations create massive obstacles to the creation of new jobs by collective bargaining. Job protection seems to be the only aspect of this policy that might have some success. Thus, the aim of the unions to make a major contribution to full employment is very likely to be proclamatory, and deprived of any significant consequence.

References

J.T.Addison et al, 'German Industrial Relations: An Elusive Exemplar', *Industrielle Beziehungen*, 2/1, 1995, pp.25-45.

K.Armingeon, 'Ende einer Erfolgsstory? Gewerkschaften und Arbeitsbeziehungen im Einigungsprozeß', *Gegenwartskunde*, 40/1, 1991, pp.29-42.

R.Bispinck, 'Stabil oder fragil? Die bundesdeutschen Arbeitsbeziehungen im Umbruch', in M.Mesch (ed), *Sozialpartnerschaft und Arbeitsbeziehungen in Europa*, Manzsche Verlags- und Universitätsbuchhandlung, Wien, 1995, pp.75-100.

C.Crouch, 'The Changing Appearance of German Co-determination: A British View', *Die Mitbestimmung*, 38, Special Issue: English Edition, 1992, pp.12-16.

G.Dörr & F.Naschold, 'Umbrüche im Werkzeugmaschinenbau – eine arbeitspolitische Betrachtung', in F.Lehner & J.Schmid (eds), *Technik-Arbeit-Betrieb-Gesellschaft*, Leske und Budrich, 1992, pp.173-190.

J.W.Henderson, *The Globalisation of High Technology Production: Society, Space and Semiconductors in the Restructuring of Modern World*, Routledge, 1989.

F.Henneberger, 'Arbeitgeber- und Wirtschaftsverbände in den neuen Bundesländern: Konfliktlinien und Organisationsprobleme', in J.Schmid et al (eds), *Organisationsstrukturen und Probleme von Parteien und Verbänden, Berichte aus den neuen Ländern*, Metropolis-Verlag, Marburg, 1994, pp.119-148.

K.Hinrichs & H.Wiesenthal, 'Bestandsrationalität versus Kollektivinteresse. Gewerkschaftliche Handlungsprobleme im Arbeitszeitkonflikt 1984', in H. Abromeit & B.Blanke (eds), *Arbeitsmarkt, Arbeitsbeziehungen und Politik in den 80er Jahren*, Westdeutscher Verlag, 1987, pp.118-132.

H.-W.Hohn, *Von der Einheitsgewerkschaft zum Betriebssyndikalismus. Soziale Schließung im System der Interessenvertretung*, Edition Sigma, 1989.

R.Hüpen, *Arbeitszeit, Betriebszeit und Beschäftigung. Produktionstheoretische Grundlagen und Beschäftigungseffekte kollektiver Arbeitszeitverkürzung* Gabler, 1994.

B.Keller, ' "Krise" Arbeitsbeziehungen: Flexibilisierung, Deregulierung, Mikrokorporatismus', in H.Hartwich (ed), *Macht und Ohnmacht politischer Institutionen*, Westdeutscher Verlag, 1988, pp.135-157.

H.Kern & C.F.Sabel, 'Gewerkschaften in offenen Arbeitsmärkten.Überlegungen zur Rolle der Gewerkschaften in der industriellen Reorganisation', *Soziale Welt*, 41, 1991, pp.144-165.

H.Kern & M.Schumann, *Das Ende der Arbeitsteilung? Rationalisierung in der industriellen Produktion*, Verlag C.H.Beck, 1994.

W.Müller-Jentsch, 'Das (Des-)Interesse der Arbeitgeber am Tarifvertragssystem', *WSI-Mitteilungen*, 46/8, 1993, pp.496-502.

W.Müller-Jentsch, 'Auf dem Prüfstand: Das deutsche Modell der industriellen Beziehungen', *Industrielle Beziehungen*, 2/1, 1995 pp.11-24.

H.Mundorf, 'Die Grenzen der Tarifautonomie', *Handelsblatt*, 214, 6.11.1995, p.2.

C.Offe, 'Freiwillig auf die Teilnahme am Arbeitsmarkt verzichten', *Frankfurter Rundschau*, 165, 19.7.1995, p.10.

M.Piore & C.F.Sabel, *Das Ende der Massenproduktion*, Fischer, 1989.

W.Riester, 'Perspektiven zukünftiger Tarifpolitik', in W.Fricke (ed), *Jahrbuch Arbeit und Technik*, Dietz, 1995, pp.122-132.

J.Schmid & S.Blancke, ' "Gelungene Anpassung" oder "prekäre Normalisierung" und "erfolgreiches Scheitern"?', *Gewerkschaftliche Monatshefte*, 46/9, 1995, pp.566-576.

R.Schmidt & R.Trinczek, 'Duales System: Tarifliche und betriebliche Interessenvertretung', in W. Müller-Jentsch (ed), *Konfliktpartnerschaft. Akteure und Institutionen der industriellen Beziehungen*, Rainer Hampp Verlag, München und Mering, 1991, pp.167-200.

C.Schnabel, 'Entwicklungstendenzen und Arbeitsbeziehungen in der Bundesrepublik Deutschland seit Beginn der achtziger Jahre. Eine Analyse unter besonderer Berücksichtigung der Arbeitgeberseite', in M.Mesch (ed), *Sozialpartnerschaft und Arbeitsbeziehungen in Europa*, Manzsche Verlagsund Universitätsbuchhandlung, Wien, 1995, pp.53-74.

J.Schregle, 'Workers Participation in the Federal Republic of Germany in an International Perspective', in A.Gladstone et al (eds), *Current Issues in Labour Relations: An International Perspective*, de Gruyter, 1989, pp.105-114.

D.Schulte, 'Anpassen oder untergehen', *Die Mitbestimmung*, 41/9, 1995, pp.35-37.

B.Seitz, *Neue Produktionskonzepte und tarifpolitische Steuerungsprobleme, Arbeitspapier des SFB 187 – Neue Informationssysteme und flexible Arbeitssysteme*, Arbeitspapier Z2-4, Bochum, 1993.

B.Smart, 'Sociology, Globalization and Post-Modernity: Comments on the "Sociology for one World" Thesis', *International Sociology*, 9/2, 1994, pp.149-160.

W.Streeck, 'The Uncertainties of Management in the Management of Uncertainty: Employers, Labour Relations and Industrial Adjustment in the 1980s', *Discussion Paper, Wissenschaftszentrum Berlin*, IIM/LKP86-26, 1986.

W.Streeck, 'The Federal Republic of Germany', in J.Niland & O.Clarke (eds), *Agenda for Change: An International Analysis of Industrial Relations in Transition*, Allan & Unwin, North Sydney, 1991, pp.53-89.

F.Traxler, 'Unternehmerinteressen, Arbeitgeberverbände und Arbeitsbeziehungen. Zum Verhältnis der Arbeitgeber zu Tarifsystem und Gewerkschaften', in O.Dabrowski et al (eds), *Tarifpolitische Interessen der Arbeitgeber und neue Managementstrategien*, Hans-Böckler-Stiftung, Düsseldorf, 1989, pp.55-72.

F.Traxler, 'Gewerkschaften und Arbeitgeberverbände: Probleme der Verbandsbildung und Interessenvereinheitlichung', in W.Müller-Jentsch (ed), *Konfliktpartnerschaft. Akteure und Institutionen der industriellen Beziehungen*, Rainer Hampp Verlag, München und Mering, 1991, pp.139-165.

U.Widmaier & S.Blancke, 'The Politics of Radical Unemployment Policies in Germany', in H.Compston (ed), *The Politics of Unemployment. Radical Policy Initiatives in Western Europe*, Routledge, 1996 (forthcoming).

Barriers to Full Employment

Jonathan Tonge
University of Salford

'Barriers to Full Employment Policies in Britain:
Problems of Ideology, Institutions and Substitutions'

Abstract

This paper examines why the development of full unemployment policies in Britain has been beset by ideological and institutional difficulties in recent years. Ideological antipathy towards regulative labour market policies has ensured an unwillingness to impose schemes such as work-sharing upon employers or employees. Tripartite policy-making institutions have been dismantled and the Department of Employment has been merged within the Department of Education. This partly reflects the new orthodoxy in employment policy, centred upon the need for greater training. Employment policy in recent years has thus been characterised by the substitution of employment-centred goals with training-oriented approaches, developed increasingly within a work-welfare framework. Economic conditions have also mitigated against the development of radical policies, as expenditure on employment-generating activity has declined during recessions. Furthermore, the implementation of schemes such as work-sharing is more problematic in low-wage economies in Britain, because of its possible adverse effect upon incomes. This paper suggests that the use of training policy, characterised by voluntary employer participation, has acted as an inadequate conventional substitute for the development of more radical employment policies.

Acknowledgements

I wish to thank Hugh Compston, University of Wales, for his comments on an earlier draft. A revised version of this paper will appear as a chapter in H.Compston (ed), The New Politics of Unemployment: Radical Policy Initiatives in Western Europe, forthcoming.

Introduction

The merger of the Department of Employment with the Department of Education in July 1995 signalled the removal of the final institutional remnants of a pro- active employment policy. That the effective abolition of the Department of Employment came as little surprise is indicative of how the Department had become perceived as an anachronism, amounting to little more than a relic of the bygone era of state responsibility for employment generation. During the 1980s, the role of the Department switched from employment promotion to the management of training schemes. The devolution of such responsibility to training and enterprise councils in the 1990s removed this function.

Concurrently, a process of substitutionism has occurred, as 'employment' policy has increasingly become training policy, A new, largely bipartisan political consensus has emerged, emphasising the utility of training over other neglected aspects of employment policy. Similarly, a political consensus is emerging over the need for greater conditionality of unemployment benefit payments. Participation by the unemployed within training schemes has become compulsory within the youth labour market and it appears likely that benefit conditions will be placed upon the adult unemployed to ensure their involvement in training. Somewhat misleadingly, this process has been labelled 'workfare', although the opportunities offered to the unemployed, upon which benefits are increasingly dependent, are defined as training rather than work.

The Political Context

An abandonment of the commitment to full employment was signalled by the Conservative Party in 1979. Elected on a manifesto devoid of specific targets in respect of unemployment, the Conservative Government's pursuit of a deflationary macro-economic strategy enshrined the control of inflation, rather than the pursuit of reductions in unemployment, as the primary economic goal.

The electability of a government presiding over a high level of unemployment was clearly demonstrated in 1983, when the Conservative Government won despite an unemployment figure approaching three million. In that contest, the Conservative Party increased its number of seats held in the 200 constituencies with the highest rates of unemployment from 33 to 44 (Grant & Nath, 1984).

Electoral survey data has indicated the continuing salience of unemployment as an issue of public importance, with the issue rated as the second most urgent item confronting the electorate during the last general election (Crewe, 1993). However, the electoral durability of Conservative Governments presiding over high levels of joblessness appears to indicate the inability of unemployment to act as the decisive factor underpinning party choice. This inability, allied to the concurrence of economic growth and high unemployment, has impaired the development of radical unemployment policies in Britain. Caution rather than radicalism has characterised employment options, although alternatives have nonetheless been preferred which reject the notion of a permanent 'acceptable' level of unemployment.

Unemployment in Britain

Unemployment in Britain between 1945 and the mid-1960s averaged only 400,000 or 1.8% of the workforce annually (Glynn, 1991). The curbing of unemployment dominated economic goals, a situation unchanged as unemployment rose to 900,000 by 1972. During that year the Conservative Government, under Edward Heath, confirmed the salience of unemployment as an economic indicator, by reflating the economy in an attempt to ensure that the total of jobless did not reach the politically sensitive figure of one million.

The trebling of unemployment to three million during the first three years of the Thatcher Government elected in 1979 was not primarily a repudiation of specific supply-side, micro-economic measures aimed at reducing unemployment. Initially at least, the approach of the Conservative Government represented an attack upon previous macro-economic reflationary responses to increases in the numbers out of work. A refusal to reflate the economy characterised governmental responses during the 1970-82 and 1990-93 recessions. Supply-side measures were partly based upon the perception that labour market rigidities, heightened by the activities of trade unions, were detrimental to economic and employment growth. Accordingly, a series of restrictions were placed upon trade unions, through legislation passed in 1980, 1982, 1984, 1988, 1992 and 1993.

Debate over the true extent of unemployment also impairs the development of radical combative policies. Over thirty changes to the method of counting the unemployed were made between 1979 to 1994, all except one reducing the unemployment register. As examples most non-working married women and unemployed males over 60 do not appear in the count. There has developed a politics of the unemployment statistics in which it is argued that the official jobless count underestimates the true extent of unemployment by nearly one million (Glynn, 1991). This uncertainty, allied to the successful application of 'scrounger' perceptions towards a section of the unemployed, has impaired the creation of any populist 'back to work' campaigns. Indeed the response of the unemployed has been far more muted than during the previous era of mass unemployment in the 1930s, as unemployed activity has moved from protest to acquiesence (Bagguley, 1991).

Until the announcement of its merger with the Department of Education, the Department of Employment was responsible for the development of labour market policy. The department also undertook the count of unemployed claimants. Financial allocations to the department were determined annually by the Treasury. Post-merger, responsibility for training, the labour market, employment and equal opportunities has been transferred to the newly-titled Department for Education and Employment, whilst the Central Statistical Office now produces employment statistics, including the monthly unemployment figures. Until 1990, employment and training schemes were run by the Manpower Services Commission (MSC) followed by the Training Commission, under the direction of the Department of Employment. Subsequently, responsibility for training the unemployed has been devolved to a network of 82 local, employer-led Training and Enterprise Councils (TECs) or Local Enterprise Companies (LECs) in Scotland. The TECs are formally accountable only to the Secretary of State for Employment (Tonge, 1993).

Stress upon the importance of training provides the new orthodoxy in

British employment policy, to an extent unseen since the mid-1960s when Industrial Training Boards (ITBs) were established by the Labour Government to improve skills training. Both the ITBs and the MSC (created in 1973) were tripartite bodies, established during a period in which employment policy was characterised by a modest veering towards neo-corporatism (Farnham & Lupton, 1994). Employment, training and labour market policies have since been government-dominated and based upon the 'empowerment of employers' (King, 1993).

Current unemployment policies

Within this restricted policy arena, employment policy has frequently been characterised by its lack of radicalism. Table 1 lists current unemployment policies.

Table 1
Unemployment Policies in Britain 1995

Policy	Policy Target
Work Training Schemes	All unemployed
Work Experience Schemes	Long-term unemployed
Childcare Assistance	Unemployed with children
Jobfinder Grants	Unemployed for two years+
Employer Incentives (for instance, direct payments to employers)	Long-term unemployed
Part-Time Workers Assistance	Long-term unemployed: 'top-up' payments if accepting a part-time job
Work Trials (Employment offered to the long-term unemployed, without contractual obligation)	Long-term unemployed

Although there thus exists a seeming plethora of employment measures, many of the above initiatives, other than training schemes, have been implemented on a trial basis only, involving only a small number of (usually 3-4) TECs. Treasury resistance to their extension remains problematic, a feature scarcely likely to be assisted by the absorbtion of the Department of Employment within a department interested in raising finance for much broader purposes.

Work training schemes are combined in a Training for Work package which displaced the previous Employment Training programme. A Youth Training programme provides training for 16-18 year olds, although fewer than half its trainees were in full time employment six months after leaving the scheme (*Hansard*, PQ, 7.7.95). Schemes of direct work experience without training were common during the first recent period of high unemployment in the 1980s, via the community programme. The Community Action scheme, involving 40,000 work placements, amounts to an attempt to combine work experience with job training. This current work experience scheme does not provide renumeration at market rates, with participants receiving their benefit plus £10 per week.

The replacement of unemployment benefit by jobseekers allowance heightens the condition that state support is dependent upon the unemployed 'actively seeking work'. The unemployed enter a 'jobseeker agreement' prior to the award of benefit. The benefit system has also been reshaped slightly in an attempt to assist those in work. Since July 1995, additional family credit has been payable to recipients taking a job of 30 hours or more weekly.

Little central state direction has been forthcoming in the promotion of childcare arrangements. Instead, the voluntary, business-led *Employers for Childcare*, with 31 large member companies, has been encouraged to promote better childcare arrangements, in conjunction with TECs (*Employment News*, October 1994). However, recent employment policy statements have indicated a switch towards work incentives for the childless, who comprise two-thirds of the long-term unemployed (Budget Statement, *Hansard*, 29.11.94). Finally, the jobfinder grant scheme is designed to assist employment prospects by facilitating greater labour mobility. Lump sum payments are provided for those out of work for the previous two years upon their return to work. Up to 25,000 grants averaging £200 each have been allocated for the scheme, at a cost of £5m annually.

Deregulatory measures have formed the major component of employment policy, with ideological support backed by a specific series of legislative measures initiated by successive Secretaries of Sate for Employment. Often aimed at curbing trade union-based influence, these Acts also reversed the major areas of employment legislation created by the Labour Government during the 1970s (Beharell, 1992). Thus the Employment Protection Act 1975 was partly neutered by the Employment Act of 1980 whilst the 1993 Trade Union and Employment Rights Acts abolished wages councils and their power to determine minimum levels of pay. The insistence of the Minister of State for Employment that 'terms and conditions of employment... are a matter for employers and employees to decide' has characterised the government's approach, with the opt-out from the social chapter providing a further indication (Michael Forsyth, *Hansard*, PQ, 5.7.95). Recently, the aim has been to create 'a bonfire of red tape' (*Employment News*, March 1994). The *Deregulation and Contracting Out Act, 1994*, was designed to effect this, whilst the Department of Trade and Industry has created a Deregulation Task Force designed to foster deregulation initiatives.

Employer incentives to hire the unemployed have increased steadily in recent years. For employers willing to hire a person unemployed two years or more, a national insurance 'holiday' has been created, in that the employer receives a full state rebate on the employer insurance contributions due for that worker for the opening year of employment. This development follows increased pressure from employer organisations, such as the Engineering Employers Federation, for such contribution exemptions, which are estimated to save employers £300 per employee (*Financial Times*, 30.11.94). The annual cost to the Treasury is estimated at £45m. For the Conservative Government, national insurance reductions represent an ideologically acceptable form of job creation, compatible with its belief that reductions in the overall burden of taxation upon employers are the most appropriate means of generating employment growth. It should be noted however, that there is cross-party consensus concerning the usefulness of national insurance holidays.

Seemingly less ideologically compatible are the small employer subsidy operations that have been exercised in recent years. The Conservative Government implemented the New Works Scheme in 1986, in which employers were given a subsidy for each unemployed 18-20 year old taken into employment. The subsidy amounted to a maximum of £20 per youth and was payable only to employers taking on workers at a rate below £65 weekly. Accordingly, the scheme was seen by critics as primarily an attempt to depress wages within the youth labour market. Since June 1993, the workstart scheme has been in operation in pilot sectors of the adult employment market, based initially in East Kent, parts of London, Devon and Cornwall and Tyneside. Under this scheme, employers recruiting workers unemployed for two years or more (four in London) receive a subsidy of £60 per week per recruit for the first 26 weeks, followed by £30 per week for the next 26 weeks, up to an annual total of £2,430. Responsibility for management of the scheme has rested with the Employment Service or, in one instance, the local TEC. The scope of the scheme has been modest, with 1,474 unemployed persons assisted in the first 18 months of operation, although an extension to 5,000 subsidies was announced in the November 1994 Budget.

Part-time workers assistance has developed in recognition that progress through secondary labour markets may be required for entry into the primary market. Under the Jobmatch pilot scheme, individuals out for work for two years or more are paid a weekly allowance of £50 for six months when they accept a part-time job. The unemployed are matched to part-time jobs by TECs. Government intentions appear to be to develop part-time jobs as 'a stepping-stone to full-time work' (*Employment News*, January 1995). TECs, as policy deliverers, believe that the acquisition of sufficient part- time jobs to act as a substitute for full-time employment is a viable approach (*Financial Times*, 30.11.94). The scope of the scheme is small, offering 3,000 such jobmatches in each of the three years 1995-96 to 1997-98. The recognition of the growth of part-time work is belated. Part-time employment actually grew faster during the 1970s than in the 1980s (TUC, 1991).

Work trials have been based upon the idea of 'selling' the unemployed to employers, whilst attracting the unemployed into work. Employers can take on people who have been unemployed for six months or more for a trial period of up to three weeks, without incurring costs, in an attempt to assess their suitability. The unemployed continue to receive their benefit during this period and may quit the job without benefit sanction. The scheme enjoys cross-party consensus and support from employer and claimant pressure groups and is being trebled in scope to cover 60,000 unemployed people by 1998.

Only a modest degree of local interventionism has developed as a policy response to unemployment. Central government remains the dominant actor in the initiation of ostensibly localist measures. However, the City Challenge Grant scheme allows local authorities to compete for funds to assist economic growth in an area. 31 central-local partnerships, based upon five-year regeneration programmes, have been created under City Challenge. Local authorities compete with private sector developers for funding. In Scotland, the fusion of the work of the Scottish Development Agency and the Training Commission in the late 1980s signalled a slight switch towards the use of local initiatives (Moore & Richardson, 1989). Such a development has been fostered by LECs, although, here, as elsewhere in Britain, debate surrounds the most appropriate set of institutional arrangements for local interventionism. Furthermore, there has been little advocacy of largescale regional approaches to curing unemployment, most common during the 1960s with the funding of assisted areas and the use of measures such as regional employment premiums.

The absence of job-creation measures

Arguably the most striking feature of the unemployment policies described above is what is not present. There are no state-sponsored schemes to reduce working hours, share jobs or introduce sabbatical leave. The Job Release Scheme introduced in 1977 was designed to encourage early retirement with replacements from the unemployed register. However, restriction of the scheme's retirees to individuals extremely close to retirement produced only a very marginal effect (Driver, 1987). The lack of radicalism in British unemployment policy has ensured that tentative pilot schemes, lacking comprehensive coverage, have characterised policy output. In explaining why, the particular balance of forces at the national level requires consideration. These include, amongst other items, current ideological direction, political and academic orthodoxies, the balance of power between political actors and the particular strengths of institutions shaping employment policies. Such balances may be influenced by levels of unemployment, the success or otherwise of particular employment policies elsewhere and the electoral salience of unemployment.

Employment policy is devoid of specific policies in respect of work-sharing. One idea in respect of helping reduce standard working time has been that the benefit system be overhauled to reflect the switch towards part-time employment. A recommendation of the Borrie Commission on Social Justice in 1994 was that a new part-time workers benefit should be introduced (Commission for Social Justice, 1994). This would allow greater proportions of other benefits to be retained in the event of part-time work being undertaken, ensuring that those undertaking such employment should be able to maintain a reasonable level of income per head. Present regulations are seen as a deterrent to part-time employment, participation in which has a punitive impact upon social security benefit. The Borrie Commission provided a redefinition of the commitment to full employment, supporting the principle but emphasising its attainment through part-time work, work-sharing and short-term contracts. These measures, allied to early retirement, are seen as the optimum solution to increasing output and employment.

The absence of proposals for work-sharing is perhaps the most glaring omission from employment policy in Britain. Suggestions to reduce unemployment by shortening the working week have been actively resisted by the Conservative Government on the grounds of their potential to reduce output and increase costs to industry. Britain's opt-out from the EU social chapter formed part of a defence of autonomy over working hours. There are no formal barriers to the instigation of a work-sharing scheme in Britain. Equally, however, government antipathy towards business regulation ensures that there is no prospect of enforcement, or even financial inducement, for such a programme. A lack of government activism concerning work-sharing is reinforced by employer hostility, labour organisation indifference and academic scepticism.

As Cripps & Ward argue, the problem associated with work-sharing is not so much how to redistribute work, but instead how to achieve the redistribution of income necessary as part of any plan (Cripps & Ward, 1994). Work-sharing is somewhat easier to implement in high income countries. In low wage economies such as that in Britain, it is more difficult to construct any populist agenda based upon the idea. Only Italy has a lower benefits to average wages rate amongst EU countries. Accordingly, any work-sharing proposal which created reliance upon payments on non-working days is unlikely to gain popular support (Layard & Philpott, 1991).

Trade union ambitions have been directed not towards work-sharing, but instead aimed at reductions in the working week without financial disadvantage. The defence of individual income conducted by citizens and representative labour organisations makes work-sharing a distant prospect. Fear of inadequate income generated by part-time employment provides an important attitudinal barrier, with only 20% of employed males willing to consider part-time work as an adequate replacement for current full-time employment (Burchell et al, 1994). Indeed, in a low-income economy such as Britain, the preference for more pay rather than shorter hours has been a persistent trend, in contrast to the situation found in, for example, Denmark and the Netherlands (Driver, 1987).

The political right suggest that compulsory work-sharing is economically damaging. Lack of support amongst the employed means that without compulsion, work-sharing would be ineffective. The centre and left fear that part-time work, without concomitant employee protection measures, increases the casualisation of labour, ensuring greater long-term vulnerability for the workforce.

Treasury opposition to work-sharing has been based upon three contentions. Firstly, there is likely to be a loss of competitiveness. Secondly, any scheme would be costly to implement, whilst increasing the marginal costs of labour. Thirdly, the Treasury has accepted the view of those economists who maintain that work-sharing is not a cure for unemployment, as it rests upon what Layard describes as the 'lump of output' fallacy (Layard, 1986, p.157). Output is not given, therefore there is no measurable amount of work that can be divided upon a more equitable basis amongst the workforce. The favoured solution therefore is to increase output and employment, by increasing demand for output through fiscal means. The Treasury has been a willing player in the subordination of a specific unemployment policy to a broader deflationary strategy. Since the demise of the Temporary Short-time Working Compensation Scheme in March 1984, a measure designed to prevent redundancies through work-sharing, there has been an absence of state attempts to utilise work-sharing to broaden the quantitative extent of employment.

The Institutional Framework

Important barriers to the development of radical unemployment policies are provided by the institutional arrangements for employment policy-making. The Department of Employment had traditionally been seen as a lower-order ministry, with its abolition long threatened prior to its absorbtion into the Department for Education and Employment in 1995. The conclusion of trade union reforms ended the Department's specific labour market role. Throughout the 1980s and 1990s, the Department was not seen as a job-creator. At best, its role was a labour market facilitator, responsible for the removal of perceived barriers to full employment. The Department of Employment was active in shifting the balance of power in labour relations decisively towards employers.

In achieving this, the last vestiges of corporatist employment policy formulation were removed during the 1980s. The replacement of the tripartite Manpower Services Commission by the Training Commission diminished trade union influence. TUC opposition to the implementation of the Employment Training Scheme in 1988 led to the abolition of the nominally tripartite Commission. The TUC opposed the scheme on the grounds that it did little to retrain the unemployed and paid only £10 above benefit levels, amounting to a form of cheap labour. Such opposition led to the transfer of the functions of the Commission to the Secretary of State for Employment. Ostensibly, this narrowing of the employment policy network concentrated great powers with the Employment Department. However, the department proved persistently vulnerable to Treasury desires for reductions in the funding of training and employment programmes, particularly during the 1990-92 recession. These reductions were criticised by employer organisations such as the Confederation of British Industry, which condemned the 'hand-to-mouth' existence of TECs (Banham, 1992).

The Dominance of Training Policy

In addition to institutional barriers to the development of radical unemployment policies, differing policy objectives have also had a negative impact. During the early 1980s, proactive employment policy, extending beyond the removal of alleged barriers to employment, largely comprised temporary work experience schemes, known as the Community Programme. These amounted to temporary public works schemes which were abandoned due to their prohibitive cost. Their replacements were training schemes, such as Employment Training, which reduced the unemployment count but achieved mediocre long-term results.

The extension of training schemes heralded the current orthodoxy in employment policy, centred upon the need to retrain the unemployed, as part of a 'skills revolution' (Department of Employment, 1988). Alongside the recurring theme of deregulation, training has become *the* instrument of employment policy, to the virtual exclusion of other supply-side measures. Changed institutional arrangements have reflected this new orthodoxy, with responsibility for training the unemployed now devolved to the creation of a local employer-led network of Training and Enterprise Councils. As Farnham & Lupton (1994) argue, the establishment of TECs represents an attempt to privatise and decentralise Britain's unemployment problem.

Political consensus over the need for training solutions to unemployment has been evident, based upon the belief in the significance of skills shortages. Specific training levies have been advocated by the Labour Party, amounting to 1% of the profits of selected companies, as part of a £900m training and employment package offered during the 1992 General Election. A similar solution has been offered by the Liberal Democrats, advocating collection of a training levy of 2% of company payrolls through the tax system. Proceeds would be hypothecated to training and allocated through regional governments to employer organisations. Outside political parties, consensus over the need for training is not total. On the right, The Institute of Economic Affairs rejects the economic utility of training (Institute of Economic Affairs, 1992). Indeed the New Right is far from united in its outlook upon the need for skills training (Evans, 1994). A thinktank of the left, the Institute for Public Policy Research, believes that cyclical recovery and full employment can occur despite skills shortages (Haskell & Martin, 1994). Amongst employers, only 2% of CBI firms reported skills shortages in 1992 (*The Times*, 8.9.94).

Governmental acceptance of the need for the retraining of the unemployed has however been characterised by the political and institutional arrangements which inhibit the development of radical unemployment policies. Henley and Tsakalotos (1995) suggest that corporatist modes of interest mediation permit the development of alternatives to the acceptance of unemployment as a crude anti-inflationary device. In Britain, the absence of such political arrangements acts against the coordination and comprehensivity of employment policy. Indeed the creation of the TEC network possesses the features of voluntarism and state detachment which characterise the broader policy arena. Participation by employers within the activities of TECs remains voluntary. Reluctance to impose employment policies upon TECs is based upon opposition from such bodies, on the grounds that compulsion does not equate to commitment. Furthermore, there is ideological antipathy to the creation of an alleged training bureaucracy.

Accordingly, there has developed a two-tier approach to employment policy. This is based upon a self-regulative institutional sphere, in which employer participation, TEC composition and innovation are self-determined at the local level. Such arrangements are juxtaposed with regulative approaches in, firstly, the financing of activity, which remains highly contingent upon national economic conditions and, secondly, in relation to the participation of the unemployed, in an increasingly work-welfare system (King,

1995). The latter feature has ensured a lack of support for aspects of the retraining programme, exemplified by the opposition of the TUC to aspects of the *Training for Work* programme (TUC, 1993) Allied to such criticisms is opposition to the use of training as a form of substitutionism, acting as a replacement for the development of more dynamic employment policies. Overall barriers to the development of radical policies are summarised in table 2.

Table 2
Constraints upon the Development of Radical Unemployment Policies in Britain

Level	Nature of Constraint
Ideological	New right conservative commitment to free economy; anti-interventionist approach
Economic	Hostility to Keynesian reflationary approach (now cross-party); dominance of supply-side Treasury opposition to pervasiveness of radical policies due to financial costs
Political	New orthodoxy centred upon training. Lack of electoral salience. Abandonment of full employment commitments. Debate over extent of unemployment
Institutional	Absence of specific department for employment. Employer domination of TECs. Non-existence of corporatist frameworks. Voluntarism of participatory arrangements

The Piloting of Radical Measures

Given the constraints upon the development of policies designed to restore full employment, how is the recent development of some such measures explained? Employer incentives and deregulation have been measures universally applied within the labour market. Both have the support of the main actors – government department; Treasury; employer organisations and TECs – within the employment policy arena. Either measure accords with the ideological direction of the government and its belief that relief of non-wage costs will facilitate employment growth. Furthermore, national insurance relief is a low-cost employment policy for the Treasury. There remains doubt over the extent to which such relief will reduce unemployment. Employers' national insurance for workers earning less than £200 is less than £10 per week. As these low-wage jobs are the type likely to be offered to the unemployed, reductions in national insurance may make little difference to employers' recruitment decisions.

The other radical policies adopted thus far have been introduced only on a localised basis. In part, this reflects the new policy-delivery arena, which, through the introduction of TECs, allows a local focus and a small measure of area innovation. For example, the introduction of the jobmatch scheme designed to help workers into part-time employment as a 'stepping-stone' to full-time work followed an experiment conducted by Lincolnshire TEC.

Furthermore, employment policies have become somewhat more radical in recent years, with the embryonic development of wage subsidies providing one example.

Indeed the former Employment Department appeared to endorse the findings of the Institute of Employment Studies which suggested that the 'Workstart' pilot subsidy programme had made a substantial difference to employment recruitment patterns. The IES found that nearly half of employers participating in the scheme would not have recruited workers without the available subsidy (IES, 1995). However, the universal adoption of such schemes is opposed by the Treasury on grounds of cost. Academic arguments that subsidy schemes could be self-financing through insurance and taxation gains have not yet held sway (Snower, 1993).

Conclusion

Few formal barriers to the development of radical unemployment policies exist in Britain. Indeed, 'flexible legalism' allows frequent changes in employment policy compared to countries such as Germany (Rose & Page, 1990, p.77). Measures can be enacted rapidly by the relevant department and given *post-hoc* legitimacy through subsequent legislation. This explains the ease why a plethora of training and employment schemes have developed and indicates how tripartite policy-making structures were so quickly dismantled.

If an absence of constitutional impediments provides a promising legislative framework for the development of radical unemployment policies, their formulation will now occur without ideological and institutional changes. In respect of the former, neo-liberal principles have been applied in that there has been state disengagement from direct responsibilty for the unemployed. A first principle underpinning the development of radical unemployment policies needs to be a reacceptance of the political and social imperative of a commitment to full employment. As Grieve-Smith (1992) declares, full employment needs to be seen as a concept no more outdated than universal suffrage. On this basis, policies can be adopted on a cost-benefit basis. A second requirement is the development of a consensus over the measurement of unemployment. There remains no guarantee that the use of different counting methods showing an alternative unemployment figure of 4 million will heighten the development of radical unemployment policies (Wells, 1995). However, statistical agreement will prevent diversion of employment solutions towards debate over the true extent of the problem.

Certainly there has been a shift away from the absolutist ideological and economic beliefs of the early 1980s. Crude monetarism has long been displaced, whilst a broader range of employment policies is utilised at the micro-level. However, the new orthodoxy that comprehensive training policy, allied to greater benefit conditionality, are the optimum solutions to Britain's employment problem has impaired the search for radical unemployment policies which could be used in conjunction. Current 'employment' policy has thus been summarised as 'the creation of a neo-liberal training regime in which employer-led training directs policy to problems of labour market disincentives and rigidities and to the short-term political need of reducing unemployment and away from the realisation of full employment'. (King, 1993, p.235).

There remains little prospect of a return to the tripartite institutional arrangements which formerly characterised employment policy-making. Trade union representatives form only 5% of the board memberships of TECs. However, this need not preclude the development of radical policies. Indeed, the conservatism of trade unions did little to assist such ideas as work-sharing, persistently favouring early retirement as the most appropriate, minimalist form of such a measure. Work-sharing policies may need to be developed via a 'snowball' effect at local or sectoral levels prior to their national application. Pilot schemes can encourage work and income sharing, but employee participants may require financial inducement.

Recent changes in institutional arrangements offer a limited scope for radicalism in employment policy. Devolution of policy-delivery to TECs may be followed by greater autonomy in policy-making. However, given that TECs possess no compulsory powers over employers, local employers may simply reject schemes such as work-sharing. There remains no guarantee that the activities or composition of a TEC accurately reflect the local labour market. Greater employee participation is required if radical employment policies are to be fostered, although the TECs may be useful in promoting local interventionism as a means of employment growth. Finally, the development of radical employment policies requires the creation of a powerful, single employment department to promote such schemes. The British experience has been precisely the reverse.

References

P.Bagguley, *From Protest to Acquiesence? Political Movements of the Unemployed*, Macmillan, 1991.

J.Banham, 'Taking forward the skills revolution', *Policy Studies*, 13/1, 1992

A.Beharell, *Unemployment and Job Creation*, Macmillan, 1992.

B.Burchell et al, 'Perceptions of the Labour Market: An Investigation of Differences by Gender and by Working-Time', in J.Rubery & F.Wilkinson (eds), *Employer Strategy and the Labour Market*, Oxford University Press, 1994.

Commission for Social Justice, *Strategies for National Renewal*, CSJ, 1994.

I.Crewe, 'Voting and the Electorate', in P.Dunleavy et al (eds), *Developments in British Politics 4*, Macmillan, 1993.

F.Cripps & T.Ward, 'Strategies for Growth and Employment in the European Community', in J.Michie, & J.Grieve-Smith (eds), *Unemployment in Europe*, Academic Press, 1994.

Department of Employment, *Employment for the 1990s*, Cmnd 540, HMSO, 1988.

C.Driver, *Towards Full Employment: a policy appraisal*, Routledge & Kegan Paul, 1987.

B.Evans, 'Neo-liberalism and Training Policy 1979-92: a Rejoinder to Desmond King', *Political Studies*, 42/3, 1994.

D.Farnham & C.Lupton, 'Employment Relations and Training Policy', in S.Savage et al (eds), *Public Policy in Britain*, Macmillan, 1994.

S.Glynn, *No Alternative? Unemployment in Britain*, Faber & Faber, 1991.

W.Grant & S.Nath, *The Politics of Economic Policy-Making*, Blackwell, 1984.

J.Grieve-Smith, *Full Employment in the 1990s*, Institute of Public Policy Research, , 1992.

J.Haskell & C.Martin, 'Will low skills kill recovery?', *New Economy*, Autumn, 1994.

A.Henley & E.Tsakalotos, 'Unemployment experiences and the institutional preconditions for full employment', in P.Arestis & M.Marshall (eds), *The Political Economy of Full Employment*, Edward Elgar, 1995.

Institute of Economic Affairs, *Training Too Much? A Sceptical Look at the Economics of Skill Provision*, IEA, 1992.

Institute of Employment Studies, *Evaluation of Workstart Pilots*, Institute of Employment Studies Report 279, 1995.

D.King, 'The Conservatives and Training Policy 1979-1992: from a Tripartite to a Neoliberal Regime', *Political Studies*, XLI/2, 1993.

D.King, *Actively Seeking Work? The Politics of Unemployment and Welfare Policy in the United States and Great Britain*, University of Chicago Press, 1995.

R.Layard, *How to beat Unemployment*, Oxford University Press, 1986.

R.Layard & C.Philpott, *Stopping Unemployment*, Employment Institute, 1991.

C.Moore & J.Richardson, *Local Partnership and the unemployment crisis in Britain*, Unwin Hyman, 1989.

R.Rose & E.Page, 'Action in Adversity: Responses to Unemployment in Britain and Germany', *West European Politics*, 13/4, 1990.

D.Snower, *The Future of the Welfare State*, CEPR, 1993.

J.Tonge, 'Training and Enterprise Councils: the privatisation of Britain's unemployment problem?', *Capital and Class*, 51, 1993.

Trade Union Congress, *Winning a better deal for part-time workers*, TUC information paper, 1991.

Trade Union Congress, *TUC Unified Budget Submission 1993*, TUC, 1993.

J.Wells, 'Unemployment, job creation and job destruction in the UK since 1979', in P.Arestis & M.Marshall (eds), *The Political Economy of Full Employment*, Edward Elgar, 1995.

T.Wilson, *Unemployment and the Labour Market*, Institute of Economic Affairs, 1987.

Ideology, Hegemony and Political Subjectivity

Glyn Daly
Manchester Metropolitan University

'Who Stole Great Britain?
Ideology and Nationalism in Psychoanalytic Theory'

Introduction

In every attempt to command the social terrain – to create an antagonism-free new order – various culprits are identified and made responsible for the original loss, or theft, of the fantastical object: Society, Harmony, Salvation, etc. Indeed the very construction(s) of the social might be understood as a never-ending attempt to solve the original crime: to identify who has possession of the lost signs which would complete 'us'.

In this respect the power of ideology is not that it reflects, or conceals, something more solid – economic interests, human nature, etc – but rather that it conceals an ephemera: an existential void. Thus ideology subsists in the fantasy of suturing the unsuturable by providing straw enemies – 'fictional' embodiments of a transcendental lack – which 'if only they could be gotten rid of' would enable the realisation of the holistic dream. The Lacanian perspective on ideology, therefore, is one which identifies its tautological character. As Žižek puts it, 'the real goal (of ideology) is the consistency of the ideological attitude itself'.[1] In this way, ideology provides a fantastical solidity against the distorting presence of the unrepresentable (the Real).

If ideology reveals any 'substance' at work it might be said to be the *jouissance*, or enjoyment, of tautology. This idea is elaborated by Žižek in respect to the constitution of nationhood:

> 'The element which holds together a given community cannot be reduced to the point of symbolic identification: the bond linking together its members always implies a shared relationship toward a Thing, toward enjoyment incarnated ... .If we are asked how we can recognise the presence of this Thing, the only consistent answer is that the Thing is present in that elusive entity called our 'way of life'. All we can do is enumerate disconnected fragments of the way our community organizes its feasts, its rituals of mating, its initiation ceremonies, in short, all the details by which is made visible the unique way a community organizes its enjoyment'.[2]

The Nation as a *jouissance*-Thing (a thing of enjoyment), cannot finally be explained or represented within the nationalist discourse. The latter, however, constantly alludes to the Thing – underlines its existence – and 'promises' that with one more sign it can fully represent it to us. The Thing,

---
[1] S.Žižek, *The Sublime Object of Ideology*, 1989, p.84.
[2] S.Žižek, *Tarrying With the Negative*, 1993, p.201.

therefore, may be regarded as a lost sign (an elusive treasure) which has to be found in the Real and which drives the symbolic-fantasy process to secure its impossible representation. To this effect, the Thing is located at a point at which the meaning(s) of the nationalist discourse collapses in upon itself – and thereby shows its tautological character – and, so to speak, reveals the surplus enjoyment in the act of inscription itself.

In this regard, Žižek is critical of the perspective of deconstruction and its attempt to 'dissolve every substantial identity into a network of non-substantial, differential relations' (1989, p.72). In respect to the nation, for example, Žižek argues that such an emphasis 'overlooks the remainder of some real, non-discursive kernel of enjoyment which must be present for the Nation qua discursive entity-effect to achieve its ontological consistency' (1993, p.202).

Taking up the argument of Jacques-Alain Miller,[3] Žižek reminds us that it is the defensive posture taken in regard to the Thing which is at the root of racism and national antagonisms:

> 'What is at stake in ethnic tensions is always the possession of the National Thing. We always impute to the 'other' an excessive enjoyment: he wants to steal our enjoyment (by ruining our way of life) and/or he has access to some secret perverse enjoyment. In short what really bothers us about the 'other' is the peculiar way he organises his enjoyment, precisely the surplus, the 'excess' that pertains to this way: the smell of 'their' food, 'their' noisy songs and dances, 'their' attitude to work. To the racist, the 'other' is either a workaholic stealing our jobs or an idler living on our labour ... The basic paradox is that our Thing is conceived as something inaccessible to the other and at the same time threatened by him' (1993, pp.202-203).

The 'other', who can never be like us and is permanently excluded from sharing our Thing, nevertheless wants to steal our special stuff: to dilute, or in Thatcher's words, to 'swamp' It. The central paradox is that '(w)hat we conceal by imputing to the Other the theft of enjoyment is the traumatic fact that we never possessed what was allegedly stolen from us' (1993, p.203)

The threat by the other is not simply that she presumes to raid the lost signs of our enjoyment, but also that the very existence of the other's enjoyment perturbs and fascinates us. In particular, it is the sexual enjoyment of the other which is most worrying and fascinating. On the one hand, this manifests itself in the fear/allure of abandoning oneself (racial identity, sexual identity, social responsibility, etc) to the mysterious enjoyment of the other – the well known themes of potent blacks, fornicating Jews, exotic Orientals, over-sexed lesbians and gays (etc). At another level this manifests itself in the fear of the reproductive capacities of the other and their 'demographic time-bomb' (Catholics, Moslems, Blacks, Palestinians, etc.).

Steven Spielberg's *Jurassic Park* is instructive. In the film, Richard Attenborough's showman has re-animated dinosaurs from their state of fossilisation to place them in the ultimate theme park (the symbolic). And then

---

[3] *Extemité*, unpublished lecture, 1985.

one dark night the dinosaurs break out (the return of the Real). The revelatory horror, however, is that despite all the best available technological expertise and methods in controlling sexual reproduction, the dinosaurs – as embodiments of the wild untamable *jouissance* of nature – find a way to reproduce themselves independently of 'us'. This presents a much deeper threat against which the universal prototypical (white) family is constituted as the guardians of 'our' enjoyment. The paradoxical message of the film might be: 'not only are dinosaurs extinct, you can't even trust them!' And this, of course, is directly homologous with numerous racist sentiments of the type: 'not only are blacks inferior, they threaten the dissolution of our entire way of life'.

It is this paranoia in the attempt to regulate/suppress the 'surplus' enjoyment of the (reproducing) other which drives ethnic antagonisms and is simultaneously fueled by it. In one of its more extreme forms, it is revealed in the systematic rape of Moslem women in ex-Yugoslavia. Not only does this rape take away the woman's dignity and her sense of herself[4] it also involves a more general theft of the sexual/reproductive enjoyment of the Moslem community as such. Rape in this sense becomes an intrusion into, and defilement of, the very 'source' of the other's enjoyment (rape as pillage): 'how can they enjoy themselves after this?' This calculation is an annihilation beyond rape/death: a shattering of a community's enjoyment so that it cannot re-make itself.

On this last point we would argue that Žižek has not paid sufficient attention to the way in which national communities are not only defensive in relation to their Thing but are also active in attempting to colonise the hidden signs of the other. In this regard, we might say that the Thing is not only a tautological distillation of incorporeal enjoyment, it also makes a gesture to the 'universal' (again revealing a constant political play between the particular and the universal). The manifestations of the Thing are paradoxically evangelical: 'our civilisation is a universal good, but you can never fully imitate or be fully part of it'. The Thing, therefore, also involves a kind of directive to bear witness, to go forth and colonise (the hidden signs) by providing 'us' with a superior 'passport'. This passport from the Thing ('I'm an American!') has not only functioned as a literal licence to explore, discover, convert and colonise but is also evident in the contemporary explosion of 'cultural tourism' – the consumption of what is of real/authentic value in the various (ancient/ecological/thematic) regions of the world even though this may be hidden from, or unappreciated by, the inhabitants themselves (they cannot enjoy their Thing as much as we can because of our Thing: civilisation, sophistication, knowledge, sensibility, etc). The other cannot penetrate/consume our Thing because they have inferior, or 'literal' passports. Indeed, many black people in Britain have experienced the frustration of not possessing the real/magical passport behind the British passport (they are frequently asked to produce their passports precisely because 'we know they don't possess the real passport').

A relevant example of the process of symbolic colonisation is afforded in the well known tale of Rumpelstiltskin. In this tale we have the figure of

---

[4] see R.Salecl in E.Laclau, *The Making of Political Identities*, 1994.

an excluded other – a dwarf – who is able to spin gold out of straw for an aspiring princess (in this sense the dwarf may be considered to represent immigrant labour). However, in exchange for this service the princess must give up her first-born child to him. Immediately we see the threat posed by the dwarf's surplus enjoyment – what does he want with the child? what is his desire? (this is the Lacanian *Che Vuoi?*) – which again insinuates itself in the domain of sexuality/reproduction. In the nick of time, however, the princess discovers his real name – the hidden sign which is the source of his power and enjoyment: his essential *jouissance*-Thing – and the threat of the desirous other is vanquished as the dwarf, in an act of symbolic castration, pulls off his leg in rage and disappears into the distance

What we see in this tale, therefore, is a process of colonising the hidden sign of the other and of re-presenting the other in a way which becomes acceptable to 'us' (that is, devoid of threat). This, of course, is the shamanism at the root of racist name-calling: identifying the inferior reality of 'their' forms of enjoyment. Representation, in this sense, may be seen as a form of symbolic 'castration' in attempting to dissolve the power of the other (and, more generally, the power of the Real: to 'castrate' the original 'castration' of the Real itself). In this way, the other is reduced to an ontological description, devoid of the power of metaphor and unable to describe 'us'.

The racist paradox, however, is that we must be constantly vigilant against the impotency and inferiority of the other. This again is illustrated in *Jurassic Park* (and much of the horror genre) where fossilisation (acceptable representation) is, in fact, a dormant menace: 'just when you thought they were a fossil they are at their most dangerous'. What if Rumpelstiltskin returns (like Freddie Krueger) with a new secret sign which re-animates the threat of his surplus enjoyment?

This also reveals the original 'impotence' of representation: the more it identifies (castrates) the more impotent it becomes; the more it tries to establish a total representation the more it fears it has not done so (this is why totalitarian regimes tend to collapse under the weight of their own paranoia: they cannot achieve Totalitarianism and the paranoia eventually 'produces' the threat (dissent, etc) they fear most). And indeed reality itself may be considered a kind of collective 'madness' in which we are always a signifier short of a full representation.[5]

The Decline of Britain

What is missing in many of the more familiar debates about 'decline' is a consideration of its phantasmic dimension and the way in which it has been variously politicised, particularly in the constitution of 'the nation'. Here psychoanalytic theory can make a positive contribution.

The themes of theft and enjoyment are clearly visible in the reactivation of British nationalism from the 1960s onwards. After the trauma of the Suez crisis, continuing economic decline and the corresponding (and unthinkable) rise of European and other foreign countries – particularly those 'who had

---

[5] That is to say, it is driven in its attempt to represent the unrepresentable: the impenetrable *jouissance* of the beyond of reality.

lost the war' (Japan and Germany), those 'who had been rescued by us' (France and Western Europe), or those 'who had not suffered like we had' (the USA) – Britain was undergoing a widespread identity crisis.

In an interesting, and revealing, article entitled 'Reviving Poffenheimer', *The Economist* addressed the issue of decline in the context of Britain's cultural baggage. This article argued:

> 'A main reason for our recent disappointments lies in the borderland between economics and national psychology: British manufacturers, representing in this the ethos of the British people, have not put so determined an effort into selling their goods abroad as European manufacturers have done.'[6]

The reason for this it argued was a kind of easy-going snobbery which was peculiarly, and forgivably, British. By contrast 'foreigners', without the burden of heritage, social status and cultural sophistication (again underlying the paradoxical forms of national enjoyment) were able to achieve increasing economic success (albeit of a purely quantitative kind: the idea of qualitative success would also have been unthinkable). The high achievement of foreigners, therefore, was the result of the fact that they did not possess the excess baggage of tradition or the cultural richness of Britain. Their enjoyment was totally inferior and yet at the same time – indeed because of this – it posed an enormous threat to our enjoyment (our just desserts, economic reward for national sacrifice, etc). This paradoxical construction is given expression in Graham Greene's description of a foreign trader's dinner in Havana:

> 'The Germans formed a group apart, rather suitably against the West wall; they carried their superiority of the deutschmark on their features like duelling scars: national honour which had survived Belsen depended now on a rate of exchange' [7]

More recently, of course, this type of sentiment persists in the intense deliberations over the activities of the Bundesbank in the European Union and the whole issue of German reunification/expansionism: 'what is their real agenda?', 'can we trust them?', 'how far will German desire/ambition go?'. And, of course, underlying this is the view that Germans may be successful but they have to remain German: to bear the indelible stain of Belsen which the mighty deutschmark tries to conceal (a substitute for inferior national enjoyment).

Against this background, *The Economist* characterised the parvenuist threat from the international economy in terms of the eponymous 'Mr. Poffenheimer'. All richness of identity is immediately subsumed under the patronising sobriquet of Poffenheimer who is clearly foreign, pushy and (implicitly) Jewish (skilfully combining a set of equivalences between anti-Semitism and a more general anti-German/European/American xenophobia). More particularly, Poffenheimer is described as 'a go getter, an orthodox and established worshipper of the Almighty Dollar, the sort of chap

---

[6] 1960, p.245.
[7] *Our Man in Havana*, 1958, p.170.

that better-class Britons devoutly hoped that they would not be obliged to invite to dinner.'

Here again we see elements of the Rumpelstiltskin myth. Poffenheimer can make gold, and is to be admired for that, but he can never become part of 'our' community or be one of 'us'. We can fully identify him, penetrate his inferior enjoyment (material wealth, ambition, etc) and thereby locate/steal his *dasein*. Thus the threat he poses is (partially) dissolved in finding his real name, his secret sign: he cannot be anything other than a Poffenheimer, no matter what he does.

However, *The Economist* is even more interesting in its prognosis for halting decline and rebuilding Britain:

> 'The need there is to mobilise the dynamic of an economic nationalism ... The policy must be produce a new race of Poffenheimers – giving to them only the honours, the royal handshakes, the social kudos which a snobbish society can bestow.'

Again, this is a paradox. In order to protect/reproduce the enjoyment of a British way of life 'we' had to become more like Poffenheimers; a double agency, which was not simply a negation, but which would enable the British to steal the enjoyment of Poffenheimers and restore Britishness. And, in this regard, we see a reversal of Žižek's formulation of the infiltrating 'body-snatching' other.[8] Britons, in order to preserve their way of life, would have to infiltrate the identity of Poffenheimers – to become the body-snatchers (or *jouissance* thieves) themselves – in order to affirm difference. Indeed, in a campaigning role, *The Economist* launched its own project in the 1960s called 'Spies for Prosperity' (actively invoking this kind of double agency) in which journalists and businessmen were encouraged to 'spy' for Britain in order to restore the national economy.

What enables the British to do this, of course, is their magical passport from the Thing which bestows the gift of infinite mutability (to be like the Poffenheimers, etc) and infinite immutability (to bear witness as part of an inimitable theft-proof culture). It therefore seems as no surprise that James Bond movies (and its genre) became so popular with the arrival of the 'global village' in the 1960s. In *You Only Live Twice*, for example, Bond actually 'becomes' Japanese and yet, for all that, his Britishness shines through all the more: his passport, 007, is rather a licence to infiltrate and steal the enjoyment of the other. Similarly, in a famous scene from the *Italian Job* we see the red, white and blue Mini Coopers soaring through the sewers of Milan – penetrating the underbelly of foreign enjoyment – to the winning sounds of 'this is the self-preservation society' (a society which is both universal and particularly British).

Under Thatcherism, by contrast, Briton's were exhorted to be more like the Germans (and the Japanese) in respect to industriousness and discipline. With John Major, on the other hand, there is the familiar argument that 'we' need to be in Europe in order to mould it in our own image.

If we look at the question of decline since the 1960s then we can see that various culprits have been identified (and sometimes combined) as re-

---

[8] 1989, p.89.

sponsible for the loss of Britain's 'Greatness'. Sometimes this has come in the shape of an external 'threat' – the Falklands crisis, which had such a powerful unifying effect on the nation. At other times it is a political force, such as the 'over-powerful' trade unions or Eurocrats. Or it may be a more nebulous identification of the 'under-class', 1960s decadence, single mothers, the enemy within (etc). And it is interesting to note that as each of these embodiments of loss have either dissolved or become unconvincing then this has undoubtedly deepened the crises of Thatcherism/Majorism (the messianism of its project is becoming eroded and 're-literalised'). To put it in the terms of Hegel, British Conservative discourse is very much feeling the effects of 'the loss of the loss'

Psychoanalytic theory is surely right in its identification of a primal loss which is subsequently projected onto the other who is made responsible for its theft ('I am incomplete/unhappy and you are responsible'), but this situation can never be simply underwritten and, moreover, there are all sorts of ambiguities which can be played out here. Indeed it appears that there is a danger of pathologising politics. For it can never be enough to simply 'go through the fantasy', because we will always be in a position of having to choose some kind of fantasy which establishes a consistency to our realities (Lacan's *points de capitons*). Now in this sense, the primal loss is also a primal gift: an opportunity to make a set of identifications which are neither pre-given nor imprisoning.

This introduces a crucial undecidability which returns the Derridean insight. Thus otherness is always less than fully embodied and the particular (historical) embodiment can never fully capture otherness. Now this type of relation in which a concrete embodiment attempts (but always fails) to capture the universal is – in the sense of Laclau and Mouffe – a hegemonic relation. This opens certain creative tensions in which the relation to otherness is not simply one of oppositional negativity but rather a relation (or *chaismus*) of active political engagement in which new possibilities can emerge. In this sense, it may be said to establish the ontological conditions of Derrida's promise of a 'to come': of engaging with the spectrality of otherness in a way which opens identity/now to the temporality of the future.[9] Indeed, capitalism may be seen as something which engages with its own negativity and otherness in constantly eradicating its own representation and (re)colonising the spaces of our (non) desire.

This perspective, however, opens greater possibilities for political and subversive practices than Žižek appears willing to allow [10] Thus otherness – in all its undecidable dimensions of antagonism and fascination – is always indifferent to its particular (incomplete) forms of embodiment and which establishes the conditions of possibility (at least) of new voices being heard and new futures being made. If there is Derrida's promise of 'democracy to come' this is always because of the constitutive possibilities of an 'otherness to come': a spectrology of political engagement.

---

[9] J.Derrida, *Spectres of Marx*, 1994.

[10] For example, Žižek's argument that the new forms of political subjectivity simply 'corresponds to late capitalism' without any 'subversive potentials', 1993, p.216.

Ideology, Hegemony and Political Subjectivity

Jeremy Valentine
Lancaster University

'Subject and Subject Position in The Concept of Antagonism'

In an essay appended to Ernesto Laclau's *New Reflections On The Revolution of Our Time* (hereafter *New Reflections*) Slavoj Žižek takes issue with the use of the category of the subject in the discourse-theoretical approach to the concept of antagonism.[1] Žižek's intervention turns precisely on the ambiguous manner in which the category of the subject is deployed in Laclau & Mouffe's *Hegemony and Socialist Strategy*, Verso, 1985.[2] According to Žižek, in this text two senses of the subject are used. Firstly, the 'post-structuralist' notion of subject-position. This boils down to the historicist thesis that individuals are constructed within historically-specific contexts, although Žižek neglects to mention the importance of the dimension of power associated with this view.[3] Secondly, the Lacanian notion of the Subject, conventionally marked by the upper case, as developed in Althusser's theory of interpellation and ideology. This boils down to the thesis that individuals are constituted by identifying with perfect representations made available by the symbolic order so as to overcome the less than perfect nature of what they really are. Derived from Lacan's theory of the 'mirror stage' this served as the basis for Althusser's theory of the specular nature of ideology which was supposed to be integrated with an insistence on the material nature of social practices.[4]

The issue is this. Essentially, the Lacanian notion of the Subject is, following Freud, a critique, or expansion, depending on how you look at it, of the Cartesian ego. In those areas of the Marxist tradition where this has been accepted the Cartesian ego is taken as the philosophical expression of the bourgeois illusion that the individual is source and master of himself, his property and his meaning (his relation to language).[5] Although this furnishes considerable resources for undermining bourgeois self-confidence, if its psychoanalytical origins are to be respected then both the ego and its critique must enjoy a universal status. For Marxists this fits in quite nicely with the universal nature of class struggle. Hence the notorious problem of the eternal nature of ideology in Althusser. Contrary to this, a 'post-structuralist' or historicist perspective would regard the bourgeois ego as merely one of any number of subject positions, although this would not be to dismiss the political and historical importance of this construct.

---

[1] S.Žižek, 'Beyond Discourse Analysis', in E.Laclau, *New Reflections On The Revolution of Our Time*, Verso, 1990.

[2] Hereafter *HSS*.

[3] On this issue see T.B.Dyrberg, *The Circular Structure of Power: Identity, Politics, Community*, Verso, forthcoming.

[4] L.Althusser, 'Ideology and Ideological State Apparatuses', in *Lenin and Philosophy*, Monthly Review Press, 1971. For a view of this opposition from the Lacanian side, see J.Copjec, *Read My Desire: Lacan Against the Historicists*, MIT Press, 1994.

[5] The paradigmatic expression of this view is found in R.Coward & J.Ellis, *Language and Materialism*, ,Routledge & Kegan Paul, 1977.

Quite rightly, Žižek points out that the two senses are incompatible and opts for the Lacanian one, claiming that *HSS* is in certain respects a regression from Laclau's earlier work which was more centrally engaged with the Althusserian problematic. This is because of the insistence that, in effect, individuals can never be who they would prefer themselves to be recognised as being, and, following the logic of psychoanalysis, are in fact constituted by the repression of this traumatic fact. This applies as much to the heroes of capital as to the innocent third world peasant deprived of his land rights. Both are equally deluded in their belief that they have a place in the symbolic order which they have determined. The consequences of this are clear. For example:

> 'The feminist struggle against patriarchal, male chauvinist oppression is necessarily filled out by the *illusion* that afterwards, when patriarchal oppression is abolished, women will finally achieve their full identity with themselves, realise their human potentials, etc.'[6]

Consequently, in Žižek's articulation antagonism is simply a 'self-inflicted impediment'[7] which occurs precisely when an external enemy is eliminated as one can no longer maintain one's unhappiness by the detour of the alibi of the other. 'The moment of victory is the moment of greatest loss'[8] or, in Hegelian terms, 'the loss of the loss'. Hence the Subject is the experience of 'pure antagonism', an empty place which prevents the closure of the symbolic field in which an individual would find a place. On the other hand, subject-positions – bourgeois, afro-American, racist, environmentalist, slacker, etc. – are simply devices designed to avoid this experience. Any antagonistic relations which they happen to enjoy with each other are merely doing the work of ideology in pluralist societies, maintaining the illusion of a stake in the symbolic order assured through a process of subjectivation which goes on behind their backs. The Subject cannot be subjectivied, cannot have a place. This is why Žižek argues that the presence of the Subject is the remainder of any symbolic order in that it constitutes its internal limit.

Two questions arise here: To what extent is Žižek's theoretical intervention justifiable, and what is the basis for it in Laclau & Mouffe's theory? The latter need not necessarily be answered by the former. All things considered it is not surprising that Žižek refers to this experience as 'pure antagonism' onto which he wishes to graft a notion of the Subject as a void which is derived from Lacan, largely because of the belief that it pre-supposes it. This is distinct from the 'social *reality* of the antagonistic fight'.[9] The former constitutes the internal limit of the social, the 'internal impossibility of the Other'.[10] The later is precisely what secures the fantasy of social cohesion, whether it be the institutionalised opposition of parliamentary democracy or

---

[6] 'Beyond', p.251, emphasis added.
[7] 'Beyond', p.252.
[8] 'Beyond', p.252.
[9] 'Beyond', p.253, original emphasis.
[10] 'Beyond', p.254.

the ritualised demonisation of the West in Muslim fundamentalist rhetoric. According to Žižek, the former is

> '*beyond or before subjectivation* [subject position, J.V.]: subjectivation designs the movement through which the Subject integrates what is given him/her into the universe of meaning – this integration always ultimately fails, there is a certain leftover which cannot be integrated into the symbolic universe, an object which resists subjectivation, and the Subject is precisely correlative to this object.'[11]

Ignoring the problems which might arise from the close proximity, not to say identity, of subject and object in this formula, we can say that for Žižek the Subject constitutes the failure of subject position. Subject position is merely an imaginary identification, to use the Lacanian vocabulary.

How then does this conflict or antagonism between Subject and subject position emerge in *HSS*? A superficial reading of the text might suggest that there are no grounds for Žižek's argument, that it might be some sort of projection. On the other hand, grounds for convergence seem to appear as well. In many respects the elaboration of the concept of antagonism constitutes the major theoretical advance of the text in that it overcomes the essentialism and reductionism entailed by reliance on either logical or dialectical contradiction or even 'real opposition' in understanding political conflict. The argument can be summarised as follows. In order to displace the myth that individuals are self-grounding and self-constituting of their identities and their social relations Laclau & Mouffe use the category of the subject in the sense of 'subject position'. Subject positions are understood to be constituted within discursive structures and any appeal to an extra-discursive vantage point in order to ground such positions is illegitimate.[12] However, in order to avoid the problem of reducing subjects to discursive structures, wherein by merely being an effect of a discursive structure the distinction between subject and structure would collapse and the dimension of constitution would become otiose, Laclau & Mouffe move to the level of the relations between subject positions in order to reveal their contingent or articulatory nature. Subject positions are further understood to be relationally constituted and these relations, although not necessarily functional, can be regarded as equivalent to the terrain of the social. To allow for this possibility all subject positions must be constitutively incomplete, polysemic, precarious. Subject positions are denied an objective status and no subject position can be regarded as separate or autonomous, howsoever dispersed. Indeed, Laclau & Mouffe insist that autonomy, as fact or ethical value, is a discursive construct.[13] To believe otherwise would be to deny the relational nature of their constitution, what Laclau calls hegemony or the political dimension through which social relations are constituted.

Hence this problem which Žižek exploits is ... Either antagonism is a property of the relations between subject positions, or it is a property of

---

[11] 'Beyond', p.254. emphasis added.
[12] *HSS*, p.115.
[13] *HSS*, p.140. See also Laclau's *New Reflections*, p.115, where this is somewhat qualified in that autonomy can only ever be 'relative autonomy'.

subject positions themselves given by their ultimately illusory character. This dilemma rests on the precise character of their incompletion. Either subject positions are incomplete because they are constituted by a discursive context which they cannot master, or subject positions are incomplete by virtue of the Subject that each really is.

Here we should consider the consequences of the denial of objective status to subject positions. Does it render all talk about subject positions subjective in the popular sense? To cut to the chase it means that antagonism is constitutive of identity. Laclau & Mouffe do not deny the fact of subject positions. If someone represents themselves as, for example, a lesbian then, all things being equal, this event is not an illusion, although it may be a lie. What is denied is the transcendental or non-discursive nature of such facts, as if lesbianism was the embodiment of some mysterious essence of the feminine and not of the discursive context in which it is constituted. Yet this would suggest that objectivity is denied to all social experience. Indeed, Žižek builds his critique on Laclau & Mouffe's infamous statement that society does not exist. Laclau & Mouffe endorse this view with one exception. This is the experience of 'the limit of all objectivity', or when the very instability of objectivity is experienced as fact. Laclau & Mouffe call this antagonism. If it looks like objectivity is simply another word for ideology in the Marxist sense, then antagonism is the rip in the ideological surface which would inscribe individuals. In other words, antagonism is characterised by rupture and dislocation, distinct from the animosity of mere name calling. Importantly, there is no privileged subject of antagonism as it effects all subject positions within a historically specific context. But in this case there is no Subject of antagonism either as it derives from the failure of the system of differences in which subject positions are constituted, and not from a failure of identification. No one is obliged to identify with the subject positions they happen to occupy in the strong psychoanalytical sense. This may occur in closed regulated societies, but even here such identifications are more likely to be cases of 'passing for'.[14] The notion of an impossible full identification as what identification really is, that is to say, failure of identification, is distinct from the more probable partial identification.[15]

So exactly what is antagonism? Laclau & Mouffe insist that the 'cause' of antagonism is not to be understood as somehow extra-discursive, like the clash of two stones or the logical incompatibility of concepts. For Laclau & Mouffe the opposition between empiricism and rationalism is a historically specific discursive construct. This is not to deny that in reality bricks collide and contradictions emerge but simply to point out that these events are not necessarily antagonistic. In this respect Laclau & Mouffe go beyond thinking antagonism in terms of a description of the conditions which cause antagonism to antagonism as such,[16] the point at which familiar narratives of antagonism break off. Antagonism derives from the intra-penetration of

---

[14] Milan Kundera's early novel *The Joke*, is a good example of the consequences of voicing this non-identification.

[15] For an interesting discussion of the implications of this see B.Arditi, *Tracing The Political Subject*, PhD Thesis, University of Essex.

[16] *HSS*, p.124.

subject positions as it is this which prevents their adequacy or correspondence to themselves as full identities. Antagonism is hetero not homo or auto. It is not reducible to the nature of the antagonistic elements as if it was a question of disposition, like the descriptions of militant workers as 'antagonistic' which one finds in the files of personnel officers. It cannot be derived from integrity. But as the relational nature of identity is constitutive something needs to be added in order to specify its antagonistic dimension. This is the experience of the failure of the system of differences in which subject positions are located, a crisis at the level of social totality which can only announce its disruptive presence indirectly, for example in the form of metaphor. Antagonism is not the impossibility of being two things at once – precisely, a Subject and a subject position – as in a logical contradiction, but the impossibility of being one thing because being anything depends on a relational context. But this means that antagonism is nothing personal.

However, instead of exploring the possible implications of this which would be consistent with its historicist assumptions Laclau & Mouffe introduce an element which somewhat undermines their reputation as having broken with essentialist or reductionist accounts of social and political phenomena. This is the assertion that 'every language and every society are constituted as a repression of the consciousness of the impossibility that penetrates them'.[17] Presumably, antagonism breaks out when the lid comes off. Yet why is this repressive element necessary, especially as in terms of both theoretical structure and political effect it reproduces the impasse reached by Althusser's doctrine of the eternal nature of ideology? In part this derives from a commitment to the artificial nature of society, yet this historicist insight is cancelled by being articulated with the psychoanalytical belief that social subjects could not bear to face up to this. Indeed, despite the attempt to replace the notion of repression with the more deconstructionist idea of a 'constitutive outside' in Laclau's later solo work this incompatibility is reproduced in the claim that it is ideology which is constitutive of the social as it furnishes the necessity of the illusion that the infinite play of difference can be fixed.[18] Apparently, this is required in order to prevent the emergence of social pathologies understood according to the most psychologistic and reductionist models. Yet simultaneously we find the assertion that 'there is no source of the social different from people's decisions in the process of the social construction of their own identity and their own existence'.[19] A cynic might conclude from this that the point of hegemony is to negotiate this paradox by mobilising the narcissism of autonomy in order to secure the discipline of denial. In short, the incompatibility of Subject/subject position is present in the concept of antagonism.

Need it be? Is repression really necessary for the constitution of society in a manner which would licence a political hermeneutic modelled on the interpretation of dreams? Undoubtedly, Žižek achieves this in his work with devastating effect. But if Laclau & Mouffe are content to dismiss the legitimacy of arguing by means of an analogy between bricks or concepts

---

[17] *HSS*, p.125.
[18] *New Reflections*, pp.92, 186.
[19] *New Reflections*, p.192.

to social antagonisms then why does the analogy from the subject specific to psychoanalysis to social relations slip through the deconstructive net? Admittedly, in a later text Laclau insisted on the provisional nature of the relation between Marxism and psychoanalysis which would be cemented through a Heideggerian 'de-struction' of the originary categories of these theories, but it is difficult to see if this has been done.[20] The effect of incorporating the necessity of repression, which is of course where Žižek comes in, is to subordinate the theoretical exploration to the assumption of an originary constitution of society. Unlike contract theorists, however, this origin takes the paradoxical form of the simultaneity of the full constitution of society and its impossibility, thereby inflating the limited force of their own stipulation that the fullness of society – its objectivity – is only a proposition designed to render social relations intelligible and does not coincide with what actually goes on in society. This domain is understood as an infinite play of difference, what people like Lefebvre and De Certeau would call 'ordinary life'.

Perhaps the issue needs to be put differently. In so far as antagonism can be described as a limit experience which can only be shown indirectly then it must be understood as constituting a moment in which the distinction between the interiority and exteriority of society is brought into question. Otherwise the objectivity of society would be assured. Yet in *HSS* Laclau & Mouffe maintain that antagonism is external to society (p.125) and then, almost immediately, go on to deny the objectivity of a beyond of society to the effect that 'the limit of the social cannot be traced as a frontier separating two territories – for the perception of a frontier supposes the perception of something beyond it that would have to be objective and positive' such that 'the limit of the social must be given within the social itself as something subverting it, destroying its ambition to constitute a full presence'. This is followed by the statement that; 'society never manages fully to be society, because everything in it is penetrated by its limits, which prevent it from constituting itself as an objective reality' (p.126, emphasis added). This vacillation is repeated in a later text, 'Why Do Empty Signifiers Matter To Politics?'.[21] Here the 'impossibility of society' thesis, society as an infinite play of difference and the attempt to limit this play, becomes subordinated to a 'logic of exclusionary limits.'[22] Now the 'authentic' moment of any limit has become exclusion because: 'The actualisation of what is beyond the limit of exclusion would involve the impossibility of what is this side of the limit' (p.169). At this point the argument jumps to the statement that 'true limits are always antagonistic' (p.169), which is to say that antagonism is relocated to the objectivity of the limit, a frontier in the most empirical sense. As exclusion is a form of actualisation the beyond is therefore objective. In which case it is no longer beyond and is deprived of any antagonistic relation.[23] This serves to

---

[20] *New Reflections*, pp.93-96.
[21] In J.Weeks (ed), *The Lesser Evil And The Greater Good*, Rivers Oram Press, 1994.
[22] 'Why Do ... ?', p.169.
[23] The beyond of a limit can now acquire objectivity largely because of the decision to echo the view attributed to Hegel that 'to think the limits of something is the same as thinking what is beyond those limits.' p.168.

reverse the position of *HSS* which simply states that '... there is no beyond' (p.126). Indeed, in 'Why Do ... ?' Laclau insists that the outside (beyond) is such a threat to the inside that it is sufficiently motivated to 'demonise' it, a gesture which domesticates antagonism within the confines of the non-exceptional, functional, institution of ritual. As things are now so apparent, as everyone knows who the enemy is, it is difficult to see what, if anything, is repressed. Of course Žižek would rubbish this as merely the 'antagonistic fight in reality'.

Taking things in this direction serves to undermine the importance of a more satisfactory formula for the constitutive nature of antagonism given in New Reflections. This is that 'it is not possible to threaten the existence of something without simultaneously affirming it' (p.27). Crucially, the element of threat is not understood in terms of exteriority but in terms of contingency, the 'element of impurity which deforms the full constitution of necessity'. With this an argument can be made which returns the question to the historicist terrain. Without the element of contingency this formula is simply abstract. This is because the category of contingency has a precise historical existence and trajectory. According to Blumenberg modernity emerged as a consequence of the circulation of this term within the economy of medieval society through the vehicle of nominalist doctrine. Contingency meant that as God did not have to give a reason for his creation of the world then the world could or could not exist. Necessity was removed from the ground of existence. Hence; 'nominalism was a system meant to make man extremely uneasy about the world.'[24] One obvious effect of this was the destruction of the legitimacy of any appeal to an extra-worldly ground of the social. Nevertheless, one thing became certain. As Bauman puts it: 'The discovery that order was not natural was the discovery of order as such'.[25] Thus the logic of the political moved from the eternal to the created, a shift announced loudly by Hobbes's *Leviathan*.[26] But the precise location of the distinction between creator and created became increasingly difficult to determine, largely because of the unavailability of anything with which to ground it.

Hence political modernity can be characterised on the one hand in almost ethical terms as an intervention which attempts to constitute the fullness of a terrain present to itself, and on the other hand, by virtue of the indeterminacy of the distinction between creator and created, as a generalised contingency. That is, the impossibility of an identity between both terms, of both terms being one thing. Thus the full presence of modern political society is constitutively incomplete, haunted by the impossibility of the self-grounding to which it aspires. Which is precisely what antagonism is. Moreover, this account is entirely commensurate with Laclau & Mouffe's assertion in *HSS* that; 'the hegemonic form of politics only becomes dominant at the beginning of modern times, when the reproduction of the different so-

---

[24] H.Blumenberg, *The Legitimacy of the Modern Age*, MIT Press, 1983, p.151.
[25] Z.Bauman, 'Modernity and Ambivalence', *Theory, Culture and Society*, 7/3, 1989, p.164.
[26] See J.Valentine, 'Artifice and Analogy in Hobbes's Leviathan: An Example of Political Modernity', *Working Papers* 3, Centre For Theoretical Studies, University of Essex, 1994.

cial areas takes place in permanently changing conditions which constantly require the construction of new systems of differences' (p.138), as distinct from the old times of traditional or closed societies when everyone knew their place and who the enemy was. It is also commensurate with the assertion, consistent over their writings jointly and severally, of 'the primacy of the political over the social.'[27] Finally, it means that far from being an abstract formula the thesis of the 'impossibility of the social' only emerges when the social becomes a question to itself. Which is in history.

---

[27] *New Reflections*, pp.33-36; C.Mouffe, *The Return of The Political*, Verso, 1993.

The Transformation of the State in Postwar Britain

Colin Hay
Universities of Birmingham and Harvard

'Labouring Under a Misconception:
The Discursive Construction of the "Winter of Discontent",'

Acknowledgements

Earlier versions of this paper were presented at the Department of Politics, Queen's University, Belfast and at the Center for European Studies, Harvard University. The author would like to thank the participants on both occasions for their helpful and encouraging comments.

Introduction

If there is indeed such a thing as a collective British political imagination then it is surely to be found in the mythology which surrounds the 'winter of discontent'. It lingers in the enduring popular resonances and connotations of a new political lexicon spawned in the winter of 1978P79. This discursive regime enlists characters as diverse as Richard III, 'Sunny Jim' Callaghan, and St Francis of Assisi in the recounting of the tale of how: the country was 'held to ransom'; of how 'the dead were left unburied' and of how the 'bins were left unemptied' during a 'winter of discontent' in which 'Britain was under siege' from 'militant trade unionists' and their 'communist leaders'; while the Prime Minister disdainfully 'abandoned the sinking ship', jetted to Guadeloupe, 'sunned himself', and complacently returned to pronounce 'crisis, what crisis?'

The 'Winter of Discontent' as Narrative, the Winter of Discontent as Crisis

In December 1978 an NOP opinion poll published in *The Daily Telegraph* gave Labour a one per cent lead. By January 1979 the same pollsters were giving the Conservatives a lead of eighteen per cent. In the intervening weeks Britain had experienced a protracted wave of industrial conflict. This was accompanied by an intense media barrage which fostered a sense of profound political crisis without precedent since the General Strike of 1926. It was to become immortalised by the then editor of *The Sun*, Larry Lamb, as the 'winter of discontent'.

Remarkable as this political turnaround was, I want to suggest that something far more remarkable and unprecedented (at least in the postwar British context) was occurring during this period. For whilst such a swing in the electoral pendulum might well account for a change in *governmental* power, it cannot in-and-of-itself provide an adequate explanation for the more significant shift in *state* power that was to originate in the winter of 1978-79. Thatcherism as a state project, though conceived long before, was born in the context of crisis during the winter of discontent.

In this paper I want to suggest that the 'winter of discontent' should be seen as a strategic moment in the transformation of the British state, a moment of state *crisis*. By crisis, however, I do not merely refer to a condition of rupture and breakdown (a condensation of contradictions to produce a ruptural unity) but, crucially, to a moment of *decisive intervention*, a moment of transformation (Hay 1994, pp. 239-242, 249-53; 1996).

For a particular conjuncture to provide the opportunity for decisive intervention it must be perceived as so doing – it must be seen as a moment in which a decisive intervention can (and perhaps must) be made. Furthermore, it must be perceived as such by agents capable of making a decisive intervention at the level at which the crisis is identified. Crises then are constituted in and through narrative. Such narratives must recruit the contradictions and failures of the system as 'symptom'-atic of a more general condition of crisis. The narrative of crisis constitutes an object (in this case the state) as in need of decisive intervention, and a (state) project (and hence a subject) through which that decisive intervention can be made. As t'Hart observes,

> 'the most important instrument of crisis management is language. Those who are able to define what the crisis is all about also hold the key to defining the appropriate strategies for [its] resolution.' (1993, p.41)

Crisis, then, is not some objective condition or property of a system defining the contours for subsequent ideological contestation. Rather it is subjectively perceived – the subject of narration. State power (the ability to impose a new trajectory upon the structures of the state) resides not only in the ability to *respond* to crises, but to *identify, define and constitute* crisis in the first place. This suggests that if we wish to understand the Thatcherite state project and its impact upon the structures, boundaries and perceived responsibilities of the state, then we must start by considering the moment of crisis itself, the winter of discontent.

What this further suggests is that crisis and failure simply cannot be equated. A given constellation of contradictions and failures within the institutions of the state can sustain a multiplicity of conflicting narratives of crisis. Such narratives compete in terms of their ability to find resonance with individuals' and groups' direct lived experiences, and not in terms of their 'scientific' adequacy as explanations for the condition they diagnose. In so doing crisis discourses operate by identifying minor alterations in the routine texture of social life, recruiting such iterative changes as 'symptomatic' of a generic condition of (state) failure. Through this process of ideological contestation a predominant construction of crisis may emerge. The crisis becomes lived in these terms.

It must then be emphasised that state projects must respond to this narrative *construction of crisis*, and not necessarily to the conditions of contradiction and failure that in fact underlie it. This would in turn suggest that Thatcherism's success was premised upon the ability of the New Right to construct the moment of the late 1970s as a moment of crisis, in which a particular type of decisive intervention was required. In so doing it proved itself capable of changing, if not the hearts and minds of the electorate, then certainly the predominant perceptions of the political context, recruiting subjects to its vision of the 'necessary' response to the crisis of a monolithic state besieged by the trade unions.

In this paper I wish to consider the processes through which the winter of discontent was discursively constructed, examining in some detail the rhetorical strategies and linguistic devices deployed within the tabloid media in framing the crisis.

Discourses of Discontent and Constructions of Crisis

> '[T]here is a difference between having power over a text and having power over the agenda within which that text is constructed and presented.' (Morley 1992, p.31)

It is the central argument of what is to follow that media influence does not reside in the power of direct ideological indoctrination, but in the ability to frame the discursive context within which political subjectivities are constituted, reinforced and re-constituted. Texts are not ideological in themselves, they only become ideological in their active appropriation. Here I refer to ideologies as discourses which in their reception have the effect of sustaining, reproducing or extending relations of domination. If we adopt such a definition then 'dominant ideologies' cannot simply be read off from the internal structure of the text itself. Ideological effects are in no sense guaranteed by processes of textual production and 'encoding'. The purpose of ideology critique must then be 'to explicate the connection between the meaning of symbolic constructions and the relations of domination which that meaning serves to sustain' (Thompson 1988, p.372; 1990). The critical inflexion of the concept of ideology is retained by considering the discursive selectivity imposed by the text: the range of different readings a given text can sustain and the discursive field or agenda thereby established. For, as Morley perceptively observes, the moment of encoding still 'exerts an "overdetermining" effect (though not a fully determined closure) on the succeeding moments in the communicative chain' (1992, p.52). The task of a critical theory of the media is to map out the contours of the discursively selective terrain within which negotiated and active decodings must be situated.

Secondly, it is crucial to emphasise that the political influence of the media is not invariant. As we have already seen the winter of discontent can be interpreted as a strategic moment in the transformation of the state. It also emerges as a moment in which the influence of the media, perhaps more than at any other point in post-war British history, was crucial. For it was predominantly through media discourses, through the process of *informediation*, that the crisis was initially constituted *as a crisis*. Moreover, the contours of political discourse and the nature of the political agenda were themselves decisively reconfigured in the narrative construction of the winter of discontent. Once again the role of the media here was central. It is to an 'integral analysis' of this reconfigured discursive space that the rest of this paper is devoted.

The Discursive Construction of Crisis: Narration and Interpellation

Media discourses work through an interpellative 'hailing'. Within contemporary cultural and media studies the notion of subject positioning or interpellation has tended to be associated with a conception of a mass audience of ideologically passified dupes, a view now rightly exposed to devastating critique. Yet the concept of interpellation, as I hope to show, need not imply audience passivity.

In the encoding of media texts, subject positions are constructed within the narrative for active readers. Yet the basis of interpellation lies in the inherently imaginative process of *decoding* through which we, the readers, inject ourselves into the narrative structure loosely framed by a media discourse. Media texts effectively construct an empty story board which recruits readers as *dramatis personae* upon an expansive stage created within the text itself. The story board comprises a basic set of characters, plot relationships, minimal relevant aspects of context and a variety of interdiscursive cues, intended associations and connotations. It invites us as readers, active decoders, and potential 'interpellates' to identify with a particular 'preferred' subject position (the victim, the hero, the heroine, the underdog...). If we do not overtly and consciously resist this interpellation by breaking or at least suspending the momentary spell of the text, then we actively position ourselves as subjects within the narrative. We recognise ourselves (as the victim, hero, heroine, underdog...) as we locate ourselves within a subject position inscribed by the text. It is in this moment of identification that we recognise our 'hailing'. In this instant we are constituted as subjects *through* the text, as we are simultaneously subjected to it.

This can be illustrated by considering extract 1. This report is taken from the front page of the *Daily Mail* on 1 February 1979 at the height of the media frenzy whipped up around the winter of discontent. The 'story' concerns the industrial dispute between Liverpool City Council and council employees, in this case gravediggers.

The banner headline

'THEY WON'T EVEN LET US BURY OUR DEAD'

carefully frames the narrative, providing a preferred subject position for the reader. 'We' are recruited through interpellation as members of a collectivity of potential victims threatened by the irresponsible, macabre and self-serving actions of a homogeneous band of militant activists, simply labelled 'they'. 'We' are invited to recognise ourselves, and the threat posed to the routine assumptions of our daily lives, by actively injecting our own subjectivities into this preferred subject position. Provided that we do not overtly resist our interpellation by either rejecting the plot construction presented to us, or by adopting the subject position of 'the other' ('them', the strikers), we become recruited to the crisis discourse. Thus hailed, we adopt the vantage point of the bereaved denied the basic human decency of being able to bury 'our' loved ones. We share in the collective revulsion at the projected 'putrefaction of the corpses of our family and friends'. Yet in so doing we do not become simply passive 'dupes' to a dominant ideology. Our interpellation is negotiated. If we are to adopt the subject position inscribed for us within the text, then we do so by 'filling out' the simple construction of the victim presented in the text. We supplement the incomplete character of the bereaved with our own experiences and thereby project ourselves into a setting framed by the media yet brought to life through our own imaginations. We join in the clamour and resistance of a community constituted and mobilised through interpellation against those who 'won't even let us bury our dead'.

To suggest the existence of textually or linguistically-inscribed subject positions within media texts is not to imply that all readers are similarly interpellated. Interpellation is an active process of recognition, misrecognition, negotiation and contestation. Subject positions are not unchallenged and readers often routinely resist preferred interpellations. Indeed, we only adopt (and supplement) a subject position inscribed within the text to the extent that it finds *resonance* with our experiences, recollections, sensitivities, sensibilities and understandings (themselves mediated both experientially and through prior interpellations).

We may resist our interpellation by either simply failing to recognise our hailing and thus remaining unpositioned, or by explicitly rejecting the preferred subject position or even the narrative structure which sets the discursive context for the interpellation itself. As Philo's work on the decoding of coverage of the miners' strike of 1984-85 clearly demonstrates, the reception of news footage is crucially mediated by lived experience (1990). Those who had found themselves on the picket lines during the winter of discontent simply could not identify with the dominant subject positions inscribed within media narratives of the miners' strike. Their experiences led them to locate themselves as striking miners within such narratives. This in turn led them to overturn the simplistic constructions of the threat posed by militant radicals which predominated in the media coverage. Similarly, Cunnison and Stageman's excellent study of the experience of women trade unionists during the winter of discontent demonstrates that trade union consciousness was in fact reinforced in part through a collective resistance to dominant media constructions of a country besieged by the labour movement (1993, pp.72-78).

Nonetheless interpellations, however resisted, define a particular subject matter as newsworthy and tend to delimit a discursive space within which such events become politically contested. It is predominantly through such primary mediation that the discursively selective terrain is defined within which political parties must compete to find resonance with popular aspirations. It is above all the media which sets the context and judges the evidence admissible in the attribution of responsibility for events such as the winter of discontent.

Distortion, Bias and Discursive Selectivity

In interrogating the media coverage of the winter of discontent we might well choose to concentrate upon the numerous descriptive errors and factual 'distortions' of reality which punctuate such media texts. We might, for instance, consider how it was that food from the Canary Islands that was being held up at Liverpool docks by pickets was apparently rotting on the quayside less than six hours after it had arrived in the country (*Daily Telegraph*, 5 January 1979). Following the prediction in *The Sun* that

'3 MILLION FACE THE DOLE QUEUE' (15 January 1979)

or that '1,000 Old Could Die Every Day' (12 January 1979) we might legitimately ask how many workers were laid off, and how many old age pensioners died during the winter of discontent. Similarly, we might recount the story, told by the Glasgow Media Group, of the week-long search for dead chickens by a TV newsreporter in early 1979. Asked if his quest for the illusive defunct poultry has proved successful,

> 'he replied that there had been twenty-five dead chickens. A camera team had been installed in a chicken coop to get shots for the story – the equipment was ready and cables installed. Finally they were ready to roll and switched on all the lights. Twenty-five chickens died of shock. To his knowledge these were the only chickens to have died in the lorry drivers' dispute.'
> (Glasgow Media Group 1982, p.8)

There are numerous other examples. Amusing and telling as such stories might be they tend to detract attention away from the crucial question of how the phenomena described (however selectively, however inaccurately) are accounted for, and of how responsibility is attributed within media narratives. This is no longer a question of bias measured against objectivity since *all* explanations and attributions of causality *abstract* from the events themselves and thus necessarily distort.

What is interesting then in the coverage of the winter of discontent is not so much the descriptive accuracy (or otherwise) of the presentation of key events. Ultimately far more significant is their narrativization, the subject positions constructed and the resulting attributions of causality and responsibility – in sum, the *discursive selectivity* imposed by such narratives upon the decoding process. The challenge for critical theorists of the media is to acknowledge that dominant media explanations for events such as the winter of discontent are not simply and unequivocally wrong (TUC Media Group 1979; Glasgow Media Group 1976; 1980; 1982). Rather these media narratives are constructed in such a way as to render their explanations adequate and sustainable in the light of the evidence they deem admissible. For those not directly exposed to the events and consequences of the winter of discontent, and many of those who were, tabloid narratives adequately accounted for their predominantly mediated understandings of the events of this period.

Crisis as Meta-Narrative

> '[T]he plot of narrative...grasps together and integrates into one whole and complete story multiple and scattered events, thereby schematising the intelligible signification attached to the narrative taken as a whole.' (Ricoeur 1984, p.x)

So far we have looked primarily at the resonances constructed by media narratives during the winter of discontent and the generic process of media interpellation. In the final sections of this paper we will consider the more distinctive rhetorical strategies and textual practices through which the winter of discontent was constituted as *crisis*.

The process of meta-narration is central to the conjuring of a sense of crisis out of the events of the winter of discontent by the tabloid media. It operates through the discursive 'recruiting' of a variety of specific events and phenomena (strikes, lockouts, confrontations, food shortages, etc.) and the experiences to which they give rise as symptomatic of a more generic condition – the winter of discontent, the crisis of the state. The discursive construction of crisis can thus be seen as a process involving the mapping together of a great variety of disparate events unified through the identification of some common essence – the overextension of the state, the holding to ransom of the country by the unions, the tyranny of the pickets, and so forth.

This process of abstraction through meta-narration is clearly illustrated in extract 2, which is taken from the *Daily Mail* on 18 January 1979. Here a series of apparently independent narratives relating to specific stories are mapped together and unified under an all-embracing banner headline which spans two pages, 'As the strike stranglehold tightens on factories...angry women pelt the men who are doing the damage'. This headline is in turn framed by two symmetrically positioned boxed headline cues, 'Tyranny of the pickets'. under this pair of headlines, a third caption which introduces the main story and which also spans two pages reads 'Shops under siege – fury of the wives'. The effect of this series of mutually reinforcing headlines and cues is to set the discursive context within which the nine separate narratives on this two-page spread are to be decoded. These at first seemingly unrelated stories (the threat posed to 'civilisation' by a shortage of baked beans, the profile of a 'militant' Scottish trade unionist, the sacking of eleven lorry drivers who refused to strike etc.) become unified in the commonly implied 'tyranny of the pickets', the sense of 'fury' and outrage that results from the unions' 'stranglehold' on the country, and the development of a 'siege' mentality. Each individual narrative is thereby recruited to this meta-narrative of siege, tyranny and crisis. The 'common sense' assumption of the tyranny of the pickets which provides the interpretative framework within which these various narratives are couched is thereby reinforced.

The crisis becomes a point of 'connotive resonance' (Hall 1980, p.174) conjured up in each picket line, each stoppage, each confrontation – each 'symptom'. The specificity and complexity of each event is thus denied as an abstracted and simplified meta-narrative capable of accounting for every 'symptom', and capable of unambiguously attributing responsibility is offered in its place.

'Newsworthy' or 'crisis-worthy' statistics, contradictions and events (industrial disputes, picket line struggles, projected food shortages, etc.) are selectively sampled and encoded with specific meaning. Notions of direct responsibility are attributed (to 'greedy labour', 'stubborn bosses', 'incompetent government', etc.) and a narrative structure is inscribed upon, and used a mechanism for ordering, the events. This is a process of *primary narration*, resulting in the construction of a series of independent narratives which still reflect (albeit to varying degrees) the specificity of each 'story'.

The discursive construction of crisis, however, is the product of a process of *secondary mediation*, abstraction and meta-narration. Here, the products of primary narration (the mediated events themselves) become the subject matter for a further process of narration. Notions of direct responsibility, causality and agency (action A leads to consequence B) are deleted, as, for instance, a strike is accounted for not in terms of the direct actions of union members, shop stewards, or managers, but in terms of the crisis of an 'overextended' state; or projected food shortages are accounted for not in terms of panic buying, but in terms of the unions' 'stranglehold' on the country. The direct agent is subsequently replaced by an abstraction linking disparate events as a new and more generic agency and causality is attributed ('trade unions hold the country hostage'). By importing such simplified and simplifying abstractions, a multitude of disparate events can be recruited as 'symptoms' within the discourse of crisis. The crisis diagnosis is confirmed in each new 'symptom' which can be assimilated within this meta-narrative.

This can be illustrated by considering extract 3, taken from *The Sun* on 23 January 1979. This is another two-page spread, which is all the more remarkable when it is considered that it displaces *The Sun*'s usual Page Three 'Girl'. Indeed, on the 15 January 1979, when this happened for the first time *The Sun* explained this unprecedented step, 'it really is a crisis'. As in the *Daily Mail* extract considered above we witness a banner headline that spans two pages, 'YOUR MONDAY OF MISERY'. This provides the discursive context and interpretative framework within which the paper's coverage is couched, whilst recruiting and positioning readers as victims of the misery produced by 'public sector strikers'. A dualistic counterposing of 'us' and 'them' is thus once again relied upon, distancing 'us' from identification with 'the wreckers'. A further rhetorical cue to the preferred reading of these individual 'crisis narratives' is provided by a map of Great Britain overlain upon a background emblazoned with the caption 'CRISIS BRITAIN 79'. The effect is to abstract from the series of independent primary narratives collected under the generic headline, recruiting these stories to an all-embracing crisis discourse.

Though characteristic of the tabloid media during the winter of discontent, such rhetorical strategies were far more widely deployed. Thus, in a particularly vivid example of abstraction and meta-narration *The Economist* commenting on Britain's 'retreat from siege', noted

'if trade unions and their pickets are allowed to be above the normal laws of contract, then a free society based on the law of contract will break down.....It will be glum if Lancastrians during a water strike have to get appalling diseases, if Merseyside children during the social workers' strike have to continue to be battered, if housewives in an island blockaded by lorry drivers have to go hungry, if patients deprived of ambulances and other emergency transport have to die, if many more small firms have to go bust, many more workers to become unemployed, more of Britain's exports and imports have to stay stuck at the docks, if sewage has to run in the streets, hyperinflation has to escalate, before Britain's politicians recognise the fact.' (20 January 1979)

Scarcely can a longer sentence or a clearer example of a crisis discourse ever have been published in *The Economist*.

Crisis as Decisive Intervention

The above analysis certainly suggests that the media were influential in the mobilisation of perceptions of profound political and economic crisis during the winter of 1978-79. Moreover, it would seem clear that within such media narratives responsibility for this crisis was attributed unambiguously to an overextended and increasingly ungovernable state held to ransom by the trade unions. Yet this is not in itself sufficient to demonstrate the existence of 'crisis' if by crisis we understand a moment of transition, a moment of *decisive intervention*. Hence it is crucial to consider the rhetorical strategies and linguistic devices used to present the principal political protagonists of the period: 'Sunny Jim' Callaghan and Mrs Thatcher.

Here it will prove instructive to examine in some detail extract 4, taken from The *Daily Mail* on 8 January 1979, during Callaghan's infamous 'junket' in Guadeloupe. What is particularly interesting about this specific example is that it provides the first usage by the tabloid media of the phrase 'crisis, what crisis?'. This was subsequently and falsely to be attributed to Callaghan by *The Sun* on his return from the Caribbean. The phrase, part of the new political lexicon which originated during the winter of discontent, was to frame *The Sun*'s continuing coverage of the events of that winter. It was reproduced on numerous occasions as a connotative cue setting the discursive context and interpretative framework within which individual 'crisis' narratives might be decoded. It was, for instance, printed in white on a black background across the top of the first three pages of the newspaper on 13 January 1979. It is interesting to reflect that this phrase so integrally associated with Jim Callaghan's return from Guadeloupe was in fact coined by a *Daily Mail* journalist almost a week before the event, whilst the Prime Minister was still complacently 'sunning himself in the tropics'.

Initially it is important to consider how such a story might be read. Here we can identify a series of discursive cues which provide the reader with an interpretative framework within which to situate the narrative. Any ideological effects of the text (which, it must be emphasised can only be secured in its active decoding) are likely to derive from the simple series of relationships between the two headlines ('As Callaghan suns himself in the Caribbean, Mrs Thatcher calls for curbs on strikers' cash' and 'BRITAIN

UNDER SIEGE'), the photograph of Callaghan sitting in the sun, and the caption ('There my be storm clouds at home, but its sunshine all the way for Premier Jim Callaghan as he studies his conference notes in Guadeloupe yesterday'). These four items feed intertextually off one another, establishing a regime of signification for the text that follows. The banner headline 'BRITAIN UNDER SIEGE' is perhaps the most immediately striking and informs the reader that this is a story about political crisis. It implies a construction of the events of the winter of discontent in which the trade unions are held responsible for the political crisis, as they have 'besieged the state' and 'held the country to ransom' through their actions. Although no explicit reference is made to the activities of the trade unions, the headline draws upon previous coverage and the interpretative frameworks by this stage well-established in the tabloid media. It hinges centrally upon implied union culpability.

This provides the context within which the actions of Callaghan and Thatcher are to be assessed. In the secondary headline, Callaghan and Thatcher are presented as actors whose actions must be judged in relation to the context of 'BRITAIN UNDER SIEGE'. Whilst the former passively 'suns himself in the Caribbean', Mr Thatcher decisively 'calls for curbs on strikers' cash'. The impression is created that Callaghan's actions are illegitimate and grossly inappropriate for a prime minister facing a profound political crisis at home, an impression apparently confirmed by the picture of a smug-looking man posing for the cameras in the sun. Mrs Thatcher's actions, by contrast, appear dynamic, befitting of a prime ministerial candidate and above all appropriate to the *Mail's* construction of the relevant context as one in which Britain is besieged by strikers 'and their pickets'.

This counterposing of the activity and decisiveness of Thatcher with the complacency, arrogance and indecision of the Prime Minister is a central feature of much of the media coverage of the winter of discontent. Thus the *Daily Express* contrasts 'INACTION MAN', 'The man in the crumpled suit who turned his back on crisis-ridden Britain', with the dynamism of 'Maggie's Crisis Challenge' (11 January 1979, 17 January 1979). Similarly, *The Mirror* proclaims, 'Jim Callaghan – THIS IS YOUR STRIKE', whilst *The Sun* asks 'WHAT THE BLOODY HELL'S GOING ON JIM?' counterposing this to 'Maggie's attack on union power' (5 February 1979). The impression firmly established is that Callaghan is incapable of the degree of decisive intervention required in 'SHUTDOWN BRITAIN', 'CRISIS-HIT BRITAIN' or 'CRISIS BRITAIN 79'. Mrs Thatcher, in sharp contrast is presented as having carefully measured up the nature of the problem and as having the charisma and panache to effect a decisive intervention in a condition of profound crisis.

Conclusion

What such an account illustrates is the importance of the mediated constructions placed upon events, and, in particular, the importance of media narratives in the constitution of crisis. Given that such representations of crisis often bear very little relationship to the failures and contradictions they purport to reflect, it is crucial that as political scientists we consider the *political and ideological mediation* of state and economic failure. State projects and the discourses of crisis on which they are premised do not compete in terms of the sophistication of their understanding of the crisis context. Indeed, their 'success' as narratives relies not on their ability to accurately reflect the complex webs of causation that interact to produce disparate effects, but in their ability to provide a simplified account sufficiently flexible to 'narrate' a great variety of morbid symptoms whilst unambiguously attributing causality (to an overextended state, to the tyranny of the pickets, and so forth).

Once the crisis of the British state in the late 1970s had been narrated as a crisis of an overextended and ungovernable state in which the trade unions were 'holding the country to ransom', the victory of the New Right was effectively achieved. With hindsight, the 'winter of discontent' emerges as the moment in which Thatcherism achieved state power.

References

S.Cunnison & J.Stageman, 'Male Power, Industrial Action and Changing Consciousness', in S.Cunnison & J.Stageman (eds), *Feminizing the Unions: Challenging the Culture of Masculinity*, Avebury, 1992.

Glasgow Media Group, *Bad News*, Routledge & Kegan Paul, 1976.

Glasgow Media Group, *More Bad News*, Routledge & Kegan Paul, 1980.

Glasgow Media Group, *Really Bad News*, Writers & Readers, 1982.

S.Hall, 'Encoding/Decoding', in S.Hall et al (eds), *Culture, Media, Language*, Unwin Hyman, 1980.

P.t'Hart, 'Symbols, Rituals and Power: The Lost Dimensions of Crisis Management', *Journal of Contingencies and Crisis Management*, 1/1, 1993.

C.Hay, 'Crisis and the Discursive Unification of the State', in P.Dunleavy & J.Stanyer (eds), *Contemporary Political Studies 1994*, Political Studies Association, 1994.

C.Hay, 'Rethinking Crisis: Narratives of the New Right and Cosntructions of Crisis', *Rethinking Marxism*, 8/2, forthcoming, 1996.

D.Morley, *Television, Audiences and Cultural Studies*, Routledge, 1992.

G.Philo, *Seeing and Believing: The Influence of Television*, Routledge, 1990.

P.Ricoeur, *Time and Narrative*, Volume 1, University of Chicago Press, 1984.

J.B.Thompson, 'Mass Communication and Modern Culture: Contribution to a Critical Theory of Ideology', *Sociology*, 22/3, 1988.

J.B.Thompson, *Ideology and Modern Culture*, Polity, 1990.

TUC Media Working Group, *A Cause for Concern: Media Coverage of Industrial Disputes*, January – February 1979, TUC Publications, 1979.

The Transformation of the State in Postwar Britain

Peter Kerr
University of Birmingham
&
David Marsh
University of Birmingham

'False Dichotomies and Failed Assumptions:
Revisiting and Revising the Consensus Debate'

Introduction

Most of the literature on Thatcherism is based upon an assumption that the Thatcher years marked an exceptional period in postwar British politics. This belief, however, tends to be ground less upon the success of the Thatcher governments in implementing their own strategies, than upon the variety of ways in which they contrived to uncouple previous ones. As a result, our understanding of the post-1979 era has been very much guided by our perceptions of the period of consensus which preceded it.

However, although the notion of 'consensus' pervades our understanding of post-war British politics, our appreciation of the essential characteristics of this period remains surprisingly partial. In large part, this is because there has been a relative lack of serious attempts at empirical analysis. Accordingly, the aim of this paper is to argue that the consensus debate needs to move beyond its present scope in order to gain a more fuller insight into the evolution of the state throughout the post-war period. Essentially, we will maintain that there is a crucial need to distinguish between the 'post-war consensus' and the 'post-war settlement' in order to gauge the impact which the policy consensus had upon the structures of the state regime. Ultimately, we hope to gain a more accurate picture, not only of the consensus period, but also of the extent to which Thatcherism constituted a distinctive phase in the evolution of the British state.

Thatcherism By Definition

It has often been remarked that Thatcherism is a diffuse phenomenon. According to Jessop et al (1988, p.5), the term has 'acquired almost as many meanings as there are people who mention it'. Consequently, the phrase exhibits a chameleon-like idiosyncrasy; lacking any precise definition, it has come to represent a variety of things to a variety of people.

Nevertheless, it is easy to exaggerate the lack of clarity in existing definitions of Thatcherism. For, if the Thatcher years are to be identified as worthy of an 'ism', then, like the chameleon, they must be distinguished from their background. As a result, they have come to be defined by their peculiarity in relation to past practices, and in particular to the 'postwar consensus'.

Thus, it is common among students of British government to claim that 1979 marked a key break with the past, which lead to a transformation of the institutions and policies of the post-war consensus. The idea that a consensual era underpinned the radicalism of the Thatcher years is embraced by the vast majority of political scientists. Therefore, as an analytical reference, the 'post-war consensus' is almost as pervasive a term as 'Thatcherism'. In our view, however, this is no small point, for it is clear that many of the assumptions which have been made about both Thatcherism and the pre-1979 era have, to a large extent, been mutually constructed. Consequently, if we are to assess the evolution of the state in post-war Britain, it is important initially to question the way in which the existing literature itself has evolved.

Constructing our Past in a Present Light

Paul Addison's (1975) *The Road to 1945* is popularly accredited as having brought the idea of the post-war consensus into common usage. However, it should be noted that the term can be traced to a scattered assortment of previous references. Nevertheless, it is true to say that Addison's thesis did not impress upon subsequent literature until after 1979. Therefore, the vast bulk of the conclusions drawn about the consensus era, have been made in the light of the Thatcher period and have subsequently been utilised to throw Thatcherism into stark relief. As a result, it is very difficult to locate a discernible literature on consensus, which, as a concept, has only recently become the focus for academic scrutiny.

To date, Kavanagh & Morris (1989) have provided the only comprehensive study of the consensus, and, by the time they did so, the concept had already been taken for granted. Thus, it is important to emphasise that the contrasts made between Thatcherism and the consensus period have generally rested upon normative assumptions rather than empirical evidence. This point has been eloquently expressed by Marlow (1995, p.7) who contends that the idea of the post-war consensus 'remains something of an unexamined assumption'. Accordingly, the author states that: 'for such a taken-for-granted notion, it is...ill-defined, poorly explicated and inadequately analysed.' (*Ibid*).

As a result, Marlow concludes that the literature displays many of the characteristics associated with the postmodernist concept of 'intertextuality'. This denotes the practice whereby an abstraction becomes defined through its repeated use within a variety of texts. If we trace the origins of the post-war consensus thesis, then it becomes clear that this process can appropriately be traced to explain why the thesis has become so overwhelmingly incorporated into our political history. Accordingly, there exists a 'universe of texts that collectively sanction the post-war consensus thesis, by dint of their sheer persuasiveness' (Marlow 1995 p 19).

Thus, if we look closely at the literature on consensus, it is clear that most commentators use the term uncritically, in order to illuminate their assumptions about the present period rather than the past. As a result, a necessary understanding of the evolution of the post-war British state is marred by the fact that a stark and often unsustainable dichotomy has been created between the pre-1979 and post-1979 eras which has invited contrast rather than comparison. The logic underpinning this dichotomy is deceptively simple but nevertheless deeply problematic. The consensus period was marked by a succession of governments seen to be pursuing pragmatic rather than radical responses to economic and political decline. According to Hay (1996), these governments are best described as 'state-accommodating' since they did not actively seek to: 'challenge the structures of the state inherited from the previous administration' (pp 129-30). In direct contrast however, the Thatcher administrations appear as 'state-shaping' since their ambitions were: 'to transform the very contours of the state itself, thereby imposing a new trajectory upon its evolution' (*Ibid*).

As a result, the election of the Thatcherites to office provides both the *appearance* and the *rhetoric* of a government which stands in antagonism to the structures of the state inherited from the early post-war period. However, as this paper will attempt to demonstrate, these appearances should be treated with caution, since a more thorough investigation into the nature of the post-war state can reveal many continuities which are not readily apparent.

The Conventional Portrait of the Post-war Consensus

The 'accepted version' (see Pimlott 1988, Butler 1993) of the post-war consensus thesis derives mainly from the work of authors such as Addison (1975), Middlemas (1986) and Kavanagh & Morris (1989). Addison's work popularised the key component of the thesis; the idea that the experience of the Second World War helped create the circumstances for the development of policies aimed at combating the deep divisions in British society. As a result, a new agenda was forged around the need for greater social security and welfare reforms. Similarly, full employment was seen as a primary ambition, coupled with more vigorous fiscal and industrial policies. Many authors view four events; the 'Keynesian' budget of 1941, the Beveridge Report of 1942, the Education Act of 1944 and the Employment Policy White Paper of 1944, as the cornerstones of the new consensus which was consolidated by Labour under Clement Attlee, and the Conservatives under Harold MacMillan.

Whilst few authors dispute the above narrative on the rise of the post-war consensus, differences remain in accounts of when this period ended. As Butler (1993) points out, 1960, 64, 67, 70, 73, 75 and 79 have all been forwarded as possible dates. However, the increased polarisation of the two main parties, coupled with the apparent breakdown of Keynesian economics and corporatist-style government, have led most authors to assume that the consensus gradually eroded throughout the 1970s, with Mrs Thatcher providing the final nail in its coffin.

The author most directly associated with the conventional portrait of consensus politics is Dennis Kavanagh. Together with Peter Morris, Kavanagh has produced, the only systematic analysis thus far, of the essential features of the supposed consensus. These authors suggest that the consensus consisted of two key elements; adherence to a particular style of government, and a shared commitment to a broad set of policies. More specifically, they define the consensus as:

> 'a set of parameters which bounded the set of policy options regarded by senior politicians and civil servants as administratively practicable, economically affordable and politically acceptable (1989, p.13)

Such a definition however, illuminates one of the major difficulties in conceptualising the post-war consensus. All policy options introduced by politicians and civil servants were thus regarded, at least to those introducing them, and can therefore be viewed as part of the consensus. Consequently, as Marlow (1995, p.36) points out: 'whatever policies came to pass (ie were adjudged at the time to be 'administratively practicable', 'economically affordable' and 'politically acceptable') are now regarded as part of the post-war consensus'. In effect then, such an argument is tautological, or at best non-falsifiable in the terms it is cast.

There are other, increasingly well-rehearsed, problems with the post-war consensus thesis which are also worth briefly mentioning. First, there is the problem of who shared in the consensus. Various answers can be identified in the literature, with very little consensus between them. Consequently, as Butler explains, different analysts tend to:

> 'pick and choose people – one minute we examine the population at large; the next we focus on parliamentary sentiment; then successive Chancellors of the Exchequer are in the frame, before we swing suddenly to "political élites" '. (1993, pp.438-9)

Secondly, the question of the depth of the consensus poses similar difficulties. According to Seldon (1994, p.506), different commentators confer 'different intensities of consensual expression'. Thus, whilst some authors refer to a consensus over policy, others argue that there was a deeper, more profound commitment to a set of common beliefs, moral values and social aspirations. Thirdly, as previously mentioned, although there is considerable agreement that the origins of the consensus lay in a cumulative process between 1940 and 1948, the question of when it ended continues to provoke a plethora of different opinions.

The conventional portrait of the rise and fall of the postwar consensus has been so overwhelmingly incorporated into our political history that it has remained a relatively uncontested thesis. According to Butler (1993, p.445): 'too many commentators find the rise and fall thesis attractively undemanding'. However, since Pimlott's (1988) influential attack on the notion of consensus, the term has been subject to an increasing number of criticisms. Unfortunately however, with political scientists seemingly unprepared to challenge conventional wisdom, the bulk of this recent work has been left to historians.

According to Seldon (1994) this fact suggests an essential difference between the priorities of historians, who tend to focus on the trees, and of political scientists whose concern is to view the whole wood. In our view however, it appears more appropriate to concur with Hay's (1996) analogy that political scientists and historians alike, have tended to *miss* the wood from the trees. Consequently, too much of the debate has thus far been bogged down in *semantic* squabbling over the meaning of 'consensus' and *pedantic* altercations over both the depth and timing of it. As a result, few authors have attempted to question the accepted assumptions about either the type of consensus which existed in post-war Britain or the nature of the state regime in which this consensus resided.

Consequently, we would argue that there is an overwhelming need to move the debate beyond its current parameters. A more salient exercise for those involved in assessing the transformation of the state in the post-war period would be to re-examine both the content of consensus and the essential make-up of the state apparatus. In order to achieve this though, it is important to distinguish between the terms 'post-war consensus' and 'post-war settlement'.

Beyond Semantics and Pedantics

As Hay (1996, p.127) points out: 'the notions of post-war settlement and post-war consensus, despite their superficial similarity cannot be conflated'. According to Hay then, the post-war 'settlement' generally refers to: 'the relationship between the state, the economy, civil society and the public sphere that was to emerge and become institutionalised in post-war Britain' (p.125). Meanwhile, the term 'consensus': 'generally refers to an implicit accord between the parties as to the nature of political responsibility and the form and role of the state in the post-war period' (p.126). For this reason, Hay emphasises the fact that the notion of 'settlement' has tended to be used by state theorists, whilst the idea of 'consensus' has been utilised primarily by political scientists and historians.

Whilst we would agree that it is crucial to distinguish between the two concepts, it must be emphasised that few attempts have thus far been made to do so. Consequently, the literature on the post-war period is infused with labels such as 'Keynesian', 'social democratic', and 'welfare state', which are randomly employed to describe both the 'settlement' and the 'consensus'. Thus, the labels which political scientists have adopted to identify the consensus have generally been the same ones which state theorists have used to describe the settlement. As a result, we are left with the assumption that the *policy* parameters set by the parties throughout the post-war period were in accord with the *institutionalised* parameters of the state regime.

In our own view, this brings us to the central problem inherent in the literature on the post-war period. For it is clear, that the majority of political commentators conflate the rhetorical and purposeful machinations of governmental actors with the structural properties of the state regime. As a result, it is assumed that the apparent pursuit of Keynesian demand management techniques and welfare policies, throughout the consensus era, provides us with enough evidence to identify a Keynesian Welfare State, or settlement. Moreover, this evidence has been regularly cited to justify the apparent radicalism of the Thatcher era, which, with its emphasis on monetarism and the freedom of the market, appears to stand in direct contrast to the pre-1979 period.

As a result of this process then, it is assumed in the literature on Thatcherism that the Thatcherites were successful in radically transforming the post-war British state. As the next section will show, this is exemplified by most authors' treatment of the contrasts between the economic policies pursued under Thatcherism and those practiced throughout the consensus.

The Limits to Keynesianism

When the Thatcherites took office, their evangelical message was that they could deliver salvation from Britain's long-term economic decline. This has provoked a broad agreement amongst most commentators, that the Thatcher 'revolution' in economic policy failed, even by its own benchmark for success. Consequently, the persistent strains on the economy caused by continual balance of payments difficulties, the lack of extensive long term investment, coupled with the bloated role of the financial sector have contributed to the fact that the Thatcher 'miracle' amounted to little more than a 'mirage' (Mitchie 1992). However, despite these various objections, 'Thatcherism' is still seen by many as marking a fundamental break with post-war economic protocol. By 'circumventing, isolating and dismantling the social democratic apparatus of intervention and representation built up over the post-war period' (Martin 1992, p.128), the Conservatives have been accredited with a move away from the practice of state intervention synonymous with the Keynesian period.

However, this claim again highlights the essential problem with much of the literature. For, as the above quote demonstrates, terms such as 'Keynesianism', viewed as a cornerstone of the *consensus*, have become conflated with labels such as 'social democracy', which imply the idea of *settlement*. This problem, of extending the idea of Keynesianism to characterise the nature of the state regime itself, is one which persists throughout the literature. Consequently, it has been argued that 'Keynesianism' represented:

> 'a vision of society which involved state efforts to harmonise interests through diverse economic and social policies, to politically regulate the market economy and to take a tutelary role in securing business and trade union approval for central economic policies'. (Krieger 1986, p.22)

In our view, attempts to stretch the notion of 'Keynesianism' to include the ideas of Beveridge and of economic corporatism, and to attribute these to an overall societal settlement, create a gross distortion of the reality of the post-war period. Thus, we would agree with Thompson's (1984) assertion, that the definition of Keynesianism must be 'limited to a fairly narrowly demarcated field of legitimate interventions', namely the stimulation of budgetary aggregates, which Keynes himself sought to legitimate. Consequently, we must accept the fact that Keynes' ideas 'did not involve any direct government interference in the economy' (Bulpitt 1986, p. 27). As Keith Smith (1984) explains:

'The "Keynesian" policy-makers have been condemned as full-scale interventionists...in fact their belief in markets was scarcely less extreme than that of the monetarists.' (p.182)

Despite this, the fact remains that the vast majority of political scientists and state theorists alike, continue to underpin their perceptions of the radical nature of Thatcherism by creating an exaggerated dichotomy between the practices of the pre-1979 and post-1979 eras. In addition, this dichotomy is heightened by the fact that a 'consensus' on applied Keynesianism is mistaken for a 'settlement' on social democratic interventions This type of conceptualisation leads to the erroneous assumption that: 'the demise of the Keynesian Welfare State represents more than the eclipse of an economic theory...it signifies also the decline in support for a kind of society' (Krieger 1986, p.31).

The Obstacles to Keynesianism

In our view, rather than extending the idea of Keynesianism to describe the institutionalised parameters of the state, it is more important to recognise that, the pre-inscribed institutions of the state served to *hamper* the full implementation of Keynesian techniques. Thus, it is essential to emphasise the need to be cautious in crediting Keynesian ideas with the success of penetrating the liberal orthodox 'Treasury View'. For it is clear that the persistence of pre-Keynesian beliefs within the Treasury served, throughout the post-war period, as a major obstacle to an effective demand-management strategy of achieving full employment. Indeed, Booth (1986) has argued that, because of the exigency of developing demand-management techniques around the needs of the bureaucracy, applied Keynesianism after 1945 reflected a more liberal version of Keynes' views prior to the war. Consequently, many of the more 'supportive' policies advocated by Keynesians during and after the war, were sacrificed, leading to the development of what Booth calls 'simple Keynesianism'. As a result, an 'oral tradition' in favour of sound monetary policies persisted within the Treasury which was reflected in both the Cabinet split over public expenditure in 1958 and continual attempts to control government expenditure and inflation.

A further obstacle to the efficient use of Keynesian budgetary policy to effect full employment proved to be the various attempts by all post-war governments to manage sterling and the exchange rate (Bulpitt 1986). As Brittan forcefully explains:

'The truth is that, for most of this period, neither the UK, nor most other countries pursued demand management policies directed to full employment. The language of such policies was often used, but so song as the Bretton Woods system of exchange rates fixed against the dollar prevailed, the overriding aim was to maintain the currency parity.' (quoted in Bulpitt, p.25)

Consequently, the attempts in the years 1957, 60, 64, 66 and 73 to protect the balance of payments meant that post-war governments were continually forced to throw their domestic policies into reverse in the defence of sterling.

These attempts at deflation rather than devaluation highlight the crucial fact that the consensus on domestic policy was, many ways, overshadowed by the persistent hegemony of the 'sterling lobby'. According to Blank:

> 'This lobby shared the belief that Britain's international position and responsibilities constituted the primary policy objectives and that the international role of sterling was vital to this position'. (quoted in Grant 1987, p.81)

Thus, the financial sector, with its ability to sanction governments by withholding investment, has played a crucial role in deflecting post-war governments from the 'Keynesian' policy of maintaining full employment. Moreover, the 'relative autonomy' of the Bank of England over monetary policy, has ensured that the 'exceptionalism' of the financial sector remained secured throughout the post-war period (Grant, 1987).

The Limits to Planned Intervention

Consequently, it is essential that we depart from the view that the post-war period was characterised by a social democratic interventionist state. In an attempt to dilute this claim, Dearlove & Saunders (1991), suggest that it is more appropriate to view the period 1945 to the early 1960s as one in which the state played a more 'supportive' role towards the private sector, as opposed to its 'facilitative' stance prior to the war. Thus, it is only from the 1960s that these authors perceive an 'increasingly directive role in economic affairs' (p 356). It is our own view however, that no such qualitative shift took place in the role of the state towards the private sector immediately after the war. Rather, 'simple Keynesianism' is best perceived as an alternative means of 'facilitating' economic growth by providing a stable climate of demand within a fixed exchange rate system in which free markets could prosper.

The tools by which governments could enact supportive measures to aid industry were severely limited. As Hall (1983) explains, the separation of the Bank of England and financial capital in general has prevented the British state from having effective control over the flow of funds in the economy. Similarly, the Treasury has traditionally remained isolated from the co-ordination of industrial policy. This has meant that the views of industrial capital have generally been subordinated to the interests of the financial sector, whilst serious attempts at planning were never implemented until the creation of the NEDC in 1962.

Thus, it is between 1962 and 1976 that it became increasingly clear to governments that the range of formerly facilitative policies aimed at budgetary management required supplementary interventionist strategies. It is during this period, therefore, that governments began to pursue policies akin to the 'supportive' type which Dearlove & Saunders equate with the early post-war period. Thus, it can be argued that it was throughout this period that a *partial* change in the management of the economy took place. However, it would be wrong to view the decade as signalling a *fundamental* change in the nature of the state regime. The extent to which the government exercised 'control' over capital has been grossly overestimated. As

Hall (1983) explains, the DEA, which had been created by Labour in 1965 as a full-blown department imbued with the responsibility of devising a long-term 'National Plan', failed to redress the short-term discretion which the Treasury exercised over economic policy. Thus, as Hall (1983, p. 387) argues: 'control over the priorities of economic policy never left the Treasury, and many of the decisions ultimately frustrated the planners' . As a result, these attempts failed when, in 1966, in the face of balance of payments crises, the Treasury forced the abandonment of economic planning and full employment in the defence of the value of sterling.

Similarly, although the Labour government from 1974-9 succeeded in enacting an Industry Act which provided for the establishment of 'planning agreements' between the government and the country's top 100 firms, coupled with the creation of the National Enterprise Board, their attempt at intervention became quickly frustrated by the imposition of the IMF conditions which signalled a return to monetarism. According to Coates (1980), Labour's programme for planned recovery suffered from, and eventually succumbed to, the constraints placed upon it by 'the centres of private power' (namely, civil servants, industrial firms, financiers, international financial agencies and foreign governments).

These points, and indeed Coates' observation in particular, serve to highlight the crucial need to distinguish between the policies around which the parties formed a consensus, and the nature and make-up of the post-war settlement. Certainly, it is clear that, whilst an early consensus had developed around Keynesian demand management techniques and a later one emerged on the need for increased intervention, both of these strategies were to find themselves at odds with the *institutionalised* practices of the existing state regime. Thus, a persistent disjuncture remained between the rhetoric of consensus politicians anxious to avoid the traumas of the pre-war years and the reality of the state intact.

Two or Three Settlements?

As such, the major problem with identifying the transformation and evolution of the post-war period lies in the fact that the decades which preceded the Thatcherite ascendancy appear contradictory in character. On the one hand, the period after the Second World War saw an unprecedented increase in the pursuit of 'statist' measures aimed at the economy and social welfare. However, on the other, many of these measures were both less ambitious than is normally assumed, and also hampered by pre-institutionalised practices. Consequently, the challenge for those who attempt to either chart or explain the events of this period must be to conceptualise and explain these types of paradox.

In our view, the most comprehensive attempts on offer have been provided by Jessop (1992) and Hay (1996) who have accounted for the contradictory nature of the era by postulating the existence of two, or even three different post-war settlements. According to Jessop then, the contradictory character of the state regime can best be explained by the suggestion of two distinct settlements:

- (i) a productivist or producers' settlement;
- (ii) a redistributive or politicians' settlement.

Thus, the producers' settlement should be seen as: 'centrally concerned with securing the conditions for economic modernisation through planning and enhanced productivity' (Hay 1996, p. 158), whilst the politicians' settlement remained 'concerned with the promotion of greater social justice' (*Ibid*).

In a more tentative attempt to develop Jessop's twin settlement thesis, Hay suggests that it may be more appropriate to refer to a third layer of settlement, namely a *financiers' settlement*. This refers to the existence of the City, Bank, Treasury triumvirate which was to continue to exercise an 'overdetermining influence on economic and industrial policy' (Hay 1996, pp.159-161). Whilst Jessop would consider the financiers' as an essential component of the producers' settlement, Hay's contention that they should be viewed as a distinct grouping appears more convincing.

The strength of both these arguments lies in the fact that they depict the post-war period as one in which the state regime displayed contradictory features. However, despite this, we believe that neither Hay nor Jessop succeed fully in their attempt to characterise these paradoxes. Essentially, this is due to the fact that their notions of 'settlement' are conflated with 'consensus' in a way which precludes any distinction between the two concepts. Certainly, Jessop's thesis, perhaps because it is more fully developed, appears most guilty of this conceptual error. Thus, the author makes little or no distinction between the ambitions of the producers and politicians on the one hand, and the reality of the institutional parameters of the state on the other. Consequently, as Hay acknowledges, Jessop's account can be criticised for overstating both the 'Keynesian' and the 'corporatist' nature of the settlement.

As a result, it would appear that, in order properly to characterise the state in post-war Britain, the notion of the existence of different 'layers' of settlement requires to be either more fully developed or abandoned altogether. In our view, however, it would appear more fruitful to follow Hay's earlier advice and attempt initially to develop the crucial distinction between the notions of post-war 'consensus' and post-war 'settlement'. By separating these two analytical references and identifying them more concretely, it is possible to locate which specific areas of policy consensus became absorbed into the institutionalised parameters of the state regime, and which ones were essentially blocked. It is only in these terms that we can begin to account for the paradox that an era of unprecedented statism occurred which failed to transform the neo-liberal structures of the British state. Thus, we may ultimately be better able to gauge the effect of the Thatcherite strategy on the post-war British state by virtue of the fact that we will gain a more accurate reading of the key characteristics of that state.

Conclusion

Once we depart from the conventional wisdom of the consensus era, it also becomes necessary to revise our accepted assumptions about Thatcherism. For, if we take seriously the charge that the post-war period exhibited many of the characteristics associated with the Thatcher years, then it becomes clear that we need to re-appraise the extent of the supposed Thatcherite transformation.

In our view, this transformation has been greatly exaggerated due to the relative lack of any critical spotlight on the nature of the settlement which emerged from the experience of the war years and the initial Attlee reforms. To us, then, the major reason why Thatcherism so readily adjusted itself to the structural parameters of the state regime is because in many ways it represented a continuation of past practices rather than a break with them.

Bibliography

P.Addison, *The Road to 1945*, Cape, 1975.

A.Booth, 'Simple Keynesianism and Whitehall 1936-44', *Economy and Society*, 15, 1983.

J.Bulpitt, 'The Discipline of the New Democracy: Mrs Thatcher's Domestic Statecraft', *Political Studies*, 34, 1986.

A.Butler, 'The End of the Post-war Consensus: Reflections on the Scholarly Uses of Political Rhetoric', *The Political Quarterly*, 64, 1993.

D.Coates, *Labour in Power*, Longman, 1980.

J.Dearlove & P.Saunders, *Introduction to British Politics*, Blackwell, 1991.

W.Grant, *Business and Politics in Britain*, Macmillan, 1987.

P.Hall, 'Patterns of Economic Policy: An Organisational Approach', in D.Held et al (eds), *States and Societies*, Open University, 1983.

C.Hay, *Restating Social and Political Change*, Open University Press, 1996.

B.Jessop et al, *Thatcherism*, Polity Press, 1988

B.Jessop, 'From Social Democracy to Thatcherism: Twenty-Five Years of British Politics', in N.Abercrombie & A.Warde (eds), *Social Change in Contemporary Britain*, Polity, 1992.

D.Kavanagh & P.Morris, *Consensus Politics: From Attlee to Thatcher*, Blackwell, 1989.

J.Krieger, *Reagan, Thatcher and the Politics of Decline*, Polity, 1986.

J.D.Marlow, *Questioning the Post-war Consensus Thesis: Towards an Alternative Account, A Different Understanding*, PhD Thesis, Dept of Sociology, University of Essex, 1995.

R.Martin, 'Has the British Economy Been Transformed? Critical Reflections on the Policies of the Thatcher Era' in P.Cloke (ed), *Policy and Change in Thatcher's Britain*, Pergamon, 1992.

K.Middlemas, *Power, Competition and the State: Volume 1 – Britain in Search of Balance 1940-1961*, Macmillan, 1986.

B.Pimlott, 'The Myth of Consensus', in L.M.Smith (ed), *The Making of Britain: Echoes of Greatness*, Macmillan, 1988.

A.Seldon, 'Consensus: A Debate Too Long?', *Parliamentary Affairs*, 47, 1994.

K.Smith, *The British Economic Crisis: It's Past and Future*, Penguin, 1984.

G.Thompson, 'Economic Intervention in the Post-war Economy', in G.McLennon et al, *State and Society in Contemporary Britain: A Critical Introduction*, Blackwell, 1984.

William Morris

Mark Bevir
University of Newcastle upon Tyne

'William Morris: Romanticism and the Rejection of Politics'

In the hundred years since his death, William Morris has inspired all the diverse strands that make up the British left. Indeed, interpretations of Morris have acted almost as a weather vain indicating the prevailing direction of the intellectual wind on the left. In the 1920s and 1930s the momentum lay with the ethical socialism that the Independent Labour Party had brought into the Labour Party. Writers such as John Bruce Glasier represented Morris as a moralist who had little interest in economic questions. Morris, they said, had told a meeting of socialists in Glasgow, 'I do not know what Marx's theory of value is and I am damned if I want to know'; 'Political Economy is not my line and much of it appears to me to be dreary rubbish.'[1] In the 1960s and 70s the momentum appeared to lie with a Marxism infused by syndicalist and humanist themes. Writers such as Robin Page Arnot and E.P.Thompson represented Morris as a Marxist who not only studied *Capital* in depth but also struggled with the problems his own political practice posed until eventually he reached the grail of Leninism.[2] From the late 1970s through the 1980s the momentum shifted once again to a libertarian outlook that drew on all sorts of counter-cultural influences. Morris then became a prophet of alternative lifestyles, even an anarcho-communist, as evidenced by the work of James Hulse, Florence Boos, and his most recent biographer, Fiona MacCarthy.[3] How has one man exercised such sway over the socialist imagination? Why have ethical socialists, Marxists, anarchists, all sorts of left-wing thinkers, returned time and time again to locate their own vision in the work of Morris? The answer to these sorts of questions lies, first, in the romantic background to Morris's own socialism, and, second, in the way his romantic socialism led him to renounce all effective forms of political action.

William Morris was born in 1834 at Walthamstow just outside of London. His father worked as a broker in the City, and even after his father's death in 1847, the family continued to enjoy a solid Victorian prosperity. Morris studied at Marlborough School before going up to Exeter College, Oxford, where he became immersed in the Pre-Raphaelite movement. During his first summer vacation he visited France where he was amazed at the beauty of the Gothic cathedrals at Amiens, Chartres and Rouen.[4] During term

---

[1] J.Glasier, *William Morris and the Early Days of the Socialist Movement*, Longmans, 1921, p.32.

[2] R.Arnot, *William Morris: The Man and the Myth, including the letters of William Morris to J.L.Mahon and Dr.John Glasse*, Lawrence & Wishart, 1964; and E. Thompson, William Morris: Romantic to Revolutionary, revised ed. Merlin, 1977.

[3] See F. & W.Boos, 'The Utopian Communism of William Morris', *History of Political Thought*, 7, 1986; J.Hulse, *Revolutionists in London: A Study of Five Unorthodox Socialists*, Clarendon, 1970; F.MacCarthy, *William Morris: A Life for Our Time*, Faber, 1994.

[4] See, for example, W. Morris, *The Collected Letters of William Morris*, edited by

time he read the works of Ruskin, and they struck him as a revelation. In the chapter on 'The Nature of Gothic' in his *The Stones of Venice*, Ruskin argued that the rough and imperfect quality of Gothic architecture is both beautiful and virtuous; it reflects the human nature of art and also the pleasure the craftsman could take in his work.[5] Gothic architecture reflected the harmony and happiness of the medieval world; an idyllic world of communal fellows who led simple, vigorous lives surrounded by beautiful, useful objects; a world in which the craftsmen could express his individual genius in his work. Contemporary society, in contrast, is a soulless beast in which isolated individuals are governed by the drab uniformity of the machine.[6]

After leaving Oxford, Morris worked for a while in an architects office, but before long he committed himself more and more to the arts and crafts movement as well as writing several successful romances.[7] Many of our museums, notably the Victoria and Albert, contain extensive collections of the objects he designed, manufactured, or both. His textile patterns provided the inspiration for those since made familiar by Laura Ashley. To Victorians, he was best known as the author of *The Earthly Paradise*, though modern readers tend to prefer the earlier poems in his *Defence of Guenevere*. One poem in *The Earthly Paradise*, 'The Lovers of Gudrun', had been inspired by the Icelandic sagas. From 1869 to 1876, Morris published a vast amount of work that drew on a more detailed study of old Norse literature. The Icelandic sagas opened to him an idyllic world akin to that Ruskin and he had found in the Middle Ages. An organic community of brave, true, genuine souls, who took a natural delight in using beautiful things in their everyday life.

Morris first became active in politics as a member of the Eastern Question Association which was formed to fight Disraeli's jingoism.[8] He joined the National Liberal League and worked hard to ensure the return of a Liberal government. Soon afterwards, however, he was horrified at the way Gladstone's second government repressed the Irish and bombed Alexandria, Egypt. He despaired of Liberalism, and in 1883 turned to Socialism, announcing his conversion whilst giving a talk at University College, Oxford with Ruskin in the Chair.[9]

It is clear that Morris approached socialism as a romantic deeply indebted to Ruskin, whom he described as his 'master' in social theory.[10]

N.Kelvin, Princeton University Press, 1984-87, Volume 1: 1848-1880, pp.19-22.

[5] J.Ruskin, 'The Nature of Gothic', in *The Works of John Ruskin*, edited by E.Cook & A.Wedderburn, G.Allen, 1903-12, Volume 10: 'The Stones of Venice' – II: *The Sea Stories*, pp.180-269.

[6] For the moral economy he therefore adopted, see in particular J.Ruskin, 'Unto this Last', in *Works*, Volume 17: 'Unto This Last, Munera Pulveris, Time and Tide, and Other Writings on Political Economy 1860-1873', pp.15-114.

[7] P.Stansky, *Redesigning the World: William Morris, the 1880s, and the Arts and Crafts*, Princeton University Press, 1985.

[8] On the background to this affair, see R.Seton-Watson, *Disraeli, Gladstone, and the Eastern Question: A Study in Diplomacy and Party Politics*, Macmillan, 1935.

[9] For the talk see W.Morris, 'Art Under Plutocracy' in *The Collected Works of William Morris*, introduced by M.Morris, Longmans, 1910-15, Volume 23: 'Signs of Change, Lectures on Socialism', pp.164-91.

[10] *Justice*, 16 June 1884.

The overlap between Ruskin's sociology of art and Marx's historical sociology should have been clear long before the 1930s, when the full extent of Marx's early concern with alienation became apparent upon the discovery of some of his early manuscripts. Morris, following Ruskin, long had argued that art reflected the conditions of labour in society; he said that the arts 'are connected with all history and are clear teachers of it.'[11] Now Morris, following Marx, also argued that different social systems represent different solutions to the necessity of humans acquiring their subsistence from nature by labour. In both cases, something like the economic base explained at least part of something like the social superstructure. Nonetheless, there are differences between a Marxist historical sociology and a romantic concern with art, even when the latter is combined with a Ruskinian sociology. The best way to understand Morris's socialism is to see how he brought them together, and the place he gave to each of them within his political thought.

Morris's broad conception of art did not cover social or political relations. His turning to Marxism meant, above all else, therefore, that he came to believe that the conditions of labour determined not only the nature of art, and so the quality of our individual lives, but also the character of our social and political relationships. Now Morris insisted on the reality of the class struggle. The conditions of labour divided civil society into classes with opposed interests. Thus, whereas earlier Morris had talked of the need 'to bridge the gap between the classes,' he now argued that 'the workman's real master is not his immediate employer but his class.'[12] His new acceptance of the reality of the class struggle brought with it a commitment to Marx's historical sociology. History consists of the struggle of classes to advance their own interests: the class struggle explains past history.

Moreover, Morris's powerful belief in the class struggle led him to condemn the state as an instrument of class oppression. People were producers, not citizens, so the notion of a shared nationality was an illusion. Parliament was just a committee of the upper classes that presented us with a facade of democracy while actually oppressing the working class. The violent repression of protesters on Bloody Sunday revealed the true nature of the state. First the police and then the judges enforced the interests of property in flagrant violation of the supposed rights of the common people.[13] The capitalist state allowed the workers to participate in their own slavery but that was all. The true nature of the state, and the reality of the class struggle, were hidden from most people by the operation of ideology. Here ideology, and especially Christianity as it was preached within the Churches, served to protect the interests of private property.

Morris's commitment to the idea of the class struggle is unproblematic. The same can not be said of the Marxist credentials of his economic analysis of capitalism. On the one hand, he clearly tried to come to terms with Capital, and some articles he wrote with Bax really do show an impressive

---

[11] Morris, *Works*, Volume 22: 'Hopes for Art, Lectures on Art and Industry', p.8.
[12] *Ibid*, Volume 23, pp.162 & 224.
[13] Morris said 'the greatest humbug which Sunday's events have laid bare is the protection afforded by the law to the humblest citizen' (*Commonweal*, 19 November 1887).

grasp of Marx's ideas.[14] On the other hand, he clearly was not comfortable with economic theory, and the articles he wrote on his own are far less impressive than those he wrote with Bax. Even if Glasier's story of what Morris told the Glasgow socialists is somewhat unreliable, nobody who reads Morris's socialist writings can fail to recognise how much he prefers to depict a communal way of life rather than try to unravel any economic logic to capitalism.[15] Crucially, however, at the same time as he published the articles with Bax, he also wrote two lectures by himself, in which he outlined a theory of surplus value based on the twin pillars of the capitalists' having a monopoly of the means of production, and wages being fixed by an iron law.[16] He called one 'Monopoly: Or, How Labour is Robbed,' and in the other he explained that:

> 'The capitalists, by means of their monopoly of the means of production, compel the worker to work for less than his due share of the wealth which he produces – that is, for less than he produces. He must work, he will die else, and as they are in the possession of the raw material, he must agree to the terms they enforce.'[17]

This theory of surplus value differs from that of Marx. Marx argued that labour-power had greater use-value than exchange-value, and this was the source of surplus value. The capitalists necessarily acquired surplus value when they purchased labour-power irrespective of any supposed law of wages or monopoly of the means of production, although the historical fact that the proletariat were a landless class helped to explain why labour-power had become a commodity for sale in the market. Given that Morris said his economic theory derived less from reading Marx than from 'conversation with such friends as Bax and Hyndman and Scheu,' perhaps we should not be surprised that his theory of surplus values incorporated the Lassallean perspective of the latter two.[18]

The fact is: Morris's commitment to the class struggle, and to socialism in general, owed far more to his earlier sociology of art than to his grasp of Marx's economic theory. He saw the class struggle as the driving force behind the dialectical movement of history, and, in this respect, it merely took over from his Ruskinian view of the history of art as an indication of the changing conditions in which craftsmen had laboured. In the feudal era, craftsmen related to their products as artists, but they did so within a class-ridden society. The rising bourgeoisie destroyed the political power of

---

[14] The articles were published in *Commonweal* throughout 1887, and republished as W.Morris & E.Bax, *Socialism: Its Growth and Outcome*, Swan Sonnenschein, 1893.

[15] Glasier's account of the Glasgow incident is considered critically by Thompson, *Morris*, pp.741-62.

[16] The easiest way to explain the greater sophistication of the articles written with Bax is surely to say the economic theory within them was the work of Bax with little help from Morris. After all, Morris himself wrote in his diary, 'Tuesday to Bax at Croydon where we did our first article on Marx: or rather he did it: I don't think I should ever make an economist even of the most elementary kind.' W.Morris, *Socialist Diary*, edited by F.Boos, Journeyman, 1982, p.32.

[17] Morris, *Works*, Volume 23, p.223.

[18] *Ibid*, Volume 23, p.278.

the landed aristocracy, but they did so on the basis of a commercial system, which denied the artistic nature of production. Morris argued that capitalism was inimical to good art. An attractive building in a modern suburb would surprise one, whereas medieval cities such as Oxford and Rouen contained almost nothing but attractive buildings. Contemporary art was in such poor condition that students of design now had to study artefacts from the past, not modern goods. Here the plight of art reflected the conditions of labour under capitalism. Capitalist production for profit had destroyed that relationship between craftsmen and their products which alone could ensure good art. Craftsmen had been replaced by wage-slaves: the growth of factories had compelled workers to labour for long hours at monotonous tasks; industrialisation had turned them into mere adjuncts of machines, thereby preventing them from expressing their individual spirit; and commercialism had forced them to make commodities that pamper to the whims of the wealthy rather than satisfying genuine needs. Craftsmen had been replaced by wage-slaves, whose conditions of work denied them the self-respect that comes from doing useful work. Moreover, these conditions of labour demonstrated the immorality of the capitalist economy. Capitalism involved a ceaseless search for profit at the expense of human values. Art was made to serve riches, not wealth. Here wealth represented 'the means of living a decent life'; riches represented 'the means for exercising dominion over other people'; and capitalism maximised the riches of the capitalist, not the wealth of the community.[19] Soon, however, a communist society would appear in which craftsmen would again be seen to be artists but in which there would be no classes. Art and fellowship would flourish as they never had before.

The key point to grasp is that even after Morris became a Marxist his ideal continued to be defined by a romantic concern with good art. Although he thought collective ownership of the means of production was essential to end exploitation, his main concern remained the place of art in people's lives. His vision of a socialist society focused on the conditions of labour that were conducive to the production of good art, and a way of life based on the use and enjoyment of good art. His romanticism committed him to a definite ethic. He wanted everyone to feel the same way that artists do about their work; for him, creativity was an ahistorical 'need of man's soul.'[20] And he wanted everyone to enjoy art in their lives; being surrounded by beautiful objects was also a need of the soul. What is more, this ethic largely defined his political strategy. It led him to disparage the struggle for higher wages, and even public ownership of the means of production, as doing nothing to end the true slavery of the working class. It led him to a purist perspective from which he denounced almost all forms of political action because they dirtied the hands of those who undertook them. It led him to emphasise the visionary content of his utopia, and to do so at the expense of political questions about how his utopia was to be created.

Morris argued that human life consisted of two dominant moods, energy and idleness. Our ethical goal was happiness in both of these moods. Art

---

[19] *Ibid*, Volume 23, p.143.
[20] *Ibid*, Volume 23, p.203.

brought such happiness. He said, 'the aim of art is to increase the happiness of men, by giving them beauty and interest of incident to amuse their leisure, and prevent them wearying even of rest, and by giving them hope and bodily pleasure in their work; or, shortly, to make man's work happy and his rest fruitful.'[21] In the mood of idleness, happiness came from using products that were works of art. This happiness was simple and natural, as exemplified by an evening in Morris's utopia:

> 'The wine was of the best; the hall was redolent of rich summer flowers; and after supper we not only had music ... but, at last we got to telling stories, and sat there listening, with no other light but that of the summer moon streaming through the beautiful traceries of the windows, as if we belonged to time long passed, when books were scarce and the art of reading somewhat rare.'[22]

In the mood of energy, happiness came from being an artist. Morris's broad view of art included all labour, so to be an artist one did not have to create a particular type of product but only to feel a particular way about the product that one did create. Certain conditions of labour would help to engender the required feeling, but the feeling, not the conditions of labour, was what mattered. Workers should have varied tasks so they would not feel compelled; they should be able to stamp their individuality on each product so they would feel the hope of creation; and they should produce goods to fulfil genuine needs so they would feel self-respect.[23] It was vital to make work enjoyable because people needed to work in order to exercise their energies. The population of Morris's utopian society were actually worried about a possible shortage of work.[24] People needed 'honourable and fitting work' to fulfil them as artists and thereby satisfy the mood of energy: their work had to be worth doing in that it produced genuinely useful commodities, 'pleasant to do' in that it allowed for individual expression, and not 'over-wearisome.'[25]

Again, people needed a decent environment in which to enjoy art during their leisure and thereby satisfy the mood of idleness. The population of Morris's utopia moved back to the countryside where they lived in simple communal dwellings and took great care to preserve natural beauty – one of the first things the Guest noticed was the cleanness of the Thames.[26] Because Morris thus allowed for the needs of both producers and consumers there inevitably arose the question of what should happen if consumers had legitimate desires that could be satisfied only if producers acted in a way that undermined their status as artists. Morris believed such conflicts would be rare because machinery would alleviate heavy and monotonous work. But if such a conflict did occur, the decision would balance the nature of the work against the social value of the product, and if the work

---

[21] *Ibid*, Volume 23, p.84.
[22] *Ibid*, Volume 16: 'News From Nowhere', p.140.
[23] *Ibid*, Volume 23, pp.164-91.
[24] *Ibid*, Volume 16, pp.91-2.
[25] *Ibid*, Volume 23, p.194.
[26] *Ibid*, Volume 16, p.6.

were particularly degrading or the product not essential, then society would just have to forego the product.

The way the workers would feel about their products was central to Morris's vision of a communist society. The market value of a commodity was unimportant. What mattered was that the workers would be like the craftsmen of old. They would create beautiful artefacts, imprinted with their own personality. Doing so would give them satisfaction, as would the knowledge that others would take pleasure in using their creations. Art would be the watchword of the factory of the future. This was why slavery would disappear. Collective ownership of the means of production was necessary primarily in order to promote god art, and so happiness, not in order to eliminate surplus value:

> 'The attractive work of our factory, that which it was pleasant in itself to do, would be of the nature of art; therefore all slavery of work ceases under such a system, for whatever is burdensome about the factory would be taken turn and turn about, and so distributed would cease to be a burden, would be in fact a kind of rest from the more exciting or artistic work.'[27]

Some commentators have suggested that Morris's concern with traditional craftsmanship made him hostile to mechanisation as such. Actually, however, he just wanted people to judge the worth of machines by whether or not they made labour more pleasant, not whether or not they made production cheaper. In his communist society, 'machines of the most ingenious and best approved kinds will be used when necessary, but will be used simply to save human labour.'[28] Because everybody would be a craftsman, they would judge the worth of the work of others and of machines in terms of beauty and use value, not in terms of profit and exchange value. The mutual exchange of useful products would replace the competitive market.

Morris's sociology of art suggested that good art required an honest, natural community somewhat similar to that of the middle-ages. Besides, 'fellowship is heaven, and lack of fellowship is hell: fellowship is life, and lack of fellowship is death.'[29] His ideal, therefore, was a society of neighbours in which people would gladly assist each other, taking pleasure in being of service. People would live rude, simple lives. They would find happiness in animal acts such as eating, loving and sleeping: Morris liked 'to think of barbarism once more flooding the world, and real feelings and passions, however rudimentary, taking the place of our wretched hypocrisies'.[30] Children would learn by play, not in schools, with an emphasis on swimming and carpentry, not on books, and they would spend the summer camping-out in the woods. Adults would be artistic producers who would eat in large communal dining-halls before sitting around telling and retelling heroic stories. At harvest time, everyone would carouse in the fields.

---

[27] W.Morris, *William Morris: Artist, Writer, Socialist*, edited by M.Morris, with 'An account of William Morris as I knew him by Bernard Shaw', Blackwell, 1936, Volume 2: 'Morris as a Socialist', p.135.
[28] *Ibid*, Volume 2, p.134.
[29] Morris, *Works*, Volume 16, p.230.
[30] Morris, *Letters*, edited by Kelvin, Volume 2, Part B: 1885-88, p.436.

Morris concentrated on the need for a new spirit of art such that the workers would relate to their products as do artists. He viewed socialism primarily in terms of the realisation of this spirit and thus good art. New social institutions, such as the collective ownership of the means of production, were required because his sociology showed them to be necessary for the growth of good art. These romantic concerns led him to a purist political strategy. Because socialism required primarily a new artistic consciousness, a change in consciousness was more important than either a change in institutions or the acquisition of political power. Morris told his fellow socialists that 'the religion of Socialism calls upon us to be better than other people since we owe ourselves to the society which we have accepted as the hope of the future.'[31] And he warned them of 'the error of moving earth & sea to fill the ballot boxes with Socialist votes which will not represent Socialist men.'[32] His desire was to make good art central to human lives in the moods of energy and idleness alike, and this meant above all else that people had to feel themselves to be artists and concern themselves with art. Both socialists and socialist action had to embody the artistic spirit.

All of Morris's arguments against parliamentary action drew on his purist concern with a new spirit of art. On the one hand, he thought it unlikely that parliamentary action would do the socialist cause much good. Parliamentary action could secure only material ends. It could not turn workers into artists. Socialist Members of Parliament could only point out what concessions may be necessary for the ruling class to make in order that the slavery of the workers may last; they could not promote the artistic spirit. On the other hand, he thought it highly likely that parliamentary action would do the socialist cause some harm. He feared that by entering Parliament socialists would weaken the purity of their example, and so hinder the growth of a socialist consciousness. He said, 'the real business of Socialists is to impress on the workers that they are a class, whereas they ought to be Society; if we mix ourselves up with Parliament we shall confuse and dull this fact in people's minds instead of making it clear and intensifying it.'[33] Besides, parliamentary action would corrupt the consciousness of the socialists who engaged in it:

> 'I really feel sickened at the idea of all the intrigue and degradation of concession which would be necessary to us as a parliamentary party: nor do I see any necessity for a revolutionary party doing any 'dirty work' at all, or soiling ourselves with anything which would unfit us for being due citizens of the new order of things.'[34]

The fact is: Morris's anti-parliamentarianism came from his moral, aesthetic ideal. No doubt his unfortunate experience of what many scholars have considered to be Hyndman's 'opportunism' strengthened his dislike of political action, but the dislike was already there, so we can not explain

---

[31] *Commonweal*, 28 August 1886.
[32] Morris, *Letters*, edited by Kelvin, Volume 2, Part B, p.693.
[33] *Commonweal*, July 1885.
[34] Morris, *Letters*, edited by Kelvin, Volume 2, Part B, p.598.

the dislike in terms of his relationship with Hyndman.[35] When he joined Hyndman within the Social Democratic Federation (SDF), he said 'the aim of socialists should be the founding of a religion, towards which end compromise is no use'; and when the SDF adopted a new programme, before his quarrel with Hyndman, he said the programme 'is better than the old one, and is not parliamentary'.[36]

A purist ethic also led Morris to doubt the efficacy of both palliatives and trade unions. He argued that if capitalism's 'wrongs and anomalies were so capable of palliation that people generally were not only contented, but were capable of developing their human faculties duly under it, and that we were on the road to progress without a great change, I for one would not ask anyone to meddle with it.'[37] He denounced palliatives because even if they provided material contentment, they would not transform the way the workers related to their products. They would not promote good art. Similarly, Morris often dismissed trade unions because they struggled for higher wages and better conditions of work, not for a mode of work that would be conducive to good art. He said:

> 'The position of the Trades Unions, as anything but benefit societies, has become an impossible one; the long and short of what they say to the masters is this: We are not going to interfere with your management of our affairs except so far as we can reduce your salary as our managers. We acknowledge that we are machines and that you are the hands that guide us; but we will pay as little as we can help for your guidance.'[38]

Instead of parliamentarianism, Morris proposed what he called 'a policy of abstention', that is, a policy based on a refusal to participate in bourgeois institutions. 'The true weapon of the workers as against Parliament is not the ballot-box but the boycott.'[39] Morris wanted socialists to provide a pure example. He wanted them to be a party of principle. He wanted them to restrict their activities to education – 'our business I repeat is the making of socialists.'[40] A new consciousness had to precede any attempt to capture power. Action had to wait until the process of education was complete, because 'until we have that mass of opinion, action for a general change that will benefit the whole people is impossible.'[41] In *News from Nowhere*, Morris described the action that he thought should follow the successful education of the workers.[42] The existence of an educated population who were aware of the ills of capitalism and who gave minimal obedience to

---

[35] The contrary position is taken by Thompson, Morris.
[36] Morris, *Letters*, edited by Kelvin, Volume 2, Part A, pp.219 & 312-13. On Hyndman and the SDF, see M.Bevir, 'H.M.Hyndman: A Rereading and a Reassessment', *History of Political Thought*, 12, 1991; M.Bevir, 'The British Social Democratic Federation 1880-1885: From O'Brienism to Marxism', *International Review of Social History*, 37, 1992.
[37] Morris, *Works*, Volume 23, p.229.
[38] Morris, *William Morris*, Volume 2, p.443.
[39] *Commonweal*, 7 June 1890. For his 'Policy of Abstention' see especially Morris, *William Morris*, Volume 2, pp.434-52.
[40] Morris, *William Morris*, Volume 2, p.518.
[41] *Commonweal*, 15 November 1890.
[42] See Morris, *Works*, Volume 16, pp.103-30.

existing authority would compel the state to adopt either a policy of force or one of fraud. At first the monopolists would try a policy of fraud by introducing state socialism in an attempt to buy the workers off. But fraud would fail because the workers would be educated to recognise it for what it was. Thus, the monopolists would turn next to force. Thereafter the workers would combine in one great federation, and when the economy next suffered from a cyclical depression, they would insist on taking control of the natural resources of the nation. This would lead to a civil war from which the workers eventually would emerge victorious and then go on to establish communism.

Why should we consider Morris's revolutionary strategy to be a purist one? For a start, he always insisted that the revolution had to represent a pure consciousness. He said:

> 'I want a real revolution, a real change in Society: Society a great organic mass of well-regulated forces used for the bringing-about a happy life for all. And the means for attaining it are simple enough; education in Socialism, and organization for the time when the crisis shall force action upon us: nothing else will do us any good at present: the revolution cannot be a mechanical one, though the last act of it may be civil war, or it will end in reaction after all.'[43]

In addition, he always insisted that suitable revolutionary action presupposed a prior change in consciousness, so there was to be no action until the workers were educated. This meant that the revolution constantly receded from view. Morris's strategy began 'with the distinct aim of making Socialists by educating them, and of organizing them to deal with politics in the end,' and this allowed him always to postpone the revolution on the grounds that the right time had not arrived yet.[44] Finally, Morris's talk of a revolution to follow education seems, therefore, to have been less a call to political action than a symbol for the vastness of the change that he hoped to see. The idea of a revolution marked the tragedy he thought necessary to ensure a total break with the present. 'The world was being brought to its second birth; how could that take place without a tragedy?'[45]

We can now answer the questions with which we began. How has Morris managed to exercise such sway over the socialist imagination? Why have ethical socialists, Marxists, anarchists, all sorts of left-wing thinkers, returned time and time again to locate their own vision in his work? Crucially, Morris has appealed to ethical socialists, Marxists, and anarchists because the bulk of his writings offer us a romantic utopia that draws on longings deeply rooted in our culture, without thereby committing us to a contentious political strategy by which to reach this utopia. Ethical socialists can applaud his emphasis on a new moral spirit without worrying about how to create such a spirit. Marxists can celebrate his avowal of communism without worrying about the haziness of his depiction of the revolution

---

[43] Morris, *Letters*, edited by Kelvin, Volume 2, Part B, p.368.
[44] *Ibid*, Volume 2, Part B, p.369.
[45] Morris, *Works*, Volume 16, p.132.

by which it is to be brought about. And finally anarchists can exult in his opposition to the state and parliamentary action without worrying about the structure of the organisation through which the change is to be realised.

Morris is the great dreamer of the British left. During the depression of the 1930s Barbara Castle tramped the Yorkshire moors overlooking the ugly, polluted, industrial towns of the valleys. Her initial despair was dispelled as she read Morris's poem 'The Message of the March Wind' with its evocation of fellowship; its old inn and roaring fire, the fiddler playing and the people dancing.[46] 'Have nothing in your houses that you do not know to be useful or believe to be beautiful,' said Morris.[47] He wanted to improve the world; to make it simpler, more enjoyable, more beautiful, more fulfilling, and more just. His romantic vision of a harmonious, beautiful world still can educate our aspirations. It gives us a glimpse of a better world, and for this we should be grateful. Nonetheless, we should not allow the grandeur of our aspirations to undermine our concern with the realisation of genuine improvements. We should not ignore the imperatives of political action.

---

[46] This story is told in the Preface to MacCarthy, *Morris*.
[47] Morris, *Works*, Volume 23, p.77.

William Morris

Ruth Kinna
Loughborough University

'William Morris: From Art to Socialism'

Introduction

This paper traces William Morris's transition from artist to socialist and examines the influence of his art on his political thought. It gives two complementary accounts of this transition: the first suggests that Morris's socialism was a natural development of his art and a result of the difficulties he encountered as a craftsman; the second sees Morris as a reluctant convert to socialism. These accounts have sometimes been seen as alternative explanations of his development[1] but here they are presented as complementary. The process of Morris's development seen as having marked his socialism in two ways. On the one hand his experience as an artist helped him to define the purpose of socialism. On the other his conception of art led him to develop an understanding of change which was constructed on the belief that there was a gulf between the real world and his aesthetic ideal. When Morris decided that the compromise imposed on his work by the market made this gulf unbridgeable he shifted his theatre of action, but he retained his theory of change.

Art and the Market

Morris was nearly 49 years old in January 1883 when he first identified himself as a socialist and joined Hyndman's Social Democratic Federation. His previous experience of public affairs had been short but intense. In 1876, suddenly galvanised by the Eastern Question, he had sided with Gladstone against Disraeli and argued the case against the Turks in an effort to stop Britain drifting into war with Russia. After becoming the treasurer of the Eastern Question Association (EQA) Morris extended his public activities by establishing the Society for the Protection for Ancient Buildings, an organisation designed to save historic monuments from what he saw as unnecessary and destructive interference. Thereafter he quickly moved through stages of left-liberalism and radicalism before finally converting to socialism.

Morris's late progression to socialism may be explained partly by a combination of changes both in his personal circumstances and in the political conditions of the period. During the 1860s and early '70s he had been so busy establishing his reputation as a craftsman and poet and reconciling himself to the failure of his marriage that he had little time to spend on public affairs. In any case, at this time the socialist movement was quiescent. Coincidentally, by the time the socialist movement revived he had resolved most of his domestic problems. Between 1874 and 1875 he managed to evict Rossetti – his wife's lover – from the family home in Oxfordshire

---
[1] See for example R.Page Arnot, *William Morris; the Man & the Myth*, Lawrence & Wishart, 1964.

and to take sole charge of the Firm, the design company which he duly re-christened Morris & Co. These accomplishments made Morris's life more settled and gave him more time to devote to public affairs. In addition, by the 1880s his work also gave him a fresh motivation.

Morris's art – and his visual art in particular – had always had a critical aspect. The purpose of becoming a co-partner in the Firm in 1861 had been to change popular taste; and as his interests expanded Morris began to realise that the commercial system hampered him in this quest. As he confessed in one of his early lectures, he began to feel that he was caught between a public who were 'set on having things cheap, being so ignorant that they do not know when they get them nasty also ...' and a manufacturing class who were 'set on carrying out competition to its utmost' and who were willing to 'meet the bargain-hunters half way, and cheerfully furnish them with nasty wares at the cheap rate they are asked for ...'.[2] Morris identified himself with 'handicraftsmen, who are not ignorant ... like the public, and who have no call to be greedy and isolated like the manufacturers or middlemen ...'. And at first he believed that, like them, he had the 'duty and the honour of educating the public' and the 'seeds of order and organisation which make that duty easier.'[3] Gradually however, Morris lost faith in his ability to educate either the stupid or the avaricious.

The watershed in Morris's development came in 1875. Free from domestic anxiety, he expanded his interest in dyestuffs and as part of this expansion he contracted Thomas Wardle, an industrialist in Leek, to help him with his experiments. The relationship was not wholly successful: Morris was continually dissatisfied with the results Wardle achieved and did not hesitate to show his impatience and irritation in his correspondence. At root the problem was that Wardle simply could not produce the quality of dyes Morris required at a price that would allow the company to retain its profit margin. Wardle's failure seemed to turn Morris against industrialists in general. As he told Rosalind Howard, his experiences in Leek had made him 'love art and manufacturers, & hate commerce and moneymaking more than ever ...'[4] Thereafter Morris's critique of commercial society gained a sharper edge. In a series of essays written between 1878-1881 he used the weakness and neglect of handicrafts as a means to discuss the poor condition of the nation.

In some ways his position was similar to Matthew Arnold's. Admittedly, Arnold wrote in very different terms from Morris and his call in *Culture and Anarchy* for a return to the Hellenic power of beauty as a corrective to the stifling and culturally stagnant Hebraic power of conduct did not have an equivalent in Morrisian language. And Morris would probably have found it difficult to reconcile this call with his own anti-classicism. Even so, Morris saw a link between the two and, though he found Arnold's work difficult to read, he shared his contempt for the 'foppish frivolity' and vulgarity of fashionable taste and he echoed his appeal for cultural renewal. Like Arnold,

---

[2] Morris, 'The Lesser Arts' in his *Hopes & Fears for Art* (hereafter *HFA*), Ellis & White, 1882, p.29.

[3] Morris, 'The Lesser Arts', p.30.

[4] N.Kelvin (ed), *The Collected Letters of William Morris* (hereafter *Letters*), Princeton University Press, Volume 1, 1984, p.262.

he saw Milton as a symbol of all he despised in middle class culture and he complained bitterly about its puritanism, its worship of mediocrity and its desire to impose order on all things.

Like Arnold's, Morris's critique also had a social and economic aspect. He argued that the ugliness of commercial society was a result of the destruction of the handicraft movement and the faulty development of fine arts since the Renaissance. Art had lost its popular base and was now being practised by specialised academicians who produced luxuries for a privileged élite. In this system, regiments of the lower classes were dragooned into factories in order to produce cheap 'makeshifts' for their own consumption whilst the minority, who made money out of their work, indulged themselves with a range of hideous, over-ornamented goods. In their struggle

> 'towards the complete attainment of all the luxuries of life ...', [Morris raged] 'the strongest portion of the race ... deprive their whole race of all the beauty of life ...'[5]

For example, though many of the rich 'buy pictures and profess to care about art...' they cannot see that their industrial activity shows that they care 'more for the image of the landscape than for the landscape itself'.[6] In Morris's view, this social and cultural deprivation was sustained by the vast economic inequalities created by the commercial system. Here he distinguished between the wealth associated with handicrafts, which signified 'the means of living a decent life', and the riches linked with mere material gain, signifying 'the means of exercising domination over other people'.[7] With this distinction in mind he argued that true wealth required that richness be overcome: in short, commerce and the distinction between rich and poor had to be abolished.

By 1883 Morris realised that the socialist movement provided him with an outlet for his increasing radicalism. Indeed, he felt compelled to take up its cause. As he told Georgiana Burne-Jones in 1884, he felt that he had been driven into socialism by the pressure of external forces. No longer could he be content to be an 'ascetic hermit of a hanger on' because 'fate or what not has forced me to feel war, and lays hands on me as a recruit'.[8] At this point, he also suggested that he had always been a socialist and that this compulsion to become involved actively was an entirely natural development of his art. Yet if his art had always been socialist, Morris also suggested that his entry into socialism marked not only the end of his career as an artist but of art in general. Even as early as 1882 he was convinced that he was 'doomed to fail' in his work. Although he continued to work 'with energy and even with pleasure and enthusiasm' he compared his endeavours to Louis XVI's lock-making: art was nothing more than a pleasant distraction. As for his greater ideas for cultural regeneration, he told Georgiana Burne-Jones that 'art must go under'.[9]

---

[5] Morris, 'The Beauty of Life', HFA, p.72.
[6] Morris, 'The Beauty of Life', p.100.
[7] Morris, 'Art, Wealth & Riches', *Manchester Quarterly*, 1883, p.153.
[8] Kelvin (ed), *Letters*, Volume 2, 1987, p.286.
[9] Kelvin (ed), *Letters*, Volume 2, p.95.

Morris's understanding of the relationship between art and socialism helped him to define the purpose of socialist activity: socialism was a collective struggle, born of a concern with the cultural well-being of the nation and directed towards the abolition of inequality as a precondition for its regeneration. But this relationship was more complex than Morris acknowledged.

Art and the Idea of Change

Notwithstanding Morris's later assessments of the relationship between art and socialism, there is evidence to suggest that his transition was neither smooth nor straightforward. Some of his friends were amazed by his conversion and saw it as a fit of madness.[10] Their reaction might have been exaggerated but it was not entirely unreasonable. After all, when Morris got involved in the EQA he had done so from a position of near political indifference; and it was not just lack of time that had prevented him from taking part in public life, for most of his youth he had balked at the idea getting embroiled in worldly affairs. He expressed this sentiment most famously and eloquently in the Prologue to The Earthly Paradise where he wrote:

> 'Dreamer of dreams, born out of my due time,
> Why should I strive to set the crooked straight?'[11]

This was not just poetic musing. In 1856, Morris told Cormell Price, one of his most intimate Oxford friends, that he could not enter into 'politico-social subjects with any interest'. Even knowing that 'things are in a muddle' he believed that he had 'no power or vocation to see them right in ever so little a degree'.[12] He maintained this position for some years. He was unmoved, for example, by the Paris Commune and whilst radicals expressed shock and fascination at it Morris merely compared Iceland's volcanic earth to 'a half-ruined Paris barricade'.[13]

Morris did not reject politics out of hand as he would do later on in his on in his career. Though he negatively associated politics with grubbing for power and self-advancement, in this earlier period he also admitted that it had a noble side. At best, he argued, politics referred to 'social' affairs (it was in this sense that he later understood socialism). The problem was that he could not see any purpose in politics, not even in this social aspect. His inability stemmed from his conception of art.

Morris's understanding of art was deeply rooted in his idea of history. He had developed an appetite for history as a boy but his study at Oxford increased it. Following the lead of three major influences – the Oxford Movement, John Ruskin and Charles Kingsley – he soon gained a sound knowledge of the medieval period. In some areas he became an unrivalled

---

[10] See J.W.Mackail, *Life of William Morris*, Volume 2, Longmans, Green & Co., 1911, p.27.

[11] Morrsi, *The Earthly Paradise*, Reeves & Turner, 1890, p.1.

[12] Kelvin (ed), *Letters*, Volume 1, p.28.

[13] quoted in F.McCarthy, *William Morris: A Life For Our Time*, Faber & Faber, 1994, p.304.

authority: Hyndman's account of how Morris filed through a pile of missals in Oxford and instructed the librarian of their date and origin stands as a testimony to his expertise in medieval illuminations. However, Morris was not really interested in charting or analysing history for its own sake and his idea of the past owed as much to literature as it did to historical scholarship: he particularly admired Walter Scott. More specifically, his view of history was intertwined with an idea of nature.

Morris understood nature in two ways. First, it was a regulator of time. Here, Morris was often quite morbid. He saw that in nature the life of all things was finite and that time was necessarily limited. Death could not be predicted precisely, but all individual lives were set on a course of inexorable decline. This aspect of Morris's understanding may well have been rooted in his own psychology and probably fed his desperation to work; he had an extraordinary sense that time was about to run out for him and felt a keen desire to leave his mark on the world before it was too late. Birthdays caused him particular anxiety and, though as he got older his bleak assessments of his mortality became more realistic, he was always obsessed with increasing age. Even when he was only 21 he told Cormell Price: 'I am too old already and there is no time to lose, I MUST make haste'.[14] Yet Morris was not fatalistic: his anxiety about time did not make him feel hopeless or lead him to think exclusively of decline and extinction. Turning back to nature as a model, he believed that the transitoriness of individual life was contained within a larger pattern of cyclical change. In nature, death was subsumed within a constant cycle of rebirth and renewal, marked by the steady ebb and flow of the seasons.

Apart from being the regulator of time, nature was also the standard of beauty. In its purest sense, Morris understood nature to be unadorned and untamed. The idea of nature was realised in woods and forests, mountains and the sea; in the 'wastes' of Salisbury Plain and in other uninhabited or uncharted territories. But Morris's sense of natural beauty also allowed for a degree of cultivation, so long as the cultivation was 'indigenous' and in keeping with the otherwise untamed landscape. This conception suggested a number of different ideas and possibilities. In particular it led him to associate natural beauty with 'character' or 'manliness'. To Morris's mind, character inhered in things which lived by hard, honest labour. This was not dull – dullness inhered in pretty, 'feminine' things – but it was everyday. One example was common language: in the Dyfi Valley he observed the pride of the people and their refusal to give up Welsh for English and he suggested that this preserved both their character and the of beauty their environment.[15]

Whether it was the regulator of time or the measure of beauty, nature, Morris believed, evoked certain sentiments and passions. These could be intangible, as his own perception of the 'strangeness' of Stonehenge and they could be depressing. But at all events the feelings engendered by nature were good and he distinguished, for example, between the sadness simply brought about by 'gloom' and that fostered by 'the melancholy born

---

[14] Kelvin (ed), *Letters*, Volume 1, p.23.
[15] Kelvin (ed), *Letters*, Volume 1, p.252.

of beauty'.[16] To an extent, Morris's understanding of cyclical change led him to believe that nature affected the emotions in a habitual way. Thus spring was classically a time of hope and autumn a time of solemnity. But Morris did not see an automatic association between the seasons and the passions. Apart from anything else, nature did not always live up to its reputation. Torquay, for example, was the one of those places that were 'always hot when they ought to be cool, and cold when they ought to be warm'.[17] But more importantly, the subjectivity of Morris's understanding implied that it was possible for individuals to feel any number of different sentiments at any given point in nature's cycle.

Morris's view of nature was an important guide for the development of his aesthetic. In general terms, he argued that art must emulate nature. He told art students in Leek, for example, that

> '... everything made by man's hands has a form, which must be either beautiful or ugly; beautiful if it is in accord with Nature, and helps her; ugly if it is discordant with Nature, and thwarts her ...'[18]

According to Morris's conception of beauty this meant that artist either drew directly from nature or that artistic creations conformed with nature's standards. He tried to follow both paths in his own work. For example, he incorporated flora and fauna in his pattern designs and created individual pieces of art in accordance with his principles of simplicity. Morris also drew on nature as a model for literature. In this respect, Morris argued that artists should give themselves over to nature and be guided by passion rather than technical skill and, unlike Arnold, he turned away from classicism. He told Edward Nicholson, a young poet who wrote to him seeking his critical advice, that his 'acquaintance with the classics ... may be rather over powering in its influence ... on your style ...' Morris wanted to see 'more weight' in his work and counselled Nicholson to 'do nothing but what you like very much yourself'.[19] For Morris the formal qualities of a piece could never compensate for a closeness to nature. He maintained this view against all writers, regardless of their reputations. He criticised Swinburne's writing, for example, because it was founded on 'literature' rather than 'nature'.[20] Taking the point to its extreme, Morris even argued that a disregard of formal criteria in the end made for the best art. The 'author-collector' of the Volsunga Saga, for example, had felt the subject 'too much to trouble himself about the niceties of art', and the result was

> 'something which is above all art; the scene of the last interview between Sigurd and the despairing and terrible Brynhild touches me more than any thing I have ever met with in literature there is nothing wanting in it, nothing forgotten, nothing repeated, nothing overstrained; all tenderness is shown without

---
[16] Kelvin (ed), *Letters*, Volume 1, p.150.
[17] Kelvin (ed), *Letters*, Volume 1, p.128.
[18] Morris, 'The Lesser Arts', pp.3-4.
[19] Kelvin (ed), *Letters*, Volume 1, p.72.
[20] Kelvin (ed), *Letters*, Volume 2, p.119.

the use of a tender word, all misery and despair without a word of raving, complete beauty without an ornament, and all this in 2 pages of moderate print.'[21]

In order to emulate nature effectively, the artist had to work with historical insight. Morris's criterion gave substance to his conception of art. For example, it enabled him to fashion a model of nature which in turn provided a foundation for him to determine acceptable levels of cultivation. In 1874 he drew history and nature together in a brief sketch of an ideal community. Suppose, he wrote,

> 'people lived in little communities among gardens & green fields ... & had few wants; almost no furniture for instance, & no servants, & studied (the difficult) arts of enjoying life ... then I think one might hope civilization had really begun ... But ... if they cannot have pleasant life ... they may at least have a history & something to think of ...'[22]

History also provided a tangible record of time and a tool for the discovery of constant and universal passions, which allowed him to distinguish between a genuine from a fraudulent emotion and a true from a false work of art. By looking back into the past it was possible to discover certain moral truths in human expression. As he told the philanthropist Thomas Horsfall, 'since the dawn of history mankind has invented no typal new stories'. The tale 'which Herodutus ... heard from an Egyptian priest was told in our fathers days by a Swabian peasant to Grimm, and two years ago by a Hindoo nurse to an English child'.[23] In his quest to create art that emulated nature Morris accordingly plundered history for guidance in both literature and the visual arts. His conviction that there were no new stories in the world led him to combine an extraordinary range of sources when he composed his own tales. But Morris did not just draw on ancient myths, legends and architecture to frame the content of his literature and design. He also looked to the past to find suitable forms of expression and he borrowed terms from ancient texts to enrich his accounts of these knightly tales. Similarly he drew on history in his visual art. His love of the Middle Ages led him to reserve a special place for gothic art. As he explained in 1867 to Morgan Watkins, one of his Oxford friends, his 'towns belong rather to the Cinque-Cento or Jacobean period than the Homeric or rather pre-Homeric, and there is more of Lincoln or Rouen than of Athens in them, let alone Tiryns or Mycenae ...'.[24] Even when he went to Verona in 1878 he confessed that the 'magnificent and wonderful towns' still left him yearning 'for the heap of grey stones with a grey roof that we call a house north-way'.[25] Morris's view of history also guided his methods of production. Specifically, it was his and the Firm's declared intention to take up the work of the gothic revivalists and in doing so to pursue those decorative arts which had flourished in the Middle Ages

---

[21] Kelvin (ed), *Letters*, Volume 1, p.99.
[22] Kelvin (ed), *Letters*, Volume 1, p.218.
[23] Kelvin (ed), *Letters*, Volume 2, p.36.
[24] Kelvin (ed), *Letters*, Volume 1, p.53.
[25] Kelvin (ed), *Letters*, Volume 1, p.487.

by the reintroduction of 'natural' methods. They did not always succeed in their aim and at times they deviated from ancient to modern techniques but Morris especially resisted modern technology.

Because of its relationship to history, Morris's conception of art was constructed on the idea that there was a gap between real world and his aesthetic ideal. Morris was aware of this and referred to it constantly in his idea of dreaming. When he spoke of dreaming he was not thinking of a sleeping activity, but of an exercise of the imagination. Dreams made images vivid; they captured an idea of reality and provided an insight into aspects of the world which were suffocated by real, drab material existence.

Sometimes, when Morris saw extraordinary images in the world, he described the experience as a dream since it was beyond his normal expectation and could not otherwise be perceived. For example, in 1871 Morris described the Faroe Islands as 'a most wonderful sight: I have seen nothing out of a dream so strange ... nothing has impressed me so much ...'.[26] On rare occasions Morris was so overwhelmed by the beauty of the real world that his imagination became redundant. But at these moments he felt as if he were dreaming. In 1878 when he first saw Lake Garda, he told Georgiana Burne-Jones:

> 'What a strange surprise it was when it suddenly broke upon me, with such beauty as I never expected to see: for a moment I really thought I had fallen asleep and was dreaming of some strange sea where everything had grown together in perfect accord with wild stories.'[27]

Dreaming also had a transformative or transcendental element and Morris felt he could alter his real experience of the world by using his imagination. In some cases, he saw dreaming as a means of reviving the past and Morris could change his impression of a particular place by using his imagination. During his first trip to Iceland in 1871, for example, he found that 'the blank, barrenness of some historical place, and the feebleness of the life ... would depress one for a while, till one remembered the lapse of years, and the courage and hope that had been there'.[28] He could also use his immediate location as a trigger to his senses in order to transport him to another time or place. He found Castle Howard to be 'one of the most poetical in England: we had a long drive yesterday all along by the border, & I sniffed the smell of the moors & felt in Iceland again. The whole country side is most poetical & full of history and legend'.[29] But most importantly, dreaming was a means of realising the future aesthetically beautiful world. When he first began to lecture on art Morris admitted that his ideal society was 'a dream ... of what has never been...' But, he added, 'since the world is alive and moving ... my hope is the greater that one done day it will be.' Moreover, he continued, 'dreams have before now come about of things so good and necessary to us that we scarcely think of them more than of daylight, though once people had to live without them, without even the hope

---

[26] Kelvin (ed), *Letters*, Volume 1, p.28.
[27] Kelvin (ed), *Letters*, Volume 1, p.484.
[28] Kelvin (ed), *Letters*, Volume 1, p.152.
[29] Kelvin (ed), *Letters*, Volume 1, p.228.

of them'.[30] Casting his mind forward, Morris imagined a world where 'our streets [are] as beautiful as the woods, as elevating as the mountainsides...' and where 'it will be a pleasure and a rest, and not a weight upon the spirits to come from the open country into a town ...'.[31] In another 'idle dream' he similarly hoped to see the 'once lovely valleys of Yorkshire in the 'heavy woollen district', with their sweeping hill- sides and noble rivers ... [become] once more delightful abodes of men ...'.[32]

In this period, Morris saw art rather than politics as the natural instrument of change: only art could help modify the natural world in accordance with his dreams. It seems significant that at precisely the moment he confided in Cormell Price that he could not take a political interest in the world he also told him that his work was 'the embodiment of dreams in one form or another'.[33] As an artist, Morris believed that he could try to realise his dreams in two ways. On the one hand, he could physically transform the real world by creating beautiful things. On the other, he could transcend the real world by developing a alternative understanding of life which was more sublime. In this respect, he described art as the 'godlike part of man'[34] It was synonymous with excellence, truth and power of expression.[35] Morris pursued the first strategy primarily in his design and the second in his literature. In the course of his 30s and 40s the project filled him with both hope and despair. At first, Morris seemed to have great hope that he could bring change about through art. In the longer term, this hope was disappointed and he was forces to revise his ideas. But though he realised that the transformation of the world could not be effected by art alone and that power would have to be conquered by collective political action, he maintained his commitment to his transcendental ideal.

Conclusion

Morris's transition from artist to socialist was the result of a combination of factors but above all of his realisation that his quest to beautify the world could not be achieved without a fundamental reordering of society. After years of failing to see the point of politics, he came to see socialism as the continuation of art by other means. Morris became a determined revolutionary from 1883 until his death but he retained elements of his anti-political sentiments. Even though he believed that change had to be brought about by struggle he also continued to see a role for dreams and visions of a better world to come.

---

[30] Morris, 'The Lesser Arts', p.37.
[31] Morris, 'The Lesser Arts', p.36.
[32] Morris, 'The Beauty of Life', p.87.
[33] Kelvin (ed), *Letters*, Volume 1, p.28.
[34] Kelvin (ed), *Letters*, Volume 2, p.119.
[35] Kelvin (ed), *Letters*, Volume 2, p.53.

Poststructuralism and Radical Politics
Iain MacKenzie
The Queen's University of Belfast
'Deleuze & Guattari's Poststructuralist Philosophy'

Introduction

At first glance, Deleuze & Guattari's *What is Philosophy?* may appear to confirm the mainstream critical opinion that poststructuralism has gone awry.[1] As Jonathan Ree suggests, what was once a radical agenda questioning the very basis of our society has become a matter of doing 'philosophy for philosophy's sake'.[2] Deleuze & Guattari, Ree believes, have at least 'come-clean' and admitted – despite all their huffing-and-puffing about 'schizoanalysis', 'total critique' and the like – that they are just old-fashioned metaphysicians glorying in the scholasticism of long dead debates. Underlying his eloquent attack is the familiar criticism that poststucturalism is an internally incoherent doctrine incapable of sustaining its own critical agenda. However, a thorough reading of *What is Philosophy?* shows that this charge is invalid. Although other problems may remain, the poststructuralist philosophy of Deleuze & Guattari is a carefully crafted account that clearly articulates a sustainable critical perspective. Showing this to be the case is the aim of this paper.

What is Philosophy?

Deleuze & Guattari give a deceptively simple answer to this question; 'philosophy', they say, 'is the discipline that involves creating concepts'.[3] At first glance this answer seems hardly contentious. The critical impact, though, is clear from the conceptions of philosophy that it excludes; namely, philosophy as 'contemplation, reflection and communication'. Philosophy as contemplation, Deleuze & Guattari call 'objective idealism' and it is clear that they have Plato in mind as the founder of this approach. For Plato, philosophy was the contemplation of 'Ideas'. In The Republic, for example, Plato is able to equate justice in the individual with justice in the community because the 'Idea of Justice' resides in neither the individual nor the community but in a separate realm of pure 'Ideas'; in the bright world outside the cave. Philosophy as reflection, Deleuze & Guattari call 'subjective idealism' and here they have both Descartes and Kant in mind. In Cartesian philosophy the doubting subject can not be sure of the objective status of ideas; Platonism, whether right or wrong, must be bracketed out of the equation. Yet, in the act of doubting, Descartes rediscovers the 'Idea', only now it resides within the subject as the 'I think'; the famous Cartesian 'cogito'. Although, Kant called into question the Cartesian 'cogito',

---
[1] G.Deleuze & F.Guattari, *What is Philosophy?*, Verso, 1994.
[2] J.Ree, 'Philosophy for Philosophy's Sake', *New Left Review*, 211, 1995.
[3] Deleuze & Guattari, *What is Philosophy?*, p.5.

the approach of reflecting upon an agent's self-knowledge was maintained (the transcendental categories replacing the activity of doubting). Philosophy, on this account, is reflection upon the subject's implicit knowledge of thought (in Descartes) or thought, space and time (in Kant). Philosophy as communication, Deleuze & Guattari call 'intersubjective idealism', a philosophical moment whose beginnings they associate with phenomenology, in particular the work of Husserl. Husserl's project was to reintroduce the Kantian subject to the phenomenal world, not in order to renounce transcendence but to put the transcendental subject on the solid empirical ground of 'actual experience'. As Deleuze & Guattari explain, the subject's transcendence via such experience has a triple root: 'the subject constitutes first of all a sensory world filled with objects, then an intersubjective world filled by the other, and finally a common ideal world'.[4] The 'transcendent Idea', on this account, is neither a pre-existing object, nor a presupposition of subjective reflection but a consequence of intersubjective interaction. Philosophical activity, therefore, becomes indistinguishable from the 'communication' (broadly defined) that takes place between subjects.

That Deleuze & Guattari take these differing accounts of philosophical activity to be variants of 'idealism' already suggests the tenor of their critique. Contemplation, reflection or communication, they argue, can not be definitive of philosophical activity because the concepts 'contemplation', 'reflection' and 'communication' must first and foremost be created. What they say of Plato in this context applies equally to Descartes, Kant and Husserl; 'Plato teaches the opposite of what he does: he creates concepts but needs to set them up as representing the uncreated that precedes them'.[5] Philosophy, they say, becomes 'idealism' when it confuses this distinction. Yet, surely treating philosophy as a form of constructivism, as the creation of concepts, is also susceptible to the charge of idealism? Is 'creation' not a concept as surely as contemplation, reflection and communication? One response would be, if creation is a concept, as a concept it must first and foremost be created, thus retaining the idea of philosophy as the creation of concepts. But this does not help. To pursue this line is to confuse the concept with the activity, to ground philosophy in a representation of the 'uncreated of creation', precisely the kind of argument that engenders the philosophical 'illusions' Deleuze & Guattari hope to avoid. Besides, to equate philosophy with creation and leave the matter at that would be to neglect the fact that other disciplines, such as science and art, are equally creative. To give substance to the idea that philosophy is the creation of concepts, and meet the charge of idealism, one must first look more carefully at what is being created; the concept.

What is a Concept?

For Deleuze & Guattari, every concept is multiple. There is no concept with only one component – the Cartesian 'cogito', for example, involves the concepts of 'doubting', 'thinking' and 'being'. Yet, neither is there a

---
[4] Deleuze & Guattari, *What is Philosophy?*, p.142.
[5] Deleuze & Guattari, *What is Philosophy?*, p.29.

concept that has infinite components – even 'so-called universals as ultimate concepts must escape the chaos by circumscribing a universe that explains them'.[6] The concept, therefore, is a finite multiplicity 'defined by the sum of its components', the component parts being other concepts. Why can there not be any singular or universal concepts? For Deleuze & Guattari, such concepts are impossible because every concept has a 'history' and a 'becoming'. Every concept has a history to the extent that it has passed through previous constellations of concepts and been accorded different roles within the same constellation. Every concept has a becoming to the extent that it forms a junction with other concepts within the same or adjacent field of problems. Given this, there can be no singular concepts to the extent that every concept implicates other concepts and no universal concepts to the extent that no one concept could survey all possible concepts.

Why does every concept have a history and a becoming? For Deleuze & Guattari, it is not so much that concepts are embroiled within changing 'social and historical contexts', though of course they are, rather it is because every concept has an 'atemporal' and 'acontextual' feature at its core. As well as 'surveying' its conceptual field, every concept inaugurates, what Deleuze & Guattari call, the 'plane of immanence' of the concept. The plane of immanence is 'neither a concept nor the concept of all concepts',[7] rather, it is a preconceptual field presupposed within the concept; 'not in the way that one concept may refer to others but in the way that concepts themselves refer to nonconceptual understanding'.[8] What is this 'nonconceptual understanding'? Ultimately, Deleuze & Guattari argue, it is: 'the image thought gives itself of what it means to think'.[9] They give the following examples: 'in Descartes [the plane of immanence] is a matter of a subjective understanding implicitly presupposed by the "I think" as first concept; in Plato it is the virtual image of an already-thought that doubles every actual concept'.[10] The plane of immanence is inaugurated within the concept (that which is created) and yet it is clearly distinct from the concept (as it is that which expresses the uncreated, that which 'thought just does'). In this sense, there is always an expression of the nonconceptual, internal to, and yet 'outside', the concept. This complex relation is characterised by Deleuze & Guattari as follows; 'concepts are events, but the plane is the horizon of events, the reservoir or reserve of purely conceptual events'.[11] We may say, for example, that 'the present happens' because there is a 'past-becoming-future horizon' presupposed within it. Without a presupposed limitless expanse of time we could not talk of the present. In the same way, without the presupposed plane of immanence concepts would never 'happen'. Moreover, as the present would never change without the existence of an 'eternal horizon' presupposed within it, without the institution of the plane – that which thought 'just does' – concepts would never change. The fact that concepts institute this 'unthinkable' plane at

---
[6] Deleuze & Guattari, *What is Philosophy?*, p.15.
[7] Deleuze & Guattari, *What is Philosophy?*, p.35.
[8] Deleuze & Guattari, *What is Philosophy?*, p.40.
[9] Deleuze & Guattari, *What is Philosophy?*, p.37.
[10] Deleuze & Guattari, *What is Philosophy?*, pp.40-41.
[11] Deleuze & Guattari, *What is Philosophy?*, p.36.

their core engenders the movement of concepts; their history and becoming. The 'contextualisation' of concepts within, say, 'ideological structures' is a secondary, though nonetheless important feature.

Two important consequences follow from this discussion. First, the claim that philosophy as 'contemplation, reflection or communication' leads philosophers to confuse the concepts they create with the activity of creation can be redeployed in a more precise way. Having explored the nature of the concept, we can see that the problem of 'idealism' is less a matter of confusing concept and creativity than a matter of confusing the concept with the presupposed plane of immanence. In 'idealist' approaches, the prephilosophical plane of immanence is always made immanent to the privileged concept (contemplation, reflection or communication). As such, the privileged concept is considered coextensive with the plane of immanence, rendering the concept transcendental – simply, 'contemplation', 'reflection' and 'communication' are privileged as that which thought 'just does'. Philosophy is contemplation in Plato, for example, because the already-thought object of contemplation extends across the plane of immanence inaugurated by the concept 'contemplation'. In other words, both the object of contemplation and the activity of contemplation are always already bound together in the transcendent 'Idea of Contemplation'. Philosophy gives rise to transcendence to the extent that it confuses the concepts it creates with the plane of immanence instituted by the concept. In general, if philosophy treats the plane of immanence as immanent to 'something', to a concept, then it creates its own 'illusions of transcendence' (in both concept and plane). Deleuze & Guattari summarise their position as follows: 'whenever immanence is interpreted as immanent "to" something a confusion of plane and concept results, so that the concept becomes a transcendent universal and the plane becomes an attribute in the concept'.[12]

A second important consequence of the distinction between concept and plane is that it helps us to see why philosophical constructivism does not fall prey to the charge of idealism; or now more correctly, the charge of attributing immanence 'to' something. For constructivism to escape the charge of idealism the concept, 'creation', must be shown to institute a plane that is immanent only to itself. Recalling that the plane of immanence is 'the image that thought gives itself of what it means to think', the question becomes; 'what is the image of thought that treats thought as immanent only to itself?'. We already know what thought can not be, for Deleuze & Guattari; an object for contemplation, a subject of reflection, or an intersubjective act of communication. But what is left? Given their critique of these idealist accounts, thought must be devoid of both subjects and objects. Yet, if there are no subjects or objects, then there can be no fixed points in thought. Without fixed reference points, thought must be viewed as an impersonal field of thought. If this is the case, there must also be no boundaries to thought, as boundaries would reinstate the plane as immanent to whatever constituted the boundary.

---

[12] Deleuze & Guattari, *What is Philosophy?*, pp.44-45.

What this suggests is that thought must be viewed as 'pure movement', where movement is taken to be 'infinite movement or movement of the infinite'.[13] As Deleuze & Guattari put it; 'thought constitutes a simple "possibility" of thinking without yet defining a thinker capable of it and able to say "I" '.[14] The 'absolute' plane of immanence, the plane which is immanent only to itself, is pure movement, pure possibility.

We must accept, argue Deleuze & Guattari, that all attempts to define thought conceptually, 'thought-as-x', will ultimately fail because all concepts must first be created. Yet, if all concepts are created, then thought itself must be 'conceptless'. The image of thought inaugurated by constructivism, therefore, is one of a 'conceptless plane'. As such, the concept 'creation' is distinct from the 'conceptless' image of thought it institutes. In other words, constructivism is that which maintains the distinction between concept and plane. The confusion of concept and plane, as noted earlier, was the source of 'idealist' approaches to philosophy. Philosophy as the creation of concepts maintains the distinction between concept and plane, and to this extent, may be said to avoid the charge of 'idealism'. Constructivism is that which institutes an image of thought, a plane of immanence, which treats thought as immanent only to itself; that is, thought as an impersonal field of thought. As noted above, this is equivalent to treating thought as a field of pure movement.

For Deleuze & Guattari, therefore, thought is not the object or 'aim' of philosophy, rather, thought is the nonphilosophical of philosophy; the nonphilosophical that is inaugurated within every act of philosophy. We are now in a position to appreciate what Deleuze & Guattari understand by 'good philosophy'. 'Good philosophy', they suggest, is that which is the most philosophical. Yet, the most philosophical approach to philosophy is that which institutes the most nonphilosophical plane of immanence, that which manages to maintain the distinction between concept and plane. Of course, every philosophy confuses the concept and the plane, constructivism included, by virtue of the fact that a 'perfect' or 'ideal' philosophy is literally 'unthinkable'. But 'good' philosophy is that which tries to grasp the plane as immanent only to itself. 'The supreme act of philosophy', they say, is 'not so much to think THE plane of immanence as to show that it is there, unthought in every plane, and to think it in this way as the outside and inside of thought, as the not-external outside and the not-internal inside – that which cannot be thought and yet must be thought'.[15] 'Good' philosophy, in other words, is that which continuously tracks down transcendence wherever it appears.

As it stands, this image of thought as pure movement may be said to 'idealise' the question of being; that is, confuse the 'mental' concept of creation with the 'physical' plane of being. Deleuze & Guattari, solve this problem by claiming that, 'movement is not the image of thought without being also the substance of being'.[16] There is, then, a 'vitalist ontology' immanent to philosophical constructivism rather than a rejection, in the manner of much

---

[13] Deleuze & Guattari, *What is Philosophy?*, p.37.
[14] Deleuze & Guattari, *What is Philosophy?*, pp.54-55.
[15] Deleuze & Guattari, *What is Philosophy?*, pp.59-60.
[16] Deleuze & Guattari, *What is Philosophy?*, p.38.

postmodern thought, of ontology per se. Without this ontology, Deleuze & Guattari's depiction of philosophy would indeed be a variant of the 'idealist' approaches discussed earlier – the plane of 'being' would be constituted as 'outside' and correlatively, the plane of immanence as immanent to thought. With a vitalist ontology, an ontology of movement as the substance of being, the charge of idealism could not be more misplaced. In short, idealism is avoided because the concept 'creation' inaugurates an image of thought as pure movement, which retains its immanence by virtue of a vitalist ontology of movement as the substance of being.

Between Concept and Plane

What exactly is the relation between concept and plane? We know that the concept and the plane are intimately connected to each other, and yet wholly distinct. For this to be the case, that which is between the concept and the plane must be 'external' to both. The relation itself, in other words, must be understood on its own terms; it must have its own logic. This idea shows the strong connection Deleuze & Guattari (and poststructuralists, in general) have with empiricism. Deleuze credits Hume with being the first to treat 'the relation' seriously: 'he created the first great logic of relations, showing in it that all relations (not only "matters of fact" but also relations among ideas) are external to their terms'.[17] This is not the empiricism so typical of first year philosophy classes, where it is taught as a theory of 'atomism' or 'individualism'. A 'pluralist' or 'radical' empiricism, is a theory of 'associationism' where between 'x and y' is 'and', not an abstract, eternal or universal 'x-ness' or 'y-ness'. The relation, 'and', is constituted as external to the terms 'x' and 'y'.

What constitutes this external relation between concept and plane? In its most general sense, it is 'a point of view'. When a concept is created it institutes a plane of immanence, but since no concept can encompass THE plane of immanence (without being indistinguishable from the plane) philosophy always simultaneously invents a 'point of view' which 'brings to life' the concept and the plane. In *What is Philosophy?*, Deleuze & Guattari characterise this 'point of view' as the 'conceptual persona' of a philosophy.[18] Their choice of phrase is revealing. The 'point of view' is neither a concept nor a plane but that which 'personalises' the absolutely impersonal plane by circumscribing a relative position on that plane. The conceptual persona, in other words, constitutes the impersonal field as a 'perspective' which then 'activates', or 'insists upon' the creation of concepts. It may be tempting to associate the conceptual persona that brings philosophy to life with the life of the philosopher. For Deleuze & Guattari, though, this would be a mistake; 'the conceptual persona is not the philosopher's representative but, rather, the reverse: the philosopher is the envelope of his principal conceptual persona and of all the other subjects of his philosophy. Conceptual

---

[17] G.Deleuze, *Empiricism and Subjectivity: An Essay on Hume's Theory of Human Nature*, Columbia University Press, 1991, p.x.

[18] Deleuze & Guattari, *What is Philosophy?*, chapter 3.

personae are the philosopher's "heteronyms", and the philosopher's name is the simple pseudonym of his personae'.[19]

While the conceptual persona, in its most general sense, is a point of view construed as external to both the concept and the plane, we can think of it in more particular ways. Deleuze & Guattari, for instance, talk of the conceptual persona as the 'territory' mapped out across the plane within the concept.[20] Such territories may be geographical or national, as when one talks about the perspective 'Italian philosophy' brings to a set of problems; or, they may also be 'normative', 'cultural', 'ideological', 'historical', 'institutional', 'global' and so on. When such territories become 'sedimented' in thought, as in the examples just given, we may talk of the formation of philosophical knowledge. Viewing philosophical knowledge in this way gives rise to a greater concern with the 'territory' upon which knowledge stakes a claim – 'how does perspective function to create knowledge?' – rather, than with the conditions which may 'guarantee' knowledge – 'what kind of knowledge transcends perspective?'. Put like this, Deleuze & Guattari's account of philosophical constructivism dovetails neatly with Foucault's account of genealogy.[21]

Conclusion

There are two accounts of poststructuralism's internal incoherence. On the first account, poststructuralism is presented as a variety of anti-foundationalism that, despite itself, continually takes certain 'foundations' for granted. As such, poststructuralism is said to steep itself in contradictions at every turn. While this may be the case for certain varieties of postmodernism, the claim is wholly inappropriate to the poststructuralist philosophy outlined by Deleuze & Guattari. On their account, poststructuralism combines Nietzsche's insight that thought is creative with both, Spinoza's insight that this demands an image of thought as immanent only to itself and, Bergson's insight that this in turn requires a vitalist ontology of movement as the substance of being. Far from constituting a lazy and insupportable anti-foundationalism, taking philosophy to be the creation of concepts rests upon very elaborate foundations with a long and complex lineage.

On the second account of its in-built incoherence, poststructuralism is portrayed as a form of relativism that rests, therefore, upon the famously paradoxical claim, 'there is no such thing as truth'. Deleuze & Guattari's 'perspectivism', though, is not the same as relativism; where relativism is taken to entail the denial of all context-independent truths. For Deleuze & Guattari, philosophical knowledge must be perspectival because of a deep-seated claim to truth – the vitalist ontology that underpins constructivism – and relativism must be refuted to the extent that it impugns the validity of this claim. Deleuze & Guattari do not deny the possibility of philosophical truths, quite the reverse; based on the claim to truth of a vitalist ontology, they show that epistemological perspectivism is an inescapable aspect

---
[19] Deleuze & Guattari, *What is Philosophy?*, p.64.
[20] Deleuze & Guattari, *What is Philosophy?*, p.69.
[21] See G.Deleuze, *Foucault*, University of Minnesota Press, 1988.

of philosophical thinking and that this perspectivism actually enables the generation of philosophical knowledge, or 'truths'. There is no theoretical problem for poststructuralism in accepting a claim to knowledge and truth from a certain perspective – thereby disregarding the issue of 'context' – though poststructuralists are exceedingly wary of claims to truth that seek to transcend all perspectives. In short, poststructuralists do not seek to deny truth, but to affirm it's complexity. As Foucault more cryptically put it, 'the task of speaking the truth is an infinite labour'.[22]

Philosophers must first and foremost be 'good philosophers'. 'Good philosophers', though, are 'critical philosophers'. Critical philosophers, in turn, are radical philosophers to the extent that they track down transcendence whenever it appears; be it in the research monograph, in the classroom, in academic institutions or in other areas of our 'public' and 'private' lives. Furthermore, to be radical in this sense, philosophers must first and foremost be creators of concepts. Whether such constructivism will have 'left' or 'right' wing consequences is a matter that can not be prejudged. Indeed, for Deleuze & Guattari, the more philosophers try to be 'left' or 'right' wing, the less critical they become; 'nothing positive is done, nothing at all, in the domains of either criticism or history, when we are content to brandish ready-made old concepts like skeletons intended to intimidate creation, without seeing that the ancient philosophers from whom we borrow them were already doing what we would like to prevent modern philosophers from doing: they were creating their concepts, and they were not happy just to clean and scrape bones like the critic and historian of our time'.[23]

---

[22] M.Foucault, *Foucault Live*, Semiotext(e), 1989, p.78.
[23] Deleuze & Guattari, *What is Philosophy?*, p.83.

Poststructuralism and Radical Politics
James Martin
The Queen's University of Belfast
'Organicism and Complexity in Gramsci's Social Theory'

Introduction

Theorists of radical politics have found in the writings of Antonio Gramsci a convenient bridge between Marxist and poststructuralist social theory. For some this bridge permits the development of a 'post-Marxist' socialism based on the recognition of the plurality of social antagonisms.[1] The key concept in this development is that of 'hegemony', a concept developed by Gramsci in his *Prison Notebooks* (1929-35).[2] Gramsci's formulation of hegemony is believed to have entailed a radical break with traditional Marxist approaches to political subjectivity to the extent that it undermined the monistic logic of economic reductionism and attempted to incorporate into revolutionary politics a 'logic of contingency' largely marginalised by more orthodox Marxists. Gramsci's innovation lay in his rejection of politics as simply a 'regional' category within a predetermined social topography and in his alternative construction of politics as constitutive of the social itself. In so doing, he formulated a theory focused on social complexity, accepting the autonomy of different subject positions from any single class antagonism.[3] Nevertheless, despite offering an opening to poststructuralist concerns with complexity, Gramsci remained wedded to a traditional Marxist concern with economic class as the necessary constituency around which a socialist hegemonic project would revolve. The result being a closure imposed on a theoretical scheme whose logic implies the interminable openness – the contingency – of political subjectivity.

The construction of Gramsci as a proto-poststructuralist follows much of the earlier humanist and structuralist readings that preceded it in foregrounding certain aspects of his theoretical analysis at the cost of obscuring the political project to which it was connected. In this paper I want to indicate how Gramsci's apparent openness to complexity was achieved whilst simultaneously expressing an organicism in his analysis. This organicism was fundamental to Gramsci's view of the socialist project as the creation of a new political order. The essentialism that certainly underlay his formulation of hegemony was not so much an inconsistency in his anti-reductionist Marxism as an integral part of his own project to theorise the conditions for establishing a socialist state.

The Constitutive Role of Politics

As a Marxist, Gramsci is distinguished by his attempt to incorporate political agency into the founding of a new social order. Going beyond Lenin,

---
[1] E.Laclau & C.Mouffe, *Hegemony and Socialist Strategy*, Verso, 1985; S.Golding, *Gramsci's Democratic Theory*, University of Toronto Press, 1992.
[2] A.Gramsci, *Selections from the Prison Notebooks*, Lawrence & Wishart, 1971.
[3] Laclau & Mouffe, *Hegemony*, p.71.

hegemony assigned to politics a constitutive role in the articulation of social orders in themselves and not merely the status of a region (the state) within a preconstituted social totality (base and superstructure). The openness to complexity lay in Gramsci's attempt to refine Marxism so as to highlight the innovative role of political action. In so doing, the conception of the social totality as a self-regulating whole was abandoned in favour of a stress on the complex plurality of antagonisms in any social formation.

Assigning politics a constitutive role was possible in Gramsci's thought by virtue of the fundamental importance he ascribed to ideology.[4] In rejecting the economistic reduction of the superstructure to an epiphenomenon of the base, Gramsci not only assigned forms of consciousness an independence from class position, he made ideology the key prerequisite for political action in so far as it served 'to cement and unify' a 'social bloc'.[5] Without consciousness, there was no action. Yet, the significance of ideology filtered down throughout Gramsci's Marxism to the point of almost abandoning the base-superstructure problematic altogether.

The key index for analysing a social formation became not so much a mode of production and its regional effects but rather the mutual interaction of economic relations with cultural, political and ideological practices. This interaction Gramsci referred to as a 'historical bloc'.[6] As a framework for socio-political analysis the concept of historical bloc foregrounded the specific linkages between a mode of production and the historically configured cultural and political formations in place of a causal analysis. As such, the interconnections between state, economy and society were viewed processually, as a mutually determining whole. The boundaries between these elements were consequently blurred, so confounding attempts to gauge their interaction from a point of absolute fixity.[7]

By emphasising the contingent configuration of the social formation, Gramsci was able to dwell on the points at which the elements of the social were linked. These linkages often became visible only in their decomposition – the moment of crisis. For instance, one of the most significant agents of linkage between the northern Italian industrial sector and the southern latifundi landlords were the high intellectuals, such as Benedetto Croce and Giustino Fortunato.[8] In legitimating the bourgeois state to the agrarian elite, the Neapolitan intellectuals were connected by what he called (long before Lacan) 'a kind of suture' to the interests of the bourgeoisie.[9] Yet that suture was beginning to unravel after the First World War causing a crisis of authority and so revealing the contingency of bourgeois dominance.

Just as bourgeois power could be analysed as a historical bloc of economic, political and cultural forces, so too should socialist revolution. Revolution was conceived by Gramsci, not as a mechanical act occurring once the proletariat's consciousness had fallen into its appropriate place, nor as

---

[4] *Selections*, pp.376-70.
[5] *Selections*, pp.328, 377.
[6] *Selections*, p.377.
[7] See R.Bertramsen et al, *State, Society and Economy*, Unwin Hyman, 1991, chapter 1.
[8] *Selections*, p.70.
[9] *Selections*, p.12.

the product of an elite carrying out the proletariat's task whilst it laboured under a false consciousness. Instead, Gramsci proffered the image of revolution as the gradual formation of a 'collective will'.[10] Substituting class sectarianism for a more broadly inclusive strategy of alliance formation, Gramsci posed proletarian hegemony as the proliferation of a world view – an intellectual and moral framework that would unite a diverse range of groups and classes. The weaving together of a wide variety of subjects into the collective will became the major task of Gramsci's politics, so placing diversity rather than homogeneity at the centre of his strategic concerns.[11]

Whilst it is true that politics played a constitutive role in Gramsci's thought, this was an innovation with roots in a specific context. Gramsci's concept of hegemony can be read not simply as a subversion of Marxist terms but also as a commentary on the possibilities for revolution in Italy. Recent scholarship has pointed to the affinities between Gramsci's thought and the problematic of state-building that characterised Italian social and political thought after unification in 1861.[12] What is often presented by the Left as an exclusively Marxist discourse (comprising questions of revolutionary rupture, class consciousness, vanguard leadership, etc) was in Gramsci's writings bound up with the historical weakness of the Italian bourgeois state and the revolutionary prospects engendered, particularly in the aftermath of the First World War, by its failure to generate a popularly legitimated authority. From this perspective, the constitutive role attributed to political action was a politics of state-building. As such, it is possible briefly to specify a number of referents for Gramsci's arguments.

Firstly, like other Italian theorists, Gramsci's political outlook had to deal with the problem of establishing authority in a country that was vastly agricultural and whose level of capitalist development was comparatively small and geographically isolated in the north. Deeply aware of the wide cultural and economic disparities in Italy, Gramsci's formulation of the concept 'historical bloc' clearly sought to grasp the bluntly empirical problem of securing the support of classes rooted in different modes of production. Secondly, his rejection of evolutionary socialism and positivist Marxism tied revolutionary strategy not to the logic of capitalist development with its inherent tendency to crisis, but rather to a gradual displacement of the connecting threads linking the bourgeoisie to its bloc of support – notably its intellectuals. This process, he believed, had already begun in 1919 with the 'crisis of authority' of the liberal state.[13] Finally, Gramsci's notion of proletarian revolution as the formation of a hegemony reflected the Risorgimento ideal of building a nation by 'consent' – a united civic consciousness – whilst simultaneously building the state. The 'collective will' was conceived as 'national-popular', the formation of distinct collective identity around the proletariat's interests.[14]

The constitutive role attributed to politics in Gramsci's thought can,

---

[10] *Selections*, p.125.
[11] *Selections*, p.324.
[12] See especially R.Bellamy & D.Schecter, *Gramsci and the Italian State*, Manchester University Press, 1993.
[13] *Selections*, pp.210, 270-1.
[14] *Selections*, p.133.

then, be associated with the more specific discourse of state-building. But does this in any way limit the poststructuralist reading of hegemony as the logic of contingency? To answer this, it will be necessary to examine one of the conceptual linkages between the discourse of state-building and that of Marxism: namely, the organicist idiom that prevailed in Gramsci's *Prison Notebooks*.

Gramsci's Organicism

The organic metaphor in Gramsci's prison writings served to delineate the rational structure of political action by emphasising the unity of theory and practice. As Franco Sbarberi has indicated, the metaphor had two broad meanings: firstly as a 'descriptive' principle of the relation between structure and superstructure, and secondly, as a 'prescriptive' account of the proper relations between elements in, or aiming towards, a future socialist society.[15] I shall give a brief outline of these uses of the organic metaphor, starting with the prescriptive use, since this is the one most closely connected to the state-building aspect of Gramsci's writings, an aspect usually left aside by his (post-) Marxist interpreters.

Organicism, as a prescriptive account of the relation between state and society, has its roots – in the modern era – in Hegelian philosophy. In Italy, Hegelian thought offered a way of theorising the role of the state as the expression of the common bonds of its citizens, rather than (as it was felt by many) an arbitrary imposition of forced obligation. For Hegel, the state could not be guaranteed its authoritative function if conceived as the outcome of a contract between preconstituted individual agents. When understood as the embodiment of a universal ideal that was only partially instantiated in finite beings, the modern state represented less an instrument and more an end that was presupposed in the individual's pursuit of self-interest. In this way, Hegel argued that the state stood to society as the apex of an 'organic' relation whereby the whole was more than the sum of its parts.[16]

Hegel's philosophy provided the Italian idealists with a method to theorise the development of a national consciousness that would reconcile state and society. In opposition to positivist thought, idealism – principally in the works of Benedetto Croce and Giovanni Gentile – sought to recover the implicit unity of Italians by affirming the creativity of human subjects (as against any predetermined scheme) and the ultimate rationality of the practical activities through which their subjectivities progressed. Gramsci was deeply influenced by this strand of idealism and incorporated it into his own socialist beliefs. In this he was particularly influenced by Gentile's radical idealism.

Whereas Croce brought his philosophy to support a conservative liberalism – refusing to permit that the creative tension between subject and object could ever be fully reconciled – Gentile argued that subject and object were united in the very activity of thought. When reality was understood as

---

[15] F.Sbarberi, *Gramsci: un socialismo armonico*, Franco Angeli, 1986, pp.77-8.

[16] C.Taylor, *Hegel and Modern Society*, Cambridge University Press, 1979, p.86.

the product of thought, the division between state and society could be eliminated by conceiving a universal consciousness as rooted in all practical activity. Subject and object were one and so, in essence, were state and society. This organic theory of the state, conceived as an implicit unity within praxis, influenced Gramsci's advocacy in 1919-20 of the industrial factory councils as a uniquely socialist form of 'ethical state'.[17] Gramsci argued that the councils would abolish the liberal distinction between public and private by grounding authority – with its concomitant requirements of order and discipline – in the praxis of factory production.[18] The worker identified his private role as producer with his public role as a citizen in the 'organism' of the factory-state. The workers' 'higher consciousness' transcended the technical division of labour by giving them an awareness of the 'spiritual unity' implicit in their discrete functions. As such they felt themselves integral parts of an organic whole.[19] The 'organic' quality of the state referred to the rational – and consequently harmonious – correspondence between citizen and authority that arose when individuals recognised their economic function as an integral part of a collective enterprise. Significantly, the 'organic unity' that issued from the factories obviated the need for an institutional realm in which public goods could be contested. Obligations would be felt to stem from the workers' own will. Political antagonism would thus be overcome when the individual's needs were no longer divided from that of the community.[20]

The failure of the factory council movement and the subsequent onset of Fascism effectively ended Gramsci's elaboration of the future socialist state. The appeal to an organic relation between leaders and led continued, however, in the *Prison Notebooks* in his account of the Communist Party as the collective agent – the 'organism' – bringing about revolution.[21] Still conceiving revolution as ultimately the creation of a state whose authority was rooted in the praxis of its subjects, Gramsci identified the intellectuals as the 'organic link' between the common sense of the masses and their universal consciousness in a new state.[22] However, aware of the frustrating gulf between the actual consciousness of the people and their potential unity, Gramsci's remarks on the future state remained speculative.[23] The abolition of the distinction between state and society was an aspiration only and much of his theoretical concerns dwelled on the question of how to properly interpret the process of transition towards the conditions in which a new state could be founded. The organic metaphor was employed again to indicate the rational correspondence between certain phenomena (ideas, events, individuals) and the economic structure.

Gramsci's factory council theory had relied on the spontaneous will of the industrial proletariat to prove the emergence of a unified subjectivity.

---

[17] A.Gramsci, *Pre-Prison Writings*, Cambridge University Press, 1994, p.50. See also D.Schecter, 'Gramsci, Gentile and the Theory of the Ethical State in Italy', *History of Political Thought*, 11/3, 1990.
[18] *Pre-Prison Writings*, p.113.
[19] *Pre-Prison Writings*, pp.120, 166-7.
[20] Schecter, 'Gramsci, Gentile and the Theory of the Ethical State', pp.506-7.
[21] *Selections*, p.129.
[22] *Selections*, pp.5-6.
[23] *Selections*, pp.268-9.

In his later writings he realised the inadequacy of this assumption both as the basis for workplace solidarity and as a foundation for a national basis of support. In his Notebooks, it was in the party rather than the new state that the unified will of the proletariat was centred. Yet Gramsci argued against the arbitrary imposition of revolution from above by a military elite. Still keeping to a conception of revolution as issuing from the immanent will of the people, he sought to make the intervention of the party an integral part of the organic formation of the state itself.

Gramsci's reconstruction of Marxism as a 'philosophy of praxis' aimed to reconcile historical materialism and historicist idealism. Marxism had fallen prey to a vulgar positivism that offered no political direction to revolutionary movements.[24] Idealism, on the other hand, had grasped the central importance of the development of human consciousness but had grounded this development in a metaphysical design.[25] For Gramsci, when shorn of their metaphysical pretensions Marxism and Idealism complemented each other in grounding human history in an immanent process of becoming. The dialectical interplay of subject and object (praxis) implied no transcendental scheme, it constituted the very process of history itself. Conceived this way, Marxism was both the apprehension of this process and its product. Marxism's role was consequently not merely to observe the historical process as if from above but to actively promote itself as the ideological basis of a new social order. It also followed that Marxism's political concepts could not be strictly causal; if base was considered to cause superstructure, then the interplay of subject and object would be replaced by a static materialism in which subjects were passive.[26] Base and superstructure were an organic unity and history could not be conceived without invoking them both.

Gramsci's construction of Marxism as the theory of the organic linkage between base and superstructure focused attention on the process of becoming rather than on the completion of an organic unity in a new state. The characteristically Marxist stipulation that the economic base is reflected in the superstructures was retained, but only by positing it as the outcome of the historical process and not a simple static requirement.[27] This organic rather than causal link permitted Gramsci to account for the possible disjuncture between base and superstructure, the fact that at any particular juncture in history the state and ideology only partially reflected the economic interests of the dominant economic class. The extent to which an economic class had a supremacy over the superstructures depended not on its empirical domination of the state but rather on the degree to which it succeeded in proliferating its own self-conscious awareness of its practical (that is, economic) activity as a universal principle. To do this a class had to move beyond an 'economic-corporate' identity and establish points of contact with other classes and groups; it had to assimilate itself to a broader, popular identity. The conditions which permitted this were not economic crises but the more profound 'organic crises' in which the various points (notably via the intellectuals) that link an economic class to this

---

[24] *Selections*, pp.434-40.
[25] *Selections*, p.444.
[26] *Selections*, p.428.
[27] *Selections*, p.408.

broader identity became weakened. The task of the revolutionary party was to identify which changes and crises represented shifts of an organic nature and those which were merely 'conjunctural'.[28] In so doing, it would have to have at hand an alternative, potentially universalising identity, drawn from the praxis of the proletariat, by which to supplant the bourgeoisie.

In some respects, Gramsci's later strategy reversed the logic of the factory council theory: the organic unity expressed spontaneously in a common 'producer' consciousness was replaced by an attempt by the party to educate the masses into seeing their implicit common bonds. The party organism would bring the disparate elements into conformity with it. What kept the party from simply imposing the will of its leaders, for Gramsci, was the imperative to act in accordance with the organic needs of its class – a requirement achievable through 'democratic centralism'.[29]

Conclusion

Gramsci's social theory is inherently ambiguous and this ambiguity stems from the organicist idiom that pervades his *Notebooks*. Organicism, whether as a theory of the state or of the historical process, offers a holistic framework in which the autonomy of disparate elements is ultimately subsumed within a unifying whole. Problems arise when it comes to determining how the parts relate to the whole. Interestingly, what occurred in Gramsci's organic theory of the factory council-state also occurred in his later organic theory of the structure: the unity that was given at an organic level was deemed ultimately to extinguish the contingent political articulation between the disparate elements. In the factory council, state and civil society were united on the basis of an assumed shared identification amongst workers with the goal of increased production. The united consciousness that arose from this common goal was deemed by Gramsci to harmonise the particular, technical differences between workers. Politics was reduced to the technical requirement of the planning of production levels.[30]

In his *Prison Notebooks*, Gramsci was clearly more aware of the complex configuration of interests, ideologies and practices that characterised a social formation. But whilst his awareness of such complexity was an advance on his earlier factory council theory, his approach was no less geared towards overcoming this plurality. The organic theory of structural development provided the justification for conceiving the harmonisation of differences as ultimately possible in a future socialist state. The result is an ambiguity in his analysis. As Sbarberi remarks:

> 'In reality, from his own conception of the world Gramsci draws two apparently contradictory orientations: as regards contemporary society, he is a theorist of *antagonism*, seeking to grasp all the contradictions in play in order to intensify them and reach a revolutionary transformation of the bourgeois system of power; as regards the future society, he proves instead

---

[28] *Selections*, pp.178-9.
[29] *Selections*, pp.188-9.
[30] Schecter, 'Gramsci, Gentile and the Theory of the Ethical State', p.507.

> to be a theorist of *cohesion*, because he aims to establish an ordered and harmonious civil coexistence where subjects live in deep sympathy with the community, according to the classical model of political organicism.'[31]

Post-structuralist efforts to incorporate Gramsci's theory of politics fail to understand this ambiguity by focusing exclusively on his anti-reductionist approach to social antagonisms. Yet the problem returns when it is noted that the logic of contingency implied in the concept of hegemony was, in Gramsci, undermined by his insistence on the single class core of hegemony. By insisting that hegemony was grounded in the ontological primacy of economic classes in historical development, he contradicted his own anti-essentialist approach to political subjectivity. If hegemony was constructed around either the bourgeoisie or the proletariat, then the political constitution of subjects through struggle was foreclosed. Hegemony was essentialised by invoking a necessary (rather than contingent) subject.[32]

Yet this recourse to essentialism is neither as surprising nor inconsistent as poststructuralists make out. For the ultimate closure to politics was already implied in Gramsci's organicism. In their failure to acknowledge the discourse of state-building in Gramsci's thought, poststructuralists have tended to see the adjective 'organic' as denoting simply a relational whole similar to the discourse theory that they advocate.[33] Yet organicism, as it was employed in the *Notebooks*, denoted conformity with economic structure, a conformity achieved when the will became conscious of its unity in praxis. Political action could then be argued by Gramsci to confront complexity not with a view to maintaining it but rather to overcoming it in a future order where state and civil society were reunited.

---

[31] F.Sbarberi, 'Introduzione' to F.Sbarberi (ed), *Teoria politica e società industriale. Ripensare Gramsci*, Bollati Boringhieri, 1988, p.22.
[32] Laclau & Mouffe, *Hegemony*, pp.70, 136-9.
[33] Laclau & Mouffe, *Hegemony*, p.67.

Do Constitutions Matter?

Richard Bellamy
University of Reading
&
Dario Castiglione
University of Exeter

'Normal Politics, Constitutional Politics and Political Constitutionalism in Bruce Ackerman's *We the People*'[1]

Liberal democrats typically regard constitutions as providing a necessary framework for democracy and the regulation of the public sphere that rests on foundations that are largely pre-political in origin. Liberal fears of the tyranny of the majority offer the prime justification for this approach. In contrast, Bruce Ackerman's *We the People* (Harvard University Press, 1991) provides one possible account of how to establish an 'overlapping consensus' on the basic structure of society by appealing to the resources of democratic politics. He argues that we must distinguish between 'normal' politics, which occurs under settled constitutional systems, and 'constitutional' politics, which arises in exceptional times and places the whole system of government in discussion. He believes that this 'dualist' scheme can overcome the liberal's fears about letting democracy out of a normative straight jacket.

Ackerman contends that the constitutionalist's objections to simple majoritarianism are valid with respect to 'normal' politics but do not hold for 'constitutional' politics. During periods of 'normal' politics, people do not speak with a single voice but are divided into different ideological factions and interest groups. Consequently, fear of a tyrannous majority during such periods are fully justified: divided representation and Madisonian checks and balances are needed to curb such tendencies as much as possible. 'Constitutional' politics, in contrast, only takes place when some national crisis manages to unite the people and leads them to transcend their own particular interests and consider the common good. On such occasions, political deliberation is Rousseauean rather than Benthamite in nature. As a result, objections to the will of the majority lose much of their force. Instead of representing the aggregate of the largest number of personal preferences, which then gets imposed on others who wanted something quite different, a Rousseauean majority reflects a general opinion on the rules and principles necessary to benefit everyone. In this latter case, voters should already have taken the rights of other individuals into account when making their decision and, when necessary, weighed them as best they could.

---

[1] An extended version of this piece is forthcoming in the *British Journal of Political Science*. Research for this paper was supported by an ESRC award for a project on 'Languages and Principles for a Constitution of Europe' (R000221170).

Ackerman identifies three instances of constitutional politics in the United States – the Founding, Reconstruction, and the New Deal. These constitutional moments established a framework for normal politics that the Supreme Court could then defend from populist incursions until such time as 'we the people' reconvened to reform it. In this way, Ackerman claims to have synthesised three different views of constitutionalism. He believes the concerns of 'rights foundationalists' can be catered for because dualist democracy gives rights special protection by making them only reformable in the context of constitutional politics. Between times they can be upheld by judicial review. He also hopes to accomodate the views of 'monist' democrats, who believe that the will of the people should always prevail. These theorists make the mistake of believing that the popular will is expressed in the ordinary law-making of 'normal' politics. In fact, at such times personal interests tend to supervene over the national interest, so that the everyday legislation of governments reflects at best majority preferences rather than the common good. However, the constraints imposed on majorities by the constitution and its judicial guardians result from constitutional politics and so do genuinely reflect the collective voice of the people. In bowing to them, therefore, governments submit not to certain elites or imposed norms but to the considered will of the demos. Finally, Ackerman also hopes to take the approach of historicist interpreters of the constitution on board. This group divides into roughly two camps: those who argue that judicial interpretation should concentrate on divining the original intent of the founders, and those who regard the constitution as an evolving document that judges need to update to reflect current conditions. Ackerman synthesises the two within his dualist perspective. The role of Supreme Court judges, he maintains, must be to uphold the intentions of the people as expressed at the last relevant moment of constitutional politics. Since the constitution has never been entirely rewritten, this will almost always involve them in a complex process of integrating various elements from each of the three moments. The Founders' intentions remain important, but have been modified by later new beginnings. The constitution does evolve, therefore, but not as a result of judicial interpretation. Indeed, Ackerman believes it would be quite illegitimate for judges to take on the responsibilty of updating it. Rather, the judges' role is to force the people to deliberate on whether they think change is necessary or not, upholding the status quo until they are sufficiently motivated to do so.

Although Ackerman's dualist democracy seems to combine the reasons underlying both constitutionalism and democracy, it might still be objected that since constitutions aim to embody universal human rights and/or rights intrinsic to the procedures of democracy, constitutional politics of the kind that Ackerman advocates is at best superfluous, at worst pernicious. Given that such rights can be justified, their democratic legitimation might be thought to add little or nothing to them whilst risking placing them in jeopardy. Although the story he tells has a decidedly Whiggish tone, with each constitutional moment leading in a progressive and more egalitarian direction, the ghost of a potential Reagan revolution haunts the pages of his book. Reagan would have radically shifted the constitution in a libertarian direction that Ackerman clearly would have deplored. Yet Ackerman appears to accept that had Reagan mobilised popular support for a counter New Deal, then the people would have spoken and he would have had to live with the result. Similarly, he regards as great wrongs the acceptance of slavery and the exclusion of women from the franchise at the Founding, the radical interpretation of freedom of contract so as to undermine all attempts at employment legislation during Reconstruction, and the absence of an adequate welfare state even after the New Deal. In his view, these policies were never acceptable. How then can he endorse the constitutional politics that gave rise to these injustices?

Ackerman's response to such attacks has been disappointing. Sometimes he seems to accept these criticisms and say that he has simply been arguing that historically the American constitution has developed in this way, not that he thinks this thesis offers the best account of how constitutions ought to be defended and devised. Indeed, he advocates the irrevocable entrenchment of social and economic rights alongside civil and political rights as an ideal conclusion to the long history of American constitution making. At other times he offers a more pragmatic defence of his theory. Constitutional moments, he appears to suggest, are in the nature of things. In the past those who have tried to entrench certain constitutional provisions have made grave mistakes, in the American case condoning slavery, the oppression of women, and grave social inequalities. Given human fallibility, similar errors are likely to occur in the future. Our best defence against oppression on the one hand and anarchic revolution on the other is to regularise the conditions and forms under which periodic constitutional review can take place. So stated, this line of argument will not do. One could equally say that the chance of periodic review provides the opportunity for even greater errors to be made in the future.

We believe a more promising case for dualist democracy can be made by taking a somewhat different tack, one which shifts our focus from the issue of justification to that of legitimation. The above criticisms assume that at the very least an overlapping consensus on certain constitutional principles can be justified. However, John Rawls has raised two difficulties with this assumption associated with the 'burdens of judgement'. First, the values and theories upon which principles of justice and rights can be based are often incommensurable. Consequently, they occasionally produce not only different rankings of basic rights but also conceiveably very diverse interpretations of what justice requires. Second, even within an agreed scheme of values rights may clash. This problem of non-compossibility, however, will become even more intractable when a political community includes individuals holding incommensurable understandings of the basis of rights and justice. There are limits to what can be justified in abstract terms when these sorts of conflicts are acknowledged. A theory of legitimacy attempts to fill the gap by finding mechanisms that allow individuals to resolve the dispute by reaching a decision all can accept even if they disagree with it.

Legitimacy so conceived supplements our conceptions of rights and justice with an account of authority. Because equally reasonable but incommensurable and non-compossible values and claims are in play, the decision cannot be resolved by deferring to 'an' authority, possessing expert moral knowledge. Instead, we need a way of placing someone or a set of institutions 'in' authority, and accepting their entitlement to generate decisions for us. Authority here rests neither on persuasion, in the sense of acceptance of the substantive truth or correctness of the decision taken, nor coercion. However, it does not supplant conceptions of rights or justice either – it could hardly prove acceptable if it did. Rather, it assumes their existence and importance and merely seeks to find ways of mediating between them.

In modern times democracy has largely filled this role of providing authoritative mechanisms that confer legitimacy. Its success in this role rests on its potential to involve relevant groups in decision making so that they feel that some account has been taken of their views. In order to understand how democracy can achieve this result, however, we need a more differentiated appreciation of the nature of democratic decision making than Ackerman's. In this respect, one main difficulty with his distinction between normal and constitutional politics lies in its being too firmly drawn. As he notes, most members of modern societies are best defined as what he calls 'private citizens'. In other words, they are neither 'perfect privatists', a term he uses to denote individuals exclusively devoted to their own personal concerns, nor are they 'public citizens', his label for persons willing to devote all their energies to the common good. Like Ackerman, we think this mixture is a good thing. A society of atomistic egoists would resemble the Hobbesian state of nature, public citizenship in the sense described by Ackerman can all too easily degenerate into the nightmare of 1984. However, Ackerman fails to develop this thesis sufficiently. He endows the 'private citizen' with a schizophrenic personality, acting as a 'perfect privatist' in normal times and as a 'public citizen' on those extraordinary occasions that define constitutional politics. He believes that only exceptional circumstances, such as civil war or the mass unemployment of the 1930s, are capable of mobilizing the citizenry and involving them in the protracted, well-focussed, public-spirited, deep and deliberative discussions that characterise higher law-making. In contrast, we wish to suggest that citizens are capable of switching between and, when appropriate, even mixing, the 'normal' Benthamite and the 'constitutional' Rousseauean form of politics most of the time. When principles are at stake, as in debates about abortion or capital punishment, discussion standardly takes a Rousseauean form and every one involved makes a genuine effort to include basic human interests in their deliberations. Even in the British Parliament – a classical example of a 'monist' democratic system – MPs are given a free vote on such occasions. However, Benthamite reasoning is entirely appropriate when one is looking simply for a decision that will maximise the general welfare. Of course, many, if not most, decisions involve elements of both sorts of consideration. When deciding on whether to build a road, for example, consideration is standardly given not only to the interests of residents and potential road users but also to more principled concerns, such as protection of the environment. A democratic majority need not be seen as riding rough shod over the values and interests of others, therefore. Rather, it may be more accurate to regard it as the best means available of weighing them and bringing them into some kind of balance.

Once the role played by democratic legitimation is recognised both in mediating between conflicting values and interests, and in promoting and transforming preferences, constitutionalism becomes a matter not of entrenching a given consensus but of devising institutions that generate a consensus that previously did not exist – albeit one that need not express any deep agreement but more often an acceptable compromise or an acknowledgement that the decision was reached in a fair manner. Within such a system, normal and constitutional politics need to be combined rather than separated. Put another way, politics has to be seen as an intrinsic part of the constitution rather than as occuring either outside or within constitutional limits.

Recognizing the constitutional role of politics also involves a break with traditional views of constitution-making processes and their self-legitimizing qualities. This At this point communitarian liberals and liberal communitarians seem to part company. The former insist, as Rawls puts it, that 'the idea of right and just constitutions and basic laws is always ascertained by the most reasonable political conception of justice and not by the result of an actual political process'. The latter subscribe to the opposite view, providing an account of periodical constitutional pre-commitments as an actual, as opposed to a hypothetical, event. Within the American context, this division reproduces the debate between Madison and Thomas Jefferson over the utility of periodic constitutional conventions. Whereas Jefferson thought they were required to avoid any living generation being bound by the decision of the dead, Madison believed they were unnecessary and potentially destabilising. From a Madisonian view point, of course, Ackerman's theory comes close to falling into the Jeffersonian error. For if you get matters right the first time, then there should be no need for any future constitutional politics. As we remarked earlier, the only reason Ackerman seems to have for suggesting we might need to keep the option of constitutional politics open is the pragmatic one that we are almost certain to get something wrong. But such a negative reason does not seem sufficient to ground the positive picture of public reason which Ackerman associates with higher law-making.

A way around this impasse can be found if we return to our earlier distinction between Benthamite and Rousseauean politics. Benthamite reasoning involves actors in a process of what Jon Elster has characterised as 'bargaining', whereby interests can either be traded or aggregated to achieve maximal welfare. This approach clearly works well for 'more-or-less' conflicts. Rousseauean democracy, in contrast, involves a form of discourse that Elster terms 'arguing'. This style of politics is probably more appropriate to 'either-or' conflicts. For, within deliberative settings, views can be transformed as opposed to simply combined in some mechanical fashion. In this way, a common view may emerge that genuinely attempts to take on board, or at least tries to weigh, the various values in play. Now, constitutional politics, which is concerned with conflicts involving both elements, does not seem to be stucturally different from normal politics. Arguing and bargaining are forms of political discourse present in both forms of politics, the only real difference being the relative predominance of one or other of the two. But the ideological picture of a constitutional dialogue where arguing prevails is partly undermined by the introduction of a third form of political debate, 'strategic arguing', through which self-interested agents often couch their political utterances in the form of impartial arguments, so as to better achieve their strategic objectives due to the efficaciousness of impartiality as a strategy for persuasion and its congruence with social norms. The diffuse presence of strategic arguing in constitutional politics may imply that impartiality and authenticity are as scarce here as in normal politics. But Elster conjectures that strategic arguing illustrates the more general phenomenon of the 'civilizing effect of hypocrisy'. Politics, in other words, forces us to take on at least the semblance of accomodating others, a necessity that in time may lead to us actually doing so.

If constitutional politics is not so different from normal politics, then the constitutionalists's belief that the enabling and facilitating of politics requires its limitation proves overstated. We may think of constitutions as embodying certain principles that stand at the heart of all just societies, without necessarily placing these basic rights and liberties within an extra-political framework on the grounds that they are prior to, pre-conditions of, or need protection from politics. Instead, their identification, specification and implementation may all best be seen as products of political processes. A constitution that takes this form consists of a complex of institutions and conventions that facilitate the various styles of political dialogue that we identified earlier as appropriate to the management of particular sorts of social and ideological conflict, rather than being a legal document that sets out specific justiciable rights and norms. We remarked above on Sunstein's observations on the part played by the separation of powers in this regard. A whole series of other measures, from the use of diverse voting systems for different representative bodies through to the vertical and horizontal articulation of the principle of subsidiarity, can also employ politics not only to achieve the traditional constitutional goal of checking arbitrary power, but also to secure informed, consensual and fair decision making. In fact, this latter objective is arguably the most important function that a constitution performs.

The issue of institutional design was a prime concern of earlier constitutional doctrines. After all, the Bill of Rights was no part of the Federalist's original project. Unfortunately, the political dimension of constitutions has increasingly given way to a reliance on judicial mechanisms. This juridification of the constitution has a number of drawbacks. As the Italian jurist Gustavo Zagrebelsky has remarked, instead of enunciating a few general norms and principles, constitutions have steadily taken on the character of ordinary legislation with an equivalent body of detailed case law. The case for handing over to judges the necessary tasks of framing, interpreting, applying and balancing the basic principles of a just social order mirrors the standard liberal argument for limiting, and suffers from parallel weaknesses. Such limitations on the self-determination of ordinary citizens imply the paradoxical belief that ordinary citizens are not fully worthy of the liberties that the proponents of such schemes nevertheless ascribe to them. Moreover, there is also a danger that decisions on such matters by an unelected body will lack legitimacy in the eyes of the population. For in this area, as we saw, no uniquely 'right' answer exists. Instead, the political process of bargaining and arguing forms a necessary aspect for generating an acceptable and authoritative solution. Democractic procedures ensure not only that decisions get made in the light of the full range of interests and values involved, but also promote a certain identification with the result on the part of the participants. To employ Hart's terminology, they create not just a 'legal system' but a 'society with law', in which citizens 'look upon [the legal system's] rules from the internal point of view as accepted standards of behaviour, and not merely as reliable predictions of what will befall them, at the hands of officials, if they disobey.'

The fragmentation of nation states has made the question of how to mediate conflict in ways that foster identification with common principles and arrangements increasingly urgent. Our argument suggests that the solution lies in restructuring political institutions in ways that correspond to the plurality and complexity of modern societies.

Do Constitutions Matter?

Cécile Fabre
Worcester College, Oxford

'Jeremy Waldron on Bills of Rights

Introduction

Jeremy Waldron's article, 'A Right-Based Critique of Constitutional Rights', *Oxford Journal of Legal Studies*, 13, 1993, challenges the claim that a bill of rights is necessary, or at least desirable, for the protection of individual rights, and argues that respect for individuals as rights bearers in fact precludes the constitutional entrenchment of rights. His main argument has two stages. First, if we respect people as bearers of rights we must accept that they will not seek purposely to harm others in their exercise of their rights, and that disagreements between them about rights are genuine and ought not to be settled by appealing to bills of rights. Second, if we respect people as bearers of rights we must accept their right to participate in the democratic process; but entrenching individual rights - even participatory rights – in a bill undermines political participation, since it gives considerable powers to the courts. I shall examine each of these two lines of argument in turn, and I shall argue that they are not wholly convincing.

(I) Settling Disputes between Rights-Bearers

According to Waldron, for someone to want individual rights to be part of the constitution implies that this person arbitrarily prefers her own formulation of rights to any other and wants to entrench it in the constitution so that it is difficult to change. More importantly, this person does not trust what other people could do with rights in the future. Waldron rejects this 'combination of self-assurance and mistrust' on two grounds.

(1) There is an inherent contradiction between entrenching rights in the name of the individual on the one hand, and the presupposition of this desire for entrenchment, to wit, our distrust of the individuals we pretend to respect. The very fact that we assume that people are able to think and act morally and therefore are bearers of rights should prompt us to trust them as 'bearers of political responsibilities', and should convince us that the fact that they disagree with us about rights does not imply that they are 'either simpletons or rogues'. We should therefore not disable them politically by entrenching one particular conception of rights in a bill.

Now, I do not think that there is any inconsistency in saying that human beings are autonomous, able to form judgements and to act morally on the one hand, and that they quite often commit appalling acts on the other hand. It is precisely because they are moral beings that we are appalled by what they can do. By saying that we should trust that people will assume political responsibilities and will not seek to crush rights, Waldron fails to see that saying that people have rights does not entail that they will always respect other people's rights. Consequently, it is not absurd to entrench rights in the constitution, in order to protect people's autonomy and morality against the majority's attempt at violating them. Moreover, the fact that someone wants fundamental rights to be protected in a bill of rights does not mean that she never trusts her fellow citizens, whatever the circumstances are. Waldron unfairly depicts such a person as a staunch individualist who is never willing to admit that she may be wrong and who is always ready to dismiss other people's views. That is an inaccurate picture.

(2) Such an attitude to other individuals downplays the existence of genuinely conflicting views about rights. We need to establish a source of authority to settle these conflicts which cannot appeal to rights. Therefore, a bill of rights cannot be such a source. One should instead rely on something like the philosophical debate, where 'openness to counter-argument is crucial', as a way of deciding upon fundamental issues.

Two points are worth making by way of reply.

(a) The underlying assumption of Waldron's argument is that there are so many different conceptions of rights that we cannot impose a given one of them. However, the very ideas of autonomy, morality, human dignity, on which Waldron rests his rejection of a bill of rights, imply that the individual has moral rights such as not being discriminated against, expressing her views, taking part in the democratic process, etc. These moral rights seem fairly uncontroversial, and widespread disagreement about the content and the foundation of rights does not constitute a reason not to constitutionalise them in particular.

(b) A philosophical debate, any debate which aim at finding the truth, cannot work if, for instance, freedom of speech is not granted, if some participants are prevented from participating because their views are not deemed worth hearing. There is therefore a reason for freedom of speech and freedom of participation to be secured constitutionally. Waldron could argue that there is after all no need for having a bill of rights: an appropriate law is sufficient. To which we could answer that since it is necessary for the debate that freedom of speech be acknowledged, it should be made more difficult to violate it; therefore, it should be included in a bill of rights the status of which is superior to the status of a statute. Waldron rejects that line of argument, which he calls the 'proceduralist gambit', and to this I now turn.

(II) Participation and Democracy

The second stage of Waldron's main argument against bills of rights is that seeing individuals as rights bearers commits us to the view that political participation is crucial. Yet political participation is undermined by a system in which a bill of rights takes some issues off the political agenda, or at least makes the terms in which they are couched difficult to alter by requiring a super-majority for constitutional amendment, and gives powers to the judiciary at the expense of the legislature. I shall first address the issue of political participation and then respond to Waldron's worries about super-majority rule and the role of the judiciary.

(II/1) Political Participation

Waldron begins by asserting that political participation is a fundamental right, which rests on a certain conception of man as a chooser, a planner. According to him, this conception not only precludes entrenching substantive rights, but it also precludes entrenching participatory rights. His claim rests on two grounds.

(1) He claims that entrenching participatory rights is wrong because it fails to acknowledge the extent of our disagreement about participatory rights themselves. That is, some of us have different views about whether we should have proportional representation, whether we should hold referenda, etc. Now I agree that there are disagreements on these issues; besides, what is desirable in one country because the particular political culture of this country is of a certain nature may not be desirable in another country. For instance, proportional representation in a country where there are several dozen parties is not desirable, whereas it could be in other circumstances. However, Waldron fails to distinguish between political participation in itself and the modalities of participation, such as referenda and types of voting. We do not have to demand that referenda be secured in a bill of rights; but we can without inconsistency demand that it be guaranteed to people that they cannot be deprived of their right of voting on grounds of their race or gender. We can also demand that their freedom of speech be protected, because it is required by their right to participate in the political decision-making process. But that does not commit us to saying that the relation between freedom of speech and, say, advertising, which is controversial, should be laid down in the constitution. In other words, the right to political participation demands that other rights be granted and that these should be included in the constitution. Those aspects of the right to political participation that are but modalities of this right or of the rights entailed by it are another matter.

(2) Waldron also claims that it will not do to divorce democratic procedures from considerations of outcomes and to argue on that basis that entrenching procedural rights is democratic, for two reasons. First, 'the same fundamental values are implicated in both spheres', with the effect that 'it will be difficult to keep constitutional jurisprudence apart from the considerations of more obviously substantive concerns'. Now, I agree that considerations about individual autonomy require both democratic participation and, say, certain distributive policies. But I really do not see why by taking a stance on the former, the judiciary will be lead to take a stance on the latter.

Second, 'we value participation not just as an end in itself but also because we think that it is one way to ensure that each person gets what is hers by right', so that 'any entrenchment of a set of putatively procedural principles would be at least in part the entrenchment of a particular view of the substantive outcomes to which each person is entitled', and thus would be undemocratic and therefore unacceptable.

Three points are worth making here.

(a) We need not value political participation for the stated reason: we may value it because it gives every one the chance of having a say about the way society should be run, irrespective of what we think people's rights are. It is thus far from clear that entrenching a particular procedure amounts to entrenching a substantive view of rights.

(b) Assuming that he is right that there is not such a clear-cut distinction between procedure and substance, that still does not entail that those rights that we can securely identify as necessary for the good functioning of the democratic procedure, such as freedom of political speech, the right to vote and to run for office, should not be put in the constitution.

(c) If entrenching any procedure is undemocratic and therefore unacceptable, it logically follows that there should be no constitution at all. Waldron nowhere addresses this rather obvious implication. But if he thinks that a constitution is desirable, he has to explain where we draw the line between enough and too much substance, and why we stop short of entrenching individual rights. On the other hand, if he thinks that there should not be a constitution, he has to show that a democratic regime without any constraints whatsoever would be more protective of individual rights than any other alternative. In particular, he has to defend the highly implausible view that citizens are less vulnerable to their government when it operates without constraint whatsoever than when it operates within a constitutional framework.

(II/2) Super-Majoritarian Rules and the Judiciary

Waldron then goes on to criticise the idea that a super-majority should be required to amend a bill of rights, on the ground that the point of such a requirement is 'to reduce the probability that any amendment will be successful'. Since it is very difficult for the legislature to alter the bill of rights, it is likely that other, non democratic procedures will be adopted to reform the constitution, through the judiciary for instance, as is the case in the United States. Now, I would like to make a few points.

First, it is true that a super-majority is normally required to amend a bill of rights because a bill of rights, being part of the constitution is meant to have a status superior to the status of a statute. However, constitutional revision need not be as difficult as it is in the United States and in Canada. In fact, one could argue that referenda by simple majority should be used, in which case a constitution-maker need not require a super-majority for constitutional amendment, and one cannot be accused of being anti-democratic. It is therefore possible to strike a balance between a desire to preserve democracy on the one hand, and a desire to protect the conditions of democracy and certain fundamental rights from being abridged. That does not refute Waldron's whole thesis about bills of rights; it simply shows that advocating the entrenchment of rights does not commit one to advocating the tyranny of the judiciary.

Second, although he is right to warn us about the dangers of giving too much power to the judiciary, he misrepresents what happens in, say, the United States, when a decision on constitutional matters is made by the Supreme Court. The Court does not make judgements out of the blue. It can make decisions on certain issues only if a citizen or a state thinks that his rights have been violated. The arguments are heard from both sides, and everybody has a chance to defend his case. It therefore does not decide arbitrarily. In fact, giving citizens the opportunity of appealing to the Court might be understood as a modality of the right to participate in the political debate.

Third, while it is a feature of Anglo-Saxon law that a high court can make judgements on particular cases by appealing to the constitution and that it can thereby modify the constitution, that is not necessarily a desirable constitutional feature. Take the case of France. Laws are examined by the Constitutional Council, which is not a juridical institution, only if the President of the Republic, or the Prime Minister or certain members of the Parliament request it. In such cases, laws are valid only if the Council agrees that they conform with the constitution. Since it is a setback for the government and the parliamentary majority to have a law struck down by the Council, they are usually more careful in drafting bills, and they engage in discussions with members of all parties to avoid violating the constitution. Debates take place mainly before the law is adopted, which satisfies Waldron's requirement that democratic debate should be preserved. Besides, a decision of anticonstitutionality by the Council does not amount to adding new rights in the constitution. Suppose that the Council strikes down a law making homosexual acts illegal. The constitution will not thereby automatically be amended to the effect that no law forbidding homosexual acts can be passed. Another government could try again and risk being defeated again. That point is important because it explains why the Constitutional Council is not accused of pre-empting the debate about fundamental rights and of robbing the people of its fundamental right to shape its institutional framework. Now, the French system has many deficiencies. But at least it offers an example of how to avoid, if only partly, some of the most acute problems posed by the American system.

This whole debate also impinges on the question of political authority. Waldron denies that the Court should be its ultimate holder, and I wholly agree with him. But that does not warrant the claim that a bill of rights always and by definition curtails the authority of the people. Arguing in favour of a referendum-based procedure for constitutional amendment enables us to locate authority without ambiguity in the hands of the people. The Court, or any institution in charge of constitutional judicial review, acts as a safeguard, as a reminder of crucial decisions made by the people concerning individual rights. What is presupposed here is obviously the claim that it makes sense for a people to bind itself into respecting individual rights. To this I now turn.

(II/3) Democratic Self-Restraint

One powerful democracy-based argument for bills of rights is that if it is decided by the democratic majority then we should accept it. Waldron seeks to refute such an argument in two stages.

Firstly, the fact that a majority adopts a law is certainly a reason for having the law but it does not entail that the law is democratic. Therefore it does not follow from the fact that a legislature adopts a bill of rights that this society shall be more democratic than a society where fundamental individual rights are not constitutionally entrenched. On the contrary, adopting a bill of rights amounts to 'voting democracy out of existence, at least so far as a wide range of issues of political principles is concerned'.

Now, it is perfectly true that the fact that a legislature votes a law does not make the latter democratic. However, it does not follow from the fact that a law voted by the majority restricts the exercise of majority rule that we should not accept it, and this for two reasons.

(1) Waldron equates democracy with the unrestrained exercise of majority rule. But that is arguable. Democracy is more than that; it requires political participation, equal political power, freedom of speech, etc. Majority rule is but one of its components, albeit a crucial one, and a lot more than what he provides us with is required to sway the balance in its favour rather than in favour of the other components. As argued above, one can combine the utmost respect for democracy with a deep seated conviction that bills of rights are desirable.

(2) Even if one accepts the contention that democracy can be equated with majority rule, one could wonder whether democracy should be valued above other values such as, for example, distributive justice and neutrality towards conceptions of the good, which could be entrenched in the constitution. Waldron implicitly assumes that democracy should be so valued, and I suspect that the right to participation, understood as the right to take part in the process and not to have one's desires thwarted if one belongs to the majority, would ground his argument if he provided one to this effect. But there are other rights than the right to political participation, which encapsulate the notions of human dignity and morality that Waldron is so keen on defending, and we need an explanation from him as to why the right to political participation is the best expression of the importance we attach to these notions, and why it should be allowed to override these other rights that protect them.

In a second stage, Waldron seeks to refute the claim that 'an electorate could decide collectively to bind itself in advance to resist the siren charms of rights violations in the future', and he makes the following analogy: when someone asks a friend to prevent her from reading books going against her religious faith, in case she came to have doubts about her faith if she read them, the friend is not bound to respect this request because, were she to do so, she would take side in an internal conflict and would not allow her friend to change her mind about her faith. The same argument can be used to argue that a democratic people cannot bind themselves to not changing its mind as to which kind of legislation should be enacted.

Now, that analogy can be contested on the following grounds. First, when the religious person changes her mind, it has consequences for her only; a majority's decision, on the contrary often affects other people than its members. A better, but not entirely satisfactory analogy would be the following: a person knows that she is vulnerable to the arguments put forward by Jehovah's witnesses to the effect that blood transfusion is forbidden by God, and is aware that should she be convinced by these arguments it could put her partner's life in danger if he has an accident and she has to make decisions about medical treatment. So she makes an informed and conscious decision to ask her friend to hide any books that might lead her to hold the views extolled by Jehovah's witnesses. Now, it seems to me that the friend ought to respect the request, because the decision was informed and carefully thought out, and because what might be at stake, the partner's life, is too important to be jeopardised.

Waldron might say that this would not be the right way to handle the arguments put forward by the Jehovah's witnesses and that it would be much better for the friend to ignore the request and to prompt the person to confront and try to refute them. I agree that it is better to face unpleasant and dangerous views than to bury your head in the sand. But it is neither a necessary nor a sufficient ground for the friend to interfere with this person's request, especially if one considers people as able to make judgements as to the way their life should be run. It would be an act of unwanted paternalism for the friend to decide what is best for the person and to act on that basis, ignoring this person's wishes. Besides, and this is where the analogy does not quite work, debates do not stop once a right is made constitutional, and there is no better example of that than the heated and raging controversies which the Roe v. Wade decision continues to arouse more than twenty years after the decision was handed down. What is hampered is changing the constitution, and we fall back on the problems discussed earlier regarding amendment procedures, which I argued could be based on referenda. The upshot of this first point is that the analogy drawn by Waldron is not very satisfactory, because it does not account for the fact that people other than the majority are harmed when the latter infringes rights, and of the fact that constitutional entrenchment does not kill any sort of political activity.

Second, and this is another respect in which Waldron's analogy is problematic, the religious woman asks another person to keep the books away from her, which means that it depends on someone else than her whether or not she will read the books. In the case of a democratic majority and the bill of rights, one could argue, here again, that the bill must be adopted and changed by the citizenry in a referendum, without these changes to be struck down by the constitutional court. Thus the citizenry constrains its representatives by laying down fundamental rights in a Bill and by having them protected by the judiciary or another institution. And the citizenry also decides whether to remove these constraints or not by referendum. This design cannot be accused of being anti-democratic since the decisions to set up or to jettison constraints on the legislature are taken by the electorate, who is the ultimate source of authority.

Conclusion

To conclude, it is not inconsistent to say that individuals are rights bearers and that they are capable of violating others' rights. The fact that there are deep conflicts about rights is not a reason for not entrenching uncontroversial rights. Having a bill of rights does not necessarily lead to the tyranny of the judiciary. The idea of democratic self-restraint makes sense. In sum, Waldron's objections against bills of rights are not very convincing.

Identities, Boundaries and Voters

Joy Squires
University of Wolverhampton

'Re-visiting "Internal Colonialism" – The Case of Shetland'

Acknowledgements

I am indebted to Jack Burgess and John Graham of the Shetland Movement for giving so generously of their time.

Some twenty years ago, Michael Hechter (1975) proposed that internal colonialism constituted the most plausible explanation for the development of nationalist sentiment in the Celtic fringe of Britain. Hechter's proposition unleashed a fervent and lengthy debate about the causes and nature of nationalism in Scotland, which left him roundly condemned for having misunderstood and misrepresented Scotland's historical and economic development within Britain.[1]

Hechter's critics focused on Scotland's industrialisation and modernisation process in the Central belt. Scant regard was paid to the periphery of Scotland, where economic, social and political experience has been markedly different to that of the Lowlands. Criticism of the cultural division of labour as the key element in the theory of internal colonialism was particularly trenchant, and the concept was generally dismissed as inappropriate to Scotland. However, an examination of the economic and political development of the remote periphery of Scotland, namely Shetland, reveals that the theory of internal colonialism and the cultural division of labour offers a highly plausible explanation for the growth of demands for greater autonomy and the politicisation of those demands through the Shetland Movement.

Hechter summarizes internal colonialism thus:

> 'Commerce and trade among members of the periphery tend to be monopolised by the core. Credit is similarly monopolised. When commercial prospects emerge, bankers, managers and entrepreneurs tend to be recruited from the core ... Economic dependence is reinforced through juridical, political and military measures ... Typically there is a great migration and mobility of peripheral workers.' (1975, p.33)

Hechter's assumption is that the periphery (Wales, Scotland and Ireland) suffers the disadvantages of uneven economic development, reinforced by the colonial relationship perpetuated by the metropolitan core (England). This relationship essentially precludes the exercise of economic, social and political power by members of the periphery, by virtue of their indigenous status. Economic development is typically either confined to basic, low value-added sectors or, where the periphery is rich in primary resources, is encouraged

---

[1] Page (1978) offers a persuasive critique of Hechter's methodology.

to the benefit of the core. In both situations the metropolitan core controls development and a division of labour, based on cultural distinctiveness, becomes operative. Eventually, exploitation and discrimination lead to a greater awareness of cultural differences between periphery and core, a growing sense of identity amongst members of the periphery and to the conclusion that only self-determination can break the exploitative colonial relationship.

Critics of Hechter point to a number of failings in his analysis, at least with regard to Scotland. Nairn (1977) and Brand (1985) argue persuasively that Hechter seems not to have noticed that Scotland has, for many centuries, produced its own economic, social and political élites operating within the context of a separate legal, religious and educational framework. These élites developed a dynamic, prosperous economy based on Scottish capital and Scottish entrepreneurial flair. Scotland flourished as part of the British Empire and Scotsmen made important contributions to the development of the technology that was to underpin Britain's dominant economic position in the world. As Nairn reminds us, Scotland

> 'is an old industrial society ... with its own cities and native capitalist class'. [For many years it developed] 'at approximately the same rate and with the same cadences as the larger society it was linked to, industrial England.' (1977, p.204).

Scotland's social-class structure was not based on a cultural division of labour as Hechter suggests, but rather it evolved from the development of capitalism within the Scottish context, linked to English capitalism but not dominated by it. (Nairn (1977), p.207, Brand (1985), p.275). It was only when industrial England experienced economic decline and the Scottish middle class recognised that Scotland could benefit substantially from the discovery of North Sea oil that the political relationship with England came to be viewed as detrimental. There was, then, no cultural division of labour in Scotland, and Scotland was not in a colonial relationship with England. As an explanation for the rise of nationalist sentiment in Scotland the theory of internal colonialism was considered interesting, but inadequate.(Kellas(1991)p.40).

A common feature of the criticism levelled against Hechter is that he failed to take account of Scotland's separate institutions and indigenous capitalist development. But, in condemning Hechter, his critics fail to recognise the wide variations of historical experience, economic development and political outlook of Scotland's own periphery.[2] Broadly speaking, over centuries Scotland's periphery suffered the ravages of uneven development. This manifested itself principally in terms of poverty, depopulation, truncated economic growth and, increasingly, a culture of dependency *vis à vis* Scotland's core. Within Scotland's periphery, Scotland was viewed as the 'coloniser', exploiting human and natural resources to fuel economic growth at the core. The peripheral 'colonies' of Scotland had little influence over their own destiny. Their land was bought, sold and managed by

---

[2] Nairn (1977) does allude briefly to under-development in the context of the Highlands of Scotland, p.203.

distant landlords who held political and economic power in Scotland and at Westminster. A cultural division of labour obtained. With few exceptions, those who lived on the periphery of Scotland were denied access to positions of influence.

Shetland provides an interesting example of internal colonialism within Scotland. Shetland was pawned to Scotland by Christian I of Norway in 1469 as part payment of his daughter's dowry on her marriage to James III of Scotland. Under Norse law, Shetland enjoyed a long tradition of local democracy which continued until 1611 when the old Shetland Law Book disappeared and Scottish law became predominant. Under Norse law, Shetlanders themselves, through an elected Lawman and in an annual assembly of freeholders, debated, interpreted and administered Shetland Law, with minimal interference from outside. (Moberg & Schei (1988) p163-164). From the time of the Stewart Earls, four sheriff-deputies were appointed to oversee the operation of Scottish legal practice, thereby removing any trace of local democracy until 1890 when the Local Government (Scotland) Act established Zetland County Council. Westminster, at least in the eyes of many Shetlanders, offered some protection against the exploitative Scots, a feeling considerably strengthened by the passing of the Liberal Government's Crofters' Act in 1886. This Act went some way to restoring the security of Shetland's many crofters following the disaster of the Clearances carried out by Scottish lairds. Scotland perpetrated the injustices, Westminster was seen as an ally. Scotland held sway in Shetland in terms of law, education and religious matters. Scottish élites decided on infrastructural investment, agricultural subsidies, support for the fishing industry and, crucially, transport levies which added to the cost of Shetland's exports and imports. By 1962, Zetland County Council, increasingly concerned at Shetland's deteriorating economic situation, sent a delegation to Faroe to investigate the reasons for Faroese economic success. The delegation concluded that the reason for its success was 'the right and power of the Faroese to manage their own affairs, and the application of special measures to special problems' (Gronneberg(1976)p.4).

Zetland County Council made representations to the Secretary of State for Scotland requesting greater autonomy of decision making for Shetland. Two responses were forthcoming, both of which dismayed Shetlanders. First, from the mid-1960s, Shetland's fire, police and water services were merged with the North of Scotland. Second, the Wheatley Commission on local government reform proposed merging Shetland's administration into the geographically vast Highland Region to be run from Inverness. The Scottish Office had not only not listened, they were proposing to exacerbate the problem by removing more control to the Scottish mainland, leaving Shetland increasingly at the mercy of remote, unsympathetic decision makers. Interestingly, frustration at these proposals did not take on a overtly political manifestation at this stage. Rather, the Scottish 'coloniser' was by-passed and appeals were made directly to Westminster on the basis of Shetland's interests not being well represented by Scotland. This suited Westminster, given that the debate on local government reform coincided with the discovery of oil in Shetland's offshore waters. Oil promised to be an economic lifeline for both Shetland and Westminster, so mutual cooperation was of benefit to both. The result was the Zetland County Council Act of 1974 which not only gave Shetland the powers of a single, all-purpose local authority but also the power to enter into virtual partnership with the oil industry, exercising considerable control over oil-related development. In direct financial terms, this enabled Shetland to negotiate a 'disturbance' payment of £5 million from the oil companies, plus harbour dues on supertankers loading up at Sullom Voe and royalties on oil pumped through the complex (Gronneberg 1976, p.24).

That Shetland embraced the oil industry enthusiastically is hardly surprising. Economically, oil has been of inestimable value to Shetland. Massive job creation ,[3] high wages and the stimulus given to retailing and the services sector more generally have kept unemployment much lower than on the Scottish mainland. Home ownership, at 67.5%, is amongst the highest in Scotland (Shetland in Statistics 1994). Average household income in 1992 placed Shetland 29th out of the 72 constituencies in Scotland (Butler & Kavanagh,(1992), p.311). Since the late 1970s, Shetland has witnessed unprecedented expansion of its infrastructure. Road, sea and air transport have developed extensively, so that even the remotest parts are accessible on a daily basis and in virtually all weather conditions. Welfare and leisure provision has expanded throughout the Islands. All these developments have helped regenerate the smaller, rural communities in Shetland so that Lerwick, the capital, although greatly dominant in terms of population, does not dominate in terms of social, cultural and welfare provision.[4]

From the beginning, the Shetland Islands Council (SIC),[5] realised that the reserves of oil in the North Sea were limited, and that Shetland would have to take advantage of the years of plenty to guard against the lean years which would inevitably follow the decline in oil production. There was the recognition that, inevitably, post-oil, Shetland would have to fall back on fishing and agriculture as the mainstay of the economy. To this end, from the late 1970s on, the SIC has made available development loans for the purchase of fishing vessels, new fishing initiatives such as Salmon farming , fish processing, farm improvements and traditional 'cottage' industries such as knitting.[6]

Rapid economic development took place against a backdrop of diminishing indigenous political control. The resurgence of the Scottish National Party in the 1970s and its influence on the political agenda of the then Labour government, caused consternation in Shetland. A devolved Scotland, as proposed by the Scotland Bill, posed a direct threat to Shetland's well-being.

'The concern in the 1970s in Shetland, was that the Scottish

---

[3] 8000 jobs, mainly unskilled, were created between 1976 and 1980 (*Shetland Economic Review*, 1993).

[4] At the time of the 1991 census, 22522 people were resident in Shetland, 7220 of them in Lerwick (*Shetland in Statistics*, 1994).

[5] Created 15 May 1975.

[6] Shetland now has the most modern pelagic fleet in Britain (*Shetland Times*, 19/1/96). Salmon farming had an output value of £33 million in 1992, exceeding that of pelagic and demersal fishing by £13 million (*Shetland in Statistics*, 1994).

Parliament would be dominated by the Central Belt of Scotland, whose representatives would not be sympathetic to Shetland's aspirations, and would, in particular, want to divert resources from Shetland to the Central Belt authorities.'[7]

Again, Scotland was seen in terms of being predatory, exploitative and unsympathetic.[8] Again, an appeal was made direct to Westminster by the SIC. The Liberal Member for Orkney and Shetland, Jo Grimond, backed an amendment to the Scotland Bill ensuring that Shetland's vote in the 1979 referendum would be counted separately and, in the event of a negative response, Shetland excluded from the devolution plans should they be approved by the mainland. Despite the opposition of the Labour government and the hostility of the SNP, the Grimond amendment was carried. On a turnout of 50.3%, 73% voted 'no' to devolution for Scotland, a clear indication that Shetland remained suspicious of the relationship with Scotland.[9]

Prior to the discovery of oil, Shetland was typical of Hechter's internal colony, exhibiting economic dependence, outward migration[10] and a cultural division of labour whereby Shetlanders, although having expressed the wish to exercise greater control over their affairs as early as 1962, were increasingly denied a larger say. After the discovery of oil, Shetland was typical of an internal colony in being rich in natural resources much coveted by the core. The cultural division of labour was heightened by the influx of (mostly Scottish) managerial and professional élites connected with the oil-industry and the commercial activity surrounding it. Although opportunities existed for Shetlanders to participate in the financial benefits of oil, pleas for opportunities to participate in deciding Shetland's future were met by the centralising tendencies of the post-1979 Conservative government and EEC fisheries policies which were deemed positively detrimental to the traditional backbone of the Shetland economy.[11] For Hechter, these would be typical circumstances in which 'nationalist' sentiment would emerge. In Shetland's case, this took the form of the Shetland Movement, originally a cross-party pressure group, later a fully fledged political party able to attract a membership of over 500 and elect a group of SIC councillors seven-strong.[12]

Intensive lobbying, together with a progressive trend in favour of devolution on the part of the Labour and Liberal Democrat parties, led the Shetland Movement to play an important part in the deliberations of the Scottish Constitutional Convention. 'Key Proposals for Scotland's Parliament' published in October 1995, specifically recognises that

---

[7] Jack Burgess, Chairman, Shetland Movement, 1996.

[8] The SIC's response to SNP demands for independence in the mid-1970s was to commission a report from the Nevis Institute to consider possible changes to Shetland's constitutional status. 'The Shetland Report' was published in 1978.

[9] Figures calculated from *Shetland in Statistics*, 1994.

[10] Shetland's population declined from a peak of 31670 in 1861 to 17245 in 1966 (Nevis Institute, 1978, p.22).

[11] Shetland delivered an overwhelming 'no' vote in the 1975 Referendum on continued British membership of the Common Market (*Shetland in Statistics*, 1994).

[12] Shetland's 26 councillors rarely declare a political affiliation. The Shetland Movement has been the largest group on the SIC since the mid-1980s. There are currently 6 Shetland Movement councillors (*Shetland in Statistics*, 1994).

'the geographical and historical circumstances of island communities warrant distinctive constitutional consideration ... Applying the principle of subsidiarity will give the Islands Councils the opportunity and responsibility to provide the services and carry out the functions appropriate to their communities ... the Scottish Parliament will take their needs into account in formulating its legislation and policy.'[13]

The Shetland Movement is content with this state of affairs. 'With general support for Shetland's aspirations evident within the Convention, we have felt no need to be outwith the scope of the Convention.'[14] Even though the SNP has revised its position and now recognises the right to autonomy of Shetland, it is interesting to note that the SNP's electoral support in Orkney and Shetland in 1992 was 11.2%, compared to an average 21.5% for Scotland as a whole (Butler & Kavanagh, 1992, p.286) This could be taken as an indication that Shetland still harbours doubts about the intentions of mainland Scotland and seeks the 'shelter' of a continuing relationship with Westminster, through the devolution plans of the Scottish Constitutional Convention.

Other explanations could be sought to account for the growth of nationalist sentiment within Shetland. Kellas (1991, p.64) has argued that the upsurge in nationalism in Scotland can be explained by the imbalance between de facto and de jure power at a time when Scotland was disenfranchised politically but growing in economic and cultural strength. This could apply to Shetland in that the imbalance between de facto economic power and de jure political power is marked. It does not, however, explain why Shetland should be seeking greater autonomy as early as 1962, when the economy was far from strong and oil a very distant prospect. Rokkan & Urwin (1983 Chapter 4) suggest that distance, difference and dependence *vis-à-vis* the central state and its dominant political culture can account for the 'territorial strain' which leads to a 'politicisation of peripheral predicaments'. The plausibility of this explanation is undermined by the fact that, since the mid-1980s, Shetland has made a positive net contribution to the Government exchequer of over £50 million per year, in addition to the oil revenues from Sullom Voe.[15] Shetland's dependence is now political rather than economic and largely created by a centralising Government.[16] Difference remains important, though not in the cultural terms implied by Rokkan & Urwin (1983), Watson (1990) and Brand (1985), for example. Shetland has a distinctive living culture, but it is not threatened by the encroachment of a dominant core culture. Shetland is a remote, island community which

---

[13]'Scotland's Parliament and Island Communities', paragraphs 1.7 & 2.1 specify that Orkney and Shetland will become two separate constituencies.
[14]Jack Burgess, Chairman, Shetland Movement, 1996.
[15]Oil revenues amounted to £700 million in 1988 (*Shetland Economic Review*, 1993). The Shetland Movement has calculated that the British government has received £100 billion in oil revenues since production began (The Shetland Movement, *Information Leaflet*, 1995). It is ironic to note that Shetland has been accorded Objective 1 status by the European Community for the period 1994-1999.
[16]The SIC is subject to the same, tight budgetary controls as Britain's other local authorities. Shetland's oil revenues are disbursed from a Charitable Trust set up in 1974.

does not fear losing its identity so much as any control it might exercise over its future economic well-being.

Hechter's theory of internal colonialism has the merit of offering a more complete explanation of Shetland's situation. The colonial relationship, primarily between Scotland and Shetland, removed local democracy as bequeathed by Norse law, exploited land and livelihoods during the Clearances and presided over the emigration of nearly half the population in the twentieth century. It established a cultural division of Labour with Scottish élites dominating the legal, educational and religious [17] structures in Shetland, as in mainland Scotland. After the discovery of oil, the uneven nature of the relationship, and the cultural division of labour became more entrenched, with mainly Scottish élites controlling economic decision-making, and the Scottish Office acting as a bureaucratic impediment to the creation of greater economic security. The resulting politicisation of demands for autonomy match the internal colonialism scenario. Whilst Hechter's theory presents genuine difficulties in the case of mainland Scotland, it would seem to bear scrutiny in the case of Shetland.

Bibliography

J.Brand, 'Nationalism and the Noncolonial Periphery', in E.Tiryakian & R.Rogowski (eds), *New Nationalisms of the Developed West*, Allen & Unwin, 1985.

D.Butler & D.Kavanagh, *The British General Election of 1992*, Macmillan, 1992.

R.Gronneberg, *Island Governments: The Experience of Autonomous Island Groups in Northern Europe in Relation to Shetland's Political Future*, Shetland Thule Print, Sandwick, 1976.

M.Hechter, *Internal Colonialism. The Celtic Fringe in British National Development 1536-1966*, Routledge & Kegan Paul, 1975.

M.Hechter, 'Internal Colonialism Revisited', in E.Tiryakian & R.Rogowski (eds), *New Nationalisms of the Developed West*, Allen & Unwin, 1985.

J.Kellas, *The Politics of Nationalism and Ethnicity*, Macmillan, 1991.

G.Moberg & L.K.Schei, *The Shetland Story*, Batsford, 1988.

T.Nairn, *The Break-Up of Britain*, New Left Books, 1977.

Nevis Institute, *The Shetland Report: A Constitutional Study*, Nevis Institute, 1978.

E.Page, 'Michael Hechter's Internal Colonial Thesis: Some Theoretical and Methodological Problems', *European Journal of Political Research*, 6/3, 1978.

S.Rokkan & D.Urwin, *Economy, Territory and Identity*, Sage, 1983.

---

[17] The current Convenor of the SIC is a Church of Scotland minister.

Scottish Constitutional Convention, *Scotland's Parliament – Scotland's Right. Key Proposals for Scotland's Parliament*, 1995.

Shetland Economic Review, *Shetland Islands Council*, Lerwick, 1993.

Shetland in Statistics, *Shetland Islands Council*, Lerwick, 1994.

M.Watson (ed), *Contemporary Minority Nationalism*, Croom Helm, 1990.